6764

PALGRAVE LAW MASTERS

Series editor Marise Cremona

Business Law (2nd edn) Stephen Judge
Company Law (3rd edn) Janet Dine
Constitutional and Administrative Law (3rd edn) John Alder
Contract Law (4th edn) Ewan McKendrick
Conveyancing (3rd edn) Priscilla Sarton
Criminal Law (2nd edn) Jonathan Herring and Marise Cremona
Employment Law (3rd edn) Deborah J. Lockton
Environmental Law and Ethics John Alder and David Wilkinson
Evidence Raymond Emson
Family Law (2nd edn) Kate Standley
Housing Law and Policy David Cowan
Intellectual Property Law (2nd edn) Tina Hart and Linda Fazzani
Land Law (3rd edn) Kate Green
Landlord and Tenant Law (4th edn) Margaret Wilkie and Godfrey Cole
Law of the European Union (3rd edn) Jo Shaw
Law of Succession Catherine Rendell
Law of Trusts Patrick McLoughlin and Catherine Rendell
Legal Method (3rd edn) Ian McLeod
Legal Theory Ian McLeod
Social Security Law Robert East
Torts (2nd edn) Alastair Mullis and Ken Oliphant

Law of the European Union

Third Edition

Jo Shaw
Professor of European Law, University of Leeds

Law series editor: Marise Cremona
Senior Fellow, Centre for Commercial Law Studies
Queen Mary and Westfield College, University of London

palgrave

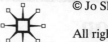
First published 1993 as *European Community Law*
Reprinted three times
Second edition published 1996
Reprinted three times
Third edition published 2000 by
PALGRAVE
Houndmills, Basingstoke, Hampshire RG21 6XS and
175 Fifth Avenue, New York, N. Y. 10010
Companies and representatives throughout the world

PALGRAVE is the new global imprint of St Martin's Press LLC Scholarly and Reference Division and Palgrave Publishers Ltd (formerly Macmillan Press Ltd).

ISBN 0-333-92491-6

This book is printed on paper suitable for recycling and made from fully managed and sustained forest sources.

A catalogue record for this book is available from the British Library.

10   9   8   7   6   5   4   3   2
09   08   07   06   05   04   03   02   01

Printed and bound in Great Britain by
Creative Print & Design (Wales) Ltd, Ebbw Vale

Contents

Preface and Acknowledgements

It remains a dangerous endeavour to 'fix' a good moment to write a textbook about the law of the European Union. It is still a quickly moving target, and this lies not only in the fact that there has been an almost unceasing routine of intergovernmental conferences. As this book was written in early 2000, another one was getting underway, preparing the way presumably for further Treaty amendments but not, please not, another large-scale renumbering exercise. Unless that is, the Member States in their infinite wisdom finally decide to go for the fundamental exercise of splitting the treaties into two, separating out the 'more' constitutional from the 'less', with a view to creating something a little more permanent by way of a constitutional charter.

This book continues to try to provide an 'introduction' to its subject, but largely in the sense of presuming no prior knowledge on the part of the reader. It does not seek to give a superficial account, but it does try to place the legal framework of the European Union, so far as possible, into its wider economic, political and historical context. Overall, the book attempts to highlight the complexities of the topics it addresses, but without giving full empirical detail. There are lists of further reading to help the reader choose among the increasing mass of secondary literature. An additional feature is a list of key websites after many chapters, although many readers are warned that web addresses often change. The availability of the Internet direct from my laptop made a tremendous difference to the task of writing this new edition.

As compared to earlier editions of this book, the emphasis has shifted in two directions, although the overall shape has been retained. I remain convinced that 'institutions are interesting' as well as that 'institutions matter', and the events and activities related in the narrative parts of this book back up that contention. The constitutional dimension built into the last edition has been rewritten and strengthened, and two new chapters on values and principles in the EU constitutional framework are included. Constitutionalism is the overarching framework for the book. But in addition, an attempt has been made to present the 'EU' as whole, rather than concentrating in practice on 'European Community law' in the narrow sense alone. Second, as appropriate more of the international dimension of the EU's work has been built in. The basic area of coverage remains the same. It is worth pointing out that the book covers the 'Constitutional and Institutional Framework' of the EU, not 'EU public law'. That, in practice, would also cover a wide area of EU substantive law, through which the socio-economic life of the Union is regulated. That will be the subject of a companion volume, under preparation by Jo Hunt, Jo Shaw and Chloë Wallace, which will be published in 2001.

The publishers have been patient with me in the preparation of this edition, at least until we reached the point where even my best friends could no longer sensibly recommend the second edition to their students. That I can count upon the series editor, Marise Cremona, as a friend as well as a respected colleague has helped tremendously in easing both the writing and the production processes. Marise has made a number of very valuable suggestions, not all of which pertained to the field of external relations. But she certainly did save me from a number of infelicities in that area, although I alone am responsible for the final product. I thank both her and the publishers especially Helen Bugler, Esther Thackeray and Tessa Hanford. I would also like to thank friends and colleagues too numerous to mention for sharing their as yet unpublished thoughts and writings with me most generously, and for responding to my requests for publication citations most promptly. The joys of e-mail attachments, and the horror when they don't seem to work! I would specifically like to thank the following for their conversations and support in relation to matters of EU law and its many contexts over recent years (some have even endured joint authorship of various pieces...): Kenneth Armstrong, Zenon Bankowski, Catherine Barnard, Gráinne de Búrca, Damian Chalmers, Sybilla Fries, Tammy Hervey, Jo Hunt, Miguel Poiares Maduro, Joanne Scott, Neil Walker, Joseph Weiler and Antje Wiener. They have made an immense contribution to my work and to this book.

On a personal note, I want to say thank you to Leo Shaw for putting up with me, and for being a great companion. A number of friends helped out by spending time with Leo when I was otherwise engaged, none more so than Zoe Collins and Carol Hussain-Dad; they and their families, as well as Sally Wheeler, have been tremendous support. Finally, I would like to say sorry to WR who has suffered more from the writing of this book than was fair.

Table of Cases

A   Cases before the European Court of Justice

1   By Case Number (in year order)

2 Alphabetical list

3 Opinions delivered pursuant to Article 300

B Cases before the Court of First Instance

1 By case number (in year order)

2   Alphabetical list

C   Cases before National Courts

1   English Courts

2   German Courts

3   Irish Courts

4 Belgian Courts

5 French Courts

D Cases before the European Commission and Court of Human Rights

Table of Treaties Establishing the European Communities and the European Union

EC (referring to the period 1993–1999)

List of Abbreviations

ABM	Activity Based Management
AC	Appeal Cases
All ER	*All England Law Reports*
BEUC	Bureau Européen des Unions Consommateurs
CAP	Common Agricultural Policy
CCT	Common Customs Tariff
CE	Compulsory expenditure
CEDEFOP	European Centre for the Development of Vocational Training
CEEP	Comité Européen des Entreprises Publiques
CELEX	Official EU document database
CESDP	Common European Security and Defence Policy
CFSP	Common Foreign and Security Policy
CIE	Committee of Independent Experts
CJHA/JHA	Cooperation in Justice and Home Affairs
CMLR	*Common Market Law Reports*
COM	Commission Document
COPA	Confederation of Professional Agricultural Organisations
CoR	Committee of the Regions
COREPER	Committee of Permanent Representatives
DECODE	Designing Tomorrow's Commission
DG	Directorate General
DTEU	Draft Treaty establishing a European Union
EBRD	European Bank for Reconstruction and Development
EC	European Community
ECB	European Central Bank
ECHR	European Convention on Human Rights
ECOFIN	Council of Economics and Finance Ministers
ECOSOC	Economic and Social Committee
ECR	*European Court Reports*
ECSC	European Coal and Steel Community
ECU	European Currency Unit
EDC	European Defence Community/European Documentation Centre (depending upon sense)

EDU	Europol Drugs Unit
EEA	European Economic Area
EEC	European Economic Community
EEIG	European Economic Interest Grouping
EFTA	European Free Trade Association
EIB	European Investment Bank
EMI	European Monetary Institute
EMS	European Monetary System
EMU	Economic and Monetary Union
EPC	European Political Cooperation
ERM	Exchange Rate Mechanism
ERTA	European Road Transport Agreement
ESCB	European System of Central Banks
ETUC	European Trade Union Confederation
EU	European Union
EUI	European University Institute
Euratom	European Atomic Energy Community
EUROPOL	European Police Office
FAO	Food and Agriculture Organization (of UN)
FYROM	Former Yugoslav Republic of Macedonia
GATT	General Agreement on Tariffs and Trade
GDP	Gross Domestic Product
GNP	Gross National Product
IGC	Intergovernmental Conference
ILO	International Labour Organization
IRLR	Industrial Relations Law Reports
MAP	Moderning the Administration and Personnel Policy
MCAs	Monetary Compensatory Amounts
MEP	Member of the European Parliament
NATO	North Atlantic Treaty Organisation
NCE	Non-compulsory expenditure
OECD	Organisation for Economic Cooperation and Development
OEEC	Organization for European Economic Cooperation
OJ	*Official Journal*
OLAF	European Anti-Fraud Office
OOPEC	Office of Official Publications of the European Communities
OSCE	Organisation for Security and Cooperation in Europe
PHARE	Pologne – Hongrie: Assistance à la Restructuration des Economies (extended to other CEECs)
PJC	Police and Judicial Cooperation
QMV	Qualified Majority Voting

RTD	Research and Technological Development
SEA	Single European Act
SEM	Sound and Efficient Management
TEU	Treaty on European Union
UN	United Nations
UNICE	Union of Industries of the European Community
VAT	Value Added Tax
WEU	West European Union
WTO	World Trade Organisation

Table of Equivalences

A Treaty on European Union

Previous numbering	New Numbering
Title I	*Title I*
Article A	Article 1
Article B	Article 2
Article C	Article 3
Article D	Article 4
Article E	Article 5
Article F	Article 6
Article F.1(a)	Article 7
Title II	*Title II*
Article G	Article 8
Title III	*Title III*
Article H	Article 9
Title IV	*Title IV*
Article I	Article 10
Title V(b)	*Title V*
Article J.1	Article 11
Article J.2	Article 12
Article J.3	Article 13
Article J.4	Article 14
Article J.5	Article 15
Article J.6	Article 16
Article J.7	Article 17
Article J.8	Article 18
Article J.9	Article 19
Article J.10	Article 20
Article J.11	Article 21
Article J.12	Article 22
Article J.13	Article 23
Article J.14	Article 24
Article J.15	Article 25
Article J.16	Article 26
Article J.17	Article 27
Article J.18	Article 28
Title VI(b)	*Title VI*
Article K.1	Article 29
Article K.2	Article 30
Article K.3	Article 31

Previous numbering	New Numbering
Title VI[b]	*Title VI*
Article K.4	Article 32
Article K.5	Article 33
Article K.6	Article 34
Article K.7	Article 35
Article K.8	Article 36
Article K.9	Article 37
Article K.10	Article 38
Article K.11	Article 39
Article K.12	Article 40
Article K.13	Article 41
Article K.14	Article 42
Title VIa[c]	*Title VII*
Article K.15[a]	Article 43
Article K.16[a]	Article 44
Article K.17[a]	Article 45
Title VII	*Title VIII*
Article L	Article 46
Article M	Article 47
Article N	Article 48
Article O	Article 49
Article P	Article 50
Article Q	Article 51
Article R	Article 52
Article S	Article 53

B   Treaty Establishing the European Community

Previous numbering	New Numbering
Paet One	*Part One*
Article 1	Article 1
Article 2	Article 2
Article 3	Article 3
Article 3a	Article 4
Article 3b	Article 5
Article 3c[a]	Article 6
Article 4	Article 7
Article 4a	Article 8
Article 4b	Article 9
Article 5	Article 10
Article 5a[a]	Article 11
Article 6	Article 12
Article 6a[a]	Article 13
Article 7 (repealed)	—
Article 7a	Article 14
Article 7b (repealed)	—
Article 7c	Article 15
Article 7d[a]	Article 16

Previous numbering	New Numbering
Title II	*Title II*
Article 42	Article 36
Article 43	Article 37
Article 44 (repealed)	—
Article 45 (repealed)	—
Article 46	Article 38
Article 47 (repealed)	—
Title III	*Title III*
Chapter 1	*Chapter 1*
Article 48	Article 39
Article 49	Article 40
Article 50	Article 41
Article 51	Article 42
Chapter 2	*Chapter 2*
Article 52	Article 43
Article 53 (repealed)	—
Article 54	Article 44
Article 55	Article 445
Article 56	Article 46
Article 57	Article 47
Article 58	Article 48
Chapter 3	*Chapter 3*
Article 59	Article 49
Article 60	Article 50
Article 61	Article 51
Article 62 (repealed)	—
Article 63	Article 52
Article 64	Article 53
Article 65	Article 54
Article 66	Article 55
Chapter 4	*Chapter 4*
Article 67 (repealed)	—
Article 68 (repealed)	—
Article 69 (repealed)	—
Article 70 (repealed)	—
Article 71 (repealed)	—
Article 72 (repealed)	—
Article 73 (repealed)	—
Article 73a (repealed)	—
Article 73b	Article 56
Article 73c	Article 57
Article 73d	Article 58
Article 73e (repealed)	—
Article 73f	Article 59
Article 73g	Article 60
Article 73h (repealed)	—
Title IIIa[(c)]	*Title IV*
Article 73i[(a)]	Article 61

Previous numbering	New Numbering
Title IIIa[(c)]	*Title IV*
Article 73j[(a)]	Article 62
Article 73k[(a)]	Article 63
Article 73l[(a)]	Article 64
Article 73m[(a)]	Article 65
Article 73n[(a)]	Article 66
Article 73o[(a)]	Article 67
Article 73p[(a)]	Article 68
Article 73q[(a)]	Article 69
Title IV	*Title V*
Article 74	Article 70
Article 75	Article 71
Article 76	Article 72
Article 77	Article 73
Article 78	Article 74
Article 79	Article 75
Article 80	Article 76
Article 81	Article 77
Article 82	Article 78
Article 83	Article 79
Article 84	Article 80
Title V	*Title VI*
Chapter 1	*Chapter 1*
Section 1	*Section 1*
Article 85	Article 81
Article 86	Article 82
Article 87	Article 83
Article 88	Article 84
Article 89	Article 85
Article 90	Article 86
Section 2 (deleted)	—
Article 91 (repealed)	—
Section 3	*Section 2*
Article 92	Article 87
Article 93	Article 88
Article 94	Article 89
Article 95	Article 90
Article 96	Article 91
Article 97 (repealed)	—
Article 98	Article 92
Article 99	Article 93
Article 100	Article 94
Article 100a	Article 95
Article 100b (repealed)	—
Article 100c (repealed)	—
Article 100d (repcalcd)	—
Article 101	Article 96
Article 102	Article 97

Previous numbering	New Numbering
Title VI	*Title VII*
Chapter 1	*Chapter 1*
Article 102a	Article 98
Article 103	Article 99
Article 103a	Article 100
Article 104	Article 101
Article 104a	Article 102
Article 104b	Article 103
Article 104c	Article 104
Chapter 2	*Chapter 2*
Article 105	Article 105
Article 105a	Article 106
Article 106	Article 107
Article 107	Article 108
Article 108	Article 109
Article 108a	Article 110
Article 109	Article 111
Chapter 3	*Chapter 3*
Article 109a	Article 112
Article 109b	Article 113
Article 109c	Article 114
Article 109d	Article 115
Chapter 4	*Chapter 4*
Article 109e	Article 116
Article 109f	Article 117
Article 109g	Article 118
Article 109h	Article 119
Article 109i	Article 120
Article 109j	Article 121
Article 109k	Article 122
Article 109l	Article 123
Article 109m	Article 124
Title VIa[c]	*Title VIII*
Article 109n[a]	Article 125
Article 109o[a]	Article 126
Article 109p[a]	Article 127
Article 109q[a]	Article 128
Article 109r[a]	Article 129
Article 109s[a]	Article 130
Title VII	*Title IX*
Article 110	Article 131
Article 111 (repealed)	—
Article 112	Article 132
Article 113	Article 133
Article 114 (repealed)	—
Article 115	Article 134

Previous numbering	New Numbering
Title XV	*Title XVIII*
Article 130l	Article 169
Article 130m	Article 170
Article 130n	Article 171
Article 130o	Article 172
Article 130p	Article 173
Article 130q (repealed)	—
Title XVI	*Title XIX*
Article 130r	Article 174
Article 130s	Article 175
Article 130t	Article 176
Title XVII	*Title XX*
Article 130u	Article 177
Article 130v	Article 178
Article 130w	Article 179
Article 130x	Article 180
Article 130y	Article 181
Part Four	*Part Four*
Article 131	Article 182
Article 132	Article 183
Article 133	Article 184
Article 134	Article 185
Article 135	Article 186
Article 136	Article 187
Article 136a	Article 188
Part Five	*Part Five*
Title I	*Title I*
Chapter 1	*Chapter 1*
Section 1	*Section 1*
Article 137	Article 189
Article 138	Article 190
Article 138a	Article 191
Article 138b	Article 192
Article 138c	Article 193
Article 138d	Article 194
Article 138e	Article 195
Article 139	Article 196
Article 140	Article 197
Article 141	Article 198
Article 142	Article 199
Article 143	Article 200
Article 144	Article 201
Section 2	*Section 2*
Article 145	Article 202
Article 146	Article 203
Article 147	Article 204

Previous numbering	New Numbering
Section 2	*Section 2*
Article 148	Article 205
Article 149	—
Article 150	Article 206
Article 151	Article 207
Article 152	Article 208
Article 153	Article 209
Article 154	Article 210
Section 3	*Section 3*
Article 155	Article 211
Article 156	Article 212
Article 157	Article 213
Article 158	Article 214
Article 159	Article 215
Article 160	Article 216
Article 161	Article 217
Article 162	Article 218
Article 163	Article 219
Section 4	*Section 4*
Article 164	Article 220
Article 165	Article 221
Article 166	Article 222
Article 167	Article 223
Article 168	Article 224
Article 168a	Article 225
Article 169	Article 226
Article 170	Article 227
Article 171	Article 228
Article 172	Article 229
Article 173	Article 230
Article 174	Article 231
Article 175	Article 232
Article 176	Article 233
Article 177	Article 234
Article 178	Article 235
Article 179	Article 236
Article 180	Article 237
Article 181	Article 238
Article 182	Article 239
Article 183	Article 240
Article 184	Article 241
Article 185	Article 242
Article 186	Article 243
Article 187	Article 244
Article 188	Article 245
Section 5	*Section 5*
Article 188a	Article 246
Article 188b	Article 247

Previous numbering	New Numbering
Section 5	*Section 5*
Article 188c	Article 248
Chapter 2	*Chapter 2*
Article 189	Article 249
Article 189a	Article 250
Article 189b	Article 251
Article 189c	Article 252
Article 190	Article 253
Article 191	Article 254
Article 191a[a]	Article 255
Article 192	Article 256
Chapter 3	*Chapter 3*
Article 193	Article 257
Article 194	Article 258
Article 195	Article 259
Article 196	Article 260
Article 197	Article 261
Article 198	Article 262
Chapter 4	*Chapter 4*
Article 198a	Article 263
Article 198b	Article 264
Article 198c	Article 265
Chapter 5	*Chapter 5*
Article 198d	Article 266
Article 198e	Article 267
Title II	*Title II*
Article 199	Article 268
Article 200 (repealed)	—
Article 201	Article 269
Article 201a	Article 270
Article 202	Article 271
Article 203	Article 272
Article 204	Article 273
Article 205	Article 274
Article 205a	Article 275
Article 206	Article 276
Article 206a (repealed)	—
Article 207	Article 277
Article 208	Article 278
Article 209	Article 279
Article 209a	Article 280
Part Six	*Part Six*
Article 210	Article 281
Article 211	Article 282
Article 212[a]	Article 283
Article 213	Article 284
Article 213a[a]	Article 285

Previous numbering	New Numbering
Part Six	*Part Six*
Article 213b[(a)]	Article 286
Article 214	Article 287
Article 215	Article 288
Article 216	Article 289
Article 217	Article 290
Article 218[(a)]	Article 291
Article 219	Article 292
Article 220	Article 293
Article 221	Article 294
Article 222	Article 295
Article 223	Article 296
Article 224	Article 297
Article 225	Article 298
Article 226 (repealed)	—
Article 227	Article 299
Article 228	Article 300
Article 228a	Article 301
Article 229	Article 302
Article 230	Article 303
Article 231	Article 304
Article 232	Article 305
Article 233	Article 306
Article 234	Article 307
Article 235	Article 308
Article 236[(a)]	Article 309
Article 237 (repealed)	—
Article 238	Article 310
Article 239	Article 311
Article 240	Article 312
Article 241 (repealed)	—
Article 242 (repealed)	—
Article 243 (repealed)	—
Article 244 (repealed)	—
Article 245 (repealed)	—
Article 246 (repealed)	—
Final provisions	*Final provisions*
Article 247	Article 313
Article 248	Article 314

Notes:

(a) New Article introduced by the Treaty of Amsterdam
(b) Title restructured by the Treaty of Amsterdam
(c) New Title introduced by the Treaty of Amsterdam

Part I

Introducing the European Union and its Constitutional Framework

1 Studying the Law of the European Union

1.1 Beginning the Law of the European Union

The purpose of this introductory chapter is to equip you, the reader, with the basic tools you need to embark upon the study of the law of the European Union, a subject which has something of a reputation for being impenetrable. It assumes that you have some knowledge of the basic components of a legal system, but very little knowledge of what the European Community (EC) or European Union (EU) can do, what they cannot do (or indeed whether and why there is a difference between these two entities), and why it is important in a specifically legal sense to understand what they can do. It offers in 1.6 a brief overview of the structure and framework of the EU legal order. That paragraph – and indeed much of this chapter – is a 'taster', providing basic pointers on to which more detailed study will be grafted in later chapters. It has three main objectives:

- to highlight at the first stage of study the pivotal roles of the Court of Justice and the EU legal and constitutional order in the system of integration based on the EU;
- to identify the basic lines of the development of the EU from the Treaties of Rome and Paris in the 1950s, through the Single European Act (SEA), the Treaty of Maastricht or Treaty on European Union (TEU) and the Treaty of Amsterdam into the 1980s and 1990s and now into the twenty-first century; and
- to present in broad outline both the basic framework of the EU as it exists today, and the contexts in which it operates.

The creation of the European Community, and latterly the European Union, has not only involved the establishment of a new type of legal order operating in the international or transnational sphere – one which can only be understood if certain basic precepts of the study of national law are set aside; it has also brought into being a legal order in which a very specific and clear purpose is dominant. This is the promotion of a process of 'integration', leading towards a 'union' of European states and peoples. This purpose operates at a number of different levels, including those of the market (the dismantling of the national barriers to trade between states to create a single market), of money and the economy (the creation of a single currency and moves towards a single economic policy and policy on employment), and of internal and external security (the creation of an 'area of freedom, security and justice' and a 'common foreign and security policy'). In addition, there are important political and legal dimensions to the integration process (the creation of political and legal institutions outside the nation state; the creation of a common political identity within the EU, particularly on the global stage). At every level, the issue of 'integration' is an underlying theme, although exactly what integration might imply varies according to circumstances. It does not, for example, automatically mean greater centralisation of decision making, legal structures and policy choices. There are principles operating in the EU precisely to prevent over-centralisation. But what it does mean is that public policy choices across the EU become, above all, a matter of common concern, as do questions such as the liberal values of a democratic constitution. The constitutional and institutional framework studied in this volume exists for the purpose of facilitating the development of this multi-faceted project of 'integration'. In addition, the Court of Justice makes frequent use of the aim of integration when it is interpreting EU law, and it will be a common theme studied in this book. 1.3 contains an outline sketch of the some key dimensions of this aim, and the concept of 'integration' is one of those which receives attention in 1.5, which attempts to demystify certain aspects of the language of European integration.

In comparison to most national legal systems, and certainly in comparison to the legal systems of the states which form its constituent members, the legal system of the EU is particularly unstable and in a state of constant flux and change. Changes mainly come about either because of a dynamic intervention on the part of the Court of Justice in the interpretation of EU law, or because the Member States have negotiated and agreed further amendments to one of the key elements of the constitution of the EU – its basic Treaties. Since the reasons for these changes lie more frequently in the field of politics than law, it will be apparent that EU law can only properly be understood in its wider political and economic context, and that the successful study of EU law presupposes the acquisition of a substantial body of contextual knowledge. The wider 'European' and 'global' contexts in which the EU is situated are sketched in 1.4. A guide to reading across the broader European studies literatures is offered in 1.8. 1.7 offers assistance in locating the treaties, legislation and official documentation of the EU, and in making a basic selection from the wealth of secondary legal literature which is available. We begin, however, with some basic facts about the European Union and the European Community.

1.2   The European Union and the European Community: The Basic Facts

What we now call the European Union started out as a Community of six in the 1950s: France, the Federal Republic of Germany, Italy, Belgium, Luxembourg and the Netherlands. In 1973 Denmark, Ireland and the UK acceded; Norway signed a Treaty of Accession, but did not join when membership was rejected by popular vote in a referendum. Further expansion occurred in 1980 with the accession of Greece, and in 1986 with the accession of Spain and Portugal, creating a Community of twelve. *De facto* expansion occurred once again in 1990, with the unification of Germany bringing the former German Democratic Republic into the Community, although not as a separate member. The most recent accession process was completed at the beginning of 1995, with Austria, Finland and Sweden becoming members. Once again the people of Norway declined through a referendum vote to take up the opportunity of membership negotiated for them by their government. In 2000, with fifteen Member States and eleven official languages, the EU had a population of just over 375 million, a GDP of over 8 billion euro and the highest share of world trade in terms of imports and exports of goods and services; all of this makes it a leading global economic and – potentially – political actor (Eurostat, 1999).

As we shall see in Chapter 3, enlargement, especially towards the east but also in the area of the Mediterranean, is a central preoccupation within the EU at present. The defining date was 1989, with the fall of the Berlin Wall and the later break up of the Soviet Union. There are numerous candidates for membership at present. In a first group of countries, with accession negotiations in progress since 1998 are Cyprus, the Czech Republic, Estonia, Hungary, Poland and Slovenia. In late 1999, there was a fundamental reappraisal of priorities in the wake of the Kosovo crisis. The violent consequences of the break-up of the former Yugoslavia generally, and the impact of the bombing of Serbia and Kosovo, in particular, including the need for physical and political reconstruction in the wake of the NATO action, have all brought home the costs in economic and human terms of *not enlarging* the EU. The costs relate to the persistence of political instability and insecurity within the continent of Europe, close on the borders of the EU. The EU – in the form of the Heads of State and Government acting on the advice of the Commission – therefore took the decision in December 1999 to start accession negotiations in early 2000 with a further group of six countries (Bulgaria, Latvia, Lithuania, Malta, Romania and Slovakia). Only with Turkey, among the group of countries which have formally applied for membership, has the EU yet to start accession negotiations, although it is now recognised as a candidate country for which a pre-accession strategy has been formulated.

The term 'European Community' was the designation commonly used up to the end of 1993 for a political entity, composed of a number of distinct legal entities with separate international legal personality, which came to be generally identified as a single unit. These are the three Communities, of which two are confined in their application to particular sectors of the economy: the European Coal and Steel Community (ECSC), formed by the Treaty of Paris concluded in 1951 which came into force on 25 July 1952, and the European Atomic Energy Community (Euratom), formed by the Treaty of Rome concluded in 1957 which came into force on 1 January 1958. Also created in 1958 by a second Treaty of Rome 1957 was the European Economic Community (EEC), the 'everything else' Community, which acquired a hegemonic position within the political and legal framework of the Community. Confusingly, since 1993 when the Treaty on European Union came into force, the European Economic Community has been redesignated as the 'European Community', leaving the other two sectoral Communities with their existing titles. The Articles of what must now be termed the 'EC Treaty' are referred to in this book as Article 1 EC, etc. Where necessary, Articles of the 'old' EEC Treaty are designated Article 2 EEC, etc. Much of the discussion in this book will be concerned with the provisions of the Treaties establishing and amending this 'general' Community, in particular those which establish and limit the powers of the institutions, which set the framework for adopting legislation and other policy measures, and which lay down general principles and frameworks for government under the rule of law. Legally, the three Communities remain distinct, although they have common institutions, formed in 1967 by the Merger Treaty. However, the powers of the institutions differ slightly between the three Communities. The ECSC Treaty also differs from the two later Treaties in that it can be described as a *traité loi*, or 'treaty-law' which itself prescribes in detail the policies to be pursued by the Community, and leaves merely issues of policy implementation to the institutions. The EEC and Euratom Treaties were developed as *traités cadre*, or 'framework treaties', which contain only the outlines of policy objectives to which the institutions must give concrete form with legislative instruments. To a large extent, this characteristic has been maintained with subsequent amendments of those Treaties. A further important distinction is that the ECSC Treaty was concluded for 50 years, and expires in 2002, whereas the Euratom and EEC Treaties were concluded for an indefinite duration. When the ECSC Treaty expires at midnight on 24 July 2002, the matters with which it deals will be reallocated to the EC and Euratom Treaties, as appropriate.

The EEC Treaty was significantly amended in 1986 by the Single European Act, which established the so-called '1992' deadline, and sought to give the institutions the powers they needed to achieve the goal of completing the internal market by December 31 1992. The Single European Act also introduced a form of institutionalised intergovernmental cooperation between the Member States regarding foreign policy, termed 'European Political Cooperation'.

The effect of the Treaty of Maastricht, or 'Treaty on European Union', has been to link the three Communities even closer together within the common structure of a European Union, a new entity built around the framework offered by the existing Communities. The Union is 'founded' on the European Communities (Article 1 TEU). The Union does not as such have legal personality, and so is not a legal body in the same way as the Communities. It is served by a single institutional framework, which is essentially that of the Communities themselves. The Treaty of Maastricht also supplemented the Communities by introducing additional policies and forms of intergovernmental cooperation in the areas of foreign affairs and justice and home affairs. It introduced what is commonly described as a 'three-pillar' structure, of which the existing corpus of law based around the Communities remains the central pillar ('first pillar'). The side pillars are:

- Common Foreign and Security Policy (which has evolved out of European Political Cooperation) (Title V of the TEU: the 'second pillar' or 'CFSP'); and
- Police and Judicial Cooperation in Criminal Matters (Title VI of the TEU: the 'third pillar' or 'PJC').

In fact this precise structure and the current designation of the third pillar are the result of a further set of amendments to the whole framework of Treaties, introduced by the Treaty of Amsterdam. This Treaty was signed in 1997 and came into force on 1 May 1999. The 'old' third pillar – Cooperation in Justice and Home Affairs (JHA) – was reduced in size and changed in scope as certain matters were transferred into the 'first pillar' or 'communitarised' (i.e. incorporated into the framework of the European Community in the strict sense). Figure 1.1 summarises the current framework and the links between the TEU and the EC Treaty. The constitutional structure of the EU will be discussed in greater detail in Chapter 5. Provisions of the Treaty on European Union are referred to in this book as Article 1 TEU, etc.

The Treaty of Maastricht was finalised in December 1991 following two intergovernmental conferences lasting one year on the subjects of economic and monetary union and political union, and was signed in February 1992. It established the framework allowing for monetary union to be achieved as of 1 January 1999, when the euro became the single currency in eleven Member States by means of the irrevocable locking of national exchange rates. The Treaty of Maastricht was due to come into force on 1 January 1993, but difficulties in the ratification process involving an initial rejection in a referendum in Denmark, ratification by only a small majority in a referendum in France, considerable opposition in the UK Parliament and a constitutional challenge in Germany delayed the coming into force of the Treaty until 1 November 1993. The Treaty of Maastricht itself provided for a further revision process to begin in 1996, with the convening of a conference

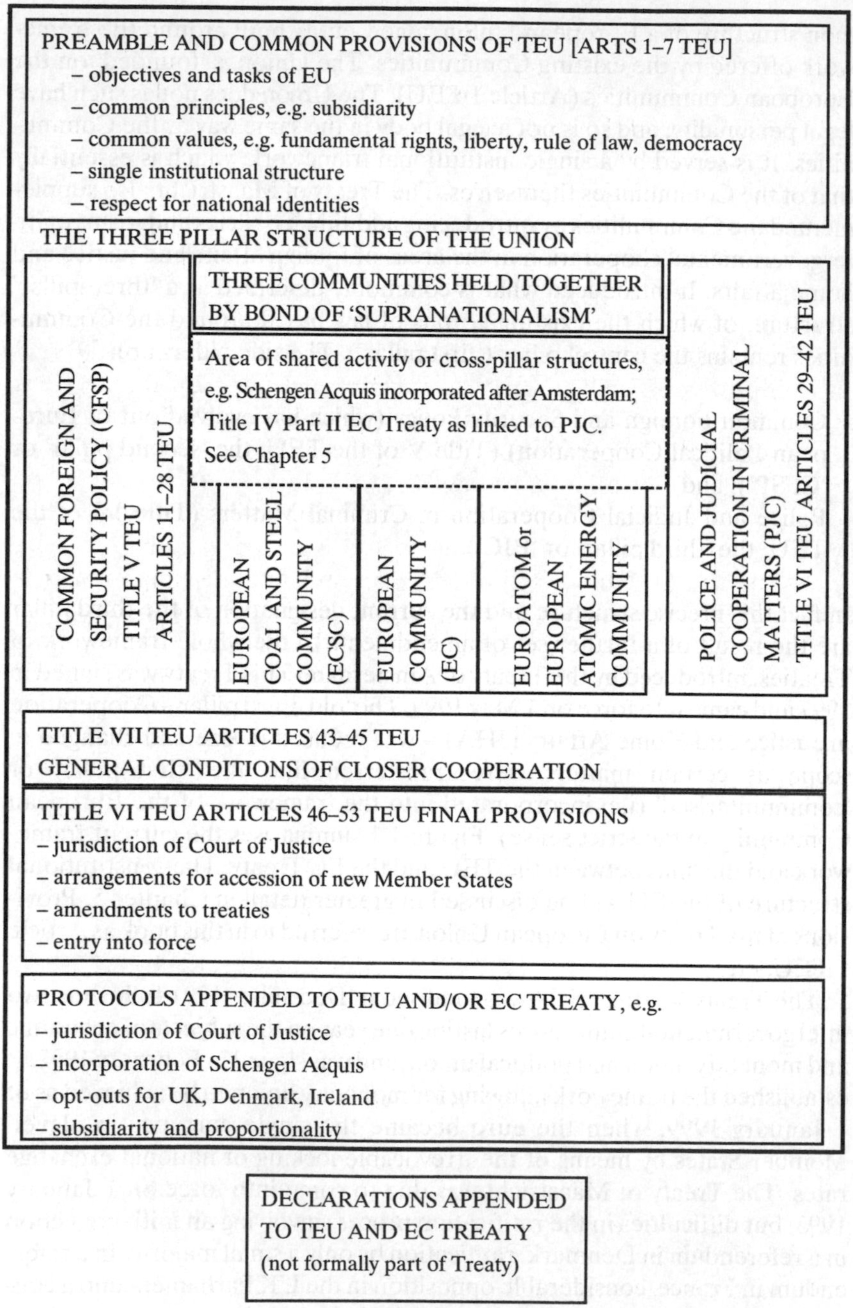

PREAMBLE AND COMMON PROVISIONS OF TEU [ARTS 1–7 TEU]
- objectives and tasks of EU
- common principles, e.g. subsidiarity
- common values, e.g. fundamental rights, liberty, rule of law, democracy
- single institutional structure
- respect for national identities

THE THREE PILLAR STRUCTURE OF THE UNION

THREE COMMUNITIES HELD TOGETHER BY BOND OF 'SUPRANATIONALISM'

Area of shared activity or cross-pillar structures, e.g. Schengen Acquis incorporated after Amsterdam; Title IV Part II EC Treaty as linked to PJC. See Chapter 5

COMMON FOREIGN AND SECURITY POLICY (CFSP) TITLE V TEU ARTICLES 11–28 TEU

EUROPEAN COAL AND STEEL COMMUNITY (ECSC)

EUROPEAN COMMUNITY (EC)

EUROATOM or EUROPEAN ATOMIC ENERGY COMMUNITY

POLICE AND JUDICIAL COOPERATION IN CRIMINAL MATTERS (PJC) TITLE VI TEU ARTICLES 29–42 TEU

TITLE VII TEU ARTICLES 43–45 TEU
GENERAL CONDITIONS OF CLOSER COOPERATION

TITLE VI TEU ARTICLES 46–53 TEU FINAL PROVISIONS
- jurisdiction of Court of Justice
- arrangements for accession of new Member States
- amendments to treaties
- entry into force

PROTOCOLS APPENDED TO TEU AND/OR EC TREATY, e.g.
- jurisdiction of Court of Justice
- incorporation of Schengen Acquis
- opt-outs for UK, Denmark, Ireland
- subsidiarity and proportionality

DECLARATIONS APPENDED
TO TEU AND EC TREATY
(not formally part of Treaty)

Figure 1.1   The EU's pillar structure after the Treaties of Maastricht and Amsterdam

of representatives of the Member States (an intergovernmental conference or 'IGC'). This IGC began in March 1996 and concluded in June 1997, with agreement upon the Treaty of Amsterdam which was signed in October 1997. One important change instituted when this Treaty was ratified and entered into force on 1 May 1999 was the renumbering of both the EC Treaty and the Treaty on European Union. In the latter case, letters have been redesignated as numbers: for example, Article N TEU, which provides for the convening of IGCs and lays down the process for formally amending the Treaties, is now Article 48 TEU. Particular confusion arises from the renumbering of the EC Treaty, as clearly older literature and case law uses the previous numbering, and some well-known legal structures within the EU have long been known by the relevant article numbers. A good example is the so-called 'Article 177 preliminary ruling procedure', under which national courts can refer questions of EU law to the Court of Justice for a ruling on interpretation or validity (now Article 234 EC). The 'new Article 177' is part of the EU's policy provisions on development cooperation policy with developing countries. Some of the number changes are quite bewildering. For example (old) Article 30 EC lays down a prohibition on import restrictions on goods imposed by Member States, subject to exceptions set out in (old) Article 36. Article 30 has been renumbered Article 28 EC, but because of deletions of intervening articles, old Article 36 is now new Article 30 EC! You are advised to consult the table of equivalences at the front of this book on regular occasions, in order to become familiar with the most important changes. Wherever appropriate, the text makes clear what the old *and* the new numbers are in specific areas.

The pattern of successive IGCs continues. At the 1996–97 IGC, the Member States were unable to agree upon the significant changes to the institutional framework long deemed necessary to permit the anticipated further enlargements, especially to the east, referred to above. Protocol No. 7 annexed to the TEU and the EC, ECSC and Euratom Treaties by the Treaty of Amsterdam in effect mandated certain institutional changes before any further enlargement and required a comprehensive review of the institutional provisions before the membership of the EU can exceed twenty countries. As accession negotiations have been proceeding with twelve countries in total since 2000 (and in some cases since 1998), swift action was clearly needed and on 14 February 2000, after the requisite Opinions from the Commission and the European Parliament, the IGC was inaugurated. Its planned conclusion was December 2000 at the Nice meeting of the European Council under the French Presidency.

This section shows that in strict legal (if not political) terms the EU is a very limited body. However, just as the strictly incorrect term 'European Community' gained widespread acceptance in the 1970s and 1980s, so the term EU is being used more and more as the general overall descriptive term, and is not limited to its narrow political or geographical connotations. As 1.1 has already indicated, this book will generally refer to the 'EU' or the 'Union' when talking about the broad institutional and constitutional structures established by the EU Treaties as a whole, although an exception is made in the historical presentation of the earlier history of the European Communities in Chapter 2. It also uses the terms 'legal order of the EU' and 'EU law' in order to highlight the relevance of law and legal institutions right across the three-pillar structure. This terminology will be applied even in Parts V and VI of the book, which look at the relationship between EU law and national law and at the judicial control of the acts of the institutions, and which are, strictly speaking, focused almost exclusively on what the Court of Justice indeed continues to call 'Community law', i.e. the legal framework of the first pillar. However, although a broad terminology of 'EU' and 'Union' will generally be used, the strict legal differences between the work of the institutions across the EC and the EU still need to be fully recognised, and appropriate distinctions will be drawn in Parts II and III of the book. For example, to assist in delimiting more precisely the powers of the EC as a legal entity, the term 'Community competence' will generally be used, especially in Part III.

As a body based on international agreements between sovereign states, the EU is in many senses a creature of international law; however, the Member States have endowed its institutions with uniquely far-reaching powers for the achievement of the objectives contained in the Treaties. It is now often described as a 'polity', an unspecific term for a political entity, or a 'polity-in-the-making'. The EU has a distinctive institutional structure, which operates across the three pillars on the basis of the principle laid down in Article 3 TEU and builds on the original institutional framework of the three Communities. In the first fifty years of its existence, the main legislative role has been fulfilled by the Council of the European Union which is composed of representatives of the Member States at ministerial level. The Member States are also represented in the European Council, a summit conference of Heads of State and Government who meet at least twice yearly to give overall policy direction to the EU. The European Parliament, while it is now directly elected by universal franchise and is therefore representative of the people, has fewer powers in the legislative field than the Council, and its role ranges between that of a consultative assembly in some policy areas and a full co-legislator in some fields. It is also the co-budgetary authority with the Council. The role of the European Commission within the EU is sometimes exaggerated by Member States hostile to extensions of the EU's competences; in fact, the Commission's role is limited to initiating policy, implementing measures adopted by the Council and ensuring that Member States fulfil their obligations under the Treaties. It is in a sense the civil service of the EU, but in many respects it is dependent upon national administrations for the actual day-to-day implementation of the policies of the Union. It is not a fully fledged executive or government. Moreover, like the European Parliament, the Commission continues to have a more restricted role in the two intergovernmental pillars of the EU, concerned with foreign policy and some areas of cooperation in home affairs.

The fourth institution is the Court of Justice which has the task under Article 220 EC of ensuring that the law is observed. It has been assisted since 1989 by a Court of First Instance, creation of which was provided for in the Single European Act. The Court has been responsible for developing the EU legal system in ways that were doubtless not imagined by the founders of the Treaties. Much of Part V will be concerned with explaining in detail those features which distinguish the European Union from an 'ordinary' international organisation, and which make the legal system operating in particular in relation to the 'Community' or 'first' pillar more akin to that of a federal state. This point will be sketched out initially in the overview of the EU legal order in 1.5. The Court has also been active in ensuring that within the 'Community' pillar itself the rule of law is applied, but it has been hitherto almost entirely excluded from exercising a judicial function within the second and third pillars. However, while it continues to play no role in relation to CFSP, since the transformation of the third pillar by the Treaty of Amsterdam from Cooperation in Justice and Home Affairs to Police and Judicial Cooperation in Criminal Matters, the Court now enjoys a restricted role in that field under Article 35 TEU. It also has a very restricted role in relation to the common provisions of the Treaty on European Union (Articles 1–7 TEU), with its scrutiny role limited to Article 6(2) TEU which provides for fundamental rights protection. This question will be discussed in Part IV on 'Values and Principles in the EU Constitutional Framework'. Part VI examines the system of judicial control of the legality of legislative and administrative acts adopted by the institutions of the Union. This is one area in which the EU can rightly claim to have emulated in large measure the characteristics of the highly evolved legal systems of its Member States.

1.3 The Mission of the European Union

Broad statements of the aims, goals and values of the European Community and the European Union are to be found in the Preambles and introductory sections of the founding Treaties. Article 1 TEU recalls the long-standing commitment in the Preamble to the EEC Treaty to the creation of an ever closer union among the peoples of Europe, and identifies the creation of the Union as a new stage in this process, one 'in which decisions are taken as openly as possible and as closely as possible to the citizen'. The task is 'to organise, in a manner demonstrating consistency and solidarity, relations between the Member States and between their peoples'. The Union has the following objectives (Article 2 TEU):

'– to promote economic and social progress and a high level of employment and to achieve balanced and sustainable development, in particular through the creation of an area without internal frontiers, through the strengthening of economic and social cohesion and through the establishment of economic and monetary union, ultimately including a single currency...;

– to assert its identity on the international scene, in particular through the implementation of a common foreign and security policy including the progressive framing of a common defence policy, which might in time lead to a common defence...;

to strengthen the protection of the rights and interests of the nationals of its Member States through the introduction of a citizenship of the Union;

– to maintain and develop the Union as an area of freedom, security and justice, in which the free movement of persons is assured in conjunction with appropriate measures with respect to external border controls, asylum, immigration and the prevention and combating of crime;

– to maintain in full the *acquis communautaire* and build on it with a view to considering to what extent the policies and forms of cooperation introduced by this Treaty may need to be revised with the aim of ensuring the effectiveness of the mechanisms and the institutions of the Community.'

The specifically socio-economic aspects of these aims are further elaborated in Articles 2, 3, 4 and 6 EC. Article 2 sets the European Community the task of achieving the promotion of harmonious, balanced and sustainable development of economic activities, a high level of employment and social protection, equality between men and women, sustainable and non-inflationary growth, a high degree of competitiveness and convergence of economic performance, a high level of protection and improvement of the quality of the environment, the raising of the standard of living and quality of life, and of economic and social cohesion and solidarity among Member States. The twin means for attaining this task are the creation of a common market and an economic and monetary union, and the implementation of common policies and activities themselves enumerated in Article 3. Article 4 outlines the goal of economic and monetary union, including the creation of a single currency. Article 6 strengthens the provisions of Article 2 and 3 relating to the environment by requiring that environmental protection 'must be integrated into the definition and implementation of the Community policies and activities referred to in Article 3, in particular with a view to promoting sustainable development'. The reference to gender equality in Article 2 is picked up by another mainstreaming provision. Article 3(2) requires that 'in all the activities referred to in this Article, the Community shall aim to eliminate inequalities, and to promote equality, between men and women.'

In the earlier stages of the EU's development, the substantive law has comprised, above all, the law of the common market, which has been developing steadily since 1958. For present purposes, we can take the common market referred to in Article 2 as practically identical to the 'internal market' defined in Article 14 EC, the achievement of which was the official central objective of the old European Economic Community between 1986 and the end of 1992. This provides that:

'The internal market shall comprise an area without internal frontiers in which the free movement of goods, persons, services and capital is ensured in accordance with the provisions of this Treaty.'

The goal appears, therefore, to be a free market ideal that, as far as possible, the territory of the fifteen Member States should resemble a single national market, where there is a level competitive playing field for all economic actors and where distortions of competition based on artificial legal barriers such as differences in consumer protection or environmental regulation will be eliminated.

Article 3(1) EC in turn gives more details on the activities that are to be pursued with a view to attaining this goal. These include the creation of a customs union, involving the abolition of internal customs duties on trade in goods and the erection of a common external tariff and a complementary common policy on external trade, the abolition of other obstacles to trade in goods, measures to achieve the free movement of services, persons and capital between the Member States and measures concerned with the entry and movement of persons. These are essentially negative measures, in that they promote integration by removing existing barriers. Positive integration measures include the establishment of common policies, in fields such as agriculture and transport; the creation of these policies also reveals a certain *dirigiste* element in the thinking of the founders of the Treaty, alongside the commitment to the free market principles inherent in the four freedoms. The commitment to a policy on the harmonisation of national legislation also demonstrates a recognition that deregulated markets alone will not bring about the creation of a single internal market which respects the interests of consumers and the environment, to name but two interests which may be sacrificed in unfettered free market competition. In addition, although subsequent amendments to the original Treaty have brought regional policy goals of social and economic cohesion and solidarity within the remit of the EU's prescribed activities, there is no clear commitment in Article 3(1) (EC) to a general social policy, as a complement to the economic policies described above. However, particularly with the effective conclusion of the substantial legislative programme to complete the internal market by the end of 1992, the focus of law making has shifted more into the fields of social policy, consumer policy and environmental policy. Article 3(1) also refers to a number of flanking policies where the EU is to make 'a contribution' or to 'promote' or 'encourage' policy, highlighting its secondary role in policy making. These include research and technological development, health protection, education and training and the 'flowering of the cultures of the Member States'.

It is useful to pause briefly to consider the extent to which the EU has achieved some aspects of this 'mission'. The basic framework of a customs union has been in place since the late 1960s for the original Six, and this is a relatively easy framework to replicate each time that the EU has enlarged through further accessions. More challenging was the task of removing the other barriers – state and non-state in origin – to the completion of the single or internal market. This was the challenge associated with the '1992' programme, along with the changes to the Treaties brought about by the Single European Act. Turning legal principle in the Treaties into empirical reality has been a lengthy process, as the Commission's ongoing strategy for the internal market makes clear.

In the economic sphere, the most significant innovation of the last decade for the EU has been the establishment of the timetable for the achievement of economic and monetary union by the Treaty of Maastricht, and the subsequent introduction of the euro as a single currency for eleven Member States on 1 January 1999 (the area often known as 'Euroland' or the 'Eurozone'). Thus far, the substantive law on these aspects of the EU's activities is not as well developed as the law of the common or internal market, along with the complementary activities highlighted in the previous paragraph. In particular, progress towards economic union has not advanced very far. An important direct correlate to EMU are new provisions committing the EU to 'the promotion of coordination between employment policies of the Member States with a view to enhancing their effectiveness by developing a coordinated strategy for employment', contained in Article 3(1)(i) EC. This is because of the need for measured responses to the fiscal disciplines and economic shifts brought about by participation by a Member State in EMU, as well as the endemic levels of high unemployment of the 1980s and 1990s in most European countries. In relation to questions of institutional and constitutional law addressed in this book, the discussion will concentrate on the institutions of monetary and economic union (4.22) and the questions raised by EMU as an instance of flexibility, as a number of Member States have opted out of 'Euroland' in the sense of the single currency, and some of the associated monetary if not economic policies (4.9).

It is interesting to note the gradual historical evolution of these programmatic provisions on the aims and goals of the European Communities and subsequently the European Union. Over the years, the list has gradually expanded, and has moved away from a primary emphasis upon the customs union and the common market towards complementary aims in relation to flanking policies such as the environment or consumer protection. In some cases, the development of a policy has preceded its inclusion in the list in Article 3(1). Environmental policy is perhaps the best example, as it was developed initially in the late 1970s and early 1980s in response to growing ecological concerns, but was only formally included in the Treaties in 1986 by the Single European Act.

1.4 The Contexts of European Union

The discussion of the aims and objectives of the EU in 1.3 has tended to reinforce the centrality of certain socio-economic goals in relation to the activities of the EU as a whole. Placing the EU in a wider context of Europe, and of the global political and economic orders more generally, highlights in addition the political objectives ascribed to the Union in Article 2 TEU. Historically, the EU has always had a broad political mission, which needs to be understood in relation to the violent history of the continent especially in the first half of the twentieth century. Joseph Weiler captured this mission very effectively, when he characterised the EC (and later the EU) as pursuing the ideals of peace, prosperity and a form of 'supranationalism' which encapsulates a departure from a narrow and debilitating nationalism, and reinforces the idea of the European Union as 'community' (Weiler, 1994a). One outcome of the crisis in Kosovo in 1999 (and in a more general sense an outcome of the Balkan conflicts throughout the 1990s resulting from the break-up of Yugoslavia, which involved four wars in eight years and countless atrocities against civilians) has been the reinforcement of these historical ideals of the Community/Union. The ideals have evolved into a more concrete policy of promoting stabilisation and reconstruction. As one Commission document puts it, 'the EU is *itself* a model for overcoming conflict and promoting reconciliation through close cooperation to achieve common goals' (Commission, 1999a: emphasis added). Newspaper comment would have it that the USA largely paid for the bombing of Serbia and Kosovo, a programme of military activity instituted for the purposes of achieving the political objective of persuading Serbia to accord political autonomy to Kosovo and to cease its policy of ethnic cleansing. In other words, the USA paid for the process of destruction. In turn, the European Union has been and will be, for the foreseeable future, paying for much of the process of reconstruction, both in economic and monetary terms but also in political terms as the EU tries to bring values of peace, democracy and respect for fundamental rights to South Eastern Europe as a whole. This has crystallised into a new type of external activity in the form of actively promoting processes of stabilisation and association with the EU of the countries of the

Former Yugoslavia (Croatia, Bosnia, the Federal Republic of Yugoslavia and the former Yugoslav Republic of Macedonia) and Albania and termed the 'Stabilisation and Association Process'. Even the long-term prospect of accession is opened up. It is an activity which ties the EU and its Member States to numerous other countries and international organisations who are 'stakeholders' in the process (a meeting of thirty-eight countries and fifteen international organisations formally endorsed the Stability Pact for South Eastern Europe). The Stability Pact is a long-term programme of conflict prevention (3.12). The Stabilisation and Association Process is the EU's main contribution to the Stability Pact.

This presentation of the work of the EU appears to give it a grandiose status in the wider Europe. The conflation of 'some aspects of the collective political and economic life of the western, northern and southern European states now organised in something rather misleadingly called the European Union' (Garton Ash, 1999: 180) with 'Europe' as a wider geographical and geopolitical entity has been the subject of criticism. Garton Ash terms this conflation somewhat ironically the question of 'EU-rope'. It is part, he says, of a historical tendency by politicians to instrumentalise 'Europe' for the pursuit of national ends. In the UK, this takes the form of rigidly separating 'Britain' and 'Europe' or 'the continent', to reinforce a 'them and us' division. In France and Germany, by contrast, the national and the European are intertwined and conflated to such an extent that 'it is almost impossible to distinguish when [politicians] are talking about Europe and when about their own nations' (Garton Ash, 1999: 181). So quite apart from debates within the EU itself about the costs and benefits of taking a more active role in processes of stabilisation and reconstruction, it is also important to note a wider discussion about the idea of 'one Europe' or indeed 'several Europes' in which the role of 'EU-rope' as it currently operates (and as it will be presented in this book) is regarded as problematic. Can the EU become a bigger 'club' without changing its nature? What of the acute diversity and sometimes painful historical legacies which need to be taken into account during the enlargement process, as well as nuts and bolts questions about redesigning the institutions for more Member States and assimilating new Member States into the internal market, the single currency, the area of freedom, security and justice and the common policies in areas such as agriculture, the environment and competition. What, indeed, about the many people to whom it is 'EU-topia' to quote the title of a TV documentary programme broadcast in the UK in April 2000, focusing upon the many migrants – refugees, asylum-seekers and others – to whom 'EU-rope' remains a promised land. What measured response can come from the EU on this question, which is more than a knee-jerk reaction against outsiders?

Beyond the specific context of identifying 'Europe' and the consequent role of the EU, there are a number of important *institutional*, *economic* and *political* contexts in which the EU is nested as an organisation based on treaties. There is, for example, an increasingly complex framework of intergovernmental organisations existing both to facilitate cooperation between states and also to pursue common political and economic goals, but stopping short of engaging in the processes of integration of states, economies and political and legal institutions characteristic of the EU. Some are 'global' in nature (although the United Nations itself is not discussed in what follows since that would shift the focus towards the domain of general international law and international relations), and others are limited to the European domain. The principal ones with direct relevance to the evolution and work of the EU are:

- The Council of Europe, established in 1949 to foster political, social and cultural cooperation between European states, and its most significant Treaty-based emanation, the European Convention on Human Rights and Fundamental Freedoms (ECHR). It is important not to confuse this body and its institutions with the EU. The institutions operating under the ECHR, to which all the Member States and the candidates for membership of the EU are signatories, are the Commission and Court of Human Rights, and these are based in Strasbourg. Membership of the Council of Europe is a minimum prerequisite for accession to the EU. Note that the Court of Justice of the European Communities, and the Court of First Instance, are based in Luxembourg.
- The Organisation for Economic Co-operation and Development (OECD), established in 1948 as the Organisation for European Economic Co-operation (OEEC), was originally based in Europe alone but now includes the other principal industrialised states. It exists to encourage economic cooperation and to coordinate development assistance to less developed countries. It is under the aegis of the OECD that the so-called G7 group of leading industrialised countries operates; it has now expanded to eight to include Russia. The OECD was responsible for establishing the European Bank for Reconstruction and Development (EBRD) in 1990 which supports the process of reconstructing the economies and infrastructures of the former communist countries. It has fostered cooperation in areas such taxation and labour market studies. Its headquarters are in Paris.
- The General Agreement on Tariffs and Trade (GATT) and the World Trade Organisation (WTO). The former was originally established in 1948 as a Treaty laying down rules governing international trade and facilitating a process of gradual dismantlement of barriers to free trade, and has been elaborated through a series of 'rounds' culminating in the Uruguay Round of 1986–93 which reformulated the old GATT into the new GATT, added some significant new agreements on services and intellectual property rights, and established the WTO itself as the institutional

basis for promoting and enforcing increased global free trade. The WTO came into being on 1 January 1995. There is an elaborate dispute settlement mechanism enforcing free trade rules which are not dissimilar to the EU's own rules, and which is gradually shifting the emphasis of this international organisation from intergovernmental cooperation towards a system of economic integration. Most significant trading countries with market-based economies are members of the WTO which had 136 members in 2000; Russia and China have been seeking membership for a number of years, but still remain outside, although the EU is sympathetic to their applications to join. The WTO is based in New York and Geneva.

- The West European Union (WEU) (1955), the North Atlantic Treaty Organisation (NATO) (1949), and the Organisation for Security and Cooperation in Europe (OSCE) (1975) are the principal organisations in the field of security and defence cooperation, and they each interact with each other and with the EU's own CFSP. The most powerful of these organisations is undoubtedly NATO, which provides the framework through which the United States is in effect the ultimate guarantor of peace and security in Europe. It has recently enlarged to include some former communist countries which are also seeking to become members of the EU (Poland, Hungary and the Czech Republic: 1999). The WEU is a more limited organisation which was originally established as an intergovernmental framework within which Germany could rearm after the Second World War, and which is partly incorporated into CFSP itself as the possible basis for increased future defence cooperation. The OSCE is a wider intergovernmental body with fifty-five members and seven partner states which is particularly concerned with promoting human rights and humanitarian values. It has played a role in dealing with conflicts in the former Yugoslavia and the former Soviet Union, and monitoring commitments by states to adhere to human rights and the rule of law. It has no enforcement powers. However, as a framework for discussion and dialogue and the promotion of liberal values it did play a role in diffusing some of the Cold War tensions through the 1970s and 1980s.

The process of economic and political integration in Europe is but one example of the wider phenomenon of 'regional integration' (see McCormick, 1999: 20–29 for a summary). Other examples are to be found in North America (North American Free Trade Association comprising the USA, Canada and Mexico) and Latin America (the Mercosur comprising Argentina, Brazil, Paraguay and Uruguay), and other parts of the world. The five Nordic countries (Denmark, Finland, Iceland, Norway and Sweden) have developed the Nordic Council, with the objectives of harmonisation of national laws, abolition of passport controls, common positions at international conferences and the development of joint ventures. The EU – as an 'experimental Union' (Laffan, O'Donnell and Smith, 2000) – is the first geographically and geopolitically significant bloc of countries displaying a higher degree of heterogeneity in economic, political and cultural terms to have taken the process so far beyond the core economic functions of constructing a common market and to have established complex supranational institutional structures. Yet as we shall see throughout this book, its capacity to expand further and even to carry forwards its current agenda is doubted by some. As the heterogeneity grows, the challenges become more complex and sometimes intractable. Moreover, the EU does not exist in isolation. For example, ideas about a 'common defence' are rendered infinitely more complex by the existence and continuing role of NATO, and the dominant American presence in guaranteeing European security.

A more general context for the EU is its relationship with the phenomena of 'globalisation' and 'internationalisation'. To some, the EU is both an incipient superpower in a political sense, contributing to emerging patterns of 'global governance' of which the intervention in Kosovo is one good example, and also a bulwark against the threatening processes of globalisation. While globalisation remains a highly contested term, it is said to be manifested by the 'ever-increasing global interconnectedness of people, places, capital, goods and services' (Axtmann, 1999: 2). Within the spheres of politics, the economy, technology, law and culture, levels of interconnectedness and internationalisation do vary dramatically, but processes such as the development of global financial markets allowing the instantaneous movement of huge capital sums across the world have called into question the capacity of nation states to exercise true economic sovereignty. The EU's own capacity to exercise economic sovereignty is in turn called into question by the development of a global trading order under the framework of the World Trade Organization (see Chapter 7).

The emphasis upon the macro political and economic contexts of EU should not conceal the continuing importance of the domestic dimension of European integration. The EU's Treaties and the activities of the EU's own institutions continue to be based upon and draw much of their legitimacy from the nation states themselves and their legal and political systems. National politics and institutions within the Member States are being 'Europeanised', but internal domestic debates, conditions and constraints are equally significant in determining the outcomes of bargaining and negotiation between the Member States, and within and between the EU institutions. In this book, the national *legal* dimension will be discussed in particular detail in Part V, and the national *constitutional* dimension will be touched upon in Chapter 5 and Part III on values and principles. The example of the controversy in Austria and across the EU generated by the inclusion of the populist Freedom Party in the governing coalition in early 2000 is drawn upon in particular in Part IV of the book.

1.5   Key Terms

It will already be apparent from the preceding paragraphs that there is a distinctive language of European integration. This section aims to demystify certain key concepts, some of which have already been mentioned, such as integration, intergovernmentalism, polity and sovereignty. It also provides a brief account of some of the main political and theoretical positions taken on the process of European integration, although clearly a detailed discussion of these questions goes beyond an introductory book on the legal framework of the EU such as this one (see the list of further reading for additional guidance). Two sets of terms should be distinguished. First there are those used to describe *political movements*, for example, in favour of, or against, more or less integration or in relation to specific dimensions of integration such as Economic and Monetary Union or a common defence policy. These offer a variety of different political readings of the achievements and current 'state' of the European Union. Second there are *academic understandings* of the process of integration and of how the European Union works as a 'polity' and as a system of governance. Such academic positions often offer theories which seek to explain what has happened in the past and to predict what might happen in the future. They are sometimes combined with a political position, which can cause confusion for those studying the EU.

Federalism has cast a shadow over the evolution of the European Union in very significant ways. The terms *federation* or *federal union* are commonly used to describe a sovereign state where power is divided between a central authority and a number of regional authorities. The basis for the division of power is generally to be found in a Constitution. Federal states are well known in the modern world: they include the United States, Canada and the Federal Republic of Germany. Sometimes federal states break up; this has happened recently in case of the Soviet Union and Yugoslavia, and, in Canada since the 1980s, *Québecois* nationalists within the Province of Quebec have argued for unilateral secession from the federation.

Within the European Union, federalism has been propounded as one of a number of different methods for achieving the goal of an integrated Europe. Commonly federalists are seen as the 'radicals' advocating the rapid transition to a sovereign United States of Europe, with the relinquishing of sovereignty on the part of the Member States. A single central government would swiftly assume responsibility for the core activities typically pursued by a federal authority: foreign policy, defence and security, external trade and representation in international organisations, internal security and home affairs, management of the currency, macroeconomic policy, and matters concerned with citizenship. Such a federal authority would incorporate the key features of the modern democratic state, including in particular a legislature elected on the basis of universal suffrage. A judicial authority would mediate conflicts within the federal authority and between the federal authority and the constituent states on the scope of their respective spheres of power, basing its resolution of disputes on a constitutional document. The term federalism has in fact never appeared in the EU Treaties, although it was suggested for inclusion in the opening article of the Treaty on European Union when it was first adopted in 1991. Eventually, the term was eradicated at the instance of the UK delegation. The pursuit of a federalist outcome to the ongoing European integration process is essentially a *political movement*, advocated by a minority of political parties within the Member States but, more often, by specialist interest groups such as the Federal Trust in the UK. As the basis for *academic understandings* of European integration, federalism comes most strongly into attempts to explain the nature of the EU legal order where the Court of Justice's *constitutionalisation* of the EU Treaties has created some akin to a federal legal order in which EU law is a supreme source of law (see 1.6). Academic statements on the 'state' of the EU today (see further Chapter 4) more frequently invoke the language of *confederation* or *cooperative federalism* (e.g. Wallace, 1994) to denote both those federal elements of the EU such as the legal framework discussed in this book, the budgetary arrangements and the role of the directly elected European Parliament, as well as the substantial interpenetration of national governments and the EU institutions which has occurred, while at the same time reinforcing the limited functional nature of the transfer of powers to a central authority.

Historically, there have been two dominant academic approaches to understanding and explaining the European integration process, both of which originated in the study of *international relations* – i.e. relations *between* nation states: *neo-functionalism* and *intergovernmentalism*. *Neo-functionalism* has played a role in both practical politics and integration theory literature. It was probably the dominant account, offered in academic literature, of early integration processes, at least up to the mid-1960s when the European Community encountered significant opposition to the deepening of integration. In the political sphere, it also underlay the decision of the founding fathers of the Community such as *Jean Monnet* and *Robert Schuman* to abandon grand federalist projects and to promote instead the adoption of the ECSC Treaty which concentrated simply on putting two strategically important commodities – coal and steel – into the hands of a central authority outside national control. Subsequently they supported the EEC Treaty which, in particular in its original form, had a remit limited to economic integration. The Treaty also gave a powerful role in the determination of policy to the representatives of the Member States in the Council of Ministers. The idea behind neo-functionalism is that sovereign states may be persuaded in the interests of economic welfare to relinquish control over certain areas of policy where it can easily be proven that benefits are likely to flow from a common approach to problem solving. Power is transferred to a central authority which exists at a level above the nation state, and which exercises its powers independently of the Member States – a *supranational* body. However, that transfer of powers is viewed as just part of a continuing process. One level of integration will lead on to the next; a sectoral Treaty dealing with coal and steel leads on to a general Treaty covering all economic sectors; a *customs union* incorporating the removal of internal customs tariffs and the erection of a uniform external tariff leads on to a *common* or *internal market*, with comprehensive free movement for all commodities and factors of production. This in turn creates demands for some mechanism to eradicate the costs and obstacles to trade which result from shifts in the value of money between the different regions of the single market, involving either irrevocably fixed exchange rates, or even a single currency managed by a single central bank (a *monetary union*). Without serious damage to the weaker economies of the union, however, this cannot be effected without a convergence of economic policies, achieved either voluntarily, or through the transfer of macroeconomic powers to a central authority (an *economic union*), and without incorporating elements of a regional policy to ensure an equitable geographical distribution of resources (economic and social cohesion).

This process was termed 'spill-over' by neo-functionalists, and as they have evolved, the European Community and later the European Union have indeed passed through a number of the stages described above, involving progressive transfers of power to them by the Member States. Spill-over has also operated in the extension of the powers of the old European Economic Community out of the purely 'economic' field into other related areas such as environmental and social policy. It has also fuelled the debate about *political union* in the EU. Two aspects of this concept can be identified, one substantive and the other procedural. According to the substantive notion of political union, the EU should exercise political powers which are commensurate with its economic powers. For example, external trade competence should be linked to the introduction of foreign policy cooperation. A concept of citizenship of the Union should be introduced and then developed into a substantive expression of membership of a supranational polity. The Union becomes increasingly the guarantor of *internal* and *external security* for the Member States and citizens, and provides the fundamental guarantees of *constitutional government*, under the *rule of law*. In its procedural meaning, political union demands that the methods by which the transferred socio-economic competence is exercised do not lead to a net decrease in democratic and popular participation in and control of decision-making processes. In the EU, this is associated with calls for the European Parliament to be given greater powers, but also for the national parliaments to be protected *vis-à-vis* the growing power of the executive (i.e. governments) at the national and supranational levels.

If the functionalist logic is followed to its conclusion the supranational authority could, at a certain point, merge into a federal or confederal authority as more and more powers are transferred, and as the mechanisms for exercising these powers become increasingly separated from the nation-state level. In this scenario the sovereign powers of the nation state are shared between the centre and its component parts, and power is exercised at the federal level not by the Member States, but by the autonomous organs of the federation, under the framework of a constitution. This means, in practice, if the traditions of Western liberal democracy are to be maintained, governance by a democratically elected legislature and a government which derives its *legitimacy* from the electoral process, as well as an active public sphere with mature political parties and an effective civil society. Within the EU, the European Parliament is in fact now a democratically elected body, but its legislative powers are still restricted, and it has little power or influence in relation to the Second and Third Pillars of the EU. Power continues, in very large measure, to be exercised by the representatives of the governments of the Member States, meeting as the Council. Pressure to alter this situation in order to remedy a *democratic deficit* within the EU is understandable and logical from a functionalist perspective. On the other hand, since the EU is not a *state* and is unlikely ever to become one in the conventional sense, but rather is a rather ill-defined *polity*, rectifying the democratic deficit at the EU level does not mean simply replicating the parliamentary and divided power systems of the Member States in the EU context. The national dimension of EU democracy will therefore remain significant.

This, in sum, brings together the various phenomena of an *integration* process, linking together institutional and policy development with the key facet of *supranationalism*. To summarise, the essence of supranationalism is found in a gradual transfer of competences to the higher level, and in the evolution of a distinctive form of decision making at the higher level where increasingly decisions are taken on a majoritarian basis, rather than by consensus. This form of supranationalism has been termed 'decisional supranationalism' by Weiler (1981), and has generally been an area in which the Community, and now the Union, has been quite weak, at least until the changes in the decision-making process introduced by the Single European Act, the Treaty of Maastricht and most recently the Treaty of Amsterdam. It can be distinguished from a specifically legal facet to the supranational nature of the Community, which Weiler has termed 'normative supranationalism'. This concerns the authority of the Court of Justice to give binding and authoritative rulings on the nature and effects of EU law, and to fashion a legal system in which EU law takes precedence over national law, often termed the *constitutionalisation of the Treaties*. In that respect, the EC has evolved more rapidly, and it is argued by some that the work of the Court of

Justice has upset the delicate balance between the supranational and *intergovernmental* elements of the Treaties by acting as a *constitutional court*.

An alternative account of the development of the EU can in fact be offered by reference to the notion of *intergovernmentalism*. This term can be used to describe a basic *political position* which stresses that the EU is primarily a creature of its component states and should limit itself either to the types of activities more commonly undertaken by international organisations founded on Treaties, which are characterised by *cooperation* between states rather than by the independent actions of autonomous bodies or institutions and the development of equally autonomous policies, subject to the (supranational) rule of law. The intergovernmental position also tends to seek limits to scope as well as the depth of cooperation, placing a particular emphasis upon the goal of creating a free trading area. It tends to be linked, politically, to support for *free market liberalism*. There have been conflicts throughout the history of the EC and the EU between the proponents of federalism and intergovernmentalism as basic positions on how these bodies should evolve. The policies of Margaret Thatcher and Charles de Gaulle towards what was then the European Community fall into the category of intergovernmentalism, although they were each propounding rather different forms of nationalism as one of the key building blocks of their policies. More recently, it is associated with *Eurosceptic* political positions in the UK, which include arguments in favour of the withdrawal of the UK from the EU. The battle lines are frequently drawn over the concept of national sovereignty, with intergovernmentalists arguing in favour of a Community of states, or at most a union of states, in which state sovereignty is preserved, not a 'union of peoples' as the Preamble to the EC Treaty puts it. Intergovernmentalists will obviously oppose any extension of the supranational powers of the EU, involving the shift of 'Union' matters into the 'Community' pillar, an increased range of Community competence (e.g. more intervention in fields such as social policy), or an enhanced supranational element in the decision-making process through the strengthening of the powers of the Parliament and the extension of majority voting in the Council. In reality, the somewhat hybrid EU – built upon the EC and the second and third pillars – combines elements of both supranationalism and intergovernmentalism in terms of its operation, as a system of integration and cooperation.

As an *academic position*, intergovernmentalism is not intrinsically hostile to the EU, but rather offers a very different explanation as to how and why integration has occurred, and of the driving forces of integration. The key similarity is provided by a focus on explaining both the EU itself and the policies it pursues as the outcomes of bargains between states rather than in terms of the actions of the autonomous institutions of the EU. In part, intergovernmental explanations of European integration need to be understood as a critique of the explanatory inadequacies of neo-functionalism. There have been periods of the history of the EC and now the EU which are hard to explain in terms of a process of incremental spill-over, notably when the French government partially withdrew from participation in the business of the EC in the 1960s until the other Member States agreed to proceed with decision making almost entirely by unanimity in the Council rather than the reaching of qualified majorities as foreseen in the Treaties (see 2.7). More generally, the *eurosclerosis* of the 1970s and early 1980s could be explained by the endemic refusal of the Member States to pursue jointly the agreed objectives of the founding treaties, and – equally – the revitalisation of the integration process after the Single European Act of 1986 and the political agreement on the Commission's White Paper on Completing the Internal Market of 1985 (Commission, 1985) are, on an intergovernmentalist understanding, best explained as a shift in the political preferences of the Member States in response to global economic challenges and domestic political priorities generated by a definitive end to the long postwar boom and rising unemployment. Interestingly, neo-functionalism as a theory of European integration also enjoyed a significant revival in the 1980s and early 1990s on the back of the single market programme, since these political events have also been explained as the product of the political entrepreneurship of the EU institutions, especially the Commission and the person of its President, Jacques Delors. Each theory claims to have the empirical evidence to support its own assertions.

As academic accounts or theories of the process of European integration, what both neo-functionalism and intergovernmentalism have in common is that they provide explanations which are framed in terms of an international relations paradigm of relationships between sovereign states, but with differing perspectives upon the EU as something quite separate from those states or something which is a mere creature of delegation by those states. An alternative approach is to treat the internal politics of the EU as if they were in fact the *domestic politics* of a state or non-state polity, and to use the insights of *comparative* or *national political science* rather than international relations as the basic tools of study. From the perspective of lawyers, what is offered by accounts such as those which characterise the EU as a 'multi-level governance system' and which focus on the various actors within the policy-making process, is an opening to insert a realistic and balanced statement of the role of law and legal institutions in the EU system (Wincott, 1995a; Armstrong and Shaw, 1998; Hunt and Shaw, 2000). Domestic politics accounts also fit well with the urgent need to provide a sound constitutional basis for the European Union, in view of its current crisis of *legitimacy* in the wake of the difficulties over the Treaty of Maastricht. Consequently, theorists of democracy and constitutionalism are increasingly turning their attention towards the European Union. Studies concentrate on the functioning of the EU as a system of governance and upon its values and principles (see Parts II and III of this book). This is often termed the *normative turn* in EU studies.

One of the generally assumed virtues of the EU legal order described in the next paragraph has been its unity, uniformity and cohesive force (Shaw, 1996). The extent to which these basic principles can be sustained in the light of the *widening* (enlargement) and *deepening* (acquisition of new areas of competence, some of which are not directly related to the original economic mission, and which fall under the intergovernmental pillars or are shared between the various pillars) is not wholly clear. An even greater challenge to the current legal order is the increasing proliferation of *flexibility* within the system, and the sustenance given to ideas about *variable geometry*, *Europe 'à la carte'*, or *multispeed Europe*, in which some Member States proceed more quickly towards closer integration than others. The Treaty of Amsterdam made a twin contribution to 'flexible Europe'. It added to the 'unplanned architectural sprawl of flexibility' (Walker, 2000). To the existing opt-out/opt-in framework of EMU in which some countries have already moved to adopt a single currency, while others remain outside through political choice or economic necessity, it added a complex system of flexibility in the field of the free movement of persons and the removal of borders between the Member States. At the same time, the Treaty sought to 'constitutionalise' the use of flexibility in the form of *closer cooperation*, limiting the circumstances in which a group of Member States may go it alone to institute new policies or measures under the Treaties. At least the Treaty of Amsterdam brought to an end one infamous 'opt-out', that negotiated for the UK in the area of social policy by the Prime Minister John Major at the Maastricht IGC.

1.6   An Overview of some Key Elements of the Legal Order of the EU

An overview of any legal system should start with its basic structure, generally to be found in a constitution and associated documents. This is all the more important in the case of a federal-type legal system, where the constitution contains important rules governing the balance between central or federal and regional or state authorities in the law-making sphere, and on the relationship between federal and state law. Neither the European Community nor the European Union is, or can be, of course, explicitly described as a federation, although the legal order which now exists displays certain of the characteristics of a federal system. Nor does it have a constitution as such, but the Court of Justice now describes the founding treaties as the European Community's 'constitutional charter' (Case 294/83 *Parti Ecologiste 'Les Verts'* v. *European Parliament* [1986] ECR 1339 at p. 1365) (see, for more detailed discussion, Chapter 5).

However, much of the 'constitutional law' of the EU is contained not in the Treaties themselves, but in the judicial pronouncements of the Court of Justice which plays a pivotal role in the legal system, and which has a commitment to the pursuit of integration through law. It has consistently given a maximalist interpretation of the authority and effect of EU law, of the regulatory and policy-making competence of the institutions and of its power to control both the institutions and the Member States to ensure that 'the law is observed' (Article 220 EC). Inevitably, therefore, the study of EU law concentrates for much of the time on the work of the Court, but that focus should be tempered by an awareness that using a picture of the EU in which the edifice of EU law as interpreted by the Court is placed at centre stage tends to give the impression that the whole system is more advanced than in fact it is. It also tends to understate the importance of the legislative and regulatory activities of the EU political institutions and the extent to which the institutional practices of those institutions can themselves create 'constitutional conventions' which form part of the corpus of EU constitutionalism. Moreover, it is somewhat misleading to focus on EU law as giving rise, above all, to a normative structure imposing duties on and granting rights to Member States and EU citizens, at the expense of its role, to give just one example, in creating a new supranational regional development policy leading to a substantial redistribution of public resources (Scott, 1995a: xi–xii). The rest of this overview is, notwithstanding these *caveats*, devoted to a brief explanation of the main areas of work of the Court in relation to the building of a constitutionalised order using the Treaties and general principles of law. It begins with a focus on the 'first pillar' – the law of the European Community, in the strict sense, for this has the most developed legal order with extensive judicial control of general constitutional principles and the rule of law.

One of the most important aspects of the Court's contribution has been its characterisation of the relationship between EU law and national law. On this topic, and on the question of the effect of EU law within the domestic legal systems of the Member States, there is little clear guidance in the Treaties themselves. Article 10 EC provides:

'Member States shall take all appropriate measures, whether general or particular, to ensure fulfilment of the obligations arising out of this Treaty or resulting from action taken by the institutions of the Community. They shall facilitate the achievement of the Community's tasks. They shall abstain from any measure which could jeopardise the attainment of the objectives of this Treaty.'

This provision has been described by AG Tesauro in Case C-213/89 *R* v. *Secretary of State for Transport, ex parte Factortame Ltd (Factortame I)* ([1990] ECR I-2433 at p. 2454) as the key to the whole system of remedies which

exists for the enforcement of EU law. In terms of specific enforcement procedures, which can be seen as an extrapolation of the 'duty of Community
loyalty' in Article 10, Articles 226 and 227 EC make it possible for the Commission and other Member States to bring infringing Member States before
the Court of Justice, and Article 228 EC gives the Court the power to make a
declaration stating that there has been an infringement and requiring the
Member State to take measures to put an end to the infringement. Financial
penalties for non-compliance were introduced by the Treaty of Maastricht,
although these have yet to be used in practice. These measures allow for the
'direct enforcement' of EU law. They give no hint, however, that the obligations undertaken by the Member States under the Treaties they have signed
are relevant at any level other than that of international law, which is primarily a law between and about states and international institutions with minimal applicability to individuals. Individuals do not have recourse to the provisions in Articles 226 and 227 either to enforce EU law directly against the
Member States themselves, or to force the Commission or another Member
State to do this on their behalf. In fact, in an exercise of remarkable judicial
creativity (Mancini, 1989), the Court of Justice has consistently distanced
the EU legal system from 'ordinary' international law, arguing that by accession to the EU the Member States have transferred sovereign rights to the
Community, creating an autonomous legal system in which the subjects are
not just states, but also individuals. The Court has given effect to this view by
enunciating four key principles:

– EU law penetrates into the national legal systems, and can and must be
  applied by the national courts, subject to authoritative rulings on the interpretation, effect and validity of EU law by the Court of Justice; in other
  words, the duty of 'Community loyalty' or 'fidelity' provided for in Article
  10 applies to courts as well as to other organs of the Member States such
  as the government and the legislature;
– in this context individuals may rely upon rules of EU law in national
  courts, as giving rise to rights which national courts are bound to protect
  (the principle of 'direct effect');
– in order to guarantee the effectiveness of this structure, EU law takes precedence over conflicting national law, including national constitutional
  provisions (the principle of 'supremacy' or 'primacy').
– the organs and constituent bodies of the Member States, including the
  legislative, executive and judiciary, are fully responsible for reversing the
  effects of violations of EU law which affect individuals. This may, for example, involve the courts ordering the government to pay damages for
  loss caused by breach of EU law.

The Court has given an extensive task to the national courts which are responsible for ensuring what is often termed the 'indirect enforcement' of

EU law at the instance of individuals. It has stressed the binding nature of EU law, including not only the Treaties themselves, but also those acts of the institutions (regulations, directives and decisions), to which binding effects are ascribed in Article 249 EC. These can, where appropriate, be enforced by individuals in national courts, if their provisions are justiciable (i.e. sufficiently precise and clear). It has also stressed that the European Union itself is bound by norms of international law, in particular where they are contained in Treaties which the EU (or in strict legal terms one of the Communities) itself has concluded with third countries or international organisations as an international actor exercising legal personality, or where the EU has succeeded to the international Treaty obligations of the Member States. Finally, it has articulated a body of superordinate principles, 'general principles of law', which govern the activities of the EU institutions and of the Member States acting within the sphere of Community competence, and which include not only fundamental rights, but also procedural principles such as proportionality and legal certainty. These are not as such to be found in the Treaties but are in fact further products of the remarkable judicial creativity of the Court which has developed a body of individual rights and principles of administrative legality which ensure the application of the rule of law within the EU legal system. The Treaties, the acts of the institutions, binding norms of international law including international Treaties, the general principles of law, and the case law of the Court itself together constitute the body of sources of EU law.

The key to the structure of indirect enforcement lies in the organic connection between the Court of Justice and the national courts in Article 234 EC. This provides that national courts may, and in certain circumstances must, refer to the Court of Justice questions on the interpretation and validity of provisions of EU law where such questions are raised in the context of national litigation and the national court considers a reference necessary in order to enable it to give judgment. National courts must refer questions of doubt regarding the application of EU law to the Court in two situations: first, where the national court is one of last resort; second, where it is the validity of a rule of EU law which is in doubt. Only the Court of Justice has the power to invalidate a rule of EU law. The preliminary ruling procedure has limits, and it depends for its effectiveness on cooperation between national courts and the Court of Justice. It is not an appeal by the parties to the Court of Justice. The power to ask for a ruling lies solely with the national court, and the legislative and political authorities of the Member States may not interfere with the exercise of discretion. Correlatively, the Court of Justice does not have the power in the context of a preliminary ruling hearing to invalidate a provision of national law. It cannot even formally make a declaration of incompatibility with EU law, as it can in the context of Articles 226–228 EC. It is limited to an interpretation of EU law. However, the manner in which the Court of Justice has often chosen to frame its rulings has given little choice to the referring court but to apply EU law in preference to national law, and in effect to invalidate provisions of national law. This duty flows from Article 10 for the national court, and it is a duty which gives rise to some difficulty in the context of the UK where the principle of parliamentary sovereignty leads judges conventionally to regard themselves as subordinate to the will of Parliament. The European Communities Act 1972 attempts, if only imperfectly, to resolve the difficulties raised by membership of the EU in conventional constitutional doctrine. In summary, therefore, the Court has constructed a system which comes close to the power conventionally held by the supreme court in a federal system, namely the power to invalidate state legislation which contravenes the federal constitution. Examples of the interaction of the various enforcement mechanisms, such as the litigation regarding the Merchant Shipping Act 1988 in the UK (*ex parte Factortame*) will be discussed in Chapters 8, 12 and 13.

In addition to controlling the exercise of sovereign power by the Member States, the Court also acts as the judge of the proper exercise of sovereign power by the European Community, and as an umpire in disputes regarding legislative authority between the institutions and between the EU's political organs and the Member States. This form of control likewise operates both directly in the Court and indirectly in litigation before the national courts. It will be seen from the above that individuals are not restricted in the national courts simply to asserting their EU law rights against the Member States. An individual may in addition question the validity of an act of an EU institution in the context of national litigation, and a national court which is minded to accept that allegation must refer a question to the Court for a ruling on validity. There are broadly two reasons why an individual might seek to challenge a rule of EU law. First, it may be unlawful because of its effects upon the complainant as an individual or part of group (e.g. a particular class of economic actors such as the producers of a particular commodity). In this context, the Court of Justice may make reference to the fundamental rights of the affected group when ascertaining the legality of an EU act. Second, the complainant may argue that the act is in breach of some more general rule of legality or constitutionality, e.g. the manner in which the act was adopted was in breach of the Treaty rules, it may fall outside the competence of the institution which adopted it, or it may fall outside Community competence altogether.

It is also possible to mount such a challenge directly in the Court of Justice itself, although there are strict restrictions on the standing of individuals under the provisions of Articles 230 and 232 EC which provide for the judicial review of unlawful acts and the unlawful failure to act on the part of the institutions. Member States, the Commission, the Council and, within limits, the European Parliament may also use Article 230 in order to seek the annulment of EU acts adopted by another institution. Through its decisions on such actions the Court of Justice has been concerned to construct a body of principles which delineate the powers of the institutions *inter se*, and of the Member States and the Community, respectively. This is another area in which the Treaty, aside from setting out procedural rules which govern the legislative process and outlining minimum prerequisites of validity for EU acts such as a statement of reasons, does not provide much assistance to the Court. The tendency of the Court has been to interpret the powers of the Community broadly: the institutions are given certain tasks by the Treaties, and the Court has consistently held that they must be regarded as having either express or implied powers to carry out these tasks. Thus there is no explicit reserved area of sovereign powers for the Member States. However, the precise delineation of the powers of the States and of the Union remains a difficult area, as Chapter 6 will show. The advent of the principle of subsidiarity as a new criterion defining the relationship between the EU and the Member States, which may be justiciable before the Court, introduces a new range of challenges for the Court of Justice.

This outline has been limited to reviewing the legal order of the first pillar, that is, the 'European Community' in the strict legal sense. It has constructed a picture of unity and cohesion running through the legal order, which is in fact partially undermined by the proliferation of systems of flexible integration such as EMU. Issues of flexibility, which have already been commented upon briefly in 1.5, will represent an underlying theme of many chapters, especially those parts of Chapter 5 dealing with the pillar system and the constitutional principles of the EU. In addition, it is important to conclude this outline by stepping beyond the confines of the first pillar, which has traditionally been the EU lawyer's primary domain. The writ of supremacy, direct effect and the 'constitutionalised treaty' more generally do not run in the second and third pillars. The forms of secondary 'law' provided for in relation to Common Foreign and Security Policy (common strategies, common positions and joint actions) and Police and Judicial Cooperation in Criminal Matters (common positions, framework decisions, decisions and conventions) cannot, for example, give rise to justiciable rights for individuals. National laws implementing such EU measures could, of course, give rise to justiciable rights, but these would arise under national not EU law. There is no equivalent to Articles 10 and 226–228 EC allowing the Commission to pursue proceedings against non-conforming Member States, although there is limited involvement of the Court of Justice in the third pillar after the Treaty of Amsterdam. The Court has limited jurisdiction under Article 35 TEU, including the possibility of references for preliminary rulings from national courts and the capacity to review the legality of as well as to interpret certain measures taken under Title VI TEU (the third pillar) which will inevitably lead the Court to review the provisions of that Title more generally. On the other hand, in relation to a proliferation of legal practices such as the evolving institutional framework, international representation and the application of general principles such as transparency, it is an oversimplification to regard the first pillar as crudely separated from the second and third pillars. It may be still be a legal order of 'bits and pieces' as Curtin famously commented in 1993 (Curtin, 1993), but it is ever more a single legal order, with unified institutions, legal structures, values and principles. In relation to that single legal order the Court of Justice performs an important cohesive, if still limited, function, operating in some domains as a constitutional court adjudicating between the various elements within the EU, including the institutions and the Member States, while upholding the 'rule of law'.

In view of all the many changes to the overall framework of the EU legal order since the early 1990s, including the institution and impact of the Treaty on European Union and the subsequent amendments in the Treaty of Amsterdam, the 2000 IGC, and the challenges of further enlargement especially towards the east, it seems wise to suggest that in ten years' time the EU legal order may appear very different to how it is at present.

1.7   Legal Literature

Primary sources (treaties, legislation, case law, other official documentation) for the study of EU law are now readily available on the Internet, via the general Europa website (see below for details of key websites; details are also given of the other websites and sources discussed in this paragraph). In practice, it is more convenient to have access to the founding Treaties of the European Communities and the European Union and a selection of the most important secondary legislation in paper format. Useful collections include Blackstone's *EC Legislation* (Foster, 1999) and Rudden and Wyatt, *Basic Community Laws* (Rudden and Wyatt, 1999). Historically, other EU official information used to be available via European Documentation Centres (EDCs), located most frequently in University Libraries. Although EDCs still exist, and will carry a vast amount of useful official information, in practice most recently published official documents are likely to be available through *Europa*, or via a commercial interface with *CELEX*, the EU's official database such as those provided by Justis or Lovdata against subscription. If you are a student at a university, you may be able to access such an interface via your university library catalogue or homepage, although the database is likely to be available on password access only. This is true also for the EU's own gateway to CELEX on *Europa*.

It is important to obtain a knowledge of the EU's own system of official documentation. Much official documentation is available through the *Official Journal* (OJ), which provides the only authentic version of documents such as new Treaties or binding legislation. The 'L' series carries the legislative acts adopted by the institutions. The 'C' series contains preparatory documents, non-binding acts such as resolutions and recommendations, reports of the activities of the European Parliament, the Economic and Social Committee, and the Committee of the Regions, brief details pertaining to the work of the Court of Justice and long lists of agricultural prices. The OJ is now available for 45 days after publication on *Europa*, and thereafter on CD-ROM through an EDC or other subscriber. Older copies of the OJ will be available in paper version through the EDC. The EDC will also carry older paper copies of other important official sources such as the *Bulletin of the European Union*, along with its supplements, and the various general and specific annual reports issued by the Commission and bodies such as the European Ombudsman. Again, recent versions will be available through *Europa*. Returning to legislation in force, an important way of accessing this is through *Eur-lex*, a searchable database available through *Europa*. Preparatory measures relating to legislation currently under discussion or recently adopted may also be accessed via the Parliament's *legislative observatory* or a new Commission database called *pre-lex*. Many policy initiatives or ideas are introduced in the form of Commission Communications, White Papers or Green Papers. Many of these are issued as 'COM Docs', i.e. documents of the Commission. The most important papers of this kind are available through *Europa*, either via the section dedicated to official documents, sources of information and databases, or via the website of the Commission Directorate General or Service responsible for the initiative. Alternatively, they will be available through CELEX, or may be available in published form in the EDC, which will also carry the publications of many subsidiary bodies or agencies of the EU (for details of these see Chapter 4). Papers originating from the Council, the European Parliament, the ECOSOC or the Committee of the Region will be found on their respective websites, all accessible via *Europa*. A number of other gateways to official, semi-official and unofficial documentation about the EU are detailed in the list of key websites below. *European Access*, an important bibliographical tool again available only online as of 2000, may be available via your university library or nearest EDC.

The official Law Reports of the European Court of Justice are the *European Court Reports*, which are likely to be held in the EDC of a university library, and/or with the other Law Reports. Since 1997 transcripts of the case law of the Court of Justice have been available via the Court of Justice's website, which also carries the weekly Proceedings of the Court (in a variety of languages although the French version is always the most up to date) and press reports on the most significant cases. In the future, the Court's website will also carry an important research and documentation facility. There remains a substantial publication delay in the production of the European

Court Reports, attributable to translation difficulties. All Court of Justice cases are eventually published in every official language of the European Union. Many of the most important cases are also published more promptly in the (privately published) *Common Market Law Reports* (*CMLR*), the *All England Law Reports* (*All ER*), especially the EC volume, and, where appropriate, specialist Law Reports such as the *Industrial Relations Law Reports* (*IRLR*). Sometimes, these may carry unofficial English language translations.

Extracts from important cases are, of course, to be found in casebooks, a number of which have appeared in the field of EU law. The most useful and up to date are Craig and de Búrca (1998) and Chalmers (1998)/Chalmers and Szyszczak (1998), both of which carry also wide-ranging and stimulating selections of secondary literature, much of which is drawn from non-legal sources.

Not all documents prepared by the EU institutions are published, or made available, of course. Since the inception of the Treaty on European Union, however, *transparency* has become an increasingly important value within the EU. There are frameworks for seeking access to the documents of every EU institution or body, and *Europa* provides details on making application for documents and the rights of EU citizens and others in this respect. Access to documents as a general principle is provided for in Article 255 EC, and those seeking redress against the refusal of access can apply to the Court of First Instance for a judicial remedy (see Chapters 9 and 10 for further details on transparency).

Turning now to *secondary literature*, you will find that in this book each chapter provides lists of selected further readings to which you should refer. As appropriate the list of readings are briefly annotated to offer more specific guidance on what is contained in each selection. There is also a general bibliography containing additional works. One of the main objectives of the book is to make the specialised literature more accessible. Much of the further reading will be found in the core journals in the field: the *European Law Review* (*ELRev*), the *Common Market Law Review* (*CMLRev*), the *Yearbook of European Law* (*YEL*), the *Cambridge Yearbook of European Legal Studies* (*CYELS*), the *European Law Journal* (*ELJ*), the *Maastricht Journal of European and Comparative Law* (*MJ*), and *Legal Issues of European Integration* (*LIEI*). Of the general English journals, the *Modern Law Review* (*MLR*) and the *Oxford Journal of Legal Studies* (*OJLS*) probably publish the most material on EU law. In the domain of international law, the *European Journal of International Law* (*EJIL*) and the *International and Comparative Law Quarterly* (*ICLQ*) both carry substantial amounts of EU law material. Many subject-specific journals now have European sections which offer more detailed coverage (e.g. *Industrial Law Journal* (*ILJ*), *Journal of Social Welfare and Family Law* (*JSWFL*)). In the specific sphere of public law *Public Law* (*PL*) and *European Public Law* (*EPL*) are important resources. Any student pursuing a research project in EU law should consult these journals, as well as the usual legal journals indexes. The European Integration Current Contents service on the Harvard Jean Monnet Chair website (see below) provides access to the tables of contents of journals relevant to work on European integration research, including journals in the fields of law, human rights, economics, history, political science and international relations.

Reference is also made where appropriate in the lists of further reading to discussions in other textbooks or more detailed works of analysis on EU law. These include Weatherill and Beaumont (1999), Lenaerts, van Nuffel and Bray (1999), Lenaerts, Arts and Bray (1999), Hartley (1998) and the books in the Longman European Law Series. Oxford University Press and Hart Publishing also produce numerous detailed works in this field, including edited collections as well as monographs. In relation to constitutionalism in the EU, Weiler (1999a) is an indispensable source. It will become apparent through this book that much of the more recent work on EU law makes use of interdisciplinary approaches to legal studies, and seeks to develop an understanding of the role of law within the wider context of European integration (e.g. Shaw and More, 1995; Armstrong and Shaw, 1998; Alston, 1999; Craig and de Búrca, 1999; Ward, 1996a, 1996b; Snyder, 1990). To this end, the final section of this chapter introduces some of the contributions in the fields of economics, political theory and policy studies which might assist you in making the most of the study of EU law.

1.8   Making the Most of Studying EU Law

In the other social science disciplines, periodical literature on the politics, governance, economics and sociology of the EU is to be found in a great variety of different journals. There are a number of more specialised journals including the *Journal of Common Market Studies*, *West European Politics*, *European Union Politics* and the *Journal of European Public Policy*. The *European Foreign Affairs Review* and *International Organization* also carry many relevant articles. In terms of online resources, the European Research Papers Archive website draws together a number of high quality series of working papers and research papers, and the European Integration Current Contents service offers a useful research resource. As with legal publishing on the EU, recent years have also seen an explosion in social science publishing. This survey can only draw attention to a number of useful basic tools, and it concentrates on work in political science and international relations alone. Works on more specific policy areas are referred to in the further reading sections of individual chapters.

Thorough historical surveys are to be found in Dinan (1999), McAllister (1997) and Urwin (1995), and a useful collection of historical documents is made available in Weigall and Stirk (1992). The relevance of integration theory is highlighted in a number of introductory and more advanced works (e.g. McCormick, 1999; Rosamund, 1999; George, 1996; Sandholtz and Stone Sweet, 1998; Marks *et al.*, 1996). Readings specifically focused on these theories are offered in Nelsen and Stubb (1998) and O'Neill (1996). Increasingly, works aim to set the 'west European experience' of regional integration into a broader European or global context (e.g. Wallace, 1990, 1994; Bulmer and Scott, 1994; Rhodes, Heywood and Wright, 1997; Laffan, O'Donnell and Smith, 2000). The internal workings of the Union and its institutions form the specific focus of a large number of books (e.g. Nugent, 1999a; Hix, 1999; Peterson and Bomberg, 1999; Greenwood, 1997; Richardson, 1996). A number of works by or for political scientists on the Court of Justice and issues of supranational adjudication should be noted (Dehousse, 1998a; Stone Sweet, 2000; compare the works by lawyers such as Arnull, 1999a and by a mixed body of scholars: Slaughter, Stone Sweet and Weiler, 1998). Good general surveys of the policies, politics and economics of the EU include El-Agraa (1998) and Wallace and Wallace (2000). Cram, Dinan and Nugent (1999) offer a summary of recent developments in the EU, with a focus on the institutions and specific policies. Topical issues (e.g. enlargement, democracy, legitimacy, specific policies) are dealt with in a number of other book series such as *Political Dynamics of the European Union* for Longman Press, the UACES series published by Sheffield Academic Press and the *European Public Policy* series for Routledge. The US European Community Studies Association series of biennial publications on *The State of the European Union* has now transferred to Oxford University Press (see Green Cowles and Smith, 2000 for the most recent volume; Hurwitz and Lesquesne, 1991, Cafruny and Rosenthal, 1993, Rhodes and Mazey and Laurent and Maresceau, 1998 are the earlier volumes). As would be expected, the anticipation of and aftermath following intergovernmental conferences and Treaty amendments are the subject of particular attention (e.g. Edwards and Pijpers, 1997; Neunreither and Wiener, 2000), as they are in law also (Winter *et al.*, 1996; Heukels, Blokker and Brus, 1998; O'Keeffe and Twomey, 1994, 1999). The normative turn in EU studies, marked by an increased consideration of issues such as legitimacy, democracy and constitutionalism, is matched by a substantial body of literature (e.g. Lord, 1998; Beetham and Lord, 1998; Føllesdal and Koslowski, 1998; Eriksen and Fossum, 2000; Bellamy and Castiglione, 1996; Weale and Nentwich, 1998).

Summary

This chapter introduces the study of EU law by providing the basic facts and introducing the key tools of analysis which students require. The mission of the EU is to promote integration in Europe, and both the legal and political systems of the EU should be understood in the context of this mission. The EU has to be seen in its institutional and global context. A basic distinction between integration and intergovernmentalism in relation to international cooperation and supranational institutions has been introduced and will be traced through the rest of the book. The EU legal order is *sui generis* and has evolved in the hands of the Court of Justice into a supranational and quasi-federal system where EU law consistently 'trumps' national law. The pillar system complements this system. The chapter also raises a number of questions and poses challenges regarding the study of the EU and its legal order. Ideas and issues raised in this chapter, about the EU institutions and constitutional framework in particular, will be elaborated in later chapters.

Questions

1 What are the 'European Community' and the 'European Union'? Why are these terms misleading and what ambiguities can arise when they are used?
2 What is the EU for?
3 Using the Preamble and introductory sections of the Treaties of Paris and Rome, as well as the SEA, the Treaty of Maastricht and the Treaty of Amsterdam, identify whether and how the basic aims of the EC and the EU have evolved since the beginning. What additional methods for promoting integration have been gradually given to the EC and the EU? To what extent is the integration function now taken over by the European Union (understood in the specific sense of the broader constitutional structure for the EU established by the Treaty of Maastricht and maintained by the Treaty of Amsterdam)? (One of the objectives of this question is to involve you in a search for the relevant documentation in the available literature and on the Internet and in the library.)
4 Define the following terms:
   – federalism
   – supranational
   – intergovernmental
   – flexibility
   What do these definitions tell us about the nature of the EU and the EC?
5 What are the key features of the legal order of the EU?

Further Reading

Full publication details for works such as Craig and G. de Búrca (1999) will be found in the Bibliography. At this stage you may find some of the works cited here difficult or inaccessible. You may find it useful to return to them once more when you have read further through this book.

P. Craig (1999a), 'The Nature of the Community: Integration, Democracy and Legitimacy', in Craig and de Búrca (1999).

L. Cram, D. Dinan and N. Nugent (1999), 'Reconciling Theory and Practice', in Cram, Dinan and Nugent (1999).

D. Curtin (1993), 'The Constitutional Structure of the Union: A Europe of Bits and Pieces', 30 *Common Market Law Review* 17.

U. Everling (1992), 'Reflections on the Structure of the European Union', 29 *Common Market Law Review* 1053.

R. Harmsen (1994), 'A European Union of Variable Geometry: Problems and Perspectives', 45 *Northern Ireland Legal Quarterly* 109.

T. Garton Ash (1999), 'Catching the Wrong Bus?' and 'The Case for Liberal Order'.

J. Hunt and J. Shaw (2000), 'European Union Legal Studies: Then and Now', in Hayton (2000).

S. Kennedy (1998), Ch. 2, 'European Organisations: Intergovernmentalism', and Ch. 3, 'European Integration: From Coal and Steel to European Union' and Ch. 7, 'Where do you Find European Law?'

T. Koopmans (1991a) 'The Birth of European Law at the Crossroads of Legal Tradition', 39 *American Journal of Comparative Law* 493.

J. McCormick (1999), *Understanding the European Union. A Concise Introduction*, London: Macmillan.

G. Mancini (1989), 'The Making of a Constitution for Europe', 26 *Common Market Law Review* 595; also published as Ch. 6 in Keohane and Hoffmann (1991).

F. Snyder (1990), Ch. 1, 'New Directions'.

S. Weatherill (1995a), Ch. 1, 'From Community to Union'.

Key Websites

The lists of websites in this chapter and the chapters that follow should be treated as guidance only. There is no guarantee that the URL given will still be correct even days after it was checked. This is meant primarily as a guide to what is available.

The EU's *Europa* website is the basic starting point:
http://europa.eu.int/
for the English language index:
http://europa.eu.int/index-en/htm

Sources of EU law on *Europa* or elsewhere:
http://europa.eu.int/eur-lex/en/index.html
http://europa.eu.int/eur-lex/en/oj/index.html
http://europa.eu.int/abc/off/index_en.htm
http://europa.eu.int/celex
http://www.justis.com/database/celex.html

Guides, gateways, starting points and research resources for EU law and EU studies:
http://www.pitt.edu~wwwcs/
http://eiop.or.at/euroint/
http://library.ukc.ac.uk/library/netinfo/intnsubg/lawlinks.htm
http://www.leeds.ac.uk/ces/cuinfo.htm
http://www.eurunion.org/cgi-bin/frames.cgi?infores/resguide.htm
http://ciop.or.at/crpa
http://www.law/harvard.edu/programs/JeanMonnet/TOC/index.html
http://www.ex.ac.uk/~pcovery/lib/eurostudies.html

2 Evolving from Community to Union

2.1 Introduction

The title and the text of this chapter and the one which follows seek to emphasise the dynamic and changing nature of first the European Community and then, later, the European Union and to highlight the fact that the processes of integration within Europe have not yet reached a conclusion or final stage of evolution. A basic knowledge of the history of the EC and the EU offers a number of benefits to the student:

- it gives a context to contemporary events, demonstrating that the current debates on the integration process have a long pedigree, and that ideas such as monetary union or political union are not simply novelties dreamt up by Jacques Delors in the late 1980s;
- it puts the EU firmly in the context of other developments within and outside Europe, recognising the significance for the EU of events such as the unification of Germany, the end of the Cold War, the break up of the Soviet Union, the emergence of new democracies in Eastern and East Central Europe, as well as the economic context of the global trading order under the World Trade Organisation;
- it highlights the ebbs and flows of the European Community and Union, which have coincided quite closely with the low and high points of the European economy since the Second World War;
- finally, the stop–start progress of political and economic integration emphasises the unparalleled contribution made by the Court at crucial points. Yet although the Court has been characterised as the 'engine of integration', when the events discussed in this chapter are reviewed subsequently in the context of developments in the EC legal system which form the main focus of this book, it will be seen that the work of the Court of Justice has not always run parallel to the political and economic evolution of the Treaties. In particular, sometimes there has been a fit and sometimes a misfit between political context and legal action; more often there appears to be a lag of some years between the point when work begins towards a new goal in the sphere of policy or politics and correspondingly significant progress in the construction of the EU legal framework.

The disadvantage of a summary account of the historical evolution of the EC and the EU is, of course, that it tends to suggest that there can be a linear account of this history. In fact, of course, different issues have evolved at very different speeds, and it is becoming increasingly difficult to provide a single account which stresses both the coherence of the effects of specific events such as Treaty amendments and the coherence of issues such as foreign and defence policy or justice and home affairs policy, which have evolved through a series of IGCs. Inevitably, the following account is severely constrained by the available space; additional elaboration upon the events and ideas discussed here can be found in the lists of further reading which follow at the end of these chapters. This chapter takes the narrative from the origins of the European integration process through to the conclusion and ratification of the Treaty of Maastricht. Chapter 3 picks up the story by presenting the key changes to the framework of European integration brought about by that Treaty, and carries on through the implementation of aspects of that Treaty to the preoccupations dominating the work of the EU in the year 2000.

2.2   The Roots of European Integration

Although it would be wrong to characterise current developments in European integration as the direct descendants of earlier ideas and proposals, it is none the less of interest that the idea of a unified Europe is by no means new. The model of a Europe brought together not by military conquest, but in common pursuit of higher goals of peace, prosperity and stability has attracted the attention of thinkers since the Middle Ages. An institutional form of federal unity in Europe was argued for by prominent intellectuals of the Enlightenment such as Bentham, Rousseau, and later, Saint-Simon. More concrete progress was made in the field of economic integration. The early period of capitalist organisation saw not only the transformation of the means of production and the shift to industrialisation, but also the integration of national markets, often achieved in parallel with national political unity. The next step was the liberalisation of trade between sovereign states, where Britain took a leading role with its commitment to free trade in the middle of the nineteenth century. However, none of the proposals for increased cooperation between states in the economic field, such as a Central European customs union between the Hapsburg empire and the German states in the 1840s, achieved real success, and there was a resurgence of nationalism and protectionism in the late nineteenth century which eventually culminated in the First World War.

The inter-war years saw continued discussion of the ideal of European integration as a better way forward for Europe than destructive interstate rivalry, most notably within the forum of the Pan-European Union founded in 1923 by the Austrian Count Richard Coudenhove-Kalergi. It is perhaps significant that among the pre-war membership of the Union were a number of politicians who played key roles in post-war Europe, including Konrad Adenauer, later Chancellor of the Federal Republic of Germany, and Georges Pompidou, later President of France. However, the influence of the Union did not succeed in saving the only initiative towards European integration of the inter-war years put forward at the governmental level, the Briand Plan of 1929–30, a proposal by the French Foreign Minister for a confederal bond linking the peoples of Europe. The logic behind French foreign policy and the Briand Plan was that of achieving security for France against Germany by tying the latter firmly into a European structure of cooperation. The theme of the 'Europeanisation' of Germany has been an enduring one which has enjoyed a renaissance since unification in 1990. Despite the modest nature of the proposals, the Briand Plan was never taken further because of scepticism and hostility in Britain, Italy and Germany.

2.3   The Postwar Climate of Change

At the end of and just after the Second World War quite different attitudes to the prospects for European unity were apparent. Even before the end of the war, voices calling for a form of unity which would prevent future wars could be heard in the Resistance movements of the occupied countries of continental Europe. Prominent figures in the Resistance movements such as Altiero Spinelli, who re-emerged much later as a champion of European federalism in the European Parliament in the late 1970s and early 1980s, argued for a federal Europe with a written constitution, state institutions such as a government and a Parliament, a judicial system and a common army. Resolutions supporting these propositions were passed at a conference of Resistance representatives held in Geneva in July 1944. It was believed at the time that support for European federalism would also come from Britain, in particular from Winston Churchill, who was popular in federalist circles after his dramatic offer to the French of the creation of a Franco–British union in 1940. The major driving force behind that offer was, moreover, Jean Monnet, who proved to be a key actor in post-war developments.

Churchill's loss of the British premiership with the victory of the Labour Party in the 1945 General Election, and the re-emergence of pre-war political leaders in many European countries at the expense of Resistance leaders, were two factors which contributed to the failure to translate the ideals of federalism into a concrete agenda for action. The immediate imperatives of national economic rebuilding took precedence over the proposal that post-war reconstruction should occur within an entirely new political framework. The danger was present, therefore, that as before the war, the ideas of unity would not take root within the institutions of the state, and that rallying calls such as Churchill's famous speech in Zurich in 1946 and the resolutions of numerous federalist groups gathered at the Congress of Europe at The Hague in 1948 would remain simply extragovernmental expressions of a desirable, but unattainable goal of integration within Europe. However, this view discounts a number of features that distinguished the two situations. These included the increasing closeness of certain key personalities such as Jean Monnet to centres of political power (Monnet had become head of the French Economic Planning Commission and thus was a senior civil servant), the willingness of federal idealists to countenance incremental strategies for achieving integration (the ideas of functionalism outlined in Chapter 1) and a greater global commitment to free trade and economic cooperation, evidenced by the adoption of the General Agreement on Tariffs and Trade (GATT) and the creation of the International Monetary Fund. Last but not least there was the need of the USA for stability in Western Europe in the context of the Cold War which followed hard on the heels of the Second World War and its consequent interest in, and partial sponsorship of, ideas of Western European integration.

In 1947 the USA committed itself to the so-called 'Truman Doctrine' which was a pledge of US support for 'free peoples who are resisting subjugation by armed minorities or by outside pressures'. The Americans had an interest in preventing a destabilising power vacuum in Europe. One outcome of this doctrine was the Marshall Plan to provide economic aid for reconstruction to countries in Europe committed to ideas supported by the USA, aid which, because of the underlying political motivation of the provider, was shunned by the Soviet Union and its allies in Central and Eastern Europe. The allocation, administration and delivery of American aid became the initial preoccupation of the first international organisation in the economic sphere set up in post-war Europe – the Organisation for European Economic Cooperation (OEEC) set up in 1948. The OEEC was a strictly intergovernmental organisation which never succeeded in achieving any of its grander ideals of economic cooperation, but none the less it had a wide membership within Europe and North America (sixteen founder members) which grew much larger when it gave way in 1961 to the Organisation for Economic Cooperation and Development (OECD) which encompasses other Western-style economies such as Australia and Japan (see 1.4).

The broad attractions of a loose intergovernmental form of cooperation were also evident at an early stage in the political field where the grandly styled but rather ineffective Council of Europe was established in 1949 (see 1.4). The proposals for the Council of Europe grew out of the resolutions of The Hague Congress. Although the nature of the Council of Europe has always been bland (Urwin, 1995: 40), and it has consistently avoided controversial issues such as defence and security, it benefits from its symbolic role within Europe, including its role as a forum for discussion, and from the particular association it has acquired with political democracy and human rights. The most significant international instrument to come into being under the aegis of the Council of Europe is the European Convention on Human Rights and Fundamental Freedoms, which came into force in 1953. Membership of the Council and signature of the Convention, while not demanding in the sense of requiring the signatory to relinquish a significant portion of state autonomy of action, have come to be benchmarks of acceptability among Western-style liberal democracies, achieved by countries emerging from dictatorship such as Spain and Portugal in the 1970s and more recently by the even newer democracies of Central and Eastern Europe. As membership of the European Union has come to appear increasingly attractive to a range of European countries, the Council of Europe has become a convenient stepping stone in the process of achieving membership. However, at no time has the Council departed from the intergovernmental consensus-based approach to international cooperation.

Finally, in the military field, cooperation took a distinctly Atlanticist turn with the conclusion in April 1949 of the North Atlantic Treaty tying together the North American states with the European parties to the 1948 Treaty of Brussels – France, the UK and the Benelux countries. Germany was later brought into the Western European Union after the failure of the initiative for a European Defence Community in 1954. In 1955 Germany joined NATO.

2.4   From Grand Ideals to Incremental Stages

A separate chapter in the evolution of integration in Europe was opened in May 1950 with the publication of the Schuman Plan, drawn up, on behalf of the French Foreign Minister Robert Schuman, by Jean Monnet. This Plan was the precursor of the European Coal and Steel Community (ECSC). The text of the Plan neatly encapsulates the small and large visions of European integration, which have marked the evolution of the European Community (Weigall and Stirk, 1992: 58–9). The plan itself was shaped around the proposal to place French and German coal and steel production under a common authority (a 'High Authority') outside national control and open to the participation of other European countries. However, although its immediate preoccupation was with supranational control of these two commodities alone, its wider agenda was evident. It declared this to be only the first step in the federation of Europe, and asserted that 'Europe must be organised on a federal basis'. However, 'Europe will not be made all at once or according to a single plan. It will be built through concrete achievements which first create a de facto solidarity'. The ECSC therefore represents a clear example of the functional approach to integration.

This French proposal, attractive to Germany because it marked the first step towards recovering sovereignty over the Saarland, still then belonging to France, while allowing the fledgling Federal Republic to regain a place in the international community, attracted also the participation of the Benelux countries and Italy. Although the UK participated briefly in the negotiations leading to the conclusion of the ECSC Treaty, the plan to transfer control away from national governments to an appointed body proved unacceptable. Only a much smaller number of countries proved ready to participate in truly supranational international cooperation than in the looser arrangements of the Council of Europe.

The ECSC Treaty was concluded in Paris in April 1951, and contained an institutional structure rather different to that envisaged by the Schuman Plan itself, in particular with less strong elements of supranationalism. The actions of the High Authority at the centre of the institutional structure of the ECSC were to be tempered by a Council of Ministers, composed of representatives of the Member States, to give a greater intergovernmentalist input into the Community and to act as a political counterweight to the High Authority. Its task was to give its opinion to the High Authority which was charged with the principal decision-making power. The triad of political institutions was completed by a Common Assembly composed in the early years of representatives chosen by the national parliaments, and endowed only with consultative powers and a minimal role in ensuring the accountability of the High Authority. Some aspects of the institutional and decision-making structures were strongly supranational: decisions were to be taken and then implemented by the High Authority independently and action did not require a consensus of the Contracting Parties; furthermore, decisions of the High Authority were binding upon the Contracting Parties. However, the potential for independent decision on the part of the High Authority was restricted by the nature of the ECSC Treaty as a *traité loi*. The four-pronged institutional pattern, which was later adopted as a model for the European Economic Community (EEC) in 1957, was completed by a Court of Justice, charged with ensuring observance of the law.

The ECSC Treaty created a common market for coal and scrap (Article 4). This comprises the abolition of internal customs duties and quantitative restrictions on imports and exports, measures and practices which discriminate between producers, purchaser or consumers, government aids and subsidies and restrictive practices tending towards the sharing or exploiting of markets. These essentially free-market principles were fetters upon the possible dirigiste tendencies of the High Authority, which might have resulted from the influence of its first President, Monnet, who was known to favour a strong element of central planning in the economy. Interestingly, unlike the later EEC Treaty, the ECSC Treaty does not provide for a complete customs union for coal and steel since it does not create a common external tariff for imports from third countries. In practice, the Member States have created a system of uniform external protection to avoid anomalies between coal and steel products and other products.

The ratification of the ECSC Treaty by the national parliaments and the entry into force of the Treaty did not inexorably lead towards closer integration. The success of the ECSC Treaty was followed closely by a serious failure – the Treaty establishing a European Defence Community (EDC) and the draft Statute for a European Political Community. This initiative was also based on a French proposal aimed at managing the re-emergence of Germany on the international stage. The Pleven Plan put forward by the French Minister of Defence proposed to apply the methods of the Schuman Plan to the field of defence, allowing German rearmament, then being vigorously urged by the USA, within the context of a European Army. The Treaty establishing the EDC was concluded by the Six in May 1952 (the UK participated in early negotiations but then withdrew from the plan, despite Winston Churchill's championship of the concept of a European army in 1950), but then encountered serious difficulties at the ratification stage. However, even before ratification, the Parliamentary Assembly envisaged for the EDC was meeting and drafting, as required by Article 38 EDC, proposals for institutional reform to guarantee the democratic character of the Community in the form of a draft Statute for a European Political Community. Both plans collapsed when the EDC Treaty did not achieve ratification by the French parliament in August 1954. Some semblance of purely European cooperation in the defence field was rescued at the initiative of the UK, with the creation in 1954 of the Western European Union (WEU; see 1.4) bringing Germany into the security framework of the West. After years of obscurity, the WEU has enjoyed a strange renaissance since the mid-1980s offering a distinctive Western European voice in defence issues and as the basis for an expansion of European integration in the defence field. It has been specifically incorporated into the Common Foreign and Security Pillar since the Treaty of Maastricht as an 'integral part of the development of the Union providing the Union with access to operational capability' (Article 17 TEU) and is charged with the implementation of decisions of the Union which have defence implications.

Despite these setbacks further concrete progress towards European integration was made in the 1950s. This time the initiative for a '*relance européenne*' came from the Benelux countries, already tied together in tighter economic cooperation than the other members of the ECSC. The key to the new initiative was that economic integration should precede political integration, but that new instruments were needed to go beyond both the ineffectual OEEC and the sectorally based ECSC. This broadening and deepening of the emphasis of economic integration is often said to be a classic example of the principles of 'spill-over' outlined in 1.5. The proposal was for a general common market, and for specific measures in the emerging field of nuclear energy. Out of a discussion at Messina in June 1955 between the Foreign Ministers of the Six came the decision to convene a committee to elaborate one or more treaties to give effect to these proposals. The report of the committee, named after its Chairman Paul-Henri Spaak, a Belgian, was submitted and approved by the Foreign Ministers of the Six by May 1956 (Weigall and Stirk, 1992: Ch. 6).

The Spaak report called for the creation of a common market, which it defined as the result of the fusion of national markets to create a larger unit of production. This, it argued, would make for greater economic growth and an accelerated increase in the standard of living. The Report foresaw three main strands to the development of this common market: the achievement of a customs union and free movement of commodities and factors of production; the creation of a policy for the common market to ensure fair competition; and the adoption of measures to facilitate the transformation and modernisation of economies and enterprises, for example through investment aid and retraining of workers. What the Report did not propose were common educational or social policies, which were not regarded as necessary for the achievement of the common market. The institutional structure was based on that of the ECSC, with a Court, a Common Assembly, a Council of Ministers, and a central supranational authority, in this case termed the Commission. Once again the Commission was to be the pivotal political institution, but endowed with rather fewer powers than the High Authority under the ECSC Treaty. The Spaak Committee accepted that the many activities to be undertaken by the institutions for the achievement of these goals could not be regulated in detail in a Treaty, and that what was needed was not a *traité loi*, but a *traité cadre*, itself giving extensive law-making powers to the institutions, in particular to the Council. This Treaty was elaborated on the basis of the Spaak Report and signed in Rome in March 1957, along with a Treaty establishing a European Atomic Energy Community (Euratom). The process of parliamentary ratification proceeded smoothly and the Treaties entered into force on 1 January 1958.

The EEC represented a reversion to the vision of a Europe created by stages, with the common market as a stepping stone towards political union. As such, it is a remarkable triumph of common interest over diversity. The Six had very different motivations and goals in seeking the creation of the Community. France had long been pursuing a policy of preventing German domination of the continent of Europe. Germany saw supranational cooperation as the means to regain self-respect and standing in the international community. The Benelux countries sought to overcome the disadvantage of smallness in an increasingly global economy. Italy was looking for a new start and respectability. All the countries saw the potential for economic benefit: in particular, the Germans sought outlets for their manufactured products, and France insisted on an agricultural policy that protected its large agricultural sector. Italy fought for the inclusion of the free movement of workers in order to capitalise on one of its greatest assets – its labour. At an institutional level, too, the document represents a compromise between federalists and intergovernmentalists, and like any document which is the result of compromise, the EEC Treaty contains inconsistencies which articulate the delicate balance between giving independence of action to the supranational institutions and retaining Member-State control over the direction of the Community.

2.5   The Non-Participants in Supranational Europe

The UK excluded itself from participation in the supranational project of the European Community from the outset of the negotiations for the ECSC Treaty. Soon after the ratification of the EEC Treaty, the UK spearheaded negotiations looking at the possibility of instituting some form of free-trade arrangement between the Six and the other OEEC countries, but without a common external tariff or arrangements for the harmonisation of laws to prevent distortions of competition. A number of Member States were anxious about the dangers of watering down their achievements; opposition was strongest from the French, and the negotiations came to an abrupt end when they were vetoed by General de Gaulle, then President of France. As a result of this rebuff a number of OEEC countries formed a separate, but looser arrangement for economic cooperation, the European Free Trade Association (EFTA), concluded by the Treaty of Stockholm in January 1960. The founder members of EFTA comprised the UK, Denmark, Sweden, Norway, Austria, Switzerland and Portugal. They were subsequently joined by Finland and Iceland, but numbers were reduced by the departure of Denmark, the UK and later Portugal to join the European Community. EFTA often sought closer economic relations with the Community, and in the 1992 these culminated in the signature of the Treaty creating the European Economic Area (EEA), which largely assimilated the relations between European Community and EFTA countries to internal European Community relations, and applied the basic principles of the internal European Community common market to those relations. This treaty, too, encountered difficulties in the ratification process when it was rejected by a referendum in Switzerland. However, the failure of one state to ratify this Treaty did not preclude it coming into force on 1 January 1994. Many of the members of EFTA were also applicants for membership of the EU, and on 1 January 1995, the accession to the EU of Austria, Finland and Sweden (the 'EFTAN' enlargement; see 3.2) reduced the participants in the EEA arrangements to Norway, Iceland, and Liechtenstein.

A change of attitude in the UK towards the European Community in the early 1960s resulted in two requests for membership in 1961 and 1967, which were vetoed or stalled by de Gaulle's opposition to British membership. Only after the departure of de Gaulle was the path opened to the enlargement of the Community.

2.6   The Early Years

The years of the late 1950s and the early 1960s were years of economic boom with unprecedented growth, which made the tasks of the nascent Community rather less daunting. The Treaty provided for a transitional period of twelve years, divided into three stages each of four years, ending on 1 January 1970. According to the original Treaty timetable, at the end of this period, the common market should have been in place. Common economic interest dictated that during the first two stages progress was smooth involving the dismantling of tariffs and quota restrictions, the erection of a common external tariff, the liberalisation of the free movement of workers and the creation of a system protecting the social security interests of migrant workers, the adoption of the initial regulations for the implementation of the Community's competition policy, and the introduction of a system of common farm prices and common organisations of the market which form the basis of the Common Agricultural Policy (CAP). Up to this point the Member States moved forward by consensus, since during the first two stages the Treaty provided for decisions to be taken by the Council acting unanimously. The Commission under Walter Hallstein, its first President, played a key role in these achievements, initiating policy and brokering agreements between the states, and there seemed little opposition at that time to its full exploitation of the supranational potential of the tasks which it had been assigned under the EEC Treaty. The Court of Justice too was busy carving out a distinctive role for itself within the Community system. In the ground-breaking cases of *Van Gend en Loos* in 1963 (Case 26/62 [1963] ECR 1) and *Costa* v. *ENEL* in 1964 (Case 6/64 [1964] ECR 585) the Court sought to distance the early Community legal order from the conventional structure of international law by identifying the importance of the relationship between Community law and individual citizens of the Member States, and by asserting the superiority of Community law over the laws of the Member States. The Court argued that there had been a transfer of sovereign powers by the Member States to the Community.

Meanwhile, however, the warning signs for the Community had been present since 1958 when General de Gaulle came to power as the first President of the Fifth French Republic on a fiercely nationalistic platform. His view that cooperation within Europe should take place within a confederal structure in which the Member States retained full sovereignty was put forward in the Fouchet Plan of 1961, an attempt to divert the process of political union to his own ends. This proposal for a 'union of states' based on strictly intergovernmental precepts came to naught after encountering opposition in particular among the smaller states. none the less it was clear that the favourable political circumstances in which the Community had flourished would not last for ever. The crisis point came when De Gaulle was faced with the prospect of the Community entering the third stage of the transitional period at the beginning of 1966 when many important decisions would be taken by a qualified majority in the Council (see Table 4.1).

2.7   De Gaulle and the Luxembourg Accords

De Gaulle objected to qualified majority voting under the EEC Treaty as he felt that it would endanger French interests within the Community. Yet majority voting was due to apply to agricultural pricing decisions – one of the issues of keenest interest for France – from 1966. De Gaulle chose to make his stand, and to precipitate the most serious crisis in the history of the Community, not over majority voting as such but over a series of linked proposals put forward by the Commission in March 1965. These concerned the financing of the CAP through a system of own resources belonging to the Community rather than through contributions by the Member States, as well as increased Parliamentary input into the making of the budget. The Commission rightly saw these matters as linked: the CAP (then as now) represents the main expenditure by the Community; 'own resources' (then coming from the revenue of the Common Customs Tariff (CCT), agricultural levies at the external borders and a percentage of the new common turnover tax levied by all Member States – Value Added Tax (VAT)) were intended to give the Community financial autonomy; and greater control by the European Parliament was a necessary democratic counterweight as control over the budget increasingly escaped the scrutiny of national Parliaments. France was not in favour of a greater role for the European Parliament, and used the lack of agreement on the package as a whole (i.e. the unwillingness of the other Member States to follow its line) to justify withdrawing from the work of the Council from June 1965 to January 1966. This period is sometimes called the period of *'la politique de la chaise vide'* (empty chair politics), and the deadlock was broken only by an agreement between the Six known as the Luxembourg Accords.

It was agreed, in the case of decisions which were to be adopted by a qualified majority, but where very important interests of one or more Member States were at issue, that the members of the Council would attempt, within a reasonable period of time, to reach solutions capable of adoption by unanimity. The French delegation added that in its view such discussion should continue indefinitely until a unanimous decision was reached. The delegations accepted that there was no common view on what should be done if unanimity could not be achieved, but agreed at that stage that this disagreement should not prevent the normal work of the Community being taken up once more. The result, in practice, of the Luxembourg Accords was that there was no voting in the Council. Just as the Member States arrived at the stage where majority voting would be introduced, they baulked at the last hurdle. Thus De Gaulle had achieved his central objective of weakening certain supranational elements of the Community. The intergovernmental mode of decision making based on consensus building prevailed over a federalist majoritarian approach as more and more of the Member States saw the attraction of maintaining the practice of unanimity. After the accession of the UK, for example the Accords allowed British politicians to maintain what they have been fond of calling the 'veto' over decisions of the Community which the UK does not like. This lies at the heart of repeated Government statements to the Westminster Parliament that British interests can always be protected by the use of the veto.

Although the Luxembourg Accords are essentially in the nature of informal understandings between sovereign states and as such have no formal status within the EC legal system, they proved remarkably enduring. No legal challenge can be mounted by any individual, institution or Member State to a refusal on the part of the Council to proceed to a vote. Even the Commission which makes the proposals on the basis of which the Council acts is impotent in such a case. The Accords were responsible for nearly twenty years of legislative stagnation within the Community where negotiations lasting up to ten years might be needed before agreement was reached on the simplest pieces of legislation. There is only one recorded instance of the Council riding roughshod over one Member State's assertion of a vital national interest in order to block qualified majority voting, and this was in May 1982 when the UK was seeking to oppose the adoption of agricultural prices. Furthermore, as the European Council became increasingly important within the Community's political structure, the practice emerged of passing on decisions which could not be taken in the Council to the European Council where their substance would be reduced to the lowest common denominator in the best traditions of political compromise. Commitments in the European Council to break the legislative deadlock by agreeing to relinquish the practice of decision making by unanimity proved to be empty rhetoric. Since provisions of the Treaty already provided for qualified majority voting in certain instances but these were being ignored, what was needed to revitalise the Community was not merely an increase in the range of decisions which could be adopted by a majority, but also a new willingness actually to vote on the part of the Council. Not until the adoption of the Internal Market Programme in 1985 and the entry into force of the Single European Act on 1 July 1987 were these two conditions satisfied. After that, remarkably rapid progress was made in many fields in the adoption of legislation required for the achievement of the single internal market.

The failure of the functionalist theory of European integration to take full account of the effects of resurgent nationalism as demonstrated by De Gaulle is one example of the deficiencies of the theory which led to its widespread rejection as a tool of analysis of the Community in the 1970s. However, it would be wrong to lay too much responsibility at the door of De Gaulle. The saga of the Luxembourg Accords and subsequent voting practice in the Council is symptomatic of how the Community has evolved, at least until the adoption of the Single European Act. The pressures of a global economy in recession, the impact of the oil crisis, the loss of confidence and prestige on the part of the Commission after the departure of President Hallstein and the effects of enlargement to incorporate countries with ever more diverse interests were all factors which contributed to the years of stagnation.

2.8　The Years of Stagnation

The years following the 1965 crisis were marked not only by a protracted legislative stalemate, but also by a general loss of momentum on the part of the Community. The politics of incremental steps to European union would normally have demanded a significant reappraisal of the direction of the Community at the conclusion of the transitional period by which time the European Community was to be one, common market. Yet creating the common market proved to be much more complicated than simply legislating for a common external tariff and prohibiting internal barriers to trade and factor movements. In fact, the hidden barriers composed of the multiplicity of national rules which govern the trading environments in each of the Member States proved resistant to removal, and, as the European economy moved into recession in the mid-1970s, underwent a revival as the Member States shifted increasingly towards national protectionism. Consequently, to say that the common market was complete at the conclusion of the transitional period would be merely an empty rhetorical statement. Attempts to move on to the logical next step – the achievement of full economic and monetary union – were entirely fruitless. The Report of the Werner Committee in 1971 setting out a timetable for the achievement of monetary union by 1980 contained unrealistic goals. Currency instabilities in the 1970s destroyed a number of attempts to peg exchange rates during that decade. The Community was too vulnerable to wider economic changes to be capable of translating any amount of goodwill into concrete progress.

Moreover, commitments such as that made at the Paris Summit in October 1972 to convert the (economic) Community into a (political) European Union proved equally worthless, as the Member States were incapable of translating words into actions. The Tindemans Report of 1975, drawn up at the instance of the European Council, was left on the table by the Member States. Much the same fate was suffered by the draft 'European Act' drawn up by Genscher and Colombo, the German and Italian Foreign Ministers, which resulted only in a Solemn Declaration on European Union adopted by the European Council at Stuttgart in June 1983. However, some of these early attempts at constructing citizenship policies were picked up again in the late 1980s and 1990s, as ideas about political union constructed around a notion of membership were revitalised.

The most significant source of progress towards political union between 1970 and 1985 was the gradual increase in the intensity of intergovernmental cooperation in the foreign policy field and its subsequent institutionalisation as European Political Cooperation (EPC) in Part III of the Single European Act. Wherever possible, the Community has sought to present a common face to the outside world. However, political cooperation of this nature has always been entirely voluntary on the part of the Member States and tended, then as now, to break down in the face of serious challenges to foreign policy cohesion such as the Argentinean invasion of the Falkland Islands in 1982 and the subsequent war between the UK and Argentina.

One proposal during this period does deserve greater attention and that is the Draft Treaty establishing a European Union (DTEU) adopted in 1984 by the European Parliament, as a counterweight to the initiatives of the diplomats and national politicians. In the climate of the time, when European Union was not high on the agenda of the Member States, the sponsorship of the DTEU by the Parliament and especially federalist Parliamentarians such as Attiero Spinelli could have been seen as a vain and impotent gesture on the part of an ineffective assembly. On the contrary, the DTEU played an important if indirect part in setting the agenda of closer integration for the second half of the 1980s.

The DTEU aimed not to sweep away the Community patrimony or *acquis communautaire*, but to build on existing achievements, albeit in an entirely new Treaty. The Treaty aimed to create a federal entity displaying the features of democratic accountability of its institutions, democracy in its decision-making processes, legitimacy through its respect for fundamental rights, and political decentralisation. The DTEU is notable for being the first semi-official Community document in which the concept of subsidiarity appeared. Article 12(2) would have regulated the case of concurrent competence held by the Member States and the Union in the following terms:

'The Union shall only act to carry out those tasks which may be undertaken more effectively in common than by the Member States acting separately, in particular those whose execution requires action by the union because their dimension or effects extend beyond national frontiers.'

There are remarkable similarities between this formulation and that ultimately inserted in the Treaty of Maastricht.

In keeping with the hybrid and mixed traditions of European integration, the DTEU envisaged a combination of 'common action' (i.e. supranational action by the institutions of the Union) and 'cooperation' (i.e. intergovernmental decisions taken by the Member States and implemented by them). The aim of the DTEU was to create a bicameral legislature with the European Parliament – elected according to a uniform electoral system – holding equal powers with the Council of the Union. The Commission was to retain the right of initiative and the right to put forward amendments. The Draft proposed the institutionalisation of the European Council. The general policy aims of the Union would have remained broadly the same, although social policies would have been strengthened.

The fate of the DTEU is discussed in 2.10 on the relaunch of the Community.

2.9   Widening and Deepening

It should not be thought that the DTEU was the only bright spot of the post-transitional period era. On the contrary, during the 1970s and early 1980s the Community went through a significant process of widening and deepening. It was widened through the process of enlargement from Six to Twelve by 1986. This would not have occurred if the candidate countries had not seen the Community as a positive force creating increased economic and political cohesion in Europe. The Community was also deepened in two dimensions – the substantive and the constitutional.

In the domain of substantive competences, despite difficulties which can be attributed at least in part to the Luxembourg Accords, the Commission was able to persuade the Council to embark upon new legislative programmes which were not envisaged in the Treaty itself. The Community developed policies on the environment and in the field of research and development without actually holding specific powers in these areas. Creative use was made in these fields of Article 235 EEC (now Article 308 EC) which provides a residual general law-making power for the purposes of the achievement of the objectives of the Community where specific powers are not granted elsewhere in the Treaty. It was not difficult to argue that the environment with its obvious cross-border dimension, and research and development where cross-border cooperation can significantly increase the level and effectiveness of investment, should thus be brought within the ambit of Community policy making, although countries such as Denmark were not wholly happy about such extensions of Community competence.

Less successful was the argument for the launch of a Community social policy. The roots of a more activist policy lay in the declaration of the Paris Summit in 1972 that the Member States attributed the same importance to energetic proceedings in the field of social policy as to the realisation of economic and monetary union, thereby seeking to give the Community a more human face. A Social Action Programme was elaborated by the Commission and accepted by the Council in 1974, but it resulted in few significant legislative measures.

In the process of the constitutionalisation of the EC Treaties, the 1970s saw a number of significant developments. The Court of Justice confirmed the supremacy of EC law, holding that national legislation may be 'disapplied' where it is contrary to Community law (Case 106/77 *Amministrazione delle Finanze dello Stato* v. *Simmenthal (Simmenthal II)* [1978] ECR 629). It also extended the concept of direct effect to directives, allowing individuals to rely upon directives in national courts in order to claim their EC rights (Case 41/74 *Van Duyn* v. *Home Office* [1974] ECR 1337). In the field of external relations, the Court developed a theory of implied powers in Case 22/70 *Commission* v. *Council (ERTA)* ([1971] ECR 263) which considerably extended the scope of the EC's competence to conclude international agreements in place of the Member States. Finally, in the context of interinstitutional relations, it was established that legislation adopted by the Council would be annulled if the Council had failed to consult the European Parliament where it was required to do so (Case 138/79 *Roquette Frères* v. *Council* [1980] ECR 3333). These are just four examples of many which illustrate that while the EC's political system partly stagnated, the Court of Justice vigorously pushed forward the development of the EC's legal system, considerably strengthening the hands of individuals claiming grievances against Member States alleged not to have observed EC law and of the supranational institutions within the Community structure, so that when the Community finally emerged into a period of positive growth in the political arena it was with a vastly changed legal system (see Chapter 5 on the constitutional development of European Union).

2.10 The Relaunch of the Community

The strong support for European Union coming from the European Parliament in the form of the DTEU was just one of the factors which lay behind the achievement of an interstate bargain needed to relaunch Europe. Indeed, the immediate impact of the DTEU should not be overestimated, since when the draft came before the European Council at Fontainebleau in June 1984 it was not accepted, but shifted off for discussion to an Ad Hoc Committee on Institutional Affairs, commonly named after its Chairman, James Dooge of Ireland. One of the first acts of the Dooge Committee was in fact to reject the DTEU as being too radical and open-ended, and proposing unacceptable levels of institutional reform.

On the other hand, the Dooge Committee was generally in favour of some reforms of the EEC Treaty, proposing, by a majority of its members (the UK opposing), the convening of an intergovernmental conference to prepare a draft European Union Treaty. The Committee also pointed out that certain very basic things could be done to further the objectives of the Community, and these included the completion of the unfulfilled tasks under the EEC Treaty. This Report alone, however, would not have persuaded the UK and the other Member States sceptical of deeper integration to agree to significant reforms of the Treaty. Pressure came additionally from a number of different sources.

By 1984 François Mitterrand, then President of France, had become a firm proponent of taking the European Community project further. In general he was supported by Helmut Kohl, the German Chancellor and the other half of the firm Franco–German alliance which has existed at the heart of the European Community since the conclusion of a Treaty of Friendship between the two states in 1963. In the first half of 1984, France assumed the Presidency of the Community, and Mitterrand was determined to leave his mark. He kept up pressure on the UK by making constant reference to the possibility of creating a two-tier Europe, with those Member States prepared to go further forging ahead in the creation of a European Union, leaving others such as the UK behind. This was opposed by the UK which did not want to risk falling behind as had happened once before in the 1950s. Mitterrand also engineered a resolution of the long-running dispute between the UK and the Community concerning the so-called British budget rebate, which recognised that the UK was a net over-contributor to the Community budget. Between the European Councils at Brussels in March and Fontainebleau in June 1984 the European Community hovered on the brink of breakdown. Eventually, at Fontainebleau, Margaret Thatcher accepted a compromise deal very similar to one she had rejected at Brussels, and she did not oppose the creation of either the Dooge Committee or a second Ad Hoc Committee on a People's Europe, chaired by Adonnino.

At the same time, a new President of the Commission was appointed, the French socialist Jacques Delors, who resolved to mark his occupation of the post by succeeding where previous Commission Presidents had failed in revitalising the Community and re-establishing the prestige of the Commission. In choosing the programme to complete the internal market as his flagship he went back to the economic and incrementalist roots of the Community to be found in the Schuman Plan and the Spaak Report, and found a proposal which offered something to everyone – Euro-sceptics, federalists, European business leaders – in its promise to bring growth to the European economy. In his task, Delors was assisted by the nomination to the Commission by Margaret Thatcher of Lord Arthur Cockfield, a committed free-market liberal. Cockfield, appointed Commissioner responsible for the Internal Market, put together at the request of the European Council the so-called 'White Paper' setting out a total of nearly three hundred measures which would need to be adopted to remove the physical, technical and fiscal barriers to trade in the Community. Already in January 1985 Delors started making speeches proposing the achievement of these objectives by the end of 1992 (two terms of office for the Commission) and when the White Paper came before the European Council at Milan in June 1985 it was unanimously accepted. Where some Member States differed from the others was with regard to the necessity for institutional reform to make the White Paper a reality. The UK argued that it was possible to complete the internal market simply through informal improvements in the decision-making processes of the Council. However, anxious to bring some concrete achievement out of the Italian Presidency, the Italian Prime Minister called for a vote on the convening of an intergovernmental conference to discuss amendments to the Treaty necessary to implement the goals of the White Paper, and, uniquely within the history of the Community, the proposal for a conference was carried by a majority vote, with the UK, Denmark and Greece opposing.

Reluctantly, the UK participated in the conference, arguing for institutional reforms including majority voting and the strengthening of the European Parliament to be limited to those measures necessary to complete the internal market. Majority voting was successfully excluded by the minimalists from the contentious areas of fiscal harmonisation, the free movement of workers and social policy. Progress towards monetary union was kept out of the main body of the Treaty, with merely a reference being made to it in the Preamble. European Political Cooperation was included in the new Treaty, but although it was given an institutional framework, it was maintained on a strictly intergovernmental basis excluding the operation of the Community rules themselves. Negotiation of what became the Single European Act proceeded exceedingly quickly, and was concluded at the European Council in December 1985 in Luxembourg, ready for signature in February 1986.

At the time, the UK believed that it had scored a significant victory in removing the impetus for a two-tier Europe, in persuading the rest of the Community of the benefits of the free market, and in minimising the impact of institutional reforms. Criticisms of the Single European Act came from the European Parliament which felt cheated of any role in the negotiations and objected to the outright dismissal of its initiative, and from pro-European commentators who feared that the SEA, being more intergovernmentalist in nature, might lead to a significant watering down of the supranational content of the Community and its legal order in particular. Subsequent events have, however, proved such pessimistic prognoses to be wrong, and now require a broad reassessment of the significance of the SEA, which claimed in its Preamble to be, and ultimately turned out to be, a stepping stone on the road to closer European integration.

2.11   The Single European Act

The provisions of the Single European Act can be divided into five categories. First, and foremost, there were provisions amending the EEC Treaty, with a view to the achievement of the goals of the White Paper. These comprised principally:

- Article 8a EEC, which contained a definition of the internal market and set the deadline of 31 December 1992 (now Article 14 EC);
- a new law-making power to be exercised by the Council acting by a qualified majority in cooperation with the European Parliament, giving the Council the necessary means to achieve the objective in Article 8a (Article 100a EEC, now Article 95 EC);
- a new legislative procedure (the 'cooperation procedure') creating a Parliamentary second reading of proposed legislation, after the Council had adopted a 'common position' by a qualified majority and the Commission had reviewed the amendments proposed by the Parliament on its first reading (now to be found in Article 252 EC).

Further amendments to the EEC Treaty were introduced by the second category of provisions which consolidated *de jure* some of the extensions of competence which had occurred *de facto* since the early 1970s, and established some important new powers associated with the Community's core activities. An example of the latter was the inclusion of a law-making power in what is now Article 12(2) EC to allow the adoption of rules designed to prohibit discrimination on grounds of nationality against nationals of other Member States. In the area of new or reinforced competences, the most important developments concerned regional development, research and technological development, and the environment, each of which was further amended by the Treaties of Maastricht and Amsterdam (see now Articles 158–176 EC). Finally, in this context, there were minor amendments to the Treaty provisions concerned with social policy, most notably the first reference to the role of 'social partners' and the 'social dialogue' (i.e. the two sides of industry, unions and employer representatives) in relation to social legislation in what was then Article 118b EEC. Article 118a EEC introduced the first law-making power in the field of social policy to be based on qualified majority voting, specifically in the area of health and safety of workers.

The third category of provisions allowed for an important addition to the institutional structure of the Community, through the creation of a Court of First Instance, to be attached to the European Court of Justice (now Article 225 EC). This Court was set up by Council Decision and commenced work in 1989.

The last two categories of provisions did not amend the EEC Treaty itself. In other words, they did not form part of the supranational corpus of EC law, but operated in the conventional realm of international law. Title I of the Single European Act consolidated and institutionalised the activities of the European Council, until then merely an *ad hoc* and informal gathering of the Heads of State or Government of the Member States. It was now required to meet at least twice a year and the leaders were assisted by their Foreign Ministers and a Member of the Commission (conventionally the President) (see now Article 4 TEU).

Finally, Title III of the Single European Act put the practice of European Political Cooperation (EPC) on a much firmer footing. Throughout this Title, the Member States were referred to as the High Contracting Parties, thereby stressing the intergovernmental nature of EPC; however, there were linkages with the Community's institutional structure in so far as the Ministers of Foreign Affairs meeting within the context of EPC were chaired by the representative of whichever Member State held the Presidency of the Council. The Commission was 'fully associated' with the work of EPC (Article 30(3)(b) SEA) and the Presidency was responsible for informing the European Parliament of the foreign policy issues currently at issue within EPC. The voluntarist nature of EPC was stressed by Article 30(1), which merely bound the High Contracting Parties to 'endeavour jointly to formulate and implement a European foreign policy' (see 3.1 for important changes to the nature of foreign policy cooperation introduced by the Treaty of Maastricht).

2.12 After the Single European Act

The immediate prognosis for the Single European Act was not good. It encountered harsh criticism on account of the vagueness of its wording, the many derogations which it allowed Member States, and its assertion that completing the internal market was somehow a new goal for a Community which since 1958 has always been committed to creating a common market (Pescatore, 1987). These criticisms, however, fail to take into account that progress for the Community in the form of Treaties must always take the form of delicate interstate bargains, which themselves may be transformed into more positive achievements by subsequent political events and by the willingness of the institutions and the Member States to implement the provisions in good faith. By 1985 the Community was suffering a serious crisis of legitimacy. It was seen by many to be a lame duck since it could never deliver on its grandiose aims, and the much-vaunted common market was quite clearly a chimera. The Community lurched from one crisis to another, beset by budgetary indiscipline, agricultural spending spiralling out of control and the lack of an obvious contribution which it could make to the pursuit of macroeconomic growth in Europe. In the event, the Single European Act revitalised the fortunes of the Community, as the Member States became involved in a project for which all had enthusiasm. The 'Christmas Tree' (i.e. overoptimistic) economic analysis (up to 5 million new jobs; an increase in 5–7 per cent of GDP) of the team of economists charged by the Commission with the task of estimating the macroeconomic benefits of the single market or, to put it another way, the 'costs of non-Europe', generally prevailed over more sober judgments of the negative effects of uncontrolled industrial restructuring on more vulnerable regions (Cecchini, 1988; Cutler *et al.*, 1989).

From most perspectives, the progress made by the institutions towards the completion of the 1992 programme was impressive. The Commission rapidly put forward proposals for the bulk of the three hundred or so measures envisaged by the White Paper. The Council streamlined its decision-making machinery, adopting an amendment to its working procedures to allow any one member of the Council, or the representative of the Commission who attends without a vote, to call for a vote on a measure. This, coupled with a new willingness not to seek to rely upon the Luxembourg Accords, led to a remarkable acceleration in the legislative process. However, very many important and contentious measures still needed to be adopted unanimously, and in this context the old practice of building 'packages' which offer something for everyone in return for compromises has continued. That was evident in July 1992 when the important fiscal harmonisation measures were agreed by the Council with the UK conceding the power of the Community to set VAT rates in return for concessions on a favourable taxation level for Scotch whisky, an important UK export.

The European Parliament meanwhile continued to make full use of the limited powers which were conceded to it, maintaining its fruitful alliance with the Commission in order to exercise maximum influence over the legislative procedure at both first reading and second reading. It sought to protect the use of the cooperation procedure by preventing the Council from using legal bases within the Treaty for measures which require a lower level of Parliamentary input. It did this by supporting Commission litigation in the Court of Justice and by bringing actions in its own name, seeking the annulment of measures enacted on the basis of the 'incorrect' legal basis. It enjoyed a mixed degree of success (on legal basis litigation see 6.8 and 7.18).

As progress was made quite rapidly towards the completion of the legislative goals set in the Single Market programme, extensive use was made of a new style of minimalist regulation by the institutions, which introduced essentially a new technique for harmonising the legislations of the Member States. In its case law on barriers to trade between the Member States, the Court of Justice had already made an important contribution to the goals of the internal market by holding that where a product is lawfully put on the market and sold in one Member State, it cannot normally be excluded from the market in the other Member States (the so-called *Cassis* principle, named after Case 120/78 *Rewe-Zentrale AG* v. *Bundesmonopolverwaltung für Branntwein (Cassis de Dijon)* [1979] ECR 649). Products must be allowed to benefit from production in one trading environment and sale in another, unless the Member State seeking to impede import or marketing can successfully argue that the rules which it is applying to the imported product (and to identical national products) are necessary for the protection of certain mandatory interests such as consumer protection, health and safety or the protection of the environment. The Commission then altered its policy on the harmonisation of national laws in order to incorporate this principle of mutual recognition. Measures put forward for adoption set only basic minimum standards for products which, if complied with, guarantee the right to free movement. This approach had obvious attractions for states such as the UK which were pursuing a vigorous deregulatory approach at national level, and which argued for the adoption of this approach at Community level. The argument is that this approach sets the stage for products to compete freely in a wider market, with consumers effectively choosing the type of trading (and, therefore, regulatory) environment in which they would like products to be produced. Consumer lawyers have countered by pointing out the risk that hard won gains at national level in the field of consumer protection may be destroyed by a Community-wide deregulatory approach.

2.13   The Social Dimension of the Internal Market

The apparent victory of free-market economics within the internal market did not wholly remain unnoticed by social policy-makers, trade unions and socialist and social-democratic politicians. For example, while sponsoring the political and economic relaunch of the Community through the internal market programme, President Mitterrand constantly made clear his interest in creating a 'Social Europe'. However, his proposal for a 'European social space' in which basic principles for the protection of workers were to be introduced at a mandatory Community level languished at the bottom of the agenda until it was picked by the Belgian Presidency in 1987 with the proposal for a 'plinth of social rights'. Soon thereafter, in February 1988, some of the problems of the anticipated differential regional effects of the internal market – one of the other central 'social' concerns of the Community – were resolved at the Community level by an agreement in the European Council to restructure the European Regional Development Fund and the European Social Fund in order to channel more EC resources into regional development measures and away from the apparently bottomless pit of the CAP.

This was followed by the adoption by eleven of the then twelve Member States (the UK dissenting) of a Community Charter of Fundamental Social Rights of Workers at Strasbourg in December 1989. It contains a declaration on the part of the signatories that the implementation of the Single European Act must 'take full account of the social dimension of the Community', and a statement of basic social rights of workers including freedom of movement, the right to fair remuneration, the importance of the improvement of living and working conditions, and the right to adequate social protection. This purely declaratory measure, to which the Commission attached an Action Programme containing a résumé of the measures which it intended to propose, was supposed to revitalise the social policy of the Community, just like the Social Action Programme of the 1970s. The results of the initiative were just as disappointing, since the political will amongst the Member States proved lacking, and the EC Treaty remained weak on the social policy front, requiring in all cases except health and safety at work a unanimous vote for the adoption of social policy measures.

The Social Charter is not binding and it introduced no new law-making powers into the Treaty. It also declares – with explicit reference to the principle of subsidiarity – that implementation of many of the rights is the responsibility of the Member States, not the EC itself. Since this accorded with the strongly held view of the UK at the time, as it wished to see the EC only minimally concerned with social policy, arguing that it was irrelevant to the achievement of the internal market and a matter for resolution at national level, it is perhaps difficult to see why the UK declined to sign such a document. However, for the UK and for Margaret Thatcher in particular, social policy became almost a symbol of its reserved sphere of national sovereignty. A new phase in the history of social policy opened up with the Social Policy Agreement which was attached to the Treaty of Maastricht, involving an opt-out for the UK between 1993 and 1997, and the subsequent re-incorporation of social policy into the Treaty mainstream by the Treaty of Amsterdam in 1999 (see 3.1, 3.4 and 3.9). In this revived story of social policy, the Community Social Charter has played a significant 'benchmarking' role.

2.14   **Towards a Treaty on European Union**

Despite the failure of the Single European Act significantly to extend the overall ambit of the Community's activities, Jacques Delors did succeed after 1986 in keeping economic and monetary union and institutional reform on the diplomatic agenda. A positive note was maintained by the February 1988 agreement on budgetary discipline and reform of the structural funds. Soon afterwards in June 1988 the Hanover European Council reaffirmed the Community's commitment to the progressive realisation of EMU, and charged a committee chaired by Delors himself with the task of identifying the concrete stages needed to realise that aim.

The Delors Committee reported in April 1989. Its report identified the three basic attributes of monetary union: full currency convertibility, complete integration of financial markets and irrevocable locking of exchange rates. The Treaties already provided for the first two attributes to be achieved. The Report therefore concentrated on the third attribute, focusing on the need not only for exchange rates to be locked, but also on the further step of the adoption of a single currency which would demonstrate the irreversibility of monetary union and remove the transaction costs of converting national currencies. However, without a convergence of economic conditions in the Member States and the adoption of certain common macroeconomic policies, even the locking of exchange rates cannot be successfully achieved. The Report therefore identified a crucial second stage in the achievement of monetary union in which budget deficits would be limited and European level institutions would be introduced which would gradually assume responsibility for monetary policy and exchange rate and reserve management. This would follow an initial stage (which began in July 1990) in which all the European Community currencies would be brought within the exchange rate mechanism ('ERM') of the European Monetary System (EMS) which controls exchange rate fluctuations, and in which fiscal coordination is gradually intensified. The final third stage would begin with the irrevocable locking of exchange rates and a European Central Bank taking over the role of national central banks.

The Report did not receive unanimous acceptance from the Member States; in particular, disagreement existed on when the various stages should begin, on whether transition from Stage Two to Stage Three would be automatic and fixed in advance, on whether all currencies would be replaced by the new currency and on whether the new Community banking institutions should be independent of control by politicians as they are in Germany. The UK favoured not a single currency, but a 'common currency' in which a hard, convertible ECU would be created which would compete with national currencies and might gradually supersede them. Against the opposition of the UK, the other eleven governments agreed at the Rome European Council in October 1990 that Stage Two would begin in January 1994, and this date was provided for by Article 109e(1) EC, as amended by the Treaty of Maastricht (now Article 116 EC – although it is of historical interest only). The UK did agree, however, to the convening of an intergovernmental conference on Economic and Monetary Union and this started work in December 1990.

Some Member States were unwilling to allow the Community to continue along the path towards EMU without significant moves towards Political Union involving the extension of the competence of the Community, and the enhancement of the democratic accountability of its institutions. Chancellor Kohl, for example, knew that a Treaty under which the Member States transferred significant competence in economic and monetary policy making to the Community would not be acceptable either to the German Parliament, the *Bundestag*, or to the *Länder*, unless the loss of democratic input into policy making at national level were at least in part matched by an increase in democratic input at the Community level. President Mitterrand also supported further moves to Political Union. Consequently, a parallel intergovernmental conference on Political Union was convened to consider the competences of the Union, in particular competences in foreign affairs, defence and collective security, and the institutions necessary to make the Union operational.

The outcome of diplomatic hard bargaining was the Treaty of Maastricht or 'Treaty on European Union', agreed by the Heads of State or Government in December 1991 and signed in February 1992. The Treaty formed the results of two separate bargaining processes, brought together only at the final stage. There was little interaction between the two conferences. After the departure of Margaret Thatcher and the arrival of John Major as British Prime Minister in late 1990, the UK was able to sign up to a Treaty laying down the stages for the achievement of EMU, while retaining the right as laid down in a Protocol not to proceed to participate in the third stage of monetary union (a similar Protocol was provided for Denmark, which would require a referendum before participation). However, in contrast to the positive progress on EMU the results of the debates on Political Union were much more modest changes. The IGC was unable to reach a single conclusion on the introduction of significantly enlarged competences and decision-making powers for the institutions in respect of social policy. Major refused to accept a new 'Social Chapter', and this was eventually concluded among the other eleven Member States as a separate Social Policy Protocol and Agreement outside the legal framework of the EC Treaty. Foreign policy also remained outside the structures of the Community proper, and, like the new field of cooperation in the internal fields of home affairs, immigration, asylum and the administration of justice, which codified existing informal arrangements, was given a separate intergovernmental 'pillar' operating alongside the supranational 'Community' pillar within the framework of an overarching European Union.

2.15   After the IGCs: the Struggle for Ratification of 'Maastricht'

The difficulties encountered in a number of Member States in gaining political and popular acceptance of the Treaty of Maastricht, as required by the various ratification processes in the different states, were unprecedented in the history of amendments to the founding Treaties of the European Communities. For a number of months, it was doubtful whether the Treaty of Maastricht would even come into force, as ratification by all Member States is required of any Treaties amending the original Treaties of Rome. These difficulties have proved extremely significant in that they have affected the progress that the 'new' European Union has made since its inception. The feeling of popular disempowerment and disillusionment felt in a number of

Member States and expressed in the ratification referendums of Denmark and France has challenged the legitimacy of the process of European integration, and its institutional forms, in a manner which crucially shaped aspects of the 1996 IGC.

The entry into force of the Treaty of Maastricht was originally foreseen for 1 January 1993. It eventually came into force on 1 November 1993, following protracted ratification procedures in particular in Denmark, France, Germany and the United Kingdom. Even in those Member States where ratification was relatively straightforward in political terms, complex constitutional amendments were required on matters such as the transfer of powers to the institutions of monetary unions, and giving effect to the concept of Union citizenship. It was the first Danish referendum in June 1992, in which – contrary to the urgings of all the main political parties – ratification was rejected by a majority of 47,000 votes, which threw the ratification process seriously off balance. For example, it was agreed in the UK to postpone further parliamentary debate regarding ratification until after a second (and then as yet unplanned) Danish referendum. Hoping to relaunch 'Maastricht', as well as to benefit from internal divisions among opposition politicians, Mitterand called a strictly unnecessary referendum in France which led to a very narrow (51.05 per cent to 48.95 per cent) popular vote in favour in September 1992. This too contributed to the feeling that something was seriously amiss both in the content of the Treaty itself, and in the procedures whereby it had been agreed among the politicians.

Responding to the malaise, the European Council meeting in Edinburgh in December 1992 under the UK Presidency attempted to meet Danish concerns about political sovereignty halfway, without actually reopening the text of the Treaty, by accepting certain declarations, particularly on Economic and Monetary Union. The compromise achieved was of dubious legal status, but the position taken has never been formally challenged in any way. It has subsequently marked Denmark's participation in the EU and aspects of the shape of the Treaty of Amsterdam. The European Council also discussed in detail the implementation of the subsidiarity concept introduced by the Treaty, stressing that part of the concept which is concerned with 'closeness of the citizen'. That has been a significant *leitmotiv* of political rhetoric on EU governance ever since then, along with the principles of 'openness' and 'transparency'.

Picking up the pieces in Denmark, a new coalition government, supported by most opposition parties, led a successful campaign for ratification in a second referendum in May 1993. The 'yes' vote was 56.8 per cent. When the matter returned to the UK Parliament, however, an atmosphere of hostility to Maastricht almost prevailed, particularly when Conservative Euro-sceptic rebels entered an unholy alliance with opposition parties which objected to Major's failure to accept the Social Policy Agreement.

Only the calling of a vote of confidence by Major on 24 July 1993 secured the passage of the Bill.

Meanwhile, in Germany a different type of ratification problem had emerged. Political ratification procedures, including extensive constitutional amendments, were completed in December 1992. However, a number of objectors to more intensive integration brought a constitutional challenge to the conformity of the Treaty with the newly amended Basic Law before the Federal Constitutional Court in Karlsruhe. This delayed ratification by some eight months, and although the Court ultimately ruled against the applicants it delivered a judgment which appears to place strict limitations upon the constitutional possibilities of European Union, when they are set against the background of the German Basic Law and the prerequisites of German sovereignty (*Brunner* [1994] 1 CMLR 57). The nature and significance of the German challenge to EU constitutionalism is discussed in 5.13.

Undoubtedly the ratification crisis faced by the Treaty of Maastricht was a turning point in the development of European integration within the framework of what was about to become the European Union. Although some of the effects have been slow to emerge clearly, it was none the less apparent that there were acute legitimacy issues which came out of the can of worms in the context of the ratification debates which could never be sidelined again. It represents, in sum, a fatal challenge to

'the traditional Monnet–Hallstein method of the "benign conspiracy". According to this method the EU operates with a process of small, gradual, technical adaptions without publicly clarifying the long-term political objectives. In the post-Cold War context the direct external threat to Western Europe has disappeared, and the whole of Europe is now involved in a democratic renaissance. In this context the old "benign conspiracy" is not only inadequate but directly counter-productive...' (Gustavsson, 1996: 223).

It will be apparent well before the end of the following chapter, which completes the historical narrative, that the old methods neither can, nor indeed are, any longer applied in the context of the evolving EU.

Summary

1   The unification of the nation states of Europe has been a consistent theme in political thinking for many centuries. Only since the Second World War has significant progress been made towards realising the ideals of a unified Europe.

2   In post-war Europe, a number of intergovernmental organisations were set up, attracting a wide membership. These included the Council of Europe, the OEEC and the WEU. Tighter supranational forms of integration attracted fewer members; the original ECSC, EEC and Euratom were composed of just six members.

3   The ECSC emerged out of a French proposal to put key strategic commodities under international control. It was followed by the unsuccessful initiative for a European Defence Community, and then the relaunch of economic integration in the form of the EEC and Euratom. The thinking behind these proposals was guided by neo-functionalism.

4   The early years of the European Community were years of economic boom and great progress was made towards completing the customs union within the agreed timetable. Less progress was made towards the completion of the common market. In 1965–66, the Community encountered a serious crisis when France withdrew from participation in protest at the move to qualified majority voting.

5   The Luxembourg Accords which brought this crisis to an end effectively committed the Community to consensus-based decision making, a pattern which was broken only after the adoption of the Single European Act in 1986.

6   Thereafter came years of stagnation, with a legislative blockage in the Council. This was exacerbated by a period of deep economic recession in Europe, and an increase rather than a decrease in protectionist measures erected by Member States. No proposals for advancing the structures of integration, for example through monetary union, had a serious chance of success.

7   Meanwhile, the Community had enlarged, and was consolidating its activities in certain areas, such as the CAP. Integration was largely led by the Court of Justice, which developed a strongly supranational case law.

8   The relaunch of the Community came in 1985–86, with a conjunction of factors, including the arrival of a new dynamic President of the Commission (Delors), the commitment of key political leaders such as Mitterrand and Kohl to further integration, and the realisation that the Community must revitalise itself in order to survive.

9   The adoption of the 1992 Single Market Programme and the amendments to the Treaty of Rome through the Single European Act 1986 have proved catalysts for a recovery of prestige and effectiveness of the Community, with a huge increase in the rate of adoption for legislation.

10   While progress continued on the completion of the single or internal market, economic and monetary union and political union returned to the agenda. A committee chaired by Delors put forward a step-by-step proposal for the achievement of monetary union.

11   Twin intergovernmental conferences were convened in 1990 on EMU and Political Union and were concluded at Maastricht in December 1991. The Treaty of Maastricht was ratified nearly a year late, after encountering significant popular opposition in the UK, Denmark and France.

Questions

1   In what ways does the early history of the Community illustrate the strengths and weaknesses of the ideas about European integration discussed in Chapter 1?

2   How did the crisis of 'empty chair politics' affect the subsequent evolution of the Community?

3   Why was the UK often described as an 'awkward partner in Europe'?

Further Reading

D. Dinan (1999), *Ever Closer Union: An Introduction to European Integration* (2nd edn), London: Macmillan.

S. Gustavsson (1996), 'The European Union: 1996 and Beyond – A Personal View from the Side-line', in Andersen and Eliassen (1996).

J. Hayward (1995), 'Governing the New Europe', in Hayward and Page (1995).

B. Laffan (1993), 'The Treaty of Maastricht: Political Authority and Legitimacy', in Cafruny and Rosenthal (1993).

P. Pescatore (1987), 'Some Critical Remarks on the Single European Act', 24 *Common Market Law Review* 9.

P. Teasdale (1993), 'The Life and Death of the Luxembourg Compromise', 31 *Journal of Common Market Studies* 567.

D. Urwin (1995), *The Community of Europe. A History of European Integration since 1945* (2nd edn), London: Longman.

W. Wallace (1994), *Regional Integration: The West European Experience*, Washington, DC: The Brookings Institution.

3 The Unfinished Union: The Treaty of Maastricht and Beyond

3.1 The Treaty of Maastricht

With the Treaty of Maastricht (also known as the Treaty on European Union), a new chapter in the evolution of European integration opened; it established the European Union and the pillar system which continues to structure the framework of European integration. Article A TEU announced that the EU is:

> 'a new stage in the process of creating an ever closer union among the peoples of Europe, in which decisions are taken as closely as possible to the citizen.'

As was noted in Chapter 1 (see 1.2 and 1.3), Title I of the Treaty of Maastricht set the structure and overall approach of the EU, and these aspects remained largely untouched by the Treaty of Amsterdam. This includes the three-pillar system outlined in 1.2 and discussed in further detail in 5.2. So far as it set an agenda regarding political union, the Treaty of Maastricht also began the slow process of introducing the principles of a liberal order into the EU, a process which continued through the Treaty of Amsterdam (3.9) and remains an important strand of a wider reform process which is still developing. In Article F(1) TEU an explicit commitment was made to the Union respecting the national identities of the constituent states. Article F(2) sought to protect citizens further by providing a (non-justiciable) guarantee of the protection of fundamental rights 'as guaranteed by the European Convention for the Protection of Human Rights and Fundamental Freedoms' and as they result from the constitutional traditions common to the Member States, as general principles of Community law'. These and the other common provisions of the Treaty on European Union did not amend the Treaties establishing the three Communities, but set out the separate framework of the EU itself. However, the unity between the EU and the Communities was maintained by the single institutional framework provided for in Article C TEU, based on the institutions of the Communities, and the commitment in Articles B and C TEU to maintain and develop the *acquis communautaire*, that is, literally, the Community patrimony. This is the body of Community law built up over the years, which forms the basis for the ongoing process of integration. Subsequent amendment by the Treaty of Amsterdam means that what is now Article 1 TEU includes a reference to decisions being taken 'as openly as possible'; the reference to decisions being taken close to the citizen is a first declaratory reference to the idea of subsidiarity, which was given further concrete form in Article 3b EC (now Article 5 EC). Article B also required the Union to achieve its objectives while respecting subsidiarity as defined in Article 3b. By virtue of Article L TEU, the grand declarations of Articles A–F TEU remained outside the jurisdiction of the Court of Justice, although that did not prevent the Court of Justice making some references in subsequent judgments to those provisions, without formally interpreting or applying them.

Titles V and VI of the Treaty of Union set out the provisions on CFSP (second pillar) and JHA (third pillar). The CFSP provisions built on Part III of the Single European Act, but with significant extensions. An element of defence and security policy was introduced within the scope of CFSP. The prospect of an eventual common defence policy and a common defence was foreseen by Article J.4 TEU, which also called upon the WEU, enjoying its late revival in importance, to implement actions of the Union which have defence implications. This was agreed by the Member States notwithstanding that some Member States have a policy of neutrality, and not all are members of the WEU. Some Member States wanted to see a formal merger of the EU and the WEU. A second innovation appeared in Article J.3 which provided for joint actions to be agreed upon where appropriate by a qualified majority. This provision had the capacity significantly to strengthen the supranational character of CFSP at the expense of intergovernmentalism. Such joint actions are binding to the extent that they 'commit the Member States in the positions they adopt and in the conduct of their activity' (Article J.3(4) TEU), although it is not clear what sanctions for non-compliance might be. The European Council was given a particularly important position in defining the 'principles' and 'general guidelines' of CFSP (Article J.8(1) TEU). A Political Committee of Political Directors from the Member States would monitor the day-to-day international situation, and provide the essential back-up to the political decision making. In contrast, the Commission and especially the Parliament were given a very restricted role in relation to CFSP. In the event, the possibilities for a more integrated CFSP after Maastricht proved to be largely unrealised, with more recent enhancements in the prospects for a genuinely 'common policy' resulting more from external forces than internal institutional or programmatic changes (3.12).

The provisions on Justice and Home Affairs were concerned with a wide range of issues relating to immigration and asylum policy, police cooperation, judicial cooperation and the residence of third country nationals within the EU. It provided for the creation of a European Police Office (Europol) for exchanging information. Interstate cooperation in this context (largely mediated through the Council, but requiring in some cases the ratification of the Member States) could involve either the conclusion of international agreements between the Member States or the formulation and implementation of joint positions or actions (Article K.3(2) TEU). The relationship with the competence of the EC strictly defined remained a difficult question, and matters were complicated by the creation of a number of bridges ('*passerelles*') allowing for the accretion of competence in this field by the EC institutions (Article 100c(6) EC and Article K.9 TEU) on the unanimous agreement of the Member States in Council, and the ratification of any such agreement by the Member States. As with CFSP, a 'Coordinating Committee' of senior national officials (Article K.4 TEU – commonly known as the 'K.4 Committee') played an important role in coordinating and guiding general JHA policy, and the Commission and the Parliament are correspondingly restricted. The Commission was to be 'fully associated' and the Parliament was to be informed, with its views to be 'taken into consideration'. As with CFSP, the Court of Justice had at first sight no role to play, although it could explicitly be given one in relation to Conventions concluded within the framework of JHA. Many felt that the second-pillar arrangements were the most unclear of all of the three pillars (e.g. Peers, 2000a), and in truth the second pillar never operated properly. For example, the European Council was not given a general role in defining the basic principles, as it was under CFSP. Thus although not originally on the agenda for the IGC at which the Treaty of Amsterdam was negotiated, fundamental reform of the system became an important issue of debate and, in turn, one of the most significant outputs of the Treaty of Amsterdam (3.6 and 3.10).

The provisions on EMU (Articles 3a, 4a, 102a–109m EC and additional Protocols) laid down the timetable for the achievement of monetary union and the convergence conditions for the national economies which need to be satisfied if irrevocable fixing of exchange rates is not to be accompanied by damage to some of the EU economies. These provisions are somewhat more detailed than was customary within the EC Treaty, which is normally regarded as a 'framework treaty' or *traité cadre*. Stage Two began on 1 January 1994, and the Treaty provided that Stage Three was to begin on 1 January 1997 or, if delayed by the Council, 1 January 1999. In the event, the latter date was chosen. It was clear from the Treaty provisions that the number of participating currencies would depend upon the achievement of the convergence criteria, and upon the decisions of the UK and Denmark to be taken under their respective 'opt-out' Protocols. The Treaty provided for a European Monetary Institute to take monetary policy forward to the third stage as a transitional institution, when it would be superseded by a European Central Bank (ECB), operating within a European System of Central Banks

(ESCB). Significantly, the Treaty opted for the 'German' approach, with an independent central bank, set apart from short-term political pressures. It was established that most decisions on progress to monetary union would be taken by majority votes.

Other amendments to the European Community Treaty itself came within the context of the rather loose notion of 'Political Union'. In the event, they included a new form of legislative procedure popularly termed 'co-decision' which further extended the powers of the Parliament, but at the expense of increasing the complexity of the already burdensome procedures (Article 189b EC; now, after partial amendment by the Treaty of Amsterdam, to be found in Article 251). Measures adopted by 'co-decision' are signed jointly by the Presidents of the Council and the Parliament. The Treaty of Maastricht provided that this procedure should apply in a significant number of cases, such measures relating to the internal market (Article 100a, now Article 95), many provisions relating to free movement (e.g. the free movement of workers – Article 49 EC, now Article 40), and measures in relation to some policies such as incentive measures in the educational field (Article 126(4), now Article 149). However, the existing procedures were also retained, with unanimity in many sensitive areas (e.g. tax harmonisation: Article 99 EC, now Article 93). The duration and mandate of the European Commission was synchronised with that of the European Parliament, and the membership of the Commission was for the first time to be approved by the Parliament. This was the approach taken with the arrival of a new Commission at the beginning of 1994, when Hearings of individual Commissioners-elect were held by the Parliament. It increased the accountability of the Commission, although there were no changes in the Treaty to the accountability of the unelected and secretive Council. The Treaty also enshrined the right of citizens to petition the European Parliament, and empowered the Parliament to set up Committees of Inquiry to investigate allegations of maladministration by the Community institutions. The appointment of an Ombudsman was also provided for, and after some delay an appointment was made by the Parliament in 1995. One final important institutional innovation was the creation of a Committee of the Regions to represent the particular interests of the Regions.

The substantive changes to the European Community Treaty outside the field of EMU were relatively modest. A concept of Union citizenship was introduced, but the attributes of citizenship are relatively insignificant in comparison to the attributes of national citizenship. They comprise principally the right of free movement, the right to stand and vote in municipal elections and elections to the European Parliament anywhere in the Union (Articles 8–8e EC, now Articles 17–22), as well as certain rights to consular protection. Social policy within the Treaty itself underwent certain minor amendments, with the more significant amendments proposed by the Dutch Presidency being relegated to a Protocol and Agreement giving the UK its so-called social policy opt-out. This delegated to the Member States other than the UK, by agreement of all Member States, the power to adopt social policy measures using the procedures and institutions of the European Community. It also involved the social partners in negotiating agreements to which the Council could give effect by Directive. Vocational training policy was for the first time regulated in more detail by the Treaty itself, and it was supplemented by general provisions on education, culture, health policy, consumer protection, industrial policy and development aid policy. Further amendments to the provisions on economic and social cohesion (including the creation of a Cohesion Fund), research and development policy and environmental policy were introduced. Legislative measures in all these policy areas, where the EC holds concurrent powers with the Member States, are subject to the principle of subsidiarity introduced by the Treaty of Maastricht. This was enshrined in Article 3b EC (now Article 5), which prescribed a test of the efficiency and necessity of EU action. It also introduced a proportionality test, and confirmed the existing principle that the power of the Community and the institutions is strictly limited, to that provided for in the Treaties.

In the final provisions to the Treaty of Maastricht, changes to the procedures for revising the Treaties were introduced, and the convening of a conference of government representatives in 1996 to review progress towards political union was provided for. While the Commission considered the progress towards Political Union contained in the Treaty to be modest, it considered it to be a worthwhile victory to persuade the Member States to commit themselves in advance to review progress.

One distinctive feature of the Treaty of Maastricht, which was perhaps explicable by reference to difficulties in the negotiating process, was the proliferation of declarations and Protocols attached to the Treaty. Some of these were strictly necessary (e.g. Protocol on the Statute of the European System of Central Banks and of the European Central Bank), but others were attached for the simple reason of appeasing certain Member States (e.g. Protocol on Ownership of Second Homes in Denmark; Declaration on the outermost regions of the EC) or, more sinisterly, of 'correcting' a Court of Justice judgment perceived by the Member States to go too far in extending the impact of EC law or to impose excessive burdens (e.g. Protocol on the Barber judgment, concerned with limiting its temporal impact upon retirement pension schemes). This trend continued when the Treaty of Amsterdam was agreed.

The Treaty of Maastricht was, of course, a compromise. Some have argued that it began a process of fatally diluting the supranational core of European integration, by formalising the three-pillar system, and by strengthening the intergovernmental dimension of the process. It was famously described as creating a Europe of 'bits and pieces' (Curtin, 1993). It did not, in any consistent way, address the issues raised by both the functional and geographical enlargement of the EU. It was certainly not a Treaty which addressed in any meaningful way the paradigmatic challenges of the 1990s, namely those brought about by the end of the Cold War and the break up of the Soviet Union. The issues raised by the ratification process suggested that the EU had a fundamental public relations problem, at the very least, on its hands, and potentially a much more serious crisis of legitimacy with the prospect of one Member State rejecting, at ratification, a Treaty agreed by its government at the IGC. These problems have not disappeared in the decade since the conference venue for the summit at Maastricht which concluded that Treaty was (physically and symbolically) shrouded in dense fog.

3.2   The EEA and the 'EFTAN' Enlargement

Hard on the heels of the changes wrought by the Treaty of Maastricht came another set of changes for the newly established EU to accommodate; a further enlargement brought in to the EU a number of countries which had previously been parties to the European Free Trade Agreement (EFTA) and which were by now closely associated with the EU by virtue of the European Economic Area Agreement (EEA) (see 2.5). By the early 1990s, the countries of EFTA were already closely assimilated, in an economic sense, to the EU. The EEA Agreement established free movement provisions and other internal market arrangements which were very similar to those in the EC Treaty itself. There was also 'close cooperation' in fields such as research and development, the environment, education and social policy. The EEA states are required to harmonise their national laws in accordance with the provisions of EU law, such as directives in the area of the environment or employee protection.

Over a period of time – partly triggered by the end of the Cold War rendering political neutrality no longer a meaningful obstacle to membership – five EEA/EFTA countries applied for membership of the EU: Austria, Finland, Norway, Sweden and Switzerland. In the event, Norway signed accession treaties, but did not ratify them; Switzerland withdrew its application before getting that far, and indeed rejected in a referendum participation even in the EEA. Austria, Finland and Sweden proceeded to accession on 1 January 1995, thus bringing about a further reshaping of the EU by extending its northern dimension and its eastern dimension. Sweden and Finland in particular have close relationships with the Baltic countries; Austria is historically and geographically closely linked to Hungary and Slovenia among the candidate countries. One byproduct of the accession process – which was largely unproblematic given the highly developed economic, political and legal orders of these three countries, which in any event had already implemented large parts of the *acquis communautaire* before accession and likely to be net contributors to the EU budget for the foreseeable future – was that the European Parliament used its role as a bargaining counter in order to obtain leverage over the IGC process foreseen in the Treaty of Maastricht to begin in 1996 (3.8). The Parliament must assent to all accessions (Article O TEU, now Article 49), and because it was dissatisfied about the compromise reached by the Member States over the management of qualified majority voting after accession and the precise threshold for a blocking minority – an issue which had threatened to derail the accession negotiations but which was a dispute *among* the Member States and not *between* the Member States and the candidates – it took the opportunity to argue for wholesale institutional reform as a pressing priority and to be given a greater opportunity to participate in future IGCs.

3.3   Managing the Internal Market after 1992

Since the end of 1992, by which time the internal market legislative programme had largely been completed on schedule bar the most controversial issues such as the free movement of persons and tax harmonisation, the emphasis in internal policy has shifted towards the management of the internal market, the continued progress towards the liberalisation of public procurement and highly regulated markets such as telecommunications specifically to enable open access to networks, and the enhancement of flanking policies such as those on economic and social cohesion, social affairs and employment, industrial affairs, the environment and transport. In addition, the legislative programme has developed to reflect the growth of the Internet and phenomena such as e-commerce, as well as other scientific, technological and commercial developments such as measures on genetically modified organisms, intellectual property protection for biotechnological inventions, and financial services, especially the protection of the small investor and pensions. However, the Commission's legislative programmes have sought to reflect the need to implement the subsidiarity principle, with an emphasis on fewer, less complex and less restrictive legislative measures. This is partly in response to the influential Sutherland and Molitor Reports on the Internal Market and Legislative Simplification, respectively (7.10). The most important omission from the legislative structure of the internal market was and remains measures related to the removal of internal border controls on movements of people, as required by Article 7a EC, and this is an issue specifically addressed by the Treaty of Amsterdam and the new EC Treaty title on the free movement of persons (3.6, 3.9 and 3.10). The Commission has also sought to ensure the concentration of the institutions on the stabilisation of the EU finances, and on the fight against fraud, which is particularly problematic in the agricultural field (7.16).

In terms of approach to the internal market and related fields, there has been a radical change in style since the late 1990s. This has two key elements. The first is a more holistic approach towards an integrated policy in promoting competitiveness and innovation in the economy, combined with measures on social exclusion and employment (a new 'Economic and Social Agenda', according to the Commission: see Commission, 2000a). This was strongly reinforced at a so-called 'dot.com' European Council meeting in Lisbon in March 2000 (the *e*Europe Initiative). The European Council showed a strong inclination to take a leadership role in this area, and to seek the closure of the Internet development gap with the United States. The second is the managerial approach of the Commission. Rather than 'old-fashioned' binding legislation, the *leitmotiv* of internal market management is now the Action Plan of 1997 (Commission, 1997), the 'strategy' (see Commission, 1999b), and the 'annual update'. This amounts to an increasing emphasis on 'soft law' and 'soft integration' (6.15).

In contrast to earlier periods of development of the European Community, the Court of Justice has been relatively cautious in its approach to the interpretation of the Treaties and secondary legislation. This may be related to the impact of the Treaty of Maastricht, particularly the clear attempts to restrict the role of the Court on the part of the Member States, and fears that an over-bold approach during the mid-1990s might lead the Member States in the 1996 IGC to impose further restrictions on the powers of the Court. There have not been wholesale revisions of earlier case law, but, as will become clear during the course of the following chapters, it has more frequently been the case that the Court has not always seized opportunities for 'pro-integrationist' or 'pro-Union' interpretations which it might have taken in the past when its case law was subject to less close political scrutiny. On the other hand, in its case law on state liability for breach of provisions of EU law, begun in *Francovich* (Cases C-6, 9/90 *Francovich* v. *Italian State* [1991] ECR I-5357) and carried through in *Factortame III* (Case C-48/93 *R* v. *Secretary of State for Transport, ex parte Factortame* [1996] ECR I-1029) (12.17, 13.6), the Court took further its judicial protection framework intended to ensure the effective enforcement of EU law, allowing individuals to bring actions for competition in national courts against Member States which have failed to implement EU law or have improperly implemented its provisions. This hardly denotes a very cautious Court, especially in the internal market arena, where the *Francovich* principle can be particularly useful for litigants.

3.4　Developing Social Policy: the Social Dialogue and the Labour Market

After Maastricht, it was anticipated that the social policy agenda would be marked by increasing fragmentation as a result of the UK's opt-out from the

Social Policy Agreement: twin-track Social Europe. It seemed unlikely to be able to play, in the medium term, a strong role in shaping EU policy as a whole. In the wake of Maastricht, the Commission issued a number of important documents relating to social policy, including a White Paper on Growth, Competitiveness and Employment (Commission, 1993a), and Green and White Papers on Social Policy (Commission, 1993b and 1994). The White Paper on Growth, Competitiveness and Employment, along with a number of Member State initiatives aimed at the flexibilisation of the labour market, notably from the UK, presaged the introduction of provisions into the EC Treaty by the Treaty of Amsterdam specifically on employment policy. These are also seen as a complement to the policy of economic and monetary union. In the field of social policy making, the role of the social partners has grown progressively. During the currency of the UK social policy opt-out, some measures did continue to be adopted under the EC Treaty proper, notably the 1993 Working Time Directive (Directive 93/104; OJ 1993 L307/18) based on the health and safety provisions, where adoption by qualified majority voting was possible. On a challenge by the UK, the Court of Justice upheld the extensive and creative use of this legal basis (Case C-84/94 *UK* v. *Council* [1996] ECR I-5755; see 6.6 and 6.8). On the other hand, a number of measures where a unanimous vote would otherwise have been necessary were pushed into the domain of the Agreement on Social Policy (SPA) where majority voting was possible by the intransigence of the UK. However, before the Treaty of Amsterdam was agreed, only two such measures were adopted under the SPA, on parental leave and European Works Councils. After the election of the Labour Government on 1 May 1997, one of its first actions was to signal its desire to opt back into all areas of social policy making. In the short term, this meant the adoption of special measures to extend the existing SPA measures, and those adopted thereafter but before the ratification of the Treaty of Amsterdam, to the UK. In the longer term, the change in the UK attitude resulted in the reassimilation of the SPA into the body of the Treaty proper by the Treaty of Amsterdam (Articles 136–141 EC), and the formal constitutionalisation of the role of social partner legislation for the EU as a whole as well as the extension of majority voting. The full capacity of the mechanisms for using social partner framework agreements as the general basis for social policy law making has yet to be tested out.

3.5 The Achievement of Economic and Monetary Union

There was – briefly – optimism, even in the midst of the ratification difficulties faced by the Treaty of Maastricht difficulties, that the path to increased integration via monetary union would prove much more solid than that offered by political union. Its optimism was blown out of the water in 1992 and 1993 by the crisis in the ERM (Exchange Rate Mechanism). This resulted initially in the withdrawal of sterling on 'Black Wednesday' (16 September 1992) as a result of international currency pressures, and then, even more seriously, in the effective collapse of the ERM in July–August 1993. Pressure specifically on the French franc forced the bands within which currencies should be circulating within the ERM to be widened from 2.25 per cent to 15 per cent. Thus, just as currencies should have been converging and becoming more closely 'locked' together in preparation for building the second stage of monetary union which began on 1 January 1994, they were effectively blown apart. Only the Deutschmark and the Dutch gilder remained tied together within narrower bands and the achievement of the timetable for the third stage provided for by the EC Treaty seemed implausible. Yet despite these setbacks, the Member States committed to the achievement of monetary union pressed forward towards the irrevocable locking of exchange rates, before the end of the century, and in December 1995 the European Council meeting in Madrid resolved to give the anticipated single currency the rather colourless name of 'euro', taking over from the ECU (European Currency Unit), and laid down a detailed third-stage timetable for switching – technically – from locked exchange rates to a single currency.

Progress on the convergence criteria other than exchange rates was equally problematic during this period. These concern budget deficits, public debts, long-term interest rates and inflation rates. Only Luxembourg and Germany, of those states most interested in monetary union, seemed likely at one stage to be able to comply. In the second stage of EMU, with the creation of the European Monetary Institute (EMI) in Frankfurt (which was the forerunner of the European Central Bank itself), the emphasis has shifted towards the analysis and management of economic policy. Member States were now being tied to ever more binding guidelines on the management of economic policy, including a power on the part of the Commission to monitor budget deficits in the Member States and to recommend to the Member States that they should remedy the position if these are deemed 'excessive'. Even so, these mechanisms seemed unlikely to deliver convergence in the face of continued economic and fiscal difficulties faced by most Member States.

1997 was abandoned as a starting date for the third stage of EMU, but the European Council continued to reaffirmed its commitment to starting the third stage in January 1999, as per the Treaty of Maastricht. The driving force was political will among governments and elites, not popular enthusiasm. The achievement of a further general election victory in Germany in October 1994 by Chancellor Helmut Kohl and his Christian Democrat/Free Democrat coalition was a key factor. Kohl staked his personal reputation on

EMU. He was joined in supporting EMU by Jacques Chirac, François Mitterand's successor as French President from 1995. A vast amount of technical and bureaucratic work on preparation and changeover strategies continued to be carried out by the EMI, the national central banks and the Commission. In addition, ECOFIN – the formation of the Council of the European Union dealing with economic and financial matters including EMU – worked on a 'stability pact' to ensure budgetary discipline even after the launch of the euro. This resulted in the agreement by the European Council in June 1997 – in parallel with the agreement on the Treaty of Amsterdam – of the Stability and Growth Pact, a budgetary austerity agreement by another name, accompanied by a commitment to implement strategies on employment by putting the measures on employment agreed in the Treaty of Amsterdam into effect in anticipation of ratification. Thus the major political event of late 1997 for the European Council was the Employment Summit of November 1997 in Luxembourg. The EU looked to be moving towards an era of 'economic government', and this was strengthened by the creation of a special formation of the Council, composed of the ministers of the participating Member States only, to look at issues such as maintaining fiscal discipline, coordinating taxation policy and setting the euro's exchange rate. This is named the 'Euro-X' Council ('x' referring to the variable number of participating Member States; it is thus presently called Euro-11 as eleven Member States participated in EMU from January 1999). Relations between such a political body and the independent central bank in the third stage of monetary union are inevitably sensitive.

The final run up to the launch of the third stage was marked by a fair amount of creative accounting on the part of the Member States wishing to participate in order to meet the convergence criteria. In May 1998 at a European Council meeting in Brussels, a decision was made by the participating Member States. In the end, despite all the speculation about EMU going ahead with only a minority of Member States or only a small majority, the participants comprised all the Member States wishing to participate apart from Greece, which was excluded on economic grounds. Denmark, Sweden and the UK opted out on political grounds. In May 1998 the conversion rates were determined. The most controversial decision at that Brussels summit concerned the appointment of the President of the ECB, which saw a row between France and Germany. In the end, Wim Duisenberg, who had taken over from the initial French appointee as head of the EMI was appointed as ECB president, against French opposition. The ECB president is a political appointment, even though the ECB is independent. The French objection was to both the ECB being in Germany (Frankfurt), and the first president being supported by Germany (although Duisenberg is Dutch). Under a compromise, Duisenberg agreed to resign early, in 2002, to be followed by a French appointee, Jean-Claude Trichet, for a full eight-year term.

The euro was launched on 1 January 1999, but its short history thus far has been marked by a dramatic collapse in its value against the US dollar, the Japanese yen and sterling. In early 2000, the euro fell below parity with the US dollar, having lost over 12 per cent in value. Once more these events call into question its long-term success, but yet again the strong political will behind EMU seems to suggest that it *must* succeed. Proponents of EMU point to indicators other than the euro's value alone, which can in part be attributed to the strength of the US economy, highlighting factors such as the positive growth rate, and levels of industrial production and unemployment within Euroland and the ECB's apparently sound and confident management of interest rates. The ECB's objective is an area of price stability, with low inflation, and politicians frequently refer to conquering inflation. Political success can be highlighted by the fact that not only has Greece continued to push to meet the economic criteria, but also that Denmark and Sweden were in mid-2000 beginning to prepare referendums which must necessarily for them precede membership of EMU.

However, the fall in the euro has complicated the British relationship with EMU. In October 1997, in a statement to the House of Commons, Chancellor of the Exchequer Gordon Brown announced that if the economic conditions were favourable and the five economic tests which he had set out were met, the Government would campaign in favour of the euro in any referendum, the holding of a referendum now being Labour Party policy. However, this was unlikely to be before the next UK general election (in other words, around 2002), barring what he called 'unforeseen circumstances'. The Chancellor's five economic tests for UK membership of EMU are:

- Cyclical convergence: are business cycles and economic structures compatible with the EU?
- Flexibility: is there sufficient flexibility in labour and product markets within the euro zone?
- Investment: would joining EMU create better conditions for inward investment into the UK?
- Financial services: would entry into EMU have a positive impact on the competitive position of the UK's financial services industry?
- Employment and growth: will joining EMU promote higher growth, stability and a lasting increase in jobs?

In reports on these tests, the UK Treasury has concluded that the UK must demonstrate that 'sustainable and durable convergence' is needed, otherwise monetary union would harm both growth and jobs. In the meantime, as the euro has fallen, previously firm business opinion in favour of joining the EMU has slipped, and popular disenchantment has continued to grow. Yet, the UK Government has formulated preparations for joining EMU, in a technical sense, with national changeover plans of February 1999 and March 2000.

3.6 Implementing the 'Third Pillar' and the Evolution of Schengen

Slow progress was made after 1993 towards the implementation of the 'third pillar' (JHA cooperation). It is important to note that the forms of largely intergovernmental cooperation foreseen in the post-Maastricht third pillar were not innovatory in themselves, but rather built upon a history of intergovernmental cooperation in areas of home affairs (especially the exchange of information relating to terrorism and organised crime) dating back to the 1970s. There had been a 'voluntary, limited and somewhat unstructured dialogue' (O'Keeffe, 1999: 272), which brought the justice and interior ministries of the Member States into the 'fold of European integration' (Dinan, 1999: 439). The most well established of these informal groupings were the 'Trevi' group of ministers and civil servants overseeing terrorism and police cooperation activities, and working groups on immigration and other related matters, especially illegal immigrants, asylum-seekers and refugees in more recent years. However, all of these activities were largely shielded from public view, and there was no attempt systemically to publish their outputs or work. Although non-binding in nature, they did influence important national policies.

Moreover, the implementation of the third pillar needs to be seen in the light of the Schengen Conventions of 1985 and 1990, which originally brought together the geographically core Member States (Germany, France and the Benelux) in what Peers has called an 'integration black market' (Peers, 2000a). Disappointed with progress on the free movement of persons within the framework of the European Community itself (despite numerous proposals in this area by the Commission, and despite the signing of the Single European Act with its commitment to the single market), these Member States determined to achieve the removal of internal frontiers through extra-EC/EU means. The Schengen system comprised measures on visas and border controls, asylum requests and the creation of the Schengen Information System, without which it would be deemed impossible to move to a system of control on the movement of persons at the external borders of the Schengen area, rather than at internal frontiers between participating states. It took some time to come into effect as a system, being delayed in most respects until 1995, as a result in part of difficulties with managing the information system. A body of secondary measures and associated agreements, often of uncertain status and not always formally published, gradually developed to implement the Schengen Conventions. This is termed the 'Schengen *acquis*'. Profound doubts about the compatibility of the

Schengen system with human rights standards and international law on matters such as asylum and the status of refugees have been raised (e.g. d'Oliveira, 1994b), not to mention concerns about the secrecy with which the activities of the Schengen system's own institutional framework were cloaked. However, by the time it was implemented, the Schengen system had gathered together all of the Member States apart from the UK and Ireland – historically connected by a passport union and separated from the Schengen system by the UK's insistence on maintaining its frontier controls – plus the other non-EU members of the Nordic passport union which have associate status (Norway and Iceland). Moreover, the UK had demonstrated its willingness to participate in some aspects of intergovernmental cooperation in the area of immigration and asylum, by joining in the negotiation of the Dublin Convention on determining the state responsible for asylum applications (in force since 1997) and a parallel convention on external frontiers which thus far has not yet entered into force, in part because of ongoing disputes between the UK and Spain over the status of Gibraltar.

Onto this framework was grafted the Maastricht system of institutions and powers, largely in the form of intergovernmental JHA cooperation, but in a limited way in the form of some additional powers within the EC Treaty itself, especially in relation to visas (what was Article 100c EC) (see 3.1). Problems with the third pillar were legion: the institutional system sidelined the Commission and the Parliament, and thus lacked the 'hub–spoke' system (Peers, 2000a) which has continued to drive progress on integration in the first pillar; the combination of unanimous voting in the Council, plus ratification procedures in the Member States for all binding measures (Conventions), placed an effective barrier to large-scale progress on implementation in the form of legislative-type measures. In view of these problems, recourse was frequently had within JHA cooperation to 'joint actions', which had uncertain legal effects and provoked hostility within national parliaments, which felt excluded from scrutiny procedures even though such instruments can have a profound impact upon national law and policy making. In relation to the Europol Convention establishing the European Police Office, one of only two conventions was signed and ratified during the Maastricht era, controversy was concentrated on the extent of judicial scrutiny. Consequently, the system was ripe for change in the context of further Treaty amendments, and it became a major item at the 1996–97 IGC and in the subsequent Treaty of Amsterdam (den Boer, 1999).

3.7   External Trade and the Conclusion of the Uruguay Round

Since the early 1990s, the external trading environment of the EU has changed dramatically with the conclusion of the GATT 'Uruguay Round', the extension of global trading regulation into new fields such as trade in services, and the creation of the World Trade Organisation. The EU and its Member States participated jointly in the international agreements relating to the WTO, which was established on 1 January 1995. For the Commission, which had sought to assert the exclusive power of the EU to participate without the Member States, a ruling by the Court of Justice confirming a largely shared competence between the European Community and the Member States was a major disappointment. Even though the final act of the WTO was concluded as a 'mixed agreement' (6.5), the European Community – acting on behalf of the wider EU – plays a full part in the WTO as a full member. Meanwhile the substantial completion of the internal market programme enhanced the EU's position as a global trading force, and 1994 saw the enactment of most of the legislation needed to complete the external dimension of the internal market in terms of creating a common external frontier in relation to third country products.

Statistics prepared for the 135 country WTO meeting in Seattle in the USA in November 1999 to launch a new 'Millennium' Round of trade negotiations highlighted that the EU was the world's largest exporter, and has had a balance of trade surplus since 1993 (3.14).

3.8 The 'Hangover' of Maastricht: the 1996–97 IGC

Internally, the greatest challenge which faced the EU soon after the ink was dry on the ratification processes for the Treaty of Maastricht was the preparation of the next Intergovernmental Conference, foreseen in Article N TEU to review the operation of that Treaty. This began in March 1996 in Turin. During the course of 1995 preparations became increasingly intense: the Council charged a Reflection Group, composed of representatives of the Member States, the Commission and the European Parliament with drawing up reports highlighting important agenda items and identifying the main areas for discussion. The European Parliament secured its place in the Reflection Group by adopting a hardline approach to the EFTAN enlargement (3.2), and in general the Parliament was a 'winner' from the IGC, especially in comparison to the Commission. Each of the institutions also submitted a separate report for the IGC. Opinions differ as to whether the Reflection Group and its reports actually effectively prepared the IGC, or were largely an irrelevance and an obstacle to effective negotiations (e.g. Dehousse, 1999). There were three strands to the evolution of the agenda for the 1996–97 IGC: the provisions of the Treaty of Maastricht itself which mandated review; the prospect of further enlargement of the EU, especially to the east; and the legitimacy gap and popular disaffection with the EU which had manifested itself most starkly in the context of the difficulties over the ratification of the Treaty of Maastricht. For the first time, an IGC became the focus for large-scale lobbying activity by interests within civil society. Moreover, in comparison to earlier IGCs, many of the negotiating documents and position papers of the Member States and the Presidencies, as well as draft treaty proposals, were made available. This was associated not only with increased pressure for transparency and accountability of politicians, but also with the overwhelming ease of transmission of documentation and information associated with the development of the Internet.

No particular political drama surrounded the formal calling of the IGC, given that it *had* to happen in accordance with the earlier Treaty, although there was no strong political enthusiasm for it at the time. Most of the Member States were at the beginning of the IGC – and still at the end – preoccupied with the pressing agenda of EMU. Moreover, there was no single 'big idea' which dominated the agenda, as happened with the earlier SEA and Maastricht IGCs. In fact, two issues did acquire a rather strong hold on the agenda: issues associated with enlargement, including the question of the role of flexibility in an enlarged and more diverse EU and the problems of efficiency and institutional effectiveness especially as regards the composition of the Commission and the weighting of votes in the Council; and the evolution and revision of the third pillar and JHA policy.

In the event, the political settlement did not make enlargement possible – in institutional terms at least. In particular, the most difficult questions about the Commission and the Council were postponed to one or more further IGCs foreseen in a Protocol attached to the Treaty, and accordingly a further IGC began in February 2000. The new 'f' word (flexibility having taken over from federalism) was extensively raked over during the negotiations, with support coming for a more flexible system from both those who saw flexibility as a way of pushing forward a hard core towards deeper integration against the opposition of states like the United Kingdom (such as the French or the Germans) and those, such as the UK Government itself, who saw a system of variable geometry and even 'pick-and-mix' options for Member States as a way of watering down the effect of the EU and its legal order. Again, the formal outcome would not have satisfied either party seeking an effective flexibilisation of the legal order, for whatever motive. In the first place, the new Treaty set (tight) general and specific conditions for 'closer cooperation' between a limited number of Member States under the first and third pillars (with little reference to flexibility in the second pillar). Second, the arrangements – especially for JHA matters – produced new layers of complexity in relation to 'actually existing flexibility', with some very complex and barely logical opt-outs for the UK, Ireland and Denmark. EMU flexibility remained untouched, and the twin-track social policy was reduced to a single track once more.

After extended preparatory work by successive Presidencies (Irish and Dutch) and by multiple meetings of senior diplomats and ministers, the final bargaining session occurred over two days in Amsterdam during June 1997. A key factor in making the successful conclusion of the IGC within the Dutch Presidency possible was the election of the (New) Labour Government in the UK on 1 May 1997. Opposition to some key questions such as integration of the social policy provisions into the main body of the Treaty immediately dissipated. The IGC itself was generally judged less confrontational than those that preceded it, and there were no particularly major political confrontations between the Member States in the context of the final summit meeting itself. The most enduring image was of a bicycle ride through the streets of Amsterdam apparently won as a race by the youthful and recently elected British Prime Minister Tony Blair. However, what was thought to be the agreed package turned out to be somewhat more problematic. One of the key lessons of Amsterdam lay in the considerable difficulties the diplomats and lawyers experienced between the date of the Amsterdam European Council meeting and the actual signing of the Treaty in October 1997 in cobbling together exactly what *were* the agreements between the Member States.

3.9 The Treaty of Amsterdam

The completion, signing and ratification of the Treaty of Amsterdam was a generally extremely low key exercise, especially if compared with the public relations exercise conducted by the Commission around the completion of the 1992 programme, the intensive press coverage sparked off by the Treaty of Maastricht's political difficulties in the ratification process, and the arrival of monetary union on 1 January 1999. Most Europeans were unaware of the Treaty at all, even though ironically many of the measures are intended to bridge the legitimacy gap and to render the EU somehow more popular with citizens. For the media, the most newsworthy EU issue of mid-1999 was not the entry into force of the Treaty of Amsterdam, but the extremely low turnout across the Member States in the European Parliament elections in June and the political issues associated with the unprecedented resignation of the Commission after a scandal of nepotism and mismanagement and the effective exercise of its powers by the European Parliament (3.11). Much of what the EU was doing was in any event overshadowed by other momentous European news, in the shape of the conflict in Kosovo. The original target date for the coming into force of the Treaty (December 1998) proved impossible, as France had some difficulties with ratification associated with necessary constitutional amendments. However, the Danish ratification through referendum proceeded reasonably smoothly, and this time round the French government eschewed the option of a referendum. One blip was a much lower level of support in the Irish referendum than ever before from this most 'communautaire' of electorates, with more than 38 per cent voting against. In the event, ratification was complete in time for the Treaty to enter into force on 1 May 1999.

The Treaty of Amsterdam makes principally piecemeal amendments to the earlier TEU and EC Treaty, along with a smaller number of wholesale changes to limited areas. Unlike the Treaty of Maastricht, it does not provide a stand-alone Treaty framework. One can group the amendments into eight principal sets of key changes, although there are other minor amendments as well which will be discussed – if they are of a constitutional or institutional nature – in the chapters which follow.

(a) The most visible change is the renumbering exercise, for both the EC Treaty and the TEU, accompanied by a moderate amount of 'housekeeping' in relation to the deletion of now redundant provisions such as the timetable for the original customs union (1.2).

(b) A number of provisions were added which are associated with the development of the EU as a type of 'liberal order', which now increasingly operates as a guarantor of liberal constitutionalism, basic democratic principles, the rule of law, and the principle of fundamental rights protection both for itself and for Member States. It is also committed to taking decisions 'as openly as possible' (Article 1 TEU). What appear to be essentially aspirational provisions were added to the general provisions of the TEU, especially Article 6(1) which provides that 'the Union is founded on the principles of liberty, democracy, respect for human rights and fundamental freedoms, and the rule of law, principles which are common to the Member States'. What was previously implicit was made more explicit by the Treaty of Amsterdam with an eye to enlargement and the still fledgling democracies of Central and Eastern Europe. The existing guarantee of fundamental rights in Article 6(2) TEU was made justiciable before the Court of Justice (Article 46 TEU), and a political process for imposing sanctions on Member States was established in Article 7 TEU. It might never be used, at least formally and fully. However, the influence of these provisions on the reaction of the fourteen other Member States to events in Austria in early 2000, with the possibility (and then reality) of the right wing and populist Freedom Party, dominated by the controversial figure of Jörg Haider, becoming part of a governing coalition with the Christian Democrats, cannot be doubted. New provisions are also added to the EC Treaty establishing a law-making power for the Council to adopt measures to combat discrimination on grounds of sex, racial or ethnic origin, religion of belief, disability, age or sexual orientation (Article 13), and laying down a principle of the right of access to documents for citizens and national and legal persons established in the EU (Article 255 EC). A new sentence was added to the main citizenship provision, confirming the arrangement reached at the Edinburgh European Council meeting in the wake of the first Danish referendum on the Treaty of Maastricht, to the effect that Citizenship of the Union is merely *complementary* to national citizenship, and does not replace it (Article 17 EC). This is one of a number of areas, including transparency or access to documents, where the changes to the Treaties do little more than concretise judge-led or informal or semi-formalised institutional arrangements. Overall, these provisions do, however, make a significant contribution to the construction of the EU's constitutional framework (see Chapter 5 and Part IV).

(c) The Treaty preserved the three-pillar system established by the Treaty of Maastricht, with some significant amendments in relation to the scope of the third pillar accompanied by the movement of matters from the third pillar to the first ('communitarisation'). The second pillar was maintained in large measure unchanged. To that extent, at least, the uneasy balance between the intergovernmental and supranational aspects of the EU remained largely untouched.

(d) Article 2 TEU established the new objective of developing the Union as an 'area of freedom, security and justice'. Among the most significant steps towards this goal (aside from those related to fundamental rights, etc. alluded to above) was the 'communitarisation' of large parts of the matters previously contained in the third pillar. In particular, there is a new Title IV of Part III of the EC Treaty concerned with 'Visas, Asylum, Immigration and other Policies related to Free Movement of Persons'. This comprises the important commitment to adopt within five years the measures necessary to ensure the free movement of persons under Article 14 EC. In addition, the Schengen Agreements and the Schengen *acquis* (3.6) were brought within the framework of the EU by means of a Protocol, with arrangements for the allocation of individual measures either to the new Title IV or the 'rump' third pillar containing provisions on Police and Judicial Cooperation in Criminal Matters (PJC). The UK and Ireland have opted out (by Protocol) of the basic goal of removing internal frontiers and achieving the free movement of persons contained in Article 14 EC and Title IV, and are permitted to preserve their own frontiers and internal passport union or Common Travel Area, notwithstanding the provisions of the EC Treaty and the TEU. A further Protocol opts them out of measures adopted under Title IV, but allows them to opt back in to any measure; these states must notify the Presidency of a desire to participate in specific measures. These opt-outs also operate in relation to the incorporation of the Schengen *acquis*, which never covered the UK and Ireland in the first place. Denmark – which is a member of Schengen – has arranged (by Protocol) a rather different form of opt out from Title IV which retains the character of 'Schengen law' and subsequent 'Title IV law' as international law in Denmark. This is because of opposition in Denmark to the deepening of EU-based integration in these fields, but it might have the ironic effect of weakening judicial control. Justice and Home Affairs law is now primarily a mix of measures under Title IV of Part III of the EC Treaty and the reworked PJC third pillar.

(e) In relation to CFSP, the Member States once again failed to agree upon the merger of the WEU and the EU, although there has been an intensification of the relationship. At the same time, greater recognition is given in the second-pillar provisions to the fact that some Member States see NATO as the primary guarantor of their security. Article 17(2) TEU incorporates into the CFSP what are known as the 'Petersberg tasks', originally conceived for the WEU as issues requiring the deployment of military forces: humanitarian and rescue tasks, peacekeeping tasks and tasks of combat forces in crisis management. In terms of making the CFSP more effective, an important innovation was the creation of the office of 'High Representative for the Common Foreign and Security Policy', termed 'Ms or Mr CFSP', who is simultaneously also the Secretary-General of the Council (Article 18(3) TEU) and who assists the Presidency in representing the Union. The voting roles were changed, with decisions still to be taken in almost all cases by unanimity, but with a possibility of what is termed 'constructive' abstention, where by a Member State can effectively opt out of a particular measure or agreement, but without preventing the other Member States from proceeding (Article 23(1) TEU). It is a 'shadow' of the concept of 'closer cooperation' introduced into the second pillar and the EC Treaty (Langrish, 1998: 13). In a further innovation, where decisions can be taken by qualified majority (adoption of joint actions and common positions: Article 23(2) TEU), Member States may apply an 'emergency brake', as a provision analogous to the (informal) Luxembourg Accords (2.7) was for the first time incorporated into any of the EU Treaties. Member States may declare that 'for important and stated reasons of national policy' they intend to oppose a policy, in which case a vote will not be taken and the Council may, by a qualified majority, request that the matter be referred to the European Council for decision by unanimity.

(f) The constitutionalisation of flexibility through the concept of 'closer cooperation' is a significant innovation of the Treaty of Amsterdam. Of course, flexibility in the framework and application of the Treaty and systems of opt-out and opt-in is nothing new, especially since the Treaty of Maastricht. The arrangements under the area of freedom, security and justice in relation to the UK, Ireland and Denmark are the natural progeny of the Social Policy Agreement and the position in relation to EMU. However, in Articles 43 and 44 TEU certain basic conditions are set down to allow groups of Member States (at least a majority) to embark upon future 'closer cooperation' which is 'aimed at furthering the objectives of the Union and at protecting and serving its interests', provided the closer cooperation complies with specific additional criteria laid down for the second pillar (Article 40 TEU) and for the EC Treaty itself (Article 11 EC). The cumulative effect of the provisions is such that it is difficult to envisage them being used, even in the circumstances for which they were apparently intended, namely the enlargement of the EU and the resultant increase in diversity.

(g) In relation to policy development, the Treaty of Amsterdam added a new task of promoting employment, and an Employment Title; social policy was, as noted above, 're-integrated' into the Treaty mainstream. In relation to gender equality in particular the Treaty of Amsterdam significantly strengthened the existing EC Treaty provisions, making 'gender mainstreaming' a task of the EC under Article 3(2) EC, and strengthening the possibility for Member States to pursue positive action measures under Article 141(4) EC. The public health policy provisions were also enhanced. The integration of environmental protection requirements was also strengthened, as this provision was moved from the Environmental Chapter to the general provisions of the EC Treaty (Article 6 EC). In terms of the making of policy, the subsidiarity principle – which affects the exercise of legislative competences – was further fleshed out by the insertion in a Protocol on the Application of the Principles of Subsidiarity and Proportionality of a selection of material developed in the Conclusions of the Edinburgh European Council. Again, this is an example of the IGC formalising informal arrangements. Article 2 TEU makes the principle of subsidiarity in Article 5 EC generally applicable to all Union activities and therefore to all three pillars. A closely associated change concerned the arrangements for Member States to seek a derogation from an agreed single market harmonisation measure (Article 95(4)–(9) EC). In political terms, the Treaty of Amsterdam has been noted as 'Blairite' in orientation, embracing more strongly a form of 'regulated capitalism', in sympathy with the 'third-way' political projects of Blair and the German Chancellor Gerhard Schröder, elected after the Treaty was agreed but before it came into force (Pollack, 2000).

(h) Finally, the Treaty of Amsterdam brought about some modest changes to the law-making process. The legislative procedure termed 'co-decision' (Article 251 EC) was extended to many further areas of the EC Treaty and the procedure was 'tweaked' to make it a more genuine partnership of equals between the Council and the European Parliament. It also enhanced aspects of the accountability of the Commission to the European Parliament, and of the overall role of the Commission President.

On institutional questions, however, the Treaty of Amsterdam was more significant for what it failed to do, rather than what it did do. Thus a Protocol was attached to the Treaty, effectively mandating a review of institutional matters such as the size of the European Parliament, the weighting of votes in the Council, the extent of qualified majority voting (extension of which in the Treaty of Amsterdam was vetoed at least in part by Chancellor Helmut Kohl of Germany under intense domestic pressures), and the composition and size of the Commission. These issues were put under review in a further IGC beginning in February 2000 (3.15).

Overall, without changing the basic framework of the Union, the Treaty of Amsterdam papered over some of the cracks evident after Maastricht, but also considerably added to the complexity and opacity of the whole structure notwithstanding the rhetorical commitment to openness and closeness to the citizen in Article 1 TEU (Gormley, 1999). The process of 'communitarisation' has confirmed the 'robustness and power of attraction of the first pillar' (de Witte, 1998: 55), while at the same time increasing the overall phenomenon of differentiation and diversity of institutional arrangements and mechanisms for decision making. But while the details might themselves – from a specialist perspective – 'improve upon' earlier solutions to institutional or policy problems, as Weatherill comments: 'in the Amsterdam Treaty, the devil is *not* in the detail' (emphasis added). On the contrary, the problem lies 'in the accumulation of texts, breeding ever deepening intransparency. Change which is not intelligible is likely to cause alienation. Both the Maastricht and Amsterdam Treaties are hard to absorb; and both have bred alienation' (Weatherill, 2000a).

3.10 The Area of Freedom, Security and Justice

The changes to the provisions on Justice and Home Affairs (3.9) have been associated with a significant shift in the political will in relation to policy making to make this area the 'new single market'. That is, the Commission and Council formulated an Action Plan approved at the Vienna European Council in December 1998 (Commission, 1999c), and devised a system of 'scoreboards' and other arrangements to enhance the process. A special summit was devoted in October 1999 at Tampere in Finland to Justice and Home Affairs policies in which common measures on asylum and immigration and police cooperation were top of the agenda, including the possibility of far-reaching harmonisation of matters such as criminal law and procedure.

One undoubted reason for this has been the continuing popularity with national electorates of policies such as combating organised transnational crime, making the EU's own structures more resistant to fraudsters, restricting illegal immigration and certain areas of transnational judicial cooperation such as making family law orders enforceable across borders. This has also allowed the Member States to pursue what has been at times a somewhat illiberal agenda in relation to civil liberties issues (Peers, 2000), and the absence of transparency in previously intergovernmental areas such as the third pillar or the Schengen framework has been a matter of concern to many civil liberties organisations and non-governmental organisations engaged with refugee or asylum issues.

3.11 Institutional Development in the 1990s and the Resignation of the Commission

Jacques Delors was succeeded as Commission President in 1994 by Jacques Santer, a former Christian Democrat Prime Minister of Luxembourg who was nobody's first choice for the role. It was a difficult act to follow in more ways than one. In the first place, Santer did not have Delors' charisma or big ideas; second, there were by the end of Delors presidency very significant problems within the Commission of work overload, under-resourcing and bad management. One very significant problem was the power of the *cabinets*, or personal advisors to the Commissioners (3.2). Santer attempted to put some of things right, for example by promising to 'do less, better', but in so doing he appears to have become the EU's Mikhail Gorbachev. That is, he has come to be characterised as someone who points out the major failings, sets in train certain reforms, and then is sacrificed as the pace of reform accelerates out of his control; he was 'swept away by the tide of reform he himself unleashed' (Peterson, 1999). The European Parliament flexed its muscles to render the Commission more effectively politically accountable, convening a five-strong Committee of Independent Experts (or 'Wise Men') to investigate allegations of nepotism, fraud and mismanagement, after refusing to give the Commission a discharge in respect of the execution of the 1996 budget. The resultant first report of 15 March 1999 was extremely critical and the Commission was forced to resign as a whole, although it was clear that it was only a minority of Commissioners who had actively done wrong. In particular, it was the French Commissioner Edith Cresson who appeared to bring down the rest. Santer was reluctant to go, and he was vilified in the English-speaking press for saying that he was '*blanchi*' by the report, literally exonerated in respect of personal accusations against him. The English-speaking press interpreted this as Santer saying that he was 'whiter than white' in relation to the whole issue, where clearly he had to bear some political responsibility (and indeed did so by resigning). In the rush to appoint his successor, Romano Prodi, who was a former Prime Minister of Italy whose political position was very akin to the European 'third way' of Blair and Schröder, Santer's own reforms were largely forgotten (Cram, 1999). Yet at the June 1998 European Council meeting in Cardiff less than a year previously, a declaration had been agreed congratulating Santer and his Commission on the progress towards improving efficiency and management, with a variety of complex programmes involved with identifying the tasks undertaken by different services and directorates-general and enhancing value for money.

During the course of mid-1999, Prodi had an unprecedented mandate to construct his own Commission, although he did not in fact veto any national nominations. He pushed the Member States hard, for example, to ensure that the representation of women among the Commissioners did not drop (it remained at five out of twenty). In the end, Prodi's Commission was evaluated as competent and suited to the job in hand, if not always charismatic, and received a strong endorsement by the vote of the European Parliament. It came into office in September 1999. The UK's Commissioners both picked up important jobs – Neil Kinnock in his second term as Vice President in charge of the Administrative Reform and newly appointed Chris Patten in charge of External Relations. Prodi also had a free hand to implement a reform programme, but in its construction he and Kinnock have drawn unashamedly upon Santer's earlier attempts at reform and half-completed projects. It also makes use of the second report of the Committee of Independent Experts of 10 September 1999 which concentrated on recommendations to prevent mismanagement, irregularities and fraud. In the short term, along with instituting measures such as using names rather than numbers for the Directorates-General and Services, Prodi has also instituted some (cosmetic?) reforms in the interests of transparency and legitimacy, such as placing his mailbag on the Internet for public scrutiny. A number of Commissioners have held 'Internet chats', thus making themselves theoretically more accessible to 'ordinary' citizens. The low turn out in the June 1999 European Parliament elections highlighted the EU's continuing tenuous grip upon claims to an underpinning of popular legitimacy for its exercise of political power; it clearly added to the urgency of the reform project.

3.12 The Development of the Common Foreign and Security Policy

As with JHA, the operation of CFSP has not entirely lived up to the challenges that the EU has faced. Since 1993, in particular with the upheaval in the Balkans, these challenges have been substantial. Largely ineffectual action in Bosnia which failed to prevent both armed conflict and atrocities against civilians including ethnic cleansing at the very borders of the EU has been accompanied by a serious challenge to the authority of the EU, and the binding force of its legal order, posed by the unilateral economic sanctions imposed by Greece on the Former Yugoslav Republic of Macedonia. Effectively it was NATO and US intervention that led to the Dayton Accords which are the basis of the still fragile peace in Bosnia. The ineffectiveness of EU action was also highlighted by the serious political problems and accompanying humanitarian crises in Rwanda and elsewhere in Africa. Frequent inability to obtain an appropriate consensus on joint action was exacerbated by difficulties regarding the funding of such action as had been agreed, with serious doubts as to whether appropriate budgetary and consultative mechanisms involving the European Parliament were in place. This was improved by the Treaty of Amsterdam, whereby Article 28 TEU now provides that most CFSP operational expenditures are to be charged to the EU budget. Overall, doubts have been raised as to whether or not CFSP is any more effective in building a common identity in foreign policy matters for the EU than the more intergovernmental approach of European Political Cooperation which preceded it was for the EC.

Despite these strictures, the prospects for CFSP in 2000 seemed distinctly better than in the last years of the previous decade. On the one hand, the long anticipated High Representative for the CFSP had been appointed; Javier Solana was the former Secretary-General of NATO and a very respected diplomat. He was also appointed as Secretary-General of the WEU, notwithstanding the continuing formal separation of the EU and the WEU. Some tentative steps towards the creation of a distinct and capable European defence identity, including the development of a direct relationship between the EU and NATO, movement involving France and the UK on the question of the EU playing a greater defence role (including an important meeting of the UK Prime Minister and the French President at St Malo in December 1998), and proposals to establish by 2003 an EU rapid reaction force of some 50,000–60,000 personnel. This could address, directly, the 'Petersberg tasks' of humanitarian military action, brought into the TEU in Article 17(2) by the Treaty of Amsterdam. The US has taken during this period a cautiously encouraging attitude. The proposal was for these activities to crystallise in a 'Common European Policy on Security and Defence' (CEPSD), highlighted by the European Council meeting at Cologne in June 1999.

At the same time, the next significant challenge for CFSP – the crisis in Kosovo – represented both threat and opportunity. Certainly, the crisis was tragically predictable, since the problems themselves had been so long in the making and what happened, in terms of Albanian nationalism and Serbian repression and ethnic cleansing, was, in so many ways, exactly what was to be expected. In terms of military action, the field was left entirely to NATO. However, alongside the launch of the CEPSD proposal in Cologne was the closely related and highly symbolic signing of the Stability Pact for South Eastern Europe, which brought together representatives from thirty-eight countries and fifteen international organisations. As commentators have noted, 'in Kosovo, [the EU's] credibility, its capacity to act and its resources were challenged to the utmost limits: the appalling mockery of those values most precious for the Euro-Atlantic community by a regime practising clandestine ethnic cleansing as a deliberate political strategy in the outgoing 20th century; the destabilisation of an entire region with incalculable consequences for the whole of Europe...' (Biermann, 1999: 5).

But crucially the Pact is not based on unilateral action by the EU alone, but on regional cooperation as well as the cooperation of the wider international community. Through the Pact the EU and others address directly issues such as the development of the democratic opposition within Serbia and the restoration of civil and civic institutions in Kosovo itself, although crucially the long-term fate of the territory is left in limbo, as it remains formally within the sovereign jurisdiction of Federal Republic of Yugoslavia although not under Serbian control. The main contribution of the EU to the Stability Pact is the Stabilisation and Association Process under which additional aid is given to five countries (Albania, Bosnia, Croatia, the Federal Republic of Yugoslavia and the former Yugoslav Republic of Macedonia) in return for compliance in relation to political and economic modernisation and liberalisation objectives. The carrot and stick approach is neatly summarised by the Commission's introduction to the policy:

'In order to develop a closer relationship with the EU, these countries will have to gear their political, economic and institutional development to the values and models underpinning the European Union: democracy, respect for human rights and a market economy. The European Union will support and assist them in introducing the reforms necessary to progress in these areas' (extracted from the introduction on the External Relations DG homepage).

The main legal mechanism for the EU is the Stabilisation and Association Agreement, which is a new form of contractual relationship with a third country, combining the lessons learnt in relation to the route to anticipated accession for the countries of Central and Eastern Europe and the other former Communist countries (3.13) with the external security imperatives of stability and peace. For all of the countries the long-term possibility of accession is offered, subject, of course, to conditions. In relation to Serbia itself, certain economic sanctions are kept in place, intended as pressure to secure democratisation in that country. Efforts at democratisation relating to political parties and NGOs/civil society in places such as Montenegro are directly supported by the EU, which takes what amounts to an intrusive interest in the internal affairs of these countries. In addition, the EU has taken a central role in the process of economic reconstruction within Kosovo itself, and established the European Agency for Reconstruction in November 1999 to organise the delivery of assistance.

3.13 Responding to Changed Political and Economic Circumstances in Europe

The crisis in Kosovo not only had the effect of galvanising and refocusing the evolution of the EU's CFSP, but it also had a dramatic effect upon one of the other major planks of the EU's current external relations policies, that related to enlargement towards the East. This issue has been on the agenda since the end of the Cold War, and in fact some of the countries involved, such as Cyprus and Turkey, have been seeking accession for longer than that. Kosovo had the effect not only of bringing about a revision of the EU's priorities in relation to countries which are in the various 'waiting rooms', devised through the course of the 1990s, but also of highlighting the need for other flexible forms of association and of the continuing utility of using membership and association as a 'carrot' in order to promote certain liberal values and approaches to market economics. The EU is, in this area, balancing its historic duty to be open to democracies within Europe, and especially the new and sometimes fragile democracies from throughout the wider Europe, against the basis on which it has worked (more or less) in the past. That is, it has always operated on the basis of a delicate balance between intergovernmentalism and supranationalism in terms of integration strategies across a relatively homogeneous band of (at least reasonably) wealthy countries.

Indeed, whatever the level of internal popular disillusionment, it remains true that the EU represents a substantial pole of attraction for many of the states of Central and Eastern Europe (as well as the states of the Mediterranean); they see membership as the logical conclusion of the process of political and economic transformation which began with the removal of the Iron Curtain and the break up of the Soviet Union. The EU cannot ignore these challenges, particularly if it wishes to avoid the accusation that it is a 'rich country club'. Faced with a total of thirteen applications for membership (ten from Central and Eastern European states and the Baltic states; three from Turkey, Cyprus and Malta), the EU has sought to draw on the experience of the past by identifying stages of cooperation and integration with the EU through which applicants may pass on the way to membership.

The key was 'pre-accession strategies' defined as a 'route plan' for associated countries as they prepare for accession (European Council meeting at Essen in December 1994). These have become steadily more complex and intensive. By 1994 a number of states had already concluded 'Europe Agreements' which are Association Agreements under what is now Article 310 EC. These Agreements, in addition to bringing about some integration between the associated state and the EU and its Member States, also contained unprecedented obligations on the associated states to harmonise their national legislation with EU law. This was at a stage prior even to accession applications having been made, and well before the EU had conceded the principle of accession as the appropriate long-term outcome to the end of the Cold War. The preambles to the Europe Agreements recognised accession as a desire on the part of the associated country, not an objective on the part of the EU. A number of states were linked with looser Partnership and Cooperation Agreements. The stance of the EU changed decisively at the Copenhagen European Council meeting in June 1993 which set the economic and political criteria for membership which have remained the keys ever since. In fact, the political criteria are now incorporated into the TEU itself, in Article 6(1) TEU. The Copenhagen criteria provide that membership of the Union requires,

> 'that the candidate has achieved stability of institutions guaranteeing democracy, the rule of law, human rights and respect for and protection of minorities; the existence of a functioning market economy, as well as the capacity to cope with competitive pressure and market forces within the Union; the ability to take on the obligations of membership, including adhere to the aims of political, economic and monetary union'.

Furthermore, it has always been intended that there should be comprehensive acceptance of the *acquis* by the new Member States and not a pick-and-choose approach based upon the capacity of the country, for example, to withstand the competitive pressures or to accept the political discipline. Of course, very long transitional periods will undoubtedly be agreed to protect interests on both sides in sensitive areas like the free movement of persons or integration of the Polish agricultural sector into the Common Agricultural Policy. Internal EU policies may well be changed as a result of the anticipation of accession, and again the CAP is a good example. But overall, double standards in terms of the acceptance of the *acquis* do sometimes seem to be applied to candidate countries, given the latitude displayed for current Member States in terms of variable geometry. In 1995, the Commission issued a White Paper on accession and the internal market, and the preparations of the associated countries (Commission, 1995). It followed this in 1997 by a set of Opinions on the applications for accession by the ten countries of Central and Eastern Europe which had applied (which it is required to provide under Article 49 TEU), which were in turn integrated into a wider package comprising proposals for the reform of key policies such as the Common Agricultural Policy and the Commission's recommendations for the Union's financial framework for 2000–2006. The integration of the two elements – accession and budget – highlights the significance of enlargement for the EU. This package is entitled Agenda 2000. It appeared soon after the conclusion of the Treaty of Amsterdam in June 1997. The Commission recommended opening negotiations with five of the ten applicants from Central and Eastern Europe (the Czech Republic, Estonia, Hungary, Poland and Slovenia), plus Cyprus. There was broad approval for the Commission's package and its opinions, apart from the disappointed applicant countries. Accession partnerships were, however, agreed with all the countries involved. The applicant states have to develop national action plans for the adoption of EU legislation and submit these to the Commission. It can be regarded as a somewhat intrusive process. With the 'five-plus-one' countries in accession negotiations with the EU and the Member States since March 1998, a process of 'screening' the applicants and their acceptance of the *acquis* has been undertaken, chapter by chapter of the *acquis*. The Commission has published regular reports on the negotiations. The pre-accession strategies have continued to become more sophisticated, and they have allowed the EU with a view to bringing together all the different forms of support within a single framework, called an Accession Partnership, for each country, and to working together with the candidates, within this framework, on the basis of a clearly defined programme to prepare for membership to familiarise the candidate countries with EU policies and procedures through their increased participation in Community programmes. Thus by 2000 the accession strategies were founded upon the following elements:

- the Europe Agreements;
- the more recently concluded detailed Accession Partnerships and the National Programmes for the Adoption of the Acquis; and
- pre-accession assistance, which comprises a number of funding programmes aimed at infrastructure and capacity building in particular.

The final element of the preparation process from the EU side was put in place in February 2000, with the launch of an IGC specifically aimed at dealing with the institutional issues which further enlargement raises such as the composition of the European Commission and the European Parliament, and the weighting of votes in the Council of Ministers and the use of qualified majority voting (3.15).

The immediate need for the IGC became more urgent when it was agreed by the Helsinki European Council in December 1999 that accession negotiations would be opened with a further six states in early 2000. This is one direct byproduct of the Kosovo crisis, especially so far as pertains to the other (Eastern) Balkan states involved (Bulgaria and Romania). Turkey has been recognised as a candidate country, but has not yet been accepted into negotiations. Enlargement is now seen under one general umbrella, rather than in a fragmented way with different categories of candidates. A general principle of differentiation is applied under that umbrella, to allow countries to proceed at their own pace through the hurdles associated with achieving accession. No specific dates are given as targets for accession, although the Commission has recommended to the European Council that the Union should be ready by 2002 to receive the first of the countries which fulfil all the relevant criteria. The role of the Commission is to manage the process, screening the activities of the candidate countries, and operating as a conduit of information. Accession will also require the unanimous agreement of the Council and the assent of the European Parliament, acting by an absolute majority of its component members (i.e. a 'yes' vote of 314 MEPs). The accession negotiations conclude with accession treaties, which also require ratification in accordance with their constitutional requirements by the candidate countries and each of the Member States. In other words, the process required by Article 49 TEU itself involves a lengthy and complex institutional and constitutional process, quite apart from the practical challenges of integrating such diverse countries into the EU.

3.14   **The EU in the Twenty-First Century**

In concluding this chapter, and the overall historical survey of the EU's development, it is important to highlight the main issues and challenges which face the EU at the present time. Most of these issues have already been alluded to, and some discussed briefly, in previous chapters or paragraphs of this chapter. Moreover, some will be the subject of more detailed discussion in later chapters. Appropriate cross-references are therefore given. It is none the less useful to provide a single global overview of the EU at the beginning of the twenty-first century, as none of these issues should be seen as distinct from the historical processes which have proceeded them. Many of them, moreover, are closely linked, especially because with the impending enlargement towards the East, the EU no longer draws a sharp dividing line between the internal and external spheres of activities.

Thus the *2000 IGC* referred to in the previous paragraph is primarily about *internal* reform for the purposes of *external* expansion and it is given more extended attention in the final paragraph (3.15). In the sense that it will result in changes to the EU's basic constitutional documents, the IGC has to be given priority as a key issue for 2000 and onwards. The changes it is likely to introduce will not be mere dry 'technical' institutional changes, but matters which go the heart of the institutional balance and the relationship between the intergovernmental and supranational themes within EU governance. The IGC may or may not incorporate the work of the Convention established in 1999 to draft a *Charter of Fundamental Rights* for the EU; the Charter may, however, merely become a non-binding declaratory document after the Convention has concluded its work in late 2000 (9.12). *Enlargement* itself (3.13) is, of course, a key issue, and it is linked to the ongoing reform processes of *Agenda 2000*, which is the name given to a number of initiatives to modernise policies such as agricultural policy and economic and social cohesion, and to give the European Union a new financial framework for 2000–2006. Without policy reform, enlargement cannot be successful. Enlargement is also closely linked to the security imperatives which led to the *Stability Pact* and the creation of the *Stabilisation and Association Process* for certain Western Balkan countries, as the EU was forced to recognise more fully its responsibilities in the wider geopolitical domain of the European continent (3.12). The internal security imperatives of developing the *area of freedom, security and justice*, moreover, have greater resonance as the prospect of moving the external borders of the EU as far east as Russia comes ever closer (3.10). It is also important for the development of the EU's own concept of citizenship (Chapter 10). External economic relations within the WTO, meanwhile, have to take account of the *WTO's Millennium Round* of trade talks, launched amidst much controversy and not a little conflict in Seattle, USA in November 1999. There has been clear public concern about talks aimed at securing further global trade liberalisation and market access, and issues about the protection of the environment and the relationships between developed and developing countries including third world debt have been brought to the fore in 2000. A more direct internal concern has been making the *euro* work as a successful currency; euro notes and coins will begin to appear after 1 January 2002, and the new currency may already be used by consumers, retailers, companies and public authorities in non-cash form. With locked exchange rates linking eleven countries, the strength of the euro and economic growth within 'Euroland' is a primary concern (3.5). Closely associated with that imperative are policies aimed at promoting employment and the development of the 'e-economy' (3.3).

3.15 IGC 2000

Article 48 TEU provides:

> 'The government of any Member State or the Commission may submit to the Council proposals for the amendment of the Treaties on which the Union is founded.
> If the Council, after consulting the European Parliament and, where appropriate, the Commission, delivers an opinion in favour of calling a conference of representatives of the governments of the Member States, the conference shall be convened by the President of the Council for the purpose of determining by common accord the amendments to be made to those Treaties. The European Central Bank shall also be consulted in the case of institutional changes in the monetary area.
> The amendments shall enter into force after being ratified by all the Member States in accordance with their respective constitutional requirements.'

This is all that the Treaties have to say about the complex process of the Intergovernmental Conference or IGC. Bearing in mind, of course, that there have been – with the inception of a further conference in February 2000 –four major IGCs (five if one counts the two which led to the Treaty of Maastricht separately) in just over fifteen years, these events have become almost part of the day-to-day life of the EU, its institutions and the Member States. IGCs appear, at first sight, to be the moments when the Member States take charge, once again, of the Treaties. But IGCs and the treaties to which they give rise should be seen in context. They are framed by periods of prior debate and negotiation which involve actors other than national governments; once in place, they are subject to interpretation by courts (especially by the Court of Justice) and 'management' by the institutions as well as the Member States. They are 'owned' by a broader interpretative community (Shaw, 2000b). Now the 2000 IGC appears, very clearly, not to be addressing *constitutional issues*, as such. It is essentially about *managing* enlargement. That may well be the correct way to begin discussing what is happening at that IGC; the UK Government Paper on the IGC was entitled 'IGC: Reform for Enlargement' (Cm 4595, February 2000). However, it is likely that the agenda for the 2000 IGC will at some point, during or after the conference itself, escape its previously limited bounds, just as the Treaty of Amsterdam – despite being the 'hangover' from the Treaty of Maastricht (3.8) – resulted in some much more fundamental changes to the overall EU constitutional settlement. After all, many institutional reforms could, if the political will were present, be pursued without Treaty amendment, such as many of the proposals from Romano Prodi for the Commission (4.2). By the same token, non-institutional questions, which do require Treaty amendments, may crowd onto the agenda.

The Protocol on Enlargement attached to the Treaty of Amsterdam provided for institutional reform in two stages. It stated that

> 'at the date of entry into force of the first enlargement of the Union...the Commission shall comprise one national of each of the Member States, provided that, by that date, the weighting of the votes in the Council has been modified...' *and* 'at least one year before the membership of the European Union exceeds twenty' a new IGC shall be convened to 'carry out a comprehensive review of the provisions of the Treaties on the composition and functioning of the institutions.'

These stages were effectively elided as a response to the widening of the enlargement negotiations. Thus the official brief for the IGC read as follows (taken from the Helsinki Presidency Conclusions of December 1999):

> [The Conference will examine] 'the size and composition of the Commission, the weighting of votes in the Council..., as well as other neces-

sary amendments to the Treaties arising as regards the European institutions in connection with the above issues and in the Treaty of Amsterdam. The [Portuguese] Presidency will report to the European Council on progress made in the Conference and may propose additional issues to be taken on the agenda of the Conference.'

This brief presupposed a narrow start and the possibility of a later widening, perhaps in the second half of 2000.

The *size and composition of the Commission* and the *weighting of votes in the Council* are, because of institutional politics and large state/small state cleavages, clearly linked. The large states currently have two members of the Commission. Such states (France, Germany, Italy, Spain and the UK) tend to take the view that a reduction of the Commission to one state/one member is acceptable so long as the votes for qualified majority voting in the Council are reweighted to pay greater heed to large state interests, giving small states fewer possibilities of blocking. However, they equally tend to say that if the members of the Commission are indeed to be limited by concession on the point about two members for the big states, then it is *just as reasonable* to think in the future about abandoning the one state/one member linkage, thus allowing for a smaller number of Commissioners than Member States. Doubtless this is because they know that it will be more likely to be the small states to miss out if the number of Commissioners is reduced, or not allowed to grow to match enlargement. Small states tend to be vehemently opposed to abandoning the one state/one member principle, and to be unable to see the merit in any reweighting of votes in the Council. Obviously they welcome the concession of the 'two state privilege' by the larger Member States. An alternative to reweighting the votes is the 'double qualified majority', whereby a qualified majority may require not only a sufficient number of votes, but also a sufficient number of Member States voting in favour. This tends to protect the smaller states as well, as it prevents outvoting by a smaller number of large states.

More *qualified majority voting* in the Council is an issue that everyone supports in principle, since with the arrival of more Member States the risk of deadlock if unanimity is required for policy making will rise exponentially. However, whether that occurs in practice is a moot point, when issues of national sovereignty in areas such as social policy and taxation are raised once again, but the possibility of ironing out some anomalies in the Treaty does remain. The Commission in its Opinion (Commission 2000d: 21) to the IGC suggests three principles for action in this field: that enlargement should have no impact on the influence of the Parliament over legislation; that unanimity should only be required where there are serious and lasting reasons for it; and decision-making procedures should be made more coherent. The extent of this challenge will become particularly apparent in Chapter 7, where decision-making processes are studied in detail.

Two other major issues are the *composition of the European Parliament*, which cannot exceed 700 members after enlargement, and so must see a proportional reduction in members and a possible reduction in the current minimum number of MEPs even for very small states (six), and changes to the *Court of Justice* and the *Court of First Instance*, to make them more effective judicial bodies after enlargement (4.21).

Possible issues to be added at a later stage of the negotiations may be the incorporation into the Treaties of the *Charter of Fundamental Rights for the Union*, being drafted through the course of 2000 by a Convention composed of representatives of the institutions and the Member States (national governments *and* national parliaments) (9.12), and the further amendments to CFSP in the light of the developments in the area of *security and defence policy*. The proposal made by a report on the *Institutional Implications of Enlargement* (Dehaene *et al.*, 1999) for splitting the Treaty into two separate parts (the basic texts and the implementing texts of less fundamental importance) is an issue which may be taken up; it could address some of the accusations of excessive complexity now levelled at the Treaties as basic documents. This is something the European Parliament, in the report of its Constitutional Affairs Committee calls 'constitutionalising' the Treaties, and is a form of halfway house to a 'true' constitutional procedure (5.12).

Summary

1   The Treaty of Maastricht introduced a new framework for European integration: the European Union. Two additional pillars concerned with intergovernmental cooperation in foreign affairs and home affairs now flank the 'Community' pillar, which itself was strengthened principally by the introduction of provisions to bring about EMU before the end of the century and enhanced legislative input for the European Parliament.

2   In 1995 the EU enlarged once more to include Austria, Finland and Sweden.

3   In the areas of internal market and social policy, the EU has made steady progress towards intensifying the level of integration. New types of measures have been introduced in both areas to reflect decentralised decision making.

4   Despite difficulties over bringing about the convergence of currencies and the economic indicators mandated under the Treaty of Maastricht, the single currency was introduced in eleven of the Member States by the irrevocable locking of exchange rates as of 1 January 1999.

5   The Schengen Convention was brought into force between a number of Member States as of 1995, bringing about a limited frontier free travel area with flanking measures such as common visa arrangements.

6   The Treaty of Amsterdam resulted from an IGC called largely because the Treaty of Maastricht required it. It was negotiated in 1996 and 1997 and

came into force in 1999. It preserved the three-pillar system, but substantially strengthened the EU and the EC by communitarising large parts of the third pillar, incorporating the Schengen system into the EU and introducing a number of provisions guaranteeing the EU as a liberal constitutional order. It introduced a new objective for the EU of creating an 'area of freedom, security and justice'.

7   In 1999 the Commission resigned as a result of pressure from the European Parliament. Romano Prodi was appointed to head up a new Commission with a reform mandate.

8   CFSP has begun to evolve in response to the challenges of the crisis in Kosovo and the implementation of the Stability Pact on South Eastern Europe.

9   Enlargement was on the agenda for the EU throughout the 1990s, with some negotiations beginning in 1999 and others in 2000. The principle of differentiation is applied to the accession process, allowing candidate countries to proceed at their own pace through the tasks associated with accession. The EU now has complex and sophisticated pre-accession strategies to assist the candidate countries.

10   In February 2000 a further IGC was opened, as required for enlargement.

Questions

1   How have the Treaties of Maastricht and Amsterdam contributed to the deepening and widening of the integration process within the EU?

2   In what ways has the external environment of the EU come to influence its internal framework and operation more directly during the course of the 1990s and early twenty-first century?

3   What are the most significant issues facing the EU at present, and how is it possible to find out more about them?

Further Reading

Further information on these developments can be found in many books and papers, but in particular the following:

Commission (2000a), Communication on *Strategic Objectives 2000–2005: 'Shaping the New Europe'*, COM(2000) 154, 9 February 2000.

L. Cram, D. Dinan and N. Nugent (eds) (1999), *Developments in the European Union*, London: Macmillan.

F. Dehousse (1999), 'The IGC Process and Results', in O'Keeffe and Twomey (1999).

D. Dinan (1999), *Ever Closer Union: An Introduction to European Integration* (2nd edn), London: Macmillan.

K. Dyson and K. Featherstone (1999), *The Road to Maastricht*, Oxford: Oxford University Press.

G. Edwards and A. Pijpers (eds) (1997), *The Politics of European Treaty Reform*, London: Pinter.

T. Garton Ash (1999), *History of the Present*, London: Penguin Press.

K.-H. Neunreither and A. Wiener (eds.) (2000), *European Integration After Amsterdam: Institutional Dynamics and Prospects for Democracy*, Oxford: Oxford University Press.

W. Rees, N. Neuwahl and P. Lynch (2000), *Reforming the European Union*, Harlow: Longman.

J. Usher (ed.) (2000), *The State of the European Union: Structure, Enlargement and Economic Union*, Harlow: Longman.

Key Websites

Website of the Millennium Round of trade talks:
htp://europa.eu.int/comm/trade/2000_round/index_en.htm

Website of the WTO: http://www.wto.org/

Key issues website: http://europa.eu.int/geninfo/key_en.htm
Economic Reconstruction and Development in South East Europe: Joint EU and World Bank Website: http://www.seerecon.org/

Links site on Southeast Europe:
http://europa.eu.int/comm/external_relations/se/various/links.htm

General IGC site: http://europa.eu.int/igc2000/index_en.htm

Parliament IGC site: http://www.europarl.eu.int/igc2000/en/default.htm

Council IGC site: http://db.consilium.eu.int/cig/default.asp?lang=en

Commission IGC site: http://europa.eu.int/comm/igc2000/index_en.htm

Dialogue on Europe: http://europa.eu.int/comm/igc2000/dialogue/index_en.htm

Part II

The Institutional and Constitutional Framework of the European Union

4 The Institutions of the European Union

4.1 Introduction

Building upon the outline presentation in 1.2 and the historical framework which has emerged through Chapters 2 and 3 in which the role of the institutions has been constantly alluded to, this chapter examines the composition, and basic powers, functions and organisation of the institutions of the EU. It is a largely static presentation, and there will be more detailed discussion of the institutions at work in Part III, which examines law and policy making in the EU. Proposed and likely reforms of the institutions in the context of the IGC 2000 were discussed in 3.15. Internal reforms, in particular of the Commission, are dealt with in this chapter, although the discussion below needs to be viewed in the light of the more detailed exposition of how the Commission works in conjunction with the other institutions in order to fulfil policy making, guardianship and executive functions under the Treaties in Part III.

The institutional structure of the European Community was, from the beginning, *sui generis*. The same institutional structure as found in the original Article 4 EEC is now embedded into the EU (Article 3 TEU), and the same institutions operate across the three pillars, albeit with differing powers and functions. This is the single institutional structure for the EU (Article 3 TEU). The institutional structure resembles neither the typical governing structure of an international organisation, in that its institutions exercise sovereign powers transferred by the Member States, nor (yet) the institutional framework of a modern parliamentary democracy. It is, for example, not possible to identify a clear separation of powers between the legislative and the executive functions (Lenaerts, 1991a). The legislative function is presently divided between the Council and the Parliament, with inputs from the Commission and from a number of subsidiary bodies. The executive function is largely held by the Commission, but often under delegated powers from the Council, which retains control through a committee structure, and such powers can only properly be exercised with the active cooperation of the Member States. There is no single legislative or executive procedure that can be described in simple terms. Reference must always be made to specific provisions within the Treaties to ensure that the institutions are acting within their powers as required by Article 4 EC. Within these limits, however, the institutions have broad autonomy of action, and may establish their own Rules of Procedure, which once created must be observed. The Court of Justice exercises a supervisory control over the division of powers between the institutions, as it does over the division of powers between the EU and the Member States.

The four-cornered structure – Commission, Council of Ministers (now renamed Council of the European Union and termed 'Council' in this book), European Parliament and Court of Justice, assisted by the Economic and Social Committee – envisaged by the original Treaties of Paris and Rome was described briefly in Chapter 1. The institutions of the three founding Treaties have been merged since 1967, although the powers conferred by each Treaty upon the various institutions continue to differ. The discussion of the powers of the institutions in this chapter is focused primarily on the powers granted by the EC Treaty, with limited discussion of the power structure under the intergovernmental second and third pillars, established under the TEU. The institutional framework has gradually evolved through the Treaties, and also in the light of changed institutional practices and the interventions of the Court of Justice. For example, under the Treaty of Maastricht the Court of Auditors, which ensures financial discipline and prudentiality within the EU, was given the status of an institution, and a Committee of the Regions was established to make an additional advisory input into the legislative process (Article 4 EC). The essential institutional structure for EMU was also established. The TEU formalised the existence and role of the European Council (Article 4 TEU).

Since the inception of the European Community, although the basic outline of the political institutions has remained largely the same, the details of the structure have altered considerably. Changes have been the product both of the enlargement of the EU, which has necessitated the enlargement of the institutions and changes in their working patterns, and of the evolution of the functions and activities of what is now the EU. The pattern of development has frequently been one of the *de facto* development of new activities and interinstitutional relationships, followed by subsequent *de jure* recognition of the changes in an amendment to the constitutive Treaties. At no point does a study of the Treaties alone give a complete picture of the institutions at work.

The new bodies that have emerged inside and outside the existing framework, while making the pattern of policy making at the EU level ever more complex, have not always brought improvements in the efficiency, transparency or accountability of the activities of the EU. Despite the frequent reference in the Treaties and documents such as the Commission's *Strategic Objectives for 2000–2005* (Commission, 2000a) to making the EU and its institutions more accessible to citizens, this seems a forlorn hope given the nature of the system. Moreover, the balance of power between the institutions has altered in significant ways. For example, the intergovernmental element in the decision-making process, represented by the Council of the European

Union, has exercised a more dominant role than envisaged in the founding Treaties, and has tended to prevail over the supranational element, represented by the Commission and the Parliament. This is not just because the Council has largely retained the core legislative power, but because its influence has been strengthened by the following key developments:

- the evolution of the European Council;
- the emergence of the distinctive role of the Presidency;
- the establishment of the intergovernmental structures of political cooperation, and cooperation in home affairs matters where the Council and its Secretariat take a leading role;
- the work of the Committee of Permanent Representatives (COREPER);
- the evolution of a structure of committees of national representatives which advise, assist and sometimes control the Commission ('comitology');
- the creation of the Office of High Representative held by the Council Secretary General.

In sum, the Council has expanded 'upstream' in such a way as to influence the initiation of policy, and 'downstream' so as to exercise more control over the implementation of policy. The expansion of its roles has been largely at the expense of the Commission.

The European Parliament, while unable to overcome the dominance of the Council, has gradually emerged as a more significant political actor. It has worked to maximise its most important powers through:

- its increasing input into the legislative and budgetary processes, which ensures an element of democratic legitimacy for the EU;
- its powers of supervision and control over the other political which promote executive accountability.

In formal terms, at least, the Commission appears to have changed the least during the existence of the EC and the EU, as there has been no compete overhaul of it or its role under the Treaties or in terms of internal administration. In practice, it is called upon to carry out many more tasks than in the early years, and up to one half of the Commission's staff are now occupied on the management of various EU funded programmes and activities. On the other hand, despite the evolution of the other institutions and the proliferation of other bodies (including in very recent years a number of regulatory and executive agencies which may in the future come to assist and even compete with the Commission in relation to the management of EU policies), the Commission still retains a pivotal role within the institutional structure. Consequently, a discussion of the political institutions needs to begin by considering the composition, duties and tasks of the Commission.

4.2   The European Commission: Composition and Basic Character

The European Commission was originally intended as the 'bonding element' within the supranational institutional structure of the EU (Urwin, 1995: 81). It would drive forward the motor of integration, recommending policies for action, administering the Treaties and acting as a guardian and watchdog of the 'Community' interest. It was intended to be a technocratic and elite body, rather than a political entity. It grew out of the High Authority, created by the ECSC Treaty, which has greater powers of decision under the more detailed provisions of that Treaty. The Commission is based in Brussels, although it has an important outpost in Luxembourg.

In legal terms, the Commission is a college of twenty Commissioners – at least one and no more than two from each Member State – chaired by a President, under whose 'political guidance' it shall work (Article 219 EC). By convention, two Commissioners are drawn from each of the five larger Member States (France, Germany, Italy, Spain and the UK), and one from each of the ten smaller states. By convention also, the UK's two Commissioners come from the two largest political parties – Conservative and Labour. Article 214(2) EC lays down the appointment procedure, which has been altered by both the Treaties of Maastricht and Amsterdam. It has weighted the system to create both a more strongly 'presidential' system, and to lend greater democratic legitimacy to the Commission as a whole by subjecting the process to parliamentary scrutiny and approval. It also politicises the Commission to a greater extent, carrying it further away from its essentially technocratic origins. It may be seen increasingly as a prototype European government. The governments of the Member States are responsible for nominating 'by common accord' the person they intend to appoint as President of the Commission. That nomination must be approved by the European Parliament. The other persons, appointed as Commissioners, are nominated by common accord with the nominee for President. Finally, all of the nominees are subject to a vote of approval by the European Parliament, and then are appointed by common accord of the governments of the Member States. The Santer Commission of 1994 and the Prodi Commission of 1999 were both subjected to reasonably rigorous hearings before a European Parliament Committee, and approved by a vote. In the case of Santer, the vote of approval was quite close, a political handicap which continued to dog Santer and his Commission throughout its period of office.

The term of office of the Commission was extended from four to five years by the Treaty of Maastricht, and synchronised in terms of inception and departure with the European Parliament. Accordingly, the newly elected Parliament of 2004 will be responsible over that summer for scrutinising the next Commission. Commissioners may be renewed for a further five years. Since the possibility of extensive eastwards enlargement of the EU has been on the agenda, it has been equally obvious that the composition of the Commission needs to be closely scrutinised. If the number of Commissioners carries on growing as the EU enlarges, it will become unwieldy and ineffective. It is already the case that the functions of the Commission barely allow meaningful portfolios to be allocated to all Commissioners. The 1996–97 IGC leading to the Treaty of Amsterdam was supposed to consider these issues, but ducked the question in the end, leaving it to a further IGC. It came under consideration again from February 2000, with the calling of the IGC envisaged in the Enlargement Protocol to the Treaty of Amsterdam (3.15).

According to the Treaty, the qualities of the Commissioners are their general competence and an independence which is beyond doubt (Article 213(1) EC). Although appointed by Member States, the Commissioners are not national representatives. Their independence is guaranteed by Article 213(2) which prohibits them from taking instructions from any government or other body, from taking any action incompatible with their duties, and from engaging in other occupations, and which enjoins them to act during and after their term of office with integrity and discretion. This includes not accepting, after ceasing to hold office, certain appointments or benefits. They give a solemn undertaking at the beginning of their term to respect the obligations of office. In return, they are protected from dismissal except for failure to fulfil the conditions required for the performance of their duties or serious misconduct, in which case the Court of Justice may compulsorily retire an errant Commissioner (Article 216 EC). The Court may also deprive a Commissioner, or retired Commissioner, of his/her benefits or pension for breach of Article 213(2). In practice, the controls upon Commissioners have normally been greater than these formalities might indicate, since the possibility of non-renewal in post at the expiry of a term of office may be sufficient occasionally to remind a Commissioner that ultimately he or she owes the appointment to the exercise of national discretion. Margaret Thatcher's well-publicised refusal to renominate Lord Cockfield, the architect of the Commission's White Paper on the completion of the internal market, for the second Commission presided over by Jacques Delors was a good example of the use of the renewal of the mandate as an instrument of discipline.

However, such sanctions may be of little assistance in controlling the actions of a Commissioner who is about to leave the Commission in any event. Such was the case of the German Internal Market Commissioner, Martin Bangemann, who came to public attention in July 1999 when it emerged that after ten years as a Commissioner he was moving directly from political responsibility for regulating the telecommunications industry to an extremely well-paid executive post with the large Spanish telecommunications company Telefónica. Bangemann received almost universal condemnation for his action, with the Commission as a college expressing 'surprise' and individual Commissioners such as Neil Kinnock being publicly critical. There were calls for him to reverse his decision to join Telefónica from bodies such as the European Parliament (see Bulletin EU 7/8-1999, points 1.9.7 and 1.9.11) and from his own political party, the German Free Democrats, who also asked him to resign from the party. All of this was despite his commitment not to represent Telefónica in its future dealings with the Commission. Many observers were surprised, none the less, when the Council took the decision – in accordance with the terms of Article 213(2) – to ask the Court of Justice to rule upon whether Bangemann was in breach of his obligations and if necessary to deprive him of his pension rights (worth in excess of £50,000 p.a.) (Council Decision 1999/494, OJ 1999 L192; Case C-290/99). Bangemann promptly counterclaimed against the Council by bringing an action for annulment of its decision before the Court of First Instance (Case T-208/99). The matter was settled by a further decision of the Council in December 1999 (Council Decision 2000/44, OJ 2000 L16/73) in which the Council agreed to withdraw its case provided Bangemann simultaneously withdrew his. The principal concession made by Bangemann, apart from a confirmation that he would remain subject to his ongoing duty of confidentiality (Article 287 EC), was that he would not take up employment with Telefónica or any other telecommunications operator until 1 July 2000, and that he would not represent any telecommunications operator in its dealings with the EU institutions until after 1 January 2002. In return, he has kept his pension.

At the beginning of the term of office, the President allocates policy portfolios to the other Commissioners. The President's nominally free hand in this task has historically been fettered by the need to balance national interests, which jealously demand the allocation of important and prestigious portfolios to their Commissioner(s), and by the general competence and reputation of the nominees. Hence the Member States appended a Declaration to the EC Treaty at the Amsterdam IGC noting that 'the President of the Commission must enjoy broad discretion in the allocation of tasks within the College, as well as in any reshuffling of those tasks during a Commission's term of office.' In his allocation of functions, President Prodi was able almost entirely to eliminate the so-called 'Frankenstein portfolios', with the exception of one of the Spanish Commissioners, Loloya de Palacio, who was allowed to keep sectoral responsibilities for energy and transport in addition to her duties as Vice President of the Commission in charge of relations with the European Parliament. Even so, not all the policy portfolios carry the same workload, or degree of policy coherence. Each Commissioner is assisted by a *cabinet* or private office, composed of officials who have been traditionally personally appointed by the Commissioner. The *cabinets* operate outside the formal bureaucracy of the Commission. The cabinets are headed by the *chefs de cabinet*, who meet on a regular basis to prepare the work of the Commission itself. These meetings fulfil something of the same role in relation to the Commission as the Committee of Permanent Representatives (COREPER) in relation to the Council (4.11).

Concerns regarding these private offices, along with the ethical questions raised by the Bangemann affair, were some of the immediate questions about the integrity and probity of the Commission as a political institution which Romano Prodi was able to deal with at the very beginning of his term of office in late 1999. Codes of Conduct for Commissioners (covering the declaration of interests, missions (i.e. travelling on Commission business) and the composition and functioning of private offices) and on Commissioners and Departments (especially the relations between them) had already been adopted even before the March 1999 resignation of the Santer Commission (van Gerven, 2000: 95), and under Prodi they were updated and revised and made available on the Internet. The Rules of Procedure of the Commission have also been revised (OJ 1999 L252/41) to reflect these principles. Private offices had become small fiefdoms within the Commission, and also were responsible for some of the abuses that attracted the criticisms of the Committee of Independent Experts appointed by the Parliament (3.11). They were 'Europeanised' by rules requiring the maximum of six advisors per Commissioner to feature at least three nationalities, and requiring either the *chef de cabinet* or his/her deputy to be of a different nationality to the Commissioner. The Commissioners and their private offices were moved out of the Commission's main building into the buildings where the Directorates-General or Services that they effectively head are based. Appointments to the private offices are now formally a task of the President. Each of the Commissioners gave an undertaking to President Prodi on entering office that he or she would resign if asked to do so because of failure to live up to high standards of conduct in public life.

The Directorates-General or Services constitute the Commission as a bureaucracy or civil service, rather than a political institution within the Treaty framework. Most of the day-to-day work of the Commission is done by a body of European civil servants who are employees of the institution. Those 'Eurocrats' are concerned with policy and executive functions and number around 10,000, assisted by a similar number in technical and support posts. Contrary to popular demonology about 'Brussels', this represents a small bureaucracy both in relation to the tasks that it is required to undertake and in comparison to the size of the national civil services. Eurocrats are normally appointed on the basis of entry examinations or, increasingly, come on secondment from national administrations. The Commission is divided into thirty-six Directorates-General ('DGs') or specialised Services, such as the Secretariat General, the Legal Service, the Statistical Office and the Translation and Interpretation Services (around one-fifth of Commission staff work in translation and interpretation, across the EU's eleven official languages). The size of the DGs and the Services varies, as does their degree of influence and input into the policy-making process. They are each headed by a Director-General. Having long been known by their numbers as often as their names, the DGs are now known solely by their names (or sometimes acronyms). Thus DGIV is the Competition DG, DGXV is the Internal Market DG (DG MARKT) and DGV is the Employment and Social Affairs DG (DG EMP). Recent 1999 reorganisations have created a more streamlined structure for issues such as industry, the distributive trades, and aspects of enterprise and competitiveness, with a single Enterprise DG. The field of external relations has also been reorganised with separate DGs for development, enlargement and trade, but a Common Service for External Relations, and two Commissioners – one for Enlargement and the other for External Relations. Even so, there are still difficulties with matching up all the DGs and the Commissioners, who have responsibility for one or more DGs. Improvements in relation to coordination should be brought about with increased cross-Commission groups of Commissioners on issues such as equal opportunities and 'growth, competitiveness, employment and sustainable development'. These changes should overcome at least some of the difficulties associated with the rigid organisational structure and the lack of overall policy oversight within the Commission, which have often meant that policy making is fragmented and lacking in coherence, at least until the more thoroughgoing reforms being pursued by Romano Prodi with the assistance of Neil Kinnock can come into effect (4.7). Within the DGs and Services, Prodi's short-term changes have also had an effect. He has insisted, once again, on Commissioners and Directors-General *not* having the same nationality, and 'flags' on specific posts such as the Director-General of the Agriculture DG who was always French have gone, appointments now being based on 'merit and experience'. Overall, of course, these are beneficial developments in a modern transnational civil service, although some of the short-term changes have been dubbed 'sub-optimal' in terms of the their effects, with talented and experienced officials with no obvious national allegiance being moved for no other reason than their formal nationality (Peterson, 2000).

As a college, decisions must be taken collectively by the Commissioners, who meet every week in private session. The Commission takes decisions by a simple majority vote, but members are bound by a principle of collective or collegial political responsibility, even if they opposed a particular decision. To facilitate the decision-making process, and prevent administrative overload, the Commission's own internal Rules of Procedures allow for a 'written procedure', whereby copies of draft decisions are circulated in advance to the Commissioners, and are adopted without discussion if there is no opposition. The Commission may also delegate the power to take 'clearly defined measures of management and administration' to individual Commissioners (Article 13 of the Rules of Procedure); sub-delegation of certain decision-making functions to senior members of the Commission staff is also permissible if expressly provided for in the delegation decision. However, some decisions cannot be delegated such as the decision to issue a reasoned opinion and to commence enforcement proceedings against a Member State alleged to be in breach of its obligations under EU law in accordance with Article 226 EC (Chapter 8). Following the *BASF* case (Case C-137/92 P *Commission* v. *BASF* [1994] ECR I-2555), where the Commission has found that undertakings have infringed the competition rules and imposes fines upon them, the undertakings in question must be confident that the operative part of the decision in question and the statement of reasons had actually been adopted by the College of Commissioners. The Court found in *Germany* v. *Commission* (Case C-191/95 [1998] ECR I-5449) that the decision to issue a reasoned opinion was not a measure of administration or management and could not be delegated. The formal requirements on the College of Commissioners are, however, limited as the issue of a reasoned opinion is merely a preliminary step which does not have any binding legal effect on the addressee (and so is not in itself challengeable), so it is not necessary for the College itself formally to decide on the wording of the acts which give effect to those decisions and put them in final form. The Court found that it was sufficient that the decisions had been the subject of collective deliberation in the College, and the information on which they were based was available to the members of the Commission.

The observance of both the Rules of Procedure, and general principles of administrative fairness and consistency, mean that the Commission must always comply carefully with the limitations set down by these procedures. This is well illustrated by the *BASF* case. In December 1988 the Commission adopted a decision finding a violation of what was then Article 85(1) EEC (now Article 81(1) EC) by a number of chemical firms alleged to be members of a cartel in the PVC sector. Heavy fines were imposed. The firms successfully challenged the decision before the Court of First Instance in Cases T-79/89, etc. *BASF* v. *Commission* ([1992] ECR II-315), which held that the decision was so vitiated by defects of form and procedure as to be 'non-existent' (15.2). It found that the measure had been altered in a way which went beyond the correction of grammatical, orthographical or typographical errors after it had been adopted by the Commission; this was a breach of the principle of the inalterability of administrative measures (Case 131/86 *United Kingdom* v. *Council (Battery Hens)* [1988] ECR 905). The Commission itself had considered only the French, German and English versions of the draft decision; it had left the Commissioner for competition policy matters to adopt text of the decision in the other languages of the case (Dutch and Italian). Finally, the Court of First Instance established that there was a problem over the timing of the taking of the decision, since some versions appeared to have been authenticated by Peter Sutherland – whose mandate expired on 5 January 1989 – at a time when there was no text ready for notification or publication. The most controversial finding of the Court of First Instance was that concerned with 'non-existence'; this could have meant that all previous decisions of the Commission could be challenged, since no time limit applies to the challenge of non-existent acts. This aspect of the case was overturned by the Court of Justice when the Commission appealed the judgment (Case C-137/92 P), which found that there was no case for applying this extreme sanction, recalling that:

> 'acts of the Community institutions are in principle presumed to be lawful and accordingly produce legal effects, even if they are tainted by irregularities, until such time as they are annulled or withdrawn' (p. 2647).

However, the Court of Justice agreed with the first instance finding of irregularities, stressing the vital importance of the collegial responsibility of the Commissioners:

> 'Compliance with that principle, and especially the need for decisions to be deliberated upon by the Commissioners together, must be of concern to the individuals affected by the legal consequences of such decisions, in the sense that they must be sure that those decisions were actually taken by the college of Commissioners and correspond exactly to its intention' (p.2650).

It rejected the Commission's view that it need only make clear its intention to take certain action without needing to be involved in the drafting and finalisation process:

> 'Since the intellectual component and the formal component form an inseparable whole, reducing the act to writing is the necessary expression of the intention of the adopting authority' (p. 2651).

The Court confirmed the primacy of the principle of inalterability, and the paramount necessity for authentication of acts in the form provided for in the Rules of Procedure (signatures of President and Executive Secretary), as a guarantee of legal certainty (9.3). Consequently, the Court annulled the decision.

The independence of the Commission makes it uniquely qualified to give a 'European perspective' upon the progress of European integration, although in practice it is of course never entirely separated from national or sectoral pressures and lobbies. It has developed a role as the mediator and conciliator between disparate and conflicting interests, in particular within the Council, and has operated as the broker in the resolution of numerous intractable disputes such as those over budgetary contributions and financial discipline within the EU.

The powers and tasks of the Commission are set out in Article 211 EC:

'In order to ensure the proper functioning and development of the common market, the Commission shall:
- ensure that the provisions of this Treaty and the measures taken by the institutions pursuant thereto are applied;
- formulate recommendations or deliver opinions on matters dealt with in this Treaty, if it expressly so provides or if the Commission considers it necessary;
- have its own power of decision and participate in the shaping of measures taken by the Council and by the European Parliament in the manner provided for in this Treaty;
- exercise the powers conferred on it by the Council for the implementation of the rules laid down by the latter.'

In practice, the role of the Commission is best described by dividing it into the four basic functions examined in the following paragraphs:

- the formulation of policy;
- the execution and administration of policy;
- the representation of the interests of the EU;
- the guardianship of the Treaties.

It does not, of course, have such extensive powers in relation to CFSP and JHA, or indeed, in relation to the post-Amsterdam Title IV of the EC Treaty, on aspects of the free movement of persons, where it will share the power of initiative discussed below until 2004 with the Member States. Thus what follows should be seen best as a general summary of the powers of the Commission, and not a comprehensive statement valid in every respect for every area of policy making.

4.3   The Policy-Making Function

There are three main mechanisms whereby the Commission develops the policy of the EU. It makes proposals for action; it drafts the budget that determines the allocation of resources; and it takes policy decisions within the limited powers that it is granted by the Treaties.

Proposals for action take either a 'small' or a 'large' form. 'Small' initiatives are draft legislative acts prepared by the Commission for adoption by the Council (acting, where, appropriate with the European Parliament) under the law-making powers of the Treaties. Almost all the provisions of the Treaty which grant a law-making power to the Council begin 'on a proposal from the Commission...'. The Commission has a broad discretion in putting forward policy proposals, although some limits are imposed by the Treaty itself. For example, when making proposals for the adoption of measures in relation to the completion of the internal market, the Commission has been required by Article 15 EC to take into account the difficulties faced by weaker economies as they prepared for the internal market. Article 95(3) EC further requires all proposals made for measures concerned with the completion of the internal market under that provision which concern health, safety, environmental protection and consumer protection to take as a base a high level of protection.

'Large' initiatives are Commission proposals for EU action within a broad field. Perhaps the best known is the Commission's White Paper *Completing the Internal Market*, but others include the *Social Action Programme* issued as the basis for action to implement the 1989 Community Social Charter and the 1995 *White Paper on Education and Training. Teaching and Learning: Towards the Learning Society.* Not all such projects necessarily envisage that all the measures to be taken will involve binding legislative action. Good examples are the 1997 *Action Plan for the Single Market* and the 1999 *Strategy for the Internal Market*, where legislative measures might be coupled with the publication of handbooks, for instance, to provide better information for citizens and those who might seek to rely upon EU law (e.g. economic operators in the field of public procurement).

In Title IV of Part III of the EC Treaty, concerned with the free movement of persons, the Commission shares the power of legislative initiative with the Member States for a period of five years. Under the third pillar, Article 36(2) TEU refers to the Commission being 'fully associated' with work in this area. More significantly, it has a joint right of initiative in relation to secondary measures to be taken by the Council under Article 34(2) TEU, reflecting its practice just prior to the Treaty of Amsterdam when it began to make third-pillar initiatives, at least informally. However, its capacity to drive policy still remains relatively weak.

The Commission has a limited power of decision under the Treaty. Some powers are granted explicitly by the Treaty, others are implicit in its system. One example is the old Article 118 EEC which gave the Commission the task of encouraging cooperation between the Member States and facilitating the coordination of their action in various fields of social policy including employment, labour relations, working conditions, vocational training and social security, and which is now in large measure replicated in Article 140 EC. In Cases 281, etc./85 *Germany et al.* v. *Commission (Migration Policy)* ([1987] ECR 3203) the Court of Justice held that where the Commission is granted a specific task under the Treaty, it must be regarded, implicitly, as having the power to take steps to achieve this task, including the power to adopt binding measures such as decisions. The Commission is also responsible for developing the competition policy of the EU, which involves not only the enforcement of the prohibitions in Articles 81 and 82 EC on anti-competitive and monopolistic conduct against individual undertakings (a function better characterised as enforcement rather than policy implementation), but also the development of general policy initiatives aimed at dismantling rigidities in public sector markets such as telecommunications. To this end it has an important power of decision under Article 86(3) EC. Use of this power to issue directives has been upheld by the Court of Justice on several occasions (Cases C-271, etc./90 *Spain et al.* v. *Commission* [1992] ECR I-5833). Other original legislative powers include Article 39(3) EC giving the Commission the power (which it has exercised) to lay down regulations establishing the principles on which retired migrant workers may continue to reside in the host state. However, the majority of the Commission's legislative or regulatory powers are not original, but are delegated to it by the Council. This has occurred extensively in the field of agriculture under Article 37 EC, in relation to customs law, and to a more limited extent in the field of competition law. The discussion of these belongs essentially under the Commission's executive and administrative function.

In the development of policy, the Commission's internal bureaucracy is assisted by internal working groups and Advisory Committees composed of national experts, or civil servants representing national interests, by networks of experts, and by 'Euroquangos' such as CEDEFOP, the EU's centre for the promotion of vocational training. Closely linked to the Commission is an ever-growing network of agencies and other similar bodies, which exercise quasi-regulatory and advisory functions (4.17). The Commission – like the other political institutions – is also subject to intense lobbying by national and EU-based interest groups.

4.4 The Executive and Administrative Function

Since the bureaucracy of the EU is extremely small, and largely centrally based, it relies for the most part for the implementation of policies upon the administrations of the Member States, and, where appropriate, the network of agencies referred to in 4.3. The examples of 'direct implementation' of EU policies by the Commission are few, and can more accurately be characterised as activities of the Commission aimed at protecting the legal fabric of the EU such as the enforcement of the competition rules and the rules on state aids (see 4.6). The Commission's role in the 'indirect implementation' of the major policy areas such as external trade, customs, agriculture and social security for migrant workers is likewise supervisory, and consists in large part in the making of rules which the national administrations must observe, and then ensuring that they are observed. The duty of loyalty to the European Community contained in Article 10 EC requires national administrations to cooperate in the implementation of EU policies. The Commission owes a duty of 'due diligence' to the Member States in its working, managing the implementation of policy or procedures under the Treaties (Case C-319/97 *Kortas* [1999] ECR I-3143).

In laying down the rules for national administrations to follow, the Commission is commonly exercising a power delegated by the Council under Article 202 EC. The Council 'may impose certain requirements in respect of the exercise of these powers'. In practice, this involves the structure known as 'comitology', under which the Commission acts in conjunction with one of a number of types of committees comprising national representatives which it chairs, which will exercise a lesser or greater degree of control over it. This is one mechanism whereby the Member States have extended their input into EU activities beyond the legislative role of the Council itself (6.7, 7.13).

In its executive role, the Commission manages the finances of the EU, and supervises both revenue collection and expenditure. More than half of the funds go to the European Agricultural Guidance and Guarantee Fund, the Guarantee Section of which is charged with implementing the agricultural price support system established under the Common Agricultural Policy. The Commission also administers the structural funds of the EU aimed at ensuring economic and social cohesion, namely the European Social Fund, the European Regional Development Fund and, more recently, the Cohesion Fund. It also manages the disbursement of funding to support research, especially the RTD framework programmes (current Framework Five). The management of smaller incentive funds, such as, for example, the programme of grants available under the SOCRATES scheme to encourage higher education student and staff mobility, is now frequently contracted out to outside bodies, which are responsible to the Commission for the proper management of the funds.

In scrutinising the implementation of policy – often with a view to developing new policies – the Commission is under an obligation to prepare a number of reports. These include the General Annual Report submitted to the European Parliament (Article 212 EC), which must contain, for example, a separate chapter on social developments (Article 145 EC) and specific annual reports on matters such as competition policy, the achievement of social policy objectives, employment policy, and equal opportunities for men and women (not all of which are required by the Treaty). It is also required to draw up reports on the application of provisions such as Citizenship of the Union (Article 22 EC) every three years and was required to report on progress towards monetary union during the second stage (Article 121 EC) under transitional provisions.

4.5   The Representative Function

The supranational composition and role of the Commission make it uniquely qualified to fulfil the function of representing the interests of the

European Union on the wider global stage. The Commission President is recognised as an important international figure, attending international conferences, acting within international organisations and speaking on behalf of the EU, often in conjunction with the leader or foreign minister of the Member State which holds the Presidency of the Council, who tends to focus on the political representation of matters falling within the Second and Third Pillars of European Union and, since the Treaty of Amsterdam, the High Representative for the CFSP who assists the Presidency. As third countries increasingly choose to deal with the EU rather than or in addition to individual Member States, the Commission's role in establishing diplomatic missions in third countries and accrediting diplomatic missions from those countries is becoming more important (MacLoed *et al.*, 1996).

The Commission also has the task of recommending the opening of negotiations with third states and of conducting negotiations leading to the conclusion of international agreements on behalf of the EC under the procedures in Article 300 EC.

4.6   Guardian of the Treaties

The Commission is the guardian of the legal framework of the Treaties, a role explicitly conferred by Article 211 EC. Its significance is such that it will be discussed fully in a separate chapter (Chapter 8). The Commission has a general power under Article 226 EC to refer to the Court of Justice alleged violations by the Member States of the Treaties and of the rules adopted thereunder. It has additional specific enforcement powers, for example in relation to state aids (Article 88 EC) and the control of the anti-competitive activities of public undertakings and undertakings entrusted with the performance of public services (Article 86 EC). It may in some circumstances authorise Member States to depart from the strict rules of Treaty; for example, it may authorise the Member States to restrict imports of third country products in free circulation in other Member States under Article 134 EC. It also supervises the right of the Member States to apply national measures to protect environmental and health and safety policies under Article 95(4)–(7), (9) EC, even where the EU has adopted harmonising measures. Under Council Regulation 17 adopted in 1962, the Commission was granted numerous enforcement powers in relation to Articles 81 and 82 EC, which proscribe anti-competitive and monopolistic conduct on the part of undertakings within the EU. In exercising these powers, the Commission is subject to the control of the Court of Justice over the legality of its procedures. A 'softer' form of enforcement against the Member States is envisaged in the new post-Amsterdam title on Employment Policy, which it exercises in conjunction with the Council (Article 128 EC).

In its 'guardianship' function, the Commission is assisted by Article 284 EC, which allows it 'within the limits and under conditions laid down by the

Council' to 'collect any information and carry out any checks required for the performance of the tasks entrusted to it.' A more specific investigative function is that given to the European Anti-Fraud Office (OLAF), established in 1999 to succeed UCLAF, the Commission's own anti-fraud unit, which had been in operation since 1987, after a negative report by the Court of Auditors. OLAF remains within the Commission, but it has an independent investigatory function. Its work is scrutinised by a Supervisory Committee of five persons who are independent of the EU institutions. It carries out internal investigations in all of the EU institutions and bodies, and coordinates with the anti-fraud authorities of the Member States. The cross-institutional framework for investigations on a common basis and with the cooperation of the staff of each EU institution or body is an Interinstitutional Agreement of 25 May 1999 between the Council, the Commission and the European Parliament. The Commission is at pains to point out on its website that OLAF is neither a 'secret service' nor a police force, but a legal instrument of administrative investigation.

4.7   Reform and review

There has been no major overhaul of the Commission as either a political institution or a bureaucracy managing policy initiation, development and implementation since its inception in the 1950s. At the same time, with the development of Community and Union competences, the Council and the European Parliament have regularly given the Commission new and additional activities to pursue, without always transferring adequate additional resources to get these done. There has always been in addition an in-built inclination in each incoming Commission – in the political sense of the College and especially the President – to be seen to be pursuing a big idea and therefore to be seen as successful in the terms of that big idea. Successive Commissions would seek to develop new areas of competence, but at the expense of developing adequate systems of internal administration and management. Because the Commission adopts its own Rules of Procedure, it has been in large measure self-regulating. The bare rules of the Treaties provide, it can be argued, an inadequate legal and constitutional framework for the operation of a supranational public service. Jacques Santer, with his 'do less, better' proposal was in truth the first President to begin to take a long hard look at what the Commission actually is and does.

When referring to 'reforming the Commission', however, a variety of different dimensions are implicated. The first is the area in which there is high level paralysis, namely the composition of the College. The formula of at least one and no more than two for each Member State might have worked well for a European Community of Six. However, it is already under considerable strain in a Union of Fifteen and will be an unworkable proposition for a much enlarged Union of anything up to twenty-eight Member States. This issue was not resolved in the Treaty of Amsterdam and was placed squarely before the Member States in the context of the IGC 2000 (3.15). Yet the unwillingness of the Member States to let go of vested interests inherent in having one or two guaranteed members of the Commission has not assisted other aspects of the reform process. Second, reform of the Commission can be taken to refer to improving the network of accountability within which the Commission exists, to reduce the possibilities for mismanagement and nepotism as occurred in the context of the Santer Commission (and doubtless many of the earlier Commissions). This is 'reform' in the sense of dealing with any whiff of corruption associated with the Commission, the Commissioners and especially their *cabinets*. These are issues that President Prodi has begun to address at the very inception of 'his' Commission with tighter rules on private office appointments, Codes of Conduct and other measures.

The third question concerns the web of control which increasingly permeates the Commission, and the absence of a management system or management paradigm oriented towards the achievement of objectives. There has historically been no effective system for prioritisation and coordination, and up to half of Commission staff are engaged with managing various programmes established by the institutions rather than the core activities of policy initiation and development and the guardianship of EU law. However, within that framework of activity, there has remarkably been evidence to indicate that no one – least of the Commission itself – actually really knows what the Commission does. This is a longer term project, one which picks up on earlier initiatives started by Santer which carry the acronyms SEM, MAP and DECODE, and on which a White Paper was issued in early 2000 under the aegis of Vice-President Neil Kinnock, who is responsible for the reform programme, but under the signature of every Commissioner (Commission, 2000b). This White Paper follows a number of earlier strategy and policy papers, putting forward options, and is nested within an ongoing process of consulting the Commission's own staff who could easily be a powerful force against change in this context.

The White Paper makes the following proposals, and enshrines the concrete ideas within an Action Plan incorporating a detailed timetable:

– The White Paper is predicated upon the strategic decision for the Commission to focus more on 'core functions' such as policy conception, political initiative and enforcing EU law. This means ceasing to take as much responsibility for managing programmes; this aspect of the work will be 'externalised', that is passed to bodies appropriately specialised in such tasks, under the supervision of the Commission as necessary.
– It puts in the foreground five principles which are central to a 'culture based on public service', namely independence, responsibility, account-

ability, efficiency and transparency, which are principles applying to the institution as a whole, the politicians who make up the College and each individual Commission staff member. These principles will allow, for example, whistleblowing by staff members concerned about improper activities, and will involve a revamped disciplinary procedure.

- The Commission is making an overall assessment of its activities and resources, building upon the earlier assessments of the Santer initiatives. It will make a hard-headed assessment as to whether the resources are sufficient for the activities, and will discontinue tasks or ask for additional resources as necessary. All institutions (and, of course, the Member States as payers) must face up to these facts.
- The internal organisation of the Commission will be restructured for optimal effectiveness, including reform of the way political priorities are set and resources allocated, changes to the policies on human resources within the Commission in order to improve the working environment, and a review of the system of financial management.
- Most specifically it develops a management tool for delivering the reforms in terms of priority setting, namely 'activity-based management' (ABM). According to the White Paper, 'this system aims at taking decisions about policy priorities and the corresponding measures together, at every level of the organisation. This allows the resources to be allocated to policy priorities and, conversely, decisions about policy priorities to be fully informed by the related resources requirements' (Commission, 2000b: 9). Effectively, the Commission is entering twenty-first century 'new public management' with a bang. ABM requires much greater strategic planning as well as prioritisation.

The timetable carries the programme through until 2002. The jury is out on the chances of its success, as the reform agenda remains remarkably similar to that which has failed to achieve sufficient political support from the Member States for more than twenty-five years to make it a reality (Spence, 2000).

4.8   The Council of the European Union: Composition and Basic Character

The Council is composed of representatives of the Member States, at ministerial level 'authorised to commit' their government (Article 203 EC). The Council represents the intergovernmental element within the institutional structure of the EU. Indeed, it is, in many respects, the main institution of the 'Union' in the strict sense of the second and third pillars, and the general treaty framework of the TEU. It meets, generally, in Brussels, where its Secretariat is based (in the recently built Justus Lipsius building). The Presidency of the Council circulates on a six-monthly rotation between all of the Member States – a long-established practice that is coming under challenge as the EU grows larger. The representative of the Presidency country sits in the chair at Council meetings (see also 4.12). The Council meets when convened by the President or at the request of one of its members or the Commission. As this implies, a member of the Commission with appropriate responsibilities normally attends Council meetings, although without a vote.

The membership of the Council is not static. Although there is a body conventionally designated the 'General Affairs Council' composed of the foreign ministers of the Member States, which discusses issues of general concern to the EC and especially the EU, much of the practical work of the EU is undertaken by the 'technical' Councils, that is sectoral and specialised Councils. These include the 'Internal Market Council', composed of trade and industry ministers with special responsibility for the completion and management of the internal market and the 'Agriculture Council', composed of agriculture ministers who oversee the development and implementation of the CAP. In the context of EMU, ECOFIN, the meeting of finance and economics ministers, has become increasingly important. There is a special meeting of the ministers of those Member States involved in EMU, termed 'Euro-11'. It acts as a political counterweight to the ECB (4.20). Exceptionally, the Treaties can provide for the Council to meet 'in the composition of the Heads of State or Government' (i.e. the European Council). This is the case in relation to decisions about whether Member States have met the convergence criteria, which are the economic qualifications for joining the single currency (Articles 121 and 122 EC) and determinations that there have been a serious and persistent breach by a Member State of the principles contained in Article 6(1) TEU, namely liberty, democracy, respect for fundamental rights and the rule of law (Article 7 TEU). The different formations of the Council meet more or less often, as required. On average, the agriculture ministers meet most often (around monthly), although at different times there have been very regular meetings of the General Affairs Council, ECOFIN and the Internal Market Council.

The fragmentation of the Council weakens its effectiveness, as there is insufficient general policy coherence within the legislative activities of the EU, although this function is fulfilled in part by the Commission, the European Council, the Presidency and even the Council's own bureaucracy or Secretariat which, while smaller than the Commission's, is increasingly influential (Article 207 EC; see Hayes-Renshaw, 1999 who describes this body as having a 'shadowy existence' until the 1990s). The Council is also assisted by its own Legal Service, which is likewise influential given, for example, that it drafted 90 per cent of the articles which formed the basis of negotiations in the 1996–97 IGC (Stubb, 2000: 165). The Treaty of Amsterdam inaugurated a post of Deputy Secretary-General responsible for administration and internal coordination (Article 207(2) EC). The Secretary-General is, of course, now 'Mr or Ms CFSP', the High Representative for the CFSP (3.12).

The tasks of the Council are set out in Article 202 EC. They are to ensure the coordination of the general economic policies of the Member States, to take decisions and to delegate implementing powers to the Commission. There is a tension between the first two tasks, in that they illustrate the sometimes irreconcilable dual role of the Council: to act as the forum for the representatives of the Member States, and to act as the principal decision-making body for both the European Community and the European Union. The Council also has the power under Article 208 EC to request the Commission to undertake any studies the Council considers desirable for the attainment of the objectives of the Community, and to submit to it any appropriate proposals. Used extensively this power could significantly limit the policy-making function of the Commission.

It is not possible to know exactly what happens within the Council. Indeed, the Council remains the least known of the EU institutions (cf. Westlake, 1995; Hayes-Renshaw and Wallace, 1997; Hayes-Renshaw, 1999). It has always deliberated in secret and no full record of its business is published. As it does not have a permanent political presence in the same way as the Commission, it has not established informational channels to the same degree. Press releases and briefings by national ministers have often been the only sources of information, apart from the published record in the *Official Journal* of legislative acts that the Council passes, or resolutions that it adopts. Like the other institutions, it now has a website, but this is not in truth as informative as the other institutions, and rarely carries materials in all official languages. Many documents appear only in French or English, and the coverage, especially under the second and third pillar, can be patchy. In the aftermath of the Treaty of Maastricht, as openness and transparency moved onto the political agenda, the Council introduced reforms to allow for limited public and/or televised sittings, publication of voting records (concretised by the Treaty of Amsterdam in Article 207(3) EC), and a policy of limited access to its internal documents. Access to documents is now subject to the general principle in Article 255 EC, and Article 207(3) requires the Council to elaborate the rules on access to documents in its Rules of Procedures, although in fact the rules are little changed since 1993 when they were first introduced. It was unsurprising that the Council should be the first institution to be the subject of an appeal before the Court of First Instance on access to documents (Case T-194/94 *Carvel and Guardian Newspapers* v. *Council* [1995] ECR II-2765), challenging the general practice of blanket refusals of documents. *Carvel* established the very important principle of the need for an individual case-by-case assessment of requests made by the public (10.8).

The members of the Council – as members of national governments – are not politically accountable to any EU institution for their acts. The Parliament can and does ask questions of the Council, but the answers given are not always full or helpful. However, a convention is developing that the Presidency presents its programme of action for the next six months for debate in the Parliament. The level of accountability at the national level varies between the Member States. The Danish Parliament – the *Folketing* – exercises the tightest control, with the Danish representatives on the Council being frequently required to delay EU decision-making processes in order to consult at a parliamentary level. Scrutiny within the UK Parliament is not as strict. This unsatisfactory situation persists although a number of governments, that of the UK included, insist that the democratic legitimacy of the EU is anchored through the role of national parliaments; the position of national parliaments has been strengthened by a Protocol attached by the Treaty of Amsterdam to the TEU and the EC Treaty on their role, entrenching the duty on the Commission to pass significant policy papers and proposals to national parliaments and enforcing a six-week waiting period for the national parliament to exercise its scrutiny function and institutionalising the Conference of the European Affairs Committees of the national parliaments which have been in existence since 1989.

The Council is subject, like all the institutions, to the rule of law. This largely leaves its legislative discretion unfettered, although there are a number of overriding principles which legislative acts may not violate (6.8). This can lead to the annulment of legislative acts adopted by the Council or to actions for damages (see Part VI). Within narrow limits the Council is also responsible for a failure to act in the legislative field. In Case 13/83 *Parliament v. Council* ([1985] ECR 1513) the Parliament successfully challenged the failure of the Council to create a common transport policy using Article 232 EC. Although the Court of Justice would not substitute itself for the legislature and lay down what form such a policy should take, the case was widely interpreted as a rap on the knuckles for the Council for dilatory exercise of its legislative function.

Article 205 EC provides for simple majority voting, unless the Treaty provides otherwise. A simple majority is constituted by the votes of eight countries out of fifteen. An example where no majority is specified is Article 207(3) which provides for the adoption of the Council's Rules of Procedure, and includes provision for the Council to lay down the conditions for public access to its documents. In practice, the Treaty almost always provides for unanimity or a so-called qualified majority, the latter becoming increasingly the norm. Qualified majority voting (QMV) means that under Article 205(2) EC, the votes of the Member States are weighted as in Table 4.1.

Table 4.1   Qualified Majority Voting

Austria	4
Belgium	5
Denmark	3
Finland	3
France	10
Germany	10
Greece	5
Ireland	3
Italy	10
Luxembourg	2
Netherlands	5
Portugal	5
Spain	8
Sweden	4
United Kingdom	10
Total	87

A qualified majority requires there to be at least 62 votes cast in favour of a measure out of 87, where the Council's deliberation is based on a proposal from the Commission. In other cases (e.g. under CFSP and CJHA where there is limited usage of QMV), the 62 votes must include the votes of at least ten Member States (so-called double qualified majority). The weighting of votes in QMV departs in part from the theory of the equality of all states in international law, although the weighting does not fully reflect population differentials – the less so, the larger the number of Member States belong to the EU. The voting power of Germany was not strengthened after unification although it is now much the biggest Member State. Before the 1995 enlargement, the weighting of the voting and the minimum requirement had the effect of allowing what would normally be at least three dissenting Member States to block a measure. In view of that enlargement, rather than remake the whole structure, the European Council adopted the so-called Ioanninou Compromise whereby a minority of Member States with a total number of votes between 23 and 25 may temporarily block a decision due to be taken by QMV. In such a case, the Council then tries to reach a solution which can be adopted by at least 65 votes. The reluctance of the Council (and the Member States) to commit themselves fully to QMV has been one of the consistent themes of institutional development in the EC and now the EU. It has returned to the agenda – as has the weighting of votes in the Council under QMW – with the 2000 IGC (3.15).

4.9 The Council Acting as an Intergovernmental Body

On certain occasions, in particular where the subject-matter of the meeting falls outside the scope of Community competence and outside the bounds of the Union's activities under the second and third pillars, the representatives of the Member States will meet on an intergovernmental basis. The best-known instance of this was foreign policy cooperation, which has gradually been institutionalised and rendered a more hybrid intergovernmental/supranational type of policy with limited QMV and a slightly increased role for the Commission under the second pillar, and a clear autonomous role for the Council as an institution in that context of the European Union. Only in the external sphere has this formula needed to be used under CFSP, bearing in mind that the EU was not endowed by either the Treaty of Maastricht or the Treaty of Amsterdam with the clear capacity to conclude international agreements with third parties. So insofar as the EU required consensual as opposed to unilateral action in the foreign and security policy field, the formula 'the Member States of the European Union acting within the framework of the Union' was adopted, for example, for the Memorandum of Understanding on the EU Administration of Mostar, in Bosnia (Dashwood, 1999: 218). Intergovernmental cooperation between the Member States also grew up to coordinate policies on immigration, asylum, police cooperation and other home affairs matters. The Trevi Group and the Ad Hoc Group on Immigration in which the Member States met to discuss these matters were replaced by the more formalised arrangements of Justice and Home Affairs in Title VI TEU (the third pillar), by virtue of the Treaty on European Union, which were then partially communitarised by the Treaty of Amsterdam (Title IV, Part III, EC Treaty).

The institutional structures have also provided a framework for intergovernmental cooperation in certain areas which once lay at the margins of Community competence such as policy on culture, education and health. Measures adopted in this field were commonly designated 'Decision of the Representatives of the Governments of the Member States, meeting in the Council'. An example is the Resolution of the Ministers for Culture Meeting within the Council of 7 June 1991, on the development of the theatre in Europe (OJ 1991 C188/3). Since the Treaty of Maastricht, such a resolution can now be adopted within the context of the EC's own limited new competence in relation to culture (Article 151 EC). Even as the competence of the Community expands, and certain areas are brought within the second and third pillars of the Union (e.g. measures on racism and xenophobia), still there are areas of cooperation and collaboration which prove themselves apt for the 'Decision of the Representatives...' formulation. One good example is the Resolution of the Council of the European Union and of the Representatives of the Governments of the Member States, meeting within the Council of June 1995 on the employment of older workers (OJ 1995 C228/1). However, after the Treaty of Amsterdam, this would probably fall under Article 129 EC. Thus increasingly the purely 'intergovernmental' role of the Council will become a historical anachronism. Measures of this nature should be characterised as 'soft law' which is not binding, but largely exhortatory in content and nature (6.15).

4.10   The European Council

The most prominent and most powerful form of intergovernmental cooperation within the EU is the European Council. The practice of summit meetings between the leaders of the Member States has long existed. Regular meetings have occurred since 1974, and the European Council was finally formalised in Article 2 of the SEA, now superseded by Article 4 TEU. This provides that the European Council should meet at least twice a year and that it should be attended not only by the Heads of State or Government, assisted by their foreign ministers, but also by the President of the Commission and one other Commissioner. It is given the task of providing the EU with 'the necessary impetus for its development' and of defining 'the general political guidelines thereof'. It is required to submit a report after each meeting to the European Parliament, and make a yearly written report on the progress achieved by the EU.

The European Council has remained formally outside the structures of the European Community (i.e. the supranational pillar), not subject to the control of the Court of Justice. Conversely it has no legal power to act in pursuance of the Community's objectives or power of decision (Case T-584/93 *Roujansky* v. *European Council* [1994] ECR II-585). Of course, there would be nothing to prevent the Heads of State or Government meeting as the Council of the European Union, and in limited circumstances the Council *must* meet in that composition (4.8). However, one of the strengths of the European Council, which has increasingly come to fulfil a troubleshooting role in pushing forward the process of European integration and resolving the conflicts between the Member States at the highest level, lies precisely in its informality. Indeed, it was originally intended as a relatively low-key meeting, and is somewhat undermined in its effectiveness by the high levels of expectation and media interest that now generally accompany its meetings. It has also been gradually co-opted in parts of the legislative process in the EC Treaty, notably in relation to the determination of the broad guidelines of economy policies under Article 99 EC and, since the Treaty of Amsterdam, the formalised consideration of the employment situation in every Member State under Article 128 EC. Many of its 'decisions', embodied in the Presidency Conclusions, have longstanding consequences for the shape and direction of the EU. Perhaps the best example is the so-called 'Copenhagen Criteria' of 1993, establishing the basis for accession to the EU and now enshrined in Article 6(1) TEU as the very liberal constitutional cornerstone of the Union itself as well as appearing in Article 49, which governs accession.

During the crisis over the ratification of the Treaty of Maastricht, the European Council probably gained an even higher status than before, with a number of skilful compromises being worked out which eventually put the ratification process back on course. Indeed, European integration processes without the European Council have now become unimaginable, although such a crucial role for the Member States in policy formulation was not envisaged by the founders of the Treaties. In practice, the European Council is not simply an opportunity, as it is sometimes portrayed in the British media, for the leaders of Member States reluctant to press further with European integration to halt the entire process. For example, Margaret Thatcher found the regular meetings of the European Council to be occasions when she could not always resist pressure for conformity, as with the agreement over the British budget rebate at the Fontainebleau summit in June 1984 (see 2.10). Furthermore, a skilful Commission President such as Jacques Delors was able to exploit alliances with pro-integrationist leaders such as President Mitterrand of France in order to carry forward the objectives of the Community. Example of this are the budgetary discipline settlement agreed at the special meeting in Brussels in 1988, or the launch of initiatives on Employment (Luxembourg in 1997), Justice and Home Affairs (Tampere in 1999) and eEurope (Lisbon in 2000) at special European Council meetings. The essence of the European Council's function, more than any other EU body, is compromise. Leaders, whose domestic fatc in elections will be judged largely according to their economic success, need to find a balance between promoting the 'good' elements of integration, while hindering the 'bad' ones. That means choosing between those EU proposals that are perceived, from the perspective of the domestic agenda, as excessively intrusive or insufficiently beneficial, and those that are not.

4.11   The Committee of Permanent Representatives (COREPER)

In addition to the help it gets from 'above' in the form of the resolution of serious conflicts at the level of the European Council, the Council also receives assistance from 'below' in the form of the preparatory work of the Committee of Permanent Representatives (COREPER), which is provided for in Article 207 EC. The Permanent Representatives are in effect the Ambassadors of the Member States to the Community, who are based in Brussels and who provide a continuity of presence which political representatives cannot. COREPER meets at two levels: COREPER I (deputy Permanent Representatives) whose remit covers more technical matters and COREPER II (Permanent Representatives themselves) who discuss the more controversial political matters, identifying the differences of view which the Council itself must settle at a political level. The workings of COREPER and the Council are further facilitated by working groups and committees, which meet on a regular or ad hoc basis to discuss policy proposals at an early stage.

Formally, COREPER facilitates Council deliberations by permitting the division of the Council agenda into two parts. Part A contains items on which a unanimous view has been obtained within COREPER. These points can be agreed without discussion. Part B contains the points on which a decision cannot be reached without further discussion and probably compromise within the Council itself. These matters are regulated by the Council's own Rules of Procedure, which themselves represent, however, a fetter on the extent to which the Council can delegate effective authority to COREPER (see Case 68/86 *United Kingdom* v. *Council (Agricultural Hormones)* ([1988] ECR 855) where the Court declared a Directive to be void, as the Council was in breach of its own Rules of Procedure in adopting a Directive by a written vote when two Member States (UK and Denmark) were known to be against it). The Court has also confirmed that COREPER, despite its increasingly significant contribution to the institutional life of the EU, is not an institution in the formal sense of the word, as its role is limited by the terms of Article 151 EC, and cannot therefore take 'decisions' in a legal sense (Case C-25/94 *Commission* v. *Council (FAO)* [1996] ECR I-1469).

Operating parallel to COREPER under the second and third pillars of European Union are two further committees which assist the Council in its work in relation to CFSP and JHA, respectively. These are:

- the Political Committee (Article 25 TEU) which monitors the international situation, contributes to the definition of policies by delivering opinions to the Council, and monitors the implementation of policies in the field of foreign and security policy generally; and
- the Coordinating Committee (Article 36 TEU – known 'pre-Amsterdam' as the Article K.4 Committee) which has a role in coordinating policy on Police and Judicial Cooperation in Criminal Matters (PJC) under the third pillar, giving opinions to the Council and preparing of the Council's discussions.

There are a number of other 'senior' committees, especially the Special Committee on Agriculture created in 1960 and the Employment Committee established by Article 130 EC, after the Treaty of Amsterdam. Beneath COREPER and these various Committees there are a huge number of

Working Groups and High Level Groups which contribute variously to the formulation and agreement of policy. They are the base of the Council hierarchy and their exact dimension is 'one of the EU's great unsolved mysteries' (Hayes-Renshaw and Wallace, 1997: 97), since hardly anyone knows exactly how many Working Groups there are at any one time. Some are temporary and ad hoc; others are permanent. Their general task is to reduce the number of problem areas to be dealt with by COREPER and the Council. They are not forums for voting, but disagreements are noted by means of minutes and the placing of reserves.

4.12 The Presidency

The Presidency of the Council of the European Union circulates at six-monthly intervals between the Member States, originally according to an alphabetical arrangement based on the title of the country in the national language (Belgique, Danmark, Deutschland, Ellas (Greece), etc.). To avoid countries always following each other, and to allow for alternation between the first half-year and second half-year slot, the Member States have resorted to various arrangements, such as reversing the names in pairs (so that Belgium follows Denmark, etc.). Historically, in the first half of the year, the everyday work of the EU used to be dominated by the CAP; in the second half of the year, it was the budget which normally dominated the agenda. Adjustments consequent upon the fourth enlargement altered the earlier arrangements to give the Presidency for the first time to Austria in the second half of 1998, to Finland in the second half of 1999, and to Sweden in the first half of 2001. During 2000 the Presidency was held by Portugal and then France, with the 2000 IGC scheduled for completion at a European Council meeting in Nice in December. The future of the Presidency in its present form has been in question for some time, as further enlargement will make the rotation principle unwieldy, reduce the influence of the larger and most internationally respected Member States, and raise the possibility of several small (or indeed exceedingly small states) succeeding each other over a period of years. However, reform has not so far been achieved and was not placed on the agenda of the 2000 IGC.

On paper the task of the Presidency of the Council is a modest one. It is to convene and chair meetings of the Council, and to sign, on behalf of the Council, legislative and other acts adopted by the Council, or by the representatives of the Member States meeting within the Council. The Presidency acts as the Chair within all the fora convened within the EU structures, in the largest sense. This includes not only the General Council, the Sectoral Councils, the European Council and COREPER I and II, and the Committees and Working Groups, but also other fora of intergovernmental cooperation such as CFSP and PJC. In practice, however, the Presidency has become a great deal more significant, usurping in part many of the policy-making and mediation functions of the Commission. The country holding the Presidency usually sees it as an opportunity to leave a distinctive mark upon the EU scene, and to be seen by the outside world as synonymous with the EU itself. It prepares and presents a programme of action for the Presidency and prioritises particular measures that it would like to see passed in the Council. This it can achieve by controlling the agenda of the Council, in conjunction with the Council's own Secretariat. It creates a certain symbolic separateness by hosting its own website away from the main Europa website. The state holding the Presidency tends to work closely with the Member States immediately succeeding it (a point expressly confirmed for the conduct of the CFSP in Article 18(4) TEU) and the one preceding it.

The key role of the Presidency can be illustrated through some examples. The Dutch Presidency of the second half of 1991 was given the onerous responsibility of brokering the outcome of the intergovernmental conferences on Economic and Monetary Union and Political Union, and the agreement within the European Council on the text of the Treaty of Maastricht. Its management of this matter was not positively evaluated by many observers, and it was felt to have achieved a much better outcome when it again managed the final stage of the 1996–97 IGC leading to the Treaty of Amsterdam. The uneven progress of the ratification process in late 1992 was influenced by the somewhat ambivalent attitude of the UK Presidency, although ultimately the Edinburgh European Council in December 1992 proved to be a triumph of diplomacy. Not all Presidencies contain such important events in the calendar of integration, but Member States do vie with each other to have the most 'productive' term of office, although not all share the same idea of what this means. It is not clear to what extent the EU has benefited from the tendency of the Presidency to match the Commission's functions as mediator and broker of compromise deals, as initiator of policies, and as representative of the EU towards the outside world (although the Presidency does have a particular role in relation to the EU second and third pillars).

4.13   The European Parliament: Composition, Basic Character and Powers

The European Parliament is composed of 626 directly elected representatives of the peoples of the Member States. The number of Members of the European Parliament (MEPs) elected in each Member State is set out in Table 4.2 (Article 190(2) EC). The total number of MEPs may not exceed 700 (Article 189 EC), raising significant problems if the current proposed enlargements take place, as the application of the current formula for allocating MEPs would carry the number very quickly over 700. They have traditionally been paid variable salaries, with rates differing between the Member States, and both the disparities and the levels of pay themselves in some Member States (e.g. Italy) have caused widespread concern. After the elections in 2004 all MEPS will be paid the same rate from the EU budget. There has also been public disapproval in some quarters about the rates of allowances for MEPs and their assistants, including travel allowances and daily *per diem* rates for attendance.

Table 4.2 Membership of the European Parliament

Austria	21
Belgium	25
Denmark	16
Finland	16
France	87
Germany	99
Greece	25
Ireland	15
Italy	87
Luxembourg	6
Netherlands	31
Portugal	25
Spain	64
Sweden	22
United Kingdom	87
Total	626

The Members of the European Parliament are elected in a five-yearly cycle, with the first direct elections held in 1979. In June 1999 the first elections for the EU of fifteen were held. Since 1989, there had been a centre-left majority in the Parliament, with the Socialists as the largest single grouping with around 220 seats, followed by the European People's Party (Christian Democrats) with around 170 seats. A significant change took place in 1999; not only were a very large number of new MEPs elected for the first time giving a significant input of 'new blood' into the institution, but there was also a clear shift towards the right of the spectrum, with the Party of European Socialists securing just 180 seats, and the European People's Party (which does not include the UK Conservative Party) more than 220. However, given the powers of the Parliament and the general institutional organisation of the EU, there is no governing party political coalition in the conventional sense, although the MEPs are grouped together in eight political groupings, covering nearly 100 parties.

There is at present no uniform electoral procedure, and for many years the UK was out of step with the other Member States in so far as it continued to elect the representatives for mainland Britain (Scotland, Wales and England) on the basis of single-member constituencies with a first-past-the-post system. Proportional representation had always been used in Northern Ireland. However, for the first time in 1999 the MEPs in England, Wales and Scotland were elected by proportional representation, with multi-member constituencies and party lists, although the turn out at 23.1 per cent was the lowest on record for a national election in the UK. There was a considerable swing towards the Conservative Party from the Labour Party (the previous elections of 1994 having been a particular low water mark in any event for John Major's Conservative Government), with the Conservative Party making opposition to the single currency a hallmark of its campaign. It is the task of the European Parliament to draw up proposals for a uniform electoral procedure or a procedure based on principles common to the Member States, and, since the Treaty of Maastricht, to give its assent to any provisions adopted for this purpose by the Council, which must act unanimously. However, any changes to the existing system will need to be ratified by the Member States according to the national constitutional requirements (Article 190(4) EC). At the Treaty of Amsterdam Article 190 EC was modified to allow for the Parliament to seek an electoral system based on the principles common to the Member States, a watering down of the 'uniformity' injunction.

The origins of the European Parliament were extremely modest. Designated the 'Assembly' in the original Treaties (a term for which Margaret Thatcher retained a great fondness), the Parliament was composed simply of delegates nominated by the national parliaments and endowed with a narrow range of consultative and supervisory powers. Until the changes introduced by the Single European Act, the only input into the legislative process which was given to the Parliament (a name which it gave itself from 1962 onwards, and which was formally recognised in the Single European Act), was to be consulted by the Council on proposals made by the Commission. It is also responsible for ensuring the accountability of the Commission (4.14). It has always had at the very least mild supervisory powers over the Commission, including the right to put written and oral questions to the Commission (Article 197 EC) and the right to discuss the annual general report submitted by the Commission (Article 200 EC). It has also held from the beginning a draconian power of censure over the Commission, namely the power, by a two-thirds majority vote, to require the Commission to resign as a body. However, although threatened, this power has never been used, and in any event there would be nothing to prevent the Member States reappointing the same Commissioners.

Since its inception, the Parliament has grown in size as consequence of enlargement, changed its character through direct elections, and acquired an important range of new powers. Clearly, there has always been a strong case for developing the role of the Parliament within the system of the EU, both in terms of its input into the decision-making process, and in terms of its control and supervisory power over the other institutions. One aspect of the 'democratic deficit' which the EU is generally held to suffer from relates to the way it exercises sovereign powers transferred by the Member States, but without the same degree of legislative input by an assembly of representatives elected by universal suffrage, and without the full executive accountability of the Commission or the Council to such a body. Ironically, so long as the Parliament remained a non-elected body with 'dual mandate' members (national parliament and European parliament), the case for more powers could be defeated, by pointing to the low calibre and the low level of commitment of its members, who were generally more committed to their role as members of national parliaments. Even now, some critics point to the absence of a coherent transnational party structure, the relatively low level of popular interest in the Parliament, and its alleged tendency to adopt positions on European integration which are out of step with popular feeling as reasons for continuing to limit the powers of the Parliament. The real reason may have more to do with the jealous protection of national sovereignty. The institution of a proper, effective European Parliament endowed with the full range of legislative and supervisory powers associated with parliaments in liberal democracies would mean acknowledging that the EU had in truth reached the stage of something approaching a federal association or even state. At present, however, democracy is suffering, since power has been effectively taken out of the hands of national parliaments, and given to Ministers who are not collectively responsible to any representative body. A step towards the enhancement of a 'European' party system was introduced in Article 191 EC which asserts the importance of political parties at the European level as a factor promoting integration, since they contribute to forming a European awareness and to expressing the political will of the citizens of the Union.

The Parliament has the power to organise its own work by adopting Rules of Procedure (Article 142 EC). It has regularly amended these Rules in order to give maximum effect to its role in the institutional structure (Nicoll, 1994); in 1999 they were in their fourteenth edition (OJ 1999 L202/1). For example, it was through amendments to the Rules of Procedure that 'congressional-style' hearings for individual Commissioners prior to the vote of approval were established. In relation to its input into the legislative process, it has maximised the effectiveness by creating a committee structure in which the range of political views within the Parliament are represented, with twenty individual Committees responsible for preparing draft amendments to legislative proposals which are placed before the plenary session.

Furthermore, to facilitate its work and in order to enable it to manage its workload, the Parliament has since 1988 been able to agree an annual legislative programme with the Commission. The Parliament also acts on its own initiative in certain policy areas. One of the best-known examples is the setting up of an (internal) Committee concerned with institutional reform after the first elections in 1979 which drew up the DTEU (2.10). In January 1999 it put together an (external) Committee of Independent Experts which effectively brought about the downfall of the Santer Commission (4.14).

The business of the Parliament is managed by its President and Vice-Presidents (now fourteen in number), who are elected for two and a half years from the MEPs (Article 197 EC), and by the Conference of Presidents, in which the President and Vice-Presidents are joined by the Chairs of the Committees. The final say is held by the plenary session of the Parliament, which meets eleven times a year. The current work of the Parliament is hampered by its geographical fragmentation: in accordance with established agreements between the Member States, plenary sessions are held in Strasbourg and occasionally in Luxembourg, but most of the Parliament's bureaucracy and support staff are located in Luxembourg, and Committee meetings are held in Brussels. There is longstanding conflict between the Parliament and certain Member States, since the Parliament would prefer to be relocated in a single city, but that desire was again frustrated by the European Council meeting in Edinburgh in December 1992 which largely preserved the status quo, as did the Protocol on the Seats of the Institutions appended to the TEU and the EC Treaty by the Treaty of Amsterdam. The Parliament's lack of autonomy in this matter was reinforced by the judgment of the Court of Justice in *France* v. *European Parliament* (Case C-345/95 [1997] ECR I-5215) in which France contested the decision of the European Parliament to hold a smaller number of sessions in Strasbourg. The Court held that it was for the Member States to determine how many sessions were held in which cities, even if this might affect the organisation of its work by the European Parliament.

At present the European Parliament holds the following powers under the EC Treaty, in addition to those with which it was endowed under the original Treaties and described above. By Articles 272–273 EC, which were amended principally by the Budgetary Treaties of 1970 and 1975, the Parliament was given the status as co-budgetary authority with the Council, although its power, in practice, to affect how the resources of the EC are spent remains limited (7.15). In practice, the provisions of Articles 272 and 273 give 'only an approximate and rather formal guide to what actually happens [in terms of budgetary decision-making]. It provides a framework which has been fleshed out and adapted over time in response to pressures, necessities, and convenience' (Nugent, 1999a: 347). The Commission is responsible to the Parliament in respect of accounting for expenditure. The Single European

Act significantly increased the powers of the Parliament by giving it the power of assent (and therefore of veto) over the accession of new members (now Article 49 TEU) and the conclusion of certain types of external agreements with third states or international organisations (now Article 300(3) EC). The Single European Act also introduced the cooperation procedure which allows the Parliament to give a second reading, and to propose further amendments, to certain legislative acts (7.4). Finally, the Single European Act extended the range of provisions where an opinion of the Parliament is required.

The Treaty of Maastricht took parliamentary involvement in the legislative procedure one step further. The assent provisions were expanded to include the adoption of a uniform electoral procedure (Article 190 EC), reorganisation of the structural funds (Article 161 EC), certain aspects of the supervision of the ECB (Article 105(6) EC) and the amendment of the Statute of the ECB (Article 107(5) EC). It gave the Parliament a power which parallels that given to the Council by Article 208 EC to request the Commission to submit proposals to it on matters which it considers EU legislation to be necessary (Article 192 EC). In addition to widening the instances in which the cooperation procedure is to be applied (e.g. environment, vocational training), the Treaty also introduced what is termed 'Council-Parliament' co-decision as a new legislative procedure (7.5). Many (but not all) provisions where the cooperation procedure previously applied were 'upgraded' to co-decision. The Treaty of Amsterdam made limited changes to the co-decision procedure (Article 251 EC) to make it a more genuine partnership of equals, and apart from the area of EMU which was untouchable in the context of the 1996–97 IGC, made considerable progress towards consolidating the co-decision procedure as the leading basis for QMV voting on legislative proposals in the Council, coupled with intensified involvement of the Parliament. The extent to which the European Parliament is now a genuine co-legislator will be discussed further in Chapter 7.5. The default position for votes in the European Parliament is that unless otherwise provided it acts by an absolute majority of its members (i.e. 50 per cent of MEPs, plus one) (Article 198 EC).

The Treaty of Maastricht also significantly enhanced the position of the European Parliament as the guardian of the interests of citizens of the Union. Article 193 EC empowered the Parliament to set up temporary Committees of Inquiry to investigate alleged instances of maladministration on the part of the other institutions or bodies established under the Treaties. The first such Committee was established in December 1995 to look at alleged contraventions or maladministration under the Community transit system and only one other Committee of Inquiry has been established, to monitor measures taken in relation to BSE (Shackleton, 1998). Article 194 EC formalised a longstanding informal right on the part of all persons resident in the Union to petition the Parliament, individually or collectively, on any matters coming within the Community's field of activity which affect them directly, a right repeated for EU citizens in Article 21 EC. That provision also refers to the citizen's right to apply to the Ombudsman, appointed under Article 195 EC (4.14), whose task it to receive and investigate complaints of maladministration by the EU institutions. Delays meant that the first Ombudsman (Jacob Magnus Söderman) was not inaugurated until September 1995; he was reappointed for a second term of four years in October 1999 notwithstanding his consistently critical stance regarding standards of administration in the institutions.

The range of powers held by the Parliament in relation to the intergovernmental activities of the EU in the sphere of foreign policy has always been very limited. Article 30(4) Single European Act merely required the Parliament to be kept informed concerning European Political Cooperation, although in practice there was a greater level of contact, channelled through the Presidency, which has reported to the Parliament regularly and held meetings with the Committee on Political Affairs. The level of involvement was little changed by the introduction of the more formalised second pillar (CFSP) and the third pillar (JHA and then PJC) by the Treaty of Maastricht and the Treaty of Amsterdam. The European Parliament is consulted by the Presidency on the main aspects and basic choices of CFSP (Article 21 TEU), and it is to be kept regularly informed by the Presidency and the Commission of the development of CFSP. It may ask questions of the Council and make recommendations, and it holds an annual debate on progress in implementing this field of policy. Under the third pillar, the Council *consults* the European Parliament before adopting certain types of measures such as framework decisions, other decisions and conventions (a significant innovation: Article 39(1) TEU), but for the rest the pattern of information, questions and debates is the same as for the second pillar (Article 39(2) and (3) TEU).

It is still not possible, even after Maastricht and Amsterdam, to characterise the Parliament as a fully operational democratic legislature. Indeed, it may well be inappropriate to take as its primary comparator national parliaments, which themselves have problems of legislative input and popular disaffection. It is, however, important to stress its symbolic role within the EU political system. It has become the platform on which statesmen and women from inside and outside the EU (e.g. President Clinton of the US or President Havel of the Czech Republic) choose to address their thoughts on European integration. The address given by Queen Elizabeth II to the European Parliament in May 1992 constituted an historic event from the perspective of both the UK and the Parliament itself in its search for greater international recognition.

Two areas of the Parliament's activities are worthy of more extensive comment in this context. First, the relationships between the European Parliament and the Commission and the extent of the latter's control over the former, in view of the momentous events of 1999; second, the evolving role of the European Ombudsman as a quasi institution in his/her own right in the EU.

4.14 The European Parliament and the Commission

The resignation of the European Commission in March 1999 was undoubtedly brought about by the activities of the European Parliament in seeking to reinforce real executive accountability. Interestingly enough, however, it occurred not because the European Parliament directly used its powers to bring the European Commission to account such as the motion of censure or the rejection of a new Commission, but because of its use of its budgetary weapon (van Gerven, 2000). In this case, it was the withholding of its discharge in relation to expenditure under the 1996 budget (Article 276 EC). A motion of censure was contemplated, but eventually the lesser – and arguably more effective – choice of convening a Committee of Independent Experts (CIE) was taken in January 1999. Even before the events of 1999, Craig and de Búrca had presciently noted the significance of the budgetary powers:

> 'The budgetary process cannot…be separated from more general issues of institutional power within the Community. History is replete with examples of legislative bodies at national level which have used their power over the purse as a lever to improve their position in the overall constitutional hierarchy. The European Parliament is no different in this respect' (Craig and de Búrca, 1998: 102).

In its work, the CIE was influenced strongly by codes of conduct and standards elaborated for example of the UK's Committee on Standards in Public Life. In regard to relationships between the Parliament and the Commission, one of the main points of initial tension was the failure of the Commission to supply the Parliament with information it deemed necessary and which it considered that it had a right to receive under Article 276(2) EC. In other words, transparency and honesty would need to characterise future relations between the two institutions. These are just two key aspects of a broader constitutional relationship of accountability between the Commission – as the head of the EU's executive structure – and the Parliament as part of the EU's legislator and the repository of representative democratic legitimacy as a consequence of being directly elected by universal suffrage. The need for individuals as well as the collective to be held to account reinforces the argument that amendments should be made to the Treaties to enable the Parliament to require the resignation of an individual Commissioner. In the event, the effective holding to account of individual Commissioners occurred because they were specifically identified by the CIE's first report. Although the internal politics of the Commission as a College resulted in a *collective* resignation in March 1999, there was an effective *individualisation* of blame onto those individuals personally responsible for mismanagement and nepotism as well as onto the President as primarily politically responsible for the whole institution. For the future, there should be a positive synergy between the reform of the Commission and its political accountability to the Parliament.

4.15 The European Ombudsman

The office of the Ombudsman was established in 1994 by a decision of the European Parliament. There were some delays in the initial appointment of the first European Ombudsman, Jacob Magnus Söderman, in 1995. In the brief time since the inception of this office, however, it has had a significant effect on approaches to administration and administrative law within the EU. Södermann was reappointed for a further term of four years. The Ombudsman has not only responded with inquiries, decisions and recommendations to specific individual complaints about maladministration within the EU institutions, but he has also undertaken 'own initiative' enquiries in sensitive issues which have often highlighted areas of resistance within the institutions (note: the male gender is adopted here when discussing the Ombudsman's work, as there has so far only been one *male* Ombudsman). Such inquiries tend to result from a consistent pattern of complaints. Areas of particular concern have been the following:

- access to documents and the general issue of transparency;
- the role of the Commission *vis-à-vis* complainants in relation to Article 226 EC enforcement proceedings which may be brought against Member States;
- the need for a preventative Code of Good Administrative Behaviour for all of the institutions and bodies of the EU, especially in relation to dealings with the public;
- the problem of late payment of its creditors by the Commission.

In relation to the latter point, the Ombudsman has highlighted the hypocrisy of the Commission in proposing harmonising national laws on late payments by undertakings and public authorities in the Commission, without learning the lessons which it points out in the proposed directive about the effects of late payment in terms of damage to the reputation of the bodies concerned and the causing of unnecessary insolvencies among creditors.

A Statute and Regulations govern the performance of the Ombudsman's duties. To be investigated, all complaints must be within the 'mandate'. That is, they have been submitted by a person or body entitled to submit a complain (any natural or legal person established in the EU), they must be against an institution or body of the EU, they cannot be against the Court of Justice or Court of First Instance acting in their judicial capacity, and they have to concern maladministration. According to the Ombudsman's Annual Report for 1997, 'maladministration occurs when a public body fails to act in accordance with a rule or principle which is binding upon it'. The office of the Ombudsman was from its inception in the Treaties linked with Union citizenship, although in fact its origins lie outside the Spanish proposals which led to what are now Articles 17–22 EC and are linked to a desire to replicate one of the most successful national Ombudsmen, the Danish one. Many of the rights laid down for 'citizens of the Union' in the Treaty are directly concerned with freedom of movement. Unsurprisingly, therefore, the Ombudsman receives a large number of complaints about free movement issues, which are inevitably found to be outside the mandate. This is because they concern obstacles – mainly based in national law or resulting from the actions of national, regional or local administrations – to freedom of movement for citizens. There are also criteria of admissibility which the complaint must satisfy before it can be investigated: it must identify the author and subject-matter of the complaint, it must be submitted within two years of the events complained of, and it must be preceded by prior administrative approaches to the institution complained of.

The Ombudsman mounts an inquiry if he finds grounds. Once the investigation begins, the institution may settle, or the citizen may drop the complaint. If no maladministration is found after enquiry the Ombudsman closes the case. If maladministration is found, the Ombudsman attempts to bring about a friendly settlement between the parties. In cases where a friendly settlement is not possible, or the basis for any settlement is not acceptable to the Ombudsman, he can close the file with a critical remark to the institution or body concerned, or make a formal finding of maladministration with draft recommendations. A critical remark is considered appropriate for cases where the instance of maladministration appears to have no general implications and no follow-up action by the Ombudsman seems necessary. In cases where follow-up action by the Ombudsman does appear necessary (that is, more serious cases of maladministration, or cases that have general implications), the Ombudsman makes a decision with draft recommendations to the institution or body concerned. The institution or body must then send a detailed opinion to the Ombudsman within three months; this could consist of acceptance of the Ombudsman's decision and a description of the measures taken to implement the recommendations. If an institution or body fails to respond satisfactorily to a draft recommendation, the Ombudsman can send a report to the European Parliament and to the institution or body concerned which may contain recommendations, a mechanism which he does not invoke very often. Important Special Reports have been made on access to documents and the adoption of Codes of Good Administrative Behaviour. Even where the Ombudsman finds no maladministration, the process of complaining and the response of the institution, which is forced to explain itself, can be salutary for the complainant.

A number of interesting facts are revealed by the statistical analysis of complaints contained in the most recent Annual Report to be published (1998). 1,360 complaints were sent directly to the Ombudsman, of which over 1,200 were from individual citizens as opposed to companies or associations. A high proportion of complaints were outside the mandate and needed to be transferred to the national Ombudsmen or to the European Parliament as a petition. Even within the mandate, there were only just over 200 admissible complaints. Within that category some 40 revealed no grounds for enquiry, so since the Ombudsman closed 185 files with reasoned decisions in 1998, it is clear that he and his office are keeping on top of the workload. Among the larger Member States, it is only from Spain where the number of complaints as a percentage of the total exceeds Spain's population as a percentage of the total EU population. This is a more common phenomenon among the smaller Member States as the number of complaints from Belgium, Portugal, Finland and Ireland as a percentage of the total significantly exceeds the population of these Member States as a percentage of the total population.

The Ombudsman has made a significant contribution to good administrative practice in relation to access to documents, although this is clearly an area where his role is subsidiary to that of the Court of Justice. He rapidly pushed through an own initiative inquiry which pushed the generalised adoption of codes of practice and rules on access to documents for all EU institutions (except the Court of Justice), and other bodies established under the Treaties and decentralised agencies (on the scope of access to documents, as opposed to the good practice of having codes, see 10.8) (Södermann, 1998).

In April 2000, the Ombudsman adopted a further Special Report to the Parliament on the adoption by the institutions and bodies of Codes of Conduct on Good Administrative Behaviour (European Ombudsman, 2000). The Special Report arose because of his dissatisfaction with progress being made on a piecemeal basis, and led to his recommendation that a general administrative law in the form of a Regulation should be adopted by the EU legislature to give effect to this principle. According to the Ombudsman,

> 'A Code which contains the basic principles of good administrative behaviour for officials when dealing with the public is needed both in order to bring the administration closer to the citizens and to guarantee a better quality of administration, thus helping to prevent instances of maladministration from arising. Such a Code is useful for both the Com-

munity officials, as it informs them in a detailed manner of the rules they have to follow when dealing with the public, and the citizens, as it can provide them with information on which principles apply in the Community administration and on the standard of conduct which they are entitled to expect in dealings with the Community administration.'

This in a sense sums up the function of the Ombudsman to take preventative action in relation to maladministration, as well as to offer recourse for citizens and others. He has been able to make a significant contribution to development of administrative law and practice in the EU (see generally Harlow, 1999a), as well as to support the evolution of fundamental rights and general principles of law, albeit that the resolution of cases which he offers remains essentially 'soft' in comparison to a judicial resolution (Bonnor, 2000). On the other hand, because of the flexibility of his responses, and his capacity to focus on all of the institutions and bodies of the EU, the Ombudsman appears to have the capacity to make change occur more quickly than might otherwise happen.

4.16　The Economic and Social Committee (ECOSOC) and the Committee of the Regions (CoR)

The idea of the ECOSOC, and, since the Treaty of Maastricht, the Committee of the Regions, is to provide for the formal representation, within the institutional structure, of disparate economic, social and regional interests. The ECOSOC originated in a similar body – the Consultative Committee of the European Coal and Steel Community (Article 18 ECSC). Under Article 257 EC the ECOSOC is given advisory status, and this in practice means being consulted by the Council and Commission where the Treaty so provides (e.g. Article 95), or where those institutions consider it appropriate (Article 262 EC). The European Parliament can consult the ECOSOC, although in practice the two bodies are more likely to be in competition for status within the system. It also issues 'own initiative' opinions (Article 262 EC). The instances of consultation in relation to legislative proposals have evolved over the years, and most recently it was given consultative status by the Treaty of Amsterdam in relation to employment policy, social policy and public health.

The 222 members of the ECOSOC are allocated between the Member States on a basis that is broadly proportionate to size and population. They are appointed by the Council, on the nomination of the Member States, for four years, with appointments renewable. The members are appointed in their personal capacity and must not be bound by any mandatory instructions. This is strengthened by Article 258 EC which insists that the members of the ECOSOC must be 'completely independent in the performance of their duties, in the general interest of the Community'.

The interests to be represented are listed, on a non-exhaustive basis, in Article 257 EC. They include representatives of producers, farmers, carriers, workers, dealers, craftsmen and professional occupations and representatives of the general public. In practice, members are divided into three categories: I – employers; II – workers; III – others, including agricultural interests, professional associations and consumers. The ECOSOC is organised in specialised sections (e.g. agriculture, transport, etc.) which prepare draft reports on legislation for consideration in plenary session.

The Treaty of Maastricht established a Committee of the Regions, composed of representatives of regional and local bodies (Articles 263–265 EC). Like the ECOSOC, the CoR has 222 members, divided on the same basis among the Member States. The provisions on the appointment of members by the Council and the organisation of the work of the Committee largely parallel those governing the ECOSOC. The Treaty of Amsterdam protected the CoR against infiltration by MEPs, forbidding a dual mandate (Article 263 EC). Like the ECOSOC, the CoR undertakes much of its work in commissions and subcommissions. It is to be consulted where the Treaty so provides, and where the Council and Commission so decide, especially in relation to matters of cross-border cooperation. It may be consulted by the European Parliament. It may also issue own initiative opinions, and is to be advised of instances where the ECOSOC is to be consulted, but it is not, with the possibility that it might then decide to submit an opinion, if it believes there to be significant regional interests affected (Article 265 EC). The provisions on EU policy in the field of culture introduced by the Treaty of Maastricht (Article 151 EC), as well as the revised provisions on economic and social cohesion (regional policy) (Articles 158–162 EC) provided for the consultation of the Committee of the Regions but the amended provisions on environmental policy did not, despite the obvious links with regional policy. This point was changed by the Treaty of Amsterdam (Article 175(1) EC). Amsterdam also extended the CoR's remit to consultation in areas such as employment, social policy, public health and transport. The provisions on the CoR are thus a mixture of the original mandate etched out by the Treaty of Maastricht, plus 'a significant if undramatic enhancement of the status of the Committee' by the provisions of the Treaty of Amsterdam (Duff, 1997: 172).

The ECOSOC and the CoR encounter a good deal of criticism as being irrelevant wastes of time and money (e.g. Weatherill and Beaumont, 1999: 169). There is already fierce direct lobbying of the political institutions by interest groups (7.9), and the institutions are regarded as relatively open to influence. In areas of particular importance, the Treaties bypass the ECOSOC by establishing bodies such as the Employment Committee (Article 130 EC), or by constitutionalising the status of the social dialogue in the area of social policy law making (Articles 138–139 EC). Certainly, in many analyses of democracy within the EU they are frequently largely ignored (e.g. Lord, 1998; Laffan, 1999a). On the other hand, within the EU viewed as a multi-level system of governance with diffuse *loci* and processes for the representation of interests as well as allowing for the citizen to have multiple avenues to express his or her identity, the CoR and ECOSOC can be viewed as part of the overall framework for the representation of the interests of citizens (Lenaerts and de Smijter, 1996).

4.17 Agencies and Other Bodies Established under the EU Treaties

Since 1990 there has been a proliferation of independent agencies endowed with specific functions or limited delegated powers under the EU Treaties. They vary greatly in composition, nature and scope of powers (although almost all have separate legal personality) (Kreher, 1997). Long disputes between the Member States over the location of some of the most important agencies have caused delays. Some, however, are longstanding such as CEDEFOP (European Centre for Development of Vocational Training, 1975) which has recently relocated from Berlin to Thessaloniki in Northern Greece, and the Foundation for the Improvement of Living and Working Conditions (1975), located in Dublin, Ireland. The most important of the new bodies are:

- European Environment Agency: Copenhagen, Denmark (largely informational, describes the present and future state of the environment);
- European Agency for Health and Safety at Work: Bilbao, Spain (provision of information of a technical and scientific nature for the EU, Member States and others);
- European Monitoring Centre on Racism and Xenophobia: Vienna, Austria (provision of objective, reliable and comparable data at European level on the phenomena of racism, xenophobia and anti-Semitism for the EU institutions and the Member States);
- European Drugs and Drug Addiction Monitoring Centre: Lisbon, Portugal (provision of objective, reliable and comparable information at European level concerning drugs, drug addiction and their consequences).

- European Training Foundation: Turin, Italy (responsible for the delivery of training aid to the countries of Central and Eastern Europe);
- European Agency for Reconstruction: initially located in Pristina in Kosovo, and using services in Thessalonika in Greece (responsible for implementing the EU's reconstruction programmes in Kosovo).

- European Agency for the Evaluation of Medicinal Products: London, UK (responsible for the coordination of an existing network of experts for the

valuation and supervision of medicinal products, and to provide scientific advice);
- Office for Harmonisation in the Internal Market (Trade Marks and Designs): Alicante, Spain (this is the Community Trade Mark Office, by another name, and it is responsible for the registration and administration of applications under the EU Trade Mark Regulation and in future a Regulation on design and models);
- Community Plant Variety Rights Office: Angers, France (responsible for the implementation of the Community Plant Variety Rights regime).

- Europol (succeeding and subsuming the Europol Drugs Unit): The Hague, The Netherlands.

The work of many of these bodies is supported by a single Translation Centre for bodies of the European Union based in Luxembourg.

The agencies listed above are grouped according to broad types of function and approach. The first group of four joins the longer established CEDEFOP and the Foundation for the Improvement of Living and Working Conditions in having largely informational tasks. The European Training Foundation is partly responsible for the delivery of EU programmes (and in that respect its work is not that dissimilar to certain private or public bodies to which the Commission in particular has already contracted out the management of programmes). It is joined by the most recently created Agency (1999), which has the time-limited objective of delivering effectively EU reconstruction aid in Kosovo. It will be wound up when the task is completed. Of the third group of three agencies, the first is essentially assisting the Commission in undertaking certain authorisation tasks delegated to it under EU legislation in relation to medicine approval, while the latter two have certain regulatory and discretionary tasks delegated to them under EU legislation. They will raise at least some of their own revenue from fees. Equally their decisions may be subject to internal appeal and, eventually, judicial review by the Court of First Instance, an imminent increase in workload which represents a serious threat to the functioning of the Community judicature (4.21). Future cases brought by rights-holders in respect of alleged infringements will come within the jurisdiction of the national courts, so the question will arise as to which Court within the Community judicature will hear references for preliminary rulings. As it stands, this will be the Court of Justice.

Finally, Europol and the Europol Drugs Unit (EDU) which it superseded on 1 July 1999 are rather different types of bodies to the others previously discussed. Europol derives its authority, and its work, from the competence of the EU under the third pillar, which now formally recognises Europol (Article 30 TEU). Europol is based on a convention adopted under the old

Article K.3 TEU, and duly ratified by the Member States. Its work is in the fields of organised crime, transnational money-laundering, drug trafficking, terrorism and similar matters. It is does not as yet have an operational role, but rather its work lies in the field of liaison between national police forces, and the exchange of information. In that context, it is important that Article 286 formally extends EU acts on data protection for individuals to the institutions and bodies set up by the Treaty.

The arrival of these new bodies marks a significant shift in the pattern of regulation in the EU, as a departure from reliance upon the current structures based on the unwieldy and opaque 'comitology' which is sometimes unable to integrate the necessary technical expertise, and upon soft instruments such as mutual recognition. However, regulatory agencies themselves give rise to difficulties such as problems of control, accountability and independence, as well as the extent to which the powers of the EC and EU may validly be delegated in this way (Everson, 1995; Lenaerts, 1993). The validity of such delegations to 'bodies established under private law, having a distinct legal personality and possessing powers of their own' has been long recognised by the Court of Justice (Case 9/56 *Meroni* v. *High Authority* [1957-58] ECR 133 at p. 151), but equally the Court has made clear that delegations to such bodies may not grant the same wide discretionary powers which may be handed to the Commission:

> 'To delegate a discretionary power, by entrusting it to bodies other than those which the Treaty has established to effect and supervise the exercise of such power each within the limits of its own authority, would render ... ineffective [the] fundamental guarantee [of] the balance of powers which is characteristic of the institutional structure of the Community' ([1957-58] ECR 133 at p. 152).

Hence, the general limitation on agencies and other similar bodies is that their work should be limited to preparatory work, gathering and monitoring of information, research and coordination. Ultimately, they should improve the effectiveness of the Commission's own work, but at this stage of their existence, their genuine autonomy is limited by the impact of the *Meroni* judgment and the concept of interinstitutional balance and they are perhaps best seen as part of wider networks, delivering better governance within the EU (Dehousse, 1997).

4.18 The Court of Auditors

Under the Treaty of Maastricht, the Court of Auditors acquired the status of an institution. Accordingly, the provisions (Articles 246–248 EC) which govern its establishment, composition, tasks and duties were shifted into the chapter on the institutions, having previously been linked solely to the budgetary provisions. It has been in existence since 1977, and consists of fifteen members – one from each Member State – who are persons qualified to serve on a body which has the task of carrying out the audit of EU finances, and whose independence is beyond doubt. They are appointed for six-year terms by the Council. The European Parliament, which has particular budgetary responsibilities, is consulted on the appointments. The protected legal status of the members of the Court of Auditors during their term of office resembles that of the members of the Court of Justice, although they can be deprived of their office by the Court of Justice (Article 247(7) EC). At the supranational level, the Court of Auditors is a rather novel institution (Laffan, 1999b).

The Court of Auditors has an auditing and supervisory task, and not, despite its name, a judicial role (see Laffan, 1997: 192–204). It is the 'financial conscience' of the EU. It extends not only to the revenue and expenditure of the EU itself, but also to all bodies set up by the EU, unless other arrangements have been made. By providing a statement of assurance regarding the reliability of the accounts and the underlying financial transactions conducted by the EU, the Court of Auditors assists the Parliament in giving the Commission a discharge in respect of the implementation of the budget. It has the important right to request and receive any document or information necessary to carry out its tasks from the institutions, any bodies managing revenue or expenditure on behalf of the EU and any natural or legal person in receipt of payments from the budget (Article 248(3) EC). Previously somewhat of a Cinderella institution within the EU structures, the role of the Court of Auditors has come increasingly to the fore as the EU budget has grown and diversified into new areas, as the fight against waste and fraud within the EU has intensified, and as the academic study of the practice of audit has evolved (Harden *et al.*, 1995).

4.19   The European Investment Bank (EIB)

The European Investment Bank has separate legal personality, although it is governed by the provisions of the EC Treaty (Articles 9 and 266–267 EC). It was established by the original Treaty of Rome, and it has a particular function to provide investment loans to assist the funding of projects aimed at promoting regional development within the EU, and projects of particular interest to two or more Member States. Its revenue is derived from money subscribed by Member States and money which it raises on the international capital markets. The management of the Bank is entrusted to a Board of Governors, a Board of Directors and a Committee of Management.

4.20 The Institutions of Economic and Monetary Union

The institutions of Economic and Monetary Union (EMU), established by Article 8 and Title VII of Part III of the EC Treaty replaced the earlier institutions such as the European Monetary Cooperation Fund. They are based in Frankfurt in Germany. Now that the third stage of monetary union has begun, the most important bodies will be the European System of Central Banks (ESCB), composed of the European Central Bank (ECB), which will have separate legal personality, and the national central banks (Article 107 EC). Details are contained in the Treaty and in the associated Protocols and Declarations. During a transitional period, preparation for the work of the ESCB and the ECB was undertaken by the European Monetary Institute (EMI) established under the transitional provisions of Article 117 EC, which took over from the existing Committee of Governors of Central Banks. The transition to monetary union, and the associated coordination of national policies, was also assisted by a temporary Monetary Committee with advisory status (Article 114(1) EC) which was dissolved and replaced on transition to the third stage of monetary union by an Economic and Financial Committee (Article 114(2) EC).

The ECB has legal personality, and it is run by its Executive Board, composed of a President, Vice-President and four other members, and a Governing Council, consisting of the Executive Board and the Governors of the national central banks (Article 112 EC). The President of the Council of Ministers and a member of the European Commission may participate in meetings of the Governing Council, but they do not have a right to vote. Thus, the institutions of monetary union under the Treaty of Maastricht are built on a model of central bank independence (Article 108 EC), but one which will not necessarily ensure adequate accountability and legitimacy for these institutions. It might, on the contrary, exacerbate the EU democratic deficit (Gormley and de Haan, 1996). The Treaty of Maastricht fitted the ECB into the system of judicial review of the EU, so that the validity and interpretation of acts of the ECB may be referred to the Court of Justice by national courts under Article 234 EC, and direct challenges can be brought against acts and failures to act on the part of the ECB under Articles 230 and 232 EC (Craig, 1999b).

The tasks of the ESCB, to be carried out by the ECB, are to define and implement the monetary policy of the EU, to conduct foreign exchange operations, to hold and manage the foreign currency reserves of the Member States, and to promote the smooth operation of payment systems (Article 105 EC). Its overall objective is price stability and the creation and maintenance of a strong currency. Most obviously, to the outside observer, the ECB sets interest rates. The ECB has the right to be consulted on certain matters related to its tasks. It will acquire the exclusive right to authorise the issue of banknotes throughout 'Euroland'. It has a limited capacity to make regulations, take decisions, make recommendations and deliver opinions in order to carry out its tasks (Article 110 EC). It has certain external powers in addition (Article 111 EC). In relation to economic policy, the Council retains certain powers.

4.21 The Court of Justice and the Court of First Instance

Since 1988 the so-called 'Community judicature' has comprised two courts sitting in Luxembourg: the Court of Justice, and, attached to it, and empowered to hear only certain categories of case, the Court of First Instance (Article 225 EC and Council Decision 88/591 OJ 1988 L319/1). The Court of First Instance is not really a separate entity from the Court of Justice (it is 'attached' to it), but to a certain extent the two courts are beginning to develop separate identities, as they work on different fields of EU law and become engaged with slightly different sets of priorities. The division of jurisdiction between the two courts has evolved gradually over the years such that the Court of First Instance now hears all direct actions brought by natural or legal persons of the EU institutions (including staff cases). Appeal lies on points of law from the Court of First Instance to the Court of Justice itself. The Court of Justice hears all references for preliminary rulings submitted by national courts (Article 234 EC; under Article 225(1) EC the Court of First Instance is explicitly denied competence in this matter), and actions brought by the institutions or Member States against each other.

Each court now has fifteen judges (one from each Member State), and the Court of Justice is assisted by nine Advocates General, who submit opinions on each of the cases heard by the Court. The Court of Justice is often influenced by the views of the Advocate General, whose opinions frequently contain detailed discussion of the background to the legal issues at issue which is not to be found in the judgments themselves, often backed up by comparative research which has been essential to the development of EC law. In some fields, important developments in the law have emerged from 'dialogue' between the Court and the Advocates General (for more details see Vranken, 1996). Advocates General have the same status and privileges as judges; they are Members of the Court of Justice. The Court held in *Emesa Sugar* (Case C-17/98 *Emesa Sugar (Free Zone) NV* v. *Aruba*, Order of the Court of 4 February 2000) that Advocates General 'are not public prosecutors nor are they subject to any authority... They are not entrusted with the defence of any particular interest in the exercise of their duties.' The Court rejected an argument based on fundamental rights which invoked the Court's new fundamental rights jurisdiction under Articles 46(d) and 6(2) TEU, and held that Article 6(1) ECHR giving the right to a fair hearing by an independent judge did not support the assertion that the applicant should be entitled to submit written observations after the Advocate General has delivered his or her Opinion, in order to reply to that Opinion. The Court of First Instance does not have Advocates General, but a member of the Court may adopt that role where the Court considers it necessary.

The Judges and Advocates General of the Court of Justice are chosen from persons 'whose independence is beyond doubt and who possess the qualifications required for appointment to the highest judicial office in their respective countries or who are jurisconsults of recognised competence' (Article 223 EC). The qualification to be a judge of the Court of First Instance is likewise independence, and 'the ability required for appointment to judicial office' (Article 225(3) EC). The members of both courts are appointed by common accord of the Member States for six years, with partial replacement every three years (Articles 223 and 225 EC). Each court elects a President. The members of both Courts are assisted by a number of *référendaires* or legal secretaries, who help with matters such as drafting and research, and typically come from more than one 'home' legal jurisdiction.

Further provisions governing the operation of the Court of Justice and the Court of First Instance are contained in the Statute of the Court of Justice appended to the founding Treaties, the Rules of Procedure of the two courts which are approved by the Council, and the Council Decision establishing the Court of First Instance referred to above. It is one of the persistent objections of the two Courts to the operation of the judicial system in the EU that they do not have the right to lay down their own Rules of Procedure, particularly in view of the fact that small changes to those rules can make a large difference to the burden which the Courts' ever-increasing workload actually places on the institutions. Procedures before the two Courts differ somewhat from those before a court in the United Kingdom (see Edward, 1995; Arnull, 1999a: Ch. 1). Among the most distinctive features of the ways the courts work are:

- a greater use of written, as opposed to oral, submissions; the written procedure is more important than the subsequent oral procedure;
- all judgments are collegiate, with no single judge benches, except exceptionally for the Court of First Instance, and no dissenting judgments;
- the advisory role of the Advocate General (before the Court of Justice);
- the role of the *juge rapporteur* appointed by the President of the Court, who draws up the Report for the (oral) Hearing and the initial draft of the decision which is then discussed by the judges in secret;
- the judgments of the Court of Justice in particular are very brief, and often lack the full reasoning associated with judgments of courts in the UK;
- this brevity is not so apparent in the judgments of the Court of First Instance where there is normally no Advocate General; moreover, one of

the particular functions of the Court of First Instance is to provide a forum which can give a detailed resolution of often complex submissions of fact and law on, for example, a Commission finding of an infringement of the competition rules;
- multilingualism: there are twelve procedural languages, one of which will be the language of the case, but the Court of Justice itself will normally work in French (Irish is added to the list of eleven EU official languages).

The Court of Justice sits in plenary session, or in chambers of five or three judges. In order to make the work of the Court more effective, and to limit the role of the plenary session to that of deciding the most important cases, it now sits in plenary session in cases to which an institution or a Member State is party, only where a request is made by one party. Most preliminary rulings are also heard by chambers. The quorum for a plenary is nine, and the Court very rarely sits of the *grand plenum* of fifteen judges. The Court of First Instance normally sits only in chambers of three or five judges. In response to a request by the Court of Justice, the Council has made it possible for single judges to hear cases in the Court of First Instance (Council Decision 1999/291 OJ 1999 L114/52). The first single judge judgment was handed down in October 1999, in a staff case brought against the EU body CEDEFOP (Case T-180/98 *Cotrim* v. *CEDEFOP*, 28 October 1999). Delegation to a single judge is not possible in the most legally significant of the Court of First Instance's areas of jurisdiction, notably direct actions in the areas of competition law and merger law, state aid and anti-dumping measures adopted to protect trade.

The basic task of the Community judicature is simple: it is to ensure that the law is observed (Article 220 EC; see also Article 31 ECSC). Articles 226–243 and 288 EC govern the most important types of action which can be brought before the courts and the types of rulings which it may give. Reference should be made to 1.6 for an outline of the basic work of the Court (Arnull, 1999a: Ch. 2). In addition, it has an important – if relatively rarely used – advisory jurisdiction, under which it can be called upon by the Council, the Commission or a Member State to give an opinion as to whether an international agreement envisaged for adoption is compatible with the provisions of the EC Treaty (Article 300(6) EC). An adverse opinion from the Court prevents the agreement into force, and if necessary the Member States must adopt amendments to the Treaties under Article 48 TEU if they wish to bring it into force. The Court can also be asked about the feasibility of amendments to the Treaties which might be needed for specific instruments to enter into force.

The Treaty of Maastricht brought a number of important changes to the jurisdiction of the Community judicature. Amendments were made to include the new institutions of Economic and Monetary Union, in particular the European Central Bank, within the system of judicial review. Judicial review was extended to cover the acts of the European Investment Bank and the Parliament which have legal effects, and formally to confer limited standing rights on the Parliament. Provision was also made for financial penalties to be imposed on Member States which fail to comply with judgments of the Court of Justice establishing an infringement of the Treaties or rules adopted thereunder (Article 228 EC), although even now this provision has yet to be fully invoked. The Court was not, however, given jurisdiction to rule over what was Article F(2) TEU, which laid down for the first time within the EU treaty system a guarantee of fundamental rights protection.

Changes to the scope of the Court's jurisdiction were also made by the Treaty of Amsterdam. However, most notably, the new Title IV of Part III of the EC Treaty on matters related to visas, asylum, immigration and other free movement issues 'communitarised' certain third-pillar issues and thus implicated the role of the Court of Justice – which was previously largely excluded from justice and home affairs policy as a whole. National courts of last resort *only* have the right (and obligation) to refer questions to the Court of Justice under Article 68 EC, and there may be costs of this limitation in terms of the lack of consistency of national case law and limited judicial protection for those involved in judicial actions related to asylum and immigration (who might frequently lack the resources to pursue the national case all the way to the court of last resort). The Court is explicitly denied the jurisdiction under Article 68(2) EC to rule on Council measures connected with the removal of controls on the movement of persons across internal borders 'relating to the maintenance of law and order and the safeguarding of internal security'. Otherwise, the Court's jurisdiction is broadly the same as elsewhere under the EC Treaty. Under the revised third pillar, Article 35(1) TEU gives the Court of Justice a preliminary rulings jurisdiction in relation to a range of measures adopted under that Title, although only at the request of the national courts situated in Member States which have declared that they accept the involvement of the Court. Again, in parallel with Title IV EC, Article 35(5) TEU prevents the Court from reviewing the validity or proportionality of national policy operations or national measures concerned with 'the maintenance of law and order and the safeguarding of internal security'. Arnull (1999a: 71) describes both Article 68(2) EC and Article 35(5) TEU as 'iniquitous' and 'designed to weaken judicial scrutiny'. These are provisions which are hard to reconcile with the principles of respect for fundamental rights and the rule of law which the EU is now founded upon (Article 6(1) TEU). In addition, measures in the third pillar provide for limited jurisdiction of the Court to rule on the validity of certain secondary measures adopted by the Council, and in relation to disputes between the institutions and the Member States over these measures. Only the Member States and the Commission can bring annulment actions.

Arnull's conclusion (1999a: 73; see also Arnull, 1999b) on these changes to the jurisdiction of the Court of Justice – notwithstanding some of these hard to justify limitations – is that they do not reflect a general dissatisfaction among the Member States with the workings of the Court of Justice, albeit that in the run up to the 1996–97 IGC a number of Member States, but most notably the UK, thought this would be a good opportunity to 'clip the wings' of the Court because of its historically activist stance. The changes are much more likely to be simply determined by the subject-matter, and to reflect an unwillingness on the part of the Member States to accept *too quickly* (as opposed to not at all) the disciplines of the judicial system and EU legal order as fashioned by the Court of Justice.

At first glance, the role of the Court of Justice, like the other institutions, is limited by the principle of 'attributed powers'. As a creature of Treaty, the Court of Justice can only hear actions and give remedies where provided for in the constitutive Treaties; however, it is arguable that with the evolution of the institutional structure and the range of competences and activities of the EU the overriding duty of the Court to ensure the rule of law should be regarded as more important than the strict limitations of the Treaties. In fact, the Court of Justice made a number of innovations within the jurisdictional structure of the Treaties, allowing acts of the European Parliament to be subject to judicial review and giving it a limited power to bring actions against the acts of the other institutions. These *de facto* developments were formally recognised by the Treaty of Maastricht. Arnull (1990a) has argued that in fact the Court of Justice has an inherent jurisdiction which requires it where appropriate to fill in gaps in the system of legal remedies under the Treaties. In his view, in extending its jurisdictional scope, the Court is acting no differently to the other institutions which have *de facto* extended their powers in response to political imperatives. Such comments must be read, however, in the light of explicit limitations on the scope of the Court's jurisdiction. Under Article 46 TEU, even after amendments by the Treaty of Amsterdam, the Court has only limited jurisdiction over the common provisions of the Treaty of European Union and the provisions on PJC – a jurisdiction which in part the Member States must explicitly accept and not all have yet done so – and no jurisdiction in relation to CFSP.

Issues regarding the reform of the Community judicial architecture have tended in recent years to concentrate less upon the scope of its jurisdiction and more upon how it will be possible in future for the two Courts to master their ever-increasing workload, especially as the EU becomes a larger and more complex polity. On this question, notwithstanding contributions from the European Parliament and both Courts, no real moves were made at the Amsterdam IGC. However, this is unsurprising in that the difficult foundational discussions relating to the other institutions were also deferred from the Amsterdam IGC to a point in the future. This future now appears to have arrived with the 2000 IGC (3.15), and the Court of Justice is firmly on the agenda.

The Court of Justice produced a report on the functioning of the Treaty on European Union which served as part of the material considered by the Reflection Group preparing the Amsterdam agenda. The Court of First Instance produced a separate report differing in certain respects from the approach taken by the Court itself. The Court of Justice was necessarily limited in any criticisms it could make of the Treaty structure under which it operates, but it did point to the unsatisfactory level of judicial protection given to individuals under the second and third pillars of the EU. Some of the most significant comments by both Courts are directed to the structure of the Community judicature. The Court of Justice opposed any suggestion that references under what was then Article 177 EC (now Article 234 EC) should be dealt with other than by itself. It did suggest, however, that some appeals from the Court of First Instance might be subjected to a 'filtering system'. The Court of First Instance advocated the limited use of single judge courts – a reform that has come to pass in the meantime without Treaty amendment. Both Courts also suggested changes to their composition. For the Court of Justice the problem arises because of the possibility that its plenary session (involving all the judges) might, as a result of further enlargements, become unmanageably large and 'cross the invisible boundary between a collegiate court and a deliberative assembly'. At some point in the future, the Member States may need to accept that not all Member States should in the future have judges – in the same way that the composition of the Commission might be revised. If this possibility is unacceptable, then other managerial possibilities could include a plenary consisting only of the President and the Presidents of the various Chambers, plus a limited number of judges, and a maximum size for the full plenary. This could make the Court a more hierarchical and less collegial institution, in the interests of the consistency of its case law and the efficiency of its operation. The Court of First Instance could more enthusiastically welcome the possibility of an increase in its membership, as it largely sits in chambers, not in plenary. Such an increase is essential, as just two years after its creation the Court of First Instance was already receiving more new cases each year than it could handle, thus leading to increasing delays in the dispensing of justice. That said, not all those who observe both EU courts would agree with the proposal for more judges. According to Koopmans (1991b: 24),

'One of the worst methods for increasing judicial productivity is to enlarge the number of Judges and Advocates-General.'

The effect of creating too large a judicial structure in Luxembourg is destabilising in the view of some. Even so, no concrete support has yet been lent to a longstanding suggestion that the Community judicial architecture should be reworked along regional lines (Jacqué and Weiler, 1990).

The strains on the Community judicature are now very plain, with the Courts reporting 'a dangerous trend towards a structural imbalance between the volume of incoming cases and the capacity of the institution to dispose of them' in a proposal which they made to the Council regarding the future influx of intellectual property cases. It now takes longer than before the Court of First Instance was instituted for a reference for a preliminary ruling to be decided within the Court of Justice (21 months). In May 1999 the Court of Justice produced a Report on *The Future of the Judicial System of the European Union* (Arnull, 1999c) and in January 2000, an independent Working Party convened by the Commission to assist it in preparing its report for the 2000 IGC, but mainly composed of ex-members of the Court of Justice, produced an extended report on *The Future of the European Communities' Court System*. Both contain cautionary words and constructive suggestions. The basic division relates to measures of reform which require Treaty amendment or changes to the Statute of the Court, and those which do not, but can be executed by Council Decision (e.g. single judge chambers in the Court of First Instance) or by changes to the Courts' Rules of Procedures, or internal reorganisation within the Courts. The two are linked, however, as Article 245 EC requires the Council to give *unanimous* approval to the Court's Rules of Procedure. One suggestion – even demand – from the Court of Justice has been to be given the flexibility to adopt its own Rules of Procedure, or at the very least to have them approved by the Council acting by a qualified majority. In that event, delays before the Council could be reduced, which is especially important as there may need to be increasingly frequent changes to the Rules of Procedure as the EU widens and deepens.

The areas to which attention needs to be paid in the very near future by the Courts, the other institutions and – especially – the Member States in the IGC include the following:

– the effects of enlargement upon the composition of the Courts;
– abandonment of the requirement that an Advocate General should give his or her Opinion on every case before the Court of Justice, with the consequent possibility to reduce the number of Advocates General and the translation burden on the administrative staff of the Court;
– the possibilities of a more streamlined preliminary ruling procedure, including an accelerated procedure for dealing with references which raise points which have already been dealt with; an amendment to Article 234 EC could help by reinforcing to national courts their task as 'Community courts' themselves capable of disposing of issues of EU law;
– a changed division of jurisdiction between the Court of Justice and the Court of First Instance, with the latter taking certain limited categories of

preliminary rulings as well as – as is currently proposed – some types of actions brought by the institutions and the Member States; eventually, the Court of First Instance could become an independent institution, rather than one 'attached' to the Court of Justice;
- the institution of a system of speedy preliminary review of appeals from the Court of First Instance to ensure that the Court of Justice deals only with important cases on appeal;
- the additional burdens to be placed upon the Community judicature by the system of appeals on points of law in relation to intellectual property cases (4.17), which could generate hundreds of additional cases each year; the possibility of specialised tribunals should be considered.

A number of proposals are currently before the Council for approval in the form of suggested amendments to the Court's Rules of Procedure on the transfer of additional areas of jurisdiction to the Court of First Instance and the management of the intellectual property case load.

What has been notable about the Court of Justice during its very nearly fifty-year history – and this point will be evident already from the previous chapters and will reappear at regular points throughout the book – has been its judicial activism. This has been most obvious in its role in 'constitutionalising' the Treaties (see Chapter 5, especially 5.21), and in 'federalising' the relationship between EC law and national law (1.6; see Chapters 12 and 13). In the 1970s in particular, commentators were fond of pointing to the Court's 'teleological' or 'purposive' methods of interpretation (see the extracts in Ellis and Tridimas, 1995: 563–569; Kutscher, 1976; Tridimas, 1996). On occasion its interpretative methods have led it to be severely criticised for being over-activist, and giving judgments which go against the text (Rasmussen, 1986; Hartley, 1996, 1999). But it is more frequently the case that academics and practitioners in the field have leapt to its defence (Cappelletti, 1987; Weiler, 1993, 1994a; Arnull, 1999a). What has intrigued political scientists more than anything about the Court has been the level of compliance on the part of Member States with its judgment which it has attracted – what some have termed 'legal integration' (Alter, 1998a, 1998b; Mattli and Slaughter, 1998). Over the years this has lent to the legal order a 'federalist' and 'constitutionalist' aura which has often stood in stark contrast to the political and economic order (Burley and Mattli, 1993). As each of the chapters of this book will make clear, the time is perhaps past for the Court to be viewed as a 'heroic' figure in the development of the EU. Its importance is probably no less than it ever was. It certainly works now in a stronger glare of not always approving publicity. But it is now the case the Court more than ever occupies a place in constantly evolving dialogue with each of the institutions, offering a specifically 'legal' voice within a ever-changing policy process.

4.22   Conclusion: the Institutions under Review

As we examine the work of the institutions of the EU, especially in relation to policy making and implementation, during the course of Part III of the book, evidence of the operation of the principle of 'institutional balance' will come increasingly to the fore. The framework set out in this chapter is the background against which this needs to be considered. The term denotes 'the complex allocation of power among the various organs established within the Community context' (de Búrca, 1999a: 58), and was first recognised by the Court of Justice back in an ECSC Treaty case in the 1950s as 'a balance of powers which is characteristic of the institutional structure of the Community' (Cases 9 and 10/56 *Meroni* [1957-8] ECR 133 at p.152). It also implies the role of some gatekeeper to keep the institutions 'in balance'; historically this role has fallen above all to the Court of Justice (Prechal, 1998a), and consequently institutional balance is almost inextricably bound up with judicial review and with the rule of law within the EU. This issue will be taken up directly in 7.18. However, the concept of institutional balance should not be understood as a 'zero-sum game'. That is, one institution's gain does not *have* to be another one's loss. The institutions demonstrate that knowledge when, for example, they choose to interinstitutional agreements in areas such as the legislative process or the budget to dissipate tensions and head off potential conflicts (7.17). It is possible that the institutional framework and the institutional balance can improve – incrementally through institutional practices or more suddenly in the form of Treaty amendments – in ways which lead to an overall improvement in relation to important values such as accountability, efficiency, independence and responsibility.

What this chapter has also sought to do is to present the 'state' of the institutions, identifying areas in particular where change has not been fully reflected in the EU's basic constitutional charter, the Treaties. An excessive divergence between the 'formal legal' constitution of the Treaties and the 'real' constitutional framework of complex interacting formal and informal bodies is damaging to the EU's relatively fragile constitutional settlement (de Búrca, 1999a). Moreover, this chapter has already highlighted a number of related themes which will need to be brought out. Much has already been done within the EU about *some* aspects of 'transparency', in the service of Article 1 TEU and its invocation of 'closeness' and 'openness'. There are formal rules about access to documents, although they are not always generously applied. A framework right of access is now enshrined in the Treaty (Article 255 EC), and it will be discussed in more detail in Chapter 10. The European Ombudsman has involved himself in pushing forward this and other issues related to good administration by the institutions. Certainly, there is no doubting the ease with which documents which were *always* available are now made available across the Internet. Yet in important areas such as Justice and Home

Affairs law it still seems that in-depth research into the institutional configuration and, especially, the development of policy cannot be undertaken unless constructive and consistent attempts are made to obtain more documents from the Council than it readily makes available (Peers, 2000a). Issues of democracy and representation have also been touched upon in this chapter. It is clearly a mistake simply to assimilate the EU institutional system with some sort of embryonic parliamentary democracy. As a supranational non-state polity, that can never be a wholly appropriate model. The democratic politics of the EU, moreover, cannot be reduced to an assessment of the European Parliament as legislature, or indeed to systems of accountability between the Council, the Parliament and the Commission. Those issues are important, but they need a detailed assessment, in particular in the light of the EU's complex multi-levelled system for law and policy making as well as its emerging albeit as yet incomplete constitutional framework.

Summary

1   The role and tasks of the institutions are not exhaustively stated in the Treaties. Regard must also be had to constantly changing interinstitutional dynamics.

2   The Commission is the pivotal political institution. It has policy-making, executive, enforcement and representative functions.

3   Since 1999 the Commission has been going through a process of reform to improve its efficiency and transparency, and to ensure that Commissioners and officials conduct themselves according to appropriate codes of conduct.

4   The Council still carries the primary legislative function, although increasingly it shares that function with the European Parliament. It is also the body which represents the national interest, and tends towards intergovernmentalist methods, relying on the achievement of consensus. It has seen an increase in its influence, in particular through related bodies and structures: the European Council, COREPER, comitology etc. The Presidency of the Council has also evolved into an important motor of the EU integration process.

5   The Parliament is gradually evolving into co-legislator with the Council, ensuring democracy and accountability within the EU, with a particular brief for protecting the interests of citizens. It exercises important powers over the Commission.

6   The Ombudsman is appointed by the Parliament and he has an important role overseeing the work of the other institutions and protecting the interests of citizens within the administrative process.

7   The interests of employers, unions, consumers and other corporate interests are protected by the Economic and Social Committee (ECOSOC). Regional interests are protected by the Committee of the Regions introduced by the Treaty of Maastricht.

8   Other institutions or bodies with increasing importance within the institutional structure include the Court of Auditors, various independent agencies endowed with a variety of delegated powers, and the institutions of monetary union.

9   The Court of Justice and the Court of First Instance ensure the rule of law in the EU. They have acquired a central role in maintaining the momentum of integration, but they suffer at present from a considerable overload of work.

Questions

1   Identify the mechanisms whereby national interests are recognised and represented within the institutional structures of the EU. To what extent does the influence of national interests extend outside the Council into other bodies as well?

2   Would you agree with the suggestion that the EU does not possess an institutional structure which easily facilitates overall coherence of policy formulation and policy implementation?

3   To what extent has the Council usurped the roles of the other institutions?

4   Which institution would you consider to have changed most since the establishment of the EU, and in what ways?

5   What mechanisms exist to enable the institutions to take the concerns of citizens seriously, and how effective are these?

6   How has the role of the Court of Justice within the institutional system evolved since the inception of the Treaties?

Workshop

Formulate a set of proposals for the reform of the EU institutions which make them:

(a) more democratic and accountable in composition and working methods;

(b) more effective in accomplishing their tasks under the Treaty.

Further Reading

K. Alter (1996), 'The European Court's Political Power', 19 *West European Politics* 458.

A. Arnull (1999b), 'Taming the Beast? The Treaty of Amsterdam and the Court of Justice', in O'Keeffe and Twomey (1999).

G. de Búrca (1999a), 'The Institutional Development of the EU: A Constitutional Analysis', in Craig and de Búrca (1999).

E. Chiti (2000), 'The Emergence of Community Administration: the Case of European Agencies', 37 *Common Market Law Review* 309.

P. Craig (2000), 'The Fall and Renewal of the Commission: Accountability, Contract and Administrative Organisation', 6 *European Law Journal* 98.

L. Cram (1999), 'The Commission', in Cram, Dinan and Nugent (1999).

A. Dashwood (1994), 'The Role of the Council of the European Union', in Curtin and Heukels (1994).

G. Edwards and D. Spence (eds) (1994), *The European Commission*, Harlow: Longman.

M. Everson (1995), 'Independent Agencies: Hierarchy Beaters?', 1 *European Law Journal* 180.

W. van Gerven (1996), 'The Role and Structure of the European Judiciary Now and in the Future', 21 *European Law Review* 211.

W. van Gerven (2000), 'Managing the European Union: For Better or for Worse?', in Markesinis (2000).

F. Hayes-Renshaw (1999), 'The European Council and the Council of Ministers', in Cram, Dinan and Nugent (1999).

J. Inghelram (2000), 'The European Court of Auditors; Current Legal Issues', 37 *Common Market Law Review* 129.

T. Koopmans (1991b), 'The Future of the Court of Justice of the European Communities', 11 *Yearbook of European Law* 15.

A. Kreher (1997), 'Agencies in the European Community: A Step Towards Administrative Integration in Europe', 4 *Journal of European Public Policy* 225.

B. Laffan (1999b), 'Becoming a "Living Institution": The Evolution of the European Court of Auditors', 37 *Journal of Common Market Studies* 251.

K.H. Neunreither (1999), 'The European Parliament', in Cram, Dinan and Nugent (1999).

N. Nugent (1999), *The Government and Politics of the European Union* (3rd edn), London: Macmillan (3rd edn).

M. Shackleton (1998), 'The European Parliament's New Committees of Inquiry: Tiger or Paper Tiger?', 36 *Journal of Common Market Studies* 115.

D. Spence (2000), 'Plus ça change, plus c'est la même chose? Attempting to Reform the European Commission', 7 *Journal of European Public Policy* 1.

Key Websites

The (multilingual) *Europa* website is a mine of information on the institutions and how they work; it carries a basic presentation, plus obvious links to all of the institutions and bodies mentioned above, with the exception of *Europol*.

Searching the *Europa* site will bring further links to legal texts on institutional development in sources such as *Eur-lex* and the Bulletin of the European Union.

The sites of the institutions themselves vary in the clarity with which they present themselves:

Council: http://ue.eu.int/en/summ.htm

European Council: http://ue.eu.int/en/Info/eurocouncil/index.htm

Presidency: http://ue.eu.int/en/summ.htm

Commission's home page: http://europa.eu.int/comm/index_en.htm
Court of Justice: http://curia.eu.int/en/index.htm
Court of Auditors: http://www.eca.eu.int/
ECOSOC: http://www.ces.eu.int/int/en/acs/fr_acs_default.htm
Committee of the Regions: http://www.cor.eu.int/
European Investment Bank: http://eib.eu.int/
European Central Bank: http://www.ecb.int/
Presentation of agencies with access to sites:
   http://europa.eu.int/en/agencies.html
Europol: http://www.europol.eu.int/home.htm
European Ombudsman: http://www.euro-ombudsman.eu.int/
European Parliament: http://www.europarl.eu.int/sg/tree/en/default.htm

5 The Evolving EU Constitutional Framework

5.1 Introduction

When the EU was first established in 1993, some observers felt that it had the capacity to lead to the fragmentation of what had been achieved, the so-called *acquis communautaire*. This could mean the effective break up of the European integration project if future developments allowed the dissipation of the unique features of the European Community, especially its supranational character in terms of the institutional framework and the evolving legal order anchored on the Court of Justice. In the late 1980s and early 1990s, the Court characterised the EC Treaty as the Community's 'constitutional charter' in several cases (e.g. in Case 294/83 *Parti Ecologiste 'Les Verts'* v. *Parliament* [1986] ECR 1339; Opinion 1/91 *Draft Agreement on a European Economic Area* (EEA) [1991] ECR I-6079), and it emphasised that this charter was based on the rule of law. Yet, in Curtin's view (1993: 67), the 'unique *sui generis* nature of the European Community, its true world-historical significance' as a 'cohesive legal unit which confers rights on individuals and which enters into their national legal systems as an integral part of those systems' was threatened by the adoption and putting into place of the TEU. Whether the developments have been as threatening as Curtin first painted them in 1993 is an issue that will be touched upon in this chapter.

The Court's Opinion on the incompatibility of certain institutional aspects of the Agreement on the creation of the European Economic Area, especially as regards the creation of a court and a separate legal order for this system, represented a high watermark in the evolution and authority of a single and autonomous Community legal order, characterised by a close link between law and legal processes and the inexorable march onwards of 'integration' (Opinion 1/91 *EEA Agreement*). According to Weatherill it marked a 'zenith' in the 'Court's description of the Treaty structure as a Constitution' (Weatherill, 1995a: 184). The accession of most of the (EFTA) countries originally involved in the EU in January 1995 (see 2.5 and 3.2) meant that the creation of the EEA lost much of its practical importance. However, as an essay in creating a novel and enhanced form of cooperation between the EU Member States and third countries partially modelled on, but not quite attaining, the level of integration within the EU, its legal importance should be underlined.

The Agreement in its original form provided for the establishment of a Court combining judges from the EEA countries and from the Court of Justice, policing a type of legal order which would have partially merged with that of the EC/EU itself, but would be no longer under the sole authoritative control of the Court of Justice. The Court took exception to this institutional configuration, when it was asked about the compatibility of the Agreement with the EEC Treaty under what was then Article 228(6) EEC. On the way to reaching its conclusion, the Court passed a number of comments upon the nature of (what was then) the European Economic Community, comparing it to the European Economic Area. Provisions of the EC Treaties governing matters such as competition policy and free movement are not ends in themselves, but mere means for attaining deeper ends, namely 'concrete progress towards European unity' (para. 17 of the judgment). The EEC Treaty, although an international treaty, is the 'constitutional charter of a Community based on the rule of law'. Moreover,

> 'as the Court of Justice has consistently held, the Community treaties established a new legal order for the benefit of which states have limited their sovereign rights, *in ever wider fields*, and the subject of which comprise not only Member States but also their nationals.' (emphasis added) (at p. 6102)

The progressive character of the Community's competence seems constitutionally crystallised by that ruling. In contrast, the EEA system is characterised as based on an 'ordinary' international treaty, which does not provide for the transfer of any sovereign rights to the intergovernmental institutions. Given the absence of homogeneity between the EEA and the EEC systems, the Court found that the proposed system of courts could have undermined the autonomy of the Community legal order 'respect for which must be assured by the Court of Justice pursuant to Article 164 of the EEC Treaty' (now Article 220 EC). The Court went on to consider whether what was then Article 238 EEC (now Article 310 EC), which provides for associations between the Community and third states, could be amended to permit the type of EEA court envisaged by the original draft Treaty. In a passage which has been widely commented upon by those working in the field the Court held:

> 'Article 238 of the EEC Treaty does not provide any basis for setting up a system of courts which conflicts with Article 164 of the EEC Treaty and, more generally, with the very foundations of the Community.
> For the same reasons, an amendment of Article 238 in the way indicated by the Commission could not cure the incompatibility with Community law of the system of courts to be set up by the agreement' [1991] ECR I-6079 at p. 6111).

It seemed, at that moment, therefore, that the Court denied that the Member States were any more the complete 'Masters of the Treaties'. That conclusion cannot, however, be formally correct, and there have been few signs of such trenchant beliefs about the irreversible and intangible nature of the EU legal order in more recent case law of the Court of Justice. As a consequence of the Court's ruling, a revised draft was submitted for the Court's approval which proposed a separate court for the EFTA states only, but with the Court of Justice itself given an authoritative role in relation to the interpretation of the EEA, even in relation to EFTA national courts. The Court was able to approve the revised but rather complex dispute settlement procedures (Opinion 1/92 *EEA Agreement (No. 2)* [1992] ECR I-2821). For this reason, among others, it is difficult to accept that the EEA achieves its aim of creating a 'dynamic and homogeneous' area 'based on common rules and equal conditions of competition' (Preamble to EEA Treaty); rather, the terms 'Byzantine structures' and 'variable geometry' (Cremona, 1994) have been coined to describe this unusual experiment in broadening the Community experience with economic integration, through a form of cooperation which is more akin to accession than other forms of association, but which still differs in both legal form and economic substance.

Notwithstanding the Court's approach to the questions it was asked in Opinion 1/91, it has in fact been possible to see increasing elements of what might be broadly termed 'variability' or 'differentiation' in the Treaty structures, legislative measures and even Court of Justice case law, probably since the adoption and entry into force of the Single European Act in 1986, and certainly since the conclusion of the Treaty of Maastricht in November 1991 (Harmsen, 1994). Taken together, the evidence would appear to indicate that while it has lost little if any of its overall authority, the EU legal order should be understood as a little less homogeneous than it was, as tolerating a wider diversity of institutional arrangements, and as requiring a lower degree of substantive uniformity in its relationship with national law.

Against the background of these comments, this chapter explores the evolving constitutional framework of the EU, observing how it has built upon the constitutional charter based on the rule of law proclaimed by the Court of Justice. Overall, it makes the case for an analysis of the EU and its legal order in *constitutional* terms. This is because constitutionalism – defined here in rather simple terms as 'limited government under the rule of law' – provides useful guidance for assessing what the EU is and what it does. It also sets some *normative standards* against which to compare the EU, not in terms of saying that it should be *like a state*. However, it does give some indications as to how apparently intractable problems about the EU's democracy, legitimacy and efficiency gaps in terms of its operation as a system of governance might be bridged.

The chapter begins by exploring directly the transformation of the European Community into the European Union, as the basis for constructing the EU's constitutional framework. In the second half of the chapter this discussion is used as the basis for arguing for an understanding of the EU as a system or model of 'multilevel constitutionalism' (Pernice, 1999), and for describing the key aspects of the EU's current constitutional framework. There is some overlap in coverage between the attempt to identify the nature of the EU and the presentation of the EU's constitutional framework, e.g. in the area of 'values and principles'. As a very broad range of issues is raised, inevitably the discussion in some places is brief. The reader will find it useful to cross-refer between this chapter and those which precede and follow it, in order to gain a better insight into how deeply these constitutional fundamentals are embedded into the institutional law of the EU.

5.2   **The Development of the Union: the Pillar System from Maastricht to Amsterdam and Beyond**

According to de Witte, 'nobody could deny that the European Union is a very capacious umbrella sheltering three quite different legal phenomena', that is, the three different pillars of the EU (de Witte, 1998: 52). Certainly the 'pillar' metaphor (and 'pillar' is a term of art developed by academics and practitioners working on the EU and not a technical term which appears in the Treaties themselves) is a relatively crude description for an entity described in Article 1 TEU as being '*founded* on the European Communities, *supplemented* by the policies and forms of cooperation established by this Treaty' (emphasis added). In other words, this is clearly not the usual 'pillared' structure, where each of the pillars provides equal support for the roof. Unsurprisingly, EU lawyers have suggested a number of different architectural metaphors. One of the most effective is that proposed by Gormley (1999: 57) who describes the EU as a cathedral with one 'great central door' (the Community Treaties) and two smaller doors (CFSP and JHA/PJC). Since the pillar structure was – despite academic criticism – retained by the Treaty of Amsterdam (albeit 'tweaked' by some changes), it seems reasonable to suppose that it will be a relatively permanent aspect of the 'legal architecture' of the EU.

Ultimately of more importance than metaphorical descriptions is the question of whether the EU is a single unit. The extent to which it is certainly possible to view the EU as a single entity from a political point of view should be clear from the previous four chapters. However, to what extent – despite the complexities of the three-pillar system – is it possible to view it as a single entity from the legal point of view? It sometimes appears that the three pillars are like chalk and cheese; the EC is 'supranational' and the structure of the EU as such, including the second and third pillars, is 'intergovernmental'. So, for example, the default decisional rule for the EC has always been simple majority voting in the Council, albeit with a multitude of exceptions. Although unanimity was the dominant mode of decision making in practice for several decades whatever was stated in the Treaty, since the Treaty of Amsterdam the EC Treaty has provided that for all but the most politically sensitive of areas (and a few anomalous areas) qualified majority voting in the Council will apply, coupled with a high degree of involvement on the part of the European Parliament, amounting in many cases to being co-legislator with the Council. The Commission is also an important partner in the legislative process. The default decisional rule in the second and third pillars is unanimity of the Member States in the Council with very few exceptions. Even so, drawing on evidence from the EC Treaty itself, de Witte suggests that the 'growing diversity in decision-making mechanisms is a global phenomenon within the European integration process, and the pillar structure is just one particularly visible example of it' (de Witte, 1998: 53), and he gives numerous examples of flexibility and institutional differentiation under the EC Treaty. This seems to suggest that the differences *between* the pillars are not sufficient, on their own, to establish that the EU is *not* a single entity. Moreover, there are powerful countervailing forces binding the system together in the shape of the many commonalities and similarities across the pillars. There are strong links between the pillars in all of the following areas: (a) the scope of coverage in terms of policy area; (b) the sharing of institutions and the principle of consistency; (c) common principles and values; (d) structuring constitutional principles and practices such as subsidiarity and flexibility; (e) rules of change and membership; (f) the capacity to adopt binding legal measures and increased decisional autonomy of the EU; (g) the external identity of the EU; and, increasingly, (h) budgetary questions.

5.3   The Scope of Coverage in Terms of Policy Area

A decade's experience with the pillar system highlights the fact that the three pillars are not discrete and closed systems for dealing with three sets of different policy problems or policy areas. On the contrary, the substantial 'communitarisation' (i.e. transfer from the third pillar to the first pillar) of policy making in the area of immigration, visas, asylum and other aspects of the free movement of persons highlights the fact that the pillars are the means to an end (i.e. the promotion of effective cooperation between states) rather than ends in themselves. Although the EU is a 'limited powers' body, restricted to acting within its objectives and in accordance with the powers which have been given to it by the Member States, those states have shown a continuing willingness both to extend those limits in areas such as defence, monetary union, employment policy, and the free movement of persons and to move issue areas between the pillars, in the context of the changes introduced by Treaties of Maastricht and Amsterdam. The Protocol on the integration of the Schengen *acquis* refers to its incorporation into 'the framework of the European Union', lending force to the argument that that the EU is a single entity. The Council was then given the task of allocating the *acquis* between the different pillars, which it completed in decisions adopted in May 1999. In other words, questions about the allocation of powers to and between the pillars should be seen in a dynamic and not static context.

Where there are borders, of course, there will be disputes. This will remain important in the EU so long as there are substantial differences in decision-making rules between the pillars. The willingness of the Court of Justice to police these disputes, where they have substantial effects upon the EC Treaty, manifested itself in a border dispute between the Commission and the Council regarding a measure adopted to regulate airport transit visas (Case C-170/96 *Commission* v. *Council (Airport Transit Visas)* [1998] ECR I-2763). By a joint action 96/197/JAI adopted in March 1996 on the basis of Article K.3 TEU (OJ 1996 L63/8), the Council sought to harmonise Member States' policies on the regulation of airport transit visas, for the purposes of combating illegal immigration. The Commission contended that this measure should have been adopted using the limited law-making power under the EC Treaty covering visa policy, introduced by the Treaty of Maastricht (Article 100c EC). The Court found for the Council on the substance of the case, concluding that the issue fell within the then third pillar, rather than Article 100c. More significant, however, was its conclusion that the action was admissible at all, for effectively it asked for the review of a third-pillar act. At that time, the third pillar was entirely outside the jurisdiction of the Court of Justice. The Court noted, however, that it is

> 'the task of the Court to ensure that acts which, according to the Council, fall within the scope of Article K.3(2) of the Treaty on European Union do not encroach upon the powers conferred by the EC Treaty on the Community' (para. 16 of the judgment).

The Court, therefore – as the arbiter of the scope of 'Community competence' under the EC Treaty and consequently the powers of the institutions under that Treaty – will effectively be the arbiter of the scope of the other pillars. That will mean the Court taking an extensive view of the scope of Article 46 TEU, which sets the limits on its own jurisdiction, in order to police the precise extent of the 'limited powers' entity which is the 'European Community' in strictly legal terms.

5.4   The Single Institutional Framework

Article 3 TEU provides:

'The Union shall be served by a single institutional framework which shall ensure the consistency and the continuity of the activities carried out in order to attain its objectives while respecting and building upon the acquis communautaire.'

Articles 4 and 5 TEU go on to amplify that statement by giving the European Council a special role to 'provide the Union with the necessary impetus for its development' and to 'define the general political guidelines' (Article 4 TEU) and by reiterating that the European Parliament, the Council, the Commission, the Court of Justice and the Court of Auditors should exercise their normal EC Treaty powers as well as their powers under the other provisions of the TEU. One construction of this provision is that the institutions of the EC are 'lent' to the EU, but with the normal roles of each institution freely varied under the second and third pillars. Other arguments speak against that interpretation: the European Council – in essence an institution of the EU since it appears in very few provisions of the EC Treaty – gives as much guidance in relation to general lines of policy under the EC Treaty as it does in respect of the policy development under the second and third pillars. Indeed, ironically, it was only in October 1999 that the European Council had its first special meeting devoted to Justice and Home Affairs matters, and that came *after* substantial areas of JHA policy had been moved into the first pillar. In its work, the Council does not appear to make sharp distinctions in practice between operating in the different pillars (although obviously it, like the other institutions, has to abide by the different rules that the Treaties provide). So, for example, the Justice and Home Affairs Council continues to sit as a single cross-pillar entity covering Title IV EC and the PJC field under the third pillar.

The European Ombudsman has successfully obtained oversight of third-pillar issues, at least in relation to access to documents questions. In relation to complaints brought to the Ombudsman about various practices of the Council in relation to access to documents brought by the UK civil liberties publication *Statewatch* and its editor, Tony Bunyan (1087/10.12.96 *Statewatch/UK/IJH against the Council of the European Union*; available from the Ombudsman's website), the Ombudsman concluded that complaints about how the Council operated its policy under its access to documents Decision (a first-pillar decision adopted in relation to its Rules of Procedure under Article 207 EC) is certainly within his jurisdiction, even if the dispute pertains to JHA/third-pillar documents. In similar terms, the Court of First Instance confirmed that it had jurisdiction to consider an action brought against a Council Decision refusing access to third-pillar documents (Case T-174 *Svenska Journalistförbundet* v. *Council* [1998] ECR II-2289), because the originating Council Decision was a first-pillar decision (10.8).

5.5   Common Principles and Values

The most visible evidence of the common framework of the EU is comprised by the liberal values laid down in Article 6(1) TEU:

> 'The Union is founded on the principles of liberty, democracy, respect for human rights and fundamental freedoms, and the rule of law, principles which are common to the Member States'.

According to von Bogdandy (2000), read together with Article 7(1) TEU, which sets up a system of internal political sanctions in the event of 'a serious and persistent breach by a Member State of principles mentioned in Article 6(1)', this provision 'enshrines unitary standards of democracy and the rule of law for all public authority' in what he calls the 'multilevel constitutional system' (adapting a definition used by Pernice, 1999). This comprises the sixteen legally independent constitutions that constitute the EU's overall constitutional system: those of the fifteen Member States and that of the EU itself. Thus the EU comes to act as a general guarantor of collective order, 'stabilising the constitution of its Member States'. The guarantee is generalised, and is not restricted by the specific limitations on the competence of the EU or the EC. The declarations in Article 6(1) TEU not only date back to the 'Copenhagen Principles' enunciated as the basis for entry into the EU by a candidate state (3.13), but much further to a Declaration on Democracy adopted at a European Council meeting back in 1978. Thus, the EU is now effectively emerging as the arbiter of how democratic Member States must be (Verhoeven, 1998). It was this framework of guarantees that lay behind the reaction of the fourteen other Member States to the impending inclusion of the populist Freedom Party, previously led by the controversial political figure Jörg Haider, in Austria's governing coalition at the end of January 2000. No formal action was taken under Article 7 TEU, but the decision to impose certain types of political 'sanctions' on Austria mainly in the form of restricting bilateral contacts with the fourteen other Member States was obviously taken in the shadow of this provision. It amounted to a 'shot across the bows' of the new coalition to remind it of its obligations under all of the EU Treaties which are now generalised *constitutional obligations* (see the Introduction to Part IV).

In addition, Article 6(2) TEU also enshrines fundamental rights in terms which 'mix' the legal order of the Union and 'Community law' in its narrow first-pillar sense. It provides:

> 'The *Union* shall respect fundamental rights, as guaranteed by the European Convention for the Protection of Human Rights and Fundamental Freedoms signed in Rome on 4 November 1950 and as they result from

the constitutional traditions common to the Member States, as general principles of *Community law*' (emphasis added).

This too implies a unity of the legal and constitutional order.

5.6   Structuring Constitutional Principles and Practices such as Subsidiarity and Flexibility

Article 1 TEU talks of decisions being taken 'close to the citizen'. This is a reference to the general political principle of subsidiarity, and as such is entirely unenforceable and merely declaratory in effect. In more specifically legal terms, the Treaty of Amsterdam introduced a general reference to the principle of subsidiarity, as it is defined in Article 5 EC, into Article 2 TEU. It operates as a general fetter upon how the EU achieves the objectives set out in that Article and how it exercises the 'powers' found elsewhere in that Treaty. Subsidiarity in relation to policy making introduces a principle of comparative efficiency: where competences are shared between the EU or the EC and the Member States, the former should only take action 'if and insofar as the objectives of the proposed action cannot be sufficiently achieved by the Member States and can therefore, by reason of the scale or effects of the proposed action, be better achieved by the Community' (6.6).

Flexibility is now a practice common to all parts of the EU, both in terms of existing arrangements such as EMU and Schengen/Title IV EC and with respect to the general conditions laid down in the Treaties. Articles 43–44 TEU govern any instances of 'closer cooperation' established under the EC Treaty or the TEU, limiting it to measures 'aimed at furthering the objectives of the Union and at protecting its interests'. It must not affect the *acquis communautaire*, and must respect the principles of both the TEU and the EC Treaty and the 'single institutional framework of the Union'. Specific provisions on closer cooperation in the first pillar (Article 11 EC) and the third pillar (Article 40 TEU) lay down additional conditions. The second pillar possesses a shadow of flexibility, in the form of 'constructive abstentionism' (Article 23 TEU).

The development of all aspects of the EU – not just instances of closer cooperation – can only proceed by reference to the concept of the *acquis communautaire* (mentioned in Articles 2, 3 and 43(1)(e) TEU and paragraph 2 of the Protocol on Subsidiarity and Proportionality). This concept is certainly not intended to ossify policies agreed in the past, and to suggest that in all areas EU policies as already developed are irreversible in every respect (Weatherill, 1998). Moreover, it is very clear that some parts of the *acquis* are more 'core' than other parts, as the Commission's approach to accession negotiations with the Central and Eastern European countries has made clear. Notwithstanding doubts about its cohesive or adhesive properties as a constitutional principle under the current framework (Weatherill, 2000a), it clearly operates as a common element linking the three pillars as a unity at present.

5.7 Rules of Membership and Change

Accession to and membership of the 'whole package', i.e. EU *and* EC, comes by virtue of the application of a single provision: Article 49 TEU. It is implicit that this must also include membership of the European Community in the reference to 'adjustments to the Treaties on which the Union is founded'. Formally, when accession actually occurs, under international law it requires an accession treaty or treaties, which must be ratified by all the states involved – candidates and Member States. Moreover, the rules of change regarding amendments to the whole framework of Treaties through the convocation of an intergovernmental conference are likewise located in the final provisions of the TEU (Article 48 TEU) (3.15, 5.11). Again, this requires one or more treaties amending the existing treaty framework.

5.8 The Capacity to Adopt Binding Legal Measures and Increased Decisional Autonomy on the Part of the EU

Article 6(4) TEU provides that

> 'The Union shall provide itself with the means necessary to attain its objectives and carry through its policies.'

Furthermore, the second and third pillars are phrased in terms of 'the Union shall define' (Article 11 TEU) and 'the Union's objective shall be' (Article 29 TEU). It seems hard to deny the ever-increasing decisional autonomy of the Union through its institutions, especially the European Council and the Council, in the context of those pillars. Under each pillar 'binding' law is produced: it was assumed in the *Airport Transit Visas* case that the joint action under challenge was legally binding and therefore produced legal effects (otherwise it could not have been the subject of an action for annulment). There is a substantial body of such 'law' covering all manner of policy activities (Curtin and Dekker, 1999). Moreover, although there remain sharp differences in terms of the nature and effects of the acts that can be adopted under the various pillars, there is an emerging similarity of instruments with the creation of the category of 'framework decisions' under PJC by the Treaty of Amsterdam. Framework decisions

> 'shall be binding upon the Member States as to the result to be achieved but shall leave to the national authorities the choice of form and methods' (Article 34(2)(b) TEU).

This is remarkably similar to the terms in which directives are described under the EC Treaty (Article 249 EC). However, Article 34 TEU goes on to say that framework decisions 'shall not entail direct effect'. One might, perhaps, speculate that framework decisions are likely to play the structuring role in promoting national legal convergence that Member States anticipated might be taken by directives; before – that is – the Court of Justice intervened with cases such as *Van Duyn* (Case 41/74 *Van Duyn* v. *Home Office* [1974] ECR 1337) to find that provisions of directives *could* under certain conditions be relied upon by individuals in national courts, at least against public authorities, in the interests of the effectiveness of EU law and the protection of the individual as a subject of EU law (1.6, see Chapter 12).

One problem relating to decisional autonomy of the EU lies in the external sphere. The Member States have not conferred upon the EU the capacity to make binding international agreements. The only measures which can be adopted in the external sphere in the areas of the second- and third-pillar competences requiring agreements with third states or international organisations (i.e. bilateral or multilateral action rather than merely unilateral action) would appear to be those taken by the Member States themselves. These need to be ratified in accordance with their respective constitutional requirements. It had been anticipated throughout the 1996–97 IGC that the new Treaty would rectify what was seen by many as an omission from the Treaty of Maastricht, namely explicit internal recognition of the formal legal personality of the EU to make international agreements, paralleling that of each of the 'three Communities' (e.g. Article 281 EC). In fact the Member States at the IGC chose a more restricted procedural mechanism which gives the Council the task of negotiating any agreements, but makes clear that these are not agreements *of the EU* (Article 24 TEU). Thus it would appear, in formal terms at least, that the EU is a Treaty regime without a legal form, and that it might be difficult to accord it, for example, the status of an international organisation under international law. This has caused difficulties, both in terms of confusion for the EU's external partners and interlocutors and the efficiency of decision making as ratification at national level can often take up to two years, leaving international agreements, in the meantime, in legal limbo. However, in practice the EU has presented itself to the outside world in CFSP terms through the Presidency, and this office is assisted since the Treaty of Amsterdam by the Secretary General of the Council, 'Mr. CFSP' Javier Solana who now provides a degree of permanence in terms of personal presence which the rotating Presidency does not have. The External Relations Commissioners (centralised in 1999 into a single office occupied by Chris Patten who is one of the UK Commissioners) have also acted as the EU's external relations 'face'. Moreover, through the Presidency in particular, the EU has participated in all manner of international 'acts'. The absence of formal legal personality conferred by the Treaties is thus not decisive in terms of determining whether the EU is a single entity, especially since the recognition of international legal personality is a question for international law not EU law, and is based on the perceptions of third parties (how do other states and international organisations perceive the EU?) and an objective assessment of the conduct of the EU itself. Curtin and Dekker (1999: 111) conclude:

> 'the legal practices of the Union with regard to its international representation and its commitment to international legal norms and rules indicate that the entity is acting in a specific fashion in international relations. Moreover there are no indications that other legal persons are not accepting the Union as a legal person'.

This point, then, is not a decisive obstacle to considering the EU as a single entity.

5.9   External Identity of the EU, the Principle of Consistency and Multi-pillar Activity

There are, on the contrary, some positive indicia of the unity of the EU in the external sphere. This is, in a sense, necessary because one of the objectives of the EU is 'to assert itself on the international scene, in particular through the implementation of a common foreign and security policy...' (Article 2 TEU), despite the lack of formal legal personality. In addition, the second part of Article 3 TEU provides that

> 'The Union shall in particular ensure the consistency of its external activities as a whole in the context of its external relations, security, economic and development policies. The Council and the Commission shall be responsible for ensuring such consistency and shall cooperate to this end. They shall ensure the implementation of these policies, each in accordance with its respective powers.'

More specifically, the Council is mandated to 'ensure the unity, consistency and effectiveness of action by the Union' in the field of CFSP (Article 13(3) TEU). The rhetoric of the EU in relation to external policy – and of the Commission in particular – is marked by an urgency to see complementarity between different external objectives, coordination of efforts, and consistency in objectives. This is to ensure that the EU's external political identity matches its economic identity. One area where the EU has been particularly successful in this has been in the 'export of standards'. Many of its complex web of international agreements, especially those providing development aid or opening up the EU market to developing countries, comprise elements of conditionality, especially human rights conditionality, or progress in the third country towards an open market economy and liberal institutions of the state.

In the context of external relations, 'multi-pillar' activity, recognising the spread of competences across the pillars, has become common. The imposition of external economic sanctions against third states, for example, requires the deployment of powers under both the TEU (the adoption of a joint action or common position under Articles 14 or 15 TEU to set the policy of sanctions under the CFSP) *and* the EC Treaty (Article 301 EC requiring the Council to take the necessary measures in relation to the EU's external economic relations). Policies on combating illegal drugs and on the export of strategic or 'dual use' goods (which have military and civilian uses) are also good examples.

5.10 Budgetary Questions

While the situation after the Treaty of Maastricht was one of considerable uncertainty, Article 28(3) and 41 TEU now largely place CFSP and PJC expenditure firmly within the central EU budget. Most expenditure will be charged to the general budget, and thus will not be reliant upon individualised Member State contributions. The exceptions are operations having military or defence implications, and cases where the Council unanimously decides otherwise.

5.11 Conclusions and Consequences

From this review, a number of important conclusions can be drawn, not just with regard to the 'unity' of the system. First, de Witte rightly highlights the 'resilience of the Community model' (de Witte, 1998: 55). The Member States appear to have experienced some regrets since the time when

'they broke the European Community mold and invented unprecedented procedures and entirely new legal instruments [in the Treaty of Maastricht]. The procedures of the second and third pillars have proved to be cumbersome and inefficient, and the new legal instruments, particularly those chosen for the third pillar, have proved to be blunt and legally ambiguous. It is out of a better understanding of their own long-term national interest that the Member States have now 'infected' the two inter-governmental pillars with an extra dose of *méthode communautaire* and have thus recognized that successful and effective cooperation between states is sometimes better served by the severe regime of institutional constraints and limitations of sovereignty practiced within the European Community than by the lax *entre nous* atmosphere of the second and third pillars' (de Witte, 1998: 55–56).

Second, elements of unity and fragmentation can co-exist quite comfortably in the paradoxical polity which the EU is increasingly becoming. While the EU is a single unit, it is composed of increasingly complex subsystems. This relates not only to the three pillars and the substructures with them, including a plethora of different decision-making techniques and provision for flexible solutions (such as Title IV EC and EMU), but also to the ever-increasing use of protocols and declarations appended by the amending Treaties such as Maastricht and Amsterdam to the EU Treaties. This serves to add, to modify, to elucidate and sometimes even to contradict apparent positions taken in or under the Treaties. All of this then begs the question raised in the next paragraph: if the EU is indeed a single entity, what should we call it?

It would be merely restating the obvious to reiterate the terms of the preamble to the EC Treaty and Article 1 TEU, namely that the EU constitutes a further stage in the creation of 'an ever closer union amongst the peoples of Europe'. Moreover, to describe the EU as an 'emerging non-state polity' largely begs the question of what features that polity might have, although confirming that the EU is a polity has the advantage of telling us what we should be looking for when we study that polity, namely institutions and structures of governance, frameworks of rights and duties, formal documentation such as a constitution, and some form of political identity. Both of these 'definitions' do, however, have the advantage of highlighting the dynamic and evolutionary character of the EU, a point that will be picked up later in this paragraph. Certainly, it seems correct to reject the suggestion made by distinguished commentators that the EU is a 'state', or should aspire to statehood (Mancini, 1998; cf. Weiler, 1998). It has not in any event taken over the sovereignty of its Member States, which continue as members of the United Nations in their own right, recognised by other subjects of international law as states. Moreover, in their own internal political and legal organisation, there is no doubt that the Member States are 'states', and could be seen as playing important 'conservatory' roles in the EU's legal and political order (Dashwood, 1998). The EU is, moreover, a limited entity, deriving its authority from the treaties, and not direct from its citizens, which is one of the classic means of determining the presence of statehood.

A variety of different descriptions have been ventured by authors and political commentators, including 'supranational federation' (von Bogdandy), federation of nation states (Delors), layered international organisation (Curtin and Dekker), European Commonwealth (MacCormick) and model of multilevel constitutionalism (Pernice). Certainly each of these terms nicely expresses the unique or *sui generis* nature of the EU, in the sense that there is only one entity in the world quite like it. The less obvious question is whether they effectively serve the purpose that such a description or designation should serve, namely to highlight its hybridity as an entity, its paradoxical relationship with the state (Shaw and Wiener, 2000), and its 'betweenness' such that it cannot be fully analysed using the tools of either international law or national law, but only with a combination of the two (Denza, 1999). Moreover, it seems best to highlight that the EU is in a state of 'becoming' and not 'being' and so static descriptions of its 'essence' are of relatively little assistance in describing or explaining it.

5.12 Describing the EU in Constitutional Terms

The advantage of the term 'model of multilevel constitutionalism' (a translation by Pernice (1999) of the German term *Verfassungsverbund*) is that it highlights the actual and potential role of constitutional ideas and practices in holding the EU together. In evaluating the EU the point is to develop a perspective which

'views the Member States' constitutions and the treaties constituting the European Union, despite their formal distinction, as a unity in substance and as a coherent institutional system, within which competence for action, public authority or ... the power to exercise sovereign rights is divided among two or more levels' (Pernice, 1999: 706).

Multilevel constitutionalism offers a useful framework for analysis, because it is a

'dynamic process of constitution-making instead of a sequence of international treaties which establish and develop an organization of international cooperation ... The Treaty of Amsterdam, seen in the light of multilevel constitutionalism, is one further step towards the progressive "constitution" of legitimate institutions and powers at the European level, which are complementary to the national constitutions and designed to meet the challenges of an evolving global society' (Pernice, 1999: 707).

Constitutionalism can be a useful means of ordering the social relationships governed by overlapping legal frameworks, because it focuses upon core values of collective liberal order such as those expressed in Article 6(1): democracy, liberty, fundamental rights and the rule of law, and also the processes by which these values can be given concrete expression within a given society or polity. Constitution-building as such has been firmly on the agenda throughout Europe, at least since the end of the Cold War. The countries of Central and Eastern Europe, as well as those of the former Soviet Union, have moved at different speeds towards systems of liberal constitutional democracy which have borrowed heavily from historical American and European models. Constitutionalism alone cannot, of course, guarantee that those values and principles are actually enforced; nor does it mean that there will be cross-EU consensus about what these terms really mean and how they should be implemented (e.g. through representative institutions or legal guarantees of rights protection). The ever-increasing diversity of the enlarging EU makes constitutionalism in a subjective sense involving 'the people' in some role a very challenging project. On the other hand, constitutional processes and ideas might form a constructive relationship with issues of political identity in order to bridge some of the EU's more prominent legitimacy and democracy gaps.

The notion of a multilevel constitution also neatly captures the complex network of legal relationships at the national and the international levels in particular within which the EU is nested. So far as the EU Treaties could be said to form the EU's main constitutional document, they have a paradoxical nature. They are, in legal form and in terms of the means by which they have been constructed, treaties governed by international law. In international law terms the Member States are the High Contracting Parties responsible for elaborating, amending, signing and ratifying the treaties before they come into force. The Vienna Convention on the Law of Treaties will apply. The work of the Court of Justice and the autonomous practices of the institutions in constructing the supranational legal and political order could logically be seen as subordinate to that international law framework. In similar terms the *national* constitutional frameworks remain, in themselves, 'sovereign'. EU law is an entity that challenges the binary divide between national law and international law and between power relations within and among states. Some commentators have observed the need for a pluralistic analysis showing how the systems of law operative on the European level are both 'distinct and partially independent of each other, though also partially overlapping and interacting' (MacCormick, 1999: 119).

In seeking to identify the nature of the EU constitutional framework, it is useful to distinguish between three separate meanings of the term 'constitution' when it is applied to states. At one level, a constitution is the bundle of legal rules and practices which underlie the exercise and control of state power, and which structure the form of government within a state. At another level, a constitution is a formal document or set of documents, achieving the same objectives. The United Kingdom has an 'unwritten' constitution in the first sense (although, of course, the vast majority of the rules are to be found in written form), but lacks a set of formally identified 'constitutional' documents in the latter sense (a 'written' constitution). However, the vast majority of modern states have such a formal constitutional document or documents. In its third meaning, the constitution has a subjective nature, related to the acceptance by those subject to jurisdiction of a given constitution as 'their constitution'. In that context, discussions of constitutions and constitutionalism tend to be closely linked to ideas about identity, especially political identity, citizenship, democracy and the conditions for the legitimate exercise of power within polities (e.g. Beetham and Lord, 1998). Studies about constitutions and constitutionalism in the EU tend to concentrate on two core questions: does the EU *have* a constitution and does it *need* one (Piris, 1999)?

However we choose to describe the EU, it is certainly incontestable that it exercises many of the traditional functions of government, albeit within limited fields; more specifically, the European Community is an entity to which, according to the Court of Justice, sovereign powers have been ascribed. The EU undoubtedly, therefore, *needs* a constitution of the first type, namely a set of basic ground rules that govern these functions and powers, which deal with the apportionment of power to various organs and the relationships between these organs. These ground rules or principles are necessary to secure the rule of law, and to create a framework for limited government in which the rights of majorities and minorities are respected appropriately. There is a danger in the EU that the gap between the 'formal/legal' constitution in the sense of the legal framework for the institutions and their powers and functions within the Treaties is increasingly losing touch with the 'real' state of governance in the EU. If that gap grows too large, constitutional values will be lost (de Búrca, 1999a). Moreover, while the mere existence of such rules will not on its own secure any significant degree of legitimacy for the EU, in the sense of popular or social legitimacy related to the acceptance of the exercise of power, thus satisfying the third meaning of the constitution, it is none the less a basic condition precedent for the EU as a lawful and legitimate polity. As we shall see, such a constitutional framework has gradually emerged in the form of what Eleftheriadis (1996: 41) has called the principles of the 'substantive constitution', although they remain as yet incomplete and fragmented in nature. In that sense, the EU does *have* a constitution.

The links between the second and third senses of the constitution can be drawn out if we examine the means whereby a 'constitution' can be brought into being or changed in the EU context. Two alternatives immediately present themselves which highlight the transitory position between 'Community' and 'Union', which the EU in its present form currently occupies. At present (3.15), the basic constitution-building process of the EU as a whole comprises international negotiations between representatives of sovereign states in an intergovernmental conference or IGC, the unanimous conclusion of a Treaty amending or adding to the existing Treaties, followed by a ratification process in which all the Member States must ratify the Treaty agreed upon according to their respective constitutional requirements (Article 49 TEU). Throughout, the process of negotiation requires 'common accord'. The formal involvement of the EU institutions is also sparse: the Commission may propose the amendment of the Treaty; the Council must deliver an opinion in favour of convening an IGC after consulting the Commission and the European Parliament (and, where appropriate, the European Central Bank), before the formal negotiation process can begin. However, once begun the negotiations are matters of intergovernmental bargaining. Moreover, at the national level, there may be little or no involvement of bodies other than the government during the negotiations themselves, so that when any amending Treaty is subsequently presented to the national Parliament or the electorate for ratification through vote or referendum, it is as a *fait accompli* on a 'take-it-or-leave-it' basis with no possibility for piecemeal change. This further distances the citizen (and the national political *fora*) from the process of change of the EU Treaties. The experiences with the Danish referendum in which the Treaty of Maastricht was rejected demonstrates that any intergovernmental consensus may not always receive the approval of national political organs. As a result the whole ratification process of the Treaty was jeopardised and only saved by very careful political footwork on the part of the Danish government and the other EU governments, in particular at the European Council meeting convened in Edinburgh in December 1992.

The lessons to be derived from this experience and from the problems encountered in relation to the ratification of the Treaty of Maastricht are clear. The 'traditional' mode of constitution-building for the EU, although firmly grounded in international diplomacy, the states system and international law, cannot necessarily deliver a satisfactory outcome because, whatever the content of Treaties agreed between governments, the process is one which excludes many interested parties, including ordinary citizens in particular. Notwithstanding that, of course, the IGC method continues to be used, as the Member States do not overtly recognise themselves as 'constitution-building'. To do so would require an express commitment to the Union as polity that would be challenging to national notions of sovereignty.

The second means of constitution-building derives from federal constitutionalism rather than international relations. Reflecting the American constitutional experience, this is often termed the 'Philadelphia' model, and would involve a constitutional convention for something like a 'United States of Europe', in which a new constitutional settlement is determined directly by the representatives of the people elected to such a convention by direct or indirect suffrage. The European Parliament has sought to promote the adoption of a variant of this method of constitution-building, sometimes by seeking to appeal to national parliaments over the heads of governments. Such a change would undoubtedly herald a quantum increase in the power and influence of the European Parliament both over the procedure of amendment (as it is the sole existing popular representative institution of the EU), and over decision-making powers in any subsequent 'state' or 'union'. A shift to such a 'federal' approach to constitution-building lies behind an initiative on the part of the European Parliament in 1994 for a European Constitution to be enacted jointly by the Parliament and the Member States (European Parliament Resolution on the Constitution of the European Union, OJ 1994 C61/155). It is true, however, that there was slightly increased transparency in the process of the 1996–97 IGC, and lobby groups, NGOs and indeed many academics took the opportunity to present a plethora of blueprints for amendments to the Treaties, many of which would have carried the EU decisively in the 'federal' direction.

Clearly the practical politics of European integration tell us that whatever the 'legitimacy dividend' of such a means of constitution-building, it would not be acceptable to the most influential actors involved at this stage. This highlights how the questions of having and needing a constitution in the EU context all too often become tied up with normative political positions on what the state of the European integration project currently is, and where it should go in the future (its 'finality'). Perhaps it is because of the difficulties of public debate on this issue, therefore, that the 'real' history of the development of European integration, and the progressive adoption and implementation of new Treaties, tends to show that it is often the apparently small steps which have offered the most realistic chance of incremental progress towards closer integration and associated frameworks of constitutionalism. This argument could be made in relation to the content and subsequent impact of the Single European Act (Bermann, 1989). It may also be one reason why in its opinion on the 1996 IGC, the European Parliament eventually renounced the earlier radical constitutionalism it was espousing and accepted that the means whereby the IGC would inevitably proceed would be through an international Treaty. However, the Parliament and many observers stressed that, whatever the form, the content of the process would involve constitution-building and must therefore take heed of relevant values of democratic participation, and openness and accountability.

In that context, it might useful for the political entities involved to take heed of the third method of constitution-building which has proved extremely important hitherto for the EU. This has been the progressive evolution of the character of the treaties and the development of constitutional practices among the institutions, fostered in particular by the role of the Court of Justice in identifying and implementing constitutional principles (what is often termed the 'constitutionalisation of the Treaties'). The work of the Court should certainly not be viewed with rose-tinted spectacles in the belief that it offers some type of general panacea for other (political) deficits in the EU. With the prominent role of the Court there is, of course, the danger of 'government by judges', who are unelected and unaccountable to the people. Furthermore the 'constitutionalisation' thesis is one that has evolved essentially in relation to the EC Treaty, and it is difficult to extend it unchanged to the TEU. As supranational judges based in Luxembourg it could be thought that the judges of the Court of Justice are even more insulated from popular sentiment. Furthermore, the reach of the Court is limited in relation to the treaties. Since the Court is still largely excluded from jurisdiction over much of the TEU, including most of its foundational principles, it has not been given the opportunity to develop a constitutional understanding of those provisions. Even more threatening to using the work of the Court of Justice to construct an understanding of the current EU constitutional framework is the fact that, as the next paragraph shows, the so-called 'constitutionalisation of the treaties' thesis using the framework of the transfer of sovereign powers is based on a rather one-dimensional reading of the EC Treaty by the Court of Justice which is not fully accepted by all the other constitutional actors in the EU, notably some of the national constitutional courts. Thus before undertaking that review, it is important to deal with one extremely important challenge to the possibility of EU constitutionalism, which has come from the German Federal Constitutional Court in particular. The next paragraph deals with this and other problems of EU constitutionalism.

5.13   Problems of EU Constitutionalism

It is an argument about sovereignty which lies to a large extent behind the strongest challenge in recent years to the possibilities of European constitutionalism, the challenge which emerged out of the decision of the German Federal Constitutional Court which formally cleared the way for Germany to ratify the Treaty of Maastricht, but which in truth raised some very difficult questions about the nature – present and future – of the European Community and the European Union (*Brunner* [1994] 1 CMLR 57 (unofficial English translation)).

The German Court opened the door to a scrutiny of the Treaty of Maastricht when it accepted the contention that the right of German citizens to participate in elections to the German parliament (the *Bundestag*) guaranteed by Article 38 of the German Constitution (the 'Basic Law') might be infringed by the Treaty. Article 23 of the Basic Law authorises the transfer of sovereign powers by the legislature to the European Union, but this is only permissible in so far as the transfer does not alter the 'identity of the constitutional order' of the Federal Republic – that is the central principles which are protected against repeal by Article 79(3) of the Basic Law. These are the principles of democracy, the rule of law, the essential content of the fundamental rights, and the federal basis of Germany. In setting the limits of German participation in the EU using these building blocks, the Federal Constitutional Court painted a picture of the EU which drew heavily on classic concepts of national sovereignty, and which saw the EU and its legal order as fundamentally a creature of international relations and international law, based on Treaties which are controlled by the Member States, and lacking the *sui generis* features of 'supranationalism' which the Court of Justice has always claimed for it. For the German court the image of the 'constitutionalised treaty' does not sustain the authority of EU law and the Court of Justice.

Democracy in the EU is guaranteed, according to the Federal Constitutional Court, not through the European Parliament, but through the national parliaments. This is because there is no single European people, and since democracy comes 'from the people', the European Parliament cannot in that sense secure democracy; it can only play a 'supporting' role ([1994] 1 CMLR 57 at p. 87). Instead, national parliaments represent national peoples. The use of the concept of 'people' in that way has been heavily criticised in some quarters (e.g. Weiler, 1995, 1996). However, from that foundation comes the limitation upon the sovereign rights that the EU may exercise. They are not the sovereign rights of a state, but of a limited 'confederation' or 'association' of sovereign states (*'Staatenverbund'*). Consequently, the Community has only limited competences – only limited competences may be transferred by a sovereign state. Authorisations given by the Member States must be given in a precise and limited way, such that the actions of the EU are foreseeable, and the EU must stay within its 'integration programme' ([1994] 1 CMLR 57 at p. 89). Most devastatingly for the Court of Justice, however, the Federal Constitutional Court held that the Community lacks what is called 'competence-competence' (*Kompetenz-Kompetenz*), that is the power to determine the scope of its competences (Kokott, 1998 for more details). That must lie elsewhere, implicitly, with the Federal Constitutional Court (and other national constitutional courts), since it confirmed explicitly that acts of the EU institutions would not be applicable within the territory of the Federal Republic of Germany if they exceeded the limits of the competences conferred upon them by the Member States. By this means, the German Court explicitly linked its judgment back to a series of earlier judgments – termed a rebellion – handed down by the German courts specifically in relation to the question of fundamental rights which appeared, by the mid-1980s, to have been quelled with the Federal Constitutional Court ceding authority to the Court of Justice (9.6). It would appear that with the larger 'constitutional' claims of European Union, the dangers of possible conflicts between the Court of Justice and the Federal Constitutional Court have emerged again with added urgency.

Many of the assertions about the EU contained in the *Brunner* judgment can, and have been, challenged by reference to the constitutional specifities or indeed sensitivities of Germany (Zuleeg, 1997), or as representing a one-dimensional picture of the EU legal order which takes insufficient account of either the dynamic nature of the EU itself (Smits, 1994), or indeed the increasingly uncertain concept of national 'sovereignty' (e.g.

MacCormick, 1995). However, it has served an essential function in giving a backdrop to serious consideration and debate about the future of European Union, in particular of an EU in which a single currency with economic and monetary union is a serious, if still relatively distant, possibility. It raises questions about the continuing need to take sovereignty and nation states seriously (de Witte, 1995) and highlights the dangers of constitutional collision in Europe (MacCormick, 1999). In that sense, it was quickly acknowledged as having 'rendered an important service to European integration' (Herdegen, 1994: 249).

The consequences of *Brunner* are felt in both the 'practical' and the 'academic' domains. Argument has been joined as to whether the EU, as the German Court conceives it, *can have* a constitution, and this has engendered lively debate among commentators (Weiler, 1995; Grimm, 1995; Habermas, 1995; Schuppert, 1995). Joseph Weiler has likened the stand-off between the Court of Justice and the German Federal Constitutional Court to the Cold War, and the threat to use the ultimate weapon, nuclear weapons, but with the knowledge that this will surely lead to mutually assured destruction (Weiler, 1997). Thus the hope is that the deterrent will be enough, with the Court of Justice and the EU's legislative organs paying sufficient attention to the concerns coming from the Federal Constitutional Court.

The conflict flared up once again in the context of the EU's external trade regime for bananas, which the EU legislature sought to reform on a uniform basis in the context of the uniform commercial policy required after 1992. There have, historically, been both huge differences in the tariff treatment of imports of bananas into the various countries of the EU and high levels of cultural sensitivity about where bananas available in particular Member States should come from. Germany was entitled to import tariff-free substantial quantities of cheap Latin American bananas under a special Protocol attached to the original EEC Treaty. Other Member States charged the standard tariff, and bananas from seventy African, Caribbean and Pacific (ACP) countries associated with the EU through the Lomé Convention entered all Member States tariff-free. Attempts to create a single external trade regime for bananas resulted in lower tariff-free quotas for imports of Latin American bananas, thus damaging their competitive position especially vis-à-vis the ACP bananas. The German Government and the importers of Latin American bananas pursued litigation strategies on many fronts: before the institutions of the GATT (General Agreement on Tariffs and Trade) challenging the legality in international trade law of the new regime; before the Court of Justice and the German courts challenging the legality of the new regime under EU law, arguing in particular that EU law had to have full regard to the requirements of the GATT as part of EU law and the GATT rendered this type of discrimination between countries which export bananas unlawful. The core of the conflict between the German courts and the Court of Justice is over the question whether the GATT (in its old pre-WTO form) could have direct effect in EU law, a point which the Court of Justice has always denied (5.14, 12.10). In other words, it cannot be relied upon directly as the basis for challenging EU legislative provisions either in the Court of Justice itself or in the national courts. It is not a generalised position on all international agreements, but one which the Court has always adhered to in relation to the GATT. This means that the Court takes a very different position on the effects of certain legal principles coming out of international trade law than it takes on the effects of EC law on national law. To date, despite the plethora of cases and judgments in this area from the Court of Justice and the German courts, including a reference from a German administrative court to the Federal Constitutional Court on the precise question of conflicts between EU law and German constitutional law, the anticipated direct confrontation has not occurred (Reich, 1996a; Everling, 1996). Meanwhile, under international pressure the EU has been forced to change some parts of its banana regime, and the terrain of debate has shifted from the more country-specific question of a conflict between Germany and the EU to a more generalised debate about the effects of international trade law within the EU legal order, and thus the extent to which the EU can lay claim to having constitutional principles in the form of international trade rules enshrined into the external dimension of its legal order in the form of general principles of law (9.3) (Peers, 1999a, 1999b; Trachtman, 1999).

The Federal Constitutional Court is not the only national court to have confronted the Court of Justice on this type of terrain. In a judgment described as 'in many ways comparable' (Høegh, 1999: 81) with *Brunner*, the Danish Supreme Court decided in 1998 that the Danish ratification of the Treaty of Maastricht was not contrary to the Danish constitution (*Carlsen* v. *Prime Minister of Denmark*, judgment of 6 April 1998; unofficial translation available from the website of the Danish Interior Ministry website). The Danish Court followed the lead of the German Court in declaring that acts of the EU institutions, including the Court of Justice, which infringed civil rights under the Danish constitution or which demonstrated that the powers transferred exceeded what could be transferred under Section 20(1) of the Danish constitution as presently drafted, would not be applicable in Denmark. In other words, it adopted the same position on 'competence-competence'.

These judicial views have been the basis for the development of arguments that the term constitution must be restricted to the fundamental legal foundations of a *state*, primarily in order to differentiate between states and other forms of political organisation. One of the objectives of this analysis is to focus upon the link between democratic rule and the *demos*, which the EU continues to lack (Grimm, 1995). But on a political level, a more appropriate and limited definition of the *demos* might be simply 'the idea of a European society that is willing across all divergence of opinion and interests to live under common rule' (Kohler-Koch, 1999). This material pre-condition for democracy might be more easy to satisfy, even though it probably has not been so far (10.2).

In addition, the consequence of such actual and potential constitutional collisions has been the development of a number of useful expositions of EU constitutionalism which take into account a more sophisticated and differentiated understanding of the EU legal order. For example, some work draws upon pluralist theories of legal authority and of the institutions of law which posit the EU's legal order within a system of overlapping and heterarchical orders in which the nation state order is not automatically privileged (MacCormick, 1999; Bańkowski and Christodoulidis, 1998). There are theories of 'multilevel constitutionalism' that draw strength specifically from the multilevel ordering of EU constitutionalism as comprising both national and EU elements (Pernice, 1999; Poiares Maduro, 2000). Finally, there are theories which are grounded in a reconceptualisation of an EU legal order based on an explicitly unitary theory of the EU as a single legal order, encompassing both the European Communities, traditionally understood as supranational and 'federalised' in nature, as well as the more intergovernmental second and third pillars where the direct dependence of the EU upon the systems of the Member States is even more evident (von Bogdandy 1999, 2000; von Bogdandy and Nettesheim, 1996).

5.14   **The Basic Constitutional Framework**

Many aspects of the basic constitutional framework of the EU have already been touched upon both earlier in this chapter and in previous chapters. The objective here is to make the different elements of the basic constitutional framework quite explicit, and also to address what would be the key questions in relation to that constitutional framework, by grouping the provisions of the EU Treaties and associated legal rules and principles into six groups:

- What is the nature of the polity?
- Is it a polity under the rule of law?
- What values, principles and norms operate within the system?
- What rules govern the exercise of power and authority?
- To what extent is there flexibility within the constitutional system?
- Finally – and in a sense most significantly – what is the EU for?

The chapter concludes with a discussion of the role of the Court of Justice vis-à-vis the evolving constitutional framework.

There are overlaps between the provisions falling into the different groups. Not all of these groups of provisions are discussed in equal depth here. Some have been the subject of study elsewhere in this or other chapters. Others, such as the issue of the function and objectives of the EU can – in large part – only be fleshed out through the medium of the study of social and economic law, which falls outside the scope of this book. Flexibility is studied here in some depth as a constitutional subject, although in practice the closer cooperation provisions, which are the subject of discussion, have yet to be applied.

It is not claimed here that the EU constitutional framework is complete. Notably there are gaps, especially in the external dimension as the 'bananas' litigation has amply demonstrated (5.13, 9.3); the constitutional framework is a rather introspective one at present. The EU is committed to respect for international law. Provisions of international agreements concluded by (or binding on) the EC are part of EU law and may, in appropriate circumstances, be invoked before national courts as giving rise to enforceable rights for individuals (e.g. Case 104/81 *Kupferberg* [1982] ECR 3659). This has been particularly the case with appropriately phrased provisions of the agreements linking the EU and other 'associated' states. The Court has also held that the provisions of the European Convention on Human Rights and Fundamental Freedoms may be enforceable within the EU legal order, as general principles of EC law, an approach now given formal constitutional sanction by Article 6(2) TEU. However, the Court has consistently held that provisions of the GATT are not capable of judicial enforcement, in order, for example, to invalidate an EC measure via the reference procedure in Article 234, because they are not of a nature to confer rights on individuals (Cases 2-4/72 *International Fruit Company NV* v. *Produktschap voor Groenten en Fruit* [1972] ECR 1219). Most controversially, the Court of Justice refused to accept the argument from Germany that provisions of the EC's importation and production regime for bananas were contrary to the (old) GATT (Case C-280/93 *Germany* v. *Council* [1994] ECR I-473), and hence faces another round of the bout of constitutional collision sketched in 5.13. It held that the same features of the GATT which precluded its direct effect (12.10), especially the fact that it was not unconditional, precluded Germany from relying upon the GATT to challenge an internal EU measure establishing the bananas by means of a direct action under what is now Article 230 EC. The only exception, the Court held, would be where the Community had intended to implement a particular obligation entered into within the framework of GATT, or if the Community expressly refers to specific provisions of GATT. In Case C-149/96 *Portuguese Republic* v. *Council* (November 23 1999), the Court confirmed the same position regarding the 'new GATT', that is the GATT 1994, other agreements, and the fundamental rules and principles of the WTO, including those relating to dispute settlement. Given the burgeoning importance of international trade law, and the changing nature of WTO law, the continuing introspective position taken with regard to international law by the Court of Justice seems increasingly inappropriate.

5.15   The Nature of the Polity

The first group of provisions is concerned with the nature of the polity, including its multilevel constitutional system, and the relations to the national polities and the international system. This is the point at which this chapter began, with an exposition of the arguments for treating the EU as a unity rather than three separate pillars. To the provisions and rules already extensively discussed in 5.3–5.9 should be added other general provisions such as Articles 312 EC and 51 TEU which establish those Treaties for an unlimited period. Beyond the conclusions drawn above about the relative strength of the elements of unity over those implying separateness, and the durability of the 'Community method' of the first pillar, it is not particularly helpful to fix upon a single designation of the EU as polity other than in terms of its evolving and multilevel constitutional framework. This limited reference point for the EU has the advantage, over other designations which draw upon terms such as 'international organisation', 'federation', or even 'Commonwealth' (5.10), that it emphasises in a functional way those elements of the EU which are essential to its construction as a *legitimate polity*. It does not presuppose that the EU is derived in its essence from either the national or the international domains, and as regards the ends of the integration process adopts a non-teleological stance that no specific objectives or end-points are necessarily in view.

5.16   The Rule of Law in the EU

For many years, one of the central reference points for the legitimation of the EU polity was idea of a 'Community governed by law'. Law has, within the constitutional system of the EU, more than a mere functional property in terms of the guarantee of legality in all its dimensions, but a stronger ideological function in expressing what some have grandly termed the 'identity and universality' of Europe (Obradovic, 1996: 196–198).

In addition to the very general statement about the rule of law in Article 6(1) TEU, central to those provisions dealing with the rule of law is Article 220 EC which provides that 'The Court of Justice shall ensure that in the interpretation and application of this Treaty the law is observed.' Building on this, the Court binds the Member States to the rule of law in particular through Article 10 EC which establishes their loyalty to the Treaties they have signed and their duty to comply with Treaty-derived obligations and sets up the Commission's primary and centralised powers of enforcement of EC law against non-conforming Member States in Articles 226 and 228 EC.

But in truth the rule of law, in the sense of the binding of the Member States to the law which they have created, is enforced as much in a decentralised way through the Court's evolutionary case law on the relationship between EU law and national law, especially the case law on direct effect and supremacy and the more recent obligation on national authorities to make good loss caused in certain circumstances by a failure to apply or properly to enforce EU law in breach of a Treaty obligation. Vital in this context is the co-optation of national courts as Community courts by the Court of Justice; they are drawn into the system of obligations under Article 10 EC and sustained by the organic link between national courts and the Court of Justice which is based upon the preliminary ruling jurisdiction in Article 234 EC. In general terms, individuals are constructed as the subjects rather than the mere objects of EU law, a notable variation from the traditional patterns of international law. Vis-à-vis the other institutions, the rule of law can seen in the provisions on judicial review by the Court of Justice of the acts and omissions of the institutions, allowing for the annulment of unlawful acts, for sanctions upon unlawful failures to act, and binding the Community to a principle of tortious liability for certain limited types of loss (Articles 230–233, 235 and 288 EC) In contrast, there is no comprehensive parallelism as regards the 'rule of law' system between the first pillar on the one hand, and the second and third pillars on the other. There is limited jurisdiction for the Court of Justice under the revised post-Amsterdam third pillar (1.6, 4.21) (Articles 35 and 46(b) TEU). The Court of Justice also has jurisdiction over Article 6(2) TEU on fundamental rights (Article 46(d) TEU). The extent of the fragmentation and limitation of the Court's jurisdiction has led to some concerns about the extent to which the 'Community of law' has become a 'Union of law', although in view of the amendments brought about by the Treaty of Amsterdam it is probably too early to draw firm conclusions.

5.17   Values, Principles and Norms

In the third group of provisions are brought together the key values, principles and norms within the system, including fundamental rights, non-discrimination, and the institutionalisation of Union citizenship (see further Part IV). This group contains, in other words, all matters related to the delivery of ideas of justice and fairness as outcomes of legal and political deliberations and related to maintaining the status of the individual as a holder of substantive rights under the system and as a sovereign subject of the legal order. Again reference should be made to Article 6(1) TEU as a foundation stone, but in this context one must refer also to two other paragraphs of Article 6, which guarantee respect for fundamental rights as they result from the ECHR and the national constitutional traditions common to the Member

States as general principles of Community law (paragraph 2) (Chapter 9) and respect for the national identities of its Member States (paragraph 3). Fundamental rights also have an explicitly political dimension since the Treaty of Amsterdam, with Article 7 TEU allowing the Council to pursue a political process to sanction Member States failing to comply with the Article 6(1) TEU guarantees, including human rights and fundamental freedoms (9.11). In addition, Article 11 TEU commits the EU to the objective of constructing a common foreign and security policy which aims 'to develop and consolidate democracy and the rule of law, and respect for human rights and fundamental freedoms. Article 29 TEU seeks the prevention and combating of racism and xenophobia as part of the search to provide citizens with a high degree of safety within an area of freedom, security and justice.

Other key provisions in this field include Articles 12, 13, 17–22 EC, respectively covering non-discrimination on grounds of (EU) nationality as a general principle, the establishment of a power for the Council to adopt measures to combat discrimination on grounds of sex, racial or ethnic origin, religion or belief, disability, age or sexual orientation (yet to be exercised), and the status and rights/duties associated with Citizenship of the Union. Notably, Article 17(2) 'attaches' to the Union Citizen all the rights and duties applying under the EC Treaty, a provision interpreted as being of significance in establishing a distinct legal figure of the Union citizen in the Court of Justice's first significant incursion into this field, the case of *Martínez Sala* (Case C-85/96 *Martínez Sala* v. *Freistaat Bayern* [1998] ECR I-2681) (Chapter 10). Also included in this category are the provisions prohibiting sex discrimination in the field of employment (Article 141 EC), and the gender mainstreaming provision pushing the Community to aim to eliminate inequalities and to promote equality between men and women in relation to all its activities (Article 3(2) EC). Furthermore, Article 6 EC now centralises environmental protection requirements in a similar way. Article 136 EC contains certain important commitments regarding the nature of EU social policy in relation to promotion of employment and improved living and working conditions and the combating of social exclusion, specifically with reference to the relevance of the social rights set out in the 1989 Community Charter of Fundamental Social Rights of Workers.

In the political domain, there are no more specific references to 'democracy' as such beyond Article 6(1) TEU (but see 6.9 and 9.5 for presentations of some of the 'democratic' elements in the EU's framework). There are, however, important general principles of 'transparency' and 'subsidiarity' (in the 'closeness to citizen' sense enunciated in Article 1 TEU, rather than the more technical sense of Article 5 EC which is covered in the next paragraph). Here, only the transparency principle has a direct significance for individuals, at least in the limited form of the right under Article 255 EC of access to documents, under conditions to be laid down by the Council and subject to the Rules of Procedure of the individual institutions (10.8). Finally, also protected as general principles of EC law under the Court's case law are principles of administrative and legislative legality such as the principles of legal certainty, non-discrimination and procedural fairness, which govern the ways in which the institutions may exercise their power (9.3). In that context, the Ombudsman appointed by the European Parliament can also make findings which individual rights in the context of criticising maladministration on the part of the institutions (Article 195 EC), emphasising the importance of extra-judicial remedies.

5.18 Power and Governance in the EU

The fourth discernible category of constitutional principles within the EU polity comprises those provisions that govern the exercise of power (see Chapter 6). Article 6(4) TEU provides that

> 'The Union shall provide itself with the means necessary to attain its objectives and carry through its policies'.

To that end, the single institutional framework provided for in Article 3 TEU, the more detailed provisions establishing and delimiting the composition, functions and powers of the institutions in the TEU and the EC Treaty, and the provisions laying out the objectives and tasks of the EU and the EC are crucial. Manifold provisions of the TEU and the EC Treaty give specific or general competences to the EU legislature – in its various different manifestations – to adopt measures to give effect to the objectives of the TEU and the EC Treaty. These are limited competences; the principle of limited powers or *pouvoirs attribués* itself is made explicit for the EC Treaty (Article 5 EC, first paragraph, for the whole EC; Article 7 EC so far as pertains to each individual institution), but it must likewise be regarded as implicit for the TEU. In addition, at least under the EC Treaty which remains the primary forum for binding legislative measures despite the development of the second and third pillars, a notion of implied powers (Article 308 EC, and the Court's case law on implied powers) operates to ensure that the institutions have the appropriate powers to achieve the objectives of the Treaty, even though specific powers have not been granted. The unwritten rule of 'interinstitutional balance' operates to structure relations between the institutions, and with the Member States, and Article 5 EC contains two fundamental principles which govern the exercise of powers under the EC Treaty: subsidiarity and proportionality (see 6.6 for the significance of these provisions for policy making). For the policing of many of these limits, reference must be made to the Court's powers of judicial review which allow it to annul an act based upon an insufficient or incorrect legal basis, and to ensure that the correct institutions participate in decision making according to the correct procedures, in particular as this may infringe the 'democratic principle' invoked by the Court on a number of occasions (6.9). There are also many provisions in the Treaties which organise the internal operation of the institutions, as well as their political and legal functioning within the system of the Treaties, through, for example, the adoption of Rules of Procedure, and the basic terms of the employment of officials and the duties they hold to the interests of the Union as opposed to national interests.

5.19　Flexibility, Variable Geometry and Closer Cooperation

The final group of provisions are those establishing instances of 'flexible integration' in the EU, and those which set the general legal conditions for what the Treaty of Amsterdam termed 'closer cooperation'. Flexibility and variable geometry within the EU have been referred to in many of the preceding chapters and paragraphs (e.g. 1.5, 1.6, 3.8, 3.9, 5.2 and 5.6), which have shown the many meanings and roles of flexibility and variable geometry within the history, politics and law of the integration process. Thus flexibility in terms of institutional and legal structures and patterns of policy making has gradually emerged as a *de facto* tool for an increasingly diverse EU where some of the key objectives of the integration process have been heavily contested by some Member States (e.g. social policy, EMU and the free movement of persons). It came to dominate many of the debates which preceded and shaped the 1996–97 IGC leading to the Treaty of Amsterdam, and offered a single language within which very different visions of the EU could be offered by politicians and practitioners within the EU institutions and the Member States. Accordingly, it was taken up as a theme in that Treaty, which not only added new instances of Treaty-based flexibility to the previous ones (especially the various opt-outs for the UK, Ireland and Denmark in relation to the free movement of persons and the incorporation of Schengen into the EU), but also 'constitutionalised' a notion of closer cooperation; that is, it introduces the formalised possibility for the future of flexible integration *under the Treaties*, subject to certain conditions.

The perspective which flexibility offers within the EU as 'a new principle and a new tool for responding to differences in the enthusiasms and capabilities of the member states of the EU to take on new tasks of policy integration' (Wallace, 2000: 173) has only become significant and visible as the EU has become gradually more all-encompassing in terms of its geographical and policy range. This was partly a product of gradual enlargement, but notably a result of the end of the Cold War and the distinct possibility that the EU might effectively encompass almost the whole of Western Europe plus very large parts of Central and Eastern Europe. The EU also became increasingly attractive in terms of its capacity to absorb other arenas of cooperation which were historically separate such as the WEU, European involvement in NATO, and the separate arrangements for a borderless zone put in place by the Schengen agreements. Within this greater ambition and reach came likewise new challenges in terms of dealing with diversity and the need to offer asymmetrical solutions. That is not to say that flexibility does not have an extended historical legacy in the EU, both in terms of its usage in successive debates about developing new areas for integration and co-operation, and in terms of its presence within the legal order (e.g. Ehlermann, 1984; Wallace, 1985). But according to Helen Wallace (Wallace, 2000: 177), specific to the debate about flexibility within and in the shadows of the 1996–97 IGC were five key factors:

- the well-defined plan to develop EMU which was 'the first flagship project in the EU which had deliberately envisaged the participation of only some of the EU members';
- previous successive enlargements had already brought within the EU 'more countries which were able, but not willing, to extend the shared agenda, as well as countries which lacked some of the capabilities to attain certain policy objectives';
- the expectation that 'two different projects of integration might be elided, namely the political economy project, developed through the EC, and the defence and security project, hitherto organised through NATO and the WEU';
- both the EU and NATO were contemplating and/or actively planning Eastern enlargement and 'the prospect of developing pan-European frames of reference'; and
- the salience of the issue of the 'permeability of borders', which brought the issue of the free movement of persons and controls on borders to the fore.

Wallace argues that together these factors 'raised major questions about the recasting of the European integration model and its methodologies' (Wallace, 2000: 178). They present in addition a constant tension between freedom and discipline for Member States, and between using flexible projects as a means of responding to both problems of management and efficiency in policy making and the ongoing task of providing a legitimate foundation for the EU polity (Shaw, 1998a).

Flexibility has spawned a complex language, as well as a wealth of debates about the future of the EU. In his work, Alexander Stubb has attempted to provide a schematic categorisation of the multiple terminologies that have emerged (Stubb, 1996; see also Ehlermann, 1996). He employs the variables of 'time', 'space' and 'matter' as a way of ordering the terminology, predicting the effects and determining the correct conditions of differentiated or flexible integration. Others have suggested that the crucial distinction is between flexible structures where the participants commit themselves to a common end, and those in which it is acknowledged that the participants in the overall integration project might have different ends.

Briefly, one might suggest that broadly three forms of variability or differentiation can now be identified, all of which can be exemplified by reference to more or less recent developments in the EC/EU. The lowest level of variability ('multi-speed') acknowledges the reality that the Member States may not all achieve what are common and agreed objectives at the same time. The use of transitional periods, particularly in accession agreements, is a good example, as are variable speeds in relation to VAT harmonisation. There is nothing constitutionally disruptive about 'multi-speed' integration. The other two forms of variability are more problematic: 'variable geometry' is a label now generally attached to a (permanent?) division within the EU between a 'hard' core and 'soft' periphery, with the hard core proceeding more rapidly towards greater integration and refusing to be held back by those standing on the periphery. This is one way of conceiving of the arrangements for Economic and Monetary Union under which there has been an irreversible locking of exchange rates for those countries which achieved the convergence criteria, leaving out those countries which did not. Yet this conclusion risks oversimplifying the degree of obligation lying upon those who were 'out' in the first round of EMU, because of the overall centrifugal impact of the duty of Community loyalty in Article 10 EC and obligations relating to convergence programmes. Such variability can also take the form of a so-called 'extra-EU solution', a characterisation which can be applied to the Schengen system, under which a core group of countries proceeded under separate international treaty to remove substantially all the internal borders between their countries. The final variant of flexibility is the 'pick-and-choose' mode which lacks even the discipline of the central core, driving forwards towards an accepted teleology of integration even if some Member States are left behind.

So much for the question of labels and terminology. Both the reality of and the ideas that underpin flexibility are more elusive – as indeed the example of EMU shows. Interestingly, flexibility seems to share many commonalities with that other rather plastic concept, subsidiarity (Shaw, 1998c; Philippart and Edwards, 1999; Wallace, 2000) (1.5 and 6.6). Like subsidiarity, it can be made to mean most things to most people, depending upon the way in which it is understood and those aspects which are given most emphasis. Substantively, it offers a mechanism for choosing the appropriate frame of reference for political and legal arrangements. In that context, it seems to be a way of satisfying the varying expectations and needs of both the Member States and the EU institutions thereby balancing various 'public' interests, as well as other 'private' stakeholders such as citizens, businesses and organisations. These expectations arise at a number of different levels, including the supranational, the national and the subnational. Overall, it is a way of balancing the dynamism of an integration process against the diffusion effects which derive from the very success of an integration project which involves already a much larger number of participants than in its original conception of the 'Six'. Likewise, subsidiarity can be seen simultaneously as meaning both 'more' and 'less', as well as a stronger and weaker 'Europe', depending upon whether it is given the 'sovereignty' or the 'federalism' 'spin'. It has been used by different political actors to buy off both the German *Länder* and the strongly Euro-sceptic wing of the British Conservative Party, even though the two groups have markedly different perceptions of the interests which need to be protected.

The provisions of the Treaty of Amsterdam including those on 'real-life' instances of flexibility such as the arrangements for the UK, Ireland and Denmark with regards to the free movement of persons and the incorporation of Schengen and those offering a system for future instances of 'closer cooperation' have been the subject of close attention by commentators (e.g. Shaw, 1998c; Weatherill, 1999; Hedemann-Robinson, 1999; Kortenberg, 1998; Philippart and Edwards, 1999). The Treaties themselves do not use the term 'flexibility' to characterise either closer cooperation or the opt-out arrangements. It remains none the less an important term of art.

The framework used for the instrumentalisation of flexibility within the EC/EU Treaties was in fact relatively straightforward. Articles 43–45 TEU provide a set of general principles for 'closer cooperation', to be supplemented by specific principles under each pillar These are to be found in Article 40 in respect of the third pillar and in Article 11 EC in respect of the first pillar. No general provision for closer cooperation was made within the second pillar, where the possibilities of introducing flexibility are limited to 'constructive abstentionism' (Article 23). In addition, a number of cases of case-by-case flexibility were preserved, enhanced/restructured and introduced by the new Treaty, most significantly EMU and the 'opt-outs' for the United Kingdom, Ireland and Denmark introduced under various conditions in respect of the new Title IV EC (visas, asylum, immigration, free movement of persons) and the incorporation of the Schengen *acquis* into the EU framework which in fact cuts across the first and the third pillars. No wonder, then, given so many instances of flexible arrangements right across the Treaty of Amsterdam that it was called the '*leitmotiv* that sounds persistently throughout the Treaty' (Editorial, 1997: 768).

The essential legal framework of Articles 43–45 TEU is to 'allow' or to 'authorise' Member States wishing to engage in 'closer cooperation' to make use of 'the institutions, procedures and mechanisms laid down' in the TEU and the EC Treaty provided that the cooperation complies with certain principles:

– It must be aimed at furthering the objectives of the Union and at protecting and serving its interests.
– It must respect the principles of TEU and the EC Treaty and the single institutional framework of the Union.
– It must be used only as a last resort and where the objectives of the Treaties cannot otherwise be attained.
– It must concern at least a majority of Member States (i.e. eight at the present time).
– It must not 'affect' the *acquis communautaire* and measures adopted under the other provisions of the Treaties.
– It must not 'affect the competences, rights, obligations and interests of those Member States which do not participate'.
– It must be open to all Member States and must allow them to become parties to the cooperation at any time, provided that they comply with the basic decision and with the decisions taken within that framework.
– It must comply with the specific additional criteria laid down in Article 11 EC or Article 40 TEU and must have been authorised by the Council.

Strikingly, 'closer cooperation' is never defined – hence the ideological issues raised about its multiple meanings remain unresolved. Furthermore it does not appear in the preambles to either the TEU or the EC Treaty, or as either an objective or a means to attain such objectives in the TEU and the EC Treaty. The criteria laid down appear to be restrictive. It is easy to interpret them as signals to those Member States which are the sceptics of flexibility, stressing that their interests are not going to be damaged. This is especially clear from the reference to not affecting 'the competences, rights, obligations and interests of those Member States which do not participate'. This is presumably a reference to competences held individually, not jointly. It prevents, along with the attributed competence principle in Article 11 EC, the cooperating Member States from overriding provisions which specifically exclude 'intrusive' harmonisation measures in areas such as education and public health policy. One might add, however, that this is yet another example of the Treaty importing undefined and very open-textured language, as it did with the reference to exclusive and shared competences in Article 5 EC which fails to define what those might be.

Article 43(2) is a statement of 'loyalty' broadly modelled on Article 10 EC, and it is capable of extensive interpretation by the Court along the lines of the latter article:

> 'Member States shall apply, as far as they are concerned, the acts and decisions adopted for the implementation of the cooperation in which they participate. Member States not participating in such cooperation shall not impede the implementation thereof by the participating Member States'.

Article 44 invokes the relevant institutional provisions of the TEU and the EC Treaty to facilitate the adoption of acts and decisions necessary for the implementation of closer cooperation. In other words, it clearly opens access to the participating Member States to make use of potentially any legal basis or competence provision within those Treaties provided the necessary conditions are complied with and provided that none of the principles in Article 43 or Articles 11 EC/40 TEU are breached. Sanguinely, but without doing the arithmetic in detail, the provision also suggests that the rules on qualified majority voting in the Council can be applied *mutatis mutandis* to closer cooperation by fewer Member States. This seems over-optimistic, given the detailed and fraught discussions (such as those leading to the Ioanninou Compromise) which the precise application of QMV and its interaction with population, territory and GDP size has given rise to at the various stages in the geographical and political evolution of the EC/EU (4.8). Expenditure – save for administrative expenditure – resulting from the application of the closer cooperation provisions is made the responsibility of the participating Member States unless the Council unanimously decides otherwise. Finally, the Council and the Commission are committed to informing the European Parliament regularly about the development of closer cooperation established on the basis of this Title. This operates in addition to the various requirements in Articles 11 EC and 40 TEU to involve the European Parliament in the decision to engage in closer cooperation, and any requirements to involve the European Parliament in individual legislative measures which implement the decision to cooperate more closely (which in the first pillar are most likely to involve either 'consultation' or 'co-decision' since the Cooperation Procedure was largely removed from the Treaty framework by the Treaty of Amsterdam: 7.3 and 7.5). Presumably it was intended to give the European Parliament scope to debate and to question the general direction of any closer cooperation which does occur.

The general conditions laid down in Articles 43–45 are subject to the jurisdiction of the Court of Justice (Article 46 TEU), but 'under the conditions provided for' in the two specific enabling clauses in the first and third pillars. Since Article 11 EC does not provide any specific conditions in relation to the Court's jurisdiction it is not wholly clear what that might mean. While some of the provisions might not lend themselves so easily to judicial enforcement (e.g. the notion of the *acquis communautaire* is relatively imprecise at the margins: 5.6), most of them are certainly capable of application by a court even if the determination of their precise meaning would undoubtedly offer a considerable challenge to any judicial instance.

Articles 43–45 TEU offer an overarching frame for the development of 'closer cooperation', rather than a separate free-standing mechanism for such cooperation. That this Title is not a separate 'pillar' is apparent from the reference in Article 43(1)(h) to the requirement that such cooperation must comply with the specific additional criteria in Articles 11 EC and 40 TEU. That said, it also seems that these provisions contain more or less all the elements to operate as a free-standing Title, should this be possible in principle.

Article 11 EC builds on Articles 43 and 44 TEU by providing the specific conditions under which forms of secondary flexibility can be put in place within the framework of the first pillar competences and methods. The areas in which closer cooperation is possible were not predetermined, but neither were any specific areas expressly excluded. In other words, there are no negative or positive lists, as was mooted during the negotiating process. Instead, Article 11 provides a set of five supplementary commandments, which in some ways replicate Article 43 TEU, but in other ways add extra and more precise conditions which closer cooperation must satisfy before it can validly be authorised (Article 11(1)(a)–(e)). They need reordering to highlight more accurately their degree of importance and their level of generality. First should come the principle of attributed powers:

'(d) remains within the limits of the powers conferred upon the Community by this Treaty...'

This reflects the centrality of that principle itself in the EU constitutional system (Article 5 EC). This provides considerable reassurance for the unity of the constitutional order since it not only requires an existing legal basis for any closer cooperation within the EC Treaty, but also requires that the existing procedures and arrangements for the adoption of legislation must be observed 'since the attribution principle has traditionally been regarded as having both substantive and procedural aspects' (Editorial, 1997: 769). However, by providing for the removal of the reluctant Member States through a decision to embark upon closer cooperation, surely this mechanism does in effect provide for the substitution of unanimity with majority voting (at least if one takes the baseline as the total number of Member States), even if it continues to require, formally, the unanimous vote of the participating Member States. Moreover, the clear impact of the attribution principle seems to be muddied by Article 11(4) which provides that 'the acts and decisions necessary for the implementation of cooperation activities shall be subject to all the relevant provisions of this Treaty, *save as otherwise provided for in this Article and in Articles 43 and 44 of the Treaty on European Union*' (emphasis added). This, however, is probably a reference to the statement on the pro-rata arrangements for qualified majority voting in Article 44(1) TEU.

Next in line comes the exclusion of areas of 'exclusive' Community competence (Article 11(1)(a)). This refers back to, but provides little assistance in clarifying, a long-standing element of uncertainty in the Community system, namely the distinction between *exclusive* and *shared* competence, which also appears in Article 5 EC (6.4 and 6.5). Closely related is the injunction in para. (b) not to 'affect Community policies, actions or programmes'. This is a reference not so much to the *existence* of competence, but to its *exercise* (6.4). The two final conditions concern the relationship between the 'ins' and the 'outs' and their citizenry. Para. (c) requires closer cooperation not to 'concern the citizenship of the Union or discriminate between nationals of Member States' and para. (e) excludes measures which 'constitute a discrimination or a restriction of trade between Member States' and 'distort the conditions of competition between the latter.' These two conditions go to the heart of the personal and material scope of the internal market and come closest to creating a 'blacklist' of untouchable areas.

Notwithstanding the innovatory character of the institutional dimension of these provisions their practical utility has to be doubted in view of the severity of the conditions which need to be satisfied. It is possible that the Article 11 arrangements will remain a dead letter until at least after the first anticipated enlargement and that they will prove to be too 'inflexible' once that rubicon has been crossed and the Union has become significantly larger and more diverse. Weatherill comments that the stiff conditions of Article 11 combined with Article 43 TEU 'are doubtless indicative of nervousness that the legal order may be tipped towards indecipherable fragmentation' (Weatherill, 1999: 27). Together these provisions manage the remarkable feat of buttressing both the 'constitutionalising' and the 'conservatory' aspects of the EU system (Weatherill, 1999: 32, applying the terminology of Dashwood, 1998 (5.11)).

The institutional arrangements for instances of secondary flexibility under the first pillar can be derived from Article 11 EC, read in conjunction with Articles 43–45 TEU. *Authorisation* is provided by the Council acting by a qualified majority, on a proposal by the Commission, after consulting the European Parliament. Article 11(2) provides an interesting and, some would say, worrying example of the importation of intergovernmental influences into the first pillar, since it effectively brings a Luxembourg Accords type arrangement into play in the event that one of the non-participating Member States is unhappy about the move to closer cooperation by the majority. The reluctant non-participant must cite 'important and stated reasons of national policy' and no vote will be taken. In that case the Council may request, by a qualified majority, that the matter be referred to the European Council which will itself decide by unanimity.

The Commission is made central to the arrangements, since it must be asked to draw up a proposal for closer cooperation on a request from the Member States which wish to embark upon this course of action, and its only obligation in the event of deciding not to submit a proposal to the Council to this effect is to 'inform the Member States concerned of the reasons for not doing so.' The Commission is also central to arrangements made by non-participants to accede to ongoing closer cooperation arrangements. It receives notification, along with the Council, and then gives an Opinion to the Council within three months of receipt of the notification. Within a further month it must decide upon the application and determine the necessary arrangements. This contrasts the failure to provide 're-accession' arrangements for the UK under the Social Policy Agreement attached to the Treaty of Maastricht.

Article 40 TEU sets out the additional conditions that apply to the development of 'closer cooperation' under the third pillar. It is a 'slimmed down' version of Article 11 EC, with just two conditions appended to Article 43 TEU. Closer cooperation must (a) respect the powers of the European Community, and the objective laid down by this Title and (b) have the aim of enabling the EU more rapidly into an area of freedom, security and justice. In other words, third-pillar closer cooperation must respect the borders of the current pillar system, and indeed would be required to do so by the Court of Justice (*Airport Transit Visas*, 5.8). Broadly similar institutional arrangements are proposed as for Article 11, although the requirement to consult the European Parliament is cut down to a duty to forward to it a request for closer cooperation.

Leaving aside the arrangements for proceeding to (probably hypothetical) *future* instances of closer cooperation under the Amsterdam rules, attention must also be paid to the examples of case-by-case flexibility instituted by the Treaty; the most significant ones were the opt-outs for the United Kingdom, Ireland and Denmark from various aspects of the 'area of freedom, security and justice', cutting across the first and third pillars.

The Treaty of Amsterdam introduced a new Title IV into Part III of the EC Treaty (Articles 61–69 EC) which 'communitarises' those parts of the old third pillar concerned with visas, asylum, immigration and other matters related to the free movement of persons, and a Protocol integrating the so-called Schengen *acquis* into the framework of the European Union, with provision for allocating parts of this *acquis* to the first or the third pillars as appropriate (hence it is annexed to both the Treaty on European Union and the EC Treaty). Hence, these arrangements not only change the contours of the pillar system, but they also bring to an end an 'extra-EU' instance of flexibility, namely the Schengen Agreements for the removal of internal borders. However, Article 69 EC declares the provisions of Title IIIa to operate without prejudice to the Protocol on the application of certain aspects of Article 7a EC (now Article 14 EC) to the UK and Ireland, and the Protocols on the United Kingdom and Ireland and on Denmark.

The effect of these Protocols in relation to the UK and Ireland is to recognise the geographical particularities of these states, and to acknowledge the continuing validity of the Common Travel Area which exists between them.

They are allowed to continue to apply border controls (and conversely the other Member States are allowed to apply border controls as against those two states). Formally, the Article 7a Protocol lays down arrangements for the UK to maintain border controls, but extends the capacity also to Ireland for so long as the Common Travel Area subsists. The reference to what is now Article 14 EC, which defines the internal market as an area without internal frontiers, is important in that it now recognises, for the future, the significance of this provision in determining the scope of the internal market. In addition, a second Protocol on the position of the UK and Ireland excluded the UK and Ireland from participating in the adoption of measures under Title IV for the future and insulated them from the effects of such measures.

The principal legal interest of such measures is as an example of case-by-case flexibility, which provides some evidence as to how Article 11 could operate if its stringent conditions were satisfied. Yet it concerns an area – namely citizenship – which is specifically excluded from the scope of future closer cooperation arrangements. These arrangements also simultaneously appear to redefine the effects of an existing Treaty provision (Article 14 EC), and to restrict the effects of the provisions of Title IV both in terms of the obligation which they lay down for the adoption of measures to remove internal frontiers and the effects of such measures in the future. Also by way of departure from Article 11 which envisages 'global in-or-out', *ad hoc* arrangements for the participation of the UK and Ireland in *individual* Title IV measures as they are adopted were made in Article 3 of the Protocol on the UK and Ireland and Article 4 provides that the Article 11(3) arrangements on *post hoc* participation after measures have been adopted can apply to *individual* Title IV measures as opposed to a *whole tranche* of closer cooperation activities (for which they appear, in a literal sense, to be intended). In other words, Article 11 provides only for opting in and out as a package, but the arrangements on Article 14, Title IV and those aspects of the third pillar concerned with free movement and Schengen appear to present the British, Irish and Danes almost with an *à la carte* menu from which to pick and choose where they wish to participate.

While the arrangements for the UK – and by implication Ireland because of the specifics of its status in this domain in relation to the UK – are regarded as more or less acceptable for geographical and geo-political reasons, and were probably also to be seen as part of a wider 'trade-off' within the overall frame of the UK participation in the Treaty of Amsterdam negotiations after the General Election of 1 May 1 1997 and especially its acceptance of the 'Social Chapter', the Danish arrangements in relation to Schengen seem to deserve a different evaluation. They have already been described as 'truly bizarre' (Editorial, 1997: 770). Although a member of Schengen, Denmark has resisted the creation of an intra-EU solution to the problems which its extra-EU status have created. Oddly, therefore, Denmark has resisted – in a manner which seems contrary to its strong adherence to Parliamentary democracy and its traditions of transparency and open government – those aspects of the integration of the Schengen *acquis* which are highly positive from precisely those points of view. At least for the future, the secrecy of Schengen may become part of a rather shameful history of executive and intergovernmental collusion in the European domain. In opting out of the integration of the Schengen *acquis* and in insisting that those elements of Schengen which it will apply will operate as *international* not as *EC* law or even as *'third pillar* law', Denmark seems to be sacrificing democracy and openness on the altar of resistance to encroachment in its state sovereignty.

Like the three-pillar system, both variable arrangements in the form of the EMU or Title IV and Schengen arrangements and the possibility (however hypothetical) of closer cooperation under the Treaty by virtue in the form of the provisions reviewed in this paragraph are here to stay. In the meantime, as a catch phrase flexibility denotes problems, not solutions (Weatherill, 1999: 40). The arrangements described here contribute to making aspects of the EU more manageable rather than more legitimate. Overall, however, the ideas and practices of flexibility have become an indelible part of the process of constitutional change and evolution in the EU and not a barrier to the development of the constitutional project (Walker, 2000; Shaw, 2000a).

5.20   **What is the EU for?**

This question returns us to the mission of the EU which was already sketched out in 1.3. To the basic provisions sketching the objectives and tasks of the EU and its 'component parts' can be added a number of provisions of a constitutional character which help to shape the direction and focus of the EU as political and socio-economic project. These include Article 12 EC (non-discrimination on grounds of EU nationality: 5.17), and Articles 23, 25, 28, 39, 43, 49 and 56 EC which lay down the basic rules on the free movement of goods, workers, establishment, services and capital. Article 61 EC lays down the goal of adopting measures to achieve – in sum – the full free movement of persons and the removal of internal frontiers, along with associated activities. Articles 81–97 EC deal with competition policy, state aid and many aspects of internal market harmonisation. Title VII (Articles 98–124 EC) establishes the basic principles and institutions of EMU, and Title VIII complements this with objectives in relation to employment policy. Articles 131–135 cover external trade policy and customs cooperation. Next the Treaty moves to social policy, with objectives and activities in that field laid down in Articles 136–145. The rest of the substantive provisions of the

EC Treaty focus on cohesion policy, transport, environmental policy, many flanking policies such as education and training, culture, public health and consumer protection. None contain dispositive rules of negative integration, comparable to the provisions on the internal market basic freedoms. The free movement provisions have a unique constitutional position within the structure of EU rules.

5.21 The Court of Justice and the EU's Evolving Constitutional Framework

In recent years, the role of the Court of Justice within the EU has been a much written about topic. As a key figure in the shaping of the EU's legal order – and consequentially in the shaping of the constitutional framework which this chapter has shown lies at the core of that legal order – it is hardly surprising that the work of the Court should have been subjected to close scrutiny in order to test it out. Those who have written about the Court have been interested in topics such as measuring the quality and consistency of the Court's decision making, testing its capacity to influence the outcomes of policy within the other EU institutions, ascertaining levels of popular knowledge, approval or disapproval of the Court's work within public opinion across the Member States, and degrees of acceptance or rejection of the Court's case law by the national courts which are another crucial element in the process of constructing a multilevel constitution. The Court of Justice is widely perceived as having been an 'activitist' court, not shying away from taking decisions based on the treaties which seek to tease the underlying purpose or 'teleology' of the integration project. As we have already seen in outline, and will consider in more detail in Chapters 6 and 12, the Court has made a 'constitutionalising' contribution especially in relation to mapping out the nature and contours of the EU's competence and the evolving relationship between national law and EU law. In the latter case, it has been reliant on the willingness of national courts to make use of the Article 234 preliminary reference procedure, which has given it the opportunity – above all – to rule upon the 'effect' of EU law (even though the 'effect' of EU law is not even mentioned in the formal text of Article 234 as one of the topics of a reference, but only questions of 'interpretation' and 'validity').

There have been distinctive phases to the Court's work. Its early role is widely recognised as having primarily effected the 'constitutionalisation' of the Treaties, and the development of the scope and effect of 'Community competence'. Constitutionalisation in this sense comprised primarily a form of 'federalisation' of the treaties by the Court of Justice through the principles of direct effect and supremacy of EC law in relation to national law, and the establishment of the duties of national courts as 'Community courts' (Chapters 11–13). The Court of Justice has also long recognised a doctrine of fundamental rights as general principles of EC law (Chapter 9), but it was effectively a limited doctrine oriented towards a goal of economic integration and the limitation of the sovereignty of the Member States. It made clear from the 1960s that it was going to exercise the classic function of a 'constitutional court', namely the constitutional review of legislation to ensure the supremacy of the terms of 'the constitution', and the scrutiny of the powers of the constituent states (i.e. the Member States) to ensure that the terms of the federal settlement based on the supremacy of EU law were properly observed. In sum, it has been involved in scrutinising the limits of government under the rule of law and this is establishing clear principles of liberal constitutionalism. In taking that stance the Court aligned itself with an emerging trend of constitutional courts and constitutional review in many European countries in the post-war years and, since the end of the Cold War, in the emerging democracies of Central and Eastern Europe. However, where the Court has also differed from those courts has been in the fact that it is not *only* a constitutional court, and the fact that it does not have a generalised function, for example, to protect individual and minorities and uphold fundamental rights, but a function limited by reference to the scope of the treaties.

In its early period, at least up until the mid-1980s, there was very little acknowledgement of the role of the Court, not even among national politicians or judges, despite its fundamental reshaping of an order based on an international Treaty. The greater visibility and public awareness of the role of the Court has coincided with the realisation that the EU as a whole faces an increasing legitimacy crisis. Yet much of the work of the Court since the mid-1980s has barely been 'constitutional' at all. It has often involved an exercise in statutory interpretation, with many preliminary references from national courts asking about the meaning as well as the effects of EU measures such as regulations and directives. Where the Court has exercised constitutional choices, as for example in some of its more recent case law on general principles and fundamental rights discussed in Chapter 9, it has faced intense scrutiny and criticism, and calls for its powers to be limited. Dehousse aptly summarises the current situation of the Court (Dehousse, 1998a: 185):

'Now that the Community political system is moving away from the international model and closer to national models, perceptions of its principal actors tend to alter. The considerable influence enjoyed by the Court during a period when the Community was seen as a distant organisation was atypical. Like all courts exercising constitutional jurisdiction, whenever it is called upon to rule on important political issues, the ECJ must come to terms with a stronger political power and more media attention. Thus, by a strange reversal of fortune, the ECJ, which worked so hard to constitutionalise Community law, seems to have lost ground in this process. Constitutional-type developments certainly complicate its own role and risk exposing it to growing criticism.'

Dehousse goes on to suggest that the Court has reacted rationally to this challenge by seeking to consolidate its own position and to avoid – as far as possible – direct fights with political actors. 'Ebbs and flows' in its case law where it has used stricter scrutiny of national law (e.g. on the procedural requirements imposed claims in national courts for breach of EU law by public authorities: Chapter 13) at particular times in order to trigger greater national judicial awareness of the demands of EU law but adopted a more hands-off stance at other times in order to protect national procedural autonomy could be said to be part of the Court's sensitivity to the overall demands of subsidiarity. The fact that an increasing number of other 'constitutional actors' compete with the Court for a role in shaping the EU's constitutional framework, including national courts, the other institutions, and the Member States is a sign of the greater maturity of the system. The Court still retains, however, a powerful adjudicatory role, with its capacity to give authoritative rulings on the meaning of the Treaties, even though some national courts have formally denied it capacity to determine the effects of those rulings within the sphere of the national constitutions. It would be correct to conclude, however, that the Court is, without doubt, increasingly aware of the complexities of its own position within a system of multilevel constitutionalism.

Summary

1 The EU is in large measure a single entity both in political and legal terms.
2 Since the introduction of the pillar framework by the Treaty of Amsterdam a number of areas of 'unity' have evolved:
   – cross-pillar policies and policy making;
   – shared institutions and the principle of consistency;
   – common principles and values;
   – structuring constitutional principles;
   – the EU's capacity to adopt binding rules;
   – shared rules on change and membership;
   – the external identity of the EU;
   – budgetary questions.
3 The Court of Justice will police the frontiers between the first pillar and the second and third pillars.
4 The concept of a model of multilevel constitutionalism is a useful framework for describing and explaining the EU.
5 The EU's constitutional framework, and notably the role of the Court of Justice, has been challenged by the German Federal Constitutional Court.

6   The EU has a basic constitutional framework comprising the following
main elements:
  – details of the nature of the polity;
  – the role of the rule of law;
  – the values, principles and norms which govern the system;
  – the rules governing the exercise of power and authority;
  – a high degree of flexibility within the system;
  – rules detailing what objectives and tasks the EU must pursue.

7   The Court of Justice operates in many areas as a constitutional court.

Questions

1   Does the EU have a constitution and does it need one?
2   What contribution has the intervention of the German Federal Constitutional Court made to the evolution of EU constitutionalism?
3   Why is the Court of Justice frequently described as a constitutional court?
4   What effect does the existence of the pillar system have upon the evolving
EU constitutional framework? Does it represent a threat to the EU legal order?

Further Reading

K. Armstrong (1998), 'Theorizing the Legal Dimension of European Integration', 36 *Journal of Common Market Studies* 155.

A. von Bogdandy (1999), 'The Legal Case for Unity: The European Union as a
Single Organisation with a Single Legal System', 36 *Common Market Law
Review* 887.

D. Curtin and I. Dekker (1999), 'The EU as a "Layered" International Organisation: Institutional Unity in Disguise', in Craig and de Búrca (1999).

A. Dashwood (1998), 'States in the European Union', 23 *European Law Review*
201.

R. Dehousse (1998a), esp. Chs. 1, 6 and 7.

P. Eleftheriadis (1998), 'Begging the Constitutional Question', 36 *Journal of
Common Market Studies* 255.

N. MacCormick (1999), esp. Ch. 7, 'Juridical Pluralism and the Risk of Constitutional Conflict' and Ch. 8, 'On Sovereignty and Post-Sovereignty'.

I. Pernice (1999), 'Multilevel Constitutionalism and the Treaty of Amsterdam:
European Constitution-Making Revisited?', 36 *Common Market Law Review* 703.

J. Shaw (1999), 'Postnational Constitutionalism in the European Union', 6
Journal of European Public Policy 579.

J. Shaw (2000a), 'Constitutionalism and Flexibility in the EU: Developing a Relational Approach', in de Búrca and Scott (2000).

J. Shaw (2000c), 'Process and Constitutional Discourse in the European Union', 27 *Journal of Law and Society* 4.

F. Snyder (2000), 'The Unfinished Constitution of the European Union: Principles, Processes and Culture', in Weiler and Wind (2000).

N. Walker (1996), 'European Constitutionalism and European Integration', *Public Law* 266.

N. Walker (2000), 'Theoretical Reflections on Flexibility and Europe's Future', in de Búrca and Scott (2000).

S. Weatherill (2000a), 'Flexibility or Fragmentation? Trends in European Integration', in Usher (2000).

J.H.H. Weiler (1999a), esp. Ch. 5, 'The Least-Dangerous Branch: A Retrospective and Prospective of the European Court of Justice in the Arena of Political Integration' and Ch. 6, 'Introduction: The Reformation of European Constitutionalism'.

B. de Witte (1998), 'The Pillar Structure and the Nature of the European Union: Greek Temple or French Gothic Cathedral?', in Heukels *et al.* (1998).

Key Websites

The website of the Walter Hallstein Institute at the Humboldt University in Berlin carries useful primary and secondary materials, along with links to other sites covering EU constitutionalism:
http://www.rewi.hu-berlin.de/WHI/english/index.htm

Part III

The European Union and its Institutions at Work

6 The Legal and Constitutional Dimensions of Policy Making in the European Union

6.1 Introduction

There is a tendency to overlook the fact that the EU is actually very constrained in what it can do and decide. The constraints are not only the internal institutional issues, such as those outlined in Chapter 4 and to be highlighted further in the next chapter which presents the legislative process in detail. It should also be clear from Chapter 5 that there exists a constitutional framework which governs the exercise of powers to make policies.

This chapter sets out the various principles involved, including the basic idea of limited powers, and issues which arise from the vertical division of powers between the EU and the Member States. It shows how and why all acts adopted can be scrutinised to see whether they have complied with the relevant principles. As the EU operates not only in the internal sphere, but also – and to an ever-increasing extent – in the external sphere, this dimension of policy making is given extensive coverage. Finally, there is a review of the outputs, of the measures that can be adopted. That section of the chapter reinforces a general point, which is that the discussion concentrates first and foremost upon powers exercised under the EC Treaty, not the wider TEU.

6.2 'Competence' and Limited Powers

The EU represents a divided power system in which different levels have responsibility for different areas of policy making. Within the first pillar, Community competence is ringfenced first and foremost by the principle of limited or conferred powers or 'attributed competences'. Article 5 EC provides that:

> 'The Community shall act within the limits of the powers conferred upon it by this Treaty and of the objectives assigned to it therein.'

In order to reinforce the point that any institution adopting an act must have competence or the legal power to act, Article 7 EC provides that:

'Each institution shall act within the limits of the powers conferred upon it by the Treaty.'

This is evidenced, on a case-by-case basis, by showing that a legal act has a valid legal basis, and reference must normally be made in the recitals (or preamble) of the act to the concrete enabling power (6.8). Moreover, Article 230 EC refers to 'lack of competence' being as a ground for judicial review by the Court of Justice of the legality of acts of the institutions. There are no equivalents to these provisions in the general provisions of the TEU, or in the specific provisions governing the second and third pillars, although it is clear from Article 5 TEU that the institutions are bound by the general principles under the EC Treaty which govern their conduct. So, under the limited jurisdiction of the Court of Justice over the third pillar (Article 35 TEU), the ground of annulment termed 'lack of competence' will apply.

These limited powers arrangements are the normal ones for an international organisation onto which specific tasks have been conferred. However, in practice, the vertical division of competences in the EU did not become a serious issue until qualified majority voting became a reality in the 1980s. Under the shadow of the veto, the growth of Community competences could be taken to be self-regulating, for such growth lay in the common accord of the Member States when they had recourse to legislative powers by unanimous vote (Weiler, 1999a: 72). That is not to say, however, that the range of policy-making activities did not grow before qualified majority voting was introduced. It most certainly did, with environmental policy being perhaps the starkest example, and the role of the EU's implied powers provisions in that growth will be explored in 6.3. But the Treaty of Maastricht made two major changes. On the one hand, it introduced the single largest one-off widening of the EU competences, with nine new areas being added to the EC Treaty, never mind the Union's activities under the second and third pillar many of which were also 'new' (even if previously pursued in purely intergovernmental cooperation fora) (Dehousse, 1994b). But in addition, at the same time it also sharpened the recognition of the limited powers principle in the EC Treaty, introduced an express proportionality principle for action by the Community (6.6) and introduced the first clear attempt to determine *which* type of competences should be exercised at the EU level, and which should be left to the national level (or indeed, within Member States which are themselves federalised, to the regional or local level). This took the form of the subsidiarity principle in Article 5 EC (previously Article 3b) (3.1). It was reflected also in Article 1 TEU, which refers to decisions being taken 'as close to the citizen as possible'. In a change introduced by the Treaty of Amsterdam, Article 2 TEU now requires the Union also to respect the Article 5 EC subsidiarity principle.

The subsidiarity principle under Article 5 only operates, however, where powers are *shared* between the Member States. In other words, it presupposes that there is not a simple binary divide between Member State competence and EU competence, but that there is an area of competence where both can act when their powers overlap. The subsidiarity principle has undoubtedly influenced the rhetoric of policy making within the EU in profound ways. The precise extent of its practical effects is a little less clear, although the adoption of the Protocol on Subsidiarity and Proportionality, which was annexed to the EC Treaty by the Treaty of Amsterdam, will continue to push clarification in this area for the future (6.5).

The limits of the subsidiarity principle highlight, however, how incomplete or underdeveloped the EU is as a federal system at least in relation to the vertical division of powers. Federal constitutions classically opt for one of two solutions to the problem of the vertical division of powers (between federal authority and constituent states). Either the powers of the federal authority are specifically defined, with the residue of powers falling to the constituent states, or the powers of the states are specifically defined with the residue of powers falling to the federal authority. In each case, some powers may be shared. Whatever principle is adopted, it can be policed by the constitutional court. Within their respective spheres, the federal authority and the constituent states will be free to exercise the powers attributed to them, subject to the respect of overarching constitutional principles. Moreover, typically a federal constitution will, as a minimum, give to the federal authority key powers relating to foreign policy, external and internal security policy, macroeconomic policy, and monetary policy (including the power to issue currency), as well as sufficient powers to ensure the preservation of an effectively functioning internal market. The EU's constitutional framework does not contain such a coherent statement of the vertical division of powers.

6.3   Implied Powers

The Treaties contain many enumerated powers, and the textual analysis of these powers forms a large component of the exercise, in any given case, of determining whether the EU will have competence to act, and under what conditions and with what effects. As a result of the sometimes rather *ad hoc* way in which the EC and now the EU have developed over a number of years, the powers now attributed to the Union, the Community and the EU institutions by the Treaties (and the manner in which they can be exercised) are partly the result of historical accident. They have also evolved in a dynamic fashion as a result of two main legal factors, which have operated in conjunction with the constant pressure from the Commission and the Parliament upon the Council to extend the range of the Community's activities. These factors are:

> – the development by the Court of Justice of a theory of implied powers, again in both the internal and external spheres;
> – the existence within the EC Treaty of a number of more general law-making powers, namely Articles 12, 94, 95 and 308 EC, and the creative use of these powers by the institutions.

The concept of implied powers, as applied in EU law, aids the effectiveness of the work of the institutions. It allows the EU to take decisions where no specific power is given, but where an obvious duty or task exists under the Treaty. Article 308 EC, which gives a residual legal basis allowing for the adoption of measures aimed at the pursuit of the objectives of the Treaty, in circumstances where the Treaty fails to provide specific powers is an example of the concept of implied powers. In addition, the Court of Justice has also applied a general doctrine of implied powers both internally and externally, to facilitate the evolution of Community competence. Although this case law predates Article 5 EC, it is suggested by the reference in that provision to the 'objectives' assigned to the Community. We shall review the internal and external dimensions here, as both have contributed to the development of the general principle (see further on external competence 6.7).

In the internal sphere, the concept of implied powers has been applied in particular to extend the scope of the Commission's power of decision. In Case 281, etc./85 *Germany et al.* v. *Commission (Migration Policy)* ([1987] ECR 3203) the Court was required to interpret the meaning of what was then Article 118 EEC. This gave the Commission the task of 'promoting close cooperation between the Member States in the social field'. On the basis of this provision, the Commission adopted a decision requiring Member States to communicate information regarding their policies on migrant workers from third states. A number of Member States challenged the competence of the Commission to adopt such a decision, arguing that such a measure should have been adopted by the Council on the basis of what was then Article 235 EEC (now Article 308 EC), if it fell within the competence of the Community at all. The Court held:

> 'where an article of the EEC Treaty – in this case Article 118 – confers a specific task on the Commission it must be accepted, if that provision is not to be rendered wholly ineffective, that it confers on the Commission necessarily and per se the powers which are indispensable in order to carry out that task.'

Accordingly, the Court found for the Commission as regards its power to adopt a binding decision, although it disagreed in some respects with that institution's interpretation of the scope of Article 118 EEC.

The Court has also applied the doctrine of implied powers in order to extend the Community's external powers and to create an extensive, if not complete, parallelism between internal and external competence. The development of implied powers in the external sphere is closely linked to the determination of the 'exclusivity' of the Community's external powers. The Community has always had an 'express' power to conclude agreements, but only in limited areas. But there are a number of principles laid down by the Court of Justice under which the Community can and has acquired external competence, even exclusive external competence (e.g. fisheries conservation), even in the absence of express powers in the Treaty. The position was summarised by the Court as follows in Opinion 2/91 *Re ILO Convention* ([1993] ECR I-1061 at p. 1076):

> 'Authority to enter into international commitments may not only arise from an express attribution by the Treaty, but may also flow implicitly from its provisions... [I]n particular ... whenever Community law created for the institutions of the Community powers within its internal system for the purpose of attaining a specific objective, the Community had authority to enter into the international commitments necessary for the attainment of that objective even in the absence of an express provision in that connection.'

The doctrine has its roots in an era when the external competences under the EC Treaty were not delineated extensively or in detail, and many of the debates originated in areas such as road transport where – given the geographical limitations of the early EEC in particular – the capacity for external action was very important. Hence in Case 22/70 *Commission* v. *Council (ERTA)* ([1971] ECR 263; often also known by its French acronym *AETR*), the Court found an implied competence to conclude the European Road Transport Agreement, based on a parallelism of internal and external competences (Cremona, 1999). The point is now generally accepted in both institutional and judicial practice, although there are limits to implied powers. In 1994 the Court of Justice annulled an anti-trust cooperation agreement with the United States concluded by the Commission, as the power to conclude such an agreement lay, under the system established by the Treaty, with the Council not the Commission, and no power on the part of the Commission could be implied (Case C-327/91 *France* v. *Commission* [1994] ECR I-3641). Second, the scope of the internal powers from which the external powers may be implied is not limitless. For example, in Opinion 2/94 *Accession by the Community to the ECHR* ([1996] ECR I-1759), the Court held that while fundamental rights are part of the legal order of the EU and respect for fundamental rights is a condition of the lawfulness of EU action, none the less there is no clear general power in the EC Treaty 'to enact rules on human rights or to conclude international conventions in the field' (para. 27 of the judgment).

In fact, the doctrine of implied powers has become less significant in the field of external relations, as amendments to the original Treaties have gradually conferred more express powers on the institutions, adding to the original primary external powers in the areas of external trade and the conclusion of Association Agreements. For example, the EC now has express powers in the fields of research and technological development (Article 170 EC) and environmental policy (Article 174(4) EC). Other new provisions, such as those on vocational training and education policy have given the Community a power to 'foster co-operation at the international level'; this appears to include implicitly again a power to enter into agreements. Thus an example of a measure originally adopted by the EU under its implied powers, but now probably covered by specific provisions of the EC Treaty is Council Regulation 1360/90 establishing the European Training Foundation (OJ 1990 L131/1) (4.17). The aims of the Foundation are to act as a vehicle for the delivery of aid in the form of assistance for vocational training from the EU and the Member States (and certain other third countries) to the new democracies of Central and Eastern Europe. The political justification for the Member States acting together in this way, rather than separately, is that it enhances the effectiveness of the aid. The legal justification was that the EU had an external competence in relation to vocational training which matched its internal competence (Article 128 EEC), but the legal basis of the regulation was Article 235 EEC (now Article 308 EC). Articles 149 and 150 EC, which have supplanted Article 128 EEC, expressly identify an external dimension to EU policy on education and vocational training respectively, making the adoption of such measures a matter of express rather than implied powers.

Article 308 EC remains the most general legislative power in the Treaty, and offers a form of structured implied power within the scope of the objectives of the Community. In terms of the measures to be adopted, it is likewise general in scope. It provides:

'If action by the Community should prove necessary to attain, in the course of the operation of the common market, one of the objectives of the Community and this Treaty has not provided the necessary powers, the Council shall, acting unanimously on a proposal from the Commission and after consulting the Assembly, take the appropriate measures.'

In Opinion 2/94, the Court of Justice turned to look at the potential of what was then Article 235 EC as the basis for the Community's possible accession to the ECHR. It concluded that Article 235 'being an integral part of an institutional system based on the principle of conferred powers, cannot serve as a basis for widening the scope of Community powers beyond the general framework created by the provisions of the Treaty as a whole and, in particular, by those that define the tasks and the activities of the Community. On any view, Article 235 cannot be used as a basis for the adoption of provisions whose effect would, in substance, be to amend the Treaty without following the procedure which it provides for that purpose' (paragraph 30).

It concluded (9.8) that the institutional and legal complexities and novelties of rendering the ECHR and its institutions effectively sovereign over the EU in relation to human rights questions would, in fact, require an amendment to the Treaties, an amendment that the Member States have yet to institute.

The extent to which Article 308 has been used as a law-making power, and the fields in which it has been invoked, are a function of the gradual evolution of the EU's range of policy-making activities coupled with the willingness of the Member States to amend the Treaties to give express powers for areas into which the EU has already moved. Again, that is not to say that Article 308 has been used to circumvent the scope of the Treaty, but rather that the range of EU activities has increased as a function of the breadth of the objectives of the EC Treaty. An example of the use of what was then Article 235 EEC in order to extend the range of EU activities is Council Regulation 2137/85 of 25 July 1985 establishing the European Economic Interest Grouping (EEIG) (OJ 1985 L199/1). The EEIG provides a specifically 'European' vehicle for companies, professional partnerships and other types of business association to cooperate with each other at a transnational level unrestricted by the limitations of any one national law. This measure would still probably require recourse to Article 308. However, in some areas the situation has shifted markedly over the years. In Case C-209/97 *Commission v. Council* (18 November 1999) the Court held that the Council acted correctly in basing a Regulation on mutual assistance between the administrative authorities of the Member States and cooperation between those authorities and the Commission to ensure the correct application of the law on customs and agricultural matters on what was then Article 235 EC. The objective of the measure was to protect the financial interests of the EU which, according to the Court of Justice, constitutes an independent objective which is placed, under the scheme of the Treaty in the provisions on financial matters in Part V of the Treaty. At the time the measure was adopted, however, there was no legal basis in what was then Article 209a EC. By the time the judgment was handed down, after the ratification of the Treaty of Amsterdam, a reworked Article 209a EC (now Article 280 EC) already contained just such a legal basis, which was used to establish OLAF, the new independent fraud investigation office.

A document prepared by the Presidency for the 2000 IGC highlighted that clusters of cases were at that time to be found in the following areas:

- the establishment of decentralised agencies forming a separate legal entity with authority to act in pursuance of one of the objectives set by the Treaty;
- economic, financial and technical cooperation with non-member countries; and
- the energy sector.

Accordingly, some parties are calling for the Member States to agree a set of provisions specifically in the energy area, which is broader than those already existing in relation to nuclear energy (Euratom) and coal and steel (ECSC).

To facilitate law-making activities under Article 308, the Court of Justice has given the individual elements of this Article a consistently broad interpretation. For example, in Case 242/87 *Commission* v. *Council (ERASMUS)* ([1989] ECR 1425) the Court held that the pursuit of a 'People's Europe' was one of the objectives of the Community. Nowhere was such a goal explicitly to be found in the Treaties then in force but the Court read it into the system of the Treaty. Moreover, it is implicit in the Court's case law that it will not seek to restrict *de facto* extensions of competence into the areas covered tangentially rather than explicitly by the EU (see Case 8/73 *Hauptzollamt Bremerhaven* v. *Massey-Ferguson* [1973] ECR 897). This is legitimate since no measure would have been adopted under Article 308 if all the Member States had not been in favour, given the unanimity requirement.

To restrict over-enthusiastic reliance upon Article 308, and to encourage the Council to make full use of other law-making powers, the Court has also confirmed the genuinely residual nature of this legal basis. The Council may have resort to Article 308 EC only when a more specific power elsewhere in the Treaty is lacking (Case 45/86 *Commission* v. *Council (Generalised Tariff Preferences)*). The Council cannot, for example, have recourse to Article 308 in order to avoid using a legal basis requiring only a simple majority of votes (see Case 242/87 *Commission* v. *Council (ERASMUS)* which concerned the relationship between what was then Article 128 EEC (vocational training) and Article 308) or one which provides for the use of the cooperation procedure (see Case C-295/90 *Parliament* v. *Council (Students' Rights)* [1992] ECR I-4193 which concerned the relationship between what was then Article 7(2) EEC (now Article 12(2) EC) and Article 308). In other words, it is notable that the Court has often paid greater attention to delineating the distinction between Article 308 and the other more specific powers under the Treaty, in order to limit recourse to this relatively restrictive legal basis, than it has to restricting the incremental growth of Community competence through the gradual adoption of novel measures such as the EEIG Regulation, or the early environmental measures based on this Article. Specific powers have now been given under the Treaty allowing for the adoption of many of the measures for which, in the early days, recourse to Article 308 was required (e.g. Articles 174–176 EC, as amended), as well as new competences in the fields of education, public health, culture and consumer protection. It is clear in light of these specific powers, and of that aspect of the principle of subsidiarity which operates as a fetter on legislative activities, that recourse to Article 308 has certainly declined, especially since the Treaty of Maastricht.

In addition, there are a number of other general powers in Articles 94, 95 and 12(2) EC, although these are more limited than Article 308. The issue here is less one of managing the outer limits of the competence of the EU, and more about internal interactions between general and specific legal bases (6.8).

6.4   Competence and Pre-emption

EU law not only supplies the competence on the basis of which the institutions may act, but it also provides the mechanisms for protecting that competence in practice. The foremost mechanism is the supremacy of EU law (1.6 and 12.3), enunciated by the Court of Justice in early 'federalising' cases such as Case 6/64 *Costa* v. *ENEL* ([1964] ECR 585) and Case 11/70 *Internationale Handelsgesellschaft* ([1970] ECR 1125). But the practical effects of supremacy, in areas where the EU has actually legislated will vary according to whether or not there is *exclusive* competence on the part of the Community or *shared* competence with the Member States, and also the extent to which and the manner in which that competence has actually been exercised.

The most restrictive solution is termed 'pre-emption'. In such circumstances, where the EU has *exclusive* competence and whether or not it has adopted measures, Member States may not validly act in that field. State powers are pre-empted. Weatherill describes the restrictive effects of pre-emption on the powers of the Member States in stark terms:

> 'National action is precluded not because the rules of Community law apply in the field and prevail in the event of conflict with national provisions but instead where, even thought there are no Community rules with which the national rules can come into conflict, the national action is impermissible. Pre-emption in this sense logically precedes supremacy. It is more clean-cut and dramatic in its exclusionary effect on national powers. But, to place this in context, Community exclusivity even where the Community has not acted is highly abnormal in the EC' (Weatherill, 1995a: 137).

In the external field, the Court of Justice has ruled that the power to implement the common commercial policy under what is now Article 133 EC is held exclusively by the Community, and there is exclusive competence also in the fields of the common customs tariff and fisheries. The particular approach that the Court has taken to exclusivity in the external sphere is examined in 6.5. In the internal sphere, the Court has never ruled *explicitly* that the Community holds exclusive powers in any policy domain, unless it has actually adopted legislation which in effect 'occupies the field'. It has been a common feature of the Court's interpretation of legislation governing agricultural markets, since otherwise the EU rules would lose their effect. In the domain of the internal market, the pre-emptive effect of legislation depends upon its drafting and the extent to which it leaves scope for national rules, e.g. those which impose stricter standards than those introduced in the EU legislation (12.13). As with the doctrine of supremacy, Article 10 EC (the 'duty of Community loyalty': 8.1 and 8.2) means that any Member State action even in a field of shared competence must be compatible with the Treaty, and the Court is the ultimate arbiter of that point.

As a simple rule, pre-emption has attractions, because it makes clear the dividing line between what the EU does and what the Member States do. It does have disadvantages. For example, if the EU is deemed to have exclusive competence and has *not* regulated (e.g. as might happen in the external sphere), then regulatory gaps might appear. In such circumstances, the Treaty provides for the Member States to be permitted to adopt measures, but with prior authorisation by the Commission. Second, the pre-emption rule is rigid and inflexible, and can mean that the regulation at the EU level is slow to react, for example, to changes in technology or scientific knowledge about the benefits or risks of products or substances. Hence, not only has the EU changed its approach to the adoption of much internal market legislation, limiting the role of many directives, for example, to stating essential safety requirements and passing the task of setting standards to standards setting bodies, but the Treaty itself has been amended such that the principal legal basis for the adoption of internal market measures (Article 95 EC) contains a mechanism allowing Member States to maintain in place more restrictive measures not withstanding rules at EU level if the Commission gives approval. Article 95 is part of the generalised trend towards greater flexibility and differentiated integration, evolving in particular since the Treaty of Maastricht. Article 10 EC continues to apply in order to police the legitimate extent of Member State action.

6.5   **External Relations and the Development of External Competence**

In Case 6/64 *Costa* v. *ENEL* the Court took an early opportunity to link the international legal capacity of the European Economic Community (as it then was) to the nature of the Community legal order as constituted by a transfer of powers from the Member States to the Community. That point is important in emphasising the parallelism between internal and external activities. In a series of cases from Case 22/70 *ERTA* onwards, the Court established that parallelism, through the doctrine of implied powers. Moreover, that parallelism is now crucial to the construction of the EU's wider identity in terms of policy making in response to, for example, global economic and environmental changes.

'Parallelism is not only a mechanism or rationale for implied powers; it is a fundamental aspect of the nature of Community competence. It is just not possible any longer – if it ever was – for the Community to pursue its objectives solely within its own internal "space" ' (Cremona, 1999: 147).

Certainly there has been no presumption that because international matters fall into sphere of 'foreign relations' which were not the preserve of the original treaties, the competence of the European Community should be commensurately restricted or narrowly interpreted.

But once there is a competence established, is it *exclusive*? The doctrine of exclusivity operates rather differently in the external sphere to the internal sphere. The issue arises most often in relation to the question whether a given international agreement should be adopted by the Community acting alone or as a 'mixed agreement' in conjunction with the Member States. In the parallel situation of shared competence in the internal sphere, the Member States and the Community may be able to continue regulating quite separately within the sphere, and in practice the Court of Justice will be able to give authoritative rulings in any disputes which come before it subject to the principle of the supremacy of EU law and the duty of loyalty on the Member States under Article 10 EC. There are few, if any, 'mixed' acts in the internal sphere (cf. 4.9). In practice, in the international domain Community and the Member States must often express the shared nature of the competence by acting together. Wherever there is shared competence, the Member States and the Community are both bound by an obligation of cooperation, both in the processes of negotiation and conclusion, and in the fulfilment of commitments entered into (Opinion 1/94 *GATT/WTO* [1994] ECR I-5267 at p. 5420). Sometimes the mixed agreement formula will be adopted because of some aspects of the way the arrangements under the international agreement are established. An example is the *International Rubber Agreement* (Opinion 1/78 [1979] ECR 2871), where the Court ruled that the Community competence was not exclusive because the financing of the arrangements made under the agreement was to be provided by the Member States, even though it could have fallen under Community competence.

The power to implement the common commercial policy – through international treaties including multilateral arrangements, and through unilateral actions by the institutions – lies exclusively with the Community (Opinion 1/75 *Re the Draft Understanding on a Local Cost Standard* [1975] ECR 1355). Although the situation of exclusive competence is very much the exception outside the field of the common commercial policy, the conservation of fisheries and (probably) competition policy, the Court is of the view that:

> 'The exclusive or non-exclusive nature of the Community's competence does not flow solely from the provisions of the Treaty but may also depend on the scope of the measures which have been adopted by the Community institutions for the application of those provisions and which are of such a kind as to deprive the Member States of an area of competence which they were able to exercise previously on a transitional basis.' (Opinion 2/91 *Re ILO Convention* [1993] ECR I-1061 at p. 1077)

For agreements lying across the competences of the EC and the Member States, the phenomenon of the 'mixed agreement' concluded by both parties has developed as the paradigm external relations instrument. The very significant agreements stemming from the conclusion of the GATT Uruguay Round and underpinning the operation of the WTO were concluded in the form of mixed agreements, following the advice of the Court of Justice (Opinion 1/94 *GATT/WTO* [1994] ECR I-5267). One of the main reasons for this was that the common commercial policy under what was then Article 113 EC (now Article 133 EC) does not include most aspects of trade in services, as opposed to goods, or the harmonisation and regulation of intellectual property rights. Exclusive competence could not be founded upon a parallelism argument derived from the relevant *internal* powers for harmonisation (Articles 94 and 95 EC), or a general provision such as Article 308 EC, because external action is not essential to achieve the internal objective of harmonisation or a single market (although doubtless it will assist). The Treaty of Amsterdam amended Article 133 EC to provide that the Council may, acting unanimously, extend this provision to cover international negotiations and agreement on services and intellectual property.

However, even where an external relations competence is expressly shared and non-exclusive, as is the case with development policy, this does not wholly preclude the possibility of the Community concluding an agreement unilaterally without the participation of the Member States. In Case C-268/94 *Portuguese Republic* v. *Council* ([1996] ECR I-6177) Portugal contested the conclusion of the Co-operation Agreement on Partnership and Development between the EC and India in 1994 as a unilateral agreement without the participation of the Member States, using the legal bases of what were then Articles 113 and 130y EC (now Articles 133 and 181 EC – the latter being a competence in the area of development cooperation policy). Portugal objected that the agreement comprised also cooperation in areas such as energy, tourism, culture and intellectual property and argued for the addition of Article 235 EC (now Article 308 EC) as an additional legal base. The Court found that the cooperation did not go beyond the scope of the objectives of development cooperation as set out in Article 130u EC (now Article 177 EC), and, most particularly, the agreement did not *pre-empt* national competence. The Member States' powers to undertake bilateral activities with India were expressly preserved by Article 4 of the agreement.

6.6   The Principles of Subsidiarity and Proportionality

The second paragraph of Article 5 EC, as introduced by the Treaty of Maastricht, provides:

> 'In areas which do not fall within its exclusive competence, the Community shall take action, in accordance with the principles of subsidiarity, only if and in so far as the objectives of the proposed action cannot be sufficiently achieved by the Member States and can therefore, by reason of the scale or effects of the proposed action, be better achieved by the Community.'

The third paragraph goes on to introduce the principle of proportionality:

> 'Any action by the Community shall not go beyond what is necessary to achieve the objectives of this Treaty.'

The introduction of the principles of subsidiarity and proportionality into the EC Treaty provoked a massive outpouring of academic comment and speculation, including work which has specifically identified subsidiarity as a constitutional principle. That situation was buttressed by the inclusion – by way of a Protocol – in the Treaty of Amsterdam of guidelines on subsidiarity and proportionality drawn from materials formulated at the Edinburgh European Council of 1993, and a specific reference to subsidiarity as a binding principle for the EU in Article 2 TEU. This brief discussion will distinguish between subsidiarity as a political principle guiding the development of the EU as a whole, and subsidiarity as a legal condition of the validity of certain types of EC measures. To that end it will attempt to tease out what exactly is meant by the phrasing in Article 5. It will review shortly the role of subsidiarity and proportionality in the legislative process, as required by the Subsidiarity and Proportionality Protocol (hereafter 'Protocol'), and the more general ways in which subsidiarity in particular is shaping the governance system of the EU. It will discuss also the extent to which subsidiarity is justiciable before the Court of Justice and how it can be used as the basis for an action for annulment of an EU act.

As a political principle, closely allied in certain respects to concepts of federalism, subsidiarity enjoys a relatively long history. Its roots lie primarily in Catholic social philosophy. Subsidiarity crystallised as a term describing a particular way of understanding social relations in Papal doctrine during the inter-war years. It expressed a specific concern with the role of the state, and postulated the individual as the base unit of society. Wherever possible individual self-determination should be ensured, and only where decisions can more effectively be taken by groups which are subsidiary to the individual (family, community, locality, region, nation state, federal union) should this occur. Within these hierarchies or networks, the collectivity holds a responsibility for the well-being of the individual (the principle of subsidiarity). The position in Catholic social doctrine is summarised by Peterson (1994: 118) in the following terms:

'Small social groups should be autonomous and sovereign in a pluralist society, yet united in a common morality which stresses duty and harmony. They should be assisted in their activities by a state which neither substitutes for social groups nor is shackled by their demands, but which serves the public good and provides legal order'.

In similar terms, van Kersbergen and Verbeek (1994: 222) argue that:

'one has to appreciate that in Catholic social doctrine subsidiarity is intrinsically linked with other fundamental principles, such as personalism, solidarity, pluralism and distributive justice, that – taken together – have found their most profound expression in the continental christian democratic version of the welfare state, the social market.'

In post-war Germany, subsidiarity, although not explicitly adopted in the Constitution or Basic Law, has constituted an underlying theme dominating the evolution of federalism as a way of breaking loose from the shackles of corporatism under national socialism, in which private interests were co-opted coercively into the processes of the state. It protects the autonomy of the *Bundesländer* in a system of cooperative federalism in which the individual states and the federal *Bund* share certain key political powers.

Subsidiarity, therefore, has a rich, complex and sometimes contradictory heritage, in which it is deeply embedded into state/society relations. So far, in both rhetoric and practice in relation to the EU, this heritage has largely been ignored as subsidiarity is primarily viewed as structuring the EU/Member State relationship. Perhaps unsurprisingly, given the strongly differing views of the Member States on the desirable extent of further integration, in the aftermath of the Maastricht negotiations, subsidiarity showed itself to be a plastic concept, offering the basis of an argument to all possible sides:

> 'The German *Länder* have used it to put pressure on Chancellor Kohl and ... Jacques Delors, in order to protect their own autonomy in the advent of increasing understandings between Bonn and Brussels. The British government led by John Major felt attracted by it, because it seemed a perfect instrument to prevent the European Community from snatching away national sovereignty. At the same time, Jacques Delors grasped subsidiarity as a means of temporarily soothing these fears, well aware that the adoption of such a dynamic and moral concept would not by definition preclude future enlargements of the Community's responsibilities' (van Kersbergen and Verbeek, 1994: 226).

However, that aspect of subsidiarity which de-emphasises the nation state, proposing models of decision making which imply radical decentralisation towards local and regional authorities, may ultimately be difficult to ignore as subsidiarity becomes increasingly well established in thinking about the European Union. Subsidiarity may come, in time, to inform not only the EU/Member State axis, but also the full range of social and political relations from the local to the transnational. At present, however, subsidiarity operates merely upon a binary divide, between the nation state and the EU.

The more limited ambition of subsidiarity within the post-Maastricht European Union is evident from the terms of Article 5 EC, which contains an essentially procedural definition focused on questions of efficiency. It will be recalled that it was introduced into the EC Treaty in the context of debates about the limits upon the growth of competence (Dehousse, 1994b), and in the shadow of the shift from almost universal unanimity in Council decision making to widespread use of qualified majority voting. It was also part of a search to assess the appropriate level for decisions to be taken. Moreover, a parallel has often been drawn with the more recently 'constitutionalised' concept of flexibility, in so far as both offer languages in which those adopting quite opposing positions can appear to communicate, while actually expressing very different ideas about the nature and purpose of integration (5.19).

The choice of a procedural rather than a political approach to reconcile these differences has undoubtedly marked the subsequent development of the concept. However, as a procedural norm, one of the significant legal functions of subsidiarity is the 'imposition of a certain onus of justification – a kind of public reason requirement – on the various EU institutions when they act' (de Búrca, 1999b). An alternative way of expressing it is as a 'regulatory principle' (Dehousse, 1994b: 109). The test of comparative efficiency for Community legislative action introduced by Article 5 EC cannot really be considered in isolation from the final paragraph of that same provision which requires Community action to be 'proportionate': that is, not to go beyond what is necessary to achieve the objectives of the Treaty. That idea can be reduced to the question of how the Community should act, and is closely linked with the subsidiary nature of Community action, that is, whether it should act. The Community is limited to taking action which seeks to achieve an objective which cannot be sufficiently achieved by the Member States, and which can be better achieved by the Community, 'by reason of the scale or effects of the proposed action'. Subsidiarity applies in this sense only to areas of shared competence. This is, as we have seen, a difficult and sometimes chameleon concept in EU law. It is perhaps more important to focus on the relationship with the *acquis communautaire*, a point clarified in the Edinburgh guidelines and the subsequent Protocol in favour of the need to 'respect the general provisions and the objectives of the Treaty, particularly as regards the maintaining in full of the *acquis communautaire* and the institutional balance.' Moreover, rather than identifying sweeping areas such 'the internal market' or 'agriculture' as areas of exclusive competence *per se*, de Búrca highlights the utility of the following loose test which looks at the two opposite ends of shared competence:

> 'the closer a particular issue is to an area of policy which is traditionally at the core of national sovereignty and far removed from the original express aims of the Community, *or* the closer it is to the core common market goals of the Community, the less room there is likely to be for serious or prolonged consideration of the subsidiarity question' (de Búrca, 1999) (emphasis added).

Understanding subsidiarity in practice is best achieved by tracing through its institutionalisation into the EU legal and institutional order after Maastricht. The detailed discussion of the instrumentalisation of subsidiarity came to the fore at an early stage in a number of documents: the Presidency Conclusions issued after the Edinburgh European Council in December 1992; various communications and reports subsequently published by the Commission, especially those concerned with inserting the principle into the legislative process (COM(93) 545; COM(94) 533); and the 1993 Inter-Institutional Agreement on Procedures for Implementing the Principle of Subsidiarity (EC-Bull, 10-1993, p119; on inter-institutional agreements see 6.11). The Presidency Conclusions offered a detailed manual on how subsidiarity should be used within the EU legal order. Indeed, the nature of the terms contained in Article 5 is such that it is more appropriate to examine the subsequent practice of the institutions, especially the Commission which plays a key role through its role of legislative initiative, rather than to subject the language of the article to an exhaustive and probably unrewarding semantic analysis. In any case, it has been suggested (Dehousse, 1994b) that there is an inherent ambiguity between the 'sufficiency' criterion and the 'better achievement' criterion, resulting perhaps from the legislative history of the provision. This suggests that too strict a textual analysis may yield little fruit, and that a study of the embeddedness of subsidiarity in institutional practice may be more illuminating. The words themselves may have been (deliberately?) ambiguous. They continue to be subject to ongoing interpretation by parties other than the Member States who constituted the IGC, and as de Búrca comments (1999b), 'usage may alter the nature of the bargain'.

That said, it is notable that in 1997 at the Amsterdam IGC the Member States returned explicitly to their bargain and added considerable amplifying detail (of a type not normally found in EU Treaties or even in Protocols). The Protocol on subsidiarity and proportionality not only links these two principles more firmly together, but it also offers a series of concrete steps which the institutions (and especially the Commission) must take to ensure that EU action conforms to Article 5. It is, therefore, highly procedural in its approach. It focuses on the need for simple and less intrusive EU action, and emphasises the scope for national decisions and national arrangements, which must be respected. The Commission's role is to insert subsidiarity fully and effectively into its proposal, and that must include consultation and demonstration of the relevance of its proposals.

Indeed it is perhaps for the Commission that the application of subsidiarity and proportionality has had the most significant and tangible consequences in terms of its legislative activities. Following its declaration to that effect at the Edinburgh Summit, it withdrew a number of proposals, and declined to submit new proposals in areas or in forms which it now considers inappropriate (i.e. too intrusive into national diversity, unnecessarily restrictive). In some fields, it has chosen since Maastricht a form of legislative measure which is less restrictive of national discretion, or opted for a 'soft' measure such as a recommendation rather than a formally binding directive. It has also engaged in a programme of 'legislative review' which has led to the simplification and codification of some legislative instruments, most notably in the field of the common external customs tariff. All this nicely reflects the preoccupations of the Protocol. The Commission is obliged to report each year on subsidiarity, in response to requests by the European Council and to the Inter-Institutional Agreement on the application of the principle of subsidiarity. After issuing two reports for 1993 and 1994, the Commission decided to extend its scope to include all action aimed at improving legislation in the broad sense, and it now terms the reports 'Better lawmaking'. It thus includes in the remit as well measures to improve the quality of drafting, the use of practices such as simplification and formal and informal consolidation and opening up access to information, and has thus collapsed this role into a wider role to maintain oversight over the legislative process more generally, thus emphasising the technocratic side of the question. These matters will be examined in more detail in 7.10. On subsidiarity, the Commission has commented that it found itself pressured by the other institutions in relation to legislation, making it difficult to comply strictly with the requirements of the Protocol (Commission, 2000c). Apparently, it is not the Commission that is now the expansive competence-grabbing institution! The other institutions remain, however, equally bound by the terms of the Protocol.

Paragraph 13 of the Protocol provides that

'Compliance with the principle of subsidiarity shall be reviewed in accordance with the rules laid down by the Treaty'.

This confirms that subsidiarity is justiciable, which is an obvious conclusion since Article 5 falls within the provisions of the Treaty which are subject to the binding and authoritative jurisdiction of the Court of Justice. However, the Court's pronouncements thus far directly upon the question of subsidiarity seem at first sight to limit both the principle and its own review. In Case C-84/94 *UK* v. *Council (Working Time Directive)* ([1996] ECR I-5755) the Court was asked to annul the Working Time Directive adopted by a qualified majority vote under what was then Article 118a on health and safety at work. One of the UK's arguments was a failure to respect subsidiarity, notably failure to respect the matters laid down in what were at the time the Edinburgh guidelines. The Court commented merely that subsidiarity concerned the *need* for Community action, not the *intensity* of it, a position which it might need to look more closely at in the light of the Protocol with its preference for less intrusive measures. The Court also rejected an argument that the directive on deposit-guarantee schemes had been adopted without proper regard to the requirement of subsidiarity, with the Court extracting from the recitals to the directive certain statements which it took to be a subsidiarity justification (Case C-233/94 *Germany* v. *Parliament and Council* [1997] ECR I-2405). Again, legislative practice and the Court's review must be seen in a different light after the Amsterdam Protocol. Even if the Court does show a continuing reluctance to invalidate EU level legislative measures, it may simultaneously recognise the influence of subsidiarity in sustaining the legitimacy of diverse national measures, showing a greater sensitivity to the interaction of subsidiarity in a more general sense with the scope and terms of EU law (de Búrca, 1998). A good example can already be taken from the field of the free movement of goods where arguably the influence of the subsidiarity principle can be seen in the Court's case law. For example, the Court has set stricter limits to the capacity of what is now Article

28 EC to provide a general all-purpose constitutional norm for challenging all types of national measures which might potentially restrict interstate trade, however vestigially (Cases C-267, 268/91 *Keck and Mithouard* [1993] ECR I-6097). Subsidiarity has also shaped the balance of enforcement powers in the field of competition law, with the Commission adopting a Notice seeking to encourage greater decentralised enforcement of Articles 81 and 82 by national courts, and with the Court of First Instance giving general support to the Commission's approach (Case T-24/90 *Automec* v. *Commission (Automec II)* [1992] ECR II-2223).

Clearly, so long as it privileges efficiency over all other criteria for assessing the appropriateness of particular levels of decision making, subsidiarity will be subject to some criticism. Yet while it is a difficult and potentially obstructive concept, subsidiarity may well prove to be enduring. De Búrca (1999b) concludes:

> 'Far from being a transitory notion whose usefulness to seal a political compromise was exhausted once the Maastricht bargain had gelled, the concept of subsidiarity continues to express, and to raise, fundamental questions about the appropriate locus of political and legal authority within a complex and multi-layered polity, which is itself situated within an increasingly interconnected international 'order''.

While de Búrca's comment may be a little overoptimistic in its assessment of current institutional practice, which is highly pragmatic in its approach, it is correct as a general statement serving to highlight the potential constitutional significance of this principle.

6.7 Delegation and Implementation: Rule-Making Powers

Legislative measures frequently require implementation. In many instances EU measures are undertaken by the national authorities alone, including many of those requiring the harmonisation of national laws, all implementation and future oversight. But in many areas of EU policy, where the EU measures are concerned with the regulation of economic activities or exchanges (including agriculture, food safety, product safety, many environmental standards), many aspects of detailed implementation and especially rule making are a matter for the EU institutions themselves. Delegation in relation to implementation is clearly foreseen by the EC Treaty. Article 202 EC (formerly Article 145 EC) provides in relation to the Council that it may confer powers for the implementation of the rules which the Council lays down on the Commission, subject to certain requirements which it must lay down in advance by unanimity. Mirroring this provision, Article 211 EC (formerly Article 155 EC) provides that the Commission shall exercise the powers conferred on it by the Council for the implementation of the rules which it has laid down. In the EU context, mechanisms for transferring the power to implement rules have proved to be necessary because of the ever-increasing range and complexity of its activities. Initially, this need was concentrated in the field of agriculture and customs, but many aspects of single market policy such as that related to food safety and health and safety issues have required complex implementing structures (Vos, 1999). Three primary mechanisms have been used for this purpose in the EU: committees (7.13), agencies (which can have only limited rule-making powers) (4.17) and private bodies, which are used for establishing technical standards based on standards of health and safety established in EU directives.

The practice of delegation of powers within the EU has long been recognised by the Court of Justice. In Case 25/70 *Einfuhr- und Vorratstelle* v. *Köster* ([1970] ECR 1161) the Court acknowledged that the Council was empowered to delegate executive powers to either the Commission, or indeed to itself. In the considering the delegation of executive powers in relation to the common organisation of the market in cereals to the Commission, to be exercised according to what is termed the 'management committee' system (7.13), the Court held:

> 'It cannot therefore be a requirement that all details of the regulations concerning the common agricultural policy be drawn up by the Council according to the procedure in Article 43 [the main legal basis in the agricultural field; now Article 37 EC]. It is sufficient for the purposes of that provision that the basic elements of the matter to be dealt with have been adopted in accordance with the procedure laid down by that provision. On the other hand, the provisions implementing the basic regulations may be adopted according to a procedure different from that in Article 43, either by the Council itself or by the Commission by virtue of an authorisation complying with Article 155' (at p. 1170).

The main feature of the emergence of the committee system, commonly known as 'comitology', is that it was marked by a strong resistance on the part of the Member States to the idea of making an unconditional delegation of rule-making powers to the Commission. Hence, it represents one way in which the Member States' tentacles have stretched into the EU institutions – in this case the Commission – effectively 'nationalising' in large measure a 'European' implementation process.

6.8 Legal Basis, the Duty to State Reasons and Other Conditions: the Principle of Judicial Control

In the context of understanding the legal and constitutional basis of policy making, it is important to observe the importance of judicial control. Under

Article 230, the Court of Justice is given the power to review the acts of the institutions:

> 'The Court of Justice shall review the legality of acts adopted jointly by the European Parliament and the Council, of acts of the Council, of the Commission and of the ECB, other than recommendations and opinions, and of acts of the European Parliament intended to produce legal effects vis-à-vis third parties...
> on grounds of lack of competence, infringement of an essential procedural requirement, infringement of this Treaty or of any rule relating to its application, or misuse of powers.'

The basic requirements can be reduced here to four core principles: legal basis, the duty to give reasons, respect for subsidiarity and proportionality, and respect for other principles and legal rules. The first requirement is that the institution adopting an act must have competence or the legal power to act. The general principle of attributed competences was discussed in 6.2. It is evidenced, on a case-by-case basis, by showing that a legal act has a valid legal basis, and reference must normally be made in the recitals (or preamble) of the act to the concrete enabling power. This is generally to be found in the Treaty itself, or, in the case of delegated legislation, located in an enabling legislative act. However, legal basis not only shows that the EU and a specific institution or institutions have competence. In addition, under the Treaty system, because of the way in which the powers of the institutions are organised, it may be that the choice of legal basis affects the degree of input of a particular institution. Consequently, the choice of legal basis is an important element in the legislative process.

According to the Court of Justice legal basis is a matter of law:

> 'the choice of the legal basis for a measure may not depend simply on an institution's conviction as to the objective pursued but must be based on objective factors which are amenable to judicial review' (Case 45/86 *Commission* v. *Council (Generalised Tariff Preferences)* [1987] ECR 1493 at p. 1520).

An incorrect reference or a general reference to the Treaty as a whole is insufficient. Although an explicit reference is not absolutely necessary, the absence of such a reference will render a measure capable of challenge if the parties concerned and the Court of Justice are left uncertain as to the precise legal basis in fact used (Case 45/86 *Commission* v. *Council (Generalised Tariff Preferences)*). Problems continue to abound in relation to the identification of the 'correct' legal basis, problems which the Treaty itself often causes, as the Court has acknowledged:

> 'Under the system governing Community powers, the powers of the institutions and the conditions on their exercise derive from various spe-

cific provisions of the Treaty, and the differences between those provisions, particularly as regards the involvement of the European Parliament, are not always based on consistent criteria' (Case 242/87 *Commission* v. *Council (ERASMUS)* [1989] ECR 1425 at p. 1452).

A number of specific inter-institutional questions raised by the problem of legal basis are discussed in 6.11. Challenges to the legal basis of measures are, of course, not the sole prerogative of inter-institutional litigation: the question of legal basis is also frequently raised by Member States in actions brought against the EU institutions (where such arguments are often closely linked to arguments about the scope of Community competence: e.g. Case 281, etc./85 *Germany et al.* v. *Commission (Migration Policy)* [1987] ECR 3203 discussed at 6.3 and C-268/94 *Portuguese Republic* v. *Council* [1996] ECR I-6177 discussed at 6.5). Litigation opposing the Member States and the institutions has also frequently raised the crucial question of the relationship between general and specific legal bases, that is, between provisions of the Treaty offering powers in relation to specific fields (e.g. agriculture), and those offering general legislative powers.

This is best illustrated using the example of Article 95 EC, the main legal basis for internal market measures. It differs from Article 94 in that it provides for QMV in the Council and involves, since 1993, the Parliament–Council co-decision procedure. Unlike Article 94, Article 95 also provides for the adoption of any type of 'measures', not just directives; it also structures the use of legislative power by requiring Commission proposals, where relevant, to be based on high levels of health, safety, environmental and consumer protection (Article 95(3) EC). However, the scope of Article 95 is limited in that it cannot be used to adopt tax harmonisation measures, or measures in the fields of free movement of persons or rights and interests of employed persons (Article 95(2)). In that respect, it is less easy to characterise it as a 'general' legal basis. The restriction on the use of Article 95(2) in relation to the free movement of workers is partly offset by Article 12(2), which provides a general power for the Council to adopt measures which eradicate discrimination based on grounds of nationality. This power, too, has been broadly interpreted by the Court of Justice, using a strand of argument drawn from its work on implied powers. In Case C-295/90 *Parliament* v. *Council (Students' Rights)* ([1992] ECR I-4193), the Court concluded that although what was then Article 7(1) EEC appears to refer, in a narrow way, to the elimination of discrimination, measures adopted under paragraph 2 of that provision

> 'should not necessarily be limited to regulating rights deriving from the first paragraph of the same article, but they may also deal with aspects the resolution of which appears *necessary* for the effective exercise of those rights' (p. 4235) (emphasis added).

Consequently, it was the correct provision to use as the legal basis for a Directive covering free movement rights for students, who, by virtue of the Treaty provisions on vocational training, fall within the scope of protection of EU law.

The delimitation of Article 95 in relation to specific legal bases, especially those concerned with environmental policy, has become intimately entangled with problems of inter-institutional balance and the relationship between different types of legislative procedure, and consequently attempts by the European Parliament in particular to use arguments about legal basis as a means for protecting its prerogatives in the form of the fullest degree of participation in the legislative process. They are discussed in more detail in 7.18. The Court's treatment of the provision has, none the less, confirmed that it is a residual legal basis. In Case C-271/94 *Parliament* v. *Council (Edicom)* ([1996] ECR I-1689), the Court refused to accept that Article 95 was the correct legal basis for a Council Decision on interadministration telematic networks for statistics relating to the trading of goods. Such networks should, since the adoption of the Treaty of Maastricht, be established using Article 156 EC (what was Article 129d), which provides for the creation of Trans-European Networks. The Court made clear its preference for Article 156 as a more specific provision than Article 95.

Furthermore, the Court has also confirmed the potential breadth of Article 95 in a case brought by Spain to challenge its use as the legal basis for a Council Regulation on the creation of a supplementary patent protection for certain medicinal products. Although there are limitations on the EU's powers to regulate property and property rights, the Court none the less concluded that this aspect of the unification of national intellectual property laws through the creation of a uniform EU system was necessary for the purposes of the completion of the internal market (Case C-350/93 *Spain* v. *Council (Patent protection for medical products)* [1995] ECR I-1985).

The legal basis of measures may also be challenged by individual litigants in cases brought against the EU institutions, or against other individuals or public authorities in actions begun in the national courts where EU measures are at issue (e.g. Case C-405/92 *Etablissements A. Mondiet* v. *Armament Islais* [1993] ECR I-6133, concerning the correct legal basis for an EU measure banning the use of driftnets of more than 2.5 km in length).

The second requirement is that every legal act must contain an adequate statement of reasons. The duty to give reasons is a principle of 'transparency', and to use the language of Article 220 EC, it is an 'essential procedural requirement'. Article 253 EC requires regulations, directives and decisions adopted by the Council, by the Commission or by the Council and Parliament jointly to refer to any proposals and opinions required to be obtained under the Treaty, and to contain a statement of reasons. A statement of reasons facilitates the process of judicial review, allowing any interested parties, and the Court where appropriate, to discover at a glance the circumstances which enjoined the adopting institution to act (see Case 24/62 *Commission* v. *Germany (Brennwein)* [1963] ECR 63). The intensity of the duty to give reasons depends upon the type of act adopted (a general legislative act requires less specific reasons than an individual act, such as one which imposes a pecuniary sanction on an undertaking for breach of the competition rules) and the circumstances in which an act is adopted. Where the institution must act urgently, a cursory statement of reasons may be sufficient (Case 16/65 *Firma Schwarze* v. *Einfuhr- und Vorratstelle für Getreide und Futtermittel* [1965] ECR 877). Similarly in complex areas like agriculture where there is frequently a highly fragmented and much amended body of legislation, the duty to give reasons has arguably been emptied of its 'substantive value' (Barents, 1994: 112). In such a field, even the objective of transparency may no longer be achieved. Closely linked to the giving reasons requirement is Article 254 EC which makes provision for the entry into force of binding acts of the institutions, and for their publication in the *Official Journal* and notification to addressees as appropriate. These principles can be similarly construed as means of facilitating review of measures.

Suggestions have been made that the giving reasons requirement might be extended beyond the essential dimension of transparency to encompass a right of participation (Shapiro, 1992; discussed in Craig and de Búrca, 1998: 119–123). Particularly as regards the executive and administrative work of the Commission, it could be argued that there is a close link between the duties which are frequently incumbent upon the Commission to hear the arguments put by those who are affected by its measures (especially, but not only in the field of competition law) (the principle of *audi alteram partem*), and the reasons then given for any measure which ensues. It is also linked to principles of participatory democracy and thus goes to the heart of the EU's legitimacy debate. Recent case law of the Court of First Instance may indicate that it is moving in the direction of pushing the Commission into greater dialogue with those concerned by its administrative actions. In Case T-95/94 *Chambre Syndicale Nationale des Enterprises de Transport de Fonds et Valeurs and Brink's France Sarl* v. *Commission* ([1995] ECR II-2651), in the context of a complaint made by the applicants regarding Commission approval for certain state aids paid by France, the Court of First Instance held that the obligation to state reasons may in certain circumstances require an exchange of views with the complainant, and this obligation had not been discharged in the present case. However, the status of the dialogue principle is not yet fully enshrined in EU law.

The third precondition for EU legal acts involves respect for the principles of subsidiarity and proportionality set out in Article 5 EC. What little evidence there exists in relation to the judicial scrutiny of subsidiarity was considered in 6.6. In contrast, the principle of proportionality, although only relatively recently formally constitutionalised, is a well-established general principle of EU law which the Court applies in a number of fields to control actions by both the EU and the Member States (de Búrca, 1993a; Usher, 1998). It means, essentially, that the means adopted should be appropriate to the end sought, such that a public authority may not impose obligations on a citizen except to the extent to which they are strictly necessary in the public interest to attain the purpose of the measure, and it is said to embody 'a basic concept of fairness which has strengthened the protection of individual rights at both the national and the supranational level' (Emiliou, 1996: 1). Proportionality is discussed further in 9.3. In the same chapter, other so-called 'general principles' of EU law are discussed. Valid EU acts must not infringe these principles. Fourth and finally, therefore, even an act satisfying the first three core principles identified here may still infringe against a range of additional principles which bind the lawmakers of the EU – as the text of Article 230 EC makes clear ('...any other rule of law...').

6.9   Democracy, Accountability and Participation in Law and Policy Making

Issues of democracy, or lack of it, in the EU can be seen from a variety of different angles: insufficient input on the part of the European Parliament because of the restrictive nature of the EU legislative process, or too great a disempowerment of national parliaments as a result of the transfer of powers to the EU and the increased use of qualified majority voting; lack of participation of 'the citizen', with alienation from an over-complex system of governance based on unelected institutions perceived as remote and inaccessible; lack of a 'European public space', with political parties, non-governmental organisations, and other associations of civil society such as unions or employer bodies still primarily organised at the national level; conversely, 'Brussels' is sometimes seen as too ready to listen to the lobbyists, indeed it is trapped by them. As Chris Lord has explained, the issue with the democratic deficit is that each person writing about it tends to identify one basic problem:

> 'The implication is plain: find some means of solving the specific problem that concerns the author in question and the democratic deficit will disappear. But what if all [these issues] form an interconnected complex? What if they relate to certain common difficulties of developing democratic politics in a political system which is both new and transnational?' (Lord, 1998: 11).

So, as Lord suggests, it may be just as important to make an inventory of those aspects of 'democratic practice' which do exist as it is to point out the self-evident gaps. For example, the Court likewise has long recognised the pivotal role of the Parliament as the only elected institution. In Case 138/79 *Roquette Frères* v. *Council* ([1980] ECR 3333 at 3359) it stated that the power of the Parliament to participate in the legislative process through 'consultation' (5.4)

> 'represents an essential factor in the institutional balance intended by the treaty. Although limited, [such power] reflects at Community level the fundamental democratic principle that the peoples should take part in the exercise of power through the intermediary of a representative assembly.'

It has repeated this point on numerous occasions since, even though the Parliament does now in certain circumstances have a more direct and effective input into the legislative process than the form of consultation at issue in *Roquette*. Despite the imperfections of the system, what this point illustrates is that each of the institutions in the EU makes some contribution to the level of democracy – including national and subnational institutions which are involved. Thus national parliaments are now linked to the system by the Protocol attached to the Treaty of Amsterdam. The system of 'partnership' in regional policy formalises the role of certain local public and private bodies in the development and implementation of policy (Scott, 1998). The Commission is increasingly indirectly democratically legitimated through the increased role of the European Parliament in the approval of the President and the Commissioners. The day might be not so far away when the political parties in the Parliament initiate the process of choosing the Commission President by 'running' their candidate via the elections for the Parliament which just precede – in the EU calendar – the choosing and investiture of each Commission. Moreover, the Parliament has effectively exercised its powers of accountability over the Commission. The Commission could become a putative government, chosen by and responsible to a democratically elected legislature. In terms of the legislative process, the co-decision procedure in its post-Amsterdam form is both simplified and more genuine (7.5). Again, it is not so far away, perhaps, from the day when the Council and Parliament appear as a true bicameral legislature.

In the view of some (e.g. Mancini and Keeling, 1994), the Court of Justice has made one of the most important contributions to the achievements thus far. So, for example, it should not be thought that power is exercised in any way arbitrarily within the EU, that there exist no checks and balances in the system, or that there is no 'separation of powers', even if there is no separation of legislative, executive and judicial roles in the classic sense. Within a system such as the EU, each institution, including the Court of Justice must play some role in relation to questions of democracy, legitimacy and also institutional efficiency. The concept of 'competence', and the system of limited powers which the Treaty establishes and the Court of Justice is required to enforce are crucial to this, as is the separation of powers between the institutions recognised by Article 4 EC.

Some examples will suffice to show the contribution of the Court of Justice to the development of concepts such as 'institutional' or 'inter-institutional balance' and 'loyal' or 'sincere' cooperation between the institutions, a principle which governs the manner in which they may exercise their powers.

In order to protect inter-institutional balance the Court recognised that the European Parliament could be both a defendant and a plaintiff in actions for annulment of illegal acts brought before it, even though the EEC Treaty before the Treaty of Maastricht made no reference to this possibility (see 6.11). The Parliament was given the power to take action before the Court in order to 'protect its prerogatives' (Case C-70/88 *Parliament* v. *Council (Chernobyl)* [1990] ECR I-2041; see now Article 230 EC). The Court has specifically recognised the contribution made by the Parliament as the representative of the people, and opted for a general principle that where genuine alternatives exist under the Treaty system, there should be a preference for the legal basis for any given measure which gives greater input from the Parliament.

Where an institution has determined in advance the way in which it will exercise a power which is conferred upon it by the Treaties or by relevant secondary legislation, it cannot retreat from the position it has publicly taken. We can take an example from the enforcement of the competition rules of the Treaty (Articles 81 and 82 EC) which prohibit various forms of anti-competitive conduct by undertakings and groups of undertakings. In the past the Commission has taken a more generous position than was strictly required by the case law of the Court in its public statements on the question of what 'access' to the 'file' which the Commission has compiled on the case an undertaking accused of a breach of the competition rules may have. The Court of First Instance held that the Commission was bound by that statement to provide the level of access it had 'promised' (Case T-7/89 *Hercules* v. *Commission (Polypropylene)* [1991] ECR II-1711.

A similar lesson emerges from the Court of First Instance's treatment of the Council's attempts, in the post-Maastricht search for greater transparency, openness and therefore legitimacy within the EU, to create a new policy of public access to its documents, appearing to step away from the almost total secrecy which had hitherto dominated its decision-making processes (4.7). It established a decision-making structure for the release of documents on request by a member of the public which allowed it a discretion in determining what was secret and what it was not in the public interest to disclose. When a journalist and his newspaper sought to put the policy to use, they were refused access to the documents they wanted. A challenge before the Court of First Instance was successful on the grounds that having established a discretion, the Council must at least turn its mind on a case-by-case basis to whether documents should be released. A continued blanket ban on public access would not be a proper exercise of the discretion (Case T-194/94 *Carvel and Guardian Newspapers* v. *Council* [1995] ECR II-2765) (10.8).

Finally, in the case of *UEAPME* (Case T-135/96 *UEAPME* v. *Council* [1998] ECR II-2335), the Court of First Instance was faced with a novel action for annulment brought by an association representing the interests of small and medium sized employers who had *not* been involved in the social dialogue between employer and employee representatives which led to the adoption of a framework agreement on parental leave and hence to a directive adopted by the Council. The Court engaged in a lengthy interpretation of the restrictive standing conditions in Article 230 EC for so-called non-privileged applicants (15.4 *et seq*) in order to assess the position of the applicant. In conclusion, it resolved that the action was inadmissible as the applicant was not directly and individually concerned, but it gave the applicant every opportunity – through the way it framed the argument – to demonstrate that it was distinguished from all other organisations of management and labour consulted by the Commission under the relevant provisions, but who were not signatories to the actual framework agreement. It indicated its awareness of the extent to which the 'social dialogue' procedure for law making differs from the EU norm, and so makes different demands with regard to 'the principle of democracy on which the Union is founded'. Thus in the absence of the Parliament's participation in this type of law-making process, it is necessary 'that the participation of the people be otherwise assured, in this instance through the parties representative of management and labour who concluded the agreement' (para. 88 of the judgment). In a general sense, therefore, the representatives of the social partners are playing a representational role within the process, although in fact the only point of direct control exercised by the Commission and the Council is to check the narrower question of their 'representativity' in relation to their status as representatives of management and labour. The case highlights, however, perhaps a growing sensitivity in the Community judicature to the issue of democratic participation.

6.10   Primary and Secondary Sources of Law in the EU

This paragraph and the ones that follow are concerned with identifying the body of legal rules which comprise the sources of law in the European Union. Sources of law are often divided into different categories; for example, there are external sources (international agreements) and internal sources (the founding treaties, general principles of law, EU legislation), as well as primary sources (treaties, general principles of law) and secondary sources (EU legislation). Of most direct interest here are secondary sources which are the outputs of policy and law-making processes involving the institutions. In brief, however, the primary sources of law which shape the EU legal order are:

- The founding treaties, comprising the ECSC, Euratom and EC Treaties, the Treaty on European Union, in each case as amended by the Treaty of Amsterdam, plus other amending or supplementing treaties such as the various Acts of Accession, the Merger Treaty and the Budgetary Treaties. All these treaties have required conclusion and ratification before entry into force.
- Conventions agreed between the Member States, such as the Judgments Convention, or the Europol Convention. In the case of the latter Convention, its status as part of 'Community law' in the narrow sense of the first pillar is a moot point. It would have the status of 'ordinary' international law.
- Other international agreements by which the EU is bound, including with one or more third states or other international organisations concluded by the Community itself in exercise of its external relations powers (6.5), of both a bilateral nature (e.g. an association or cooperation agreement with a third state) and a multilateral nature (e.g. a trading arrangement regarding a particular commodity, such as the Multi-fibre Agreement). This category also contains agreements predating the foundation of the EC/EU under which it has succeeded to the rights and obligations of the Member States. An important example is the (old) General Agreement on Tariffs and Trade (GATT), which represents the basic framework for the evolution of global free trade now found in the new WTO Agreements. Finally, there are international conventions which form part of the legal patrimony of all states and organisations which claim respect for the rule of law, including, within Europe, the European Convention on Human Rights and Fundamental Freedoms (ECHR), as well as truly international human rights instruments such as the International Covenant of Civil and Political Rights. The Court of Justice will enforce the EU's international legal obligations within the EU legal system, so far as those international treaties touch upon Community competence, including in some circumstances treating the provision of international law as a reason for invalidating an EU act (although see the approach to the GATT: 5.13, 15.13). In limited certain circumstances, individuals may also be able to rely on provisions of international agreements by which the EU is bound as creating rights which they may invoke in national courts; in other words, such provisions may have direct effect (12.10).
- International law generally: EU law must comply with international law, and even if the relevant provisions do not have direct effect, EU law must

be interpreted so far as is possible in conformity with international law (Case C-53/96 *Hermès International* v. *FHT Marketing Choice BV* [1998] ECR I-3603, para. 28).

– General principles of law, which comprise a body of superordinate rules of law, for the most part 'unwritten' (in the sense of not contained in any formal constitutional document) and derived by the Court of Justice by reference to its general duty to ensure that the law is observed (Article 220 EC). General principles of law are discussed at length in Chapter 9.

Turning to secondary sources of law, many of these are helpfully brought together by the Treaties in one provision. The acts of the institutions within the framework of the EC Treaty are classified and described in brief terms in Article 249 EC:

> 'In order to carry out their task and in accordance with the provisions of this Treaty, the European Parliament acting jointly with the Council, the Council and the Commission shall make regulations and issue directives, take decisions, make recommendations or deliver opinions.
>
> A regulation shall have general application. It shall be binding in its entirety and directly applicable in all Member States.
>
> A directive shall be binding, as to the result to be achieved, upon each Member State to which it is addressed, but shall leave to the national authorities the choice of form and methods.
>
> A decision shall be binding in its entirety upon those to whom it is addressed.
>
> Recommendations and opinions shall have no binding force.'

The legislative processes whereby EU measures may be adopted will be considered in the following chapter, and the basic requirements for the lawful adoption, entry into force and publication of such measures including the duty to give reasons, and the requirement of a legal basis have already been highlighted in this chapter. It remains here to describe in brief terms the basic nature of each form of EU act, leaving for Chapters 12 and 13 the detailed consideration of the effects of such acts within the domestic legal systems of the Member States. As a preliminary point it should be noted that although there is a crude hierarchy of EU acts, with regulations ranking as the strongest form and non-binding recommendations and opinions as the weakest, there is no very clear logic as to where the Treaty will mandate, in a particular provision, the adoption of one or more specific forms of legislation, or where it leaves it open to the adopting institution to adopt any necessary 'measures'. Furthermore, the Court has consistently held that it is the content of a measure which is decisive as to its nature, not the form which it is given by the adopting institution. In Cases 41–44/70 *International Fruit Company* v. *Commission* ([1971] ECR 411) the Court held that a measure labelled a regulation was in truth a bundle of individual decisions. This finding was crucial as it affected the ability of the applicant company to bring a challenge to the measure in question under the EU's system of judicial control (see Chapter 15). It is therefore necessary to scrutinise in all cases both the concrete enabling provision (legal basis) to ensure that the relevant institution has acted within its power and the substance of the act adopted to ensure that it is what it purports to be.

The system used in Article 249 EC, although replicated in Article 161 Euratom, did not adopt that already used in the ECSC Treaty. Under the ECSC Treaty only three types of measure are envisaged; these are decisions, recommendations and opinions. An ECSC decision is broadly equivalent to either a regulation or a decision under the EC Treaty, depending upon whether it is general or individual in nature. An ECSC recommendation can be equated to a directive under the EC Treaty, and ECSC opinions, like their counterparts under the EC Treaty, have no binding force. The analysis throughout this book follows the EC schema. Finally, it should be noted that no detailed analysis is offered of the types of measures which can be adopted under CFSP and PJC (joint actions, common positions, conventions and, in the case of the latter 'framework decisions'). In the future, some PJC measures will be the subject of litigation before the Court of Justice, and thus an interesting practice of comparison may develop in the future between first- and third-pillar measures. At this stage, it is rather too early to offer any detailed comments. Suffice it to say that while these measures do not have exactly the same effects as measures adopted under the EC Treaty, in particular with regard to their capacity to bind the institutions, the Member States, and even, in the case of some first-pillar measures such as Regulations, individuals, they are none the less binding legal measures. At the very least, they may have effects in international law and as international law must be part of the EU legal order; the most obvious comparison with the 'sources' of law under the EC Treaty would be with forms of 'soft law' (6.15).

6.11 Regulations

Regulations are like EU 'Acts of Parliament'. Regulations have 'general application', are binding in all respects and 'directly applicable'. Thus they are general, non-individualised legislative measures which take effect directly in the national legal order, without need for national implementing measures. Indeed national re-enactment is not permitted, unless it is required by the terms of the regulation (Case 34/73 *Variola* v. *Italian Finance Administration* [1973] ECR 981). The Court held (at p. 990):

> 'the direct application of a Regulation means that its entry into force, and its application in favour of or against those subject to it are inde-

pendent of any measure of reception into national law... Member States are under a duty not to obstruct the direct applicability inherent in Regulations. Strict compliance with this obligation is an indispensable condition of the simultaneous and uniform application of Community Regulations throughout the Community.'

Examples can be given of regulations which are explicitly stated to be dependent upon national implementation. The Tachograph Regulation (Council Regulation 1463/70 OJ 1970 (Sp. Ed.) p. 482) provides:

'Member States shall, in good time and after consulting the Commission, adopt such laws, regulations and administrative provisions as may be necessary for the implementation of this Regulation.'

In crude terms, the existence of a regulation in a particular field adopted by the EU normally acts as a 'keep out' sign to the national legislature (Usher, 1981: 17). The pre-emptive effect of EU legislation will be examined further in the context of the discussion of supremacy in 12.3 and 12.13.

6.12   **Directives**

The specific character of directives lies in the type of obligation which they impose upon addressees. Directives contain essentially obligations of result, not obligations of conduct. However, the implementation of directives is a positive obligation for the Member States, and the effective implementation of directives is one of the keys to the realisation of the EU's objectives in the internal market sphere. Since the beginning of the 1990s, enforcement proceedings under Article 226 EC have been begun automatically by the Commission in the event of failure by a Member State to implement a directive by the time limit which it is set in each measure (usually between one and three years) (8th Annual Report by the Commission to the European Parliament on the Monitoring of the Application of Community Law, OJ 1991 C338/1).

The Member States have discretion as to how they implement directives. They are 'not designed to breed uniformity' (Weatherill, 2000c), as they may 'be applied by the Member States in different ways' (Case C-293/97 *R* v. *Secretary of State for the Environment and Minister of Agriculture, Fisheries and Food, ex parte Standley and Metson* [1999] ECR I-2603) especially where Member States are granted a wide discretion in a field involving complex assessments. In limited circumstances under Article 95(4) EC, a Member State can notify the Commission that in respect of a directive adopted under that provisions (which relates to the completion of the internal market) it deems it necessary to maintain a national provision on grounds of 'major need' (such as environmental protection or public health). Since the Member State cannot apply the derogating measure until after it has received approval from the Commission, in the meantime the effect of the directive remains unconditional (Case C-319/97 *Kortas* [1999] ECR I-3143) (8.12). Implementation normally involves either adopting or changing legislation, but exceptionally nothing need be done if existing legislation is sufficient. They may also be given alternatives within the directive itself. In practice, the mis-implementation of directives is as serious a problem as the failure to implement, and the Court of Justice is frequently faced with preliminary references regarding the interpretation of particular directives where national courts are required to decide upon the adequacy of national implementing measures. Specific examples of this and related problems will be discussed in 12.11, where the important question is often whether the provisions of directives can themselves be invoked in national courts as giving rise to rights for individuals and, if this is not possible, the scope of the duty upon the national court to achieve a harmonious resolution of apparently conflicting provisions in the directive and the national implementing measures (12.14 and 12.15). An additional element in enforceability of directives emerged in Cases C-6, 9/90 *Francovich* v. *Italian State (Francovich I)* ([1991] ECR I-5357) where the Court held that a Member State could be liable for the damage which results from its failure to implement a directive (12.17 and 12.18).

6.13 Decisions

These are measures of an individual nature which may be addressed either to individuals or undertakings, or to Member States. Article 134 EC, for example, gives a power to the Commission to adopt decisions addressed to the Member States authorising them to restrict imports of third country products from other Member States, in derogation from the normal principle that third country products, once they have entered the EU, may circulate freely. Decisions adopted by the Commission under Regulation 17 in application of Articles 81 and 82 EC (the competition rules) offer an example of decisions addressed to individuals or undertakings. Decisions are not normally normative, in the sense of creating generally applicable EU law; this is certainly the case with competition decisions which do not create general rules of conduct for undertakings, but merely bind those to whom they are addressed. On the other hand, decisions adopted by the Commission in pursuance of a policy objective laid down by the Treaty such as that of coordinating cooperation between the Member States in a field of social policy are more akin to a general normative act. A good example of this was the former Article 118 EEC, which was interpreted by the Court of Justice as implying a power of decision (see Cases 281, etc./85 *Migration Policy*).

One of the difficulties which arises with the identification and interpretation of 'decisions' is that the effect of Article 230(4) EC is to lend a special status to decisions as individual measures which are capable of challenge by so-called non-privileged applicants before the Court of Justice. By non-privileged applicants is meant the natural and legal persons whose activities are affected by the regulatory activities of the EU institutions, who have only limited standing to challenge EU measures in the Court of Justice (15.4 *et seq.*). In this sense, the concept of 'decision' has been refined in two ways. The first is in contradistinction to regulations – i.e. general measures not amenable to individual challenge. The second is in contradistinction to measures that have no legal effects at all. This is in the sense of a 'reviewable act' (see 6.14 and 15.2; Greaves, 1996). For example, the Court has gone so far as to characterise as a 'decision' the conclusion of the Commission that it had no jurisdiction in relation to a particular merger between two airlines, made public entirely informally by the spokesman for the Commissioner responsible for competition policy (Case T-3/93 *Société Anonyme à Participation Ouvrière Nationale Air France* v. *Commission (Air France)* [1994] ECR II-121). In that context, the characterisation of a measure as a 'decision' is a policy measure intended to ensure the efficacy of judicial review (cf. Toth, 1995).

6.14   Sui Generis Acts

Not all binding legal acts of the institutions are readily capable of inclusion within the categories set out in Article 249 EC. The Court has recognised a further category of so-called *sui generis* acts. These include in particular internal management measures of the EU institutions, such as measures establishing committees, or allocating funds for European Parliament elections (see Case 294/83 *Parti Ecologiste 'Les Verts'* v. *Parliament* [1986] ECR 1339). This category also includes certain measures which might be thought, at first sight, to fall within the 'soft law' category of non-binding acts such as recommendations and opinions. An example of this is the 'resolution' adopted by the Council determining the format for Community participation in the negotiation of the European Road Transport Agreement. In Case 22/70 *ERTA*, the Commission successfully established that such a measure could be challenged under Article 230 EC which provides that the 'Court of Justice shall review the legality of acts ... *other than recommendations or opinions*' (emphasis added). The important point in such a case is the binding nature of the act, which must in some way change the legal position of those affected by it. In contrast to the position in *Air France* described in 6.13, the applicant in *ERTA*, as a privileged applicant with no restrictions on standing, had no formal need for a characterisation of the measure as a 'decision'.

Challenges to resolutions of the Parliament have also been declared admissible: in Case 230/81 *Luxembourg* v. *Parliament* ([1983] ECR 255) Luxembourg brought the first of a number of cases in which it has challenged resolutions concerned with the geographical relocation of the Parliament. The full range of reviewable acts is considered in 15.2.

6.15 'Soft Law'

'Soft law' has been defined as 'rules of conduct which, in principle, have no legally binding force but which nevertheless may have practical effects' (Snyder, 1993b: 32) In the EU soft law takes a multitude of forms: recommendations and opinions (which are explicitly recognised by Article 249 EC), as well as 'communications', 'conclusions', 'declarations', 'action programmes' and 'communiqués'. In recent years, particularly since the advent of the subsidiarity principle, the EU has resorted to regulation through soft law, in preference to binding measures such as directives or regulations. Moreover, the role of these types of measures should be seen as part of a general shift in administrative or regulatory culture, in which the EU is by no means isolated from other regulatory authorities, such as states (Snyder, 1994). On this view, soft law is being used 'to embrace those features of a mature legal system which give that system its flexibility and dynamic character' (Beveridge and Nott, 1998: 290). On the other hand, it is a term and a concept 'borrowed' from international law, and as such it is often thought to bring its strongly intergovernmentalist heritage with it (Beveridge and Nott, 1998: 288).

The contents of such measures may be used as persuasive guides to interpretation of other measures adopted by the EU or the Member States, and may influence the conduct of those parties (Wellens and Borchardt, 1989). We shall see in 12.15 that the Court has held that EU soft law measures may need to be used by national courts for the purposes of interpreting national legislation (see Case C-322/88 *Grimaldi* v. *Fonds des Maladies Professionnelles* [1989] ECR 4407). On the other hand, the Court has always consistently held that soft law measures cannot prevail where they contradict other 'hard' measures. The Court has reached that conclusion twice in recent years in relation to one particular form of soft law which is distinct from the types of published measures cited above, namely 'entries' in the margins of Council minutes. This technique is often used as a way of defusing political tensions surrounding the adoption of particularly contentious measures by the Council (see 5.9) (Case C-292/89 *R* v. *Immigration Appeal Tribunal, ex parte Antonissen* [1991] ECR I-745; Case C-25/94 *Commission* v. *Council (FAO)* ([1996] ECR I-1469). What was at issue in the *FAO* case was an inter-institutional agreement on voting within an international organisation, the Food and Agriculture Organisation (7.13). This highlights a type of measure which is capable of having internal binding effects within the EU legal order but may have no impact on the national legal orders in the manner that regulations, directives and decisions, as well as Treaty provisions, will often do. In that case, the Council had inserted an entry in its minutes stating that notwithstanding the decision to allow the Member States to exercise their voting rights in the FAO Council in that particular case, it had not by that means resolved questions relating to future voting rights or issues of competence under the Agreement thereby to be concluded in the FAO. The Court held on the contrary that the decision on the exercise of the voting rights in relation to the conclusion of the Agreement did have a future 'message' to third parties about the scope of Community competence. The Council could not deny that by reference to its statement in the minutes which could not be read into the text of the decision.

Another notable feature of EU soft law has been its progressive nature. Where a policy field lies at the margins of Community competence, the evolution of a common Community policy may well shift from the soft to the hard over a period of time, with non-binding measures such as those cited above forming a useful prelude to the adoption of more rigorous measures. Such a development has taken place in the field of vocational training. Less positively, soft law can also be the refuge of the Council when it is unable to agree upon binding measures. This has occurred in particular in the social policy field, where some of the proposals put forward by the Commission under the Social Action Programme agreed in 1974 (see 2.9) were watered down from directives to recommendations.

6.16   The Case Law of the Court of Justice and the Court of First Instance

Although the task of the two EU Courts is to interpret and not to make the law, and although the Courts themselves are not bound by their own previous decisions, it is none the less true that in a practical sense the case law of the Courts (especially that of the Court of Justice) is an important source of law within the jurisdiction of EU law. We have noted already the unwritten general principles which the Court of Justice has distilled from national and international traditions as being 'inherent' in the EU legal order, as an important example of the contribution of that case law to 'making' EU law (see Chapter 9). EU case law is, of course, binding upon national courts; nowhere is this clearer than in the UK where s.3(1) of the European Communities Act 1972 states:

'any question as to the meaning or effect of any of the Treaties, or as to the validity, meaning or effect of any Community instrument, shall be treated as a question of law (and, if not referred to the European Court, be for determination as such in accordance with the principles laid down by and any relevant decision of the European Court or any court attached thereto).'

Following the case law of the Court of Justice is made easier by the fact that the Court is generally consistent in its judgments, and, since 1973, has frequently referred to its earlier judgments as one, or even the sole line of argument in a subsequent judgment. The various phrases used by the Court to indicate that a case is located within an established line of case law reveal on occasion an element of impatience that a particular point is not in fact seen as established law. Thus it sometimes states '... as the Court has repeatedly held ... ' (Koopmans, 1991a: 504).

The element of *stare decisis* in EC law has now become so strong that when the Court occasionally changes its mind it makes it clear that it is doing so (e.g. Case C-70/88 *Parliament* v. *Council (Chernobyl)* [1990] ECR I-2041 in which the Court reversed its finding in Case 302/87 *Parliament* v. *Council (Comitology)* [1988] ECR 5615 that the Parliament did not have standing under what is now Article 230 EC to challenge the acts of other institutions) (see Arnull, 1993, 1999a).

Summary

1 The EU is a divided power system subject to the principle of limited powers.

2 Principles of exclusive competence and implied powers assist the EU institutions in making full use of the powers conferred upon them. Article 308 EC provides the institutions with a broad general law-making power to pursue the objectives of the EC Treaty.

3 These principles operate in the internal and external spheres alike.

4 The principles of subsidiarity and proportionality enshrined in Article 5 EC provide a test for ascertaining the legality of EU measures adopted in the area of shared competences.

5 In principle, powers may be delegated to the Commission acting with a committee system, to agencies, or to private parties to carry out certain tasks of implementation of policy.

6 The basic conditions for the legality of EU acts are a statement of reasons, a valid and correct legal basis, and respect for the principles of subsidiarity and proportionality and other EU legal principles.

7 Democratic input into and control over the policy-making process in the EU is represented by a patchwork of complementary measures. A parliamentary model is difficult to apply to the EU.

8 The following are the main sources of EU law:
   – the constitutive treaties and other international instruments binding the EU;
   – general principles of law;
   – the acts of the institutions, including where relevant, non-binding measures (soft law);
   –the case law of the Court of Justice.

Questions

1   Why is the concept of competence important? How limited is the competence of the EU?

2   What have been the most important innovations in the area of external relations to facilitate effective action on the part of the EU?

3   Where do you think the EU's democratic deficit is chiefly located?

4   What are the important features which distinguish regulations, directives and decisions.

5   Using the material discussed in this and earlier chapters identify some examples of creative 'law making' by the Court of Justice. Would you agree with the argument that the Court sometimes oversteps the limits of acceptable judicial interventionism?

Further Reading

F. Beveridge and S. Nott (1998), 'A Hard Look at Soft Law', in Craig and Harlow (1998).

G. de Búrca (1999a), 'Reappraising Subsidiarity's Significance after Amsterdam', Harvard Jean Monnet Working Paper no. 8/99.

M. Cremona (1999), 'External Relations and External Competence: The Emergence of an Integrated Policy', in Craig and de Búrca (1999).

R. Dehousse (1994b), 'Community Competences: Are there Limits to Growth?', in Dehousse (1994a).

D. McGoldrick (1997), Chs. 3–5.

F. Snyder (1994), 'Soft Law and Institutional Practice in the European Community', in Martin (1994).

S. Weatherill (1994), 'Beyond Pre-emption? Shared Competence and Constitutional Change in the European Community', in O'Keeffe and Twomey (1994).

S. Weatherill (1995a), Ch. 5, 'Pre-emption and Competence in a Wider and Deeper Union'.

7 Legislative, Administrative and Budgetary Procedures

7.1 Introduction

This chapter examines the various processes of decision making provided by and under the Treaties. The EC Treaty in particular lays down an extraordinary number of different instances where a decision can or must be taken, primarily but not solely by the Council. These decisions are to be taken according to the processes set out in the Treaties, and again there is an extraordinary variety. Nor is there a single *legislative* process for the adoption of legislative acts under the EU Treaties, which the Commission has recently defined as 'rules of general scope, based directly on the Treaty and which determine the fundamental principles or general guidelines for any Community action' (Commission, 2000d: 26). Indeed, nowhere in the Treaties is the *legislative* power as such strictly separated from other aspects of decision making, although in Article 207(3) EC the Council is required, for the purposes of transparency, to determine those cases in which it is acting in a legislative capacity. The Commission's Report to the Reflection Group for the 1996–97 IGC identified 22 different decision-making processes, highlighting a situation of excessive complexity which has not been reduced since that time. A complete picture of decision-making processes can only be derived from a detailed study of the Treaties. This chapter concentrates on legislative, certain executive rule-making and budgetary procedures.

7.2 Varieties of Legislative and Decision-Making Processes

There are three basic patterns to which the majority of provisions in the EC Treaty which grant a decision-making power to the Council of Ministers conform, and each of these is relevant to the adoption of *legislation*. The simplest procedure involves the Council acting, either by a qualified majority, or unanimously, on a proposal from the Commission, and after consulting, where required, the Parliament and/or the Economic and Social Committee (ECOSOC). This model dates from the original Treaty of Rome, but is still used for certain provisions, and has been introduced in new areas of competence where the Member States have sought to minimise parliamentary input or maintain maximum national control. It is termed here the 'old procedure', and is discussed in 7.3. It could also be termed the single reading procedure, although there are variants in which the Parliament is not consulted at all. The Single European Act introduced the cooperation procedure and this is examined in 7.4. It is largely of historical interest outside the field of EMU. It was retained for EMU by the Treaty of Amsterdam because those provisions were treated as politically untouchable and so could not be 'modernised' alongside much of the rest of the Treaty. It will presumably disappear in due course, most probably after the 2000 IGC. Most recently, the Treaty of Maastricht introduced what is popularly termed 'Council–Parliament co-decision', a form of joint legislative action by the Council and the Parliament. This is discussed in 7.5. In 7.6 the small number of cases where the assent of the Parliament is required will be discussed. Finally, in 7.7, a fourth form of legislative process is discussed, namely the use of the social dialogue between management and labour for the purpose of elaborating framework agreements which are subsequently turned into binding legislation by the Council. The section of the chapter on legislative processes moves to a conclusion with a review of the processes and of 'post-Maastricht' approaches to legislating.

Both the cooperation and co-decision models, as with most cases under the 'old' procedure, require the Commission to initiate legislation. The right of proposal is important. The Commission maintains considerable control over the proposal until its adoption or rejection by the Council. This is confirmed by Article 250 EC. The Commission may amend its proposal at any point during the law-making process, and the Council requires unanimity in order to amend a Commission proposal, except in certain limited circumstances under the co-decision procedure, where the matter is before the Conciliation Committee (7.5). In Case 355/87 *Commission* v. *Council (Italo-Algerian Maritime Transport)* ([1989] ECR 1517) the Commission objected to what it saw as the abuse of the Council's right of amendment. It argued that the Council had reversed the effect of its proposal. The Court found for the Council by holding on the facts that both the measure adopted and the proposal were designed to achieve the same objective, without ruling on the greatly differing submissions made by the two institutions on the scope of the right of amendment. The Commission can, of course, prevent the Council from adopting an amended version of its proposal to which it objects by withdrawing it from consideration, although under the revised co-decision procedure, the Commission does to a much greater extent lose control of its proposal. There are some provisions requiring the Council to act on a *recommendation* from the Commission, especially in the area of EMU (e.g. Article 99 EC regarding the broad guidelines of economic policy). This technique has clearly been adopted to give the Commission input into the legislative process, but no 'ownership' of a proposal.

Away from the legislative process, there is a minority of decision-making powers under the Treaties which differ significantly from these patterns;

these are generally, but not solely, concerned with the institutional configuration of the Union, and with arrangements relating to Economic and Monetary Union. For example, the Council has some powers to adopt legal measures without the need, apparently, for the participation of any of the other institutions in the decision-making process. Two examples are Articles 284 EC, which requires the Council to lay down the conditions under which the Commission may collect any information and carry out checks required for the performance of the tasks with which it has been entrusted, and Article 290 EC, under which the Council shall determine by unanimity the rules governing the languages of the institutions.

Alternatively, a provision may give an institution other than the Commission the right of initiative. For example, Article 225(2) EC makes provision for the transfer of additional categories of cases to the Court of First Instance. It requires the Council to act, on the request of the Court of Justice, and after consulting the European Parliament and the Commission. Here the Commission's role is merely consultative. Likewise, it is the European Parliament which is responsible for drawing up initial proposals for parliamentary elections according to a uniform election procedure in all Member States or according to principles common to all the Member States, to be decided upon by the Council acting unanimously after obtaining the assent of the Parliament itself, although any such decision would require ratification by the Member States according to their constitutional requirements (Article 190(4) EC).

In an important innovation, under the new Title IV of the EC Treaty on visas, asylum, immigration and other matters related to the free movement of persons, a special transitional period of five years is instituted during which the right of initiative is shared between the Member States and the Commission (Article 67 EC). This is because of the origins of this Title in the old JHA third pillar and hence within the domain of intergovernmentalism. It has been criticised for watering down the supranational dimension of the decision-making procedures under the EC Treaty. Exceptions are provided in relation to measures on visas which were within the former Article 100c EC, not the JHA third pillar (Article 67(3) and (4)). After five years, the right of initiative reverts to the Commission alone, although it must continue to 'examine any request made by a Member State that it submit a proposal to the Council', and the Council – presumably on its own initiative – can decide unanimously to move all the decision-making processes under that Title to the co-decision procedure under Article 251. It must consult the European Parliament. It may also use the same procedure without initiative from the Commission to decide to adjust the controversial provisions relating to the Court of Justice under this Title (4.21). Paralleling an earlier 'bridge' between the third and first pillars instituted by the Treaty of Maastricht, Article 42 TEU now provides for the Council acting unanimously on an initiative of either the Commission or a Member State to move matters from the PJC third pillar into Title IV, and to decide upon the voting conditions after transfer. It must consult the Parliament. Such a decision has to be ratified by the Member States according to their constitutional requirements. It is, in effect, a simplified Treaty amendment procedure.

The procedures relating to closer cooperation (especially Article 11 EC) are likewise a special case with regard to their provisions on decision making (5.19).

7.3   The 'Old' Procedure

The simplest form of the old procedure involves a Commission proposal and a Council decision with no involvement by the Parliament. For example, Article 57(2) EC allows the Council, acting by a qualified majority on a proposal from the Commission to adopt measures on the movement of capital to or from third countries in relation to a number of types of transactions. If the measures introduce *restrictions* (i.e. they are a step backwards from the current level of integration), Article 57(2) requires a unanimous vote from the Council. The European Parliament has never been accorded its normal 'legislative' status in relation to external commercial policy, and has no right to be consulted in relation to measures adopted under Article 133 EC, except in the relation to the newly instituted power on the part of the Council to extend the application of Article 133 to international agreements and negotiations on services and intellectual property. In practice, the Parliament is normally consulted under an informal procedure (Luns-Westerwerp Procedure: OJ 1982 C66/68) (7.11). In the sensitive field of culture, the Council may adopt recommendations acting unanimously on a proposal from the Commission (Article 151(5) EC), although in the field of public health, such recommendations may be adopted under the same procedure by a qualified majority (Article 152(4) EC). Likewise, in an area which links the first and third pillars, namely the adoption of economic sanctions against third countries, Article 301 provides for the Council to take the necessary measures on a proposal from the Commission and acting by a qualified majority. Urgency here could dictate also the non-involvement of the Parliament.

Not infrequently, measures adopted using, for example, the cooperation procedure also make provision for certain types of technical amendments to the original measure to be adopted by the Council acting alone and by a qualified majority, on a proposal from the Commission, thus excluding the European Parliament. Since these are implementing measures, the non-consultation is more understandable, as it is for Article 26 EC, which provides for the fixing of the Common Customs Tariff duties by the Council acting by a qualified majority on a proposal from the Commission.

More frequently, consultation of the European Parliament, and/or ECOSOC, the Committee of the Regions, and in a few cases even the European Central Bank, is mandated by the Treaty. Despite all the changes introduced by the Single European Act, the Treaty of Maastricht and the Treaty of Amsterdam to the role of the Parliament as legislature, it is still the case that a remarkably high proportion of the work of Parliament comprises its involvement in these *consultation* procedures where its role is merely advisory. Examples include cases of both qualified majority voting and unanimity in the Council. The old-style procedure retains a strong attraction for the Member States as evidenced by a number of fresh instances introduced by the Treaties of Maastricht and Amsterdam. Examples include:

- Article 175(2) EC, which provides for some measures in the field of the environment (e.g. those of a fiscal nature) to be adopted by the Council acting unanimously on a proposal from the Commission and after consulting the Parliament and the ECOSOC;
- Article 19(1) and (2) EC which provides for the laying down of the detailed arrangements for the exercise of citizenship voting rights by Council unanimity after consulting the Parliament;
- Article 13 EC which introduced a law-making power to be exercised by unanimity by the Council, after consulting the Parliament, to adopt measures to combat discrimination based on sex, racial or ethnic origin, religion or belief, disability, age or sexual orientation;
- Article 137(2) EC which provides a law-making power in the social policy field in relation to certain matters where there is greater Member State sensitivity, such as social security and social protection or the employment conditions of lawfully resident third country nationals, again mandating just consultation of the Parliament;
- Article 172 EC which provides for the establishment of joint undertakings or other structures necessary for the efficient execution of EU programmes in the field of research and technological development, after consultation of the Parliament.

The old style procedure is also employed for another simplified Treaty amendment procedure akin to that discussed in 7.2. Article 22 EC can be used for the purposes of extending the rights of citizens of the Union laid down in Part II of the Treaty. Here, unlike Article 42 TEU, the Council acts unanimously *on a proposal from the Commission*, after consulting the Parliament.

The old style is used for two of the Treaty's important general law-making powers, Articles 94 and 308 EC, which both require a unanimous decision of the Council. There are still instances within the core of the EC Treaty's provisions relating to the establishment of the internal market where the old style procedure is used in conjunction with a qualified majority (Article 37 EC – agricultural policy; Article 52 – liberalisation of specific services; Article 133 EC – external trade policy), but in most instances law-making powers requiring only a qualified majority in the Council were altered by the SEA to increase parliamentary input from consultation to cooperation.

Consultation of the Parliament or other bodies means just that; there is no obligation on the part of the Council to follow the opinion. However, the Council must actually receive the opinion, not simply ask for it (Case 138/79 *Roquette Frères* v. *Council (Isoglucose)* [1980] ECR 3333). A measure adopted by the Council before it receives the Parliament's opinion can be annulled for breach of an essential procedural requirement; but the fact that the Council definitively adopts a measure just five days after receiving the Parliament's opinion in circumstances where it has indicated that there is a degree of urgency and the Parliament itself has taken several months over delivering the opinion does not of itself make that consultation a 'sham' (Case C-417/93 *Parliament* v. *Council (TACIS)* [1995] ECR I-1185).

None the less, the Parliament must normally be given sufficient time to adopt its opinion; this can take some time, since the draft opinion is first worked on within the Parliament's committee structure, before it comes to the plenary session for adoption. In one case the Court of Justice was asked to consider the impact of 'urgency' on the consultation process: must the Council always wait for the Parliament to deliver its opinion? The answer is 'not always'. Case C-65/93 *Parliament* v. *Council (Generalised Tariff Preferences)* ([1995] ECR I-643) involved a proposal to extend into 1993 the 1992 system of generalised tariff preferences, which was sent to the Parliament on 22 October 1992. The Council requested urgency, and the Parliament accepted this request, setting the matter down for debate and decision at a plenary session on 18 December 1992. However, the session was adjourned before the matter could be discussed, and since there was no possibility of reconvening an emergency Parliament session before the end of the year, the Council went ahead and adopted the Regulation on 21 December 1992 in order to meet the end-of-year deadline. The Parliament failed in its action for annulment, since, although there had been no consultation in a formal sense, the Parliament itself had failed to observe the essential duty of 'sincere cooperation' which structures inter-institutional relationships, as much as it does those between the Member States and the institutions. Consequently, the Parliament was not entitled to complain of the Council's failure to await its opinion before adopting the contested Regulation.

As this shows, effective consultation always depends on the goodwill of the parties. Relations between the Council and the Parliament are not perfect. Despite the *Roquette* case, the Parliament regularly documents instances where the Council takes at least a preliminary decision before receiving the Parliament's opinion, although its failure to win the *TACIS* case may indicate that it has little hope of successfully taking action before the Court on this matter. The Council does reconsult the Parliament in cases where it proposes to change the legal basis of a measure, in particular where this changes the procedure under which it is adopted. An example is provided by the Titanium Dioxide Directive which gave rise to litigation discussed in 7.18, where the legal basis was changed from what was then Article 100a EEC (internal market – then cooperation procedure) to what was then Article 130s EEC (environment – then simple consultation).

Reconsultation must likewise occur where the Council departs markedly from the text on which the Parliament has given its opinion. The Court has expressed the requirement to reconsult thus:

> '[The duty to consult] includes a requirement that the Parliament be reconsulted on each occasion when the text finally adopted, viewed as a whole, departs substantially from the text on which the Parliament has already been consulted, except where the amendments essentially correspond to the wishes of the Parliament itself' (Case C-388/92 *Parliament v. Council* [1994] ECR I-2067 at p. 2085).

This point has been tested in a quite few cases arising in the field of road transport policy, beginning with Case C-65/90 *Parliament* v. *Council (Cabotage Regulation)* ([1992] ECR I-4593) where the Court held that where there was a lapse of three years between the Parliamentary opinion and the adoption of the regulation, and the Council had adopted a substantially different proposal, reconsultation was required. In a case such as *Harmonised Road Taxes* (Case C-21/94 *Parliament* v. *Council* [1995] ECR I-1827), where the Parliament went back as far as 1989 to identify a Directive on the harmonisation of road transport taxes which was adopted on the basis of a text substantially different to the one on which an opinion was given, it was through its actions making little concrete difference to the policies which are being adopted. Instead the Parliament was giving notice of its serious intention to ensure the protection of its prerogatives, however uncomfortable that might be for both the Council and the Commission in a sensitive and highly politicised field like road transport.

7.4 The Cooperation Procedure

For future reference, the procedure dealt with in this paragraph is likely to of essentially historical interest only. Since the ratification of the Treaty of Amsterdam, its usage is confined to policy on EMU and it can be anticipated that in the future it will be eliminated in this area also. None the less it is important for several reasons, related to the fact that it was the procedure on which the Parliament 'cut its teeth' as a 'serious' legislator, and first began the process of learning to use intensified input into the legislative process as an opportunity to have a real influence upon the pattern and content of policy making. Hence studies on how the Parliament learnt to use the cooperation procedure to its fullest effect will continue to be relevant both in explaining the history of the Parliament but also in understanding its orientation towards the co-decision procedure (e.g. Westlake, 1994; Earnshaw and Judge, 1993, 1997). As Earnshaw and Judge (1997: 561) put it:

'The operation of the co-operation procedure provided Parliament with the opportunity to revise its internal rules both to maximise its legislative impact, and also to demonstrate its wider legislative "responsibility"'.

It thus created the expectation of more institutional innovation, leading on to greater parliamentary involvement. In essence, the introduction of the cooperation procedure appended a second reading of proposed legislation in the European Parliament onto the existing consultation procedure. This not only gave the Parliament a 'second bite at the cherry' in the process of formulating EU legislation, but it also involved it in a more complex interactive process with the Council, with the Commission in the middle. The details of the cooperation procedure, originally introduced by Articles 6 and 7 SEA and now to be found in Article 252 EC, are set out in Figure 7.1.

The principal law-making powers in the EEC Treaty covered by the cooperation procedure after the adoption of the Single European Act included Article 100a (measures for the completion of the internal market) Articles 49, 54(2), 56(2) and 57 (measures for the achievement of free movement of workers, providers of services and the self-employed), and Article 118a (health and safety of workers). The Treaty of Maastricht began the process of 'upgrading' many of these powers to co-decision, but also added more in the form of measures relating to the achievement and management of EMU. After the Treaty of Amsterdam, all extant cooperation procedure powers were further 'upgraded', leaving only five powers under the EMU provisions. Table 7.1 sets these out.

Table 7.1   The Cooperation Procedure under Article 252 EC

EC Treaty Article	Nature of power
99	Multilateral surveillance of economic policies to ensure closer coordination
102(2)	Equal access to financial institutions
103(2)	(a) Prohibition on overdraft facilities at ECB or national central banks and (b) non-assumption of liabilities of Member States
106(2)	Issuing of coins

The introduction of the cooperation procedure was important because it revealed the first signs of Council accountability to the Parliament. The Council has the obligation under Article 252(b) EC to inform the Parliament of the reasons which led it to adopt its common position. The Parliament has objected on numerous occasions that the Council has adopted a cavalier attitude towards this vitally important aspect of the cooperation procedure.

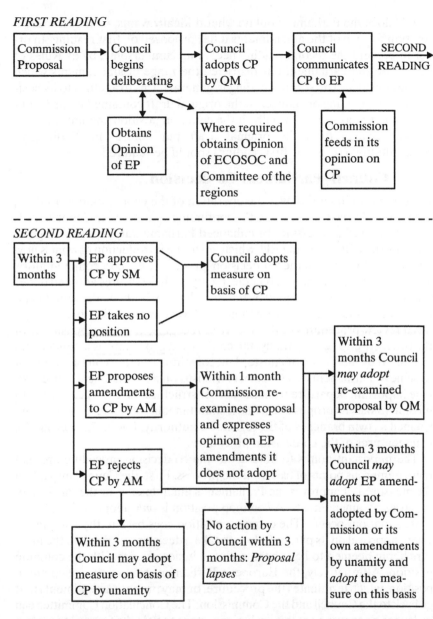

Figure 7.1   The Cooperation Procedure – Article 252 EC

Rarely does the Parliament obtain what it ideally wants, namely a specific reaction to each of the amendments it has proposed on first reading. In order to prevent the second reading becoming cumbersome, by its Rules of Procedure the Parliament has restricted the range of amendments which can be considered on second reading in general terms to a return to its position on first reading or changes to the original draft contained in the Council's common position. Formally, if the common position amounts to a significant change from the original draft put before the Parliament, reconsultation (i.e. a new first reading) should be required.

7.5   Council–Parliament Co-decision

It was in part difficulties over the operation of the cooperation procedure, such as the absence of a veto and the continuing opacity of the Council's procedures, as well as pressure for enhanced Parliamentary input as a sign of the maturity of the evolving EU, which led to the introduction of what is now Article 251 EC, termed the 'co-decision' procedure by most commentators. This is a 'term of art', not used in the Treaty itself. Measures adopted under the new procedures are signed by the Presidents of both the Parliament and the Council, and consequent amendments have been introduced into the judicial review procedures of the Treaty to recognise the co-responsibility of the two institutions. Essentially, the co-decision procedure as amended and simplified by the Treaty of Amsterdam constitutes a more complex attempt to achieve Parliament and Council consensus on a common legislative text. One important departure from the earlier structures is that when the Commission makes its proposal it sends it simultaneously to the Parliament and Council as twin branches of the legislative authority. Figure 7.2 sets out the main features of the co-decision procedure.

The important points to note about the co-decision procedure are that there numerous points of exit from the process. First, the Council may adopt the measure if it approves the Parliament's amendments, or the Parliament proposes no amendments. A common position is *only* adopted if neither of those situations occurs. The common position goes back to the Parliament, where approval on its part or failure to take a decision will result in the measure being deemed to have been adopted in accordance with the common position. Alternatively, the European Parliament may reject the common position, which terminates the procedure, or may propose amendments that go back to the Council and the Commission. The Conciliation Committee can no longer be convened at this preliminary stage to help the Council to explain its position to avert rejection of the Common Position. It was an option little used. Still in the second reading, the Council can approve the amendments to the common position, with the procedure depending upon the Commission's position on the Parliament's further amendments. Alternatively, together with the President of the Parliament, the Presidency may convene the

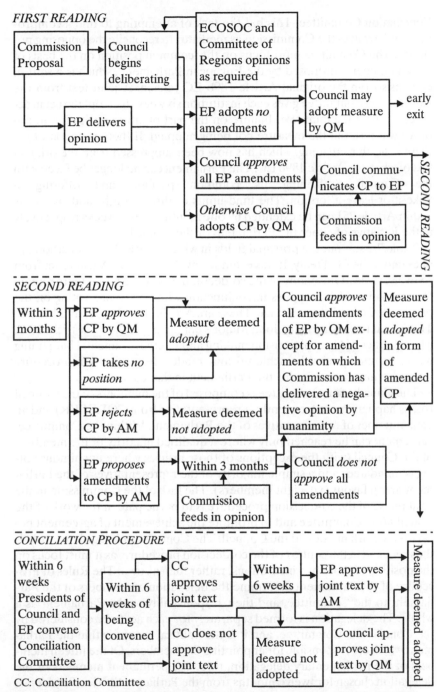

Figure 7.2 Council/European Parliament Co-decision – Article 251 EC

Conciliation Committee. This has the task of attempting to find a compromise and involves the Commission as mediator to reconcile the opposing positions. The Committee must focus on the 'common position on the basis of the amendments proposed by the European Parliament', which is a shift in emphasis from the original Article 189b EC version. A joint text from the Conciliation Committee gives each institution six weeks to adopt the act in accordance with the joint text. Failure on the part of either institution to approve will result in the measure not being adopted. If there is no joint text, there is no third reading, which has now been suppressed from the original text of what was Article 189b EC. The Parliament can no longer be faced with the Council confirming its common position and offering a 'take-it-or-leave-it' option. The time limits of three months and six weeks within Article 251 can be extended by one month and two weeks respectively at the initiative of either the Parliament or the Council.

Table 7.2 sets out the principal fields in which Article 251 co-decision applies under the EC Treaty. It was extended by the Treaty of Amsterdam from 15 to 38 articles. One oddity of the co-decision procedure is that there remain four fields in which it applies in conjunction with *unanimous* voting on the part of the Council at every stage. These are Articles 18, 42(5), 47 and 151 EC. This is said to be a legacy of John Major's bargaining at the Maastricht IGC. The rigidities of Council decision making and intergovernmental bargaining where unanimity must be achieved may render the co-decision procedure rather a fruitless exercise for the Parliament in that context.

The Conciliation Committee is composed of the members of the Council (or, as happens more frequently, a representative from COREPER) and an equal number of representatives of the Parliament. Within the Committee, agreement can be reached only where a qualified majority of the members of the Council (with the exceptions of those articles where unanimous voting is mandated) and a simple majority of the representatives of the Parliament are in favour (i.e. eight members). The task of the Commission in the final phase of the co-decision procedure is to participate in the work of the Conciliation Committee and to promote the achievement of agreement between the Parliament and the Council. The Commission's legislative role is thus reduced in the context of the co-decision procedure, as it must focus on the position of those two institutions, rather than its own. The Rules of Procedure of the Parliament determine the delegation of members of the Parliament to the Committee, and their responsibility to the Parliament as a whole. The delegation is formed separately for each act to be considered by the Conciliation Committee, and it is the political groups within the Parliament which are responsible for appointing the members. Of the fifteen members of the parliamentary delegation, three are permanent members of the delegation chosen for twelve months from the Parliament's Vice-Presidents, two are the Chair and rapporteur of the parliamentary committee responsible for the legislation, and the remaining ten are chosen from the members of the various parliamentary committees responsible for the legislation.

Table 7.2 The Co-decision Procedure under Article 251 EC

Note: inclusion of a policy area in this list does not indicate that every measure can be adopted using the Article 251 procedure. In other cases, the 'old procedure' may apply.

EC Treaty Article	*Nature of power*
12	Measures to prohibit discrimination on grounds of EU nationality
18	Implementation of right of residence (subject to other provisions in the Treaty)
40, 42, 44, 46(2), 47(1) and (2)	Aspects of the achievement of free movement of workers and services and freedom of establishment
67(2)	After five years from May 1999, Council may adopt co-decision for certain Title IV measures
67(4)	After five years from May 1999, certain aspects of measures on visas
71	Common transport policy
95	Internal market
129	Employment incentive measures
135	Customs cooperation
137	Certain areas of social policy
141	Equality of men and women
148	Implementing decisions for European Social Fund
149	Education: incentive measures
150	Vocational training policy
151	Culture
152	Public health
153	Consumer protection
156	Trans-European networks
162	Implementing decisions for the European Regional Development Fund
166, 172	Research and technological development multi-annual framework programme
175(1) and (3)	Some environmental measures
179	Development cooperation
255	Implementation of access to documents provision
280	The fight against fraud and protection of EU's financial interests
285	Collection of statistics

The details of the work of the Conciliation Committee were established following an inter-institutional conference held in Luxembourg in October 1993, involving all three political institutions. The arrangements are contained in an inter-institutional agreement of 25 October 1993 on 'the phase preceding the adoption of a common position by the Council and on the arrangements for the proceedings of the Conciliation Committee under Article 189B' (OJ 1993 C331/1). These arrangements determine that the chair at meetings of the Conciliation Committee is shared between the Presidency of the Council and the President (or Vice-President) of the Parliament. The Committee is also serviced jointly by the secretariats of the two institutions. It meets in camera, and seeks, within six weeks, to draw up a joint text representing a compromise version of the legislation over which the two institutions have disagreed. In practice, up to 130 persons could be present at a meeting, if all assistants and other participants were present, and so the practice grew up of informal preparation of Conciliation Committee meetings involving a trialogue of the chair and rapporteur of the relevant Committee of the Parliament, the chair of COREPER and the responsible Director-General or Deputy-General of the Commission (Neuhold, 2000). This was institutionalised after the Spanish Presidency in 1995.

The Parliament retained a veto under the first version of the co-decision procedure, although it was used sparingly. Of 275 draft legislative acts submitted to the Parliament under co-decision up to March 1999, 177 were adopted. Two cases failed as no agreement was reached in the Conciliation Committee and only in the case of the legal protection of biotechnological inventions in March 1995 did the Parliament in plenary reject a compromise agreement. According to Peterson and Bomberg (1999: 218–9), what the rejection of that draft directive showed was the relative indiscipline of the Parliament's political groupings when faced with vigorous lobbying by environmentalists and others on the emotive issue of gene patenting for specific biotechnological processes, the lack of expertise and technical support within the Parliament which meant that the Parliament found it hard to decide what was safe, and – equally – that there are powerful pressures for uniform legislation within EU hi-tech industries. Thus eventually in 1998 a modified version of the directive was adopted.

The introduction of the co-decision procedure was very much the result of political compromise. Even so, and despite the intense complexity of the procedures introduced and the consequential criticism that it received from commentators, experiences with co-decision have been largely judged positively (e.g. Boyron, 1998). There has been a marked intensification of dialogue between the Parliament and the Council, with contacts now in relation to every legal act under consideration at the level of Council Working Groups and European Parliament rapporteur, as well as COREPER chair and chair of the relevant Parliament Committee. During the latter half of

1999, after the entry into force of the Treaty of Amsterdam, some initial evidence regarding the simplification of the co-decision procedure emerged. Four legal acts were concluded at the very first reading, taking advantage of the early exit points from the process (Neuhold, 2000: 6). This could be said to be a small number, since figures from November 1993 until June 1999 indicated that 55 per cent of procedures could have been concluded after the first reading as the Parliament either did not put down any amendments, or the Council accepted all of the proposed changes.

Christopher Lord's assessment on co-decision and democracy in the EU is worth quoting extensively. He assumes:

> 'first, that Union legislation will often be instigated (but not formally initiated) by governments with pressing and particular needs they want addressed at the Union level; secondly, that the commitment of governments to decision-making by consensus means that decisions have to be painstakingly negotiated in the Council; and, thirdly, there will, accordingly, be a sunk investment of around one to two years of intergovernmental negotiation before a proposal enters a final showdown with the Parliament under the co-decision procedure. What this means is that Council members will have a strong incentive to adopt an accommodating attitude to parliamentary amendments, rather than risk an outright rejection by the EP: not only would they lose a great deal of time by 'returning to go', they might not even be sure of obtaining a new intergovernmental agreement under constantly shifting conditions of domestic politics. Knowing that the EP will be powerful in the 'end game', the Council might even attempt to anticipate parliamentary opinion from the early stages of its own bargaining process' (Lord, 1998: 63).

As the co-decision procedure could be said to provide the Commission with an incentive to behave in the same way (see Peterson and Bomberg, 1999), this effectively turns the EU into a 'strongly bicameral' legislature, at least in comparison with many of the national democracies of Western Europe (Lord, 1998: 64; see also Dehousse, 1998b on the parliamentary model as the basis for the EU).

7.6 The Assent Procedure

There has been a gradual increase in the number of fields in which the assent of the Parliament is required before a specific measure can be adopted. This procedure was first introduced in relation to Association Agreements and the accession of new Member States under the Single European Act, and has now been extended to 'legislative' fields outside external relations (see Table 7.3). In all cases except Article 190(4) EC on the uniform or common electoral procedure and Article 49 TEU on the accession of new Member States, where an absolute majority of component members is required, assent requires a simple majority of members present and voting. A double requirement is imposed on the parliamentary assent under Article 7 TEU, which provides for measures to be taken against a Member State which has acted in serious and persistent breach of the principles laid down in Article 6(1) TEU, namely absolute majority, *plus* two-thirds of the votes cast.

Table 7.3   The Requirement of Parliamentary Assent

EC Treaty Article	Nature of Power	Nature of majority
105(6)	Granting to ECB of tasks relating to the prudential supervision of credit and other financial institutions	Simple
107(5)	Amendments to Statute of the ECB	Simple
161	Definition of the tasks, priority objectives and organisation of the Structural Funds	Simple
190(4)	Electoral procedure for the Parliament	Absolute
300(3)	Association agreements and other international agreements establishing a specific institutional framework, with significant budgetary implications or entailing the adoption of an act falling to be adopted under Article 251 (co-decision)	Simple
TEU Article		
7	Determination of the existence of a serious and persistent breach by a Member State of the principles of Article 6(1) TEU	Absolute, plus two-thirds of votes cast
49	Accession of new Member States	Absolute

7.7 Legislation and the Social Dialogue

By Articles 138 and 139 EC, instituted by the Treaty of Amsterdam, the social partners have been elevated to the 'role of political and institutional actors in the decision-making process' (Szyszczak, 1999: 148). Alongside the move to qualified majority voting and the use of the co-decision procedure for many (but not all) fields of social law and labour law policy making which social lawyers had long clamoured for (Article 137 EC), the EC Treaty now containsa mechanism whereby the representatives of management and labour meeting within the social dialogue under Article 138 EC can adopt contractual agreements under Article 139 EC, and a special simplified procedure exists for these to be turned into EU level legislation. So far as the agreements are covered by the scope of the competence laid out in Article 137, the parties may make a joint request for the Commission to make a proposal and for the Council to adopt a decision giving legal effect to the agreement (by qualified majority or unanimity, as appropriate, depending upon the matter covered). This is the procedure originally included in the Social Policy Agreement appended to the Treaty of Maastricht, which was the basis for some social policy making – minus the UK – between 1993 and 1999. One issue is that not all representatives of labour and management are involved in the bargaining process. The *UEAPME* case (Case T-135/96 *UEAPME* v. *Council* [1998] ECR II-2335) involved a challenge by a federation representing small and medium sized employers against the Parental Leave Directive, based on their non-inclusion in the social dialogue. There is no requirement that the dialogue need be inclusive, and the Court of First Instance upheld the approach to assessing the representativity of the parties used by the Council and the Commission, finding the action inadmissible (6.9). This procedure operates in addition to 'conventional' law-making processes in Article 137 EC.

7.8 Common Foreign and Security Policy (CFSP) and Police and Judicial Cooperation in Criminal Matters (PJC)

There are no 'legislative' processes under the second and third pillars of the EU in the sense in which we have discussed here the various structures under the EC Treaty and the different types of inputs which the institutions may make. The processes are largely, but not entirely intergovernmental in nature, with most direct inputs coming from the Member States and structured through the institutional framework of the Council, the European Council and, especially, the Presidency. The 'outputs' of the policy-making processes, although capable of having binding effect in certain circumstances, are not subject in the same way to the jurisdiction of the Court of

Justice, although the position has evolved somewhat with regard to the third pillar since the Treaty of Amsterdam (4.21).

The policy-making process in the context of CFSP is principally based on processes of mutual information and consultation among the Member States leading, in appropriate cases, to coordination of international action, the taking of common positions and the adoption of joint actions. The default voting arrangement is unanimity. QMV may be used as the basis for votes in the context of joint actions under Article 23(2) TEU. For the purposes of ensuring continued cooperation between the Member States, the Political Committee (4.11) plays a key role. The European Council and the Presidency – again representing in various ways the interests of the Member States – also play key roles in the processes. The former determines general guidelines of policy and common strategies to be implemented by the EU (Article 13 TEU), and the latter has a representative role (Article 18 TEU), the task of negotiating international agreements under Article 24 TEU, as well as the task of consulting the Parliament – which is consigned to a minor institutional role in the context of CFSP (Article 21 TEU). It may ask questions of the Council and make recommendations and is required to hold an annual debate on the progress in implementing the CFSP. The role of the Commission is rather more substantial: it is entitled to be 'fully associated' with the work under the CFSP (Article 27 TEU) especially with the task of representing the EU (Article 18 TEU), it can refer questions and submit proposals relating to CFSP to the Council along with the Member States (Article 22(1) TEU), and it may be involved in the negotiation of agreements under Article 24.

The provisions governing PJC represent a kind of halfway house in *institutional* terms between the first and the second pillars. On the one hand, there are strong elements of intergovernmentalism with references to a focus on 'common action among the Member States' (Article 29 TEU), a dominant role for unanimous voting (Article 34(2) TEU), a special list of types of legal act differing from the EC Treaty norm under Article 249 EC and more akin to international law soft law, and a sharing of the power of initiative between the Commission and Member States. On the other hand, there is a limited role for the Court of Justice (Article 35 TEU), limited consultation of the Parliament as an element of decision making (Article 39 TEU), and provision for Conventions once ratified by half of the Member States to come into force for those states. The European Council plays no role in this Title, other than in relation to issues of potential closer cooperation, as a backstop decision-maker. That raises the question of which institution would be the motor of policy making in those circumstances, although the default position appears to be the Council (Article 34(1)).

7.9   The Legislative Process Reviewed

Whenever there is an IGC, there are inevitably calls that this, finally, will be the occasion when some logical system is imposed upon the provisions of the EU Treaties which deal with decision making in general, and legislating in particular. Since the 2000 IGC's formal basis lies in the composition of the Commission and the weighting of votes in the Council, and only secondarily in other institutional questions needed to facilitate enlargement, it is not necessary that there should be radical change in this field. However, extended coverage is given in the Commission's Opinion, which bemoans (without being too directly critical) the fact that every time an attempt is made to impose logic on the decision-making procedures, it appears to be stymied by the Member States, such that changes are reduced to being completed on a case-by-case basis (Commission, 2000d). It can be assumed that these result from trade-offs within each IGC. In any event, it is already the case that a large proportion of the legislative measures adopted by the EU involve co-decision, and it is now the dominant mode shaping many inter-institutional interactions.

The issues which could be taken on board at a full review of the legislative and decision-making procedures at the IGC are the following (based on Commission, 2000d):

- A definition is needed of what constitutes a 'legislative act', for the purposes of delineating the most appropriate role for the Parliament.
- Recourse to Article 308 EC (which should retain unanimity as the voting procedure) could be reduced by some new specific law-making powers, e.g. in the area of energy policy.
- Adoption of qualified majority voting as the default position for legislative acts and most other decisions in the Council; several means for promoting this might be adopted:
  - In some cases the price of moving from unanimity to qualified majority voting may be the acceptance of the 'double qualified majority' used in the second and third pillars; this is a specified number of weighted votes in the Council, plus a minimum number of Member States voting in favour;
  - An alternative means of encouraging the Member States to include more qualified majority voting in the Treaty might be to accept a greater role for the European Council in the decision-making process in appropriate cases, just as it has in relation to EMU and employment policy;
  - Some areas of unanimous voting such as social security and taxation should be subdivided, with only those issues which are not, for example, directly related to the proper functioning of the internal market remaining under unanimity.

- Quasi-constitutional decisions, such as those under Articles 22 or 190(4) EC requiring national ratification should continue to be adopted unanimously.
- Co-decision between the Parliament and the Council should become the default position for legislative acts.
- An important step would be the removal of the anomaly which combines co-decision with unanimity in the Council (7.5).

It must be concluded that while the legislative processes of the European Union are now vastly different and more complex than those established in the original Treaties, they remain strongly intergovernmental in nature. Even the Court of Justice admits that the EU legislative process is 'characterised by a certain flexibility necessary for achieving a convergence of views between the institutions' (Case C-280/93 *Germany* v. *Council* [1994] ECR I-4973 at p.5054), although it does not formally admit the role of the Member States in this question. This contributes to the generally high level of secrecy which still surrounds the law-making process, and to the absence of transparency. The increase in complexity has not overcome the lack of accountability on the part of the Council for the manner and type of decisions it takes. EU legal acts are bargained for and negotiated, rather than debated openly. The Conciliation Committee has not increased openness – in that it meets in secret – although it does offer increased efficiency (arguably) and increased legitimacy (definitely) by making the Parliament into something closer to a co-legislator. Moreover, one of the practices which the Council has used over the years to 'resolve or circumnavigate difficulties and disagreements' (Nicoll, 1993: 562) is that of inserting 'entries' or declarations 'in the minutes'. Very often these are simply a way of giving some recognition to a strongly held position taken by one delegation which is not directly reflected in the formal public output of a Council meeting. Rarely are these declarations made public, and they have a very uncertain legal status. However, they do have a significant impact upon the work of the Council, one that does not enhance the status or accountability of the EU legislature. The transparency of the legislative process is only slightly enhanced by the cooperation which now occurs between Commission and Parliament in relation to the former's 'work programme' each year. This programme is now formally submitted to the Parliament, and is combined with a review of the work of the previous year (The Commission's Work Programme for 2000, COM(2000) 155; Parliament Resolution on the Commission's Annual Work Programme for 2000, 16 March 2000). Moreover, there are now several databases (*PreLex* on the Commission website and the Parliament's *Legislative Observatory*) available through the *Europa* website which make the tracking of legislative proposals easier for the outsider.

Some areas such as environmental policy or research and technological development policy still have a confusing plethora of different procedures which apply to different areas of EU activity in that field, ranging from simple parliamentary consultation to co-decision. Significant areas of Community competence are also still excluded from the more intensive Parliamentary input, including agricultural policy, many aspects of external trade policy, indirect taxation and the system of Community own resources, as well as the general legislative powers in Articles 94 and 308 EC. The general lack of agreement between the institutions on essential elements of the law-making process has resulted in a proliferation of disputes being submitted to the Court of Justice for resolution in the judicial sphere, in particular in the matter of legal basis (7.18).

The democratic deficit is only very partially offset by alternative mechanisms whereby different interests can ensure input into the legislative process (6.9). Moreover, the 'diffusion of leadership' in relation to decision making (Nugent, 1999b) means that it is difficult for interest groups to know always where to aim their efforts. Although the intensity and effectiveness of lobbying in the EU has increased dramatically since the early 1980s, it remains only a partial substitute for a 'genuinely' democratic and legitimate legislative process (Harlow, 1992b, 1999b). As the EU has grown in importance, as a policy-maker and producer of legislative outputs, so it has become the target for ever-larger numbers of lobbyists, operating through a variety of private and public channels for interest representation. In some ways, the involvement of different interests in the EU policy-making process is structured or channelled, either through ECOSOC and, more recently, the Committee of the Regions, through the Social Dialogue (7.7), or through the huge network of advisory committees where national interests are represented, often through the work of experts on whom the Commission relies quite heavily (Buitendijk and van Schendelen, 1995). There also exist numerous more or less effective European level interest representation groups, of which the best known are UNICE (representing employers and business), ETUC (representing employees and their organisations), CEEP (representing public sector enterprises), BEUC (representing consumers) and COPA (representing agricultural interests).

These groups, along with numerous other bodies such as the EC Committee of the American Chamber of Commerce (one of the most effective lobbyists), European level organisations in particular sectors (e.g. chemicals, the car industry, pharmaceuticals), individual firms, local and regional government, the voluntary sector and charities all seek to exercise influence upon the Commission, Members of the European Parliament, Council delegations and even the Economic and Social Committee (Mazey and Richardson, 1999; Greenwood, 1997). Involvement of a variety of actors in the policy process is in many ways extremely healthy; the Commission often relies upon its contacts for particular types of technical expertise. Inevitably, however, an urgent debate has arisen in recent years over the management of interest representation, to ensure some degree of fairness, probity and transparency. Progress in the management of interest representation has been slow, with the Parliament perhaps showing more willingness than the Commission to order the situation through a register of lobbyists. Some of the most concrete proposals for an informal code of conduct have come from lobbyists themselves, who are anxious not to lose credibility (see McLaughlin and Greenwood, 1995).

Even a brief discussion of the issue of private interest representation at the EU level serves to emphasise how misleading it is to analyse the legislative processes of the EU in isolation from a broader view of the policy-making process, extensively investigated by political scientists and policy analysts in particular (e.g. Peterson and Bomberg, 1999; Nugent, 1999b; Hix, 1999). The workings of supranational governance remain, in many ways, a puzzle (Sandholtz and Stone Sweet, 1998). While recalling the continuing debates between those who ascribe varying degrees of importance to the respective roles of the EU institutions and the sovereign Member States (see 1.5), it is useful to point out a growing tendency among those who concentrate upon the institutions not only to show the Commission as pivotal, in particular in its capacity to show leadership, but also to acknowledge the types of inputs into the policy-making process that the Court may have and how the process is often shaped by an interaction between the Commission and the Court. The *cause célèbre* in this context tends to be the Court's decision in *Cassis de Dijon* (Case 120/78 *Rewe-Zentrale AG* v. *Bundesmonopolverwaltung für Branntwein* [1979] ECR 649) in which it developed an important 'mutual recognition' principle in the context of the free movement of goods which played a not inconsiderable role as an underlying factor in the effectiveness of the single market programme. Another high profile example is the Court's decision in the *Philip Morris* case (Cases 142 and 156/84 *BAT and Reynolds* v. *Commission* [1987] ECR 4487) on the application of the EC competition rules to mergers between companies, which was undoubtedly an important factor in the Council reaching a long postponed agreement on a Regulation giving the Commission special powers on the supranational control of mergers (Armstrong and Bulmer, 1998).

7.10   Legislation and Policy Making Post-Maastricht: 'Simplification' and Better Law Making

As Weatherill (2000b) points out, the emphasis post-Maastricht is not 'building a market', but 'managing a market'. This has a number of causal effects upon the whole arena of legislation and policy making, not to mention many areas of implementation (7.11, 4.17). As a sea change in the way things are done, it can be closely linked to the introduction of the subsidiarity principle, which rapidly spawned as an offshoot a programme of legislative review and 'simplification' (Maher, 1995; Wainwright, 1994). The work of the Commission in this area can also be traced back to the Sutherland Report, the independent report sponsored by the Commission to examine how the full benefits of the internal market could be secured in practice after 1992 and to the Commission's White Paper on Growth, Competitiveness and Employment of 1993 (Bull. EC Supp. 6/3). The application of the subsidiarity principle questions whether the EU should legislate in certain areas at all: hence after Edinburgh, a number of proposals were withdrawn, and others were changed in nature. The Commission has also radically reduced the numbers of proposals that it makes. Subsidiarity can also be linked to transparency, and to the argument that EU legislation needs to be 'recast' or 'simplified' (and occasionally 'repealed') to make the EU more transparent and therefore accountable in its work. There has also been a programme of 'consolidation', which has occurred in areas such as customs and agricultural law where multiple amendments not always coupled with the necessary repealing measures have left an excessively complex tangle of legislative measures. Other areas to which the Commission turned its attention in the search for simplification have included the EU regulation of water, foodstuffs and vocational qualifications. Since December 1994, an Inter-Institutional Agreement between the three political institutions specifically to ensure an accelerated working method for the official codification of legislative texts has been in place (OJ 1996 C102/2) (for further details on such agreements see 7.17). The annual 'Better Law-Making' reports of the Commission deal not only with subsidiarity and proportionality, but also with the quality of drafting (on which an inter-institutional agreement was adopted in December 1998 (OJ 1998 C73/1), simplification and consolidation, as well as access to information for citizens (see COM(98) 715 and COM(99) 562).

The internal market, being a field with a marked volume of legislation, much of which was in need of codificiation, has been a prime target for law reform work. One initiative of the Commission in this area was termed the 'SLIM initiative' (Simpler Legislation for the Internal Market), formally launched in March 1996. The initiative was fine-tuned into the *Action Plan for the Single Market* (CSE(97) 1) and, most recently, the *Strategy for Europe's Internal Market* (COM(1999) 624; see also COM(1999) 464) in November 1999. Quite apart from the clear influence of the Commission's post-Prodi shift to objective-driven management (4.2), visible in the plethora of 'target actions' and 'operational and strategic objectives', the *Strategy* document is marked by a mix of proposals for legislative action, along with reports, reviews of policy, codes of conduct, handbooks, communications, dialogues and monitoring exercises which have become the characteristic modes of governance in the EU and much of which is marked by the *leitmotiv* of greater 'transparency' (Weatherill, 2000b).

7.11   **Procedure for Negotiating, Approving and Giving Effect Internally to International Agreements**

6.5 presented the nature and development of the EU's external capacity. This paragraph carries the discussion further by detailing some specific external powers, looking briefly at the procedures for negotiating, approving and giving effect internally to international agreements. A number of provisions of the EC Treaty provide explicitly for the formulation of policies in the external sphere, including those involving the conclusion of international treaties. The common commercial trade policy (Article 133 EC) is an obvious example; Title XVII of Part III (development cooperation) and Part IV of the EC Treaty (association of overseas territories and countries with special relationships with Member States, including ex-colonies and dependencies) could also usefully be cited in this context. Article 310 provides for the conclusion of associations with States or international organisations 'involving reciprocal rights and obligations, common action and special procedure'. In practice, with the parallelism of internal and external competence and the principle of implied powers, the existence or otherwise of a specific internal power is not an obstacle to external relations activity, and consequently the EU has also undertaken important initiatives in areas as varied as culture, research and technological development and the environment.

Where international agreements are to be concluded, Article 300 EC provides for a single method for negotiation and conclusion, although there are exceptions such as Article 133 EC for trade policy and Article 111 EC for EMU. Article 300, as amended by the Treaties of Maastricht and Amsterdam largely fills out 'in the light of the Council's practice, the initially somewhat meagre provisions ... on the procedure for negotiating and concluding international agreements' (Dashwood, 1999: 205). The essential structure requires the Commission to negotiate on behalf of the EC, acting under authorisation from the Council, with the Council itself concluding the agreement. In many fields the Council will act by a qualified majority, unless an equivalent internal act would require unanimity, in which case parallelism is preserved. Parallelism is not, however, the principle governing the treatment of the European Parliament, which is normally only consulted on the conclusion of agreements (Article 300(3) EC). Article 133 EC does not even provide for that, although practice has seen the Council normally consulting the Parliament. A number of exceptions are made to the normal practice, of which the most important cover agreements with important budgetary implications for the EU and agreements entailing the adoption, internally for the purposes of giving effect to the agreement, of a measure falling under the procedure of Parliament–Council co-decision. These are subject to Parliament assent, and a new arena of conflict between the Parliament and the Council has been opened up by the delimitation of those terms (7.18). The Parliament is also entitled to be informed of decisions on the provisional application or suspension of agreements, an important right as the simplified procedure noted below operates by way of derogation from the Parliament's consultation rights.

The Treaty of Amsterdam fleshed out some issues that had previously not been covered specifically by the Treaty. Notably, it highlights the role of a decision of the Council in concluding the agreement (although a more informal process involving mere signature may also be used), and allows for the Council to decide upon the provisional application of international agreements pending ratification (Article 300(2) EC). Normally, the decision is published, with the agreement attached to it (e.g. Council Decision approving the results of the Uruguay Round on behalf of the Community, Decision 94/800 OJ 1994 L336/1). That same subparagraph sets up a 'simplified procedure' (Dashwood, 1999: 207) which is especially useful for decisions to suspend the application of an agreement (e.g. for breach of human rights conditionality clauses by other party) and decisions in relation to the position to be taken by the EU in decision-making bodies (such as Association Councils) established under international agreements (on the effects of their decisions, see 12.10).

In terms of ensuring the constitutionality of external actions, Article 300(5) confirms the obvious point that agreements cannot be concluded which go against the terms of the Treaty; for such agreements to be adopted, prior Treaty amendments must be brought about under Article 48 TEU. The role of the Court of Justice at an early stage is guaranteed by Article 300(6) which allows any Member State or institution to obtain the opinion of the Court of Justice on an, as yet, unconcluded agreement (a number of examples are discussed in 6.3 and 6.5). Agreements once concluded (or, more precisely, the acts of the Council which give effect to them internally) must be challenged using the Article 230 annulment procedure (Opinion 3/94 *Framework Agreement on Bananas* [1995] ECR I-4577). In Case C-122/95 *Germany* v. *Council* ([1998] ECR I-973) the Court confirmed that the measure concluding a Treaty on behalf of the EU, notwithstanding that the international agreement in question may have entered into force, could still be challenged. Although international agreements become part of EU law, it may be necessary – to give full effect to them and in order to satisfy the EU's obligations under international law – for the EU legislature or executive to adopt additional implementing measures.

7.12 Cooperation in International Organisations

There are particular problems of cooperation which will result from the joint participation of the Member States and the Community in an international organisation which stems inevitably from the limited nature of the latter's external competence (see Sack, 1995). These were discussed by the Court of Justice in Case C-25/94 *Commission* v. *Council (FAO)* ([1996] ECR I-1469). The United Nations Food and Agriculture Organisation (FAO) was the first international organisation of which the EC formally became a 'member organisation'. The management of the right to vote in the FAO Council – which deals with subjects which cut across both national and Community competences – is dealt with in an unpublished Arrangement dating from 1991 between the Council and Commission 'regarding preparation for FAO meetings, statements and voting'. This establishes a coordination procedure between the Commission and the Member States to decide on the exercise of responsibilities or on statements on a particular point. Section 2.3 deals with questions where there is shared competence: the respective roles of the Member States and the Community are determined according to where the 'thrust' of the measure lies. In the absence of agreement between the Commission and the Member States the matter will be decided according to the procedure provided for in the Treaty and the agreed practice. In the absence of agreement on this basis, the matter will be referred to the Committee of Permanent Representatives (COREPER). In the FAO case, the Court found that Arrangement to be binding on the institutions, and concluded that in the particular instance which concerned fishery conservation matters (covered by Cases 3/76 etc. *Kramer* [1976] ECR 1279), the Council had acted in breach of that Arrangement by opting for a Member State vote. In contrast to the form of cooperation organised for participation in the FAO, specific procedures for the organisation of cooperation in relation to the WTO are laid down by Council Regulation (Council Regulation 356/95 OJ 1995 L41/3).

7.13   Implementation, Rule Making and the Role of Comitology

The legislative process cannot be examined in isolation from the extensive structures of 'comitology' which determine the manner in which many powers arising under primary legislative instruments are exercised in practice (Joerges and Vos, 1999). These structures were introduced in 6.7. The term comitology refers to the practice within the Council of delegating in the primary legislation certain implementing powers (typically aspects of secondary rule making) to the Commission, to be exercised in conjunction with committees (*'comités'* in French: hence the term) of national representatives chaired by a representative of the Commission. These committees of national representatives – some of whom are civil servants, but many of whom are scientific experts or even representatives of interest groups – wield varying degrees of influence over the executive process. There are over 200 such committees in existence. Whether one regards the practice of comitology as an enhancement of both the effectiveness of the EU's institutional structure and the quality of its decision making because it can facilitate deliberation at the supranational level and brings expert knowledge into the system, or as a bureaucratic mechanism which rids EU decision making of its last vestiges of democratic accountability is a moot point. What cannot be doubted is its importance, as well as the inevitability in practice of some sort of delegated powers system to enable effective rule making and execution of EU policies, as we saw already in 6.7. Most observers agree that comitology is 'possibly one of the most significant organic developments in the EU's institutional structure' (Bradley, 1992: 720). According to Weiler, comitology is central to 'the democratic life of the Union', and thus the task of addressing the challenges it raises in terms of the exercise of power within a 'complex and hazy landscape' is of fundamental importance (Weiler, 1999b: 2, 9).

The amendment to what is now Article 202 EC by the Single European Act was introduced to begin the task of matching legal form and practice. Comitology was well established in the system when Article 202 was redrafted in terms which leave much discretion with the Council:

> '[The Council shall …] confer on the Commission, in the acts which the Council adopts, powers for the implementation of the rules which the Council lays down. The Council may impose certain requirements in respect of the exercise of these powers. The Council may also reserve the right, in specific cases, to exercise directly implementing powers itself. The procedures referred to above must be consonant with principles and rules to be laid down in advance by the Council, acting unanimously on a proposal from the Commission and after obtaining the Opinion of the European Parliament.'

More detailed rules were enacted in a framework measure (Council Decision 87/373 OJ 1987 L197/33) which established that comitology could take three basic forms, with a number of variants. The least intrusive Committee is the Advisory Committee (Procedure I), to which the Commission submits a draft of the measures it proposes to adopt. The Commission must take 'the utmost account' of the opinion delivered by the Committee, but is not prevented by a negative opinion from adopting the measure. Under Procedure II, the draft is considered by a Management Committee, which has the power, by a qualified majority, to delay the adoption of the measure by the Commission, during which time the Council itself can adopt a different decision by a qualified majority. The most restrictive type of Committee is the Regulatory Committee (Procedure III), where the support of a qualified majority of the committee is required for the Commission draft. If there is not sufficient support, the power of decision reverts to the Council, but if this institution does not act within three months, the Commission may adopt the act. The three procedures themselves incorporate a number of variants, and the delegating power granted by the Council will specify which procedure and variant applies in each case.

Comitology in this form is not supported by the Commission, which feels its discretion is excessively limited by Member State interference; this argument derives strength from an argument that the intention of the third indent of Article 202 was to intensify the separation of powers within the EU by consolidating the executive function within the Commission, not to intensify the powers of the Member States. The Parliament likewise has remained implacably opposed since it fears that its prerogatives under the legislative process are restricted by forms of delegation of powers to the Commission under which the Council and the Member States retain control, but which bypass the legislative role of the Parliament. The sidelining of the Parliament had, of course, been enshrined by the Court ever since the *Köster* case (Case 25/70 *Einfuhr- und Vorratstelle* v. *Köster* [1970] ECR 1161) which explicitly acknowledged that the original legislative procedure need not be followed for any implementing measures taken under the original measure. Despite that precedent, the Parliament attempted to challenge the Council's Decision formalising the structures of comitology (Case 302/87 *Parliament* v. *Council (Comitology)* [1988] ECR 5615), but its attempt failed on the procedural question of its standing to bring annulment actions under what was then Article 173 EEC before the Court of Justice (a position on standing the Court later reversed), rather than an examination of the merits of its arguments. There matters rested for some time, although to protect the Parliament's interests, the Commission agreed that draft measures going before the Committees will be forwarded to the Parliament for information.

The comitology question returned to the institutional agenda with added force in the wake of the introduction of the co-decision legislative procedure by the Treaty of Maastricht. As a 'co-legislator' the Parliament was able to argue very forcefully that it should not be wholly excluded from the executive process, given that the Council, as the other co-legislator, is intimately involved in it, by virtue of the terms of Article 202. Using what powers it had under the Conciliation Committee process in the context of co-decision to seek improvements in its situation, the Parliament rejected the draft directive on voice telephony precisely over its dissatisfaction with the way the comitology issue was dealt with in the draft. Indeed, during the first year of applying co-decision, the Parliament systematically made use of its powers to highlight the comitology question. This drastic action led the Council to the negotiating table to produce a *modus vivendi* agreed in December 1994 between the three institutions on comitology and measures adopted using the co-decision procedure (OJ 1996 C102/1) (a form of 'inter-institutional agreement': see 7.17). This put on a more formal footing the Parliament's 'right' to receive all draft general implementing acts at the same time and under the same conditions as to the relevant committee. The Commission committed itself to take account of the Parliament's comments and to 'keep it informed at every stage of the procedure of the action which it intends to take'. The Council's commitment, in the event of the matter being referred to it, was not to adopt an implementing measure without first consulting the Parliament, and taking due account of its views. It should seek 'a solution in the appropriate framework' with the Parliament.

This was a matter set down for review at the 1996 IGC, both because of inter-institutional conflicts and also because the Council continued to spend an inordinate amount of debating time choosing the committee procedure to include legislative measures, something which the 1987 Decision was supposed to prevent. In the event, the IGC disappointed all expectations, and agreement was not reached. However, a declaration was annexed to the Treaty of Amsterdam calling on the Commission to propose an amendment to the 1987 decision, and it duly did so, with the measure being adopted in June 1999 (Decision 1999/468 OJ 1999 L184/23). The legislative procedure surrounding the adoption of that act was again marked by significant action on the part of the Parliament, which chose to wait until its final legislative session before the elections of June 1999 and managed to block half of the budgetary appropriations for committees using its budgetary powers, in order to express more firmly its opinion on the matter than its 'simple' consultation under Article 202 would have seemed to warrant. The old framework of committees is essentially preserved. However, the Parliament is given a scrutiny power to alert the Commission if it considers that an implementing measure intrudes into the legislative sphere. The Decision also brings some limited transparency to the field, by applying to comitology the principles and conditions on access to documents which apply to the Commission. That would have been the position anyway, regardless of the Council's formalisation of the rule, as it was the conclusion reached by the Court of First Instance in a judgment handed down shortly after the Decision was adopted (Case T-188/97 *Rothmans* v. *Commission*, 19 July 1999). The Court found that comitology committees came, for the purposes of access to documents, under the Commission itself. The Commission could not deny 'authorship' of the documents. Overall, the new decision is regarded as a step forward, but many commentators favour further reform, including Treaty amendments (Lenaerts and Verhoeven, 1000)

It is perhaps worth noting as a footnote to these comments that the situation is even more opaque in relation to the matter of policy formulation and implementation in the area of Justice and Home Affairs than in, say, the agriculture or internal market fields. Peers (2000b) charts the complexity of working groups and committees, the conflicts between justice ministries and interior ministries in the Member States, and the interaction between COREPER and a newly created Strategic Committee on Immigration,

Frontiers and Asylum, created to cover the five-year Title IV transitional period where special rules on decision making apply).

7.14   The Financing of the EU

The finances of the EU, and the expenditure of those finances, involve much more than dry legal rules and procedures (for a good summary see Commission, 1995b). Both the income and expenditure sides of the EU budget have proved to be sites of intense political conflict which have mirrored the overall debates about the direction of European integration. For example, the crisis of the 'empty chair' in 1965–66, which came closest to precipitating a complete breakdown in the work of the European Communities, was to a large extent a clash about the question of financing (see 2.7). The political conflicts have generally been viewed as reducible to two key issues: the division of the 'cake' between the Member States, and the relationships between the poorer and richer Member States; and the struggle for power between the various institutions, in particular between the Parliament – representing the 'federal' element in the EU – and the Council – representing the governments of the Member States.

The regime for financing the European Communities envisaged by the original Treaties of national contributions – the traditional method of funding international organisations – is now entirely supplanted by later measures. These have included the 1970 and 1975 Budgetary Treaties, the 1984 agreement on the UK budget rebate, the 1988 agreement between the Member States on the restructuring of the budget and the reallocation of revenues (the so-called 'Delors I package' – see 2.13), and the 1992 decisions reached at the Edinburgh European Council which were based on the so-called 'Delors II package' (see Bull.-EC 12/92). That package was devised to update the financial structure and resourcing of the EU in order to make it possible to achieve the goals of Maastricht, providing a financial perspective from 1993 to 1999 (From the Single Act to Maastricht and Beyond: the Means to Match our Ambitions COM(92) 2000). The limit of spending up to 1999 was 1.27 per cent of GDP in the EU, and in 1998 the budget stood at 85.66 billion ECUs, that is 1.15 per cent of GDP. The rapid rise in the EU budget since the Treaty of Maastricht tends to give the lie to claims that subsidiarity means less intervention by the EU. What it probably means is intervention in different forms, and a widespread recognition that the move to economic and monetary union requires the EU to have something which approximates a little more closely to a 'pre-federal' budget.

Since 1988, the Member States and the EU institutions have sought to defuse conflict over the question of how much money is available to spend by adopting the method of medium term 'perspectives', based on political decisions about how the activities in the EU are likely to change within that time period. The method worked quite well between 1988 and 1992, to the extent that there was sufficient slack and flexibility in the system to allow the EU to respond quite effectively to the challenges posed by the changes in Central and Eastern Europe where it has sought to play a lead role in delivering and coordinating aid aimed at facilitating transformations to liberal constitutionalism and market capitalism. The financial perspective for 1992–99 was set at the Edinburgh European Council. The debates over the most recent financial perspective for 2000–06 proved somewhat more painful, particularly after the German Chancellor Helmut Kohl declared in 1998 that Germany – now unified and relatively poor – should withhold its budget payments unless a fairer system was devised. The new financial perspective also had to be seen in the context of Agenda 2000, which comprises a focus specifically upon policy adjustment with a view to enlargement. The result of the conflict, which included the Commission suggesting that the UK's prized budget rebate should be scrapped, was hard bargaining, resulting in an agreement at the European Council in Berlin and embodied in an inter-institutional agreement (Inter-Institutional Agreement of 6 May 1999 between the European Parliament, the Council and the Commission on budgetary discipline and improvement of the budgetary procedure, OJ 1999 C172). Begg suggests that although the Berlin deal kept the budget show on the road, it made it even harder than before to see an underlying logic to the budget, and represented a catalogue of missed opportunities in relation to reform especially in relation to the CAP (Begg, 1999).

The European Union is now financed by a system of 'own resources', that is revenue to which it is entitled as of right, rather than national contributions. Contributions can, of course, be withheld; own resources cannot. This should mean that the money accrues to the EU automatically, irrespective of the relative wealth or poverty of the Member States. The EU's revenue has four components:

- customs duties charged on goods at the EU's external frontiers;
- levies charged on agricultural products at the external frontiers;
- a proportion of the VAT levied by the Member States up to a ceiling of 1 per cent;
- since the 1988 budget agreement between the Member States, a fourth resource calculated according to national GNP, which makes up the shortfall between the three 'traditional' own resources and the Community's necessary expenditure.

Unlike the VAT element, the fourth resource is progressive, not regressive; that is, it is a tax proportionate to the wealth of the Member States, whereas the VAT element has a tendency to penalise the poorer Member States where the VAT base on which it is calculated gives rise to disproportionately high contributions from poorer Member States. Such states have a greater level of consumption in relation to production. The fourth resource was also needed as the proportion of customs duties and levies within the total EU revenues has been dropping as customs duties have gradually been reduced in the move towards global free trade, and as the EU has become increasingly self-sufficient in agricultural resources. Consequently, there was a need to find additional resources for additional EU activities (especially policies on economic and social cohesion) without adding (and indeed reducing) the VAT element. Proposals for a fifth resource, based on a tax directly levied by the EU perhaps on energy consumption, have not as yet been accepted by the Member States.

The legal basis for an alteration to the basis of the EU's revenues is Article 269 EC. It is for the Council to lay down provisions on revenue, acting unanimously on a proposal from the Commission and after consulting the Parliament. However, such provisions are merely themselves recommendations to the Member States, which must then be ratified or accepted by them according to their respective constitutional requirements. As noted above, the revenue side of the budget also depends heavily upon the conclusion of inter-institutional agreements between the three political institutions despite the formal limitations on the involvement of the Parliament.

In addition to the Common Agricultural Policy (CAP) and the structural funds, the EU spends its revenue on the buildings, staff and other administrative costs of the EU institutions and other policies including development aid, research and technological development support, and educational and vocational training support programmes. The 1988 overhaul affected expenditure as well as revenue. It brought a major shift in emphasis from the CAP towards the structural funds, a shift mandated both by the increasingly widespread acceptance that the level of support going to the CAP was now too great, and by the commitment in the Single European Act to the development of regional policies. Limitations on spending on the CAP have been brought about both by structural reforms within the CAP itself (especially controls on production levels) and by cutting down on the price support system on which it is based. Agriculture now accounts for rather under 50 per cent of the expenditure of EU, although this is as much a result of growth elsewhere in the budget, as real constraints on agricultural spending.

One area where the financing of EU activities gave rise to particular problems was that of the Common Foreign and Security Policy (CFSP). Formally, there is a budgetary process only for each of the 'Communities'. In reality, certain activities falling under the 'Union' pillars do require expenditure. Only since the Treaty of Amsterdam has operational expenditure for most aspects of CFSP work been attributable directly, by Treaty authorisation, to the budget (Article 28 TEU; see also Article 41 TEU on PJC). Before that time administrative expenditure for CFSP-related institutional activities was charged to the EC budget (what was Article J.11(2) TEU). Operational expenditure (e.g. for joint actions) could either come from contributions from the Member States, or – perhaps – be attributed to the EU budget. The former solution took the EU back to the old problem of contributions: Member States may be slow to pay their dues, as occurred in relation to EU aid to Bosnia, thus reducing the effectiveness of CFSP actions. An alternative which was used in the past, but which has caused great friction between the Commission and the Parliament, has been the redirection of EU funds already committed elsewhere to CFSP purposes. An effective budget line for CFSP was only entered into the EU budget for 1995, and the situation regularised in 1999 with the entry into force of the Treaty of Amsterdam.

7.15 The Budgetary Process

It is one of the constant complaints of the Parliament that there is no formal institutional parallelism between the revenue and expenditure sides of the Community finances. Revenue raising remains largely in the hands of the Council and the Member States, with Parliamentary input limited to consultation (Article 269 EC) combined with informal interactions based on the relevant inter-institutional agreement; expenditure falls under the joint control of the Parliament and the Council. The budgetary process is governed by Article 272 EC, as amended by the Budgetary Treaties of 1970 and 1975. The present provisions need to be read in the light of the 1999 inter-institutional agreement, replacing the earlier 1988 and 1993 agreements. These have introduced an element of medium-term financial planning into the budgetary process and thereby significantly reduced the potential for conflict between the institutions in the context of agreeing each annual budget. In each agreement the basic outlines of the next four budgets (financial perspective) were agreed in advance, and any revisions required the cooperation of the Commission and the consent of the Council and the Parliament.

Under the provisions of Article 272 the Commission draws up a preliminary draft budget for the next calendar year on the basis of expenditure estimates made by each of the institutions. The draft budget – and all amendments that follow – must be within the relevant financial perspective. This draft is then sent to the Council for amendment and approval, on a qualified majority, before 5 October. The Parliament then has 45 days to consider the draft budget as established by the Council.

For these purposes, a distinction must be made between compulsory and non-compulsory expenditure within the budget. Compulsory expenditure (CE) is that which results necessarily from obligations under the Treaty or acts adopted thereunder – for example, spending on the CAP. Non-compulsory expenditure (NCE) is other, discretionary, expenditure. In considering the budget, the Parliament has more restricted powers over CE than over NCE. It can, by a majority of members, propose amendments to NCE. These amendments will stand if they are not rejected or modified by the Council, acting by a qualified majority, within 15 days. In the latter event, when the budget returns to the Parliament for second reading, it can, within 15 days, in effect reinstate its amendments by a majority of its members and a three-fifths majority of the votes. In the case of CE, the Parliament can merely propose modifications, acting by a majority of votes. Where these increase the total expenditure of an institution, the modifications will be included in the budget only if they are positively accepted by the Council within 15 days. Modifications, which do not increase the total expenditure of any institution, must be positively rejected by the Council within 15 days; otherwise they are included in the budget. It will be apparent, therefore, that the Parliament's real control over the content of the budget is not so great as might appear from its designation as joint budgetary authority. However, the distinction between CE and NCE needs to be read in the light of changes first introduced in the 1993 Inter-Institutional Agreement. Most significantly for the Parliament, this Agreement provided for a conciliation procedure between the Council and the Parliament in relation to CE, in the event that the Council wished to depart from the preliminary draft budget. It also redefined the concept of CE, specifying that all expenditure on structural policies including the Cohesion Fund, and internal policies is NCE where the Parliament has the final say. Finally, it ring-fenced NCE, protecting it against encroachment in the event of increases in the level of CE.

In the event of great dissatisfaction with the draft budget, the Parliament does have the power to reject it as a whole for 'important reasons', provided it acts by a majority of its members and two-thirds of the votes cast. It has done this twice – in 1979 and 1984. In this event, a new draft budget must be prepared by the Commission. Provision is made in the budgetary process for the spending to continue on a pro rata basis in the event of the non-adoption of the budget before the beginning of the year – a problem endemic in the mid-1980s. Supplementary budgets also sometimes have to be adopted, if unexpected contingencies cannot be covered out of the commitment appropriations.

The President of the Parliament also has the final power to declare the budget adopted at the conclusion of the budgetary process. This can in turn lead to disputes, since in 1985 the Parliament adopted a budget for 1986 containing what the Council considered to be proposed expenditure in excess of the 'maximum rate' set each year by the Commission, and used as a rule to restrict expenditure growth. The act of the Parliament was successfully challenged by the Council before the Court of Justice, the budget annulled, and the 1986 budgetary process reopened in the middle of the year (Case 34/86 *Council* v. *Parliament* [1986] ECR 2155). In 1995, the Council once more successfully sought the annulment of the adoption of the budget by the

President of the Parliament (Case C-41/95 *Council* v. *Parliament* [1995] ECR I-4411). The budget adopted in December 1994 for 1995 contained a higher increase in non-compulsory expenditure than was possible without an agreement between the Council and the Parliament. The Council also argued that the Parliament had exceeded its powers regarding compulsory expenditure by introducing amendments, and that it had violated the principle of sincere cooperation between the institutions. The Parliament's argument rested on the alleged apparent acquiescence of the Council to the Parliament's actions, through verbal assurances and behaviour, which apparently approved the approach taken by the Parliament. The Court did not share the Parliament's view of the actions of the Council, and in particular its President. It annulled the act approving the budget, on the grounds that it was taken at a time when the budgetary procedure had not yet been concluded, holding that the Parliament had indeed violated the principle of cooperation with the institutions by which it is bound.

7.16 Financial Oversight and Budgetary Control

As the financial resources available to the EU have become greater, so the problem of ensuring the protection of those resources against fraudulent misuse has become more urgent. Areas of particular concern are the CAP, VAT and customs, and the misuse of monies allocated under EU programmes such as the structural funds or development aid. The role of the Court of Auditors has increased in recent years somewhat, particularly in highlighting financial irregularities. According to Laffan (1999b), it has constructed itself – in an emerging agenda of financial management – as a 'living institution'. All of this has heightened awareness of the need for financial oversight and budgetary control.

The first point of control is the requirement of a dual legal basis for any significant expenditure. This means that there must be – in relation to any given head of expenditure – both an entry in the budget itself and secondary legislation authorising the expenditure, duly adopted under the Treaty. This was confirmed by the Court of Justice, which found that the Commission's 'Poverty 4' programme lacked such a dual basis (Case C-106/96 *UK* v. *Commission (Poverty 4)* [1998] ECR I-2729). The point is backed up by an Inter-Institutional Agreement of October 1998, subject to allowance being made for experimental and pilot projects up to a maximum of some 30 million euros.

Second, the Parliament gives the Commission a discharge in respect of the implementation of the budget (Article 276 EC). Its refusal to do so in respect of the 1996 budget in early 1999 led to the appointment of the Committee of Independent Experts and to the eventual resignation of the Commission in March 1999, because of allegations of impropriety against some Commissioners.

Third, Article 280 EC, introduced by the Treaty of Maastricht, expressly assimilates the financial interests of the EU to the financial interests of the Member States, but until the provision was enhanced by the introduction of a specific legal basis by the Treaty of Amsterdam progress was quite slow in this area. For example, the lack of a secure legal basis within the EC Treaty for securing the financial interests of the EU resulted in the adoption of a convention under the third pillar Article K.3(2)(c) TEU on criminal penalties which required separate adoption by the Member States (Council Act of 26 July 1995 drawing up a Convention for the Protection of the Financial Interests of the European Communities OJ 1995 C316/48), supplemented by reference to matters falling directly within Community competence (administrative controls and penalties) by a Council Regulation of December 1995 on the same topic (OJ 1995 L312/1) (adopted on the basis of what was then Article 235 EC). The amendment to Article 280 introduced a decision-making process based on qualified majority voting, and involving co-decision with the European Parliament. In record time, this led to the adoption of the measures establishing OLAF, the EU Anti-Fraud Office.

7.17   The Role of the Institutions in Law and Policy Making

Much of this chapter and chapter 6 has sought to show that law making and policy making in the EU often owe as much either to high-level political agreements achieved within the European Council or between the various institutions, or to day-to-day structures of informal cooperation between and within the institutions as they do to the formal texts of the Treaties. In an evolving EU, disputes between the institutions are as inevitable as disputes between the EU and its Member States. Comitology is just one example of an evolving institutional structure which continues to 'set institution against institution' (Bradley, 1992: 721). In so far as disputes exist between the EU's more and less supranational institutions (e.g. between the Commission and the Council), disputes between the institutions may also conceal an element of dispute between the interests of the Member States and those of the EU.

This was clearly the case with the dispute which arose between the Commission and the Council – representing the Member States – concerning voting arrangements in the United Nations Food and Agriculture Organisation (FAO) (Case C-25/94 *Commission* v. *Council (FAO)* (on the involvement of the EU in FAO see 7.12). The dispute arose because the Council insisted that for the purposes of a vote in the FAO on certain fisheries conservation measures the Member States should exercise their votes through the Presidency rather than the Community voting as a single member of the FAO. In an area (as here) where there is shared competence between the Member States and the Community, the institutions and the Member States 'must take all necessary steps to ensure the best possible cooperation' on the management of the right to vote. Here, that duty to cooperate had been fulfilled through an arrangement between the Council and the Commission on the exercise of the right to vote, and the Court essentially committed the Council to observing the provisions of that arrangement. It found the Council to be in breach of the provision which determined that the 'thrust' of an FAO measure would determine whether the right to vote would be enjoyed by the Community or the Member States. Consequently, in formal terms a dispute between the EU institutions and the Member States was subsumed into a dispute about the terms and effect of an 'agreement' between two of the institutions representing the 'intergovernmentalist' and 'federalist' elements of the EU.

A number of corrective mechanisms have emerged within the EU's political and legal systems whereby disputes may be resolved. These exist in addition to the normal channels of compromise and negotiation which mark the activities of any complex political organisation. A general duty of inter-institutional cooperation which is capable of being derived from Article 4 EC, and which was obliquely referred to by the Court in the *1995 Budget* case (Case C-41/95 *Council* v. *Parliament*), is of great importance in this context (Bieber, 1984). The following paragraphs examine in more detail two of the most important corrective mechanisms: the proliferating phenomenon of inter-institutional agreements, and the tendency to 'legalise' certain aspects of inter-institutional relations by submitting them to the Court of Justice for resolution according to the provisions of the Treaties. In this context, disputes about the legal basis of legislation represent perhaps the most important – but not the sole – trigger for such litigation.

Inter-institutional agreements involving the Council, the Commission and the Parliament are not a new phenomenon. They date back to the early 1960s, in the form of various types of practical measures agreed upon bilaterally between the Parliament and the Commission, and the Parliament and the Council, to increase the effectiveness of the Parliament's work. Trilateral agreements date back to the mid-1970s, with a joint declaration on the institution of a conciliation procedure between the Parliament and the Council in relation to legislation (OJ 1975 C89/1). It is, however, since the mid-1980s and especially since the adoption of the Treaty of Maastricht, that the practice of adopting such agreements and declarations has accelerated rapidly. Overall, it is difficult to be exact about the precise number of such measures, since not all have been officially published and there is no exact definition of what actually constitutes an 'inter-institutional agreement', nor any fixed procedure by which an inter-institutional agreement comes into being.

In addition to the inter-institutional agreements on the work of the Conciliation Committee (see 7.5), on legislative codification and the quality of drafting (7.9), on comitology (7.13) and on the budgetary process and EU finances (see 7.14 and 7.15) already specifically discussed in this chapter, the most important agreement of the 'new' generation is that on implementing the principle of subsidiarity (Bull. EC 10/93), which was supplemented by an inter-institutional declaration on democracy, transparency and subsidiarity (Bull. EC 10/93). Large parts of the important aspects of these measures are now enshrined in the Amsterdam Protocol (6.6). As the very recent Inter-Institutional Agreement May 1999 on internal investigations by the European Anti-Fraud Office (OLAF) (OJ 1999 L136/15) shows, however, inter-institutional agreements can sometimes be used to reinforce the gravity and solemnity of an issue as well as to diffuse conflict.

Inter-institutional agreements fall within the category of 'soft law' (see 6.15), and as such are more akin to political declarations of intent than formal legal commitments binding in a precise textual sense. That is not to say that they lack all legal effects, but it may be that they operate quite satisfactorily in the political realm as the basis of inter-institutional cooperation even while doubts exist as to their exact legal relevance or status. What is certain is that inter-institutional agreements cannot alter or modify the basic Treaties or secondary legislation (i.e. they are subject to the rule of law), but they may operate to complement existing procedures. They may also be internally binding on the institutions (Case C-25/94 *Commission* v. *Council (FAO)*), or binding externally in the sense of generating a legitimate expectation on the part of third parties such as international organizations or other states.

7.18   Inter-Institutional Litigation

The most drastic, public and formal way of bringing about the resolution of an inter-institutional dispute is to submit it to the Court of Justice. The legalisation of inter-institutional relationships in this manner is illustrative of the key role which the Court of Justice has played in the policy-making process. The involvement of the Court will normally take the form of an action brought under Article 230 EC for the annulment of an act taken by one or more institution (measures adopted by co-decision are signed jointly by the Presidents of the Council and the Parliament, and are seen as acts of the Council: Case C-259/95 *Parliament* v. *Council (Home Accidents)* [1997] ECR I-5303). Exceptionally, however, circumstances may arise where one institution takes action against another for failure to act, where there is a duty on the latter to act (Article 232 EC) (e.g. Case 13/83 *Parliament* v. *Council (Transport Policy)* [1985] ECR 1513). Much of the litigation between the institutions is concerned with the legal basis of EU measures (6.8), but some cases have raised other principles of EU law such as the duty of cooperation between the institutions, and the requirements of 'consultation' in the context of the legislative process.

One important obstacle to the involvement of the Parliament in inter-institutional litigation was that it was not cited as a potential plaintiff or defendant in the original version of Article 173 EEC, as it then was, although it was, from the beginning, given standing under Article 175 EEC (now Article 232 EC) to bring an action for failure to act. In order to extend the scope of judicial protection, the Court of Justice was required to recognise the standing of the Parliament to bring an annulment action based on what was then Article 173 EEC (15.3). Although this point is now of largely academic interest following the alteration of this Article by the Treaty of Maastricht to extend *locus standi* to the Parliament, it is worth reconsidering briefly the two contradictory cases in which the Court first denied and then accepted the principle that the Parliament had the right to pursue an action before the Court, at least in order to protect its prerogatives – notwithstanding the strict wording of the Treaties. It should be noted that neither the Court, through its judicial legislation, nor the Member States in their amendments to the Treaty, have recognised a generalised right of action on the part of the Parliament in order to protect the general interest such as was accorded by Article 173(1)(now Article 230(1)) to the Council, the Commission and the Member States.

In Case 302/87 *Parliament* v. *Council (Comitology)* the Court dismissed the Parliament's action as inadmissible, refusing to draw parallels between Article 173 and Article 175, or between the right of others to bring the Parliament before the Court in respect of allegedly unlawful acts (which it had already recognised in Case 294/83 *Parti Ecologiste 'Les Verts'* v. *Parliament* [1986] ECR 1339) and the right of the Parliament itself to bring an action. It suggested that the interests of the Parliament could be adequately protected by the Commission's ability – in the general interest – to take action in respect of any measure. The Court's decision was heavily criticised by commentators (Weiler, 1989; Bradley, 1988). Just over a year later the Court reversed its position (Case C-70/88 *Parliament* v. *Council (Chernobyl)* [1990] ECR I-2041), allowing the Parliament to bring an action, this time to challenge the legal basis used by the Council to adopt a measure regarding the marketing of foodstuffs affected by radiation. The Parliament successfully argued here that the measure should have been adopted on the basis of Article 100a EEC (now Article 95 EC) rather than Article 31 Euratom. The Court acknowledged its right to bring an action in order to protect its prerogatives (e.g. involvement in the cooperation procedure, or the right to be consulted). In *Chernobyl* it was the right to be involved in the cooperation procedure which was at issue (Article 31 Euratom requires merely consultation of the Parliament; Article 100a was then based on the cooperation procedure) and it must have been significant for the Court's judgement that in this case the Commission did not support the Parliament's views and therefore had no incentive to protect the rights of the Parliament, as the Court had suggested in *Comitology* was the appropriate course of action. The Court held:

> 'The absence in the Treaties of any provision giving the Parliament the right to bring an action for annulment may constitute a procedural gap, but it cannot prevail over the fundamental interest in the maintenance and observance of the institutional balance laid down in the Treaties establishing the European Communities' ([1990] ECR 2041 at p. 2073).

The effect of the *Chernobyl* judgment was to recognise more fully the specific identity of each of the institutions, and to acknowledge the need for a legal mechanism to be available to each institution in order to ensure that its prerogatives are not harmed in the dynamic process of integration. It is the logical conclusion to the process of recognition of the Parliament in the institutional structure of the EU begun in the *Isoglucose* cases, which concerned the issue of consultation (7.3). However, it should not be thought that even now the Parliament has an unlimited right of standing. In Case C-156/93 *Parliament* v. *Commission (Micro-organisms)* ([1995] ECR I-2019) the Court held that the Parliament has no right of standing under Article 230 to attack the reasons on which the Commission's proposal is based, unless it can show that these in some way affect its prerogatives.

The phenomenon of inter-institutional litigation also illustrates how the intensely political issue of the choice of a legal basis can be reduced in large measure to the scenario of a legal dispute between institutions, where procedural rules rather than substantive political choices appear to predominate. The most dramatic example of this scenario is offered by the Court's shifting approach to the interrelationship between what were then Articles 100a and 130s EEC (now Articles 95 and 175 EC) as legal bases for measures in the field of environment. In Case C-300/89 *Commission* v. *Council (Titanium Dioxide)* ([1991] ECR I-2867) the Commission (with the support of the Parliament) challenged the decision of the Council to use Article 130s EEC as the legal basis for Directive 89/428/EEC approximating national programmes for the reduction and eventual elimination of pollution caused by waste in the production of titanium dioxide. The Directive had an admittedly dual function, namely to protect the environment (Article 130s) and to harmonise national measures which had an impact upon the completion of the internal market. From the latter perspective the measure would fall within the remit of Article 100a, thus requiring only a qualified majority vote in the Council and the use of the cooperation procedure (at that time). In contrast, Article 130s was an 'old-style' legislative power, requiring unanimity in the Council and involving only the consultation of the Parliament. The Court ruled out a dual reference to both articles, since this would in practice defeat the very purpose of the cooperation procedure, which is to expand the influence of the Parliament, and held that such a measure must be based on Article 100 alone. The effect of this decision appeared very significantly to limit the scope of application of Article 130s, and to assert the dominance of the procedural imperatives of the cooperation procedure over the substantive resolution of the appropriate content of an environmental protection measure.

In Case C-155/91 *Commission* v. *Council (Waste Directive)* ([1993] ECR I-939), however, the Court took a different view of the precise focus of Directive 91/156 on waste disposal. Again the legal basis chosen by the Council was Article 130s, but this time the Court held that the chief purpose of the Directive was to safeguard the management of the environment through the safe disposal of waste throughout the EU. Questions of free movement (and hence the issue of the internal market for waste) were merely ancillary to the central focus of this Directive. The Court reached a very similar conclusion in a subsequent case brought by the Parliament to challenge the use of Article 130s as the legal basis for Council Regulation 259/93 on the supervision and control of shipments of waste within, into, and out of the EU (Case C-187/93 *Parliament* v. *Council (Transport of Waste)* [1994] ECR I-2857). Since these cases were decided, of course, the relationship between what are now Articles 95 and 176 has changed somewhat: both provisions now provide for qualified majority voting and the use of the co-decision procedure, although there are complexities and conditionalities surrounding the precise scope of both provisions. These changes, coupled with the modification of the Court's approach in the two *Waste* cases indicates that in future decisions involving Article 100a may be less motivated by procedural factors (see Case C-271/94 *Parliament* v. *Council (Edicom)* discussed in 6.8), and that the main arguments used will be whether the 'internal market question' is merely ancillary to the measure, and whether there exists a *lex specialis* which should be used as the legal basis.

As the Court repeated its arguments on the protection of the cooperation procedure, when discussing the relationship between what were then Articles 7(2) and 235 EEC in Case C-295/90 *Parliament* v. *Council (Students' Rights)* [1992] ECR I-4193 (6.3), it seems that the argument of institutional balance will always retain some relevance to the question of legal basis. Yet the mere fact that an institution wishes to be more involved in the adoption of an act is no reason for the Court to overturn the choice of legal basis (Case C-269/97 *Commission* v. *Council*, 4 April 2000, para. 44). But recent cases do show that the centre of gravity argument developed by the Court continues to feature largely in the steady flow of legal basis literature (a flow noted by the Court of Justice in every annual report it issues). In Case C-42/97 *Parliament* v. *Council* ([1999] ECR I-869) at issue was the multi-annual programme to promote the linguistic diversity of the EU in the information society, and the choice was between a legal basis under what is now Article 157 (industry) or what is now Article 151 (culture). The Parliament sought a dual legal basis, but the Court found that the 'thrust' was more towards industry and the benefiting of enterprises through concrete action. The effects on culture were merely incidental and indirect in comparison. Accordingly the Court found for the Council.

A different perspective upon legal basis is opened up by the emergence of the three-pillar system. In Case C-170/96 *Commission* v. *Council (Airport Transit Visas)* ([1998] ECR I-2763) the Court in effect reviewed a third-pillar act for the purposes of ensuring that the third pillar was not encroaching upon the first pillar. Given the very different allocation of powers to the institutions, especially the Parliament, under the second and third pillars, such border disputes are likely to be important. The failure to give the Parliament standing to challenge framework decisions adopted under the third pillar (Article 35(6) TEU) recalls neatly the original drafting of what was then Article 173 EEC. It will be interesting to see how the Court interprets this provision, given its earlier approach to questions of standing in the interests of the institutional economy.

Finally, in Case C-189/97 *Parliament* v. *Council* [1999] ECR I-4741, the Court was called upon for the first time to interpret the term 'agreements having important budgetary implications for the Community', which is used in Article 300(3) as the basis for according the right to assent to an international agreement to the Parliament. To determine what were such 'important' budgetary implications, the Court rejected an approach which compared the appropriations to the whole EU budget, and adopted three criteria:

- the period of time over which the expenditure was carried out; over a period of years modest expenditure can become quite significant;
- a comparison with budgetary outlay on the EU's overall external programme; and
- where appropriate for a particular sector, a comparison with internal and external expenditure on that sector.

The Court concluded that the disputed fisheries agreement with Mauritania was not 'important' in that sense. It was concluded for only five years, and involved only one per cent of the whole of the payment appropriations allocated for the external operations of the EU, even though it was more than five per cent of expenditure on fisheries.

Summary

1   Under the EU Treaties there are a wide variety of decision-making processes, making it very difficult to draw general conclusions about how the EU acts in order to achieve the objectives of the Treaties.

2 Three legislative procedures can be seen as the most important:
- the 'old' procedure;
- the cooperation procedure;
- the co-decision procedure.

3 Despite the continuing importance of the 'old' procedure, under which the Parliament is at most merely consulted on proposed legislation, co-decision is gradually establishing itself as the EU's default legislative procedure.

4 The Commission's right of initiative in relation to most legislative proposals remains its most powerful weapon in shaping policy outcomes.

5 Under co-decision, the Parliament is gradually emerging as a genuine co-legislator, particularly through judicious maximisation of its powers.

6 Bargains between Member States continue to shape much EU legislation, but these bargains are increasingly structured by the constraints of the institutional framework.

7 The Treaty of Amsterdam amended the co-decision procedure in significant ways to give the Parliament more powers and to simplify the latter stages.

8 In limited circumstances the Parliament must assent before a decision can be taken.

9 A different system of law making may apply in the field of social policy, based on framework agreements between representatives of management and labour under the framework of the social dialogue.

10 Decision making in the areas of CFSP and PJC is more akin to intergovernmental bargaining than the law-making processes of the first pillar.

11 The legislative process reveals the ongoing democratic deficit of the EU. Non-governmental interests compete through lobbying the institutions in order to seek to influence the legislative process.

12 The introduction of the subsidiarity principle combined with the need to manage the internal market has resulted in programmes of simplification and 'better law making' being introduced by the Commission.

13 In the external relations domain, the Commission normally negotiates agreements which are concluded by the Council on behalf of the European Community.

14 The system of 'comitology' is an important institutional innovation within the EU structure which allows the Member States to retain much control over the process of policy implementation. The Parliament objects strongly to the use and extent of comitology. Comitology may make a contribution to the effectiveness of decision making.

15 The EU derives its revenue – termed 'own resources' – from customs duties, agricultural levies, a proportion of the VAT collected by the Member States, and a fourth resource based on Member State GDPs. The budget amounts to under 1.5 per cent of total EU GDP.

16 The budgetary process involves the Council and the Parliament as joint authorities, and has given rise to considerable inter-institutional conflict especially in the 1980s. Since the 1990s, longer-term financial perspectives have been introduced to reduce year-on-year conflict and to assure EU financing. Financing of the EU needs to be seen in the context of Agenda 2000 and impending enlargement.

17 Disputes between the institutions are inevitable in an evolving EU. Litigation and inter-institutional agreements are two of the mechanisms, apart from negotiation and compromise, most commonly used for the settlement of inter-institutional disputes.

Questions

1 Why does the EU have so many different decision-making processes? What impact does the lack of a single law-making process have upon the effectiveness of the institutions?

2 In what significant ways have the law-making processes changed since the original Treaties were introduced?

3 Is the co-decision procedure still too complex to work properly?

4 Is the Parliament correct to complain about comitology?

5 Does the Parliament have sufficient control over the collection of EU revenues and the allocation of expenditure?

6 What does inter-institutional litigation tell us about the nature of the EU? In that context, why has the concept of legal basis become so important?

Further Reading

S. Boyron (1998), 'The Co-decision Procedure: Rethinking the Constitutional Fundamentals', in Craig and Harlow (1998).

T. Burns (1996), 'Law Reform in the European Community and its Limits', 16 *Yearbook of European Law* 243.

H. Cullen and A. Charlesworth (1999), 'Diplomacy by Other Means: The Use of Legal Basis Litigation as a Political Strategy by the European Parliament and Member States', 36 *Common Market Law Review* 1243.

D. Earnshaw and D. Judge (1997), 'The Life and Times of the European Union's Co-operation Procedure', 35 *Journal of Common Market Studies* 35.

J. Garman and L. Hilditch (1998), 'Behind the Scenes: An Examination of the Importance of the Informal Processes at Work in Conciliation', 2 *Journal of European Public Policy* 271.

K. Lenaerts and A. Verhoeven (2000), 'Towards a Legal Framework for Executive Rule-Making in the EU? The Contribution of the New Comitology Decision', 37 *Common Market Law Review* 645.

D. McGoldrick (1997), Ch. 6, 'Practice and Policy on EC competence'.

I. Maher (1995b), 'Legislative Review by the EC Commission: Revision without Radicalism', in Shaw and More (1995).

S. Mazey and J. Richardson (1999), 'Interests', in Cram *et al.* (1999).

J. Monar (1994), 'Inter-institutional Agreements: The Phenomenon and its New Dynamics after Maastricht', 31 *Common Market Law Review* 693.

C. Neuhold (2000), 'Into the New Millennium: The Evolution of the European Parliament from Consultative Assembly to Co-legislator', *Eipascope*, issue no. 1, p.3.

J. Neyer (2000), 'Justifying Comitology: The Promise of Deliberation', in Neunreither and Wiener (2000).

E. Vos (1997), 'The Rise of Committees', 3 *European Law Journal* 210.

Key Websites

Two websites allow the monitoring of drafts through the legislative process:
PreLex:
http://europa.eu.int/prelex/apcnet.cfm?CL=en
which is accessible from:
http://europa.eu.int/geninfo/info-en.htm
The Parliament's legislative observatory:
http://www.europarl.eu.int/r/dors/oeil/en/default.htm

8 The Implementation and Enforcement of EU Law

8.1 Introduction

Two of the most important factors which distinguish the EU legal order from that of other international legal orders are the complexity of the regulatory structure and associated implementation mechanisms and the relative effectiveness of the enforcement mechanisms available. It is crucial that the binding legislative measures envisaged by the Treaty should not only be passed, but also implemented and enforced. However, the EU largely lacks the means and personnel whereby it can itself implement EU law, in the sense of applying it to individual cases or policing its application by individuals. It cannot, for example, police and enforce the external borders and collect customs duties and agricultural levies, or carry out the detailed implementation of the Common Agricultural Policy (CAP). Only exceptionally is direct implementation by the EU envisaged, although where it is, it is the Commission that is the institution charged with this task (see 4.4). The EU is therefore in large measure dependent upon the effective implementation of EU law by the national administrations, in accordance with detailed procedures laid down in individual EU measures and the general duty of 'Community' loyalty or fidelity incumbent upon the Member States by virtue of Article 10 EC (formerly Article 5 EC). This is termed 'indirect implementation' or 'indirect administration' (Daintith, 1995a), and to a great extent the successful implementation of EU law will be intimately linked to the structures, regulatory cultures and values of national law.

In recent years, in part as an aspect of its strategy for implementing the internal market but also within related policies, the Commission has shifted its focus away from an exclusive emphasis on post hoc correction of non-implementation through litigation towards encouraging vertical (EU/Member State) and horizontal cooperation (between Member States), often concentrating on the exchange of information and the creation of 'partnership' structures (e.g. in relation to EU Structural Funds disbursing regional and other aids). A Commission Communication on the development of administrative cooperation in the implementation and enforcement of EU legislation in the internal market (COM(94) 29) led to the adoption of a Council Resolution on coordinating information exchange between the national administrations (OJ 1994 C181/1) and on developing administrative cooperation between the national administrations (OJ 1994 C179/1). Inevitably, the involvement of the EU will at times be intrusive, and will entail changes in the way national regulatory structures are organised (Daintith, 1995a; Weatherill, 1995b). This is so for the system of prior notification to the Commission of draft technical standards and regulations, required under rules dating back to 1983, but now consolidated in Directive 98/34 (OJ 1998 L204/37, as amended by Directive 98/48 OJ 1998 L217/18). The drastic effects of this requirement of notification on national technical regulations which are *not* notified is apparent from Case C-194/94 *CIA Security International SA* v. *Signalson SA and Securitel SPRL* ([1996] ECR I-2201; 12.16) where the Court of Justice held that such national rules were unenforceable against third parties in national courts (see Weatherill, 1996a on the significance of this legal framework of notification for the management of the internal market).

Beyond the facilitation of cooperation, with the internal consequences which this will entail, the Commission's role will principally be that of supervising the Member States in order to ensure the effective enforcement of EU law (see 4.6). To this end, the Treaty provides a mechanism in Article 226 EC (formerly Article 169 EC) which permits the Commission to bring alleged Treaty violations by the Member States before the Court of Justice for a declaratory judgment. A similar procedure is also available to Member States in Article 227 EC (formerly Article 170 EC), which can themselves pursue the interests of the EU by taking defaulting states before the Court of Justice. This can be termed the 'direct' enforcement of EU law, in contradistinction to its 'indirect' enforcement through the medium of actions in the national courts, at the instance of aggrieved individuals (see Chapter 12).

This chapter examines the effective implementation and enforcement of EU law by reference, in particular, to Articles 10 and 226–228 EC (formerly Articles 5 and 169–171). It also reviews other means of enforcement provided by the Treaty – as Articles 226–228, although the most important, are by no means the only enforcement mechanisms available to the Commission – and assesses the problem of enforcement as a challenge to the EU institutions in ensuring the 'effectiveness' of EU law. It is concerned with the enforcement of EU law and obligations against the *Member States*, not individuals.

8.2   The Role of Article 10 EC in the Implementation and Enforcement of EU Law

Article 10 EC provides:

'Member States shall take all appropriate measures, whether general or particular, to ensure fulfilment of the obligations arising out of this

Treaty or resulting from action taken by the institutions of the Community. They shall facilitate the achievement of the Community's tasks. They shall abstain from any measure which could jeopardise the attainment of the objectives of this Treaty.'

The role of Article 10 – which has never been amended since its original EEC Treaty form – in the system of the Treaty has grown over the years. It is a general statement of the duties of Member States in relation to the achievement of the tasks of the EU which are in any case implicit in the binding force of the Treaties, and in the obligation under international law upon the Contracting Parties not to hinder the operation of the Treaties. Until relatively recently it was thought that Article 10 took effect only when read in conjunction with the objectives of the Treaty, and other provisions of EU law which set out the EU's policies (Temple Lang, 1990). However, in recent years, the Court of Justice has shown a markedly increased tendency to refer to Article 10 as a separate source of Member State obligations within the Treaty system (e.g. Case C-374/89 *Commission* v. *Belgium* [1991] ECR I-367). It is therefore appropriate to analyse it as a distinct feature of the EU's constitutional structure, emphasising here its particular importance in the context of implementation (see Chapter 12 for the role of Article 10 in the context of the relationship between EU law and national law).

In Cases 205-215/82 *Deutsche Milchkontor GmbH* v. *Germany* ([1983] ECR 2633 at p. 2665) the Court stated:

'According to the general principles on which the institutional system of the Community is based and which govern the relations between the Community and the Member States, it is for the Member States, by virtue of Article 5 of the Treaty, to ensure that Community regulations, in particular those concerning the common agricultural policy, are implemented within their territory.'

Thus what is now Article 10 imposes the obligation on the Member States to adapt their national provisions and practices to the requirements of EU law. The Court has held that the obligations under EU law fall upon all organs of the state, including the legislature, executive and judiciary, and apply at all levels of authority. As Temple Lang notes (1998: 109), every national authority is in effect an EU authority now. The Court amplified this point in Case C-8/88 *Germany* v. *Commission* ([1990] ECR I-2321) when stressing that, while all state authorities must ensure observance of the rules of EU law within their sphere of competence, the Court was not empowered to rule upon the division of competences made by national rules (e.g. between federal and regional levels), but could merely verify whether internal supervisory and inspection procedures were effective to ensure that EU law is applied.

The duty on national courts is to ensure the effective application of EU law for individuals (Case 14/83 *Von Colson and Kamann* v. *Land Nordrhein Westfalen* [1984] ECR 1891). This point will be addressed in Chapter 12.

Temple Lang summarises the duty on national authorities as comprising:

> 'a duty when necessary to make Community institutions, laws and policies work the way they are intended to work, and a general duty, which applies in every case, not to interfere with the way they are intended to work. This is a duty to apply and to supplement Community law and policy, when the occasion arises in the course of the authority's usual activities and when this is necessary for Community policy to be adequately applied' (1998: 111).

As Temple Lang notes, this can comprise a duty to take action against private parties as necessary. This point was made very clear in Case C-265/95 *Commission* v. *France* ([1997] ECR I-6959) when the Court of Justice found that the French authorities were in breach of their obligations under Article 10 read in conjunction with what is now Article 28 EC, which guarantees the free movement of goods, for failing to take adequate action to prevent blockades by private parties, especially farmers, of lorries carrying goods from other Member States. The Commission noted that it had been receiving complaints for more than a decade about the passivity of the French authorities in the face of violent acts committed by private individuals. Thus EU law can render private acts a matter of public concern, even if at the national level political expediency cautioned against taking action (because of the strength of the French agricultural lobby). Likewise, Article 10 has the effect of conflating the national and the EU interest. In Case C-186/98 *Nunes* [1999] ECR I-4883 the Court held that Member States must take all appropriate steps under Article 10 EC to safeguard the financial interests of the EU.

Individual/administrative authority relationships at national level can also be structured by the operation of Article 10. This occurs most frequently in relation to the instrumentalisation of the fundamental freedoms. In Case 222/86 *UNECTEF* v. *Heylens* ([1987] ECR 4097), the Court held that an individual who was exercising his right of free movement as a worker had a right to a judicial remedy to challenge an administrative determination denying him recognition of a foreign diploma. Building on this, the Court held in Case C-340/89 *Vlassopoulou* v. *Bundesministerium für Justiz, Baden-Württemberg* ([1991] ECR I-2357) that Article 10 required the German authorities to set up some form of system whereby they could assess the individual elements of the applicant's Greek legal training, such that she could be given recognition for those elements which were relevant to the practice of law in Germany.

Finally, as Temple Lang implies, Article 10 contains a duty of cooperation; the Member States have the duty to facilitate the achievement of the Commission's tasks under Article 211, and this includes, where necessary, providing requested information. The Commission has a general right to obtain information from the Member States about their implementation of EU law, quite apart from any specific reporting requirement contained in EU legislation (Case C-33/90 *Commission* v. *Italy* [1991] ECR I-5987). Where Member States persist in refusing to provide information, even to the Court of Justice itself, this constitutes a 'serious impediment to the administration of justice' (Case 272/86 *Commission* v. *Greece* [1988] ECR 4875 at p.4903).

The duty of loyalty is mutual, and applies also to the EU institutions. In Case C-2/88 Imm *Zwartveld* ([1990] ECR I-3365) the Court used Article 10 as the basis for a duty on the Commission to respond to a request for mutual assistance made by a Dutch examining magistrate in which he asked for information regarding fisheries inspections carried by Commission inspectors, which he required to pursue an investigation into alleged violations of EU fish marketing Decisions. It has also applied these principles in the context of what is now Article 81 EC; it held in Case C-234/89 *Delimitis* v. *Henninger Bräu AG* ([1991] ECR I-935) that the Commission must, where requested, assist the national courts in their task of applying EU competition law. It must not only supply information about the state of any relevant proceedings before the Commission itself, but also make available any information of a legal and economic nature which might assist the national court in resolving the case before it.

Overall, to assist Member States in relation to their duties under Article 10 EC, Temple Lang has suggested a 'Community code for national authorities', setting out their duties, with national authorities also taking proactive steps to audit themselves the principles of EU law which are relevant to their work (Temple Lang, 1998: 125). This will require a significant culture change within most national authorities and public services.

8.3   Enforcement Proceedings under Articles 226–228 EC

It is in pursuit of the Commission's obligation under Article 211 EC to 'ensure that the provisions of this Treaty and the measures taken by the institutions pursuant thereto are applied' that the primary obligation of direct enforcement of Member State obligations falls upon that institution. The principal instrument of enforcement is Article 226 EC (formerly Article 169 EC) which provides:

'If the Commission considers that a Member State has failed to fulfil an obligation under this Treaty, it shall deliver a reasoned opinion on the matter after giving the State concerned the opportunity to submit its observations.

If the State concerned does not comply with the opinion within the period laid down by the Commission, the latter may bring the matter before the Court of Justice.'

Article 227 EC (formerly Article 170 EC) gives a similarly framed power to the Member States which they may use against each other. It has been rarely used, and is practically a dead letter. The successful challenge by France to the UK's unilateral fishery conservation measures (Case 141/78 *France* v. *United Kingdom* [1979] ECR 2923) is one of the few examples of the invocation of this procedure. The use of the Article 227 procedure will always increase the tension and conflict between two states that are in dispute. The Member States prefer to leave the enforcement role primarily to the Commission, although in appropriate cases they are prepared to intervene in support of the Commission before the Court.

Remedies under the enforcement procedures of Articles 226 and 227 are set out in Article 228 EC. Prior to the Treaty of Maastricht, the Court of Justice was limited to a 'finding' of breach of the Treaty and the obligation which fell upon the Member State in breach was merely to take the necessary measures to comply with the judgment of the Court. However, although failure to comply with Court judgments has never been as serious a problem as non-compliance in general, a new paragraph was inserted in Article 228 by the Treaty of Maastricht which provides as follows (8.15):

'If the Commission considers that the Member State concerned has not taken such measures [i.e. to comply with a judgment of the Court] it shall, after giving that State the opportunity to submit its observations, issue a reasoned opinion specifying the points on which the Member State concerned has not complied with the judgment of the Court of Justice.

If the Member State concerned fails to take the necessary measures to comply with the Court's judgment within the time limit laid down by the Commission, the latter may bring the case before the Court of Justice. In so doing it shall specify the amount of the lump sum or penalty payment to be paid by the Member State concerned which it considers appropriate in the circumstances.

If the Court of Justice finds that the Member State concerned has not complied with its judgment it may impose a lump sum or penalty payment on it.'

A number of preliminary points can be made about the enforcement procedures of Articles 226–228. First, Articles 226 and 227 both divide the enforcement process into an administrative and a judicial phase. Opportunities for settlement exist throughout the administrative phase, but once the Commission has brought the matter before the Court at the conclusion of the period for compliance laid down in the reasoned opinion, it may continue with the proceedings, notwithstanding compliance by the Member State during the course of the proceedings (Case 240/86 *Commission* v. *Greece* [1988] ECR 1835), for the purposes of obtaining a clarification of the law by the Court. The Court indicated that such a declaratory judgment would still be useful, since it would clarify the possible liability of the Member State at national level for breach of the Treaty, and make it unnecessary for a national court to make a subsequent reference under Article 234 EC. This point may be increasingly important in view of the decision of the Court in Cases C-6, 9/90 *Francovich* v. *Italian State (Francovich I)* ([1991] ECR I-5357) regarding the award of damages against Member States for loss stemming from the failure to implement a directive.

Secondly, the Commission cannot take binding measures under Article 226 to order the compliance of the Member State, or to state the nature of the infringement. In this context, the enforcement of EU law and obligations against *Member States* under Articles 226–228 should be contrasted with the enforcement of the competition rules against *individuals* under Articles 81 and 82 EC and Regulation 17. In that context, the Commission may issue binding decisions that are enforceable against individuals unless successfully challenged in the Court. The Commission also has similar powers under Article 86(3) EC which enables it to address decisions or directives to the Member States in order to enforce the provisions of Article 86 on the application of the competition rules to public undertakings (4.3, 8.12). General enforcement proceedings under Article 88 ECSC also consist of a decision taken by the High Authority, which may be challenged before the Court.

The basic elements of a successful action by the Commission are the following:

(a) The Commission takes the view that a Member State is in breach of its obligations; the relevant obligations include those flowing from the constitutive treaties and any other international instruments which impose obligations upon the Member States, and from secondary acts of a binding nature. Failure to apply a general principle of law in the interpretation of provisions of EU law would probably also engage Member State responsibility under Article 10 and give rise to an Article 226 action, although the Court has not stated this explicitly (Temple Lang, 1990: 655).

(b) The Commission informs the state of its view and gives it an opportunity to answer the allegation or to end the offending practice or to repeal the offending law (*letter of formal notice*).

(c) The Commission delivers a *reasoned opinion* demonstrating the existence of the infringement.

(d) The state fails to comply with its Treaty obligation within the time limit laid down by the Commission. *[End of the administrative phase.]*

(e) *[Beginning of the judicial phase.]* The Commission brings the matter before the Court.

(f) The Court finds a violation.

(g) In the event of failure to comply, the procedure in Article 228 may be engaged.

8.4   The Range of National Conduct Capable of Engaging State Responsibility

The defendant in an enforcement action is the state, not the government, although it is conventionally the government that conducts the defence on behalf of the state. It is 'state conduct' which engages state responsibility, and the Court has defined this category broadly. It includes the following:

- acts or omissions on the part of the legislature, including the maintenance in force of an infringing statute, even if it is not applied (Case 167/73 *Commission* v. *France (French Merchant Seamen)* [1974] ECR 359);
- acts or omissions on the part of the executive, including the maintenance in force of an infringing administrative measure, even if it is not applied;
- even a single incident can form the basis for an enforcement action: in Case C-431/92 *Commission* v. *Germany (Environmental Impact Assessment)* ([1995] ECR I-2189) the Court held that proceedings under Article 226 do not need to be brought in respect of failure to implement a particular directive in general; they may instead concentrate on a failure in a specific case to apply a directive which has not yet been implemented;
- actions of constitutionally independent public authorities, such as local or regional authorities (Case 1/86 *Commission* v. *Belgium (Water Pollution)* [1987] ECR 2797), the constituent states within a federation (Case 9/74 *Casagrande* v. *Landeshauptstadt München* [1974] ECR 773) or law enforcement agencies (C-265/95 *Commission* v. *France*);
- decisions of national courts, which are subject to the duty of Community loyalty under Article 10. It was suggested by AG Warner in Case 30/77 *R* v. *Bouchereau* ([1977] ECR 1999) that mere judicial error should not engage state responsibility, but only the deliberate flouting of EU law by a national court. In fact, the Commission has been extremely hesitant to take proceedings in respect of judicial conduct citing 'the universal principle

of the independence of the judiciary' as the reason (6th Annual Report by the Commission to the European Parliament on the Monitoring of the Application of Community Law, COM(89) 411, p.95). Such proceedings have been started by the Commission, but have never actually been brought before the Court.

More contentiously, the Court has extended state responsibility to cover the acts of a private party under the control of the state. In Case 249/81 *Commission* v. *Ireland (Buy Irish)* ([1982] ECR 4005), Ireland was held responsible for the actions of the Irish Goods Council, a private limited company funded by the government, with a management appointed by and policies determined by the government, which was charged with the running of a 'buy Irish' campaign which contravened EU rules on the free movement of goods.

A large part of the business of the Commission in relation to enforcement actions arises automatically, so to speak, as a result of non-communication by the Member States of measures adopted to implement EU directives. These 'infringements' are logged and followed up automatically, and need to be seen in addition to infringements under investigation as a result of complaints from third parties or because the Commission itself has detected them (e.g. through the press, or as a result of a parliamentary question).

8.5   The Administrative Phase

The administrative phase is more than just a necessary precondition for the engagement of an action before the Court of Justice. From the perspective of the Commission, it is probably the most important phase, as it engages in the vital process of negotiation with Member States, seeking to achieve compliance without recourse to law, and establishing practices with which it hopes in the future Member States will comply. Snyder describes its role as in part 'playing for rules' (Snyder, 1993b: 30), in a context where

'the main form of dispute settlement used by the Commission is negotiation, and litigation is simply a part, sometimes inevitable but nevertheless generally a minor part, of this process.' (Snyder, 1993b: 30)

In similar terms, Mendrinou (1996) argues against viewing enforcement in isolation from the Commission's other roles:

'through its monitoring function, the Commission may reinforce policy priorities while taking into account general balances, sensitivities and issues in the policy environment. In this way, the Commission itself and the handling of its monitoring role become critical factors in determining the impact of non-compliance on integration ... Not only is the

Commission's role central in understanding the impact of non-compliance on integration, but the analysis of the Court's role would have to take into account the Commission's strategies.'

The administrative phase is itself subdivided into an informal and a formal phase. In the informal phase, the Commission investigates the possibility of a breach, and attempts to settle matters informally. The Commission then requests the Member State to submit its observations, stating the alleged infringement and laying down a time limit for the submission of observations (the formal letter of notice or 'Article 226 letter'). If it is not satisfied by the replies it may deliver a reasoned opinion which opens the formal phase. Article 226 EC incorporates the principle of *audi alteram partem* (the right to a fair hearing). Consequently, it is incumbent upon the Commission to ensure that the Member State is told in clear terms exactly what constitutes the alleged violation in order that it may submit its observations (Case 211/81 *Commission* v. *Denmark* [1982] ECR 4547).

In recent years, the Commission has instituted a notable overhaul of its procedures in relation to the administrative phase. This is unsurprising given the volume of complaints and alleged infringements, especially since the early 1990s (see Table 8.1), with some 3,311 cases under examination in the Commission's services as of 1 April 2000 (Figures 8.1 and 8.2). The Commission needs to make best use of the multi-stage procedure, ensuring settlement at an early stage. Thus in 1996 it initiated a series of reforms (reported in Commission's 14th Annual Report on Monitoring the Application of Community Law (1996), OJ 1997 C332/1) to enable the quicker processing of cases, the simplification of internal procedural rules and the transparency of Commission decision making in infringement cases. The latter is a matter relating primarily to the treatment of complainants and complaints, and is dealt with in 8.16. It is significant, however, that the Commission set itself certain priorities for dealing with infringements, which will inevitably impact upon the treatment of complaints. Its priorities are:

- infringements which cause the greatest harm for the EU legal order, i.e. failure to transpose directives and failure of national measures to comply with EU law in general;
- horizontal cases of incorrect application, particularly those detected from a series of specific complaints by individuals;
- infringements that seriously violate the interests that the relevant legislation is supposed to protect;
- infringements in relation to Community co-financing.

These are priorities in relation to interests at issue not the sectors implicated (cf. Figure 8.2).

Table 8.1   Statistics on enforcement proceedings under Article 226 EC: administrative phase to Court referral

Type of measure or statistical indicator	1998	1997	1996	1995
Complaints	1128	957	819	955
Detections by the Commission services	396	261	257	297
Letter of formal notice/ Article 226 letter	1101	1461	1168	1044
Reasoned Opinions	675	334	436	195
Referrals to the Court of Justice	123	121	93	72

Sources: Commission's Annual Reports on Monitoring the Application of Community Law

Fourteenth Annual Report (1996), OJ 1997 C332/1

Fifteenth Annual Report (1997), OJ 1998 C250/1

Sixteenth Annual Report (1998), COM(1998) 301

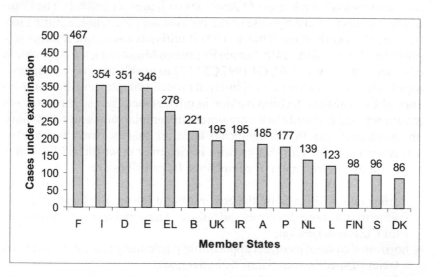

Source: Website of Commission Secretary General

Figure 8.1   Break down, by Member State, of the 3,311 cases under examination as of 1 April 2000

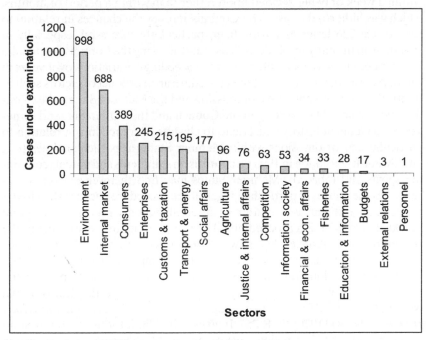

Source: Website of Commission Secretary General

Figure 8.2 Break down, by sector of the 3,.311 cases under
examination as of 1 April 2000

The most important internal administrative reform related to the formal letter of notice, which the Commission has 'dedramatised' and restored to its original function 'to facilitate veritable dialogue with the Member State in full respect of its rights, and to do so at the earliest possible opportunity.' Thus the letter is meant to seek observations, not begin an adversarial procedure forthwith, and the changes returned the letter to the informal stage of proceedings. The Commission also highlighted that it would insist, for the future, on stricter compliance with deadlines to respond to such letters and to reasoned opinions. The Commission has shifted from regarding the one-year time limit for the informal stage as a guideline to a rule. In 1998 (see the Commission's 16th Annual Report on the Monitoring of Community Law (1998), COM(1999) 301) it looked again at the achievement of these objectives, instituting further enhancements such as prioritising business on enforcement actions within fortnightly Commission meetings on the application of EU law traditionally devoted to state aid issues, and ensuring that Article 226 letters and reasoned opinions are served on Member States within a week of being decided upon rather than within a period of months, which was hitherto the case. The Commission saw the changes in relation to the Article 226 letter as having been particularly successful, especially in speeding up the early resolution of cases and allowing the Commission to take quicker decisions to open enforcement proceedings. Variations over years in relation to the various stages of the procedure are a product of factors such as political priorities within the Commission and the Member States, the calendar and rhythm of law making in the Council and the Parliament, and sometimes accidents of history which lead to clusters of complaints in relation to particular acts or omissions within Member States at particular times (e.g. new Swedish legislation in 1998 on controls on shipments and parcels containing spirits and tobacco). Member States may find themselves over-represented in the figures at particular stages of the procedure because they find it particularly difficult as a matter of internal political process to respond quickly to Commission proceedings. The overall trend in every aspect of the procedure under Article 226 is upwards, which is hardly surprising in a larger and more complex EU (on the problem of non-compliance see further 8.17).

The alleged violations must be defined by the reasoned opinion: the Commission cannot subsequently raise matters before the Court which were not contained in the reasoned opinion (Case 31/69 *Commission* v. *Italy (Export Rebates)* [1970] ECR 25). It gives a time limit for the Member State to comply with EU law, which must be reasonable. This may vary according to the circumstances of the case. In Case 85/85 *Commission* v. *Belgium* ([1986] ECR 1149), the Commission required Belgium to remove a property tax imposed on EU officials resident in Belgium within two weeks of the reasoned opinion. The Court held that the time limit was reasonable because the Belgian Government knew of (and had not contested) the Commission's position long before the Article 226 procedure was initiated. However, in Case 293/85 *Commission* v. *Belgium* ([1988] ECR 305) two weeks was considered an unreasonably short time limit for Belgium to remove discriminatory fees imposed on foreign nationals studying within the Belgian higher education system. In Case 74/82 *Commission* v. *Ireland (Imports of poultry)* ([1984] ECR 317) the Court even accepted a five-day time limit. The principle of collegiality within the Commission constrains the drawing up of the reasoned opinion (4.2) (Case C-191/95 *Commission* v. *Germany* [1998] ECR I-5449). The Commission's decision to issue a reasoned opinion must be the subject of collective deliberation by the College of Commissioners, which implies that the information on which those decisions were based must be available to the Commissioners. However, it is not necessary for the College of Commissioners itself formally to decide the wording of the acts which give effect to the decision to issue a reasoned opinion and to put them in final form (Case C-272/97 *Commission* v. *Germany* [1999] ECR I-2175).

The reasoned opinion cannot be challenged by an aggrieved private party (or indeed a Member State) by way of Article 230 EC annulment proceedings, as it is not an act which produces legal effects; it is merely a step in the proceedings (Case 48/65 *Lütticke* v. *Commission* [1966] ECR 19) (see 9.2). However, a Member State which is subject to proceedings will have an opportunity in the context of the judicial phase to raise irregularities in the reasoned opinion, such as the failure to state reasons, just as it can with any other procedural irregularities that have occurred during the course of the administrative phase. No party can force the Commission to take enforcement proceedings; failure to act is not actionable under Articles 230 or 232 EC (Case 247/87 *Star Fruit* v. *Commission* [1989] ECR 291). The Commission's discretion is likewise unfettered as to when it may wish to bring enforcement proceedings. In Case 7/71 *Commission* v. *France (Euratom Supply Agency)* ([1971] ECR 1003) – an action brought under the materially identical Article 141 Euratom – the Court held:

> 'The action for a declaration that a state has failed to fulfil an obligation … does not have to be brought within a predetermined period, since, by reason of its nature and purpose, this procedure involves a power on the part of the Commission to consider the most appropriate means and time-limits for the purposes of putting an end to any contraventions of the Treaty.'

Of course, Member States can have recourse to Article 227 if they are dissatisfied with the conduct of the Commission, but in terms of formal proceedings an aggrieved private party can only seek to bring proceedings in the national court which have the effect of enforcing EU law against the national authorities (for further discussion of the status of complainants, see 8.16).

The Commission's discretion is also not restricted by any form of 'estoppel' whereby it is deemed to have consented by previous informal or even formal approval of the Member State's conduct. It may at any point revise its view and take infringement proceedings (Case 288/83 *Commission* v. *Ireland (Potatoes)* [1985] ECR 1761). Nor will the Commission's action be 'time-barred' by delay in bringing proceedings. This is well illustrated by a rather strange enforcement action brought by the Commission against Germany in respect of failures to implement certain EU directives on waste more than six years after the entry into force of the basic German legislation on the shipment of waste, and at a time when the EU had in fact changed its policy in that field along the same lines as those followed by that legislation. The Court expressed the view that the Commission's decision to institute and pursue the action was 'surprising'. However, it went on to conclude that:

> 'It is settled law that the rules of Article 226 of the Treaty must be applied and the Commission is not obliged to act within a specified period. The

Commission is thus entitled to decide, in its discretion, on what date it may be appropriate to bring an action and it is not for the Court to review the exercise of that discretion' (Case C-422/92 *Commission* v. *Germany (Waste Directives)* [1995] ECR I-1097 at p. 1131).

8.6   The Judicial Phase

In the judicial phase, the Court will examine both the procedural propriety of the action as so far conducted by the Commission, as an issue of the admissibility of the action, and the substance of the alleged violations. The Commission must prove its case, of course, and on rare occasions the Court will find for the Member State on the question as to whether there has in fact been an infringement of EU law (e.g. Case C-300/95 *Commission* v. *UK (Product Liability Directive)* [1997] ECR I-2649). Although the Commission has an extensive discretion in relation to the decision whether to bring an action, it is strictly bound by the procedural formalities of Article 226. This has often been the most fruitful area for Member States when searching for a defence (for a recent example, see Case C-266/94 *Commission* v. *Spain* [1995] ECR I-1975, where the Court declared the Commission's action inadmissible because of its failure to take into account the observations made by Spain in response to the Commission's letter). In contrast, the following paragraphs set out the arguments put forward by the Member States which have consistently been judged by the Court to be ineffective defences to enforcement actions.

8.7   Questions of National Law in General

No matter pertaining to the status of the national measure in question can hinder a finding of infringement by the Court. In Case 48/71 *Commission* v. *Italy (Art Treasures II)* ([1972] ECR 527) Italy cited as a defence the difficulties of parliamentary procedure it had experienced in abolishing a tax on the export of artistic and historical treasures to other Member States, owing to the need to observe the relevant constitutional requirements. Attributing the obligation to comply to the supremacy of EU law, the Court stated that:

'the attainment of the objectives of the Community requires that the rules of Community law established by the Treaty itself or arising from procedures which it has instituted are fully applicable at the same time and with identical effects over the whole territory of the Community without the Member States being able to place any obstacles in the way. The grant made by Member States to the Community of rights and powers in accordance with the provisions of the Treaty involves a definitive limitation on their sovereign rights and no provisions whatsoever of national law may be invoked to override this limitation.'

8.8 Legislative Paralysis and Change of Government

The ineffectiveness, permanent or temporary, of the national political system cannot be used as a defence. There is no element of fault contained in a finding of infringement of the Treaty under Article 226; the finding is a simple objective statement of fact concerning the failure of the Member State to fulfil its obligations, and it is irrelevant whether the failure stems from inertia or opposition (see Case 322/82 *Commission* v. *France* [1983] ECR 3705, per AG Rozès). In Case 77/69 *Commission* v. *Belgium (Pressed Wood)* ([1970] ECR 237) the Belgian government was unable to secure the passage through the legislature of a bill revising a law which imposed a discriminatory tax upon imported pressed wood. The constitutional separation between the legislature and the executive did not preclude the responsibility of Belgium for infringement. In Italy, frequent changes of government have often hampered the effective implementation of EU directives, but this has not been accepted as a defence by the Court (e.g. Case 136/81 *Commission* v. *Italy* [1982] ECR 3547 – failure to implement directive harmonising provisions of company law).

8.9 Defences Related to the Nature of the Relevant Provision of EU law

The obligation upon Member States under Article 10 and more specific provisions of the Treaty is to implement EU law in full and proper form. Thus it is insufficient and no defence to adopt a circular binding only upon the administration but with an uncertain effect *vis-à-vis* third parties in order to implement a directive on atmospheric pollution (Case C-361/88 *Commission* v. *Germany* ([1991] ECR I-2567). Similarly the Member State may not rely upon the direct effect of a directive as a substitute for implementation. It was held to be no defence in proceedings against the Netherlands for failure to implement a Council Directive on the quality of drinking water that regional and local authorities were in any case directly bound by the Directive, provisions of which were justiciable before national courts, and that the authorities had in fact implemented the Directive in the practical management of water quality (Case 96/81 *Commission* v. *Netherlands* [1982] ECR 1791).

It is not clear whether the alleged unlawfulness of the EU measure with which non-compliance is alleged is an effective defence. Case 156/77 *Commission* v. *Belgium* ([1978] ECR 1881) and Case 3/59 *Germany* v. *High Authority* ([1960] ECR 53) are usually cited as demonstrating that if a Member

State has failed to challenge a EU measure directly under the relevant provisions of the EC or ECSC Treaties, it cannot raise the unlawfulness of the measure in enforcement proceedings brought against it. The two sets of provisions are separate, with different objectives. However, there may be an exception for measures which contain such serious and manifest defects that they can be regarded as 'non-existent' (Case 226/87 *Commission* v. *Greece* [1988] ECR 3611) (see 15.2).

8.10   The Principle of Reciprocity

The EU legal order differs sharply from the general public international legal order in that there is no defence of reciprocity. A Member State cannot escape a finding of infringement by claiming that another Member State is also failing to comply (Case 232/78 *Commission* v. *France (Lamb Wars)* [1979] ECR 2729). The same principle applies to the claim that the EU institutions are in breach of their obligations. In Cases 90 and 91/63 *Commission* v. *Luxembourg and Belgium (Dairy Products)* ([1964] ECR 625) the Court declared:

> 'except where otherwise expressly provided, the basic concept of the Treaty requires that the Member States shall not take the law into their own hands. Therefore the fact that the Council failed to carry out its obligations cannot relieve the defendants from carrying out theirs.'

8.11   Expedited Proceedings

Expedited proceedings, which allow the Commission to bring an alleged infringement before the Court without observing the procedural requirements laid down in Article 226, are provided for *inter alia* in Articles 88, 95(9) (see 8.12), and 298 EC. Articles 87 and 88 EC charge the Commission with the task of reviewing state aids, and where necessary, with issuing decisions requiring Member States to abolish, to alter or not to bring into force aids which are incompatible with the common market. A Member State which fails to comply with such a decision may be brought directly before the Court by the Commission, without prejudice to Articles 226 and 227 (Gil Ibáñez, 1998b).

Article 298 EC allows the Commission to bring before the Court a Member State which it considers is abusing the powers it is given under Article 297 to derogate from the Treaty rules in event of a threat to internal or external security (after consulting with the other Member States). If it considers that the derogation from the rules of the Treaty applied by the Member State is having the effect of distorting competition in the common market, the Commission (or a Member State) may bring the matter before the Court of Justice, which will give its ruling in camera. The Commission made its first use of this provision in 1994, when it brought an action against Greece for applying unilateral sanctions against the Former Yugoslav Republic of Macedonia (FYROM). Greece alleges that Macedonia has territorial ambitions in relation to the creation of a 'greater Macedonia' which threaten Greek territorial integrity. The Court dismissed the Commission's application for interim measures (8.14; Case C-120/94R *Commission* v. *Greece (FYROM)* [1994] ECR I-3037).

8.12 Enforcement and the Internal Market

Although actions brought under Article 226 EC remain numerically by far the most important, it is interesting to note the development of a greater variety of means of enforcement specifically concerned with the evolution of the internal market (cf. 8.1). In particular, there has been a marked shift in this area away from the use of individualised litigation as the basis for the enforcement strategy. Evidence for this comes from the use of Article 86(3) EC which allows the Commission to issue directives or decisions aimed specifically at the deregulation or restructuring of highly regulated markets, such as the telecommunications market (4.3; Flynn, 1995: 224–227). According to Emiliou (1993: 314) this 'is a provision of a hybrid nature where the supervisory and administrative functions of the Commission merge'. Clearly it may be more efficient for the Commission to make use of its own powers of decision, rather than relying on either a negotiation or litigation strategy based around Article 226.

Then there is the Commission's role in relation to the operation of Article 95(4)–(9) EC, which represents potentially a very significant element of variability in the operation of the internal market. Member States may be able to continue to apply, after the adoption of harmonisation measures by QMV under Article 95, national provisions justified by reference to a 'major need' such as health and safety or protection of the environment. It must notify them to the Commission. The Commission must verify that the national provisions are not excessive or arbitrary, and must then approve or reject them, under a time limit of six months. It may also bring the offending Member State before the Court of Justice through expedited proceedings for improper use of the powers (8.11). The Commission's own activities here are, however, subject to challenge in a way which its discretionary role in relation to Article 226 is not, for its consideration of the measures will result in the taking of a decision. In Case C-41/93 *France* v. *Commission (PCP)* ([1994] ECR I-1829), which was decided under an earlier pre-Amsterdam version of the rules, the Court accepted a challenge by France to a Commission decision confirming German rules on pentachlorophenol which were more restrictive than the relevant EU harmonisation measures. The Court ruled that the reasoning given by the Commission was inadequate (6.8), in particular because it had proved sufficient to state what reasons of health and safety justified the preservation of the German rules.

Internal market measures themselves may construct mechanisms for their own supervision and enforcement. This was the case with the Product Safety Directive (Directive 92/59 OJ 1992 L228/24), which was based on Article 95. Germany mounted an unsuccessful challenge to the legal basis of this measure, focusing its attention specifically on Article 9 of the directive which establishes a process whereby the Commission can, after following a specified procedure, take temporary measures to ensure the free movement of a product against which one or more Member States have taken restrictive measures. Such measures can take the form of decisions addressed to the Member States. The Court rejected an argument that such individual measures cannot be regarded as a form of harmonisation, and therefore could not be validly adopted on the basis of Article 95 (Case C-359/92 *Germany* v. *Council (Product Safety Directive)* [1994] ECR I-3681). The case demonstrates an elision of the policy making and enforcement functions which operate to enhance the effectiveness of the work of the Commission.

The procedures for pre-notification of national technical standards, including measures relating to services within the information society (*per* the most recent amendment) (8.1) are clearly a part of an overall framework of EU law enforcement (12.16). This framework may in future be significantly strengthened. At the Amsterdam European Council in June 1997 the Commission was asked to examine ways and means of guaranteeing in an effective manner the free movement of goods, and it has proposed a Council Regulation giving the Commission power to take mandatory legal decisions requiring the removal of obstacles to the free movement of goods, and if the Member State fails to comply the Commission will be able to bring expedited proceedings under Article 226 EC.

8.13   **Enforcement and Economic and Monetary Union**

In an amendment to the scope of the jurisdiction of the Court introduced by the Treaty of Maastricht, what is now Article 237(d) EC gives the Court jurisdiction in disputes concerning

> 'the fulfilment by national central banks of obligations under this Treaty and the Statute of the ESCB. In this connection the powers of the Council of the ECB in respect of national central banks shall be the same as those conferred upon the Commission in respect of Member States by Article 226. If the Court of Justice finds that a national central bank has failed to fulfil an obligation under this Treaty, that bank shall be required to take the necessary measures to comply with the judgment of the Court of Justice.'

While this provision is presently largely of academic interest, as the level of monetary integration becomes greater – at least as between certain Member States – and the stringent duties on national central banks under Articles 98–124 EC start to apply, it may become a great deal more important. It might be of assistance, where a national bank bows to public pressure and gives special credit facilities to a public authority in breach of Article 101 EC (Craig, 1999b: 115).

Notably, however, in relation to the mechanism for avoiding excessive government deficits (Article 104 EC), the use of Articles 226 and 227 is explicitly excluded from parts of the process (Article 104(10) EC). The Council is constructed in the main in this part of the Treaty as the guardian of EU law, rather than the Commission (Gil Ibáñez, 1999: 109).

8.14 Interim Measures

Article 243 EC states:

> 'The Court of Justice may in any cases before it prescribe any necessary interim measures.'

This possibility applies both to Article 226 proceedings (e.g. Case 61/77R *Commission* v. *Ireland (Fisheries)* [1977] ECR 937) and to expedited proceedings, such as those brought under Article 88 (e.g. Cases 31 and 53/77R *Commission* v. *United Kingdom (Pig Producers)* [1977] ECR 921). An application for interim relief may be made at any time once the administrative stage has been completed. Applications for interim measures are heard generally by the President sitting alone, without the assistance of an Advocate General. Interim measures may be awarded if two conditions are satisfied; the Commission must show:

– a *prima facie* case (i.e. the case must not be manifestly ill-founded);
– urgency, which is assessed in relation to the necessity for interim measures in order to prevent serious and irreparable damage to the interests of the EU.

At first sight it might appear that the powers of the Court are greater in interim proceedings than they are in the main proceedings. This is because the Court's judgments are framed in more trenchant terms (e.g. the order to suspend the application of the Merchant Shipping Act 1988 in Case C-246/89R *Commission* v. *United Kingdom* [1989] ECR 3125); however, the judgment remains declaratory in effect.

In a departure from the usual practice, the dismissal of the Commission's application for interim measures in the *FYROM* case (Case C-120/94R

Commission v. *Greece*) was given in a judgment handed down by a full Court of thirteen judges. The Court concluded that the Commission had failed to show that Greece had committed a 'manifest' breach of EU law (although it was prepared to accept that it had shown a *prima facie* case). More serious was the Commission's failure to show that there would be 'serious and irreparable' damage to the interests of the EU. It was not sufficient to show that there was damage to FYROM.

8.15   Sanctions

The declaratory nature of the Court's judgment under Article 226 means that the Court does not have the power to declare national measures void. On the other hand, it would be inconsistent with the principle of the supremacy of EU law for a national court which was aware of such a finding on the part of the Court to apply an infringing national rule: national law is thus in effect rendered 'inapplicable' (Case 106/77 *Amministrazione delle Finanze dello Stato* v. *Simmenthal (Simmenthal II)* [1978] ECR 629; see 12.13).

The declaratory judgment under Article 228 is binding, and thus failure to comply with a Court judgment is itself a Treaty obligation and can therefore be the subject of further enforcement proceedings. In Case C-291/93 *Commission* v. *Italy* ([1994] ECR I-859) the Court held that although Article 228 does not specify the period within which a judgment must be complied with, compliance as soon as possible is required in the interests of the immediate and uniform application of EU law.

For a number of years, the Commission argued that there was a need for more effective sanctions, and it put before the Intergovernmental Conference (IGC) on Political Union convened in 1990 proposals for the imposition of financial penalties for failure to give effect to a judgment. These proposals attracted the support in particular of the UK, and consequently, amendments to what was then Article 171 EC were introduced by the Treaty of Maastricht. The initial proposal to impose a penalty comes from the Commission, but the discretion to fine lies with the Court. Members of the Court of Justice were known to be reluctant to be given the entire responsibility for fining Member States. The question remains open whether fines will need to be high to bring about compliance and to deter recidivism, or whether the simple fact of the imposition of a fine, however small, and the associated political opprobrium, will be sufficient. The Commission has already on numerous occasions taken a decision to seek such penalties, and fixed the proposed level. Most cases in which the Commission has proposed sanctions have settled, and one case has recently reached a conclusion before the Court of Justice (Case C-387/97 *Commission* v. *Greece*, 4 July 2000). The Court of justice ordered Greece to pay a penalty payment of 20,000 euros per day until it complied with an earlier judgment of 1992 regarding compliance with waste disposal directives. According to the Commission (Commission's 16th Annual Report on the Monitoring of Community Law (1998), COM(1999) 301), the arrangements do have a significant deterrent effect:

> 'The effectiveness of the mechanism has been borne out, since Member States responded to most penalty decisions by rapidly coming into line with Community law, either before the case was referred to the Court or shortly afterwards.'

The Commission's practice is governed by a published *Memorandum on applying Article 171 of the EC Treaty* (OJ 1996 C242/6) and a statement laying down its *Method of calculating the penalty payments provided for pursuant to Article 171 of the EC Treaty* (OJ 1997 C63/2). The Commission interprets Article 228 as meaning that it must, when referring a case back to the Court of Justice, either ask for a penalty, specifying the amount or – if the infringement is sufficiently minor not to merit asking for a penalty – give reasons why it is not doing so (see Bonnie, 1998). There are three fundamental criteria the Commission applies in deciding the amount of the penalty to ask for:

– the seriousness of the infringement;
– the duration of the infringement; and
– the need to ensure that the penalty itself is a deterrent to further infringements.

There were other proposals to enhance the sanctions system put before the IGC, including the suggestion that the Court should be given the power to strike down infringing (i.e. unconstitutional) national legislation, a power held by the constitutional courts of many federal states. An alternative suggestion was that the Court should have the power to award compensation to the victims of an infringement in the context of enforcement proceedings, but the Court has come closer to giving effect to this suggestion by articulating the responsibility of Member States for damage caused by failure to implement a Directive in *Francovich I*, and subsequent cases applying the principle of State liability (see Chapters 12 and 13).

Under Article 88(2) the Commission has a policy of requiring Member States to reclaim monies paid to the beneficiaries of state aids which are found to be incompatible with the Common Market (OJ 1983 C318/3). However, the Commission has to take care to observe the procedural rights of the interested parties. This is illustrated by the Rover/British Aerospace 'sweetener'. In 1988 the Commission issued a decision authorising certain capital aids by the UK to Rover in connection with its acquisition by British Aerospace. It later came to the conclusion that certain financial concessions had been made which were not authorised by the decision, and it issued a further decision ordering the UK to reclaim the payments. This was successfully challenged by British Aerospace and Rover (Case C-294/90 *British Aerospace and Rover Group Holdings plc* v. *Commission* [1992] ECR I-493). The Court held that if the Commission objected to the granting of a new aid, it was obliged to follow the procedures laid down in Article 88 once more in order to respect the rights of the defence of interested parties, in particular the right to be heard. It could not short-circuit these procedures by simply requiring the aid to be reclaimed.

8.16   The Individual and the Commission's Enforcement Powers

The 'direct' and 'indirect' enforcement processes for EU law should exist and function in a manner which is complementary and cooperative. One point which is notable about EU law has been its construction of the individual as a subject of law – particularly in the context of actions before the national courts. In one field, that of public procurement, a Remedies Directive has been adopted precisely for the purposes of enhancing the enforcement possibilities of individuals in national courts. In contrast, although considerably improved in recent years, the individual still has a rather much more vestigial position in relation to the Commission's own direct enforcement powers, a point already referred to in the context of Article 226 proceedings (Case 247/87 *Star Fruit* v. *Commission* [1989] ECR 291; 8.5), but equally relevant in the context of other enforcement mechanisms. Yet as the figures show, complaints form a very substantial percentage of the cases of alleged infringements which come before the Commission, and massively outweigh the Commission's own 'detection' of complaints (Table 8.1). Thus the Commission has always had a rather paradoxical relationship with the complainants and the idea of complaints, seeing them as 'indispensable instruments' (13th Annual Report on Monitoring the Application of Community Law (1995), OJ 1996 C303/1), and yet not wanting to be seen as a type of 'Community Supercourt' with overhigh expectations among complainants about the Commission's capacity to pursue all individual infringements (14th Annual Report).

The point was discussed in some detail by the Court of First Instance in Case T-84/94 *Bundesverband der Bilanzbuchhalter eV* v. *Commission* ([1995] ECR II-101), when it dismissed an action for annulment of a Commission Decision rejecting the applicant association's complaint seeking a declaration by the Commission that German legislation on tax advisors infringes Articles 49 and 82 EC (free movement of services; abuse of a dominant position by an undertaking). The Court repeated the well-established principle that the Commission has full discretion in relation to Article 226 proceedings, and then applied this principle to Article 86(3), which might have offered an alternative means of proceeding in such a (competition policy) case for the Commission. It concluded that this provision too implies 'a wide margin of discretion' for the Commission in deciding whether to take action (p. 112). The judgment was confirmed on appeal to the Court of Justice (Case C-107/95 P *Bundesverband der Bilanzbuchhalter eV* v. *Commission* [1997] ECR I-947), and while the Court's dismissal of the Article 226 point was brief and to the point, Advocate General La Pergola's opinion contains an extended discussion of the position of Article 226 in the institutional system. He concentrated on the role played by Article 226 in *inter-institutional* relations (rather than directly in 'citizen-EU' relations), highlighting that the benefits to individuals from this provision may well be indirect and that they are excluded from challenging judicially the exercise of discretion.

In its 1996 reforms of the administrative procedure, and then again in 1998 (8.5), the Commission directly addressed the situation of the complainant. Much of that change in approach can be attributed to the wider trend toward changes in relation to access, transparency and the general openness of the Commission *vis-à-vis* the individual. However, it has also been firmly pushed in this direction by the Ombudsman, who was faced with many complaints regarding the Commission's unresponsiveness to complaints made about the building of the Newbury Bypass in Southern England, which became a *cause célèbre* for environmental campaigners. The intervention of the Ombudsman has highlighted the potential of *extra-judicial* remedies in improving the situation of individual complainants within the EU administrative framework. He urged that the complainant be seen as 'citizen of the Union', not as a kind of informer (Södermann, 1998: 16). He emphasised that the Commission has *discretionary* not *dictatorial* power in relation to the administrative procedure – strong language indeed. Consequently, the Ombudsman conducted an own-initiative enquiry into the status of complainants, looking to improve the quality of the Commission's administrative procedures (303/97/PD, closed on 13 October 1997 and reported in the Ombudsman's Annual Report for 1997). The Commission was pushed into acknowledging that it must register complaints and keep complainants informed about the treatment of the case, which it now does, although in some cases through block acknowledgements in the *Official Journal*. The Commission also routinely informs complainants where it plans to terminate a case, giving them the opportunity to make observations. An improved complaints form is in use.

Another possible avenue for complainants to pursue will be to use the Commission's rules on access to documents, in order to obtain materials which reveal something more about the Commission's approach in a case than is clear from the published materials such as press releases or direct communications to complainants. The applicants in Case T-303/97 *Bavarian Lager Company* v. *Commission* (14 October 1999) objected to rules on tied houses in the UK which, they alleged, made it difficult for them to market the beer they imported from other Member States. A specific rule, termed the Guest Beer Provision was at issue, and the Commission considered taking action against the UK and drew up a 'reasoned opinion' which it never sent to the UK. The applicant requested a copy of that document from the Commission, but was refused on grounds that disclosure could undermine the protection of the public interest, in particular Commission inspection and investigation tasks, as foreseen in the 1994 Code of Conduct on access to documents (10.8). The Court of First Instance held that that 'not all documents linked to infringement procedures are covered by the exception relating to protection of the public interest' (para. 41). However, it concluded that the document sought by the applicant was not in truth a reasoned opinion as it was never sent, but merely a preparatory document. It had been misclassified by both the applicant and the Commission. The Court then concluded that:

> 'it is clear that the procedure under Article [226] of the Treaty was still at the stage of inspection and investigation. As the Court stated in the *WWF* judgment [Case T-105/95 *WWF UK* v *Commission* [1997] ECR II-313], the Member States are entitled to expect confidentiality from the Commission during investigations which may lead to an infringement procedure (para. 63). The disclosure of documents relating to the investigation stage, during the negotiations between the Commission and the Member State concerned, could undermine the proper conduct of the infringement procedure inasmuch as its purpose, which is to enable the Member State to comply of its own accord with the requirements of the Treaty or, if appropriate, to justify its position … could be jeopardised. The safeguarding of that objective warrants, under the heading of protection of the public interest, the refusal of access to a preparatory document relating to the investigation stage of the procedure under Article [226] of the Treaty' (para. 46).

Thus the Court confirmed its earlier reasoning in relation to preparatory documents respecting Member State confidentiality, but left open the possibility that a 'true' reasoned opinion might be obtained through the access to documents rules.

Only in the areas of competition policy, merger control and state aid control is a different pattern of treatment of the individual visible (see also Chapter 15). Under Article 88(2) EC, which provides for the Commission to take decisions applying in specific cases the substantive standard of legality of state aid contained in Article 87 EC ('incompatibility with the common market'), interested parties – which may include individuals or undertakings – do have consultation rights. If they disagree with the final decision taken by the Commission, they do have a right to challenge it before the Court of First Instance under Article 230 EC (Case C-198/91 *William Cook plc* v. *Commission* [1993] ECR I-2486). Likewise, those who submit complaints to the Commission about alleged violations of Articles 81 and 82 EC, under Article 3 of Regulation 17, are entitled to a basic investigation of the issues of fact and law raised by their complaint, followed – it would appear – by a determination on the part of the Commission which they can challenge before the Court of First Instance (Case T-24/90 *Automec* v. *Commission (Automec II)* [1992] ECR II-2223). They are not entitled to force the Commission to undertake a full investigation of their complaint, or to begin proceedings under Articles 81 and 82. Total inaction on the part of the Commission in relation to the complaint, however, can be sanctioned by an action for failure to act under Article 232 EC (Shaw, 1995; Vesterdorp, 1994). Complainants may also challenge substantive determinations by the Commission (Case 26/76 *Metro-SB-Großmärkte* v. *Commission* [1977] ECR 1875), as can complainants under the Merger Control Regulation (Case T-3/93 *Société Anonyme à Participation Ouvrière Nationale Air France* v. *Commission (Air France)* [1994] ECR II-121).

8.17 The Problem of Non-compliance

Non-compliance can take numerous forms, including non-implementation, non-application and non-enforcement (van den Bossche, 1996). There are also problems of 'competitive under-implementation' as the Member States see advantages in restricting the effects of EU rules, either because they are observing closely the activities of others, or because under-implementation of, say, environmental measures, leads to competitive advantage at home, and environmental damage in another state (Weatherill, 2000c). The risks attendant upon under-implementation mean that enforcement of the law is taken very seriously within the EU legal order. The pursuit and prosecution of violations of the Treaty is viewed as one aspect of the application of the rule of law. Non-compliance is therefore a challenge to the fabric of the legal order, as well as a failure to give effect to the intentions of the drafters of the Treaty and of the framers of legislation. The Commission has responded to this challenge by monitoring national compliance and it submits Annual Reports on Monitoring the Application of Community Law to the Parliament (see most recently the 16th Annual Report for 1998, COM(1999) 301). It has adopted measures to improve the effectiveness of the enforcement procedures. For example, the Commission has clearly distinguished between two separate situations: actions arising from national *failures* to implement directives and actions arising in respect of other breaches of the Treaty. The issue of non-communication is dealt with automatically. The latest transposition figures (Table 8.2) highlight very high rates of formal compliance, and much less differentiation between individual Member States, with a minimum of 94.5 per cent (Greece) and a maximum of 97.1 per cent (Denmark). Interestingly, in the last edition of this book which contained figures highlighting the situation in relation to directives due to be transposed by 31 December 1994, rates at the end of 1994 varied between 86.7 per cent (Greece) and 97.6 per cent (Denmark). Somehow the Danish have slipped in their compliance! The average has risen from 91.89 per cent to 94.53 per cent. Difficulties in one of the main trouble spots, Italy (88.4 per cent in 1994 and 94.1 per cent in 2000), were alleviated by the adoption of a new procedure in 1988 whereby an annual EU law is passed implementing *en bloc* all applicable EU legislation. The UK has traditionally prided itself in on a high level of compliance – whatever its political difficulties with the obligations of membership. This is better borne out by 2000 figures (95.4 per cent, against an EU average of 94.5 per cent) than by the 1994 figures, which put the UK at below the EU average, with only 89.4 per cent notification to the Commission of measures transposing directives which were due for transposition.

Table 8.2   Report on the application of directives (1 January 2000)

Rank	Member States	Directives applicable at the date of reference	Directives for which measures have been notified	Percent of notification, at the date of reference
1	Denmark	1499	1456	97.13%
2	Spain	1502	1449	96.47%
3	Netherlands	1505	1447	96.15%
4	Finland	1498	1436	95.86%
5	Sweden	1500	1437	95.80%
6	Germany	1507	1439	97.49%
7	UK	1504	1435	95.48%
8	Austria	1501	1425	94.94%
9	Belgium	1505	1428	94.88%
10	Italy	1504	1416	94.15%
11	Ireland	1499	1411	94.13%
12	France	1505	1412	93.82%
13	Portugal	1507	1407	93.36%
14	Luxembourg	1503	1402	93.28%
15	Greece	1503	1383	92.02%
Total/Average EC		**1508**	**1426**	**94.53%**

Source: Website of Commission Secretary General.

Each year the Commission opens well over 1,000 new proceedings by issuing formal letters of notice. Its procedures in relation to directives have led to a sharp rise in the number of reasoned opinions delivered (up from 279 in 1990, via 546 in 1994, to 675 in 1998 with a small dip in 1997: Table 8.1). The number of referrals to the Court has risen more slowly (from 78 in 1990, via 89 in 1994, to 123 in 1998), with a sharp dip to 44 in 1993 and a dip again in 1995 to 73. Even so, Article 226 actions do occupy a good proportion of the Court of Justice's available time. In 1995 it decided over 30 such actions brought by the Commission. By 1998 that had risen to 54 Article 226 actions, although the figure dipped in 1999 to 46 actions. Since the Court decided 378 cases in total in 1999, that represented some 12 per cent of the total judgments. However, apart from monitoring the implementation of directives, the Commission is very greatly indebted to the vigilance of the public to enable it to uncover infringements of the Treaty. It tends to receive more than 1,000 complaints per year from private parties, and since 1989 has made available a standard complaint form to facilitate the process of making a complaint. It also receives information about alleged infringements via parliamentary questions, and petitions sent to the Parliament by aggrieved citizens.

There is a multitude of reasons for non-compliance; only rarely is it outright opposition to a particular measure or the protection of national sovereignty which lies behind a failure to comply. Of course, being outvoted in the adoption process is one reason why a Member State might very well drag its heels over the implementation process, but it may equally be the fact that a EU measure is badly drafted, subject to misinterpretation or just very complex or that representatives of the Member States were not fully and properly involved in preliminary negotiations within the Commission. Reasons which are internal to the Member States themselves are often significant; legislative paralysis has been a particular problem where there are coalition governments or frequent changes of government. If a measure requires active and expensive steps to be taken (e.g. the building of a water treatment plant), there may be a natural tendency for Member States to drag their feet (Azzi, 2000: 57). Executive inefficiency with no clear line of authority determining who is responsible for ensuring the implementation of EU law, and the particularities of the national division of power within each state can also be contributing factors. The alleged infringement may also result from a measure which previously the Commission has shown no particular inclination to enforce, but for which compliance is now required following a change in policy.

The enhancement of sanctions for non-compliance with a Court judgment is just one mechanism aimed at solving a more general problem. It may be that in addition to its perennial need for more resources, the Commission also needs a clear order of priority for the pursuit of cases of non-compliance. Much of this was achieved with the 1996 and 1998 reforms. Finally, it has often been suggested that the task of bringing about compliance could be hived off to a separate service, thus separating the enforcement role from the policy-making role. In view of the comments made in 8.5 about the relationship between policy making and enforcement this seems an undesirable development from the point of view of the Commission.

The enforcement proceedings contained in the Treaty need to be viewed in the context of the alternative mechanisms available for the enforcement of EU law against the authorities of the Member States in the form of proceedings brought before the national courts. Direct and indirect enforcement need to be seen as two aspects of one overall structure; indeed, frequently they will run side by side, with the same issue coming before the Court for decision in the context of different proceedings. This occurred with the litigation surrounding the restrictions on non-national fishing boats introduced by the Merchant Shipping Act 1988, which has recently reached a final culmination in the UK courts. In Case C-246/89R *Commission* v. *United Kingdom*, the Court awarded interim measures against the UK at the behest of the Commission, who had received complaints from Spanish fishing boat owners based in the UK. Just a few months later, in Case C-213/89 *R* v. *Secretary of State for Transport, ex parte Factortame Ltd (Factortame I)* ([1990] ECR I-2433) the Court gave a judgment making it clear that the House of Lords should give an interim remedy in the national proceedings concerned with the same dispute. Finally, in Cases C-46, 48/93 *Brasserie du Pécheur and Factortame III* ([1996] ECR I-1029), the Court concluded that the UK Government could in principle be liable for damages suffered by the private individuals in such circumstances, depending upon the severity of the breach to be determined by the national courts. The proceedings have thus continued in the UK courts, with the House of Lords deciding in 1999 that there had indeed been a sufficiently serious breach of the relevant EU provisions, leaving only the matter of causation to be decided (*R.* v. *Secretary of State for Transport, Ex parte Factortame Ltd. and Others (No. 5)* [1999] 3 CMLR 597). Press reports assess the likely level of damages payable to the many plaintiffs at around £80 million.

Private or indirect enforcement is efficient in the sense that it does not use EU administrative resources. It also emphasises the relationship between the EU citizen and the EU legal system. The disadvantage is that such an approach depends upon the vagaries of individual decisions to litigate and upon the varying attitudes of national courts to EU law. Part VI will examine the grounds for bringing actions based on EU law in national courts, addressing the status of EU law within the national legal order and the range of sanctions for non-compliance which courts must make available for failure to observe the Treaty. As a first step, however, the organic connection in the form of Article 234 EC between the national courts and the Court of Justice has to be examined (Chapter 11).

Summary

1   EU law and EU policies are principally implemented by the Member States, rather than by the Commission. Article 10 EC imposes a duty of loyalty upon the Member States in the implementation of EU law, breach of which may give rise to an enforcement action under Article 226 EC by the Commission. In effect, national authorities are now 'EU authorities'.

2   Enforcement proceedings may be brought by the Commission or by a Member State under Articles 226 and 227 EC. They comprise an administrative and judicial phase. It is during the administrative phase that the Commission is often able to achieve compliance by the Member States, without recourse to the Court.

3   The Commission has reformed the administrative phase to improve the effectiveness of its enforcement procedures.

4   Failure to comply with any obligation arising under EU law, by any organ of the state, may engage the responsibility of the Member State.

5   The Court of Justice will not accept defences to enforcement proceedings based on national law.

6   The sanctions available under Article 228 EC prior to the adoption of the Treaty of Maastricht were solely declaratory. Article 228 has now been amended to provide for the possibility of financial penalties being imposed upon Member States which fail to comply with a declaratory judgment of the Court which states that they are in breach of their EU obligations.

7   Individual complainants may not force the Commission to take enforcement proceedings under Article 226, but changes to the Commission's internal procedures as a result of intervention by the Ombudsman have improved the status of the complainant.

8   The availability of stiffer sanctions is one means by which the problem of non-compliance with EU law can be dealt with. The procedures for enforcement can also be made more effective. The Commission rigorously monitors the application of EU law and produces regular reports. These indicate that the level of compliance is gradually improving.

Questions

1   What obligations does Article 10 EC impose upon Member States in relation to the implementation and enforcement of EU law?

2   What is meant by the direct and indirect administration of EU law?

3   How could the system of enforcement mechanisms available under the EC Treaty be made more effective?

4   Why is the administrative phase of the enforcement process so important to the Commission?

5   Why has the Commission been slow to enhance the status of complainants under Article 228 EC? What difference has the intervention of the Ombudsman made?

6   Identify the key differences between the direct and indirect enforcement of EU law.

Workshop

In June 1999 the Council adopted a directive which required, on grounds of the protection of the consumer, that all milk sold in the European Union should be packaged in cylindrical 1.5 litre cartons. Measures were to be brought into force by the Member States to give effect to the directive before 31 December 1999. The measure was adopted by a qualified majority with the states of Ajax and Zeno voting against. The Parliament, when consulted, had been unhappy about the measure, but the Council ignored its objections. In July 1999, the Parliament brought an action for annulment against the measure arguing that the directive should be declared void because it was adopted using the wrong legal basis: Article 95 should have been used instead of Article 37. This action is still pending. Zeno agrees with the proceedings brought by the Parliament, but has neither joined the Parliament as a co-applicant, nor intervened in the case.

In Zeno, instead of implementing the directive in the Parliament, the Minister of Agriculture and Consumer Protection issued an instruction to all Trading Standards Officers ordering them not to enforce the directive. Cowcrop, a company which already sells its milk in cylindrical cartons, challenges the validity of these instructions in the Zeno administrative courts, arguing that they give a competitive advantage to companies which are not adopting the EU standard and are in breach of EU law. The matter proceeds quickly to the Zeno Supreme Administrative Court, which refuses to refer the matter to the Court of Justice on the grounds that directives cannot give rise to rights which individuals may enforce. It also doubts whether the directive is lawful, on the grounds that it has been adopted on an incorrect legal basis.

Cowcrop has also complained to the Commission. After a period of informal consultation in which Zeno has shown itself unwilling to compromise or accept the Commission's objections, the Commission issued a reasoned opinion on 4 February 2000, stating as the basis of Zeno's violation the instructions issued to Trading Standards Officers. It gave Zeno fourteen days in which to bring its conduct into line with the Treaty, and then on 19 February, brought the matter before the Court of Justice, citing as an additional ground of objection the refusal of the Zeno Supreme Administrative Court to refer the matter to the Court of Justice. It is now seeking the award of interim measures by the Court.

Zeno objects that Ajax is also not enforcing the directive, and that the Commission has not brought proceedings against Ajax. In addition it points out that another Member State (Kenjo) has unilaterally stopped all imports of milk from Ajax and Zeno on the grounds that the latter two Member States are in flagrant breach of EU law. Zeno argues that while there is a clearly a political issue which needs to be settled in the Council of the EU, this is not an appropriate matter for the Court of Justice.

Discuss.

[Note: It would be useful to review again this Workshop after you have completed work on Chapters 11–13.]

Further Reading

G.C. Azzi (2000), 'The Slow March of European Legislation: The Implementation of Directives', in Neunreither and Wiener (2000).

A. Bonnie (1998), 'Commission Discretion under Article 171(2) EC', 23 *European Law Review* 537.

A. Dashwood and R. White (1989), 'Enforcement Actions and Article 169 and 170', 14 *European Law Review* 388.

U. Everling (1984), 'The Member States of the European Community before their Court of Justice', 9 *European Law Review* 315.

A.J. Gil Ibáñez (1998a), 'A Deeper Insight into Article 169', Harvard Jean Monnet Working Paper 11/98.

A.J. Gil Ibáñez (2000), 'Exceptions to Article 226: Alternative Administrative Procedures and the Pursuit of Member States', 6 *European Law Journal* 148.

M. Mendrinou (1996), 'Non-compliance and the European Commission's Role in Integration', 3 *Journal of European Public Policy* 1.

R. Rawlings (2000), 'Engaged Elites: Citizen Action and Institutional Attitudes in Commission Enforcement', 6 *European Law Review* 4.

F. Snyder (1993b), 'The Effectiveness of European Community Law: Institutions, Processes, Tools and Techniques', 56 *Modern Law Review* 19, pp. 19–40.

F. Snyder (1998), 'General Course on Constitutional Law of the European Union', esp. pp. 80–99, 105–120.

J. Temple Lang (1990), 'Community Constitutional Law: Article 5 EEC Treaty', 27 *Common Market Law Review* 645.

S. Weatherill (1995b), 'Implementation as a Constitutional Issue', in Daintith (1995b).

S. Weatherill (2000b), 'New Strategies for Managing the EC's Internal Market', *Current Legal Problems*, forthcoming.

J.H.H. Weiler (1988), 'The White Paper and the Application of Community Law', in Bieber et al. (1988).

Key Websites

Information on Article 226 and 228 actions and the Commission's reports on the monitoring of the application of Community law can be obtained from:
http://europa.eu.int/comm/secretariat_general/sgb/infringements/index_en.htm

Part IV

Values and Principles in the European Union Constitutional Framework

Introduction

There has been much explicit and implicit reference to the question of values and principles in the EU throughout the first two parts of the book. If two issues could sum up the usefulness and relevance of gathering these questions for purposes of explanation and amplification, they would be the controversy over the entry of Jörg Haider's populist Freedom Party into the Austrian governing coalition in early 2000 (5.5) and the development of the EU's external role in the context of the multilateral Stability Pact for South East Europe concluded at the end of NATO's bombing campaign in Kosovo and Serbia in June 1999 and intended to bring peace, liberal values and a process of reconstruction to the area (1.4, 3.12). Both of these issues have reinforced the fact that there is now a complex network of provisions and policies related to questions of fundamental rights, citizenship and other aspects of constitutional and democratic governance which form a type of 'EU backbone'. In many cases these provisions do not offer justiciable rights for individuals. They are often little known about at national level, and in some cases there is a serious lack of any type of effective enforcement mechanism. But none the less this framework of provisions incorporating certain values and principles does undermine the frequent assertion that what the EU really needs for it to become more legitimate and more popular is 'more rights' for citizens. It may certainly need better enforcement of what rights do exist and a great deal more transparency. As a system of governance its effectiveness and efficiency leave a lot to be desired. But what follows in the next two chapters does suggest that laying claim to 'more rights' to be included in the EU Treaties is not necessarily the best approach to ensuring that the EU takes seriously the principles of a liberal order (Garton Ash, 1999).

Part IV

Values and Principles in the European Union Constitutional Framework

Introduction

9 Fundamental Rights and General Principles of Law

9.1 Introduction

In this chapter we chart the increasing significance of fundamental rights for the EU. The original treaties – focused functionally upon economic integration albeit with the wider project of an 'ever-closer Union' in the background – made no reference to fundamental rights. That did not prevent the emergence of a 'market' in ideas, practices, policies and rules relating to fundamental rights, as in practice the implementation of rules of economic integration and the associated rights and claims which these generate has cut across existing international and national fundamental rights regimes. The presentation in this chapter is essentially historical and institutional in nature, working outwards from the role of the Court of Justice to examining the development of a variety of binding and declaratory sources of fundamental rights within the EU. These include both 'written' sources clearly set out in the Treaties and the 'non-written' sources comprising general principles of law formulated by the Court of Justice. It begins by presenting the emergence of 'general principles of law' as sources of law within the EU legal order, moves on to consider the current state of fundamental rights policy in the EU, and touches along the way upon the process of negotiating a Charter of Fundamental Rights for the EU triggered by the Cologne European Council in June 1999 and due for completion before the end of 2000. It should be noted that this chapter uses the terms fundamental rights and human rights interchangeably, although it is acknowledged that in some circles a distinction is drawn between the two. The reason why the term 'fundamental rights' is used so commonly in EU discourse is that it includes a number of rights which can quite properly be invoked for the protection of legal as well as natural persons. Fundamental rights are defined in simple terms here as the most deeply entrenched and morally important value statements of a given social grouping.

9.2 The Emergence of General Principles and Fundamental Rights in EU Law

In 6.10 we viewed in brief the main primary sources of law within the EU legal order. One of these is 'general principles of law', which comprise a body of superordinate rules of law, for the most part unwritten and derived by the Court of Justice by reference to its general duty to ensure that the law is observed (Article 220 EC). These principles bind the EU, its institutions, and, within the sphere of Community competence, the Member States and individuals. 'General principles of law' are a familiar source of law within those Member States with 'civil law' systems based on the traditions of Roman law. They offer a background statement of values and basic standards which courts can use to inform their interpretation of rules of written law and to fill gaps in the written law. General principles comprise above all rules which are sufficiently general, such as 'the right to equality' or 'the principle of legal certainty', to be widely accepted. It is the application of such principles to specific fact situations which is more likely to cause controversy than the principles themselves.

The International Court of Justice is explicitly called upon to apply general principles of law in its case law. Article 38(c) of its Statute provides:

> 'The Court ... shall apply ... the general principles of law recognised by civilised nations.'

In contrast, the EU treaties offer no equivalent statement, although general support for the practice of the Court in using general principles can be derived from the treaties. In addition to Article 220 EC, referred to above, Article 230 EC gives as one of the grounds for review of the legality of EU acts:

> 'infringement of this Treaty or *any rule of law relating to its application*' (emphasis added).

More explicit reference to general principles, albeit within a more limited remit, is to be found in the second paragraph of Article 288 EC which governs the tortious liability of the EU for wrongful acts. The Court is to decide disputes:

> 'in accordance with the general principles common to the laws of the Member States.'

The reference to what is 'common' to the laws of the Member States highlights the comparative method which has frequently marked the Court's search for general principles. This comparative method appears most clearly in the Opinions of the Advocates General rather than the judgments of the Court itself (see for example A-G Warner in Case 17/74 *Transocean Marine Paint Association* v. *Commission* [1974] ECR 1063 – the right to a fair hearing in competition proceedings, and the excursus given by Usher, 1976: 370; see more recently Usher, 1998: 73 *et seq.*). For a principle to be 'common' does not necessarily mean that it must be recognised in all the Member States in precisely the same form. It is sufficient that a general trend can be discerned among the Member States. As an alternative to comparative methodology, the Court may find inspiration for a general principle of EU law in international instruments such as the European Convention of Human Rights and Fundamental Freedoms and the International Covenant of Civil and Political Rights. However, whatever the source of inspiration, the Court invariably stresses the 'Community' nature of the principle once expressed. The general principles of law are principles of EU law, elaborated in the specific context of the EU and its legal order with its particular mission and subject to the authoritative interpretation of the Court of Justice alone.

Four main groups of general principles can be identified although a number of important general principles such as 'equality' straddle the first two categories and the final one in various guises. These are:

– certain rules and standards which operate as restrictions upon the exercise of EU administrative, executive and legislative powers either by the EU itself or by the Member States where they are required to implement EU measures;
– the economic freedoms contained in the EC Treaty, which the Court has consistently elevated to the status of 'general principles' and given constitutional force to (5.20), and which act principally as fetters upon the Member States. For example, in Case 240/83 *Procureur de la République* v. *Association de défense des brûleurs d'huiles usagées* ([1985] ECR 520) the Court stated (at p.531):

> 'It should be borne in mind that the principles of free movement of goods and freedom of competition, together with freedom of trade as a fundamental right, are general principles of Community law of which the Court ensures observance';

– an emerging group of 'political' rights, within which the principle of transparency or 'openness' is both the most powerful and the most clearly formed, even though its status as a general principle of EU law is not yet completely assured;
– an as yet relatively ill-defined body of fundamental rights. In view of the general importance of fundamental rights and of the specific and continuing history of the protection of those rights within the EU it is, however, essential to analyse them as a separate category of general principle of law.

To a certain extent, these divisions are arbitrary; for example, there is little 'space' between a principle of administrative or legislative legality, and a fundamental right, as the title of a paper called 'Administrative Justice: A Developing Human Right?' makes clear (Bradley, 1995). Moreover, it has been the Court's failure to draw a conceptual distinction between 'economic' rights guaranteed as part of the market-building process and fundamental socio-economic or humanistic values which has given rise to some of the controversy in this field, as the discussion below of the Irish Abortion Case (*Grogan*) will show (9.6; see the criticisms of Phelan, 1992). Furthermore, the general principles of law represent a product of judicial activism and creativity which is typical of the Court. The proactive role taken by the Court in this regard has been used as one basis for the claim that the Court has exceeded its judicial role and trespassed into the realm of politics (Rasmussen, 1986: 4.18). In some cases, such controversies have provoked one or all of the Member States to make a response, by adopting specific provisions in amending Treaties, Protocols or Declarations appended to the Treaties.

9.3   Principles of Administrative and Legislative Legality

The comparative methodology referred to above has been particularly useful for the Court in the context of the development of those general principles which can be characterised as principles of administrative and legislative legality. A number of pointers to the development of this group of principles are to be found in the Treaty itself. For example, Article 230 EC cites 'lack of competence' and 'infringement of an essential procedural requirement' as well as infringement of the Treaty and 'any rule of law' as grounds for review. Article 253 EC also requires all regulations, directives and decisions to be accompanied by a statement of reasons (6.8). However, there are also many unwritten principles of administrative and legislative legality, and these have evolved through the case law of the Court which has drawn much of its inspiration in this field from the national administrative systems of the Member States. The most important are the principles of legal certainty and proportionality, and the rights to non-discrimination and procedural fairness.

Procedural fairness is particularly important in those areas of EU law where the EU institutions must enforce the law directly against individuals, such as competition law and anti-dumping law. The *Transocean Marine Paint* case provides an example of the development of the right to a hearing in the competition law field for those whose trading activities come under the scrutiny of the Commission on the grounds of alleged anti-competitive or monopolistic effects. Case C-49/88 *Al-Jubail Fertiliser* v. *Council* ([1991] ECR I-3187) extends this principle to companies which are required to pay anti-dumping duties imposed on allegedly subsidised imports into the EU. A rather different principle of procedural fairness was developed in Case 155/79 *A.M. & S.* v. *Commission* ([1982] ECR 1575) where the Court of Justice recognised the confidentiality of communications between lawyer and client in the context of Commission competition investigations. This right of legal professional privilege extends only to independent lawyers established within the EU; it does not apply to communications with lawyers outside the EU, or with in-house lawyers. *A.M. & S.* provided the first significant instance of the Court drawing more heavily upon the common law heritage offered by English and Irish law. Likewise in the field of competition law, the Court of First Instance has articulated a general principle of 'equality of arms' in administrative procedures, which requires the Commission to make available to those under investigation so-called 'exculpatory documents' which may assist them in their defence (Case T-30/91 *Solvay* v. *Commission* [1995] ECR II-1775).

Other procedural rights have been developed by the Court of Justice as fetters upon the investigatory activities of the Commission which are more akin to fundamental rights, such as the right to be protected against arbitrary administrative action; this will be considered below.

The principle of legal certainty has been cited by the Court in a number of diverse contexts. For example in Case 43/75 *Defrenne* v. *SABENA* ([1976] ECR 455) legal certainty was used as a justification for imposing a temporal limitation upon the effects of a preliminary ruling under what was then Article 177 EEC (Article 234 EC). In that case, the Court concluded that what was then Article 119 EEC (Article 141 EC) could have direct effect; in other words, individual women and men could bring equal pay claims in national courts on the basis of Article 119 itself. The Court held that this applied only for the future, so that with the exception of claims already submitted at the date of the ruling, back pay could not be claimed in respect of periods of service at an unequal rate of pay prior to that time. The Court has made it clear that the limitation of the temporal effects of a ruling is a wholly exceptional measure imposed on grounds of legal certainty because of the seriously disruptive effects of the ruling. Such reticence is desirable since the imposition of such a limitation on a Court ruling represents one of the most blatant examples of judicial legislation within the EU legal system, and wholly abandons the pretence that the Court is merely interpreting, as opposed to making, the law.

Furthermore, legal certainty has a particular role to play as EU legislation becomes ever more complex, and in particular where the EU shifts from one system of regulatory control to another (as has occurred in the field of customs law, following widespread international developments). The EU lacks a principle of implied repeal, whereby later enactments are regarded as implicitly taking precedence over contradictory earlier provisions. Instead, legal certainty may require the EU institutions to repeal provisions to ensure that individuals know their rights, and consequently earlier and now redundant provisions should not be applied by national administrative authorities or courts (Case C-143/93 *Gebroeders van Es Douane Agenten BV* v. *Inspecteur der Invoerrechten en Accijnzen* [1996] ECR I-431). It operates as an additional fetter upon the national authorities, because according to the Court in Case 257/86 *Commission* v. *Italy* ([1986] ECR 3249)

> 'the principles of legal certainty and the protection of individuals re-quire, in areas covered by Community law, that the Member States' legal rules should be worded unequivocally so as to give the persons con-cerned a clear and precise understanding of their rights and obligations and enable national courts to ensure that those rights and obligations are observed' (at para. 12).

Legal certainty in this sense equates closely to 'clarity'.

Legal certainty may also take the form of the protection of 'legitimate ex-pectations'. Since the EU is actively involved in the customs and agricultural fields in the management of the market by intervening to set prices, levies and duties, it must take care not to violate the legitimate expectations of those concerned which it might previously have aroused. This is illustrated by Case 74/74 *CNTA* v. *Commission* ([1975] ECR 533). Here it was held that the Commission was not permitted to abolish without warning so-called 'monetary compensatory amounts' ('MCAs') granted to exporters of agri-cultural products to compensate them for fluctations in exchange rates since:

> 'a trader may legitimately expect that for transactions irrevocably under-taken by him because he has obtained, subject to a deposit, export licen-ces fixing the amount of the refund in advance, no unforeseeable alter-ation will occur which could have the effect of causing him inevitable loss, by re-exposing him to the exchange risk' (p. 550).

There are a number of alternative scenarios on which a successful claim for breach of the principle of legitimate expectations may be based. For exam-ple, there may have been a course of conduct undertaken by the EU authori-ties (e.g. the construction of an EU scheme to persuade milk producers to cease production for a number of years: Case 120/86 *Mulder* v. *Minister van Landbouw en Visserij* [1988] ECR 2321; see the damages claims resulting from this finding of an infringement of the principle of legitimate expecta-tions: 17.9). Alternatively, the structure of EU legislation may specifically require particular interests to be taken into account in future measures (e.g. a Commission power allowing it to prohibit certain imports from third coun-tries but requiring it to take into account the specific position of those with goods in transit: Case C-152/88 *Sofrimport Sarl* v. *Commission* [1990] ECR I-2477). However, the Court of First Instance has stressed that in a field where the EU institutions have broad discretion in the framing of policy – such as agriculture – the institutions must retain the ability to modify the regulatory framework in particular markets without facing challenges based on the principle of legitimate expectations. The principle cannot, according to the Court, be extended to the point of generally preventing new rules from applying to the future effects of situations which arose under earlier rules (Case T-466/93 etc. *O'Dwyer* v. *Council* [1995] ECR II-2071).

Finally, legal certainty operates in the guise of the principle of non-retroactivity. Legislation is presumed not to take effect retrospectively unless this is expressly stated, and retroactivity will not be permitted unless it is essential for the purpose of the measure to be achieved and the legitimate expectations of the persons affected have been protected. In Case 108/81 *Amylum* v. *Council* ([1982] ECR 3107) the conditions for retroactivity were met. This concerned a Council Regulation imposing a system of quotas and levies on the production of isoglucose (a sugar substitute) intended to equalise the production conditions of the two products (isoglucose and sugar). Since an earlier Regulation to the same effect had been annulled on procedural grounds (failure to consult the Parliament: see 7.4), it was permissible to pass a second Regulation imposing the same system with retrospective effect. The objective of equality could not otherwise be achieved, and the isoglucose producers were presumed to be put on notice about the scheme by the earlier abortive Regulation.

Equality and non-discrimination themselves operate as important general principles governing the legality of EU action. This is expressed most clearly in Article 34(2) EC (formerly Article 40(3) EC) which demands that the common organisations of the market set up under the Common Agricultural Policy (CAP) must 'exclude any discrimination between producers or consumers within the Community', and there are many cases in which this principle of equality has been successfully invoked to challenge EU legislation in the agricultural field (see for example the *Skimmed Milk Powder* case – Case 114/76 *Bela Mühle Josef Bergman* v. *Grows-Farm* [1977] ECR 1211). The principle also has a wider impact as the principle that the EU legislature may not treat similar situations differently unless differentiation is objectively justified. In Case 41/84 *Pinna* v. *Caisse d'allocations familiales de la Savoie* ([1986] ECR 1) the Court held that the Council was not permitted, when legislating to determine the conditions under which migrant workers enjoy family benefits, to differentiate between those who were subject to French legislation and those who were not (a differentiation created on the insistence of France which has a particularly generous system of family benefits). This legislative intervention by the Council had the effect of accentuating the existing disparities between the national systems and was not permitted. In a move applauded by a number of commentators (e.g. Peers, 1999a, 1999b), the Court extended the coverage of the non-discrimination principle into the arena of international trade in its review of the legality of the Framework Agreement on Bananas, drawn up in response to initial disputes over the EU's first common market regime for bananas (see 5.13) (Case C-122/95 *Germany* v. *Council* [1998] ECR I-973; Cases C-364 and 365/95 *T. Port GmbH & Co* v. *Hauptzollamt Hamburg-Jonas* [1998] ECR I-1023). The focus of the claim was upon measures which awarded differential country quotas to states exporting bananas to the EU and measures differentiating between different categories of exporters, exempting some from an export licence requirement. As to the differential treatment of countries, the Court expressly confirmed that the EU is not obliged, as a matter of EU law to accord all third countries equal treatment (and in this respect the compatibility of EU law with the GATT's so-called 'Most Favoured Nation' clause requiring equal treatment has been called into question). As to the differences in treatment between certain categories of traders, the Court found this was not justified as the Council had not supplied the Court with sufficient information why the other measures taken were not sufficient to achieve the objectives of the Framework Agreement regarding trade in bananas. None the less the Court largely upheld the banana regime, as it had done in an earlier case (Case C-280/93 *Germany* v. *Council* [1994] ECR I-4973).

The principle of equal treatment is, however, multi-facetted, as we shall see (de Búrca, 1997). In this context, it is playing a 'market-regulating' role, according to the classification adopted by Gillian More, constraining legislative action within the market, although subject to a principle of objective justification allowing for differentiated treatment if objective and uniform criteria are used for that making the difference (More, 1999: 530).

Proportionality is a concept which has entered EU law primarily out of German law, where it is given constitutional status. Essentially it requires a measure to be no more burdensome than is necessary to achieve its objective. Once the legitimate aim or objective of a measure is identified, a threefold test can be applied: is the measure a suitable or useful means of achieving the objective; is the measure necessary for the achievement of the objective; and is there a reasonable relationship between the measure and the objective? The latter, and most controversial limb, of the test essentially requires a measure not to have an excessive or disproportionate impact upon a person's interests (de Búrca, 1993a: 113). Where there is a choice between two effective means to achieve an objective, recourse should be to the least onerous or intrusive.

An example of proportionality operating is offered by Case 181/84 *R* v. *Intervention Board for Agricultural Produce, ex parte Man (Sugar) Ltd* ([1985] ECR 2889) where the Court held that it was disproportionate for a Regulation to require the forfeiture of the entire security deposited by a company, where the security is intended to ensure that goods for which an export licence is to be obtained will actually be exported (the primary obligation), for failure to satisfy a secondary obligation, namely the duty to submit the licence application within a certain time period. The sanction was particularly harsh since the applicant was only four hours late in submitting the application.

On the other hand, in the field of general legislative discretion, the approach taken by the Court of Justice does not appear to involve strict scrutiny of institutional action. In Case C-331/88 *R* v. *Minister for Agriculture, Fisheries and Food, ex parte Fedesa* ([1990] ECR 4023), a challenge was mounted to a 1988 Directive prohibiting use of certain hormonal substances in livestock farming, on the grounds of a breach of the principle of proportionality. It was argued that the ban would be ineffective, that it would lead to the growth of a black market, that consumer anxieties could be allayed by means of an informational campaign, and that the effect on traders would be disproportionate. All aspects of the claim failed, although the Court reiterated the principle that proportionality can affect legislative discretion. The Court held, however:

> 'It must be stated that in matters concerning the common agricultural policy the Community legislature has a discretionary power which corresponds to the political responsibilities given to it by Articles 40 and 43 of the Treaty. Consequently, the legality of a measure adopted in that sphere can be affected only if the measure is manifestly inappropriate having regard to the objective which the competent institution is seeking to pursue' (p. 4063) (note: now Articles 34 and 37 EC).

Proportionality has become an extremely important principle in the economic law of the EU. Not only is it used to assess the legality of the measures of EU law and implementing measures of the Member States in the context of customs and agricultural law but, like the principle of equality, it has also become a vital component in assessing interferences by the Member States in the economic freedoms guaranteed under the EC Treaty which have been elevated to the status of general principles.

The operation of these general principles of law as the basis for actions for the annulment or invalidity of EU legislation, or for actions for damages against the EU institutions, is reviewed again in Chapters 15 and 17, and it is important to note that the application of principles in any judicial review or damages action can be nuanced by the particular conditions in which such action arose. In other words, it can be somewhat misleading to discuss them in isolation from the judicial contexts in which they are applied.

9.4　The Pillars of Economic Integration as General Principles of EU Law

The Court of Justice has consistently repeated its view that the four basic economic freedoms under the Treaty (free movement of goods, persons, services and capital), along with the general right to non-discrimination on grounds of nationality contained in Article 12 EC are protected not just as written rules within the Treaty system, but also as general principles of EU law. The breadth of protection now offered by EU law is illustrated by cases such as *Cowan* (Case 186/87 *Cowan* v. *Le Trésor public* [1989] ECR 195). The Court of Justice held that a British tourist attacked, robbed and injured while on holiday in Paris was entitled to make a criminal injuries compensation claim under French law under the same conditions as a French national. As a recipient of services (tourism), Mr Cowan fell within the scope of the application of the Treaty, and he was therefore entitled to the protection of what was then Article 7 EEC (now Article 12 EC). The Court stated (at p. 222) that:

'[national] legislative provisions may not discriminate against persons to whom Community law gives the right to equal treatment or restrict the fundamental freedoms guaranteed by Community law.'

Article 12 EC is an important – but residual – legal provision. According to the Court in Case C-18/93 *Corscia Ferries* ([1994] ECR I-1783), it

'applies independently only to situations governed by Community law in respect of which the Treaty lays down no specific prohibition of discrimination' (para. 19).

In Case C-291/96 *Grado and Bashir* ([1997] ECR I-5531) the Court of Justice was asked whether it was contrary to Article 12 EC for a public prosecutor before a German court to refuse to use the courtesy title '*Herr*' in criminal proceedings against a national of another Member State where it was used in similar proceedings against German nationals. The Court found, however, that the principle was not relevant as the national court when referring the question had failed to provide any evidence that EU law in general, or the free movement rules in particular, were relevant. In Case C-274/96 *Bickel and Franz* ([1998] ECR I-7637), criminal proceedings were brought in Bolzano, Italy against a German national and an Austrian national, neither of whom were resident in Italy. Bickel was a lorry driver, and had been stopped by the police and charged with driving under the influence of alcohol. Franz was present in Italy as a tourist, and he was found at a customs inspection to be in charge of a knife, and charged with possession of a type of knife that is prohibited. Under Italian laws applying in Bolzano for the protection of the German-speaking community, the German minority is entitled to use its own language in relations with the judicial and administrative bodies. These rules were not extended to Bickel and Franz, because they covered only those German speakers permanently resident in Bolzano, and the point was raised that this infringed the non-discrimination principle. As the Court confirmed, Article 12

'requires that persons in a situation governed by Community law be placed entirely on an equal footing with nationals of the Member State' (para. 14).

It found that both Bickel (service provider) and Franz (receiver of services as tourist) were in situations governed by EU law (i.e. the right to move), and consequently Article 12 could apply. The Court went on to find the refusal to extend the rules discriminatory on the part of the Italian authorities, not-withstanding the fact that in general criminal legislation and the rules of criminal procedure are matters for which Member States are responsible.

Equality and non-discrimination are also of considerable importance when read in conjunction with the citizenship provisions (10.3). The Court of Justice held in Case C-85/96 *Martínez Sala* v. *Freistaat Bayern* ([1998] ECR I-2691) that a Spanish national who was lawfully resident in Germany could rely upon Article 12, in conjunction with her status as a citizen of the Union to whom all rights under the Treaty are 'attached' (Article 17(2) EC) to claim equal treatment with German nationals in relation to the provision of a child raising benefit in Germany (10.4). This, and the previous cases, high-light the point at which the equal treatment principle slides from being a 'market-unifying' principle into being a 'constitutional' principle under EU law (More, 1999).

Finally, in a number of cases the Court has stressed the importance of as-sociated procedural rights to due process without which the exercise of the fundamental freedoms is meaningless. For example, where a public author-ity takes a decision which impinges upon an individual's rights under EU law, he or she has the right to be given reasons, to make it possible to chal-lenge this decision in court. In Case 222/86 *UNECTEF* v. *Heylens* ([1987] ECR 4097), Heylens' application for the recognition in France of his Bel-gian diploma as a football trainer was rejected on the basis of an adverse opinion given by a special committee which gave no reasons for its decision. Without that recognition Heylens could not work in France. The Court held that reasons must be given for such a decision to enable effective judicial re-view, since the adverse opinion affected a fundamental right conferred by the Treaty on EU workers, namely the right of free access to employment.

EU legislation has been held to confer a right to judicial review on benefi-ciaries of EU rights. In the field of sex discrimination, the Court held in Case 222/84 *Johnston* v. *Chief Constable of the Royal Ulster Constabulary* ([1986] ECR 1651) that an alleged victim of sex discrimination bringing a claim for equal treatment guaranteed by the Equal Treatment Directive (76/207) could not be denied access to a judicial remedy by a ministerial order. In this context, the Court has also relied on the importance of Article 6 ECHR as conferring a right to judicial process (on the role of the ECHR see the discussion of fundamental rights below).

These cases are expressions of a general principle that individuals must be given effective remedies against the Member States, which allow them to protect or assert their rights under EU law. In Cases 6, 9/90 *Francovich* v. *Italian State (Francovich I)* ([1991] ECR I-5357) the Court held that it is for national courts to ensure the full effect of the provisions of EU law, and to protect the rights which EU law confers on individuals. This principle will be examined in more detail in Chapters 12 and 13.

9.5   Political Rights: Democracy and Transparency

The extent of recognition of political rights within the EU legal order has been limited. On a number of occasions, both the Court of Justice and the Court of First Instance have made reference to the 'fundamental democratic principle that the people must share in the exercise of power through a representative assembly' (Case T-135/96 *UEAPME* v. *Council* [1998] ECR II-2335). Referring in *UEAPME* to cases such as Case 138/79 *Roquette Frères* v. *Council* ([1980] ECR 3333), the Court of First Instance noted that the participation of the Parliament in the legislative process reflects this principle, and gives democratic legitimacy to measures adopted by the Council (or – one might add – by the Council *and* the Parliament jointly). So, in the context of the social dialogue based legislative procedure envisaged in the Social Policy Agreement of 1993–99, and now enshrined in Article 139 EC,

> 'the principle of democracy on which the Union is founded requires – in the absence of the participation of the European Parliament in the legislative process – that the participation of the people be otherwise assured, in this instance through the parties representative of management and labour who concluded the agreement...' (para. 89).

In practice, however, the case law has always demonstrated that this is not a free-standing general principle of law, but needs to be combined with some procedural principle, such as infringement of one of the Parliament's prerogatives.

Thus far the interpretation of the subsidiarity and proportionality principles enshrined in Article 5 EC has not demonstrated that the Court has plans to elevate them into general 'political' principles. Rather, once again, the Court's scrutiny seems to be focused on the question of whether – in the circumstances – the institutions did the right thing. In other words, it becomes a question of the institutional economy (6.6; Case C-233/94 *Germany* v. *Parliament and Council* [1997] ECR I-2405).

In broad terms, the case law of the Court of Justice and the Court of First Instance thus far on the principle of transparency has operated through the prism of the interpretation of written texts put in place by the Member States and the institutions, rather than via the derivation of a general principle of law. To put it another way, those bodies rather than the Court were the *original* agenda setters in this field. So far they are required to elaborate a measure giving effect to the new Article 255 EC added by the Treaty of Amsterdam, the institutions must continue to engage directly with that question. To that end, the interpretative case law will be examined in more detail in Chapter 10, as it should be viewed as part of a process of the construction of constitutionalism and citizenship in the EU. In its Code of Conduct on access to documents the Commission declares that the public should have the widest possible access to documents. Thus when it overturned both the judgment of the Court of First Instance and the underlying Commission decision refusing access to documents prepared by the Commission for a national court hearing a case under the EU competition rules (Cases C-174 and 189/98 P *Netherlands and van der Wal* v. *Commission*, 11 January 2000), the Court was essentially following the lead of the *other* institutions when it reiterated the principle of the 'widest public access possible' (para. 27) (on the facts in *van der Wal* see 9.6).

The most pertinent *general* discussion comes from its judgment in the case brought by the Netherlands to challenge the legal basis of the Council's access rules within its Rules of Procedures (Case C-58/94 *Netherlands* v. *Council* [1996] ECR I-2169). The Netherlands sought a more general legal basis for such a fundamental measure, befitting its status within the framework of the EU legal order. In reviewing the relevant legal background, the Court held:

'the domestic legislation of most Member States now enshrines in a general manner the public's right of access to documents held by public authorities as a constitutional or legislative principle.
In addition, at Community level, the importance of that right has been reaffirmed on various occasions, in particular in the declaration on the right of access to information annexed (as Declaration 17) to the Final Act of the Treaty on European Union, which links that right with the democratic nature of the institutions. Moreover, (...) the European Council has called on the Council and the Commission to implement that right' (paras 34 and 35).

The Court also referred to a 'trend, which discloses a progressive affirmation of individuals' right of access to documents held by public authorities', and a departure from the Council's previous working practices based on a principle of 'confidentiality' (para. 36). The approach of the Court is somewhat less affirmatory of such democratic rights than that taken by Advocate General Tesauro, who refers approvingly in his Opinion to 'openness of decision-making processes' as:

> 'an innate feature of any democratic system and the right to information, including information in the hands of the public authorities .... (as) a fundamental right of the individual' (para. 6 of the Opinion).

He finds the basis for the right to information:

> 'in the democratic principle, which constitutes one of the cornerstones of the Community edifice, as enshrined now in the Preamble to the Maastricht Treaty and Article F of the Common Provisions. In the light of the changes which have taken place in the legislation of the Member States, the right of access to official documents now constitutes part of that principle. It is the essential precondition for effective supervision by public opinion of the operations of the public authorities' (para. 19).

Building on this declaration, and materials derived from further case law and from the objectives of the Treaties especially the reference to openness in Article 1 TEU, O'Neill argues that

> 'now is the perfect time for the (Court) to recognise the individual's right of access to Community-held information as a general principle of EC law. The need is clearly pressing, there already exists an extensive and strong legal foundation upon which to ground this right and the time is ripe – when the Member States have formally affirmed, in the Amsterdam Treaty, their desire to see this right advanced' (O'Neill, 1998: 431)

9.6   Fundamental Rights in the Court of Justice

The EU constitutional framework still lacks a clear and identifiable catalogue or charter of fundamental rights protecting the interests of those who fall under the jurisdiction of EU law. Instead, under EU law as constructed by the Court of Justice, which has taken the lead in this context in developing a framework of binding rights, fundamental rights are protected as general principles of law. Notably, this point is articulated not only in the Court's case law but also in the TEU's affirmation of fundamental rights protection (Article 6(2) TEU). In view of this, it is important to review the doctrinal construction of the scope of fundamental rights protection as the basis for later developments.

The emergence of a specific category of general principles termed 'fundamental rights' is widely regarded as attributable to the need on the part of the Court of Justice to assert the supremacy of the EU legal order, even in the face of national constitutions, such as that of the Germany, which enshrine the protection of fundamental human rights; however, Arnull describes the attribution of the Court's conversion to human rights doctrine to expediency rather than conviction as 'churlish' (Arnull, 1999a: 219). In effect, the Court has read into the EU legal order an unwritten Bill of Rights, drawing on both national constitutional expressions of fundamental rights and international human rights instruments (especially the European Convention on Human Rights and Fundamental Freedoms) as the sources of inspiration for EU fundamental rights. The articulation of a specific category of rights termed 'fundamental' was in part forced upon the Court by the reluctance of certain national courts, notably German and Italian courts, to acknowledge the full supremacy of EU law. In particular, these courts were reluctant to accept that the superior nature of EU law precluded them from testing provisions of EU legislation against national constitutional guarantees of fundamental rights.

The German Federal Constitutional Court held in the case of *Internationale Handelsgesellschaft* ([1974] 2 CMLR 549) that so long as an adequate standard of fundamental rights protection was not offered under EU law itself, it would not regard itself as precluded from scrutinising measures of EU law for conformity with German fundamental rights, and where necessary, invalidating or disapplying such measures within Germany. Recognising the progress made by the Court of Justice, however, the Federal Constitutional Court decisively shifted its position in the case of *Wunsche Handelsgesellschaft* ([1987] 3 CMLR 225) indicating that an effective level of protection was now generally ensured, and scrutiny by the national court was no longer required, so long as that was maintained.

The position previously taken by the German court, and still maintained by the Italian Constitutional Court (Gaja, 1990; Schermers, 1990; Ruggeri Laderchi, 1998), is in fact inconsistent with the position taken by the Court of Justice on the supremacy of EU law (12.3). However, in practice, the Court felt constrained to defend its position by developing a line of case law beginning with Case 29/69 *Stauder* v. *City of Ulm* ([1969] ECR 419) in which it has proclaimed the existence of fundamental rights enshrined within the EU legal order which are protected as general principles of law. To reassure the national courts, it was stressed in *Internationale Handelsgesellschaft* (Case 11/70 [1970] ECR 1125) that human rights in EU law are inspired by the constitutional traditions common to the Member States. That source of inspiration was extended in Case 4/73 *Nold* v. *Commission* ([1974] ECR 503) to include 'international treaties for the protection of human rights on which the Member States have collaborated or of which they are signatories'. In Case 44/79 *Hauer* v. *Land Rheinland Pfalz* ([1979] ECR 3740) the Court made an extensive examination of the right to property as protected in a number of the national constitutions, as well as Article 1 of the First Protocol to the ECHR, before concluding that there had been no human rights violation by the Community when it adopted an agricultural Regulation which prohibited the planting of new vines for three years. In 1989 the Court referred for the first time to the International Covenant of Civil and Political Rights as a potential source of EC fundamental rights (Case 374/87 *Orkem* v. *Commission* ([1989] ECR 3283). However, whatever the sources of inspiration for its case law, the Court has always stressed that EU fundamental rights, like the other general principles of law, become specifically EU rights, subject to interpretation 'within the framework of the structure and the objectives of the Community' (Case 11/70 *Internationale Handelsgesellschaft*).

This frank admission of the influence of the objectives of the EU upon the interpretation of fundamental rights, when viewed in the light of the specific purpose of the Court when it first introduced the doctrine of EU fundamental rights protection, has led some commentators to doubt the real effectiveness of EU human rights protection (Coppel and O'Neill, 1992). This is a claim which represents just one of several areas of criticism which the Court of Justice has encountered in relation to its fundamental rights jurisprudence (cf. the defence offered by Weiler and Lockhart, 1995a, 1995b).

The claim that adequate respect is not ensured derives some support from the paucity of cases in which the Court has in fact held that there has been a human rights violation by the EU institutions. Successful claims are largely confined to the realm of administrative law enforcement by the Commission, especially in the field of competition policy where the cases are closely linked to those on principles of administrative legality discussed in 6.5, and to staff cases. In Case 46/87 *Hoechst* v. *Commission* ([1989] ECR 2859) the Court held that undertakings which are under investigation by the Commission for alleged infringements of the competition rules have the right to be protected against arbitrary or disproportionate interventions on the part of public authorities in their sphere of activities. This means in practice that before conducting surprise searches of the premises of undertakings under investigation the Commission is obliged to observe whatever procedural formalities apply within the Member State where the undertaking is established, such as the duty to obtain a search warrant before a judge. In similar vein the Court declared in Case 374/87 *Orkem* v. *Commission* that an undertaking under investigation should not be required to answer leading questions about its activities, although it declined to recognise a formal right of protection against self-incrimination under Article 6 ECHR (see 9.9). One question that does arise about the case law of the Court in this context is whether it represents a sufficiently strict application of the standards contained in the ECHR which represent the essential judicial benchmark in this field. We shall return to this point below.

Staff cases – a rather *sui generis* body of EU case law – offer some of the very few examples of protection being sought successfully for individual civil or political rights under EU law. In Case 100/88 *Oyowe and Traore* v. *Commission* ([1989] ECR 4285) the Court held that the duty of allegiance owed by all staff to the EU institutions they are employed by cannot be interpreted and applied in such a way as to conflict with the principle of freedom of expression. The issue of the administration of HIV tests on EU officials without their effective consent was raised in Case C-404/92 P *X* v. *Commission* ([1994] ECR I-4780), and the Court of Justice, annulling the judgment of the Court of First Instance, found a violation of the applicant's right to respect for private life protected under Article 8 ECHR.

Reviewing recent case law reveals that the catalogue of EU fundamental rights and its usage within the Court's case law remains relatively unsophisticated, although it is gradually evolving. Perhaps of greatest significance is that so far the Court has not had occasion to declare a general principle based on the right to non-discrimination on grounds of race, ethnic origin or nationality (as opposed to EU nationality, guaranteed by Article 12 EC) (de Búrca, 1995). In other areas of equality jurisprudence, the Court has sometimes been less cautious in developing a more generalised principle. In Case C-13/94 *P* v. *S and Cornwall County Council* ([1996] ECR I-2143) the Court accepted an argument derived from its earlier case law on pregnancy discrimination to the effect that discrimination against a male to female transsexual was discrimination based 'essentially if not exclusively, on the sex of the person concerned.' Having undergone gender reassignment, P was dismissed from her post in Cornwall County Council. She was found to have been discriminated against in comparison with a person of the sex 'P' was deemed by the authorities still to belong to (i.e. a male), and thus able to based an action on the Equal Treatment Directive, which covers sex discrimination. The judgment contains strong language on such discrimination, saying that 'to tolerate such discrimination would be tantamount, as regards such a person, to a failure to respect the dignity and freedom to which he or she is entitled, and which the Court has a duty to safeguard.'

Unsurprisingly, in view of such language, some commentators suggested that this marked the emergence of a general constitutional principle of equality in EC law, based on essential moral and ethical groundrules about the treatment of one person by another (Barnard, 1997). Might such a principle then give rise to the inclusion of sexual orientation discrimination within the ambit of EC sex equality law? In fact, this promise was very short-lived, as the first attempt to rely upon *P* v. *S* showed. It came in a case that did indeed seek to extend sex equality protection to cover sexual orientation discrimination. The applicant in Case C-249/96 *Grant* v. *South West Trains Ltd* ([1998] ECR I-621) was a lesbian employee of a railway company in the UK, who had been denied travel benefits for her same sex partner, where such benefits had been given to her predecessor in the job, a man with an opposite sex partner. The Court refused to accept the logic of a 'but for' test ('but for' her sex, Grant would not have been discriminated against); instead it compared her situation to that of a man with a same-sex partner. He too would have been denied benefits, and there was nothing in that denial which fell within the scope of EC law as presently constituted. The Court developed its argument in deference to the development of a legislative power (Article 13 EC) under the Treaty of Amsterdam which had not yet come into force, but had been agreed at the date of the judgment. In so doing, it went against the Opinion of Advocate General Elmer, who applied the *P* v. *S* reasoning of 'essentially but not exclusively based on sex' to the sexual orientation question as well.

Finally, the judgment of the Court of Justice in Cases C-174 & 189/98 P *Netherlands and van der Wal* v. *Commission* highlights the delicate interaction between fundamental rights under the EU legal order, especially those of ECHR origin, EU based rights such as transparency, and the multi-levelled nature of the EU legal order. The applicant in that case was a lawyer practising in the field of competition law, who asked the Commission to disclose to him a number of documents which it had prepared in response to questions put to it by national courts seized of actions under the EU competition rules, under a framework of cooperation elaborated since the case of *Delimitis* (Case C-234/89 *Delimitis* v. *Henninger Bräu* [1991] ECR I-935; 8.2). The applicant had no specific interest in the proceedings enquired about. He was refused access by the Commission, the Director General for Competition replying on behalf of the Commission that

'When the Commission replies to questions submitted to it by national courts before which an action has been brought for the purposes of resolving a dispute, the Commission intervenes as an *'amicus curiae'*. It is expected to show a certain reserve not only as regards acceptance of the manner in which the questions are submitted to it but also as regards the use which it makes of the replies to those questions.

I consider that, once the replies have been sent, they form an integral part of the proceedings and are in the hands of the court which raised the question.... [T]he decision whether to publish that information and/or make it available to third parties is a matter primarily for the national court to which the reply is sent...'

In a subsequent formal decision confirming that refusal, which the applicant contested in the Court of First Instance, the Secretary General of the Commission confirmed the Competition DG's decision:

'on the ground that disclosure of the replies could undermine the protection of the public interest and, more specifically, the sound administration of justice ... [T]here is a risk that disclosure of the replies requested, which comprise legal analyses, could undermine the relationship and the necessary cooperation between the Commission and national courts. A court which has submitted a question to the Commission would obviously not appreciate the reply being disclosed, particularly where the question is relevant to a pending case.'

Before the Court of First Instance (Case T-83/96 *Van der Wal* v. *Commission* [1998] ECR II-545), the right to a fair hearing under Article 6 ECHR was regarded as fundamental to the issue. The Court held:

'The right of every person to a fair hearing by an independent tribunal means, *inter alia*, that both national and Community courts must be free to apply their own rules of procedure concerning the powers of the judge, the conduct of the proceedings in general and the confidentiality of the documents on the file in particular' (para. 47).

It concluded that the public interest exception in the Commission's access to documents rules invoked by the applicant was intended to ensure respect for that principle, which covers the procedural autonomy of the national and EU courts. It therefore upheld the Commission's decision. The essence of the appeal by both the original applicant and the Netherlands (which had intervened to support the applicant and which – under the Rules of Procedure of the Court – is then able to mount an appeal) was that allowing a blanket public interest exception was not appropriate; rather there should be a case-by-case review. This was in essence the position taken by the Court of Justice which allowed the appeal and then decided the case for itself and annulled the Commission's decision. A case-by-case review would allow the Commission to take into account the national court's specific position on access to such documents, bearing in mind the need to allow the 'fullest public access possible', without endangering Article 6 ECHR. The Court also noted that the power to grant access to documents was not directly deducible from Article 6 ECHR, contrary to the conclusion of the Court of First Instance. The Commission could not, therefore, automatically disclaim responsibility for making available documents which it had produced by pointing to the national court to which they had been sent, as the Director General for Competition had originally sought to do. The documents supplied to national courts under the cooperation arrangements may range very widely in nature, and may not pertain to that specific case, but be general legal or economic analyses. The public interest worthy of protection under the access to documents rules was the procedural rules of the relevant national court on disclosure of documents, and these had to be taken into account on a case-by-case basis by the Commission in determining requests for access to documents. This is the essence of the Commission's duty.

9.7   The Scope of EU Fundamental Rights Protection

A second area of difficulty which arises in relation to fundamental rights protection is the question of the 'reach' of EU law, and the extent to which national law is subject to scrutiny by reference to EU fundamental rights (de Búrca, 1993b). Although it was thought in the early stages of the evolution of fundamental rights doctrine in the Community that the Court would apply its analysis only as a means of testing the validity of measures adopted by the EU institutions themselves, in more recent cases it has applied a fundamental rights argument across the range of Community competence, whether measures are adopted by the institutions or by the Member States. To understand the case law, it is important to note that the Court has frequently made reference instrumentally to fundamental rights in its case law in order to enhance, in general terms, the socio-economic foundations on which the EU is constructed (e.g. the reference to the fundamental right of access to employment in *UNECTEF* v. *Heylens*; the reference to the fundamental right of sex equality as one of the general principle of EU law in Case 149/77 *Defrenne* v. *SABENA* [1978] ECR 1365; the subsequent construction of that principle in Case C-13/94 *P* v. *S and Cornwall County Council*). Frequent reference to fundamental rights reinforces the legitimacy which the EU can claim as a body subject to the rule of law, as the Court asserted in Case 294/83 *Parti Ecologiste 'Les Verts'* v. *Parliament* ([1986] ECR 1339).

It is in the light of these generalised assertions that the principles developed by the Court in cases such as Case 5/88 *Wachauf* v. *Federal Republic of Germany* ([1989] ECR 2609) should be viewed. In *Wachauf* the Court reiterated the principle of fundamental rights protection in the EU legal order, applying it specifically to a case in which a tenant farmer might, under the rules of the CAP, be deprived, without compensation, of his livelihood, on expiry of his lease. Such rules would infringe fundamental rights protection, as required by the EU legal order, and:

> 'since those requirements are also binding on the Member States when they implement Community rules, the Member States must, as far as possible, apply those rules in accordance with those requirements' (p. 2639).

It seems perfectly acceptable that where the Member States are acting effectively in an 'agency' situation, on behalf of the EU albeit in some cases exercising a discretion, that Member State actions should be subject to scrutiny under EU fundamental rights. Although this may mean that a form of fundamental rights protection through judicial action and interpretation enters a Member State 'by the back door' as a consequence of membership of the EU (Grief, 1991), this seems to be an incontrovertible consequence of the transfer of sovereign rights entailed by membership.

A more contentious situation arises where the Court of Justice has applied fundamental rights scrutiny to the actions of Member States taken within the realm of the derogations from the fundamental (economic) freedoms guaranteed by the Treaty. The first case where this approach was taken was Case 36/75 *Rutili* v. *Minister for the Interior* ([1975] ECR 1219) where the Court examined the limitations which bind Member States when they seek to rely upon what was then the Article 48(3) EEC public policy derogation which allows them to exclude migrant workers exercising their rights of free movement under Article 48 (now Article 39 and 39(3) EC). Reviewing the various limitations upon the national discretion, the Court concluded that they were all specific manifestations of a more general principle, enshrined in a number of provisions of the ECHR, that

> 'no restrictions in interests of national security or public safety shall be placed on the rights secured by [Article 39] other than such as are necessary for the protection of those interests "in a democratic society"' (p. 1231).

In Case C-260/89 *Elliniki Radiophonia Tileorasi* v. *Dimotiki Etairia Pliroforissis (ERT)* ([1991] ECR I-2925) the Court expressed a similar principle in much broader terms, by stating when it was examining the acceptability national public policy derogations (under what were then Articles 56 and 66 EEC – now Articles 46 and 55 EC) from the principle of free movement of services (then Article 59 EEC, now Article 49 EC), it was applying fundamental rights standards to national measures falling 'within the scope of Community law'. It held that the prohibition in Greece on the broadcasting of television programmes by all undertakings apart from the State Television Company, which Greece sought to justify by reference to important public policy interests protected by Articles 56 and 66 EEC, had to be assessed in the light of general principles of law, notably fundamental rights. In particular, the principle of freedom of expression, enshrined in Article 10 ECHR, could be invoked before the national court which is called upon to assess the validity of the purported justification for the derogation from principles of EU law.

The point was confirmed in essence by Case C-368/95 *Vereinigte Familiapress Zeitungsverlag* v. *Bauer* ([1997] ECR I-3689), another case which illustrates how often fundamental rights cases become delicate balancing acts involving competing interests for courts. The reference to the Court of Justice concerned the compatibility with EC Treaty rules on the free movement of goods of an Austrian law preventing the sale of periodicals containing prize competitions. The asserted aim of the national legislation was to protect press diversity, and thus it was justified under the relevant EU rules as an 'overriding requirement'. Such an attempt to derogate from the EU rules by means of a prohibition had, however, to face the addi-

tional obstacle that it must be shown that it did not infringe general principles of law and fundamental rights, including freedom of expression under
Article 10 ECHR. The national authority would have to show that the prohibition was a proportionate means of achieving the stated aim of protecting
press diversity, or could it be achieved by means less restrictive of intra-EU
trade in goods and of freedom of expression. Yet the overriding requirement invoked by the Austrian government, namely press diversity, is *also* a
value protected under Article 10 ECHR. Thus the case is actually about balancing two sides:

> 'of the same fundamental right of freedom of expression: the right of
> publishers to sell their products regardless of frontiers (combined with
> the right of readers to receive that information), as opposed to the value
> of protecting press diversity so as to allow for freedom of expression.
> What appeared to be a banal trade restriction is thus transformed into a
> delicate balancing act of opposed aspects of an important fundamental
> right, to be performed by the national courts under the guidance of the
> European Court of Justice' (de Witte, 1999a: 872).

The logical corollary of the point that EU fundamental rights protection extends into certain areas of national law affected by EU law is that EU fundamental rights protection does not extend to areas which fall within the jurisdiction of the Member States, rather than the EU (see Cases 60-1/84
Cinéthèque v. *Fédération nationale des cinémas français* [1985] ECR 2605).
This pattern is in marked contrast to the scope of human rights protection
afforded by the Supreme Court of the USA under the US Constitution,
where creative judicial interpretation of the Fourteenth Amendment which
guarantees the right to due process has allowed extensive federal judicial
oversight over how the states manage their residual legislative and administrative competences (see Lenaerts, 1991b). That side of the equation has
been confirmed also by the Court of Justice. In Case C-299/95 *Kremzow* v.
Austria ([1997] ECR I-2629) the applicant in the national proceedings had
been convicted of murder in Austria, but the criminal proceedings had subsequently been held to be in breach of the ECHR by the European Court of
Human Rights. He argued in an action for damages against the Austrian
State brought before the Austrian courts that the national court was bound
by the judgment of the European Court of Human Rights because of Austrian membership of the EU. The Court of Justice refused to accept jurisdiction under Article 234, because of the lack of any connection with situations
envisaged by the EC Treaty. He had argued that the prison sentence prevented him from exercising free movement by moving to other Member
States, but the Court found that the deprivation of liberty was not sufficiently closely connected with free movement to bring him within the scope
of EU law.

The widest formulation of EU fundamental rights protection so far proposed comes from AG Jacobs in Case C-168/91 *Konstantinidis* v. *Stadt Altensteig* [1993] ECR I-1191 (3.6). The case involved the transliteration of a Greek name by the German authorities, whereby it lost its cultural and religious significance, on being transformed from 'Christos' into 'Hrestos'. Konstantinidis fell within the scope of EU law, as a self-employed migrant worker of Greek nationality working in Germany, and the Court found that any change in his name which was liable to confuse customers constituted an infringement of his economic rights. AG Jacobs suggested a more radical approach to the problem. An EU national who goes to work in another Member State is:

> 'entitled to assume that, wherever he goes to earn his living in the European Community, he will be treated in accordance with a common code of fundamental values, in particular those laid down in the European Convention on Human Rights. In other words, he is entitled to say "civis europeus sum" and to invoke that status in order to oppose any violation of his fundamental rights' (p. 1211).

As this broad approach was not accepted – or even referred to – by the Court of Justice, it must be assumed at present the 'Citizen of Europe' status remains – at least within the scope of the Treaty – a market and socio-economic, rather than a civic status (10.5).

The intervention of the Court of Justice into the field of fundamental rights protection has raised some very sensitive issues involving potential conflicts between different rights, where the very economic orientation of the EU has left the Court open to the challenge that it does not pay adequate attention to other values and principles. The potential for conflict is amply illustrated by Case C-159/90 *Society for the Protection of Unborn Children (Ireland) Ltd (SPUC)* v. *Grogan* ([1991] ECR I-4685). The applicants, SPUC, had relied upon Article 40.3.3 of the Irish Constitution which guarantees the right to life of the unborn, in order to obtain an injunction prohibiting the distribution of information about abortion clinics in the UK by the defendants, who were officers in a students union. They argued that what was then Article 59 EEC (now Article 49 EC) precluded the application of the Irish Constitution in such a way as to hinder the free movement of services. EU law required the free availability of the information required by Irish women if they were to take advantage, as recipients of services, of abortions lawfully available in other Member States. On a reference by the Irish High Court concerning these points the Court of Justice held that abortion – at least where it is provided for remuneration – is a service for the purposes of Article 49 EC. It should follow that any measures taken by Ireland which hinder the free movement of such services and of the recipients of such services should be capable of scrutiny under EU law, including fundamental rights, in this case freedom of expression protected by Article 10 ECHR. However, the Court avoided the need to consider the issue by holding that the distribution of abortion information by the students union fell outside the ambit of the Treaty. Since there was no economic link between the provider of the service (the UK clinics) and the advertiser of the service (the students union), the situation fell outside the scope of Article 49. No charge was made to the UK clinics in respect of the advertisements contained in the handbooks.

This distinction is, of course, a tenuous one, and could easily be circumvented in a future instance by the imposition of even a small charge for the advertisements. The Court would then have to confront the issue of the availability of information about abortion in a Member State where abortion itself is unlawful and, consequently, the possible conflicts between the freedom of information of the service recipients and providers and the right to life of the unborn which underlies the prohibition on abortion in Ireland. For having classed abortion as a service, the Court will logically be faced with the question of whether national variations in the conditions under which abortion is available, including a constitutional prohibition, represent restrictions on the free movement of services, in the same way that variations in product standards are categorised as potentially restrictive of the free movement of goods (Case 120/78 *Rewe-Zentrale* v. *Bundesmonopolverwaltung für Branntwein (Cassis de Dijon)* [1979] ECR 649). This could lead to the undermining of what is an important constitutional value in one Member State, and tends in general to indicate that those Member States which assert constitutional values which are not shared by the others may find them under attack from the imperatives of the internal market which requires the sweeping away of restrictions on trade. At the very least it requires Ireland to justify the operation of its prohibition on abortion, at least in so far as that has effects outside the Irish jurisdiction – a requirement that many might consider beyond the limits of a body such as the EU (Phelan, 1992). It might furthermore bring about a concrete conflict between the EU's economic law and the guarantee of respect for national identity now contained in Article 6(3) TEU – one of the non-justiciable provisions of the Treaty on European Union.

In reviewing the approach taken by the Court of Justice in *Grogan*, it is necessary to take into account also the decision of the European Court of Human Rights in a parallel case on abortion information, where it found that a prohibition on advertising does contravene Article 10 ECHR as a disproportionate interference in freedom of expression (*Open Door and Dublin Well Woman* v. *Ireland* (1992) Series A, no 246; (1993) 15 EHRR 244). Even though the Court of Justice side-stepped the problem of conflicts between differing constitutional values by drawing an 'economic/non-economic' distinction in *Grogan*, it is clear that a future case may require application of the ECHR in circumstances where the Member States find it politically unacceptable for provisions of their constitutions to be adjudicated upon by the judges of the Court of Justice, or even judges of other national courts.

9.8 Accession to the ECHR?

The significance of the ECHR in the framework of fundamental rights protection under the framework of general principles of EU law will be apparent from what has gone before. It is not surprising therefore that on a number of occasions, the Commission and the Parliament have both suggested that a solution to the problems of identifying a catalogue of justiciable rights for those subject to EU law, and of ensuring that the ECHR and EU systems operate in tandem, could be found if the EU (or, more precisely, the Community) could accede to the Convention itself (e.g. EP Resolution on Community Accession to the ECHR, OJ 1994 C44/32). This raises a number of problems, from both the EU and the ECHR perspectives. The latter at present only provides for the accession of 'states', and it is not clear how the EU would become involved in the judicial structure (one judge or fifteen involvement in all cases or only those involving the EU?). To endeavour to find a resolution to the problems on the EU side, the Commission submitted a request for an Opinion by the Court of Justice under what was then Article 228(6) EC on the question of accession (Opinion 2/94 *Accession by the Community to the ECHR* [1996] ECR I-1759).

The Court's Opinion profoundly disappointed those in favour of accession. The Court did make some general comments on fundamental rights which have attracted attention. For example, it confirmed that:

> 'respect for human rights is … a condition of the lawfulness of Community acts' (para. 34).

However, dealing with the specific questions posed in rather a technical manner, it largely declared the Opinion inadmissible. The only concrete question it considered was whether – in the absence of a Treaty amendment under what was then Article N TEU – the Community could have the competence to accede by means of an instrument based on what was then Article 235 EC (Article 308). For it found on reviewing the Treaty that:

> 'No Treaty provision confers on the Community institutions any general power to enact rules on human rights or to conclude international conventions in this field' (para. 27).

Hence the potential applicability of Article 308. Perhaps with one eye on the *Brunner* judgment of the German Federal Constitutional Court ([1994] 1

CMLR 57; 5.13) the Court was at pains to stress that the Community operates upon the basis of conferred and limited powers, supplemented where appropriate by implied powers (6.2, 6.3). Reiterating likewise the importance of fundamental rights as an integral part of EU law, the Court argued that accession to the ECHR would make a difference to institutional (rather than the substantive) basis of human rights protection and enforcement. Consequently, it would fall outside the scope of Article 308 EC to use it for accession:

> 'That provision, being an integral part of an institutional system based on the principle of conferred powers, cannot serve as a basis for widening the scope of Community powers beyond the general framework created by the provisions of the Treaty as a whole and, in particular, by those that define the tasks and activities of the Community ... (para. 30).
>
> Accession to the Convention would, however, entail a substantial change in the present Community system for the protection for the protection of human rights in that it would entail the entry of the Community into a distinct international institutional system as well as integration of all the provisions of the Convention into the Community legal order' (para. 34).

On the other hand, having denied the present competence of the Community to accede, the Court of Justice then unfortunately did not go on to say whether the EC legal order could accommodate – in the event of the necessary Treaty amendments – its own incorporation into a superordinate system, on the grounds that the question was essentially premature. Yet this was precisely the question which the Court of Justice did address on Opinion 1/91 *EEA Agreement* ([1991] ECR I-6079) where the Court found that the arrangements involved there would have led to a compromising of the autonomy of EU law. If states are able to submit to the jurisdiction of the ECHR and its Court, however, there seems no reason, institutionally, why the EU cannot do likewise. The question remains open, however. What the Court's Opinion did at least provide was a comprehensive review of the various positions taken by the Member States on this question, the opinions of all of them having been canvassed by the Court in the course of the proceedings. Because of the manner in which the questions were raised and dealt with by the Court it is not entirely clear as to the views taken by the Member States, but it would appear that a majority, but not all, are in favour of accession. The judgment in the *ECHR Opinion* was handed down on the very eve of the beginning of the IGC in late March 1996, and so the initiative to take matters forward on the basis of the Opinion immediately devolved to the national governments.

9.9 Fundamental Rights Authority in Europe

Before turning to the question of how fundamental rights issues have developed in the Treaty of Amsterdam, bearing in mind that the ECHR and EU systems still remain quite institutionally separate, it is important to consider the question of fundamental rights authority in Europe. The Council of Europe, along with the ECHR in particular, is, as we noted in 1.4, a basic liberal constitutionalist cornerstone of state-building and polity construction in Europe. Moreover, it appears by virtue of its position within the international legal order to be the supreme arbiter of fundamental rights protection in Europe. Certainly all the Member States are signatories of the ECHR and recognise the right of individual petition to the institutions of the ECHR which may pronounce upon alleged fundamental rights violations within those states. In each case, moreover, the ECHR is recognised as a superior authority even to fundamental rights authorities within the domestic jurisdiction, although ECHR rulings do not have the same effects, necessarily, as rulings on EU law do by virtue of its supremacy.

There have already been a number of cases of conflict between Court of Justice and Court of Human Rights jurisprudence. The cases of Case C-159/90 *Grogan* and *Open Door* have been highlighted. The ECHR case of *Funke* v. *France* (Series A, No. 256-A. [1993] 16 EHHR 297) undermined the earlier ruling in Case 374/87 *Orkem*, because the Court of Human Rights did indeed find that Article 6 ECHR includes the right to remain silent and not to incriminate oneself in contrast to the conclusions of the Court of Justice. These highlight the potential for future conflict. Yet up to 1999, all attempts by applicants before the Court or the Commission of Human Rights to argue that they should consider complaints against acts adopted within the legal framework of the EU were rejected. In *M & Co.* v. *Germany* (Appl. 13258/87, 9 February 1990), the Commission confirmed that:

- the ECHR does not prohibit states from transferring powers to international organisations;
- such a transfer does not necessarily excludes the state's responsibility under the ECHR with regard to the transferred powers; and
- the transfer to powers to an international organisation is not incompatible with the ECHR provided that within the organisation fundamental rights will receive equivalent protection.

In *Matthews* v. *United Kingdom* (Appl. 24833/94, 18 February 1999, [1999] 28 EHHR 361) the Court of Human Rights was faced for the first time with an act taking effect within the EU legal framework which was not reviewable before the Court of Justice. One might pause here to note that there are now countless such acts, especially since the burgeoning activities under the second and third pillars, and the restricted role of the Court of

Justice. Matthews, a citizen of Gibraltar, which is a dependent territory of the UK, complained that she was not permitted to register as a voter for the European Parliament elections of 1994. This, she alleged, was a breach of Article 3 of Protocol No. 1 ECHR. The relevant UK legislation on direct elections did not include Gibraltar within the franchise for these purposes. Yet Gibraltar's situation with regard to the EU is anomalous. It is not part of the customs territory and is treated as a third country for the purposes of the common commercial policy. On the other hand, many EU legislative acts in the areas such as the free movement of persons, services and capital and the protection of the environment and consumers do apply to Gibraltar and become part of the legal order of Gibraltar in the normal way.

The Court of Human Rights found that the UK was in principle responsible for any violation, that Article 3 could be applied to the European Parliament even though it was not envisaged when the ECHR was originally drafted, and that the European Parliament should now be viewed as a 'legislature' which was an essential precondition for applying Article 3. Most significantly it concluded that the UK could not invoke its 'margin of appreciation' in deciding that in order to apply its European Parliamentary electoral system it had to exclude Gibraltar, because its population was too small to be a full European Parliament constituency (at the time there was single constituency, first past the post voting). The case in *Matthews* was not about the type of electoral system – which the Court of Human Rights leaves to the state to determine – but about the very essence of the right to vote.

Commentators have noted the potential ramifications of this amplification of its position by the Court of Human Rights (King, 2000; Canor, 2000) in terms of the review of acts within or on the margins of the second or third pillars, especially under the many organisations established by conventions such as Europol. It also raises again the urgent need for appropriate institutional arrangements, with the accession of the EU to the ECHR being the best outcome in view of many commentators.

9.10   Fundamental Rights Outside the Court of Justice

Arguments in favour of ECHR accession have, however, been only part of the fundamental rights debate which was taken place outside the Court of Justice. This could be divided into three elements:

> – The creation of a strengthened fundamental rights presence within the EU Treaties themselves, perhaps involving
> – an EU Charter of Fundamental Rights, all of which is part of
> – a comprehensive EU human rights policy.

These issues will be dealt with in 9.11–9.13.

So far in the political sphere 'soft law' (see 6.15) measures have been the dominant outcome of the fundamental rights debate. The three political institutions adopted a Joint Declaration on Fundamental Rights in 1977 (OJ 1977 C103/1), and a number of joint declarations and resolutions of the institutions are specifically concerned with racism and xenophobia (e.g. Resolution of the Council and the representatives of the Member States of 29 May 1990 on the fight against racism and xenophobia OJ 1990 C157/1). The Parliament has played a particular role in relation to fundamental rights, drawing up a series of influential reports and initiating many of the joint initiatives. It has prepared annual reports on human rights in the EU and elsewhere, being prepared to point the finger at, for example, Member States which have failed to implement important conventions such as the UN Convention on the Rights of the Child. In other words, it has been little bothered by the formal confines of Community or Union competence (Bradley, 1999), a point foreshadowing, in a sense, the controversy over Austria and Jörg Haider's Freedom Party in early 2000 (9.11). This was one of the possible goals that the EU (effectively the Council) committed itself to in a noticeably vague Declaration drawn up in Vienna to mark the fiftieth anniversary of the UN Declaration on Human Rights in December 1998, and the first such report was published in October 1999 (Doc. 11350/99). It promised to consider strengthening the relevant EU structures.

The initial insertion of fundamental rights into the Treaty framework, through the Treaty of Maastricht, resulted in the non-justiciable Article F(2) TEU, building on the Court's treatment of fundamental rights as general principles of law. As it was phrased in the same terms as the Court's own case law, it was hard to see what it might add to that. There were references to the respect for fundamental rights also to be found in Article J.1(2) TEU and Article K.2(1) TEU, in the context of CFSP and JHA. These likewise fell outside the 'Community' sphere making them non-justiciable within the EU legal order. Only Article 130u(2) EC (now Article 177 EC) made reference within the EC Treaty to fundamental rights, but this provision is limited to ensuring that EU policy in the area of development cooperation contributes to the objective of respecting human rights and fundamental freedoms.

9.11 Fundamental Rights in the Treaty on European Union

One issue placed on the agenda for the IGC in 1996–97 was the possibility of 'reversing' Opinion 2/94, for example by creating possible mechanisms for EU accession to the ECHR. This option was not pursued, ruling out the possibility of accession in the very near future, although as an item on the agenda it is unlikely to go away, given the issues raised in 9.8 and 9.9. In the event, several changes were made to the Treaty framework, none of which *directly alters* the work of the Court of Justice, except that the fundamental rights guarantee in what is now Article 6(2) TEU has been formally and explicitly rendered justiciable before the Court of Justice by the addition of a new provision, Article 46(d) TEU. However, given that this provision is modelled on the wording of the Court's case law, it is difficult to see how it can lead to significant changes in practice. Moreover, the scope of the protection appears to be narrower, in any event, because Article 46(d) limits the scrutiny of the Court under Article 6(2) to issues raised 'with regard to action of the institutions'. This might be an invitation to the Court to look carefully at the scope of its case law, but if so it is an invitation which is likely to be declined. In Case C-17/98 *Emesa Sugar (Free Zone) NV* v. *Aruba* (Order of the Court of 4 February 2000) the Court was asked to invoke the Articles 46(d) and 6(2) TEU jurisdiction for the first time in the context of a request by one party to an action to submit observations 'replying' to the Advocate General's Opinion in its case. It invoked – unsuccessfully – the right to a fair trial under the ECHR.

The communitarisation of large parts of the old third pillar in Title IV of the EC Treaty, the incorporation of the Schengen *acquis*, and the creation of limited judicial review of measures adopted under the third pillar, including a preliminary reference procedure should Member States accept jurisdiction, does open up the possibility of using both Article 6(2) TEU and the Court's general case law as the basis for scrutiny of fundamental rights. This may limit the potential difficulties arising from the decision of the Court of Human Rights in *Matthews*.

In addition, the liberal underpinnings of the EU have been strengthened by the general guarantee clause contained in Article 6(1), committing the Union to the principles of liberty, democracy, respect for human rights and fundamental freedoms, and the rule of law, gathering together the so-called Copenhagen principles. These are made conditions of accession (Article 49 TEU), and through the procedure under Article 7 TEU, coupled with Article 309 EC, the possibility exists for the Council to sanction serious and persistent breaches by an *existing* Member State by suspension of voting rights and the benefits of membership. The procedure is triggered by the Council meeting 'in the composition of the Heads of State or Government' (i.e. as the European Council), and 'acting by unanimity on a proposal by one third of the Member States or by the Commission' to determine 'the existence of a serious and persistent breach by a Member State of principles mentioned in Article 6(1)' (Article 7(1)). There is scope for 'constructive abstention'. Abstentions do not prevent the adoption of the determination by the Council (Article 7(4)). The Parliament must give its assent by an absolute majority of its members and a two-thirds majority of those present and voting, and the

Member State in question must be given the opportunity to submit its observations. It is, however, excluded from voting on the issue (Article 7(4)). Obviously the scope of this procedure extends beyond the formal reach of human rights, but it is worth amplifying the point in this specific context.

The 'bâton' then passes to the Council (which need not involve in this context, one assumes, the European Council formula) to decide by a qualified majority on sanctions such as suspending voting rights or other rights under the TEU. It is required to have regard to the 'possible consequences of such a suspension on the rights and obligations of natural and legal persons'. The obligations under the TEU continue to be binding on the delinquent Member State (Article 7(2)). Article 7(3) allows for variation or revocation of such measures in response to changes in the underlying political or legal situation. Article 309 EC mirrors and extends the procedure into the EC Treaty. It confirms that voting rights under the EC Treaty are likewise suspended if such a decision has been taken under Article 7 TEU. Rights under the EC Treaty can be revoked by the Council acting by a qualified majority, taking into account the consequences for natural and legal persons. The only implication of these provisions for the Court of Justice would be that if the Council were to exercise its power under Article 309(2) EC to withdraw certain benefits, it would take a decision which could be challenged under Article 230 EC before the Court. The 'decisions' under Article 7 TEU are not subject to the jurisdiction of the Court.

While these rights are unlikely to be applied in their full rigour often if ever, even though the voting arrangements provide where appropriate for qualified majorities adjusted for the fact that one Member State is the subject of the vote (Article 7(4)), they cast a shadow under which hard bargaining can take place and political pressure can be exercised in order to bring a delinquent Member State back into the liberal fold. It could be called an 'insurance policy' (Hall, 2000). The events of early 2000 in relation to Austria clearly illustrate this point. When it became obvious towards the end of January 2000 that negotiations to form a coalition government in Austria following the General Election in 1999 were likely to involve a partnership of the conservative People's Party and the populist and allegedly xenophobic Freedom Party, then led by the controversial figure Jörg Haider, there was a negative international reaction. This was mainly because of previous public statements by Haider which had indicated that he was not within the liberal mainstream of European politics in which suggestions of support for any aspects of Nazi Germany and its policies and politics are utterly condemned. He had also made negative statements about immigrants. Despite the argument that any action by the other fourteen Member States would amount to interfering in the internal politics of a Member State, a statement was issued on 31 January 2000 instituting what amount to bilateral sanctions imposed on Austria by each of those states. These comprised the following actions:

- a refusal by the Governments of the other fourteen Member States to promote or accept any bilateral official contacts at political level with an Austrian Government integrating the Freedom Party;
- a denial of support for Austrian candidates seeking positions in international organisations; and
- Austrian Ambassadors in EU capitals would only be received at a technical level.

Notwithstanding these threats, the Austrian President was put in a position where he had no alternative but to invite the two parties to form a coalition government in early February, with a representative of the Freedom Party as Vice Chancellor under a Chancellor from the People's Party. The 'sanctions' – such as they were – remained in place, intended to ensure that the Austrian Government at least remains on probation. At the supranational level the EU institutions are not involved in the issue, since this would have required a formal invocation of the Article 7 procedure. On the other hand, the fact that Haider was a member of the Committee of the Regions – nominated by the Austrian Government long before the immediate controversy arose in early 2000 in his capacity as Governor of the Austrian Province of Carinthia – could be seen as an irony and almost a provocation.

In April 2000, in the context of the ongoing negotiations within the IGC and with the 'sanctions' continuing, Austria's President Thomas Klestil – who had reluctantly invited the formation of the controversial government – looked for an 'exit' strategy for Austria. He suggested that this might involve not only looking to see whether there was a genuine threat to the principles of freedom, democracy and human rights coming from Austria, but also examining (at the IGC) the formal procedures in Article 7 to see whether they should be expanded in order to create a monitoring system triggered in the event that those principles were under threat in any Member State. Soon afterwards, Belgium – a keen supporter of the 'sanctions' as a message to its own far right parties – proposed a broadening of the procedure in Article 7 TEU to include the possibility of an enquiry process more appropriate to the Austrian case. This has been discussed in the IGC 2000 but seems unlikely to result in Treaty amendments.

The reference to fundamental rights in CFSP was retained by the Treaty of Amsterdam. Article 11 TEU now provides that it is an objective of the common foreign and security policy 'to develop and consolidate democracy and the rule of law, and respect for human rights and fundamental freedoms'. This links neatly to the development cooperation provision (Article 177(2) EC), originally inserted by the Treaty of Maastricht. In view of the reduction and shift in the tasks covered by the PJC third pillar, the reference to fundamental rights has disappeared, although a specific task under Article 29 TEU is the prevention and combating of racism and xenophobia, in order to provide 'citizens' with a high degree of safety. The phrasing of this is unfortunate, because it tends to undermine the universality of the need for security against offensive racist or xenophobic actions. Article 6(2) TEU applies, of course, to the third pillar making fundamental rights a general condition of the constitutionality of action, if not an objective of the policy.

Finally, as noted in 9.6, a new law-making power was introduced in Article 13 EC allowing the Council to act on a proposal from the Commission, by unanimity and after consulting the European Parliament, to take appropriate action to combat discrimination based on sex, racial or ethnic origin, religion or belief, age or sexual orientation. The potential coverage of such measures is specifically limited to matters falling 'within the limits of the powers conferred by [the Treaty] upon the Community'. This does not create a new competence outside the *existing* objectives of the EC Treaty and reiterates the principle of conferred powers in Article 5 EC (see further 9.13). This complements also a reference in Article 136 EC, in the context of the social policy objectives of the EU, to the Charter of Fundamental Social Rights for Workers, originally drawn up in 1989.

9.12　Drafting a Charter

It might be thought that the answer to many of the questions raised in previous paragraphs would be for the EU to have its own free-standing Charter of Fundamental Rights. It could provide definitive guidance on issues such as the rights to be protected, the scope of the protection, and the standard of protection. It would certainly raise the profile of the EU generally, and in particular the existing body of rights. It could deal with the relationship between the ECHR and the EU, and it might potentially both strengthen the supremacy of EU law and provide one basis for the evolving constitutional framework of the EU.

The political will among the Member States to see some form of EU Charter of Fundamental Rights adopted received concrete endorsement in the Presidency Conclusions following the Cologne European Council of June 1999, although it is obviously not a new idea. It has been a political hot potato within the EU for a number of years. Work in the Parliament, and the development of the EU's own Human Rights Report, are initiatives which have been cited already. The Commission has sponsored research on this question, and the drawing up of a number of experts' reports, most recently a 1999 report on *Affirming Fundamental Rights in the European Union: Time to Act* published by DG V, the Employment and Social Affairs Directorate General, which built in turn upon the so-called *Comité des Sages* report of 1996 entitled *For a Europe of Civic and Social Rights*, produced by a committee of distinguished experts. Many of these papers have concerned questions internal to and external to the EU in relation to fundamental rights.

The German Presidency in the first half of 2000 resuscitated the narrower question of fundamental rights *within* the EU, giving it a prominent place on the Agenda of the European Council in Cologne. The Presidency Conclusions contain a decision on establishing a body with the task of drawing up a Charter of Fundamental Rights for the European Union.

The most interesting questions concern not the timing or scope of this initiative, both of which could be said to be driven by primary considerations of expediency rather than pure moral imperative, but rather *process*. First, the elaboration is taking place outside an IGC. In fact, through the course of 2000 it took place *alongside* an IGC, which began in February 2000. It has always seemed likely that the status of the Charter would be declaratory, like the Community Charter of Fundamental Social Rights for Workers, which was originally adopted – without the UK's participation – in 1989, but perhaps be incorporated later in some way into the Treaty. That point has been explicitly left open, although the Convention doing the drafting has taken the view that it must produce something which could be enshrined in a binding instrument. But might its outputs, like those of that first Charter, at some stage in the future, be formalised in a Treaty, or quasi-Treaty document such as a Protocol? The Social Charter was originally made an explicit inspiration by the Social Policy Agreement attached to the Treaty of Maastricht, from which the UK opted out, and is referred to now in Article 136 EC as the basis for the EU's reformulated social policy provisions, so a similar usage of the Fundamental Rights Charter could be a possibility as a minimum level of treaty incorporation. Moreover, any Charter – whatever its status – would inevitably become part of the fundamental rights 'heritage' inspiring the Court of Justice in its interpretation of fundamental rights as general principles of law under Article 6(2) TEU.

Second, in its Cologne Decision the European Council determined the framework for the elaboration of the Charter:

> 'a draft of such a Charter of Fundamental Rights of the European Union should be elaborated by a body composed of representatives of the Heads of State and Government and of the President of the Commission as well as of members of the European Parliament and national parliaments. Representatives of the European Court of Justice should participate as observers. Representatives of the Economic and Social Committee, the Committee of the Regions *and social groups as well as experts should be invited to give their views*. Secretariat services should be provided by the General Secretariat of the Council' (emphasis added).

The Presidency Conclusions of the Tampere European Council of October 1999 formalised this further in an Annex regarding the Composition, Method of Work and Practical Arrangements for the Body to Elaborate a Draft EU Charter of Fundamental Rights, with 'other bodies, social groups and experts' to be invited to give their views. Moreover, 'in principle, hearings held by the Body and documents submitted at such hearings should be public', and a 'complete language regime' should be applicable to meetings, making them accessible in all the official languages of the EU. Non-governmental interests were not slow to respond to such an initiative. Within a few days, a response from the Platform of European Social NGOs and the European Trade Unions Confederation welcoming the initiative and insisting that they should be fully consulted had appeared on the Platform website, and was given quasi-official sponsorship when it appeared also on the website of the Social Affairs Directorate of the European Commission. This was the first of many hundreds of submissions, complemented by public hearings at which NGOs were given the opportunity to present their ideas.

Third, as is apparent from the list given above, those participating in the body (which gave itself the title 'Convention') drafting the Charter were drawn from a much wider range of bodies and institutions than the normal IGC participants. Specifically, the Parliament has made much of this being the first drafting group of a constitutional nature in which its representatives have participated as equals. A comprehensive website was set up within the Council's website, and the European Parliament complemented this with a further site. Submissions to the Convention from governments, institutions, members of the Convention, and non-governmental interests were all logged, given a number and placed on the website. The minutes of the Convention's meetings were made available.

Fourth, the Convention decided to elaborate a preliminary draft Charter for consideration by the European Council at the Feira summit in Portugal in June 2000, with a final draft to be ready by the Nice European Council in December 2000, where the IGC was expected to close. Between June and December one possibility would be the incorporation of the Charter into the work of the IGC, with the possibility, therefore, of binding effect potentially on the agenda. Its drafting committee comprised the Chair, plus representatives from the Commission, the Parliament, the national parliaments and the Council Presidency.

Unsurprisingly the issues of the content and effects of the Charter dominated debate in and around the Convention. In the early part of its work programme, the Convention concentrated on 'classic' civil rights, working synthetically with sources such as the constitutional principles common to the Member States, the ECHR and the Social Charters of the EU and the Council of Europe. It grappled with the issue of whether this should be a Charter for 'citizens' or for others, including legal persons and third country nationals resident in the EU. Wider issues regarding social and economic rights have been raised by many interlocutors of the Convention, and it appeared that at least some wider rights such as a right to education would be included in the final draft. As to the question of effect, it has been unsurprisingly pointed out in many quarters that the drawing up of a non-binding Charter is a rather pointless exercise. Yet a binding Charter is problematic as to the potential scope of its effects, its relationship with the ECHR and the national constitutions, and the continuing 'limited powers' status of the EU which makes a universally applicable Charter in the style of the ECHR not a feasible option at the present time. In February 2000, the Parliament adopted a resolution calling upon the Charter to be incorporated into the Treaties and given binding legal status, although it seemed to assume that Article 6(2) TEU would continue to exist and apply. Moreover, it assumed that it would be given the opportunity to 'assent' to the Charter; this simply serves to highlight the fact that nothing relating to the Charter has had any formal legal basis in the Treaties, but rather it represents in effect an example of 'extra-Treaty' informal and *ad hoc* integration, albeit involving all of the Member States and all the institutions.

9.13   **An Evolving Human Rights Policy**

Joseph Weiler has been the most vociferous long-term proponent of the EU having a 'human rights policy' (for a recent restatement of his views see Alston and Weiler, 1999). That is, the EU should have more than just a statement of fundamental rights enshrined in the Treaties, or a negative commitment not to infringe rights, but also have a positive, institutionalised programme to improve the status and effects of human rights in all dimensions of its work. In one sense that could be said to be shifting to seeing human rights as an objective of the EU rather than merely a matter to be taken into account in pursuing other objectives (McGoldrick, 1999). The development of some sort of 'policy' is unavoidable, given the ever-greater involvement on the part of the EU in human rights related matters. From recent years, one could list the following developments as just some examples of emerging policies:

– The adoption of the Data Protection Directive (Directive 95/46 on the protection of individuals with regard to the processing of personal data and on the free movement of such data, OJ 1995 L281/31), the commitment in Article 286 EC to extend the principles contained in this Directive to cover the EU institutions, and the Commission's consequential proposal for a Regulation on this matter (COM(1999) 337 OJ 1999 C 376). The data protection rules contain principles governing the collection, storage and use of personal data.
– The development of policies on human rights in the field of development cooperation with third countries, especially *vis-à-vis* third world countries which have emergent or vulnerable democratic systems of government and a sometimes tenuous hold on the rule of law. Case C-268/94 *Portugal*

v. *Council* ([1996] ECR I-6177) confirmed the legality of the EU placing human rights clauses into development cooperation agreements allowing for the suspension of aid, for example, in the event of serious breaches of human rights. This has been the EU's practice since 1995, although it has been accused of seeking to export its own standards in a culturally insensitive manner, and being inconsistent in its approach to 'big players' in the trade field. In two Regulations adopted in 1999, the Council concretised and made more specific its integration of human rights questions in relation to development cooperation and other external activities (Regulations 975/1999 and 976/1999, OJ 1999 L120/1 and L120/8). These were adopted under the commitment to human rights in development policy in Article 177 EC.

– The implementation of Article 13 EC. The Commission quickly made a series of proposals for a general equal treatment directive applying to all grounds cited in Article 13, but covering only employment issues, for a wider race discrimination directive covering other issues such as the supply of services which would fall within the scope of EU law, plus a proposed action plan on discrimination and a Communication on policies (COM(1999) 564–7) (Barnard, 1999; Flynn, 1999). Closely linked is the EU's developing policy on racism and xenophobia, also based on a proposed action plan (COM(1999) 183) (Hervey, 1999). In June 2000 the Council unanimously gave approval for adoption of the race discrimination directive.

Some of these activities might be thought more 'rhetorical' than real at present. Certainly, in the case of racism the Commission is looking at a subject which public opinion surveys tell the politicians is something that people think 'Europe' should do something about. But linked to the Charter development, the overall programme is clearly something that the EU will take more and more seriously during the coming years. From the perspective of the potential effectiveness of such a policy, its institutionalisation within the framework of the Commission (where presently responsibilities are scattered across many Directorates General) would be a desirable step.

Summary

1 The important body of general principles of law can be sub-divided into four groups:
   – principles of administrative and legislative legality and of due process of law;
   – the economic pillars of the internal market;
   – political rights such as democracy and transparency;
   – fundamental rights.

2   General principles of law bind the EU and, in so far as their activities fall within the scope of the EU's competences, the Member States.

3   Under EU law, the application of fundamental rights as general principles of law by the Court of Justice and national courts often involves delicate balancing exercises between competing rights and interests.

4   Although accession by the EU to the ECHR has been suggested as a means of securing the status and protection of fundamental rights in the EU and avoiding possible conflicts with the ECHR, this option is unlikely to be taken in the near future following the Court's ruling that accession will not be possible without a formal treaty amendment.

5   In appropriate cases the Court of Human Rights will review acts of the Member States within the field of EU law, scrutinising them for compatibility with the ECHR.

6   The TEU contains important provisions guaranteeing fundamental rights, in particular Article 6(2), plus a procedure for sanctioning Member States which commit persistent and serious infringements of rights contrary to the liberal principles guaranteed Article 6(1).

7   In 1999 the EU decided to begin drafting a Charter of Fundamental Rights, possibly to be incorporated into the Treaties in the context of the 2000 IGC. The Convention elaborating the Charter draws its members from a wide range of bodies and institutions, and conducts its business largely in public.

8   The amendments to the Treaties introduced by the Treaty of Amsterdam may be the starting point of a comprehensive human rights policy in the EU.

Questions

1   How does the Court of Justice identify and protect general principles of law?

2   Why and how has the protection of fundamental rights in the EU evolved?

3   To what extent should the actions of the Member States be controlled under the framework of EU fundamental rights protection?

4   Does the EU need a Fundamental Rights Charter?

5   What advantages or disadvantages would result from the establishment of a comprehensive human rights policy?

Workshop

Draft a 'human rights code' for the European Union, covering not only a body of formal fundamental rights but also safeguards to ensure that EU action protects and promotes fundamental rights in all circumstances.

Further Reading

P. Alston and J.H.H. Weiler (1999), 'An 'Ever Closer Union' in Need of a Human Rights Policy: The European Union and Human Rights', in Alston (1999).

A. Arnull (1999a), Ch. 6, 'General Principles of Law and Fundamental Rights'.

C. Barnard (1997), '*P* v. *S*: Kite Flying or a New Constitutional Approach?', in Dashwood and O'Leary (1997).

C. Barnard (1999), 'Article 13: Through the Looking Glass of Union Citizenship', in O'Keeffe and Twomey (1999).

K. Bradley (1999), 'Reflections on the Human Rights Role of the European Parliament', in Alston (1999).

G. de Búrca (1993a), 'The Principle of Proportionality and its Application in EC Law', 13 *Yearbook of European Law* 105.

G. de Búrca (1993b), 'Fundamental Human Rights and the Reach of EC Law', 13 *Oxford Journal of Legal Studies* 283.

G. de Búrca (1995), 'The Language of Rights and European Integration', in Shaw and More (1995).

G. de Búrca (1997), 'The Role of Equality in European Community Law', in Dashwood and O'Leary (1997).

I. Canor (2000), '*Primus inter pares*. Who is the Ultimate Guardian of Fundamental Rights in Europe?', 25 *European Law Review* 3.

T. King (2000), 'Ensuring Human Rights Review of Intergovernmental Acts in Europe', 25 *European Law Review* 79.

D. McGoldrick (1999), 'The European Union after Amsterdam: An Organisation with General Human Rights Competence?', in O'Keeffe and Twomey (1999).

G. More (1999), 'The Principle of Equal Treatment: From Market Unifier to Fundamental Rights?', in Craig and de Búrca (1999).

C. Turner (1999), 'Human Rights Protection in the European Community: Resolving Conflict and Overlap between the European Court of Justice and the European Court of Human Rights', 5 *European Public Law* 453.

B. de Witte (1999a), 'The Past and Future Role of the European Court of Justice in the Protection of Human Rights', in Alston (1999).

Key Websites

The Council, Commission and the Parliament all established websites on the Convention drafting the Charter of Fundamental Rights:
http://db.consilium.eu.int/df/default.asp?lang=en
http://www.europarl.eu.int/charter/en/default.htm
http://europa.eu.int/abc/cit1_en.htm
The Employment and Social Affairs DG of the Commission also maintains a fundamental rights website:
http://europa.eu.int/comm/employment_social/fundamri/index_en.htm
A good gateway to NGO activity around the Charter proposal is:
http://www.socialplatform.org/

10 Citizenship and the European Union

10.1 Introduction

The second dimension of 'values and principles' in the constitutional framework is citizenship. However, the discussion is not phrased in terms of 'Citizenship of the Union', although this limited notion enshrined in Part II of the Treaty will be a subject of some discussion (10.2). Note that the danger with the concept of citizenship is that it is highly contested in its meaning and scope. A useful comparison with the question of fundamental or human rights can be drawn. There are certainly significant definitional questions about what 'rights' are and when they are 'fundamental' and 'basic' in some way, and important issues about the proper scope of protection, the avenues of redress, the effects of rights on third parties, as well as the balancing of competing rights and interests in the context of determining the appropriate standard of protection. It is none the less probably reasonably clear to all what – broadly – would be meant when we talk about an 'EU human rights policy' (9.13). There is not even that degree of clarity or agreement were we to talk about a 'citizenship policy'.

There are many ways to approach the citizenship issue in the EU context. This much is apparent from the vast array of different takes on the question in the secondary literature, even just restricting the choice to legal scholars (see the list of further reading and other papers and articles referred to in this chapter). Consequently, the approach taken here is necessarily to some extent personal. It seeks to highlight in an exemplary rather than a comprehensive way the main significance of citizenship for the EU. It takes a particular interest in the link between citizenship and the constitutional framework of the EU and the emergence of the EU as a 'polity'. That link could, equally, be drawn between fundamental rights and polity building, and there is some overlap in coverage between this chapter and the previous one. Citizenship raises rather different questions to fundamental rights. To that end, the first step in the process of demonstrating its importance is the question of definition.

10.2 Defining Citizenship in the EU Context

The story of citizenship is intimately linked to the emergence of the nation state as a dominant form of political organisation. A legal concept of 'nationality', more or less loosely connected to an ethnic sense of the 'nation', is frequently invoked to distinguish between the citizen insiders and the alien outsiders. One key factor has historically been the boundaries of suffrage: who can vote in any given polity? But the formal legal concept is an inadequate description of the meaning of 'citizenship' as it is currently constituted. Since the Second World War in particular it has become almost as common to use the language of citizenship as a framework for understanding and investigating the extent to which individuals can lay claim to full membership of any given social grouping or polity (including, but not limited to, states). The classic formulation of that notion of membership has been in terms of a triad of different groups of rights, acquisition of which will feed into an underlying status of equality:

- civil rights (basic freedoms from state interference);
- political rights such as electoral rights and other rights to participate in government;
- social rights including rights to health care, protection against unemployment and old age.

The sociologist T.H. Marshall identified a historical progress through these stages of rights, at least in England where he rooted his analysis, from the eighteenth to the twentieth centuries (Marshall, 1950). Useful as this categorisation remains, in the context of assessing what might constitute 'membership' in any given time or place, citizenship scholarship within the social sciences today would be more likely to refer to a wider variety of factors including:

- demographic and other pressures on the modern welfare state, and issues of social inclusion and exclusion, especially related to unemployment and an ageing population;
- the increasingly multi-cultural nature of many Western societies;
- the complex identities of individuals where issues of gender, race, sexual orientation or other 'difference' are factors in determining 'who we are' as much as nationality or social class;
- issues of regionalism, nationalism and statehood, including – but not limited to – the legal concepts of nationality and/or citizenship which may be enshrined in the constitution or basic laws of a polity;
- questions of global responsibility, relating particularly to the environment and issues of development.

Citizenship has therefore become a rather plastic concept, capable of supporting arguments that a status of membership must be universal (we are all equal) but also capable of recognising differentiation (we are all different). This analysis serves to reinforce the highly complex nature of citizenship as a prism or lens through which to examine aspects of the human condition and suggests that any given notion of citizenship cannot simply be transplanted from one economic or political location to another without full regard to context.

If one defines citizenship in such broad terms, there seems no particular obstacle to it being applied at the EU level. The link – however strong histor-ically – with nation state formation would appear to be broken. But citizen-ship also implies belongingness. It comprises not only the bonds that link a person and the state/polity/society in which she lives, but also her relation-ship with others who live in the same dimensions of time and space. Thus the task in relation to any attempt to apply citizenship ideas at the EU level is not just to show how citizens are connected to the system of multi-level constitutionalism outlined in Chapter 5, by sets of rights and duties, but also to identify what might hold them together in terms of cultural identity or sense of civic obligation. The evolution of a public sphere or political space in which citizens within the EU understand themselves as mutually involved with and obligated to each other as exercising political sovereignty would prob-ably be a minimum condition for that part of a bond of citizenship to exist. It does not mean that the nation states have disappeared as objects of identifi-cation and loyalty, but that those who vote for the European Parliament and have a stake in the exercise of governmental powers by the Council, the Commission, the Parliament and the other relevant public institutions do at least see these questions as an object of mutual concern. Some have termed this idea 'postnational membership' (Soysal, 1994; Shaw, 1998a, 1998b). The key problem for many is the so-called 'no-*demos*' problem: there is no European people, and under the current conditions of integration within the EU, with widespread alienation from a polity seen as remote, inefficient and even corrupt, it is not immediately obvious how there might become one. The rest of this chapter will illustrate both the limitations and potential-ities of citizenship for the EU. The situation is well summarised by Ulrich Preuss (1995: 280):

'European citizenship does not mean membership in a European nation, nor does it convey any kind of national identity of 'Europeanness'. Rather, by creating the opportunity for the citizens of the Member States of the European Union to engage in manifold economic, social, cultural, schol-arly, and even political activities irrespective of the traditional territorial boundaries of the European nation-states, European citizenship helps to abolish the hierarchy between the different loyalties ... and to allow indi-viduals a multiplicity of associative relations without binding them to a specific nationality. In this sense, European citizenship is more an ampli-fied bundle of options within a physically broadened and functionally more differentiated space than a definitive legal status.'

10.3 Citizenship of the Union in the EC Treaty

In formal terms, citizenship finds a place in Part II of the EC Treaty. It takes the form of a concept defined as 'Citizenship of the Union', another sign – perhaps – of the growing unity of the legal order discussed in Chapter 5. This concept was introduced by the Treaty of Maastricht (what were then Articles 8a–e EC, now Articles 17–22). Article 17 now reads:

'1. Citizenship of the Union is hereby established. Every person holding the nationality of a Member State shall be a citizen of the Union. Citizenship of the Union shall complement and not replace national citizenship.
2. Citizens of the Union shall enjoy the rights conferred by this Treaty and shall be subject to the duties imposed thereby.'

The reference to the nationalities of the Member States is important. It states clearly the limited nature of EU citizenship. It links back directly to one of the framework 'constitutional' provisions of the TEU itself, Article 6(3) TEU:

'The Union shall respect the national identities of its Member States, whose systems of government are founded on the principles of democracy'.

Moreover, the reference to the complementarity of citizenship was an innovation added by the Treaty of Amsterdam. It refers back to a concession made to Danish sensibilities in the aftermath of the first Danish referendum rejecting the Treaty of Maastricht in 1992, which was a declaratory confirmation in the Edinburgh Summit conclusions by the European Council that nothing in the provisions of the Treaty of Maastricht in any way displaced national citizenship. As a form of membership, it is not an independent status, since citizenship of the Union is derived directly from citizenship or nationality at national level, which remains for the Member States to determine according to national law (10.4).

The statement of the rights and duties of EU citizens begins with the confirmation that these are those which are conferred or imposed by the EC Treaty (Article 17(2) EC) (i.e. including rights and duties to be found elsewhere in the Treaty). The following provisions then go on to confer some specific rights including:

– the 'right to move and reside freely within the territory of the Member States, subject to the limitations and conditions laid down in this Treaty and by the measures adopted to give it effect' (Article 18(1)); Article 18(2) lays down that the Council may adopt measures to facilitate the ex-

ercise of that right, in co-decision with the European Parliament unless other provisions in the Treaty would require otherwise; however, the Council must act unanimously;
– the right to vote or stand in municipal elections for those citizens residing in Member States of which they are not nationals (Article 19(1)); this right has been implemented by Council Directive 94/880 on the exercise of the right to vote and stand in municipal elections (OJ 1994 L368/38); there have been considerable difficulties in some Member States in implementing this Directive effectively (or at all), especially in Belgium where there have been constitutional difficulties;
– the right to vote or stand in European parliamentary elections for the same group of citizens (Article 19(2)); this right has been implemented by Council Directive 93/109 on the exercise of the right to vote and stand in European parliamentary elections (OJ 1993 L329/34) and two sets of parliamentary elections (1994 and 1998) have now passed with the provisions in place without them having a major discernible effect;
– EU citizens finding themselves in the territory of a third country where their own country is not represented have the right to diplomatic or consular protection by any Member State which is represented there (Article 20);
– the right to petition the European Parliament under Article 194 and to apply to the Ombudsman established under Article 195 (Articles 21(1) and (2)).

It should be noted that closer examination of the rights conferred in Articles 194 and 195 EC reveals that these political rights are ones which can be exercised by any citizen of the Union or 'any natural or legal person residing or having its registered office in a Member State'. In other words, they are not strictly 'citizens' rights' in the sense of being held *exclusively* by the class of person defined as the members of the polity in Article 17(1). It is immediately apparent that this is a very limited and specific catalogue of citizenship rights and it is hardly comparable with domestic (generic) conceptions of citizenship. Indeed, the provisions are as notable for what they do not say as for what they do. In particular, the original Memorandum from the Spanish Government, which initiated the inclusion of Part II of the EC Treaty at Maastricht, referred to the human rights foundation of citizenship. Of course, as we have seen, the Treaty of Maastricht did build a fundamental rights element into the TEU, namely what was then Article F(2) TEU, but it made no cross-reference between that provision and the citizenship provision other than the generalised reference to other rights in what is now Article 17(2).

An evolutionary element is built into the provisions. The Commission is required by Article 22 to report every three years to the Parliament on the implementation of the provisions, and in its Second Report in 1997 (COM(97) 230) it concentrated on the need for effective information campaigns to make citizens aware of their rights, notably in the case of the electoral rights under Article 19. In relation to free movement, the problem remains much the same as ever: whatever the theoretical status of free movement rights under the Treaties and the relevant secondary legislation, the greatest obstacle to exercising them is obstructiveness on the part of some Member States and their failure to observe many of their obligations. Part of the problem stems from the complexity of the system of free movement rights, and the fact that it has never conferred universal protection, but remains a system defined by reference to a person's status in the marketplace (worker or self-employed), by his or her capacity to provide for him or herself, or by membership of the family of such a person. Article 22 also provides for the possibility of the Council extending the catalogue of rights in Part II of the Treaty, but it must act unanimously, and any changes recommended in that way must be adopted and ratified by the Member States according to their respective constitutional requirements. In other words, it is a truncated Treaty amendment procedure, and has yet to be invoked.

Two issues emerge most strongly from this framework of provisions. The first is the centrality of the definition of membership by reference to nationality or citizenship of a Member State, and the consequences for those who fall either inside or outside that category. The second concerns the intimate link between the citizenship provisions and free movement rights.

10.4 Defining the Citizen: Member State Nationals and Third Country Nationals

It was not surprising that when drafting the citizenship provisions the Member States should choose to link Union citizenship and Member State nationality in Article 17. Article 12 EC restricts the right to non-discrimination on grounds of nationality implicitly to nationalities *of the Member States* alone. Article 39 on the free movement of workers benefits only the nationals of the Member States – although again this is not explicitly stated but must be deduced from the case law of the Court of Justice (e.g. Case C-355/93 *Eroglu* [1994] ECR I-5113). Furthermore, Articles 43 and 44 EC expressly provide for the abolition on restrictions on freedom of establishment for *nationals* of a Member State only.

The Member States have very different rules on matters of citizenship and nationality, and these are in essence fully protected by Articles 17–22. Some have separate concepts of citizenship (essentially the internal term, under which national law 'recognises' those who belong to the polity) and nationality (a term rooted also in international law, as it is a status which other states must recognise). Some use *ius soli* (place of birth) to determine the acquisition of citizenship and/or nationality, and others *ius sanguinis* (based on a historical connection to the territory). Many countries have a combination of both these principles. There are more or less restrictive approaches to changes of civil status through naturalisation or marriage, and more or less restrictive approaches to dual nationality. These differences do have consequences in terms of understanding how a superimposed EU citizenship which makes use of the definitional power of national law in relation to the acquisition of Union citizenship will operate. The Member States attached a declaration to the Treaty of Maastricht explicitly restating the right of the Member States to determine who are to be considered their nationals. This is not illogical or unreasonable in view of the position in international law that the capacity of each state to define its own nationals by its own legislation is a component of sovereignty.

However, the position needs to be viewed in the light of Case C-369/90 *Micheletti* v. *Delegación del Gobierno en Cantabria* ([1992] ECR I-4329), which effectively restricted the right of Spain to apply its own legislation on dual nationality. Micheletti was an Argentine national holding an Italian passport issued on the basis of his Italian parentage. Under Spanish law he was regarded as possessing Argentine nationality alone, but EU law now requires Spain to accept his Italian passport as well. In *Micheletti*, the Court of Justice declared that the competence of the Member States to determine who are their nationals must be exercised

> 'having due regard to Community law.... [I]t is not permissible for the legislation of a Member State to restrict the effects of the grant of the nationality of another Member State by imposing an additional condition for recognition of that nationality with a view to the exercise of the fundamental freedoms provided for in the Treaty' (at p. 4264).

This definitional question is not only important in terms of how it positions EU citizenship in relation to the nationalities or citizenships of the various Member States, but also because of the consequential knock-on effects for third country nationals. Whatever their formal or *de facto* status within the countries in which they are resident, third country nationals are excluded from benefiting from EU citizenship, and the rights which it confers, including the right of free movement. Also excluded from EU citizenship are third country nationals who are entitled to entry and residence by virtue of national laws governing family reunion or by virtue of EU law, which gives free movement rights to the family members of EU nationals who themselves exercise their Treaty rights (Article 10 of Regulation 1612/68). Nor does it give EU citizenship to those benefiting from the Court of Justice's interpretation of the free movement of services provisions which allow for a form of free movement for third country nationals moving as employees of a service provider (Case C-43/93 *Van der Elst* [1994] ECR I-3803) or those benefiting from international agreements linking the EU and its Member States with third countries some of which grant limited residence rights.

10.5 The Link between Citizenship and Free Movement

It is in the area of free movement generally that the whole arena of citizenship is most developed. This is for three reasons:

– On reading Articles 17–22 EC, it would appear that the emphasis of the citizenship rights is on constituting the strong transnational citizen who holds and exercises rights *vis-à-vis* the Member States which are set up as the obstructive parties. There is relatively little, on the face of it, to constitute either a vertical relationship between the EU and 'its' citizens (with the exception of the non-judicial remedies before the Parliament and the Ombudsman), or a horizontal relationship between the citizens *inter se*. It suggests little or nothing about the essentially reciprocal nature of citizenship, or about the problem of 'duty'.
– This link is not accidental. It is out of the field of free movement that the concept of citizenship in the EU context largely emerged. In fact, lawyers have been referring to 'Community citizenship' in the free movement context since the 1970s.
– In turn, it is only the free movement aspects of the citizenship provisions which have thus far received any detailed consideration by the Court of Justice, notably in Case C-85/96 *Martínez Sala* v. *Freistaat Bayern* ([1998] ECR I-2691) and Case C-378/97 *Wijsenbeek* [1999] ECR I-6207.

Dealing with the first two points first, a powerful line of case law can be traced in which the Court of Justice has given quasi-constitutional status to aspects of free movement law. Not only has the Court given extensive interpretations to key concepts such as the notion of 'worker' under Article 39 EC, but it has also extended the protection of EU law to a number of other categories of persons not specifically named in the Treaties. Article 12 EC, the guarantee of non-discrimination on grounds of (EU) nationality, has played a vital role in this context as a constitutional principle, and there is a substantial overlap between this construction of the question and the Court's preferred approach to reasoning via the medium of general principles of law (9.4). Two key cases will highlight the point amply. The plaintiff in Case 186/87 *Cowan* v. *Le Trésor public* ([1989] ECR 195) was, as we saw in Chapter 9, mugged on the Metro when he was visiting Paris as a tourist. He was denied compensation from the French criminal injuries compensation scheme, on the grounds that he was a UK national. The Court of Justice brought Mr Cowan within the scope of the protection of the Treaty, finding that as a tourist he was a recipient of services who had exercised his right of free movement, and therefore was implicitly covered not only by the provisions on the free movement of services, but also by the general right to non-discrimination in Article 12. Hence a compensation scheme which arbitrarily excluded non-nationals was contrary to the principles contained in the Treaty.

The second example concerns migrant students: the plaintiff in Case 293/83 *Gravier* v. *City of Liège* ([1985] ECR 593) was a French national who wished to study strip cartoon art at university in Belgium. The Court held that by virtue of (what was then) Article 128 EEC which established an outline competence for the Community in relation to vocational training, she too fell within the scope of the Treaty (wishing to undertake a vocational training course in another Member State), and was therefore entitled to the protection of what was then Article 7 EEC (now Article 12 EC). Hence she was entitled to access to the course on a non-discriminatory basis and could not be charged a fee that was imposed by Belgian universities on non-nationals. In these cases, provisions of the Treaty which originally had a 'market' orientation, have been used for a broader constitutional purpose. Cowan and Gravier are constituted not only as 'market' citizens of the European Union but are also conceived in broader constitutional terms or beneficiaries of the evolving polity.

The Court of Justice has not, however, been entirely consistent. In 9.7 we reviewed the approach taken by Advocate General Jacobs to Case C-168/91 *Konstantinidis* v. *Stadt Altenstieg* ([1993] ECR I-1191), concerning the self-employed masseur of Greek nationality living in Germany who complained that the German authorities were infringing his EU rights in their official mistranslation (transliteration) of his name (from Greek letters into Roman ones). The Court of Justice concluded that in such circumstances the German authorities were not entitled to insist on a spelling of the applicant's name in such a way as to misrepresent its pronunciation since 'such distortion exposes him to a risk of confusion of identity on the part of his potential clients'. What is notable about this case is that the Court focused specifically on the economic considerations, highlighting the role of Konstantinidis within the EU system as a 'market' citizen. In contrast, AG Jacobs, in a very wide-ranging opinion, concentrated on a fundamental rights argument in which he argued that the migrant worker (or professional) should be able to rely on a prima-facie claim as a 'European citizen' to a basic standard of rights protection, irrespective of whether the protection he or she received was granted on a non-discriminatory basis. AG Jacobs' approach has not been taken up, as the Court of Justice in Case C-274/96 *Bickel and Franz* ([1998] ECR I-767) followed the narrow approach of linking Article 12 to a specific provision in the Treaty conferring a right to free movement.

It is in the context of this line of case law that Case C-85/96 *Martínez Sala* must be studied. The Court held that a Spanish national who was long-term resident in Germany – although on what precise basis her lawful residence in that country could be deduced was not entirely clear – could rely upon the non-discrimination principle in Article 12 EC as the basis for claiming equal access to a Germany child-raising benefit for her new born child. In economic terms her status might best be categorised as marginal to the labour market, but not wholly excluded. It was many years since she had worked in Germany, almost certainly as a result of her ongoing childcare responsibilities. The Court concluded that she could not be obliged to produce a residence permit in order to obtain the benefit, when nationals merely had to prove that they were permanently settled in Germany. It offered two ways to the national court of approaching the case. Either it could consider whether Martínez Sala should be classed as a worker under Article 39 or an 'employed person' under Community social security regulations (Regulation 1408/71), which was a distinct possibility on the very broad constructions of those terms which it gave. But the novelty of the Court's judgment lay in its invocation of Citizenship of the Union, notably Article 17(2) which 'attaches' to the citizen the rights and duties existing under the EC Treaty. Martínez Sala could claim equality of treatment, the Court found, even if she was solely dependent upon welfare and could bring herself within the personal scope of Community law by no other means than that she was a Union citizen lawfully resident in another Member State. The only material condition was that the benefit that she claimed must fall within the scope of EU law. The Court of Justice found that it was within that scope using its own earlier interpretation of a legislative measure which had expressly conferred social advantages on *economic* migrants and their families (Article 7(2) of Regulation 1612/68).

One interpretation of the Court's approach to the intersection of the material and personal scope of EU law, in combination with the non-discrimination principle, is that it gives something close to universal right of access to all manner of welfare benefits to all those who are Union citizens and who are lawfully resident in a Member State (Fries and Shaw, 1998). No longer, it would appear, are those benefits only going to be available to those able to point to a particular economic or family status protected under EU law. *Martínez Sala* has a significant impact, therefore, upon the welfare sovereignty of the Member States and mandates, in effect, that the community of concern and engagement by reference to which citizens of the Union must define themselves is, indeed, in certain welfare respects all those other citizens of the Union who have equal access to welfare benefits. In that respect, perhaps, the Court has gone significantly outside the confines of market citizenship in its early construction of the citizenship provisions.

Case C-378/97 *Wijsenbeek* deals with a different dimension of free movement, namely the question of borders. Disregarding the question of Schengen, and without looking ahead to a future after the Treaty of Amsterdam in which it is intended that free movement of persons across internal frontiers should become a reality within five years of its entry into force, *Wijsenbeek* addressed the legal situation under the EC Treaty after the expiry of the deadline in what is now Article 14 EC for creating the internal market by the end of 31 December 31 and after the entry into force of the Treaty of Maastricht with its consequential changes to the EC Treaty including the insertion of the citizenship provisions. In December 1993 Wijsenbeek was prosecuted in the Netherlands for refusing to present his passport and prove his Dutch nationality when flying into Rotterdam airport from Strasbourg in France, which is an airport where all flights come from or go to other Member States. The justification given by the Dutch government for requiring the production of a passport was that in the absence of common external frontiers it could not otherwise be certain that any person passing through Rotterdam airport had a right to be there, for third country nationals do not have a right of free movement within the EU, but may require visas in particular countries. The case thus turned on the interpretation of Article 14, which contains the deadline of 31 December 1992 and the relevance and applicability of what is now Article 18 EC, giving citizens of the Union a right to reside and move freely within the EU. Article 14 also needed to be read in the light of a Declaration appended by the Single European Act when the '1992' deadline was set. The Member States declared that while they were politically committed to adopting the necessary measures by the deadline, none the less 'setting the date of 31 December 1992 does not create an automatic legal effect'.

The Court gave the expected interpretation of Article 14, which it said:

> 'cannot be interpreted as meaning that, in the absence of measures adopted by the Council before 31 December 1992 requiring the Member States to abolish controls of persons at the internal frontiers of the Community, that obligation automatically arises from expiry of that period... [S]uch an obligation presupposes harmonisation of the laws of the Member States governing the crossing of the external borders of the Community, immigration, the grant of visas, asylum and the exchange of information on those questions.'

In other words, a 'frontier-free' Europe cannot be attained by mere 'deregulation', but presupposes a network of other controls. Typically, of course, frontier controls simply move to another place, perhaps in the form of more regular and random internal checks on forms of identity, or requirements to register a domicile. Likewise in relation to Article 18(1), while the Court accepted that this did contain a free movement right, it none the less held that it was one which could only be exercised by persons with the nationality of a Member State who must therefore be able to *prove* that they were entitled to benefit. This would be the case at least until there were harmonised rules among the Member States on matters relating to the external frontier of the EU. Consequently, it was acceptable for the Netherlands not only to require Wijsenbeek to show his passport, but also to prosecute and punish him for failing to do so, provided the punishment was not so disproportionate to the offence as to create an obstacle to free movement.

10.6 Citizenship Rights under EU Law

The discussion in the previous paragraphs has highlighted the fact that citizenship rights are not only to be found in the 'citizenship provisions' in Part II of the EC Treaty, but are scattered across the Treaties and also the case law of the Court of Justice. This point is true not only in relation to that major segment of citizenship issues and policies which is directly related to the question of free movement, but also if an approach to citizenship is taken which takes the classic 'triad' of civic, political and social rights introduced by Marshall in his work in the 1950s and attempts to apply it to EU law. This is an approach to citizenship which looks not at the formal rights under the Treaty identified as specifically 'citizenship related', but rather undertakes an audit from the perspective of asking what dimensions of a concept of 'membership' currently exist in the EU. Potentially, this could involve looking at a very large part of EU law through the lens of citizenship – which would be an impossible undertaking in this context. So what follows is, instead, a very brief sketch. Moreover, it goes back over old ground already addressed in this chapter and the previous chapter. The merit lies in presenting a *different* way of recording the problem of assessing the state of citizenship in the EU. It also offers a well-established 'ideal type' against which to measure what level of citizenship exists at present in the EU, at least as regards the issue of rights. An important point to note is that in view of the functional evolution of the EU out of a system of market integration, in one sense the order of Marshall's triad is reversed. What came first was a form of 'social citizenship', but specifically as a socio-economic concept of market citizenship. Civil rights and political rights have followed thereafter.

The *civil rights* of EU citizens are primarily constituted through the existence of the European Community as a 'community of law' (5.16). So, according to Curtin (1993: 67):

> 'the unique sui generis nature of the Community, its true world-historical significance [is constituted by its character] as a cohesive legal unit which confers rights on individuals.'

As we have seen, it is customary to credit the Court of Justice with the achievement of 'constitutionalising' the EC Treaties, principally by upholding the authority of EU law in relation to national law. But in addition to this, the Court is also responsible for a substantial case law on fundamental rights reviewed in Chapter 9. While it has been suggested that in part the motivation for that case law lay in the need to enforce the superior status of EU law *vis-à-vis* national law, this field of law has probably now developed a life of its own in upholding a teleology of integration and a 'Community of law' on behalf of a rather activist Court of Justice. Moreover, although the ECHR remains a vital source in relation to the construction of a framework of civil rights, it needs to be seen in the light of the EU's own construction based on Article 6(2) TEU and the case law of the Court. The narratives presented in Chapter 9 make this very clear.

Turning to *political rights*, it is worth repeating the point that many of the elements of 'political structure' in the EU lag some way behind the relatively sophisticated edifice of the legal system. Both the practice of democracy, and the associated political rights for citizens, remain pale shadows of the national 'versions' of democracy. The EC Treaty itself concentrates upon limited electoral rights in local and European Parliamentary elections, and upon forms of non-judicial access to the political institutions through the medium of petitions and complaints. Democratic participation in the form of European Parliament input into legislative decision making has been growing at a steady rate, but the absence of a cross-European culture of political parties maintains a dislocation between the laudable work of MEPs to ensure democratic accountability and to enhance the quality of legislation and the basis upon which people actually vote in European parliamentary elections. The role of the European Parliament in the March 1999 resignation of the European Commission, in the wake of the Report of the Wise Men, marks a new transition on the political muscle of the European Parliament, but the rupture between the exercise of political power and popular representation remains as strong as ever. A key area of development is that of transparency, especially the right of access to the documents of the EU institutions, which will be discussed in 10.8.

At first blush, in view of the rather fragmentary 'social dimension' of the EU up to now, one might be tempted to conclude that the *social rights* of EU citizens are exceedingly sparse. However, if one reads social citizenship in the EU against a broader canvass of socio-economic citizenship this suggests that these social rights can divided into three distinct categories: market citizenship, industrial citizenship (i.e. participation in the enterprise), and welfare citizenship. Perhaps the strongest message of a review of social citizenship rights in the EU is how the market order established by the framework of 'fundamental freedoms' to be found in the EC Treaty simultaneously both empowers and constrains the EU citizen. It offers new possibilities and rights in relation to the domains of employment, production and consumption, where the exercise of individual 'choice' can in some senses be seen as contributing to the process of building the EU as a political as well as economic entity. But it also constructs a limited market-oriented picture of the citizen in which welfarist principles have found it hard to establish a foothold in hostile territory. For instance, in relation to sex discrimination law – long lauded as a 'success' of EU social policy – the Court of Justice draws a stark distinction between employment-related discrimination, and issues which arise directly out of (traditional) divisions of labour within the domestic household or the family (Case 184/83 *Hofmann* v. *Barmer Ersatzkasse* [1984] ECR 3047). In other words, social citizenship thus far has been substantially led by market citizenship. At the same time, the rhetoric of social policy remains strong. The Commission is a forceful proponent of the idea of a 'European Social Model'; moreover, the 1996 report of the independent *Comité des Sages* on a *Europe of civic and social rights* also contains a powerful defence not only of the need for such rights in a 'People's Europe' but also of the empowering nature of bottom-up processes of constitution building in which individuals and social groups are involved in the formulation of key statements of citizens' rights (9.12).

10.7 The Link between Citizenship and Constitution Building

Thus far there has been a very strong emphasis on the link between citizenship and rights. And yet, as was suggested in the Introduction to Part IV, the thesis that EU law should necessarily go further with rights for citizens (or others) is not necessarily the best way to enhance constitutionalism and liberal order within the EU. The case can be made instead (or at least in addition) for linking the evolution of citizenship and the policies which have promoted development (such as the creation of a uniform format for passports, as well as the issues relating to free movement highlighted already) with the shift towards seeing the EU as a constitutionally based polity (Chapters 5 and 6) (Shaw, 2000b; Wiener, 2000). Examples can be drawn from the Treaty of Amsterdam, including not only the issues around fundamental rights highlighted in Chapter 9 but also the strengthening of the social dimension of the EU. It also includes policies for the first time on employment and strengthened competences to adopt social policy measures, including measures on social exclusion, by qualified majority voting in the Council under the Article 251 EC co-decision procedure, or by means of the legislative process in Article 139 EC involving the social partners. The opening of policies (not just those which are rights-based) on all forms of discrimination and especially racism and xenophobia are important developments in this area. However, perhaps the most important area of intersection between citizenship and constitutionalism has been in the area of transparency, and the possibilities which transparency offers in addressing the noticeably weak political dimension to citizenship in the EU.

10.8   Transparency: Citizenship in Action?

The legal framework of what is conventionally termed transparency has evolved relatively quickly in the EU. It became an issue in the aftermath of the Treaty of Maastricht, when the Member States attached a Declaration to the TEU signed in 1992 on the right of access to information:

> 'The (IGC) considers that transparency of the decision-making process strengthens the democratic nature of the institutions and the public's confidence in the administration. The (IGC) accordingly recommends that the Commission submit to the Council no later than 1993 a report on measures designed to improve public access to the information available to the institutions.'

From this it can be deduced that transparency in the EU comprises two main elements. The first is access to information by the public, who can, if properly informed, participate more fully in political debate. The second concerns the fact that the main decision-making body in the EU, the Council, continues to operate almost entirely *behind closed doors*. It continues to *legislate* in secret, although it has introduced a very limited number of public sessions. Little precise information is put into the public domain about the legislative process, with mandatory publication even of voting records introduced only in 1993 (Article 7(5) of the Council's Rules of Procedure: now in Article 207(3) EC). The position is eloquently summed up by Twomey (1996: 831):

> 'At present the work of the Council is carried out in a culture of secrecy, tempered by leaks, official and unofficial, and ministers putting inflections on Council proceedings for consumption by domestic electorates.'

Moreover, in spite of certain changes, as a general statement this remains essentially true: 'The novel idea of transforming diplomacy into democracy faces considerable barriers' (Laffan, 1996: 93). The Ombudsman defines transparency in the following terms (Södermann, 1998: 6):

- the processes through which public authorities make decisions should be understandable and open;
- the decisions themselves should be reasoned;
- as far as possible, the information on which the decisions are based should be available to the public.

In terms of 'soft legal' development matters progressed reasonably quickly once the first initiative had been taken, with the elaboration of several communications by the Commission (e.g. OJ 1993 C156/5). These included comparative surveys of access to documents in different Member States, and culminated in the adoption of a Code of Conduct by the Council and the Commission on public access to Council and Commission Documents in December 1993 (OJ 1993 L340/41). The Code of Conduct took the principled position that 'the public will have the widest possible access to documents held by the Commission and the Council'. It went on to define both a 'document' (any written text containing existing data held by the Council or the Commission) and also certain reasons for refusing access to a document, such as public interest including public security, international relations, court proceedings, and privacy and confidentiality of the individual. The Council and the Commission and later the Parliament adopted Decisions giving effect to this Code of Conduct and they were joined by all the other EU institutions and bodies such as ECOSOC, the Committee of the Regions and the various agencies, in many cases responding to an own initiative enquiry undertaken by the Ombudsman in the existence of basic access rules (see OJ 1993 L304/1 and OJ 1993 L340/43 (Council); OJ 1994 L46/58 (Commission); OJ 1997 L263 (Parliament)).

This would seem to suggest that transparency has indeed come to the top of the agenda for the institutions, responding to one of the perceived legitimacy deficits identified during and after the Maastricht IGC. This perception would also seem to be supported by the adoption of Article 255 EC at the Amsterdam IGC. It provides:

> 'Any citizen of the Union, and any natural or legal person residing or having its registered office in a Member State, shall have a right of access to European Parliament, Council and Commission documents ...'

Paragraphs 2 and 3 provide for the general principles and limits on grounds of public or private interest regarding access to documents to be laid down by a measure adopted by the Council, acting by co-decision with the Parliament under Article 255, within two years of the Treaty of Amsterdam coming into force (i.e. May 2001). Each institution will then elaborate its own rules of procedure to give effect to this general instrument. Article 255 applies to the second and third pillar by virtue of Articles 28(1) and 41(1) TEU.

In fact, the apparent ease with which transparency has leapt to the top of the political agenda belies a story which has involved documented institutional unwillingness, at least at the start, to give any form of 'real' access to documents (e.g. very high rates of refusal in the Council in the early years), attempts to give as wide as possible an interpretation to the exceptions contained in the existing rules, and consequentially extensive disputes between the institutions and individuals which have involved more than ten cases brought before the Court of Justice or the Court of First Instance, and numerous complaints to the Ombudsman many of which have been adjudicated in favour of the complainants. The conflict over this question has carried on into the post-Amsterdam era, with controversy over the publication of the Commission's proposal for a Regulation under Article 255 in January 2000 and a very public disagreement between Romano Prodi, the President of the Commission and Jakob Södermann, the Ombudsman, in the pages of the *Wall Street Journal* shortly thereafter.

The issues over which disagreement is rife can be seen from a more detailed review of the developing legal framework for transparency. For the Council, implementation of the Code of Conduct took the form of a change to its Rules of Procedure, Article 22 of which now provides that:

> 'The detailed arrangements for public access to Council documents disclosure of which is without serious risk of prejudicial consequences shall be adopted by the Council.'

Acting on the basis of Article 151(3) EC, which empowers it to adopt its Rules of Procedure, and Article 22 of the Rules, the Council then adopted a Decision setting out detailed modalities for public access (Council Decision 93/731 OJ 1993 L340/43). That Decision laid down a general principle of the 'professional secrecy' of the deliberations of the Council, unless it decides otherwise, and then set out cases where the Council 'shall not' disclose documents, and cases where it 'may' do so. In particular, under Article 4(2) it provided that access to a document may be refused in order to protect the confidentiality of the Council's proceedings. In sum, the rules were not generously worded. Applications for documents must follow a procedure laid down in the Decision, including the making of a confirmatory application in the event that the Council intends to refuse access.

Legal challenges were not long in arriving before the Court of First Instance. In Case T-194/94 *Carvel and the Guardian* v. *Council* ([1995] ECR II-2765), an application brought by a journalist and his newspaper, who were refused access to certain Council documents including minutes of meetings and had followed the procedures laid down in Article 7 of the 1993 Decision, the Court of First Instance chastised the Council for the 'blanket' way in which it was operating its self-imposed rules, requiring that the discretion which the Council has arrogated to itself be exercised on an individual basis. The Council had to balance confidentiality with the interests of the applicant. This precipitated some limited changes to the procedural rules operated by the Council. Case T-610/97 R *Carlsen and others* v. *Council* ([1998] ECR II-485) was an Order of the President of the Court of First Instance in an application for interim measures stemming from the refusal of the Council to disclose documents written by its Legal Service which had advised that certain pieces of draft legislation which were later adopted by the

EU legislature were beyond the scope of Community competence. The applicants wanted these materials in the context of the action that they brought before the Danish courts to challenge the Treaty of Maastricht as contrary to the Danish Constitution (5.13). The interim measures were refused, with the President of the Court of First Instance ruling provisionally that the Council was entitled to treat opinions of its legal service as internal and so refuse access to them. In its decision, the Council had cited the need to protect the public interest in 'the maintenance of legal certainty and *the stability of Community law*', and the words emphasised – although not specifically approved by the President of the Court of First Instance – have made a reappearance in the Commission's draft Regulation which will be discussed below.

Inevitably, of course, the rules on access to documents have been used deliberately to test out the system, and in order to raise test case litigation on serious points of conflict. This occurred in Case T-174/95 *Svenska Journalistförbundet* v. *Council* ([1998] ECR II-2289) where the applicants had requested certain third-pillar documents related to Europol, many of which they had already received from the Swedish Government by making use of Swedish freedom of information legislation. The Council refused most of the documents, so the applicants embarrassed the Council by placing many of them on the Internet at the same time as making the application to the Court. This case is one of the applications under the access to documents rules which could be said to have been brought broadly in a spirit of the 'public interest'. The Council has objected to such uses of the access to documents rules almost on principle, and one of the objections it raised in the *Svenska* case was that the applicants had no interest in seeking the documents since they had obtained them from another source. The Court held that because of the 'public interest' nature of the access to documents rules the very fact that a person has been refused access is sufficient to establish an interest in the annulment of the decision refusing access (para. 67). The Court also made it clear that the current access to documents rules do extend to third (and indeed second) pillar documents (a point which is clarified beyond all doubt in relation to Article 255 EC). It indicated that the confidentiality and public security exceptions, invoked by the Council, should be narrowly defined, and insisted that it had the power to review the merits of a decision by the Council to invoke the public security exception. It annulled the Council's decision to refuse access. The applicants' decision to place the Council's statement of defence on the Internet in order to put pressure on the Council was, however, treated by the Court as an abuse of procedure.

The principle of partial disclosure was applied in a further case to be decided in relation to the Council was brought by an MEP. In Case T-14/98 *Hautala* v. *Council* (19 July 1999), the application for disclosure had been made for a Council report on conventional arms exports drawn up by a working group operating within the framework of CFSP. The Council invoked the international relations head of the public interest exception. The Court held that the Council was wrong to fail to consider the possibility of disclosing certain passages contained within the document, removing those which were sensitive.

It should not be thought that it is only the Council which has been challenged and found wanting in the Court of First Instance on the question of access to documents. In a letter to the President of the European Parliament in March 2000, in the context of his disagreement with Romano Prodi about the Commission's proposal for a Regulation implementing Article 255, Jakob Södermann noted almost caustically:

> 'you should remember that most of the complaints which are within the mandate of the European Ombudsman concern the European Commission and that one of the main reasons for complaint to the Ombudsman over the years has been a lack of transparency of the Commission.'

However, in the present state of evolution of the EU political system, its activities are less likely to be of direct concern to individuals or organisations involved in the civil liberties field. Rather the litigation against the Commission has been brought by firms, environmental organisations, and a lawyer in private practice. In Case T-105/95 *WWF* v. *Commission* [1997] ECR II-313 the Court annulled the Commission's decision to refuse access to documents relating to a possible enforcement action under what was then Article 169 EC which it had been considering bringing against Ireland in relation to breaching certain provisions of EU environmental law. It decided in the end not to bring the enforcement action. Although the Court upheld the Commission's wish to bring such documents under a mandatory exception to access for 'investigations', it none the less found that the Commission had failed to explain the reasons for its decision. In Case T-309/97 *Bavarian Lager Co* v. *Commission* (14 October 1999), the Court upheld the refusal to disclose a draft reasoned opinion which was never sent to the UK Government regarding an alleged infringement of the competition rules (8.16). Perhaps the most significant decision with regard to the Commission concerned 'comitology' documents (7.13). The applicants in Case T-188/97 *Rothmans International* v. *Commission* (19 July 1999) wanted access to the minutes of the Customs Code Committee, which assists the Commission in the management of the Common Customs Code. The Commission refused access to the documents, arguing that it was not the author of the documents. However, the Court found that making this claim in relation to comitology documents amounted to an exception that needed to be strictly interpreted. Moreover, 'comitology' committees were not 'another Community institution or body', as they have no real separate existence, with no administration, budget, archives or premises. The Council, in response to a question from the Court, denied responsibility for them. Finally, in view of the need not to place a considerable restriction on the right of access to documents by allowing the committees to fall into a gap between two institutions, the Court concluded that for the purposes of applying the access to documents rules the system of comitology comes under the Commission.

In addition to these specific findings, which have almost universally gone towards tightening up the rules and limiting the exceptions, the Court of First Instance has adopted a broad phrasing in relation to its general approach to the question. Thus, in its decisions it has consistently stated that the measures are:

> 'intended to give the widest possible access for citizens to information with a view to strengthening the democratic character of the institutions and the trust of the public in the administration' (Case T-309/97 *Bavarian Lager*, para. 36).

It is the reinforcement of this principle, which effectively takes the first declaration attached to the Treaty of Maastricht at its word, and the clear differences of views about what exactly should be done to ensure that it is applied in practice, that go to the heart of a cultural conflict about 'openness' within the EU. It is illustrated by the frequency with which different Member States have intervened on behalf of applicants and the institutions in the cases, clearly pitting Member State against Member State, and also by the action which the Netherlands brought in the Court of Justice to challenge the legal basis of the Council's access decision.

The Court of Justice upheld the legal basis of the transparency rules (Case C-58/94 *Netherlands* v. *Council* [1996] ECR II-2765). The Netherlands challenged the use of legal bases concerned with the internal organisation of the Council's work for the purposes of giving effect to what it saw as a fundamental right. It suggested that this manner of proceeding also infringed the balance between the institutions, because it excluded the European Parliament – which in many important areas is now a co-legislator, and at the very least has the right to be consulted in most other fields. Although the Court did acknowledge the existence of the principles of open government which underlay the arguments made by the applicant government but without going as far as to decree that transparency is a general principle of law (9.5), it rejected the application on the merits, finding that:

> 'so long as the Community legislature has not adopted general rules on the right of public access to documents held by the Community institutions, the institutions *must* take measures as to the processing of such requests by virtue of their power of internal organisation, which authorises them to take appropriate measures in order to ensure their internal operation in conformity with the interests of good administration' (emphasis added) (para. 37).

Thus, far from acting wrongfully, the Council had in fact acted as it should. The irony of the Court's finding lay in the fact that for purposes such as the adoption of document disclosure rules or a basic rule of freedom of information under the Treaties as they then were, the *Community legislature* would, for all practical purposes, be the *Council* given that such a measure would undoubtedly have required adoption by unanimity under what was then Article 235 EC. The Council as an *institution* therefore escaped censure because of the failure of action on the part of *legislature*.

As Curtin (1996: 103) has commented, there is an ongoing (and still unresolved) dispute about:

> 'the legal nature of the principle of freedom of information in the Union context: the Dutch emphasise the fundamental (at least from the perspective of democratic philosophy) nature of the principle and maintain that the primary purpose of the Decision was to regulate the openness of the administration for third parties. On the other hand, the other members of the Council (with the probable exception of the Danes) are convinced that the Code of Conduct and Council Decision constitute a simple policy orientation adopted by the Council in the interests of its own good administration, subject as a matter of course to the other rules of its Rules of Procedure as well as the stringent and discretionary exceptions outlined in the Decision itself.'

Clearly there are many interests within the institutions and among the Member States which remain reluctant about taking a rights-based approach to the question of transparency. But at least the judicial language in transparency actions has changed markedly since the first case of *Carvel*, in which Kenneth Armstrong found it hard to 'find' the citizen in the Court's judgment. He commented that:

> 'There is (...) a paradox at the heart of the concept of Union citizenship. The concept of citizenship has been invoked as a counterbalance to the seemingly remote institutions of the EU in order to attach political legitimacy to EU governance. However, the essentially inter-institutional nature of EU governance has not changed leaving the Union citizen as a rather ambiguous identity within the Union's political and legal systems. (...) At no point does John Carvel as a Union citizen ever become constructed in the Court's mind' (Armstrong, 1996: 588).

That accusation is certainly more difficult to make in the light of the Court of First Instance's case law since *Carvel*, which has given restrictive interpretations of the various exceptions, has insisted upon the centrality of this principle in view of the requirements of democracy and the need for trust in government, and has required that each institution individually balance the interests of the applicant in seeking access to the document and its own interest in withholding that document (Österdahl, 1999). Despite this, however, formal judicial resolution of disputes over access can only ever be marginal to the day-to-day exercise of citizens' rights and to the capacity of a principle such as transparency to contribute to constitutionalism and citizenship within the EU. In that context, informal forms of settlement such as the right to apply to the Ombudsman can make a constructive contribution (Öberg, 1998). But, more importantly, there needs to be a culture change to make access to documents more than an inconvenience to the institutions or a mere way of trying to make them seem more accessible to the general public and therefore more popular.

In January 2000, the Commission published its draft Regulation based on Article 255 EC, without putting it out for prior consultation with interested parties as promised (COM(2000) 30). This was not a formal requirement, but the Commission has done little thereby to endear itself to observers, including the Ombudsman. The draft Regulation draws more upon institutional practices and wishes than it does upon the case law of the Court. In one positive step, the draft proposes that the access rules (which will be those for the Council, the Commission and the Parliament once adopted) will apply to all documents held by the institutions, not just those which they have produced, subject to the possibility that the author of the document may assert confidentiality. In other words, there will be no need for the applicant to be turned away and sent elsewhere to make a second application if he or she discovers after applying that the document was written by another party. Of most concern are a definition of 'document' which excludes documents for internal use (in other words, does not make the with-holding of internal documents an exception to the principle, but rather builds it into the definitional framework of the Regulation) and a rather broad statement of exceptions, drawing upon, for example, the infamous statement about the 'stability of the Community legal order' drawn from Case T-610/97 R *Carlsen*. This is an example of the Commission seeking to push institutional practice rather than the principles of open government into the transparency rules. Curtin (2000: 39) notes that:

> 'the Commission focuses exclusively on its own administrative convenience as justifying a retrogressive exception regarding (its) internal documents. It does not look, for example, at the Council's different structure and the fact that such an exception could have a very far-reaching scope in that different context.'

Open government has the capacity to make a positive contribution to the construction of the public space which the Commission in its rhetoric on such questions so obviously desires to see developing. The shame of it is, that the only real 'citizenship practice' happening at present is that coming from those who are constantly testing the limits of the document access rules and being disappointed by the lack of openness on the part of the institutions.

Summary

1 Citizenship is a contested concept that can be defined in many ways. It is useful in the EU context to concentrate upon the idea of 'full membership' of the EU, and a cluster of civil, political and social rights.

2 The concept of citizenship of the Union is very limited and the full range of EU citizenship rights can only be identified with the assistance of a more wide-ranging review of EU law and policy.

3 Free movement remains an important foundation stone of the citizenship concept in the EU, and the Court's approach to the free movement rules may gradually be shifting from a primary concern with market issues to welfare citizenship issues.

4 In the context of constitution building and the role of citizenship as a constitutive policy, principles and practice of transparency can play a key role.

5 An evaluation of institutional practices in this context does not indicate that as yet a real culture of openness has taken root in the EU.

6 The Court of First Instance and the European Ombudsman have received many cases and complaints, and have been required to adjudicate on matters relating to document access often in favour of claimants and applicants.

Questions

1 Why has the EU developed a concept of citizenship?
2 What meanings does citizenship have in the EU context?
3 Who or what is a market citizen?
4 What issues are raised by the law and practice on transparency and access to documents?

Further Reading

D. Curtin (1996), 'Betwixt and Between: Democracy and Transparency in the Governance of the European Union', in Winter *et al.* (1996).

D. Curtin (1999), 'The Fundamental Principle of Open Decision-Making and EU (Political) Citizenship', in O'Keeffe and Twomey (1999).

D. Curtin (2000), 'Citizens' Fundamental Rights of Access to EU Information: An Evolving Digital *Passepartout*?', 37 *Common Market Law Review* 7.

S. Douglas-Scott (1998), 'In Search of Union Citizenship', 18 *Yearbook of European Law* 29.

P. Dyrberg (1999), 'Current Issues in the Debate on Public Access to Documents', 24 *European Law Review* 157.

M. Everson (1995), 'The Legacy of the Market Citizen', in Shaw and More (1995).

S. Fries and J. Shaw (1998), 'Citizenship of the Union: First Steps in the Court of Justice', 4 *European Public Law* 533.

C. Harlow (1999b), 'Citizen Access to Political Power in the European Union', EUI RSC Working Paper 99/2.

C. Lyons (1997) 'A Voyage around Article 8: An Historical and Comparative Evaluation of the Fate of European Union Citizenship', 17 *Yearbook of European Law* 135.

D. O'Keeffe (1994), 'Union Citizenship', in O'Keeffe and Twomey (1994).

H.J. d'Oliveira (1994a), 'European Citizenship: Its Meaning, its Potential', in Dehousse (1994a).

U. Preuss (1995), 'Problems of a Concept of European Citizenship', 1 *European Law Journal* 267.

J. Shaw (1998a), 'Citizenship of the Union: Towards Postnational Membership', in Academy of European Law (1998).

J. Shaw (1998b), 'The Interpretation of European Union Citizenship', 61 *Modern Law Review* 293.

J. Shaw (2000b), 'Constitutional Settlements and the Citizen after the Treaty of Amsterdam', in Neunreither and Wiener (2000).

J.H.H. Weiler (1999a), Ch. 10, 'To be a European Citizen: Eros and Civilization'.

Key Websites

Information on applying for access to the documents of the Commission:
http://europa.eu.int/comm/secretariat_general/sgc/acc_doc/en/index.htm
and the Council:
http://register.consilium.eu.int/isoregister/frames/introfsEN.htm

The Ombudsman's own initiative special report on access to documents:
http://www.euro-ombudsman.eu.imt/SPECIAL/EN/Default.htm

Citizens' rights websites include:
http://europa.eu.int/abc-en.htm
http://europa.eu.int/comm/internal_market/en/cp/cit/intro.htm
(contact points for citizens wanting more information about their rights in the single market):
http://citizens.eu.int/
(EU's 'dialogue' with citizens)

On secrecy and freedom of information see:
http://www.statewatch.org/
http://www.rz.uni-frankfurt.de/~sobotta/FOI.htm

Part V

The EU Legal Order and the National Legal Orders

11 Article 234 EC – The Organic Connection Between National Courts and the Court of Justice

11.1 Introduction

An American political scientist looking at the European Union legal order commented that:

> 'an exclusive focus on the ECJ's case law gives us an incomplete, and at times erroneous, picture of the dynamics of constitutionalization. The construction of a constitutional, rule of law Community has been a participatory process, a set of constitutional dialogues between supranational and national judges' (Stone Sweet, 1998: 305).

Since the decision of the German Federal Constitutional Court in the *Brunner* case (5.13), as well as the popular discontent with the Treaty of Maastricht, which has never truly dissipated in full, it is more true than ever that the Court of Justice must be aware that it operates within a series of dialogues. Within the constraints of this book, it is not possible to look in detail at these dialogues, even though they represent 'a historical record of legal integration' (de la Mare, 1999: 215). However, as we examine the principal organic link between national courts and the Court of Justice, which has provided the mechanism for these dialogues to occur, it is important to remember these cautionary words.

Article 234 EC (formerly Article 177) makes provision for national courts to ascertain from the Court of Justice its views on the status and meaning of EU law. It provides:

> 'The Court of Justice shall have jurisdiction to give preliminary rulings concerning:
> (a) the interpretation of this Treaty;
> (b) the validity and interpretation of acts of the institutions of the Community and of the ECB;
> (c) the interpretation of the statutes of bodies established by an act of the Council, where those statutes so provide.

Where such a question is raised before any court or tribunal of a Member State, that court or tribunal may, if it considers that a decision on the question is necessary to enable it to give judgment, request the Court of Justice to give a ruling thereon.

Where any such question is raised in a case pending before a court or tribunal of a Member State, against whose decisions there is no judicial remedy under national law, that court or tribunal shall bring the matter before the Court of Justice.'

The grand objectives of the EU legal order, which include the intermeshing of EU law and national law, could not be achieved without some organic mechanism for ensuring the uniform application of EU law, in which the Court of Justice can give authoritative rulings on the meaning of EU law. The Court of Justice frequently reminds us that it is the purpose of Article 234 to provide such a mechanism:

'[Article 234] is essential for the preservation of the Community character of the law established by the Treaty and has the object of ensuring that in all circumstances the law is the same in all States of the Community' (Case 166/73 *Rheinmühlen-Düsseldorf* v. *Einfuhr- und Vorratstelle für Getreide und Futtermittel* [1974] ECR 33 at p. 43).

With this purpose in mind, the Court has been able to use Article 234 preliminary rulings as the centrepieces for the construction of a legal edifice in which EU law can be uniformly interpreted and enforced within the national courts of the Member States in the same terms as it is within the Court of Justice itself. To this end, of course, Article 234 references have given the Court the opportunity to articulate the principles on which it is possible for individuals to enforce EU law against infringing Member States and, where this is permitted under EU law, against infringing individuals. In addition, however, Article 234 is a key element in the system of judicial control over the acts of the institutions within the EU, and its role in this context will be reconsidered in Part VI. For Article 234 provides a mechanism for indirect challenges to the validity of EU legal acts in national courts, using the medium of direct challenges to national implementing acts based on an allegedly invalid 'parent' EU act.

As Article 234 provides a 'reference procedure' in the hands of the referring court and not an 'appeals procedure' in the hands of parties who consider their rights under EU law to be infringed or feel themselves to be the victims of an invalid EU act, its success has always rested on the willingness of national courts to collaborate by making references and by accepting the subsequent judgments of the Court. The Court has based its approach on a philosophy of the separate functions of national court and 'Community' court, a philosophy which can be derived from the views of AG Lagrange in the first case submitted under what was then Article 177 EEC. In Case 13/61 *Bosch* v. *de Geus* ([1962] ECR 45 at p. 56) he asserted that:

'applied judiciously – one is tempted to say loyally – the provisions of Article 177 lead to a real and fruitful collaboration between the municipal courts and the Court of Justice of the Communities with mutual regard for their respective jurisdictions. It is in this spirit that each side must solve the sometimes delicate problems which may arise in all systems of preliminary procedure, and which are necessarily made more difficult in this case by the differences in the legal systems of the Member States as regards this type of procedure.'

A similar view emerges from the ruling of the Court itself in Case 16/65 *Firma Schwarze* v. *Einfuhr- und Vorratstelle für Getreide und Futtermittel* ([1965] ECR 877 at p. 886):

'[Article 234 establishes] a special field of judicial cooperation which requires the national court and the Court of Justice, both keeping within their respective jurisdiction, and with the aim of ensuring that Community law is applied in a unified manner, to make direct and complementary contributions to the working out of a decision.'

The 'separate functions' conception gives the national court a broad discretion to formulate the questions which it believes to be appropriate. However, as the Court put it in the early case of *Costa* v. *ENEL* (Case 6/64 [1964] ECR 585), the fact that a question is 'imperfectly formulated' does not deprive the Court of the power to extract from that question those matters which are relevant to the interpretation of the Treaty. It will pull in provisions of EU law that it considers pertinent, even though these were not raised by the national court. A good example of this is Case C-85/96 *Martínez Sala* v. *Freistaat Bayern* ([1998] ECR I-2691) (10.5) in which the national court did not raise the possibility that citizenship of the Union might be relevant to the case, but phrased its questions in terms of 'traditional' free movement law. In fact, the Court rarely hesitates to rephrase questions posed by national courts where it deems this necessary. On the other hand, it has frequently used the separation of functions argument in order to evade the argument that it is overstretching its remit as the EU's court, stressing that it has no jurisdiction to interfere with the discretion of the national court as to what to refer, or indeed when to refer. When challenged about the nature of its case law, the Court insists on the fine line between the interpretation and application of EU law, maintaining it is restricted in the Article 234 context only to the former. It frequently insists on the right of the national court to judge the relevance of the questions which it poses to the litigation before it when it determines the issue of 'necessity' in Article 234 (e.g. Case C-186/90 *Durighello* v. *INiPS* ([1991] ECR I-5773)). In that case it held:

> 'A request from a national court may be rejected only if it quite obvious that the interpretation of the Community law or the examination of the validity of a rule of Community law sought bears no relation to the actual nature of the case or to the subject-matter of the main action' (p. 5795).

In Case C-343/90 *Lourenço Dias* v. *Director da Alfândega do Porto* [1992] ECR I-4673 the Court put it slightly differently:

> 'the national court, which is alone in having a direct knowledge of the facts of the case, is in the best position to appreciate the necessity for a preliminary ruling, having regard to the particular features of the case, so as to enable it to give judgment' (p. 4708).

Apart from its interpretation of the text of Article 234 EC (e.g. when is the answer to a question 'necessary'? which courts may refer? etc.), the only requirements that the Court places upon the questions that it receives are that they arise out of a 'genuine dispute' before the national court, that they are not purely hypothetical questions, and that the national court should furnish sufficient factual and legal context to permit the Court to address the questions put to it.

11.2 Court Controls on the Preliminary Reference Procedure

In the two *Foglia* v. *Novello* cases, the Court articulated and applied the requirement of a genuine dispute. In Case 104/79 *Foglia* v. *Novello (No. 1)* ([1980] ECR 745) the Court was asked by the Italian court, before which the case had come, to assess the compatibility with EU law of a French tax imposed on imported wine. It appeared that the parties were in agreement that the tax was in breach of EU law, and that they had artificially constructed the litigation before the Italian courts, involving an action by Foglia (a dealer) to force Novello (an importer) to pay the French tax, knowing that an Italian court was more likely than a French court to expose the tax to the scrutiny of the Court of Justice by making a reference. The Court unexpectedly refused to answer the questions, sending the case back to the Italian court in the following terms (at p. 759):

> 'It thus appears that the parties to the main action are concerned to obtain a ruling that the French tax system is invalid for liqueur wines by the expedient of proceedings before an Italian court between two private in-

dividuals who are in agreement as to the result to be attained and who have inserted a clause in their contract in order to induce the Italian court to give a ruling on the point...
The duty of the Court of Justice under Article 177 of the EEC Treaty is to supply all courts in the Community with the information on the interpretation of Community law which is necessary to enable them to settle genuine disputes which are brought before them. A situation in which the Court was obliged by the expedient of arrangements like those described above to give rulings would jeopardise the whole system of legal remedies available to private individuals to enable them to protect themselves against tax provisions which are contrary to the Treaty.'

Quite why the Court chose to argue that such allegedly apocalyptic consequences would result from the 'misuse' of the reference procedure in these circumstances is not clear. The expedient of friendly litigation is practised and tolerated in many countries including the UK. It would seem bizarre – and excessively intrusive – if the result of EU law were that non-hostile litigation involving, for example, a test case, could not result in a reference to the Court of Justice (see the comments of AG Jacobs in Case C-412/93 *Leclerc-Siplec* v. *TFI Publicité* [1995] ECR I-179 at pp. 183–4). What is more, judges in many of the Member States find themselves subject to a prohibition on refusing to give judgment. In keeping with the view that the judge's role is to interpret the law, not to judge the appropriateness of litigation or to interfere in the political sphere, the so-called *déni de justice* (refusal to judge) is a violation of the judge's duty and a criminal offence in France (Article 4 of the code civil). On the other hand, the Court's position is not the same as the conventional national judge. It has claimed a unique and highly political position within the EU legal order, and it is arguable that fictitious litigation (as opposed to friendly litigation, if a distinction can be drawn) is damaging to the gradual evolution of the supranational system in that it may unnecessarily bring into conflict the courts and governments of different states. In that case, it may be legitimate to argue that the rights of the defence of states that find their laws impugned before the courts of other Member States will be undermined. The Court may well have been concerned to avoid handing down a decision which the French Government would be unwilling to execute, and thereby to endanger the system of enforcement of EU law. The decision in Case 104/79, and its follow-up in Case 244/80 *Foglia* v. *Novello (No. 2)* ([1981] ECR 3045) where the Court reproduced the substance of its views when re-questioned by the Italian court and reinforced the point that it is not subject to a duty to give advisory opinions at the request of national courts, has divided academic commentators and the arguments for and against can be found in Barav (1980), Wyatt (1981) and Bebr (1982).

However, while the *Foglia* v. *Novello* case law was never formally over-ruled by the Court of Justice, for a number of years it did not in practice show a great readiness to apply it. For example, it has accepted implicit challenges to the validity of legislation in the court of another Member State, such as the challenge to an Italian law in the German courts in Case C-150/88 *Eau de Cologne* v. *Provide* ([1989] ECR 3891). In that case it stated that there was a genuine dispute and that the Court is under a duty to provide the national court with the answers to questions of interpretation which it needs to settle the dispute. It made it clear that it did not by any means intend to exclude the possibility that the courts of one Member State may determine the compatibility of the laws of another Member State with EU law, and that it will participate by providing any necessary interpretations of EU law.

The Court has since moved onto a slightly different tack with a new approach to certain types of preliminary references. In a series of cases since 1992 it has started to subject some of the references it receives to the following enquiries before concluding whether or not they are admissible:

– are the questions purely 'hypothetical'? and
– has the national court supplied the Court of Justice with sufficient information of a factual and legal nature to enable it to answer the questions which the former has posed?

It is not hard to see these questions as an expression of the Court's exasperation with its ever-growing workload, and its perceived need to place some sort of control on the numbers of references which are now reaching it from national courts (11.9).

In Case C-83/91 *Meilicke* v. *ADV/ORGA* ([1992] ECR I-4871) the Court refused to answer certain questions regarding the interpretation of the Second Company Law Directive, and the compatibility with this Directive of certain German case law. The Court characterised the questions referred by the German court as 'hypothetical', and, with a passing reference to *Foglia* v. *Novello* and other cases on the cooperative structure of the reference procedure, reached the conclusion that it could not answer the questions otherwise it would be exceeding its proper function under Article 234. One of the difficulties which the Court faced when assessing the relationship between the litigation in the German court and the questions referred to it by that court, was that if the Court of Justice had given the interpretation of EU law which the plaintiff sought, he would in fact have lost his case in the national court. He would, however, have succeeded in his ulterior goal, which was to establish the incompatibility of the German case law that he had challenged in the domestic litigation with EU law. Unlike the Court itself, AG Teasuro did not decline to answer the rather convoluted questions referred by the national court, but rather found a way to reformulate them so they could be answered. This reasoning has been applied in further cases: in Case C-343/90 *Lourenço Dias* the Court refused to answer six out of the eight questions which were put to it, commenting that they bore no relation to the case as set out in the order for a reference; in Case C-428/93 *Monin Automobiles* v. *France (Monin II)* ([1994] ECR I-1707) it denied that an interpretation of EU law was objectively necessary in the case.

Subsequently, the Court went a step further and demanded a certain minimum level of information from national courts. In Cases C-320-322/90 *Telemarsicabruzzo* v. *Circostel* ([1993] ECR I-393) it declined to answer questions on the EU competition rules posed by an Italian court in the context of proceedings brought to prohibit a group of television broadcasters from using certain broadcasting frequencies, on the grounds that it was essential to have precise details of the situation at issue before the national court before the Court of Justice was able to give a useful interpretation of EU law. Strangely it took the Court of Justice more than two years after the reference was lodged to reach this conclusion, and it did so despite the availability of full information – if not in the order for a reference itself, at least in Report for the Hearing and the Opinion of the Advocate General (see Tesauro, 1993: 14). A similar line of reasoning has been employed since by the Court in Case C-157/92 *Pretore di Genova* v. *Banchero* ([1993] ECR I-1085), Case C-386/92 *Monin Automobiles* v. *France (Monin I)* ([1993] ECR I-2049), and Case C-167/94 *Grau Gomis* ([1995] ECR I-1023). In other words, neither the *Meilicke* nor the *Telemarsicabruzzo* approaches represented isolated cases in the way that the *Foglia* v. *Novello* cases appear to have been, and may be interpreted as one response by the Court of Justice to its burgeoning workload problem and as a possible attempt to impose a quality control on national courts (11.9).

On the other hand, the approach of the Court of Justice has been questioned, because it may lead to national courts deciding questions themselves, resulting in divergent applications of EU law, or it may discourage national judges from using the preliminary reference procedure (Arnull, 1999a: 58). It has been said to threaten the very spirit on which the reference procedure is based (O'Keeffe, 1998). There also seems to be some inconsistency in the Court's approach, as in some cases it has successfully managed without a full statement of facts and issues (e.g. Case C-316/93 *Vaneetveld* [1994] ECR I-763). In the spirit of dialogue under Article 234, it is therefore a positive move for the Court to have proposed amendments to its Rules of Procedure in July 1999 to allow it to make requests back to the national court for clarification in circumstances where the reference documents provide an inadequate description of the factual and/or legal context of the reference or insufficient information concerning the relevance of the questions put to the Court. This procedure will supplement a guidance note for national courts making references for preliminary rulings, published by the Court in 1996 ([1997] 1 CMLR 78).

11.3   **Provisions of EU Law which may be the Subject of Reference**

Article 234 itself defines those provisions which may be the subject of a reference. These are provisions of the Treaty, acts of EU institutions (including the ECB) and the statutes of bodies established by an act of the Council (for an example of the latter category see Case 44/84 *Hurd* v. *Jones* [1986] ECR 29). Acts of the EU institutions, which can be the subject of a reference, include non-binding acts such as recommendations and opinions. In Case C-322/88 *Grimaldi* v. *Fonds des Maladies Professionelles* ([1989] ECR I-4407) the provisions referred were contained in Commission Recommendations on the adoption of a European schedule of occupational diseases, and on the conditions for the granting of compensation to those suffering from such diseases. The fact that agreements with third countries are concluded by the Council has provided a convenient justification for the acceptance of references on the interpretation of such agreements (e.g. Case 12/86 *Demirel* v. *Stadt Schwäbisch Gmund* [1987] ECR 3719 – a reference on the Association Agreement between the European Community and Turkey). The Court has also accepted references on international agreements to which the European Community has never formally adhered, but where it has succeeded to the rights and obligations of the Member States, such as the [old] GATT (Cases 267-269/81 *SPI* [1983] ECR 801). This is because such agreements are binding upon the EU, and the Court regards the provisions of these agreements as penetrating the EU legal order and as therefore being part of the body of legal rules in the light of which national law must be interpreted. However, the Court will not rule on the interpretation of the Agreement establishing the European Economic Area where the question arises not with regard to the EU or a Member State but *with regard to one of the EEA states*, as it has no jurisdiction either by virtue of EU law or the EEA Agreement itself. In Case C-321/97 *Andersson* v. *Swedish State* [1999] ECR I-355, the situation was complicated: the facts arose as a matter of 'EEA law' before Sweden was a Member State of the EU (as of 1 January 1995) but was a contracting party to the EEA, but came before the Court of Justice after its accession. The fact of subsequent accession did not have the effect of attributing to the Court jurisdiction to interpret the EEA Agreement as regards an EEA state.

General principles of law alone do not appear to be capable of forming the basis of a reference, although in practice a national court may request a ruling from the Court of Justice on how other provisions of EU law should be interpreted in the light of general principles of law recognised in the EU legal order (Case 44/79 *Hauer* v. *Land Rheinland Pfalz* [1979] ECR 3740).

11.4 Courts and Tribunals of the Member States Capable of Making a Reference

The whole range of bodies that embody the judicial power of the state may make references, regardless of what title they are given. For example, in Case 61/65 *Vaassen* ([1966] ECR 261) the Court accepted a reference from a Dutch arbitral tribunal or *Scheidsgericht*, pointing to those features which brought it within the ambit of Article 234. It was a permanent body instituted by the law, with members appointed by a Minister; it was given compulsory jurisdiction over the cases assigned to it by law, used a form of adversarial procedure, and applied the law in its decisions. A Dutch general practitioners' registration appeal committee was also held to fall within Article 234 in Case 246/80 *Broeckmeulen* ([1981] ECR 2311). The Court stated that:

'in the absence, in practice, of any right of appeal to the ordinary courts, the Appeals Committee, which operates with the consent of the public authorities and with their cooperation, and which, after an adversarial procedure, delivers decisions which are in fact recognised as final, must, in a matter involving the application of Community law, be considered as a court or tribunal of a Member State within the meaning of Article 234 of the Treaty' (at p. 2328).

A judicial body exercising investigatory functions within an inquisitorial system of criminal law is likewise capable of making a reference, even at a preliminary stage of the investigations where the potential defendants have not yet been identified. In Case 14/86 *Pretore di Salò* v. *X* ([1987] ECR 2545) the Court accepted a reference from the Italian *pretore* or examining magistrate, which requested an interpretation of EU pollution legislation precisely with a view to identifying the potential defendants in criminal pollution proceedings. However, in Case C-24/92 *Corbiau* ([1993] ECR I-1277), the Court found that the *Directeur des Contributions* who exercised an appellate function within the Luxembourg taxation authorities was not a 'court or tribunal' because the Director did not have an independent 'third party' relationship with both parties to the proceedings. Where a national body is multi-functional, and has both judicial and administrative functions, it can be a 'court or tribunal' for the purposes of the first, but not the second (Cases C-192 & 440/98 *ANAS and RAI*, Order of 26 November 1999).

Commercial arbitration is also excluded from the scope of Article 234. This was decided by the Court in Case 102/81 *Nordsee* v. *Reederei Mond* ([1982] ECR 1095). Although the decision of an arbitrator has force of law between the parties, and although the arbitrator must apply the law, it is more significant that the jurisdiction is contractual and therefore not compulsory and that, as a private arrangement, does not involve the public authorities. The Court therefore concluded that the link between the arbitration procedure and the organisation of legal remedies through the court structure was insufficiently close for the arbitrator to be deemed a 'court or tribunal'. The importance in practice of avoiding incorrect applications of EU law in national arbitration proceedings is emphasised by the indication given by the English Court of Appeal in *Bulk Oil* v. *Sun International* ([1984] 1 WLR 147) that the existence of a point of EU law for decision before an arbitrator should become a ground for giving leave to appeal to the court against the decision of an arbitrator.

11.5　The Discretion to Refer: Article 234(2)

Article 234 is concerned with two separate scenarios for national courts. The first is the discretion to refer, which is held by all courts faced with questions of EU law. The second is the obligation to refer, imposed only on courts of last resort.

The discretion to refer given to lower courts is entirely unfettered – subject to the principles set out in 11.2. References are not precluded by, for example, the existence of a prior ruling by the Court of Justice on a similar question (Cases 28-30/62 *Da Costa en Schaake NV* [1963] ECR 31). However, in its 1999 proposals for changes to its Rules of Procedures, the Court of Justice has suggested a special simplified procedure to enable it to give rulings by way of an order where the question is manifestly identical to a question that the Court has previously ruled upon. Nor may internal rules governing the hierarchy of the court structure limit the discretion of inferior courts. An inferior court which regards itself as internally bound by a rule of law stated by a superior court either in the same case or in an earlier case (e.g. the common law system of binding judicial precedent) is not prevented from making a reference to the Court of Justice if it believes applying the internal rule would lead it to a violation of EU law (Case 166/73 *Rheinmühlen*).

In the light of this conclusion in *Rheinmühlen*, it was therefore somewhat surprising that in the same case the Court went on to hold that as a matter of EU law nothing precluded an internal appeal against the decision of an inferior court to refer, and that such appeals were to be regulated by national rules on procedure. However, where a reference has been made but is under appeal, the Court will proceed to the hearing of the reference, which will be regarded as valid and effective until such time as it has actually been revoked. In this decision the Court went against the view of AG Warner who argued that appeals against orders to refer should not be available as a matter of EU law, and this is the view which has been espoused by the Irish Supreme Court in *Campus Oil* v. *Ministry for Industry and Energy* ([1984] 1

CMLR 479). It held that appeals against orders to refer are precluded within Ireland by the terms of Article 234, which it held to be part of Irish law.

The discretion to refer also extends to a discretion as to when to refer. We have noted already the early reference made by an Italian *pretore* (Case 14/86), and the Court will not reject a reference on the grounds that it is too 'early'. However, the Court has suggested that it might be convenient for the national court to decide the facts and issues of purely national law before making the reference, in order to enable the Court itself to take fuller cognisance of the relevant circumstances of the case (Cases 36, 71/80 *Irish Creamery Milk Suppliers Association* v. *Ireland* [1981] ECR 735). This is presumably in order to increase the effectiveness of the reference procedure from the perspective of the Court of Justice.

Finally, although the question of EU law must be necessary in the sense of being relevant to the resolution of the dispute, the Court has not placed any restrictions on the meaning of such a question. In Cases C-297/88 and C-197/89 *Dzodzi* v. *Belgium* ([1990] ECR I-3763) the Court asserted the primary importance of the uniform interpretation and application of EU law when it held that it had jurisdiction to give a ruling on a preliminary reference made by a national court in circumstances where national law had extended the ambit and application of certain EU law provisions beyond the scope required by EU law itself. In other words, the Court gave a ruling in an area that was beyond the scope of Community competence, because the national law made reference to the content of EU law. The overwhelming need to ensure uniformity required the Court to be able to interpret EU law for the purposes of the interpretation of national law. In contrast, AG Darmon did advise that the Court should have no jurisdiction in that case, or in one raising similar questions which was decided shortly thereafter (Case C-231/89 *Gmurzynska-Bscher* v. *Oberfinanzdirektion Köln* [1990] ECR I-4003). Once again in Case C-28/95 *Leur Bloem* ([1997] ECR I-4161) and Case C-130/95 *Giloy* ([1997] ECR I-4291), the Court confirmed its approach in the context of domestic rules on the imposition of tax:

> 'where, in regulating internal situations, domestic legislation adopts the same solutions as those adopted in Community law so as to provide for one single procedure in comparable situations, it is clearly in the Community interest that, in order to forestall future differences of interpretation, provisions or concepts taken from Community law should be interpreted uniformly, irrespective of the circumstances in which they are to apply...' (para. 28 of *Leur Bloem*).

Although the English inferior courts remain free to exercise their discretion to refer, subject to appeals (under Rules of the Supreme Court, Order 114, r.6 in the case of the High Court and above), in fact Lord Denning MR purported in the early stages of UK membership of the European Community to give some guidance on the question of references. In *Bulmer* v. *Bollinger* ([1974] Ch. 401; [1974] 2 All ER 1226) he argued that before a reference is made the judge must be certain that the point is conclusive of the case and that there is no previous ruling of the Court of Justice or no grounds for applying the doctrine of *acte clair* (see below 11.6, although this point is not strictly relevant to the exercise of the discretion to refer). Finally, he or she should decide the facts first, and should bear in mind the delay caused by a reference and the workload of the Court of Justice. These guidelines have been criticised as encouraging courts too strongly not to refer (Arnull, 1990b: 382).

A much more positive attitude towards the Court was displayed by Bingham J in *Commissioners of Customs and Excise* v. *Samex ApS* ([1983] 3 CMLR 194) who pointed out that the Court of Justice is much better equipped than an English court to decide matters of EU law, as a consequence of the linguistic advantages it enjoys in the scrutiny of the various different language texts, the oversight it has over the whole field of EU law, and its particular understanding of the highly purposive methods interpretation which it is necessary to apply to EU law.

Subsequently, in *R* v. *International Stock Exchange of the United Kingdom and the Republic of Ireland, ex parte Else* ([1993] 1 All ER 420) the guidelines were further refined by the same judge, this time in the first case in which the Court of Appeal overturned the decision of a lower court to make a reference to the Court of Justice. Three factors must be present: the facts must be clarified; the judge must be satisfied that the provision of EU law is critical to the final determination of the case; and the judge must consider whether he or she can resolve the question of EU law, with complete confidence. Once these factors have been addressed, it will 'ordinarily' be appropriate for a lower court to make a reference (for further details see Dwyer, 1994).

11.6   The Obligation to Refer: Article 234(3)

The obligation to refer falls upon a court against whose decisions there is no judicial remedy under national law. The Court of Justice has given no definitive interpretation of what this phrase means, although in 2000 it was finally asked the question directly by a referring Court (Case C-99/00 *Lyckeskog*, pending OJ 2000 C149/26)The formulation contained in Article 231(3) has led to the development of two different theories of the scope of the obligation. First there is the abstract or organic theory whereby the court of last resort within the judicial hierarchy against which there is never a judicial appeal carries the obligation to refer. This would cover the House of Lords, the Irish Supreme Court and other comparable courts. Support for this theory can be obtained from the wording of Article 234(3), which refers in plural to the 'decisions' of such courts. The opposing theory is the concrete or specific case theory that considers the case in question, not the court in abstract. This would obviously, in appropriate cases, cover the English Court of Appeal, or even inferior courts where the right of appeal is restricted by the nature of the case. Support for this view comes from Case 6/64 *Costa* v. *ENEL* ([1964] ECR 585) which involved a reference from an Italian *guidice conciliatore*, a magistrate who is the judicial authority of last resort for certain minor cases; the Court stated (at p. 592) that:

> 'by the terms of [Article 234], however, national courts against whose decisions, as *in the present case*, there is no judicial remedy, must refer the matter to the Court of Justice' (emphasis added).

The adoption of this position, however, still leaves the English Court of Appeal in a rather ambiguous position, since it is not clear until the end of any particular case – i.e. after the decision not to refer to the Court has been taken – whether an appeal to the House of Lords will be possible. In *R* v. *Henn and Darby* ([1978] 3 All ER 1190 (CA); [1980] 2 All ER 166 (HL)) the question was not discussed in the Court of Appeal, which refused to refer and refused leave to appeal. The House of Lords granted leave to appeal, and made a reference to the Court of Justice. The matter was addressed again in what has been described as the 'peripatetic' case of *Chiron* v. *Murex* ([1994] FSR 187 (CA); [1995] All ER (EC) 88 (HL)) (Demetriou, 1995: 628). In that case, the applicants failed on two occasions to persuade the Court of Appeal to refer or to give leave to appeal to the House of Lords; it also failed to persuade the House of Lords to give leave to appeal. It is not surprising that the applicants' attempts, in effect, to have the Court of Appeal override the House of Lords failed, but it is perhaps regrettable that the House of Lords failed to refer this difficult question to the Court of Justice for resolution subject to the principles of EU law. It is all the more disappointing because the House has in the past used its ability (and indeed obligation) to refer in order 'to protect its neutrality and impartiality' within the UK's complex constitutional framework (Maher, 1995a: 312).

There are three sets of circumstances in which there is no obligation to refer on a court of last resort (although, of course, there remains a discretion to refer). First, there is no duty to refer a question of interpretation in interlocutory proceedings providing that the findings of law are subject to review in main proceedings. In Case 107/76 *Hoffmann-La-Roche* v. *Centrafarm* ([1977] ECR 957 at p. 973) the Court held that Article 234(3):

> 'must be interpreted as meaning that a national court or tribunal is not required to refer to the Court a question of interpretation ... mentioned in that Article when the question is raised in interlocutory proceedings for an interim order, even where no judicial remedy is available against

the decision to be taken in the context of those proceedings, provided that each of the parties is entitled to institute proceedings or to require proceedings to be instituted on the substance of the case and that during such proceedings the question provisionally decided in the summary proceedings may be re-examined and may be the subject of a reference to the Court under Article 177.'

Interlocutory proceedings involving challenges to the validity of EU legislation are discussed in 11.7.

The second category of cases in which the obligation to refer lapses is where the Court has previously answered a materially identical question. This point emerges from Cases 28-30/62 *Da Costa en Schaake* where the Court referred to the authority of a previous ruling which it had given on a materially identical question as in effect depriving a subsequent preliminary reference of its *raison d'être*. A similar situation arises where the Court has already declared an act of one of the EU institutions void. This is sufficient reason for a court in another Member State to treat that act as void and to be exonerated from the duty to refer (Case 66/80 *International Chemical Corporation* v. *Amministrazione delle Finanze dello Stato* [1981] ECR 1191).

Finally, it is argued that the doctrine of *acte clair* can override the obligation to refer. This doctrine, espoused in particular by certain French courts in the early stages of development of the EU legal order, holds that a sufficiently clear legal provision does not require interpretation, but only application. Since the matter of 'application' falls within the remit of the national court under the principle of the separation of functions, it should follow that there is no question of interpretation to be referred. This doctrine was eventually accepted by the Court in Case 283/81 *CILFIT* ([1982] ECR 3415), but in such a qualified and watered-down form that it is questionable whether the Court was not also seeking simultaneously to destroy its substance. In its judgment the Court referred to *Da Costa*, and indicated that further circumstances in which references might be meaningless included those where the previous rulings of the Court effectively decided a point of law even though the questions at issue were not materially identical, and where the correct application of EU law is so obvious as to leave no scope for any reasonable doubt as to how the question raised is to be resolved.

However, the Court went on to say (at p. 3430) that:

'before it comes to the conclusion that such is the case, the national court or tribunal must be convinced that the matter is equally obvious to the courts of the other Member States and to the Court of Justice. Only if those conditions are satisfied may the national court or tribunal refrain from submitting the question to the Court of Justice and take upon itself the responsibility for resolving it.'

The Court then indicated the factors to be taken into account by the national court in deciding this point. These include the characteristic features of EU law, and the particular difficulties to which its interpretation gives rise: the fact that EU law is drafted in several languages and that the different language versions are all equally authentic; the existence of difficulties relating to terminology and legal concepts, the meanings of which may vary significantly between Member States and between national and EU law; and finally the fact that EU law must be interpreted in its context, having regard to its purpose and object. It would be rare that a provision of EU law would satisfy these requirements of simplicity and clarity, or indeed that a national court would feel itself equipped with the resources for the comparative analysis which ought to underlie a faithful application of the *CILFIT* criteria. Notwithstanding this ruling, there have been subsequent instances of the application of *acte clair* by national courts, including examples from case law in the UK (see *SA Magnavision NV* v. *General Optical Council* [1987] 1 CMLR 887 and [1987] 2 CMLR 262 (Div. Court). Even more worrying, perhaps, was the decision of the House of Lords in *R* v. *London Boroughs' Transport Committee, ex parte Freight Transport Association* ([1991] 3 All ER 915) in which it declined to make a reference in circumstances of uncertainty over the precise interpretation of certain Directives (which the Court of Appeal and the House of Lords interpreted quite differently), without referring to what other judges have called the 'cautionary comments' in the Court of Justice in *CILFIT* (see for a contrast *R* v. *Secretary of State for Transport, ex parte Factortame Ltd* [1989] 2 CMLR 353 (HL)) (for a general discussion see Weatherill, 1992). However, the complexities of faithfully applying the *CILFIT* criteria may be such that the ruling must be regarded as 'unrealistic and unworkable in practice' (Bebr, 1988: 355).

Failure by a court of last resort to make a preliminary reference where unresolved issues of EU law remain crucial to the resolution of a case is, of course, a breach of a Treaty obligation by the judicial arm of the state which could potentially form the subject matter of an action under Article 226 EC. There is no individual redress available against the failure to refer.

11.7   Rulings on Validity

Only the Court of Justice has the power to declare an act of an EU institution invalid. In Case 314/85 *Firma Foto-Frost* v. *Hauptzollamt Lübeck* ([1987] ECR 4199) the Court acknowledged that this point was not definitively settled by the Treaty itself. It concluded that while national courts have the power to decide that there are no serious grounds for impugning the validity of EU legislation without recourse to the Court of Justice, it would be contrary to the objective of ensuring the uniform application of EU law by national courts, which underlies Article 234, to allow them to decide on the invalidity of an EU act. In this context, divergences in national interpretation would be intolerable from the perspective of the unity of the EU legal order, the cohesion of the system of remedies under the Treaty and the imperatives of legal certainty. It follows from this decision that there is in effect an obligation on all courts to refer issues of (doubtful) validity to the Court of Justice.

In *Foto-Frost* the Court explicitly left open the question of how national courts should deal with the problem of the alleged invalidity of an EU act in the context of interim proceedings, where the urgency of matters would tend to render a reference to the Court meaningless. In Cases C-143/88 and C-92/89 *Zuckerfabrik Süderithmarschen & Zuckerfabrik Soest* ([1991] ECR I-415), the Court was confronted directly with this issue, but again it refused to allow the national court the power to declare EU measures invalid. Instead it stated that the national court should, in interim proceedings, invalidate the national implementing measures which are based on the impugned EU act, if there are factual and legal matters brought by the applicants before the national court which suggest that there are serious doubts about the validity of the EU measure (in that case, a regulation). There must also be evidence that the matter is urgent and that the applicant is threatened by grave and irreparable harm if no action is taken by the national court, and the national court must not act before it has taken into account the interests of the EU. With respect to the latter point, the Court indicated that some form of guarantee could be required from the applicant against loss, which might be suffered by the EU if the national measure is suspended in these circumstances.

The matter was taken a step further by the Court in Case C-465/93 *Atlanta Fruchthandelsgesellschaft mbH* v. *Bundesamt für Ernährung und Forstwirtschaft* ([1995] ECR I-3761) where the Court concluded that a national court may also under the same conditions issue a positive order granting interim relief. The Court stressed the importance of the parallelism between interim relief in respect of allegedly unlawful EU measures, and interim relief in respect of national legal provisions alleged to be in breach of EU law (Case C-213/89 *R* v. *Secretary of State for Transport, ex parte Factortame Ltd (Factortame I)* [1990] ECR I-2433) (13.3). It also referred to a close link to the Court's own power to issue interim relief under Article 243 EC, in proceedings brought under Article 230 (15.12).

Interim relief should be available under the same conditions, and the national court was reminded that it must take into account the interest of the EU in such questions and that it could no longer grant or maintain in place interim relief in circumstances where there remained no real doubt that the EU measure in question was in fact valid.

We shall review the role of Article 234 in the system of judicial review of EU acts in Chapter 15.

11.8 The Authority and Effects of Rulings of the Court of Justice

No provision in the Treaties prescribes the effects or authority of rulings of the Court of Justice within the national legal orders. However, the Court has evolved an extensive case law on the effects of Article 234 rulings *vis-à-vis* the parties to the case, third parties and national courts.

A ruling of the Court of Justice in proceedings in which a reference has been made is binding on the national court, at least in so far as it chooses to resolve the case on the basis of EU law (Case 29/68 *Milch- Fett- und Eierkontor* v. *HZA Saarbrücken* [1969] ECR 165). On the other hand, a ruling on the interpretation of EU law does not have the effect of *res judicata* (decided issue) in other proceedings raising similar or identical questions (Cases 28-30/62 *Da Costa*). This means that the Court will not dismiss as inadmissible references made on points which it has already decided although, of course, the referring court may choose to withdraw the questions. The key question is whether a national court is bound to follow the rulings of the Court of Justice, or, where it disagrees with the ruling given by that Court, to ask it to reconsider its case law. This happened in Case 28/67 *Molkerei Zentrale Westfalen* v. *HZA Paderborn* ([1968] ECR 143) when the referring court asked the Court to review its interpretation of what was then Article 95 EEC in Case 57/65 *Lütticke* v. *HZA Saarlouis* ([1966] ECR 205) (now Article 90 EC). Although the point is not made explicitly, however, it must follow from Article 10 EC that all national courts are bound to decide cases in accordance with the case law of the Court of Justice. In the UK, section 3(1) of the European Communities Act 1972 removes all remaining doubts, in that it provides that questions of EU law, if not referred to the Court of Justice for a ruling, must be decided in accordance with the principles laid down by any relevant decision of the Court. In other words, the Court is inserted at the apex of the system of binding judicial precedent in the UK.

The position *vis-à-vis* other courts has been articulated more clearly by the Court in relation to the effects of rulings on invalidity. Although such a ruling is not strictly binding *erga omnes*, it is none the less 'sufficient reason for any other national court to regard that act as void' (Case 66/80 *International Chemical Corporation* v. *Amministrazione delle Finanze dello Stato* [1981] ECR 1191 at p. 1216). It follows from a finding of invalidity that a national court must not apply any national provisions based on the invalid EU act (Case 162/82 *Cousin* [1983] ECR 1101).

Using Article 231(2) EC as a starting point, the Court of Justice has shown itself prepared to modulate the effects of a preliminary ruling according to the circumstances. Article 231(2) provides, in the context of the annulment of acts by means of direct actions under Article 230, that:

'In the case of a regulation ... the Court of Justice shall, if it considers this necessary, state which of the effects of the regulation which it has declared void shall be considered as definitive.'

The Court has implicitly claimed a similar power in the context of preliminary rulings, holding in Case 4/79 *Providence Agricole de la Champagne* ([1980] ECR 2823) that it may rule that an act is valid for the past but invalid for the future. It has likewise asserted the power to place a temporal limitation upon the effects of an interpretative ruling under Article 234 (Case 43/75 *Defrenne* v. *SABENA* [1976] ECR 455 – the direct effect of what was then Article 119 EEC (now Article 141 EC); see more recently Case C-262/88 *Barber* v. *Guardian Royal Exchange* [1990] ECR I-1889 – the application of Article 141 to occupational pensions, where the ruling on limited temporal effects itself required further clarification: Case C-109/91 *Ten Oever* v. *Stichting Bedrijfspensioenfonds* [1993] ECR I-4879). However, it is clear that only the Court itself may place a temporal limitation upon the effects of a ruling, and that it must place that restriction in the context of the actual judgment in which it rules upon the interpretation or validity of the relevant provision (Case 61/79 *Denkavit Italiana* [1980] ECR 1205).

11.9   Title IV and Third Pillar: Limited Preliminary Reference Systems

Under Title IV of the EC Treaty, on visas, asylum, immigration and other policies related to free movement of persons, the Court will receive references from national courts under the normal rules in Article 234, subject to the following conditions laid down in Article 68(1) EC:

'where a question on the interpretation of this Title or on the validity of interpretation of acts of the institutions of the Community based on this Title is raised in a case pending before a court or tribunal of a Member State against whose decisions there is no judicial remedy under national law, that court or tribunal shall, if it considers that a decision on the question is necessary to enable it to give judgment, request the Court of Justice to give a ruling thereon.'

The Court has no jurisdiction to rule on 'any measure or decision taken pursuant to Article 62(1) relating to the maintenance of law and order and the safeguarding of internal security'. This differs noticeably from the existing general 'public security' rules (Articles 296–298 EC) which seek to preserve the sovereignty of the Member States without explicitly ousting the jurisdiction of the Court. Indeed, under Article 298, there is an expedited enforcement process to bring a Member State abusing the rules before the Court of Justice (8.11). Title IV contains no such equivalent.

To offset the limited preliminary reference procedure, an advisory jurisdiction on the part of the Court is established in Article 68(3), enabling the Council, the Commission or a Member State to 'request the Court to give a ruling on a question of interpretation of this Title or of acts of the institutions of the Community based on this Title', save only that the response of the Court does not apply to judgments of national courts which have already become *res judicata*. In other words, it will apply for the future only. It will be interesting to see whether the price paid through the limited reference procedure in terms of restricting civil liberties is worthwhile in view of the need not to overload the Court of Justice or to make it impossible for the Member States to operate efficient systems for reviewing requests for asylum.

Under the third pillar, the limited preliminary reference jurisdiction is laid down in Article 35 TEU. It is restricted to references on the validity and interpretation of framework decisions and other decisions, on the interpretation of conventions established under Title VI, and on the validity and interpretation of measures implementing such conventions. However, jurisdiction only applies if the Member State has made a declaration to that effect, and it must also make a declaration about whether or not to limit the possibility of referring to courts of last resort or not. It may impose an obligation on courts of last resort to refer. By the date of entry into force of the Treaty of Amsterdam declarations had been made by all Member States except France and, less surprisingly in view of their semi-detached status, Denmark, Ireland and the UK, accepting jurisdiction (OJ 1999 C120/24). Under Article 35(4) the Court is in any event denied jurisdiction to:

> 'review the validity or proportionality of operations carried out by the policy or other law enforcement services of a Member State or the exercise of the responsibilities incumbent upon Member States with regard to the maintenance of law and order and the safeguarding of internal security.'

In sum, these provisions represent a begrudging acceptance on the part of the Member States to allow some judicial review – as an essential element of the rule of law – into the third pillar, rather than leaving its outputs to be dealt with simply as if they were 'ordinary' public international law measures.

11.10 The Assessment of the Preliminary Reference Procedure

The Article 234 reference procedure has been described as a specific expression of the duty of mutual cooperation between the EU and its Member States contained in Article 10 EC, creating a system of judicial cooperation which has worked remarkably well and in which the Court has delivered numerous judgements of constitutional significance for the EU legal order (Slynn, 1992: 9–10; de la Mare, 1999). This is in part attributable to the manner in which the Court has chosen to frame its interpretative role, breaking down the barrier between interpretation and application, and phrasing its judgements on some occasions in terms which leave little doubt to the national court as to how it should apply the ruling. Equally important it has construed the task of giving interpretations of provisions of EU law as allowing it also to determine the effect of those provisions. This can be seen, for example, in the many rulings delivered by the Court since the groundbreaking case of Case 26/62 *Van Gend en Loos v. Nederlandse Administratie der Belastingen* ([1963] ECR 1) in which it has held that in certain circumstances provisions of EU law give rise to individual rights which national courts must protect.

The most important factor has, however, been the willingness of national courts to refer questions to the Court. Although 'reference rates' vary considerably between the Member States with, for example, German, Dutch, and Belgian courts showing themselves among the most ready to refer, and UK judges closer to the bottom of any reference 'league table' (particularly by head of population), the success of Article 234 in terms of volume of cases which have been generated cannot be denied (see the detailed figures and statistics in Stone Sweet and Brunell, 1998 and de la Mare, 1999). The Court now receives over 250 references each year from national courts, and decides around 200. Although this disparity can in part be accounted for by cases dealt with other than by the rendering of a judgment (e.g. withdrawal of the reference by the national court, order other than a full judgment, joining of two cases), it inevitably means that the average length of proceedings has risen and now hovers around twenty-one months for preliminary references. Thus in many ways, the Court has become a victim of its own success, since by interpreting Article 234 in such a way as to expand its jurisdiction and to encourage national courts to refer it has a created a flood of cases with which it is barely equipped to deal, even after the transfers of jurisdiction in other areas to the Court of First Instance. Yet in principle the reference procedure should be a relatively light procedure for the Court. It does not decide cases, but merely answers questions. It does not decide the facts, or take a position (at least in principle) on matters of national law. When it made its report to the Reflection Group preparing the 1996 IGC agenda (see 4.21), the Court commented upon the need for further procedural simplifications in relation to 'cases of lesser importance', and expressed a wish to be given the power to approve its own Rules of Procedure to enable more flexible responses (it took until December 1994 for the Court's revised Rules of Procedure following the entry into force of the Treaty of Maastricht to be approved by the Council). However, the Court continued at that time to express its opposition to any suggestion that all or part of the preliminary ruling jurisdiction should be given in the first instance to the Court of First Instance. A preliminary ruling procedure is not apt for resolution under a two-tier judicial structure.

That opposition had, however, melted away by the time the Court prepared its report for the 2000 IGC. That Report contemplated the conferring of jurisdiction on the Court of First Instance to take references for preliminary rulings in 'certain circumscribed, specific cases in which the Community interest would not require the Court of Justice to have exclusive powers'. While the Court would not wish to see an appeals procedure from such rulings by the Court of First Instance, it would like to have a power to review, in certain circumstances, preliminary rulings given by the Court of First Instance where it was necessary 'to safeguard the unity and coherence of Community law'. A working party established by the Commission to advise it in the context of making proposals to the 2000 IGC also recommended very limited changes to the preliminary rulings jurisdiction; the types of area which might be appropriate would be intellectual property cases, where the issues can be tightly circumscribed.

Extensive academic work has been done on proposals to reform Article 234, both structurally and procedurally (Schermers *et al.*, 1987; Watson, 1986, de la Mare, 1999: 246–249) and the Court itself has mused extensively on the future of its jurisdiction as a whole in a report published in 1999 (Court of Justice, 1999). Procedural proposals to reduce delays have included making the Article 234 procedure entirely written, with no oral argument. The Court has recently proposed a simplified procedure for 'simple questions' (11.2). Structural reforms have concentrated on considering the reconciliation of two objectives: that the Court of Justice should continue to hear and to decide the important cases which develop the law and that national courts should increasingly decide the less important cases without recourse to the Court itself. Judicial education is widely recognised as a vital component in such a strategy. The efficiency of the Court's own work might also be increased by encouraging specialisation among its own judiciary – a move which has been resisted in the past, which appears increasingly attractive as the areas covered by EU law range across ever-wider fields of public and private law, calling for a 'multifunctional' court (Weatherill, 1995a: 282–284). Other suggested measures include 'docket control' (the Court chooses the cases it wishes to take) and a simplified procedure under which the Court can give a 'green light' to an interpretation proposed by the national court. While it may be that the Court is moving towards a stricter control of the question of admissibility (11.2), as yet no firm proposals have been tendered on docket control. Commentators have always stressed that docket control cannot be cost-free, at the very least in terms of tampering with sacrosanct principles such as the right to a judicial hearing. An additional method of reinforcing the level of cooperation between the national courts and the Court of Justice may be to institute lines of communication to seek to ensure that the Court does not receive multiple, essentially similar but slightly different, sets of questions which all require separate resolution.

Lawyers and political scientists agree about the significance of the Article 234 reference procedure: it has contributed greatly to the widespread acceptance of the authority of EU law and of the Court of Justice's rulings in particular. Exactly how this has occurred is not so clear (Alter, 1996, 1998a; Wincott, 1995b). After all, there is a slight paradox in the suggestion that involving more courts in the judicial hierarchy by, in effect, making national courts into 'Community courts' (Maher, 1994) will have this effect. It seems equally probable that this could lead to a watering down of the authority of EU law, through a loss of uniformity, not to its strengthening. The 'political' explanations tendered include the use by the Court of its 'mask of law' (Burley and Mattli, 1993), or 'legal formalism', behind which it has brought about a startling political agenda; and the effect of 'intercourt competition', both vertically between courts within the same state and between the courts of different Member States, which has enhanced the status of EU law, as national courts 'compete' to achieve compliance. Equally, lawyers would point to the Court's astute harnessing of the resources of national law to achieve compliance. Just as the EU lacks powers of direct implementation in the administrative sphere, but can effect through other means considerable changes in regulatory culture in the Member States (8.1 and 8.2), so it lacks the powers of national courts to issue and enforce injunctions, and to make and enforce compensation orders. As the next two chapters will show, building on the opportunities provided by the Article 234 reference procedure, the Court has ensured that the rules of EU law now shape to an astonishing extent, from inception to conclusion, from issues of constitutional principle to procedural minutiae, any action before the national courts in which EU rights and duties are at issue.

Summary

1   Article 234 EC provides an organic connection between national courts and the Court of Justice, enabling national courts to obtain authoritative rulings on the interpretation and validity of provisions of EU law.

2   The preliminary rulings procedure is based on a separation of functions between the national court and the Court of Justice, and its effectiveness depends upon the cooperative application of this distinction by all courts.

3   In general the Court of Justice does not interfere with the discretion of the national court in referring questions. However, it will not answer abstract or hypothetical questions, and has imposed the requirement that there be a genuine dispute in the national court. The national court must supply the Court of Justice with sufficient information of a factual and legal nature to enable it to answer the questions.

4 Article 234 provides for references on questions of the interpretation (and, implicitly, the effect) of:
– provisions of the Treaty and other international agreements binding the EU;
– provisions of EU legislation, including non-binding acts.
References on validity can be made in respect of binding legal acts of the EU.

5 The concept of a 'court or tribunal' of a Member State is interpreted broadly as any body representing the judicial power of the state.

6 Inferior courts have a discretion to refer; orders for references may be appealed within the national juridical structure. The obligation to refer is imposed on courts of last resort, and is qualified in only three cases:
– in interlocutory proceedings, where the issues of EU law can be reconsidered at trial;
– where the Court has already answered materially identical questions;
– where the limited doctrine of *acte clair* as laid down by the Court in *CILFIT* applies.

7 Only the Court of Justice may rule upon the validity of EU acts. The Court has indicated that in cases of urgency a national court should invalidate the national measures implementing an EU act which is allegedly invalid, or adopt other appropriate interim measures, making a reference on the validity of the EU act.

8 The authority of rulings of the Court of Justice is such that in general no national court should depart from a position taken by the Court of Justice. The Court has asserted the power in limited circumstances to restrict the temporal effects of its rulings.

9 Title IV of Part III of the EC Treaty and Title VI (third pillar) of the TEU provide for limited preliminary ruling jurisdiction on the part of the Court of Justice. In the case of the third pillar, the Member States must each accept jurisdiction.

10 The preliminary rulings procedure has been effective in generating a flow of cases to the Court of Justice in which it has laid down many of the central constitutional precepts of the EU legal order. In some ways, Article 234 has proved too successful, with increasingly long delays before the Court is now able to give judgment on references for preliminary rulings. It has been suggested that the Court's increased rigour in examining the admissibility of some references for preliminary rulings is the first signs of a new policy of 'docket' control.

Questions

1 What purposes does Article 234 serve within the EU legal order?

2 What is meant by the 'separation of functions' in the context of Article 234?

3 Which bodies may refer questions to the Court of Justice?

4 Why did the Court refuse to answer the questions posed by the Italian court in *Foglia* v. *Novello*?

5 Was the Court correct to refuse to answer the questions posed by the German court in *Meilicke*?

6 Does the Court's recent case law on the admissibility of preliminary references from national courts represent an attack upon the 'spirit of Article 234'?

7 In what circumstances is a national court obliged to make a preliminary reference to the Court of Justice?

8 Why does the Court maintain that it has sole authority to declare invalid provisions of EU law?

Workshop

1 'In providing for references on questions of the interpretation and validity of EU law from national courts to the Court of Justice, the authors of the Treaty settled on a compromise solution to the problem of developing a uniform application of EU law within the EU under the control of a single supranational court.'
Discuss in the light of the detailed provisions and conditions which govern the operation of Article 234.

2 Refer back to the text of the workshop in Chapter 7. What would be the appropriate action for the Supreme Administrative Court of Zeno to take if it believes that the EU Directive is unlawful?

Further Reading

D. Anderson (1994), 'The Admissibility of Preliminary References', 14 *Yearbook of European Law* 179.

A. Arnull (1990b), 'References to the European Court', 15 *European Law Review* 375.

A. Arnull (1999a), pp. 49–69.

G. Bebr (1988), 'The Reinforcement of the Constitutional Review of Community Acts under Article 177 EEC', 25 *Common Market Law Review* 684.

K. Lenaerts (1994), 'Form and Substance of the Preliminary Rulings Procedure', in Curtin and Heukels (1994).

G.F. Mancini and D. Keeling (1991), 'From *CILFIT* to *ERT*: The Constitutional Challenge Facing the European Court', 11 *Yearbook of European Law* 1.

T. de la Mare (1999), 'Article 177 in Social and Political Context', in Craig and de Búrca (1999).

D. O'Keeffe (1998), 'Is the Spirit of Article 177 under Attack? Preliminary References and Admissibility', 23 *European Law Review* 509.

H. Schermers *et al.* (eds) (1987), esp. G. Bebr, 'The Preliminary Proceedings of Article 177 EEC – Problems and Suggestions for Improvement', p. 345.

G. Tesauro (1993), 'The Effectiveness of Judicial Protection and Co-operation between the Court of Justice and the National Courts', 13 *Yearbook of European Law* 1.

Key Websites

The Court of Justice's website offers not only its own case law, but also its Note of Guidance for National Courts, statistics on its judgments indicating the numbers of rulings given in Article 234 cases, and various proposals for changing the EU's judicial architecture:

http://curia.eu.int/en/index.htm

12 EU Law and the Legal Systems of the Member States

12.1 The Nature of the EU Legal Order and its Impact upon the National Legal Orders

The problem we shall consider in this chapter is how the evolving EU legal order has established itself as a superior legal order operating within, but none the less independently of, the national legal systems. It demonstrates how the Court of Justice has used the organic connection offered by Article 234 EC both to assert its own ability to give authoritative interpretations of the meaning and effect of EU law, and to emphasise that where EU law applies, national courts themselves must act as 'Community courts' (Maher, 1994), interpreting and applying EU law subject to the authority of the Court of Justice. Once the general principles have been identified in this chapter, Chapter 13 will focus on certain key aspects of the way in which they have been instrumentalised, with a particular focus, as necessary, upon the Member States, and especially the UK.

The edifice of rules and principles set out in this chapter has been built out of relatively unpromising material. The constitutive treaties themselves contain little indication of the precise nature of the relationship between EU law and national law or of the extent to which, if at all, the legal order created by the Treaties of Paris and Rome should be regarded as differing from the system of international law in general. Reference can be made, of course, to Article 10 EC (the duty of Community loyalty applying to Member States and institutions alike) and Article 220 EC (the duty of the Court of Justice to ensure that 'the law is observed'). With the exception of these provisions, the principles of a unique supranational legal order have evolved entirely through judicial action.

A cautionary note about the role of the Court is sounded in a 'political science' analysis of the 'constitutionalisation' process, which it would be useful to bear in mind here:

> 'On reading some of legal literature it would be easy to come to the conclusion that this process of constitutionalization inevitably followed on once the initial steps had been taken. As ... political scientists come to

take the Court of Justice seriously in the analysis of European integration, there is a danger that this sense of a teleological legal process of ever closer union will be swallowed whole. The fact that the Court has often acted as a protagonist for integration, and that its interpretation of Community law often sought to bring about the ever closer union of Europe, should not be allowed to cover over the fact that even these foundational doctrines of Community law had to be constructed' (Wincott, 1995b: 590).

This chapter will describe the essential features of an effective supranational legal order, in which the law and the institutions entrusted with the tasks of enforcing and applying the law have indeed claimed a central role as motors of the integration project. The key features have commonly been termed the direct effect and supremacy of EU law, and these concepts have been referred to already in earlier chapters. They will be considered in greater detail here, within a constitutional framework that identifies the different levels at which EU law impacts upon the national legal orders. They will also be located within the broader notion of the 'effectiveness' or '*effet utile*' of EU law. In a classic exposition of the doctrine of direct effect, Pescatore (1983) argued that it is fundamental to any legal system that the institutions responsible for its stewardship should seek always to render the law operative. In keeping with this pragmatic philosophy, the approach taken here of describing the important legal concepts and principles is buttressed by the attempt, in Chapter 13, to identify the practical mechanisms evolved by the Court of Justice in order to make the EU legal order fully and uniformly effective throughout the Member States, and to do this in the context of the type of fundamental constitutional dialogue between the different legal orders highlighted as important by Stone Sweet (1998) (11.1).

In two early statements of principle, the Court laid down the markers for establishing the parameters of the EU legal order. In Case 26/62 *Van Gend en Loos* v. *Nederlandse Administratie der Belastingen* ([1963] ECR 1 at p. 12) it asserted that:

'the Community constitutes a new legal order of international law, for the benefit of which states have limited their sovereign rights, albeit within limited fields, and the subjects of which comprise not only member states but also their nationals.'

It continued in similar vein the following year in Case 6/64 *Costa* v. *ENEL* ([1964] ECR 585 at p. 593):

'By contrast with ordinary international treaties, the EEC Treaty has created its own legal system which, on the entry into force of the Treaty, became an integral part of the legal system of the member states and which their courts are bound to apply.'

These remarkable statements by the Court of Justice are now accepted as commonplace – although they were radical at the time. Rather than being mere descriptions of what the EU legal order then was, they constituted at the time normative assertions by the Court about what it wished that order to resemble. It is remarkable not only that the Court expressed itself in those terms in the early 1960s in cases of first impression on the relationship between EU law and the national legal orders, but also that it has experienced astonishing success in fashioning a legal order after the model put forward in those cases – even though the progress of the case law does not always follow a linear model. From these statements can be extrapolated four elements which are often taken to provide a full explanation of the EU law/national law interface:

(a) the EU legal order is a separate and autonomous system distinct from the general order of public international law; the Court has therefore been able to claim a free hand in evolving the substance of that legal order;

(b) EU law is part of national law, which means that national courts can and must apply it in accordance with the authoritative rulings of the Court of Justice;

(c) the EU legal order is based on a transfer of sovereign powers by the Member States to the EU; Member States can no longer exercise those powers which have been transferred to the EU, and must abstain from any acts which hinder the EU in its exercise of these powers;

(d) Member States and EU citizens are the subjects of EU law, and as subjects have rights and obligations flowing from and under the Treaties.

On closer examination, however, these explanations cannot be regarded as adequate on their own. What they do not provide is a framework for distinguishing between four different aspects of the EU law/national law interface:

1   The 'policies' which structure the overall approach of the Court, and which result from its understanding of what the role of the law and of the judicial apparatus should be within the EU.

2   The constitutional qualities which distinguish EU law as a species of 'federal law', within a federal-type legal order.

3   The techniques – of a more or less novel nature – which the Court of Justice has devised and developed to give effect to those constitutional qualities.

4   The principles which the Court has developed to ensure a degree of supervision over national courts when they give effect to the techniques when faced by individual cases arising within the national legal orders which raise issues of EU law.

This chapter characterises points 2–4 as different levels of impact of EU law upon national law, which are structured by the three policy objectives identified under point 1 that the Court of Justice pursues more or less consistently:

– ensuring the 'effectiveness' of EU law; this has not only occurred in relation to the EU law/national law interface, but also, as Chapter 8 has shown, in relation to administrative processes for the enforcement of EU law; it is a consistent underlying theme of the case law which is examined throughout Part V, as will already be apparent from Chapter 11;
– pursuing the uniform application of EU law, already discussed in relation to Article 234 references, but equally apparent in the degree of precision regarding the duties of national courts which emerges in many of the cases discussed here;
– constructing the individual within a framework of legal protection; this is not just a question of ensuring that individuals can rely upon (economic) EU rights, but also of reinforcing the symbolism of an EU legal order 'close to the citizen'.

Looking in more detail at the three levels of impact, it is perhaps important to note that this scheme differs somewhat from the approach conventionally adopted in much of the literature on these questions. In particular it will be seen that it places 'supremacy' and 'direct effect' at different levels, although many have characterised these notions as twin 'pillars' of the EU legal order. The following discussion will show why they should be regarded as essentially quite different notions. Some commentators have used a similar frame of analysis when they talk of 'second' and 'third' generation EC rights. These correspond broadly to the second and third levels identified here (e.g. Docksey, 1995, Curtin and Mortelmans, 1994).

1   EU law has certain distinctive constitutional qualities, as a superior source of law (the supremacy of EU law), and as a source of law that penetrates into the national legal orders notwithstanding its 'international' origins or the particularities of the various national constitutional orders (the direct applicability of EU law).
2   In order to guarantee these constitutional qualities, in the spirit of the policy objectives already identified, the Court of Justice has developed a number of techniques for ensuring that EU law can be enforced; some

will already be familiar from earlier chapters; others will be introduced and explained in this chapter:

- EU law can in certain circumstances be relied upon directly in national courts as giving rise to rights, duties and, perhaps, interests which those courts must protect ('direct effect', or the 'justiciable' quality of EU law);
- a closely related idea is that EU law generates responsibilities which are imposed on national public authorities (and, in certain circumstances, individuals), leading, in particular to the notion that Member States are subject to compensatory obligations where they fail to give effect to EU law, operating for the benefit of individuals (often termed the principle of state liability);
- as a superior source of law, EU law has a pre-emptive effect on national law and national legislative competence;
- as EU law is part of national law, in any event national courts are subject to an interpretative obligation to give effect to EU law.

3   However, the EU lacks a complete 'federal' order, comprising judicial, remedial and procedural structures to give effect to these principles of EU law. Hence it must borrow from national law, requiring national courts to give effect to EU rights using the techniques of national law, and upholding in that context a principle of national procedural autonomy, but subject to two overriding principles:

- national remedies must be no less favourable than those available for the enforcement of equivalent national rights (the principle of non-discrimination);
- national remedies must not operate in such a way as to render the enforcement of EU rights impossible in practice (the principle of effective remedies). Clearly the articulation of this principle by the Court of Justice is very closely related to its overall policy objective of ensuring the effectiveness of EU law.

Figure 12.1 sets out these concepts in the form of a figure. The main objective of this figure is to show the different levels of analysis along a horizontal plane. However, it does hint at certain vertical links between the constitutional qualities of EU law, and the techniques for the enforcement of EU law which derive in main from those two qualities. Justiciability and responsibility owe perhaps more to the direct applicability of EU law; pre-emption and interpretation can more easily be seen as deriving from the superior nature of EU law. However, each of the four techniques is ultimately dependent upon the existence and respect for the twin constitutional qualities of EU law.

Policy objectives of the Court of Justice	Ensuring the effectiveness of EC law: *effet utile*		Uniformity of EC law	The legal protection of individuals as legal subjects	
Constitutional qualities of EC law (level one)	EC law penetrates into the national legal orders			EC law is a superior source of law within the national legal orders	
Techniques for individual protection (level two)	Justiciability (direct effect)	Responsibility (State liability)	Interpretation (indirect effect)	Pre-emption	
Principles governing (*prima facie* autonomous) national remedies (level three)	National remedies must be made available on a non-discriminatory basis		National remedies must be sufficiently effective to ensure protection of EC rights		

Figure 12.1 Framework for analysing the different levels at which EC law impacts upon national law

The review of the case law in these chapters will make clear that the emphasis of legal development at present lies in a number of specific fields:

- the refinement of a number of detailed questions relating to the scope of direct effect, the principle itself having been already long settled;
- in that context, the particular interaction with the national court's interpretative obligation – indirect effect – has raised questions about the extent to which directives can be relied upon in national courts;
- settlement of the scope and nature of the pre-emptive effect of EU law, responding in particular to certain changes in the regulatory pattern of EU law;
- continued development of the notion of 'responsibility', and of the conditions under which it can apply;
- more detailed articulation of the contours of the non-discrimination and (especially) the effective remedies principles, as the Court's attention is drawn to an ever-wider range of potential national fetters upon the effective enjoyment of EU rights, and as the Court examines the detailed implications for national legal orders of giving effect to the principle of responsibility.

To return to the point about the difference between supremacy and direct effect, it will now be seen that supremacy is a constitutional quality of EU law, whereas direct effect is now increasingly seen as one of a number of techniques for giving effect to those constitutional qualities (albeit in the early years probably the most important).

12.2   The Penetration of EU Law into the National Legal Orders

The first constitutional quality of EU law that we will examine is that it becomes part of the national legal order. From the perspective of the Court, this follows simply from the nature of EU law combined with the fact of accession. The strict logic of the transfer of sovereign powers thesis is that the Treaties themselves and any legal acts adopted by the EU institutions within the scope of their competence take their place within the domestic legal order and form part of the sources of law which the national judge must apply. Within the sphere of EU competence, EU law must take precedence. Moreover, as the Court emphasised in Opinion 1/91 *Re the Draft Agreement on a European Economic Area* ([1991] ECR I-6079), the transfer of competence has occurred 'in ever wider fields' (para. 21 of the judgment).

The structure is akin to a federal legal system, with the federal and state authorities acting within their respective spheres of competence, and with courts adjudicating over the boundaries between those spheres. In this chapter we shall refer to this quality of EU law as its 'direct applicability'. For the avoidance of terminological confusion, two points of explanation must be made.

First, the use of 'direct applicability' in this sense accords well with the terminological usage of the Court, which has referred to this concept as meaning:

> 'that the rules of Community law must be fully and uniformly applied in all the Member States from the date of their entry into force and for so long as they continue in force' (Case 106/77 *Amministrazione delle Finanze dello Stato* v. *Simmenthal SpA (Simmenthal II)* [1978] ECR 629 at p. 643).

It is to be distinguished in this context from the justiciability of provisions of EU law, that is, from the question of whether a particular provision is capable of giving rise to rights and obligations enforceable by a court of law. This is the concept of 'direct effect', and is one which, in the framework set out in this chapter, operates at a 'lower' level of the EU law/national interface.

Second, confusion need not arise from the fact that Article 249 EC refers to regulations, and apparently only regulations, as being 'directly applicable in all the Member States' (formerly Article 189 EC and referred to as such in many of the quotations from older cases which follow below). The Court has made it plain on numerous occasions that it is not only regulations which are directly applicable in the sense of being part of the national legal system. Directives are undoubtedly also part of the national legal system. However, this does not detract from the fact that regulations do have certain special qualities, amounting in the view of Usher (1981) to a 'stop sign' to national legislatures which make them particularly useful instruments for the EU law-maker in fields where absolute uniformity of the rules applied is of paramount importance (e.g. customs, agriculture, social security of migrant workers). Direct applicability in this sense is a matter of legislative technique. In this chapter we use a broader notion which includes but also transcends the 'stop sign' argument, and extends to cover also the wider 'pre-emptive' qualities of EU rules of law generally (see 12.13).

12.3   EU Law as a Superior Source of Law

Nowhere in the constitutive Treaties is it stated that EU law takes precedence over national law, although such a position can be derived from the duty of 'Community loyalty' contained in Article 10 EC. None the less, the supremacy of EU law has been broadly accepted since the early 1960s. Like the penetration of EU law into national law, this constitutional quality is drawn by the Court of Justice from the 'transfer of sovereign powers' thesis which makes it:

> 'impossible for states, as a corollary, to accord precedence to a unilateral and subsequent measure over a legal system accepted by them on the basis of reciprocity' (Case 6/64 *Costa* v. *ENEL* [1964] ECR 585 at p. 593).

In Case 11/70 *Internationale Handelsgesellschaft* ([1970] ECR 1125), the Court held that EU law prevails over all forms of national law, including national constitutions and fundamental rights enshrined in those constitutions. EU measures derive their validity solely from EU law, and thus the validity of an EU measure or its effect within a Member State cannot be affected by objections that it runs counter to either fundamental rights as guaranteed by the constitution of that State or the principles of a national constitutional structure. The Court made the point very strongly:

> 'The law stemming from the Treaty, an independent source of law, cannot because of its very nature be overridden by rules of national law, however framed, without being deprived of its character as Community law and without the legal basis of the Community itself being called into question' (p. 1134).

In order to counter the objection that it is not reasonable to replace the sovereignty of nation states which offer citizens constitutional guarantees of fundamental rights with an EU which does not, and in order to head off possible rebellions by the German and Italian Constitutional Courts, the Court has evolved the doctrine of EU fundamental rights (see 9.6). So it would seem that the justification for supremacy in this form is that it is inherent in the ideal of creating a new 'federal-type' legal order which lies at the heart of the project of economic integration in Europe, which has always had as its ultimate objective a 'Union of Peoples' (see the Preamble to the EC Treaty). The process of economic integration would be much less effective if Member States were able to hinder the attainment of EU goals by denying the superiority of EU norms.

12.4   National Constitutions and the Reception of EU Law

The attraction of basing the penetration of EU law within the domestic legal systems upon its own inherent qualities, rather than upon some constitutional mechanism for giving effect to EU law, is that it prevents the effectiveness of EU law being contingent upon the vagaries of national constitutional and judicial attitudes to incorporating the provisions of a 'foreign' legal system. In other words, it should enhance the uniform application of EU law. In reality, of course, as the Treaty itself recognises in its references to national mechanisms for ratification of international instruments (e.g. Article 48 TEU which provides for amendments to the Treaties to enter into force after ratification), the incorporation of EU law into the domestic legal system usually depends upon the creation of the appropriate 'gateway'. In the UK, where courts will refuse to take account of Treaties until they have been translated into domestic law by Act of Parliament, that gateway is to be found in the European Communities Act 1972, in particular sections 2 and 3. This will be examined in 13.8. Moreover, the point has already been made (11.1), that the constitutionalisation of the Treaties has not been an entirely unilateral endeavour on the part of the Court of Justice. It has also been the result of a number of constitutional dialogues, in which it continues to be involved. It is therefore appropriate to look briefly at the constitutional reception which Member States have given to EU law.

The written constitutions of some of the other Member States create models for the transfer or delegation of sovereign powers to international organisations which are more or less perfectly in accordance with the simplicity of the Court's own transfer thesis. For example, Article 92 of the Dutch constitution and Article 25*bis* of the Belgian constitution provide for the possibility of the transfer or attribution of sovereign powers to international organisations. Article 28(3) of the Greek constitution is rather more detailed. It provides that:

'Greece may freely proceed, by virtue of an Act passed by the votes of the absolute majority of the total number of members of Parliament, to limitations on the exercise of national sovereignty, provided that this is dictated by an important national interest, does not affect human rights and the foundations of democratic government and is effected in conformity with the principles of equality, and on condition of reciprocity.'

As we shall see, it is not possible for the domestic constitution to place riders such as these upon its transfer of powers to the EU, although in practice national judges may be unwilling for a variety of reasons to recognise the full force of EU law in the domestic system. Such provisions may also be important in a wider political context, in so far as they may express particular national aspirations in relation to the EU, or may reflect the experiences of a country relatively recently emerged from dictatorship.

Since the introduction of changes in connection with the ratification of the Treaty of Maastricht, Germany now has a detailed constitutional provision specifically concerned with the problems of German involvement, as a democratic and federal state under the rule of law, in the autonomous legal order of the EU (Article 23 of the Basic Law). Of particular interest is the fact that special provision is made for the political participation of the *Länder*, and of the *Bundestag*, the Upper Chamber of the Parliament where the *Länder* are represented.

12.5   Conceptions of International Law in the Member States

The second factor conditioning the reception of EU law is the conception of the relationship between public international law and national law. Classically, there are two conceptions: monism and dualism (Jackson, 1992; de Witte, 1999b: 200). Under monism, international law and municipal law are conceived of as part of one single legal system, with international law taking precedence. A dualist conception views international law and municipal law as two separate systems, each supreme within its own sphere. For example, since Parliament in the UK is sovereign, a dualist position on international law must necessarily be adopted by the UK courts which can recognise international obligations only once, and to the extent that, they have been incorporated into national law by Parliament in the form of a statute (*British Airways* v. *Laker Airways* [1984] 3 All ER 39). No account was taken of the EEC Treaty after agreement by the Crown on behalf of the UK but before the passing of the European Communities Act 1972 (*Blackburn* v. *Attorney General* [1971] 1 All ER 1380). In contrast, both the Dutch constitution (Articles 91–94) and the French constitution (Article 55) provide that duly ratified international obligations take precedence over municipal law. The Belgian courts have also achieved the same constitutional position in the absence of an explicit provision by proclaiming that international obligations have an effect superior to domestic law in the Belgian legal system (*Fromagerie Le Ski* [1972] CMLR 330).

Ostensibly since the ratification such as that referred to in the Dutch and French constitutions will often require some form of parliamentary approval, there is little difference between the monist and dualist positions in terms of the formalities required before international law can be recognised domestically. Where a difference does remain is in judicial attitudes subsequent to incorporation. The UK judges consistently betray their dualist heritage, either because they treat the application and enforcement of EU law principally as a matter of construction of the European Communities Act 1972 (see, for example, *Duke* v. *GEC Reliance* [1988] 1 All ER 626 discussed in Chapter 13), or because they treat the rules of EU law which they do apply as if they were statutes, interpreting them accordingly (see for example the interpretation of breach of Articles 81 and 82 EC as if it were a breach of statutory duty in *Garden Cottage Foods* v. *Milk Marketing Board* [1984] AC 130). In contrast, even the French *Conseil d'Etat* (Supreme Administrative Court) – long resistant to the claims of EU law – has now begun to refer to the basis for the authority of EU law in France as being the transfer of sovereign powers (*Boisdet* [1991] 1 CMLR 3).

12.6   EU Law and the Sovereignty of Parliament

There remain substantial obstacles to the successful reconciliation of the implications of membership of the EU with the classic Diceyian thesis of the sovereignty of Parliament. The sovereignty of Parliament is to be distinguished from the sovereignty of the UK as a nation state. The sovereignty of all the Member States is limited, or perhaps better 'pooled' or 'shared' by accession to the EU. However, the existence of a set of rules governing the conduct of the UK courts in relation to Parliament, under which the latter is recognised as the supreme law-making body, does present particular difficulties for the reception of EU law in the UK. Of most significance are the rule that Parliament may do anything except bind its successors and the universally accepted principle that courts may not call into question the validity of Acts of Parliament. From the first principle, it would appear that future Parliaments could not be restrained from legislating expressly in a manner that is inconsistent with the UK's Community obligations. If this principle is coupled with the doctrine of the implied repeal of Acts of Parliament, it is arguable that the European Communities Act 1972 would be vulnerable to change as a result of subsequent inconsistent enactments, regardless of whether a repudiation was intended or not. Upholding the sovereignty of Parliament thus comes into conflict with the loss of national sovereignty inherent in accession to the EU. This is expressed most clearly by the Court of Justice in Case 6/64 *Costa* v. *ENEL* (at p. 594):

'The transfer by the States from their domestic legal systems to the Community legal system of the rights and obligations arising under the Treaty carries with it a permanent limitation of their sovereign rights, against which a subsequent unilateral act incompatible with the concept of the Community cannot prevail.'

The transfer of sovereign powers thesis denies the effectiveness of unilateral repudiations of EU obligations. Such repudiations would be seen merely as violations of the Treaty system. In the absence of a negotiated return of the powers originally transferred, a state will not be released from its obligations under the Treaties. Such a position is also in conformity with the international law principle of *pacta sunt servanda*.

At the time of the accession of the UK to what was then the European Communities, a position emerged on the sovereignty of Parliament which contrasted somewhat with Diceyian absolutism. Authors such as Mitchell (Mitchell, Kuipers and Gall, 1972; Mitchell, 1979) argued that British constitutional history has always demonstrated a capacity for constitutional change, in recognition of changes in political circumstances. It is precisely out of political circumstances that a convention of Parliamentary sovereignty has arisen. Now that the UK has acceded to a political entity within which absolute Parliamentary sovereignty is no longer tenable, it must be regarded as abrogated, with legislative and judicial sovereignty passing to the European Community, within its spheres of competence. However, many British constitutional lawyers still adhere to the orthodox position that the binding effect of EU law in the UK flows only from the European Communities Act 1972, an Act which Parliament remains as free to repeal as any other Act, although for the time being it chooses not to (e.g. Munro, 1987).

Not surprisingly, the courts have for the most part declined to pass comment on theoretical conflicts between Parliamentary sovereignty and EU obligations. The essential problem is, of course, whether the UK judges now owe their allegiance to the EU authorities in respect of matters falling within the competence of those authorities, just as they undoubtedly owe allegiance to the Westminster Parliament in respect of matters falling within the jurisdiction of that body. According to Lord Denning MR in *Macarthys* v. *Smith* ([1979] 3 All ER 325 at p. 329):

'If the time should come when Parliament deliberately passes an Act with the intention of repudiating the Treaty or any provision of it or intentionally of acting inconsistently with it and says so in express terms then I should have thought it would be the duty of our courts to follow the statute of our Parliament. I do not envisage any such situation ... Unless there is such an intentional and express repudiation of the Treaty, it is our duty to give priority to the Treaty.'

For the most part, however, the judges have contented themselves with resolving, in generally satisfactory terms, the specific practical problems thrown up by the penetration of EU law into the UK legal system. For example, Craig (1998: 204) describes the judicial response in the litigation in *Factortame*, especially before the House of Lords (*R* v. *Secretary of State for Transport, ex parte Factortame (No. 2)* [1989] 2 All ER 692 and [1990] 3 CMLR 375) as being about the principled endeavour to work through the consequences of the UK's membership of the European Union. Some of these problems will be examined, using examples, in Chapter 13.

12.7   The Instrumentalisation of the Constitutional Qualities of EU Law

The next level of detailed analysis involves the four techniques developed by the Court of Justice for the purposes of giving effect to these two principal constitutional qualities. They have not all been accorded equal attention. By far the largest proportion of cases have been concerned with the question whether provisions of EU law can give rise to rights in national courts which individuals may rely upon, the conditions in which this can occur, the range of provisions which are so covered, and the duties which they cast. Pescatore described 'direct effect' as an 'infant disease' of EU law (Pescatore, 1983). The justiciability of provisions of EU law was an instrument devised at an early stage in the history of the EU legal order for maximising the effectiveness of EU law. Historically, it has proved most important in those Member States such as the Netherlands and the UK where, as a matter of national law, EU law appears capable of overriding national law only where it generates rights enforceable by individuals (see Chapter 13). Partly as a consequence of some of the tensions which have been thrown up by the Court's own case law on direct effect, it has increasingly emerged not as an isolated centrepiece of the EU law/national law interface, but as one of several techniques each deserving of separate and equal attention.

12.8   The Justiciability of EU Law in National Courts

The principle that provisions of EU law may be justiciable in national courts provided they satisfy certain conditions has been recognised since the landmark case of *Van Gend en Loos*. In that case, the Court held that an importer could rely upon the standstill clause in Article 12 EC, prohibiting any increases in customs duties between the Member States after the coming into force of the Treaty, in order to challenge such an increase by the Dutch authorities in the Dutch courts. The self-executing nature of Treaty provisions is a phenomenon not entirely unknown in international law generally (Jackson, 1992; Wyatt, 1982; de Witte, 1999b) and flows from the principle of direct applicability as enunciated in this chapter. The most powerful justification for the doctrine of direct effect, as it is known, is that it enhances the effectiveness or '*effet utile*' of binding norms of EU law. As a doctrine that principally protects the individual, and often gives individuals rights that they can rely upon as against Member States, it sets up a mechanism for the individual or indirect enforcement of EU law. In practical terms, this relies upon the operation of the preliminary rulings procedure examined in Chapter 11. The existence of a centralised enforcement procedure in the hands of the Commission under Article 226 EC has never been considered an argument for preventing the decentralised enforcement of EU law.

However, the doctrine of direct effect is not simply limited to the Member State/EU citizen interface. Although the principle that states should not be able to rely upon their own failure or inefficiency in implementing EU law in order to deny to individuals the rights and benefits which flow from EU provisions – the so-called 'estoppel argument' (Curtin, 1990) – is a powerful argument for direct effect, it is not the only one. The need to ensure the effectiveness of EU law in some circumstances applies to relations between private parties. In appropriate cases, EU law is also justiciable in disputes between individuals. In other words, certain provisions of EU law may be horizontally as well as vertically directly effective.

12.9 Prerequisites of Direct Effect

To be directly effective, a provision of EU law must constitute a complete legal obligation capable of enforcement as such by a court. This means that it must be sufficiently precise and unconditional (Cases C-6, 9/90 *Francovich* v. *Italian Republic (Francovich I)* [1991] ECR I-5357). In its early case law the Court appeared to limit direct effect to negative obligations, such as that contained in what was then Article 12 EEC (now Article 25 EC), which prohibited Member States from raising their customs duties or introducing any new customs duties after the coming into force of the Treaty. It was held in *Van Gend en Loos* (at p. 13) that:

'the wording of Article 12 contains a clear and unconditional prohibition which is not a positive but a negative obligation. This obligation, moreover, is not qualified by any reservation on the part of States which would make its implementation conditional upon a positive measure enacted under national law. The very nature of this prohibition makes it ideally adapted to produce direct effects in the legal relationship between Member States and their subjects.'

That limitation has since been dropped, and the Court has subsequently held that numerous provisions of the EC Treaty are capable of judicial enforcement, including Article 28 (prohibiting non-tariff barriers to interstate trade in goods erected by Member States), Article 39 (guaranteeing free movement of workers), Articles 43 and 49 (guaranteeing freedom of establishment and freedom to provide services), Articles 81 and 82 (prohibiting anti-competitive conduct by undertakings) and Article 90 (prohibiting taxation by the Member States which discriminates against imported products). Articles 81 and 82 provide a perfect example of Treaty provisions that are horizontally directly effective. The prohibitions on anti-competitive agreements and the abuse of a dominant position enacted in these provisions are by their very nature aimed at economically active individuals, defined as 'undertakings'. The obligations inherent in the provisions can be enforced against infringing undertakings, at the instance of other individuals injured by anti-competitive conduct, in national courts. Some provisions, such as Article 12 EC (the general prohibition on discrimination on grounds of nationality) are judicially enforceable in the main in combination with another provision of the Treaty. This is because the prohibition only applies in 'situations governed by Community law' (Case C-274/96 *Bickel and Franz* [1998] ECR I-7637). For example, Article 128 EEC, as it was drafted prior to the Treaty of Maastricht, established an outline competence on the part of the Community in relation to the creation of a Community vocational training policy. Article 128 read in conjunction with what was then Article 7 EEC created a right to non-discrimination on grounds of nationality for vocational training students who move to study in another Member State, at least as regards matters of educational access (Case 293/83 *Gravier* v. *City of Liège* [1985] ECR 593 – e.g. they cannot be charged fees when domestic students are not). Read in conjunction with Article 293 EC and the Brussels Judgments Convention, Article 12 has been applied to discriminatory provisions of national civil procedure law (Case 398/92 *Mund & Fester* v. *Firma Hatrex International Transport* [1994] ECR I-467).

Those Treaty provisions which have been held not to be capable of judicial enforcement are those which are worded in conditional or contingent terms. The pre-1994 formulation of the provisions on the free movement of capital provided a good example. For example, Article 71 EEC provided that:

> 'Member States shall endeavour to avoid introducing within the Community any new exchange restrictions on the movement of capital and current payments connected with such movements, and shall endeavour not to make existing rules more restrictive.'

In Case 203/80 *Casati* ([1981] ECR 2595 at p. 2616) the Court noted that:

'by using the term "shall endeavour", the wording of that provision departs noticeably from the more imperative forms of wording employed in other similar provisions concerning restrictions on the free movement of goods, persons and services. It is apparent from the wording that, in any event, the first paragraph of Article 71 does not impose on the Member States an unconditional obligation capable of being relied upon by individuals.'

Since 1 January 1994, this provision has been superseded by stricter obligations in relation to the free movement of capital (what are now Articles 56–60 EC), linked to the move towards Economic and Monetary Union. Even before that date, one of the key directives of the 1992 programme had largely given unconditional force to this aspect of the internal market (Directive 88/361). In two cases in 1995 concerned with exports of banknotes out of Spain, the Court held that the relevant provisions of both the Directive and the Treaty were capable of giving rise to rights which individuals may enforce in national courts (Cases C-358, 416/93 *Bordessa* [1995] ECR I-361; Cases C-163/94, etc. *Sanz de Lera* [1995] ECR I-4821).

Similarly there are certain provisions of the Treaty which grant a discretion to Member States which make it impossible to identify a specific obligation to which they are subject or a dispositive requirement imposed upon them. An example is Article 142 EC which states:

'Member States shall endeavour to maintain the existing equivalence between paid holiday schemes.'

12.10 Provisions of EU Law Capable of Judicial Enforcement

All provisions of EU law containing a binding obligation of conduct or of result are capable of direct judicial enforcement, providing they are sufficiently precise and unconditional. No category of legal acts is *a priori* excluded. Thus in addition to Treaty provisions, the Court has held that provisions of regulations (Case 43/71 *Politi* v. *Italian Minister of Finance* [1971] ECR 1039), directives (Case 41/74 *Van Duyn* v. *Home Office* [1974] ECR 1337), decisions (Case 9/70 *Grad* [1970] ECR 825), agreements with third countries (Case 104/81 *Kupferberg* [1982] ECR 3641), and decisions adopted by bodies set up under international agreements such as Association Councils which oversee the implementation of Association Agreements with third states (Case C-192/89 *Sevince* v. *Staatssecretaris van Justitie* [1990] ECR I-3461) are all capable of giving rise to rights which individuals can enforce in national courts.

However, in the category of international agreements, the Court has ascribed direct effect only to certain types of international agreements. The test for direct effect in the context of an international agreement is set out in Case 12/86 *Demirel* v. *Stadt Schwäbisch Gmund* ([1987] ECR 3719):

> 'A provision in an agreement concluded by the Community with non-member countries must be regarded as being directly applicable when, regard being had to its wording and the purpose and nature of the agreement itself, the provisions contains a clear and precise obligation which is not subject, in its implementation or effects, to the adoption of any subsequent measure.'

The Court has faced arguments that since it has held provisions of its 'own' international treaty (i.e. the EC Treaty) to be directly effective in the national courts, it ought, if it were being consistent, to be prepared to contemplate ascribing that characteristic to a wide range of provisions in other international agreements, so far as they are a binding part of EU law. In replying to those arguments the Court has consistently compared the objectives and scope of many such agreements (e.g. Association Agreements, Free Trade Agreements, as well as the GATT) to the EC Treaty itself, commenting that their nature and purpose is not to create a single market (e.g. Case 270/80 *Polydor Ltd and RSO Records* v. *Harlequin Record Shops* [1982] ECR 329). In particular, it refused to accept that the GATT in its old pre-WTO could have direct effect because of its flexibility in particular in relation to enforcement, even though it does 'bind the Community' (Cases 2-4/72 *International Fruit Company NV* v. *Produktschap voor Groenten en Fruit* [1972] ECR 1219; Cheyne, 1994). This has rendered the internal impact of GATT within the EU somewhat 'ineffectual' (Scott, 1995b: 149). There has been no explicit finding as yet in relation to the GATT 1994, and the other WTO arrangements, although the Council Decision concluding the WTO Agreements explicitly rules it out, stating that 'by its nature' the GATT/WTO 'is not susceptible to being directly invoked in Community or Member State Courts' (OJ 1994 L336/1). It is also implicit in Case C-149/96 *Portugal* v. *Council* (23 November 1999), although that case directly pertains to the use of the WTO agreements as the basis for reviewing the legality of EU measures in the Court of Justice (15.13).

In the case of regulations there was little doubt that they should be capable of enforcement in national courts, since they are expressed to be 'directly applicable', which, according to the Court in *Politi* (at p. 1048), means that:

> 'by reason of their nature and their function in the system of the sources of Community law, regulations have direct effect and are as such capable of creating individual rights which national courts must protect.'

Occasionally, however, regulations will not be capable of judicial enforcement, because of the nature of the obligations which they contain (e.g. they are too vague, or are contingent upon action by a third party). This point was recognised by AG Warner in Case 131/79 *R* v. *Secretary of State for Home Affairs, ex parte Santillo* ([1980] ECR 1585). An analogy can be drawn with Acts of Parliament in the UK, not all provisions of which are enforceable by the courts. For example, section 23 of the British Telecommunications Act 1981 expressly provides that no action in tort shall lie against British Telecom in respect of failure to provide or delay in providing a telecommunications services. If this line of argument is pursued it is clearly possible to maintain a conceptual distinction between direct applicability and direct effect, as suggested by Winter (1972) and as argued in this chapter, even though the terminology used by the Court has had a tendency to confuse the two concepts.

An extended controversy surrounding the direct effect of directives was finally resolved by the Court in *Van Duyn*. It had been argued that since directives contain obligations of result, and not of conduct (see 6.12), and since only regulations are expressed to be 'directly applicable' in Article 249 EC, they could not be capable of judicial enforcement. The Court refuted these arguments in the following terms (at p. 1348):

'If ... by virtue of the provisions of Article 189 regulations are directly applicable and, consequently, may by their very nature have direct effects, it does not follow from this that other categories of acts mentioned in that article can never have similar effects. It would be incompatible with the binding effect attributed to a directive by Article 189 to exclude, in principle, the possibility that the obligation which it imposes may be invoked by those concerned.'

The Court showed itself prepared, therefore, to overlook the fact that the binding obligation in a directive is principally an obligation to implement, not a substantive obligation. While that may originally have represented a slender foundation for arguing the direct effect of directives, it cannot be denied that subsequent developments have rendered this doctrinal shift irreversible. In *Van Duyn* the Court held that the applicant, who was threatened with exclusion from the UK on the grounds of her membership of the Church of Scientology – an organisation which attracted official disapproval in the UK, but was not actually proscribed – could rely upon the provisions of Directive 64/221 in order to claim certain procedural rights which limited the exercise of the UK's discretion to exclude Member State nationals on public policy grounds.

Consequently, as with other provisions of EU law, the question is one of construction, based on a test defined in Case 8/81 *Becker* v. *Finanzamt Münster-Innenstadt* ([1982] ECR 53) in the following terms:

'wherever the provisions of a directive appear, as far as their subject matter is concerned, to be unconditional and sufficiently precise, those provisions may, in the absence of implementing measures adopted within the prescribed period, be relied upon as against any national provision which is incompatible with the directive or in so far as the provisions define rights which individuals are able to assert against the state' (para. 25).

Applying this test, the fact that the directive gives a choice to Member States as between alternative methods of attaining a given result does not necessarily mean that the provisions in question are not capable of judicial enforcement. In Case C-271/91 *Marshall* v. *Southampton and South West Hampshire AHA (Marshall II)* ([1993] ECR I-4367), the Court was faced with a request for the interpretation of Article 6 of the Equal Treatment Directive (76/207), which guarantees an effective judicial remedy to those who suffer discrimination in the employment context. In an earlier case (Case 14/83 *Von Colson and Kamann* v. *Land Nordrhein Westfalen* [1984] ECR 1891; see 12.14), the Court had held that this provision was insufficiently precise to give rise to a specific obligation on Member States to choose a particular method of sanctioning discrimination (damages or (re)instatement by the employer). It had, however, held in Case 222/84 *Johnston* v. *Chief Constable of the Royal Ulster Constabulary* ([1986] ECR 1651) that this provision could be relied upon at least to the extent of giving rise to a right to a judicial remedy (in that case purportedly denied under the UK system by a ministerial certificate). Building on this conclusion, the Court held in *Marshall II* that once a state had chosen pecuniary compensation as the means by which it would instrumentalise this provision, it was then bound to provide an effective compensatory remedy (i.e. compensation matching the loss suffered, and not limited by law to some arbitrarily low amount). It had 'no discretion in applying the chosen solution' (para. 36). To reach this conclusion, the Court stretched the doctrine of direct effect, and combined it with the doctrine of effective remedies (13.4).

The time limit given for the implementation of a directive is, however, crucial. Before the time limit has expired, the provisions cannot be regarded as containing perfect legal obligations (Case 148/78 *Ratti* [1979] ECR 1629).

12.11 Horizontal and Vertical Direct Effect

Having held that directives can have direct effect, the Court was then faced with a subsidiary question of scope, namely whether directives could be horizontally directly effective. This matter was initially decided in Case 152/84 *Marshall* v. *Southampton and South West Hampshire AHA (Marshall I)* ([1986] ECR 723). The Court held (at p. 749):

'With regard to the argument that directives may not be relied upon against an individual, it must be emphasised that according to Article 189 of the EEC Treaty the binding nature of a directive, which constitutes the basis for the possibility of relying on the directive before a national court, exists only in relation to "each Member State to which it is addressed." It follows that a directive may not of itself impose obligations on an individual and that a provision of a directive may not be relied upon as such as against such a person.'

In relation to the direct effect of directives, therefore, it appears that the so-called 'estoppel' justification has prevailed. The objective sought by allowing individuals to rely upon directives is to deny to Member States the benefits that they might derive from their failure to implement directives. This being so, it would be inconsistent to allow horizontal as well as vertical enforcement. Since *Marshall I* never fully silenced those holding the opposing view (and taking a formalist view, the position taken by the Court was strictly *obiter dicta*, since the plaintiff in that case was relying on the Directive *vis-à-vis* a public authority), the Court took the precaution in a subsequent case of explicitly revisiting the issue. In deciding once more against the horizontal direct effect of directives in Case C-91/92 *Faccini Dori* ([1994] ECR I-3325), the Court stood out against the strongly held views of at least three of its own Advocates General (AG van Gerven in Case C-271/91 *Marshall II*; AG Jacobs in Case C-316/93 *Vaneetveld* v. *SA Le Foyer* [1994] ECR I-763; AG Lenz in *Faccini Dori*), and numerous academic commentators. However, it went with the views of the majority of Member States – whose opinions it had taken the precaution of canvassing in a series of questions submitted to national governments in *Faccini Dori*. The caution displayed by the Court in *Faccini Dori* is notable:

'The effect of extending [the case law on the direct effect of directives] to the sphere of relations between individuals would be to recognise a power in the Community to enact obligations for individuals with immediate effect, whereas it has competence to do so only where it is empowered to adopt regulations' (at p. 3356).

Consequently, the plaintiff in *Faccini Dori* could not take the benefit of Directive 85/577 on the protection of the consumer in respect of contracts negotiated away from the business premises. The plaintiff was approached in Milan railway station, and prevailed upon to purchase an English language correspondence course. She changed her mind about the purchase, and sought the right to cancel the contract within seven days, which is guaranteed by the Directive in such a case. However, at that point the Directive had not been implemented in Italian law, and there was no such right in Italian law. Nor, in the absence of the horizontal direct effect of directives, could Dori rely directly upon the Directive as against the seller (another private party). In basing its decision on a formalist distinction between directives and regulations, drawing on the wording of Article 249 EC, the Court now appeared to be distancing itself slightly from the 'estoppel' theory, which has been heavily criticised particularly as the Court has given an increasingly broad view of what can constitute 'the state' against which a directive may be relied upon (12.12). Regarding entities such as health authorities (as in *Marshall I*) as the state may be convincing at one level, but they cannot in any real sense be held responsible for a failure to implement the directive. But given that the Court has previously done much to undermine the validity of a formalist reading of Article 249, for example, by recognising the direct effect of directives, it seems odd that it should now retreat behind that same provision. Consequently, the Court's judgment in *Faccini Dori* has failed to convince all (e.g. Arnull, 1999a: 140). In the view of Tridimas:

> 'Where it comes to relations between individuals, the reason why directives should be able to produce horizontal effect is not that a Member State must not be allowed to derive an advantage from its own failure to implement Community law but that the effective protection of Community rights must be guaranteed unless overriding principles (for example, legal certainty, non-retroactive application of criminal laws) require otherwise' (Tridimas, 1994: 633).

12.12   The Notion of an 'Emanation of the State'

The effect of the restriction on the direct effect of directives is, of course, to create an important borderline which is not based upon the nature of the provision to be enforced, but upon the actual nature of the dispute between. the parties. In fields where EU law frequently takes the form of directives, and where it is aimed ultimately at altering the conduct of individuals as well as states (e.g. environmental law, labour law and social law) the potential for injustice is clear. For example, a public sector employee may rely upon the guarantee of equal treatment as regards sex in employment matters contained in the Equal Treatment Directive (76/207) in order to challenge alleged sex discrimination on the part of his or her employer, whereas a private sector employee may not. Injustices could also emerge as between the Member States given that the numbers and types of public sector jobs do vary greatly between the different states. Three mechanisms have consequently emerged which soften the harshness of this distinction. The first is concerned with the interpretation of the notion of the 'state' and constitutes a further extrapolation of the scope of direct effect; the latter two (indirect effect and state liability) go beyond the scope of direct effect, and reinforce the point made in 12.1, and by Figure 12.1, that direct effect is just one mechanism of several aimed at ensuring the effective enforcement of EU law. So, in *Faccini Dori*, the Court of Justice reminded the national court of the availability of the principle of interpretation or 'indirect effect' (12.14), and the principle of state liability for failure to implement a directive (12.17), as alternatives to relying on direct effect.

The Court has developed a broad interpretation of precisely what is this 'state' which is not allowed to benefit from its own wrong in failing to implement the directive. In *Marshall I* the Court held that the state includes the state as employer as well as the state as public authority. In Case C-188/89 *Foster v. British Gas plc* ([1990] ECR I-3313) the Court provided general guidance on the concept of the 'emanation of the state', holding that the definition of this concept is a matter of EU law, not national law. It is, none the less, for the national court to decide whether a given body falls within the criteria offered by the Court of Justice. *Foster* involved the question of whether certain women employees made redundant by (pre-privatisation) British Gas in circumstances in which they would not have been made redundant had they been men, could rely upon the Equal Treatment Directive as against their employer. The Court summarised the bodies previously held to be emanations of the State: tax authorities (Case 8/81 *Becker*); local or regional authorities (Case C-221/88 *ECSC v. Acciaierie e ferriere Busseni* ([1990] ECR I-495; see also Case 103/88 *Fratelli Costanzo v. Milano* [1989] ECR 1839); the police (Case 222/84 *Johnston v. Royal Ulster Constabulary*; and bodies responsible for state-funded health care (*Marshall I*). It then went on to say (at p. 3348) that:

> 'a body, whatever its legal form, which has been made responsible pursuant to a measure adopted by the State, for providing a public service under the control of the State and has for that purpose special powers beyond those which result from the normal rules applicable in relations between individuals is included in any event among the bodies against which the provisions of a directive capable of having direct effect may be relied upon.'

The categories of 'emanation of the state' are clearly, therefore, not yet closed. Moreover, on this interpretation it is not clear that a post-privatisation utility would necessarily be held not to be an emanation of the state if it retains sufficient special statutory powers. Since *Foster*, the Court has had occasion to treat an Italian university as an emanation of the state, but that leaves open the question as to how universities in other Member States which may be funded and organised along different lines should be treated (Case C-419/92 *Scholz v. Opera Universitaria di Cagliari* [1994] ECR I-505).

12.13　**The Effect of EU Law on National Law and National Legislative Competence**

Just as the 'penetrative' quality of EU law has direct and intrusive consequences for the national legal order in the form of the judicial enforceability of provisions of EU law in national courts, so its superiority as a source of law has an impact upon the validity of national law and the exercise of national legislative competence.

In Case 106/77 *Simmenthal II* the Court deduced from the principles established in Case 6/64 *Costa* v. *ENEL* that the supremacy of EU law logically must limit national law-making powers. It held ([1978] ECR 629 at p. 643):

> 'Furthermore, in accordance with the principle of the precedence of Community law, the relationship between provisions of the Treaty and directly applicable measures of the institutions on the one hand and national law of the Member States on the other is such that those provisions and measures not only by their entry into force render automatically inapplicable any conflicting provision of current national law but – in so far as they are an integral part of, and take precedence in, the legal order applicable in the territory of each of the Member States – also preclude the valid adoption of new national legislative measures to the extent to which they would be incompatible with Community provisions. Indeed any recognition that national legislative measures which encroach upon the field within which the Community exercises its legislative power or which are otherwise incompatible with the provisions of Community law had any legal effect would amount to a corresponding denial of the effectiveness of the obligations undertaken unconditionally and irrevocably by Member States pursuant to the Treaty and would thus imperil the very foundations of the Community.'

In practice, of course, these principles can be put into effect only by the domestic institutions themselves. The Court has no power to invalidate national legislation, although it may state in a preliminary ruling that national legislation of the type at issue in a given case is inconsistent with EU law, or make a declaration under Article 228 in proceedings brought under Articles 226 or 227 EC that a given provision of national law is incompatible with EU law. It elaborated upon the consequences of *Simmenthal II* for national courts in Cases 10-22/97 *Ministero delle Finanze* v. *IN.CO.GE'90* ([1998] ECR I-6307), making clear that the effects of that ruling are not that:

> 'incompatibility with Community law of a [measure adopted after the EU measure] has the effect of rendering that rule of national law non-existent. Faced with such a situation, the national court is, however,

obliged to disapply that rule, provided always that this obligation does not restrict the power of the competent national courts to apply from among the various procedures available under national law, those which are appropriate for the protecting the individual rights conferred by Community law (para. 21).

However, as C-213/89 *R* v. *Secretary of State for Transport, ex parte Factortame Ltd (Factortame I)* ([1990] ECR I-2433) makes clear, the coupling of these principles with the principle of effective national remedies may mean that national courts need to set aside a national rule – such as a procedural limitation upon their ability to award interim relief – in order to make an appropriate ruling (13.3).

As was noted in 6.4, there is a strong link between the effects of EU law and the nature of competence. The so-called pre-emptive effect of EU law is particularly apparent in those areas where EU legislature has exhaustively regulated the field, in particular using legislation in the form of regulations. This is so, in particular, under the rules governing the Common Agricultural Policy (CAP). In Case 16/83 *Prantl* ([1984] ECR 1299 at p. 1324) the Court stated that:

> 'once rules on the common organisation of the market [in wine] may be regarded as forming a complete system, the Member States no longer have competence in that field unless Community law expressly provides otherwise.'

However, in areas of 'shared competence' the position is not always so clear-cut (Weatherill, 1994). It depends upon the Court's interpretation of the type of EU measures – such as harmonisation directives – which have been adopted. One example of the loss of national regulatory competence is offered by Case 60/86 *Commission* v. *UK (Dim-dip headlights)* ([1988] ECR 3921) which was concerned with whether the UK could validly require motor vehicles sold in the UK to be fitted with 'dim dip' devices for their headlights. In view of the effect of the relevant Directive which contained an exhaustive list of permissible lighting devices, the Court concluded that the UK:

> 'cannot unilaterally require manufacturers who have complied with the harmonised technical requirements ... to comply with a requirement which is not imposed by that directive' (at p. 3935).

In sharp contrast, in Case C-479/93 *Francovich* v. *Italian Republic (Francovich II)* ([1995] ECR I-3843) the Court reached quite a different conclusion about the effect of the Insolvency Directive. It concluded that the Directive in question constituted only a partial harmonisation of the issues raised by the protection of the employee in the event of the insolvency of the employer. It found in this instance that previously existing differences in national insolvency regimes – which had the result of making any protection offered by the directive exceedingly uneven in coverage – were not affected by the provisions of the Directive. Ironically, therefore, this would seem to rule out the possibility that the applicant Francovich – to whose endeavours in the courts we owe the doctrine of state liability for failure to implement a directive (12.17) – of receiving compensation precisely because of the effect of Italian insolvency law is to place his employer in a category of insolvency which does not fall within the scope of Article 2(1) of the Directive (proceedings 'to satisfy collectively the claims of creditors'). No principle of direct effect, indirect effect or state liability will assist an applicant whose situation is ultimately regulated by national law.

12.14　**The Development of the Interpretative Obligation**

The second way in which the Court has sought to alleviate the consequences of the limitation it has placed upon the direct effect of directives has been through its promotion of the principle of construction which requires national courts, in conformity with their duty under Article 10 EC to give full effect to EU law, to interpret all national law in the light of relevant EU law, regardless of whether it has direct effect. Although this principle of construction is sometimes called *Von Colson* effect, following the case in which it was first discussed (Case 14/83 *Von Colson and Kamann* v. *Land Nordrhein Westfalen*; see 12.10), it is now more generally termed 'indirect effect' (Fitzpatrick, 1989) (and occasionally the 'duty of sympathetic interpretation' or the doctrine of 'substantive effectiveness' (Meads, 1991)).

It flows in general terms from the duty on Member States to enforce EU law, inherent in the constitutional principles articulated at the beginning of this chapter, and clearly stated in Cases 314/81, etc. *Procureur de la République* v. *Waterkeyn* ([1982] ECR 4337 at p. 4360) that:

> 'all the institutions of the Member States concerned must … ensure within the fields covered by their respective powers, that judgments of the Court are complied with.'

For example, contravention of national legislation which breaches EU law may not be prosecuted by the domestic authorities as a criminal offence (Case 269/80 *R* v. *Tymen* [1981] ECR 3079). Conversely, Member States have a duty to prosecute breaches of EU law using national criminal legislation as diligently as they would in purely domestic circumstances (Case 68/88 *Commission* v. *Greece* [1989] ECR 2965). This duty also comprises the duty on national courts to interpret national law in the light of EU law and the duties on national courts to give effective remedies in respect of breaches of EU law.

The duty on the national court to apply the law in such a way as to facilitate the achievement of the EU's objectives flows directly from the penetration of EU law into the national legal system, and is expressed most clearly in Article 10 EC. It is not limited to giving effect to EU rules that are judicially enforceable as such, but also extends to the development of a range of interpretative devices that derive their force from EU law. In other words, EU law does not have to be directly effective in order for it to benefit from the general doctrine of supremacy.

In *Von Colson*, where the doctrine first emerged, the Court found itself unable to hold that a particular provision of the Equal Treatment Directive was sufficiently precise and unconditional to support the implication alleged by the plaintiff (12.10). It none the less held that (at p. 1909):

> 'the Member States' obligation arising from a directive to achieve the result envisaged by the directive and their duty under Article 10 of the Treaty to take all appropriate measures, whether general or particular, to ensure the fulfilment of that obligation, is binding on all the authorities of Member States including, for matters within their jurisdiction, the courts. It follows that, in applying the national law specifically introduced in order to implement Directive No. 76/207, national courts are required to interpret their national law in the light of the wording and purpose of the directive in order to achieve the result referred to in the third paragraph of Article 189.'

The Court held that Article 6 of the Equal Treatment Directive, which guarantees the victims of sex discrimination in employment matters the right to a judicial remedy, is not sufficiently precise to support the implication that a particular sanction (in that case the obligation on the discriminating employer to conclude a contract of employment with the victim) must be applied by the national court. In general terms, however, it does include the right to a sufficient remedy, which constitutes an adequate deterrent against future acts of discrimination. It is in the light of this general interpretation that the national court was required to interpret the German Equal Treatment Act, passed to implement the Directive.

Von Colson left two matters undecided. First, it was not clear what categories of national law had to be interpreted in the light of EU law. *Von Colson* itself contained an ambiguity, with the Court appearing to refer at some points (such as the paragraph cited) only to national legislation specifically introduced to implement an EU obligation, but at other points to cast the net wider to include potentially all national law. On this point of doubt, the Court repeated, but had no need to apply, the wider formula in Case 222/84 *Johnston* v. *Chief Constable of the Royal Ulster Constabulary*. The same formula also found strong words of support from AG van Gerven in Case C-262/88 *Barber* v. *Guardian Royal Exchange* ([1990] ECR I-1889).

The second uncertainty concerned the scope of the rule of construction: how far, precisely, were national courts required to go in order to ensure conformity between national law and EU law? Was there in truth any difference between giving effect to EU law through the direct effect doctrine, which would mean where necessary overriding conflicting national legislation (12.13), and construing it in conformity with EU law (including, if necessary, reading words into a statute or reconstructing the intention of the legislature)? If not, that would appear to reduce greatly the consequences of the rules on the justiciability of EU law.

Both difficulties appeared to have been resolved by the Court in favour of the widest possible ambit of the indirect effect principle. In Case C-106/89 *Marleasing SA* v. *La Comercial Internacional de Alimentación* ([1990] ECR I-4135) the Court repeated its formulation from *Von Colson* on the responsibilities of national courts, going on to say (at p. 4159) that:

> 'in applying national law, whether the provisions in question were adopted before or after the directive, the national court called upon to interpret it is required to do so, as far as possible, in the light of the wording and the purpose of the directive in order to achieve the result pursued by the latter and thereby comply with the third paragraph of [Article 249 EC].'

There seemed to be no limitation in this judgment that the national provisions subject to interpretation in the light of EU law should be those intended or deemed to implement EU law. Potentially, therefore, UK courts could be required to reconsider the rules of the common law in the light of EU obligations. Second, courts must seek 'as far as possible' to achieve a resolution of EU law and national law. Does this mean that national courts must depart from national canons of construction when performing their interpretative duties under Article 10? Must UK courts abandon their preference for the literal rule of statutory interpretation and their adherence to the convention of *stare decisis* when applying EU law? Certainly, the methods of interpretation used by national courts must match those preferred by the Court of Justice, looking for the purpose of a measure, and going beyond its literal meaning (Millett, 1989; Kutscher, 1976). Overall, it must be possible to discern a difference in practice between the obligation to achieve conformity 'as far as possible' with a directive, and the approach of the Court in *Simmenthal II* to a regulation which required the national court to do all that was 'necessary' to achieve enforcement of EU law, including the disapplication of national law.

The Court of Justice has made it clear since *Marleasing* that there are clear limits to the interpretative obligation on national courts. In *Marleasing*, the Court itself reached the conclusion that the Spanish court in question was precluded from interpreting national law other than in a way that achieved conformity with the company law Directive at issue. In Case 334/92 *Wagner Miret* v. *Fondo de Garantía Salarial* ([1993] ECR I-6911), it reached the opposite conclusion, this time in relation to the interpretation of Directive 80/987 on the protection of employees in the event of the insolvency of their employer. The Court found that the terms of the Spanish provisions intended to implement that Directive were not in conformity, as they excluded company directors from making a claim for unpaid salary against the guarantee fund set up to protect employees. Although the Court explicitly recognised the existence of the indirect effect principle, stating that it was particularly relevant to the situation where a Member State deemed its pre-existing legislation to be an adequate implementation for a subsequent directive, it acknowledged and accepted the conclusion of the national court that an interpretation in conformity with the Directive, as interpreted, could not here be achieved by applying the interpretative obligation – an apparent change from formulation used in *Marleasing* (Bettlem, 1995: 17–18). Instead of insisting on the national court's duty to achieve a 'conforming interpretation', the Court instead reminded the court of the possibility of applying the state liability principle, introduced in Cases 6, 9/90 *Francovich I*, which had concerned Italy's failure to implement the same Directive. In the view of Tridimas (1994: 533), in *Wagner Miret* the Court revealed the weakness of the indirect effect principle.

12.15 The Scope of the Indirect Effect Principle

The interpretative duties of national courts apply also in relation to certain non-binding measures of EU law. In Case C-322/88 *Grimaldi* v. *Fonds des Maladies Professionnelles* ([1989] ECR I-4407) the Court applied the indirect effect principle to the Commission Recommendations on the adoption of a European schedule of occupational diseases and on the conditions for granting compensation to persons suffering from occupational diseases. Such (non-binding) Recommendations had to be taken into consideration by a national court in order to enable it to decide disputes, in particular where they are capable of clarifying other provisions of national or EU law.

However, the application of the indirect effect principle by national courts is limited by reference to other general principles of the EU legal order, such as the prohibition on retroactivity and the principle of legal certainty. This point is made by AG van Gerven in *Marleasing* and is illustrated by the judgment of the Court in Case 80/86 *Kolpinghuis Nijmegen* ([1987] ECR 3969) where the use of the principle of indirect effect would have come into conflict with the principle of *nulla poena sine lege*. A national judicial authority could not rely upon an unimplemented directive in order to 'sharpen' existing domestic sanctions on the marketing of unfit goods. The Court stated (at p. 3986):

> 'A directive cannot, of itself and independently of a national law adopted by a Member State for its implementation, have the effect of determining or aggravating the liability of persons who act in contravention of the provisions of that directive.'

In other words, the state could not in such circumstances benefit from the operation of the principle of indirect effect. *Kolpinghuis* was applied in Case C-168/95 *Arcaro* ([1996] ECR I-4705), a case involving an alleged breach by an Italian trader of national rules on industrial discharges of dangerous substances into the aquatic environment from his plant. The difficulty arose because it was unclear whether or not the Italian rules covered Arcaro's plant, but they should have done if the relevant EU directive had been properly implemented. To reinforce the point in *Kolpinghuis* the Court held that the interpretative obligation on the national court:

> 'to refer to the content of the directive when interpreting the relevant rules of its own national law reaches its limit where such an interpretation leads to the imposition on an individual of an obligation laid down by a directive which has not been transposed' (para. 42).

This seems consistent with applying direct effect and indirect effect coherently together, because the alternative scenario of interpreting the national legislation in the light of the directive would be, in fact, to impose an obligation upon an individual in the absence of implementation. It seems unconscionable to allow the Member State, in those circumstances, to benefit from the interpretative obligation on the national court, having failed to implement the directive (Arnull, 1999a: 132).

12.16　Direct Effect and the Effects of Directives not Applied by the State

It will be recalled from 12.1 that four techniques were identified having been developed by the Court of Justice to ensure that EU law is effectively and uniformly enforced in national courts, in the context of providing protection for individual rights. A line of case law is emerging which may amount to the development of a fifth distinctive technique of enforcement which focuses on wider public interests in the effective enforcement of EU law beyond the 'rights' of the party seeking to rely upon the directive (Hilson and Downes,

1999). It has been suggested that it is a widening of direct effect shading effectively into the horizontal direct effect (Craig and de Búrca, 1998: 206), or a form of 'incidental effect' (e.g. Arnull, 1999a: 140).

In Case C-194/94 *CIA Security* v. *Signalson and Securitel* ([1996] ECR I-2201), the proceedings before the national court involved a claim by the plaintiff that the defendants had libelled it by claiming that it had marketed an alarm system which did not comply with Belgian legislation on security systems. The plaintiff conceded that it had not sought approval of the alarm system, but based its case on an argument that the Belgian legislation was contrary to EU law and had not been notified to the Commission in breach of Directive 83/189 (8.1). Asked whether the Belgian legislation should have been notified to the Commission, whether the provisions of the Directive were sufficiently precise and unconditional to have direct effect, and whether a national court should refuse to apply a national technical regulation not notified to the Commission, the Court gave a positive answer to each of these questions. It concluded that the provisions of the Directive satisfied the 'precise and unconditional' test and that the effect of applying it would be to conclude that the breach of the obligation to notify amounted to a procedural defect rendering the technical regulations inapplicable and unenforceable against individuals. That much is, in a sense, an incontestable consequence of the supremacy of EU law. It is the applicability of these principles in a case involving two private parties which is the novelty. Yet while the plaintiff was able to benefit from the Belgian state's failure in relation to the Directive, it would not be wholly true to say that the defendants were required to carry a burden under the Directive which they would not otherwise have done. They were required to stop certain trading practices which they had previously been using. This situation is very different to the one in Case C-91/92 *Faccini Dori*, involving unimplemented EU legislation aimed at harmonising national law. Directive 83/169 is a very different type of EU legislative intrusion into the regulatory lives of the Member States, and in any event its primary objective is not to create new rights or duties for individuals once implemented, but to improve the effective enforcement of the free movement rules and the development and management of the single market. Coincidentally, the Commission is seeking to replace or complement this Directive with a regulation, in which case such questions would not arise in relation to its effects *vis-à-vis* national law (8.1). In no circumstances could it be envisaged that the consumer protection directive invoked by the plaintiff in *Faccini Dori* could be replaced by a regulation.

Arnull (1999a: 142) distinguishes *CIA* from *Faccini Dori* by pointing out the positive steps which the state had taken by adopting legislation which did not comply with the procedural conditions laid down in the Directive. The effect of the Court's decision was to prevent the defendants from relying upon that measure, which he views as an incidental effect upon individuals which would not have arisen in a 'simple' case of the Member State failing to implement a directive. Hilson and Downes (1999) in turn highlight the 'public law' element of this (and similar cases where the Court has applied parallel reasoning such as Case C-441/93 *Pafitis* v. *TKE* ([1996] ECR I-1347), another explanation which coincides with the need to highlight the very different regulatory frameworks of *CIA* and *Faccini Dori*.

12.17   The Responsibility of the State in Respect of Breaches of EU Law

The possibility of the responsibility of the State in respect of breaches of EU law giving rise to a compensatory obligation has long been envisaged, but for many years the issues were not taken forward by the Court of Justice. For example, in Case 199/82 *Amministrazione delle Finanze dello Stato* v. *San Giorgio* ([1983] ECR 3595), the Court held, as a matter of EU law, that unlawfully levied charges and taxes must be reimbursed to aggrieved importers and exporters, subject to principles of national procedural autonomy, non-discrimination and effective remedies (Figure 12.1). Furthermore, in Case 60/75 *Russo* v. *AIMA* ([1976] ECR 45 at p. 56) the Court held that:

> 'if ... damage has been caused through an infringement of Community law the state is liable to the injured party of the consequences in the context of the provisions of national law on the liability of the state.'

Since Cases C-6, 9/90 *Francovich I*, the possibilities raised by this principle have come under detailed scrutiny. The claims in *Francovich I* were brought by workers in Italy made redundant when their employers became insolvent, who received no compensation or redundancy payments. No funds were available from the employers themselves, and Italy had failed to implement Directive 80/987 which requires Member States to set up guarantee funds to cover the compensation claims of employees made redundant in the event of their employers' insolvency. The employees claimed that the Italian State was responsible for payment of the compensation, either by virtue of the direct effect of the Directive, or on grounds of liability for a failure to act.

Having considered the provisions of Directive 80/987, the Court reached the conclusion that those provisions concerned with the creation of a minimum guarantee were not sufficiently precise in themselves to support a claim for the lost wages against the Italian State. In particular, the failure to implement the Directive meant that the state had not chosen what form the guarantee would take, and how it would be funded. The argument that the relevant provisions of the Directive were directly effective therefore failed since the Directive gave a discretion in the implementation process to the Member States. The only remaining remedy, therefore, was a right to damages for non-implementation.

In its judgment the Court offered two alternative bases for the right to damages. First it returned to basics in deriving the right to damages from the specific nature of EU law, its justiciability and superior nature, going on to hold:

> 'that the full effectiveness of Community rules would be impaired and the protection of the rights which they grant would be weakened if individuals were unable to obtain compensation when their rights are infringed by a breach of Community law for which a Member State can be held responsible' (p. 5414).

This repeats, in similar terms, the position already reached in *Russo*, and highlights the availability of damages for breach of a substantive EU obligation by a Member State. It then continued:

> 'The possibility of obtaining redress from the Member State is particularly indispensable where, as in this case, the full effectiveness of Community rules is subject to prior action on the part of the State and, consequently, in the absence of such action, individuals cannot enforce before the national courts the rights conferred upon them by Community law' (p. 5414).

The alternative basis for the damages obligation given by the Court is Article 10 EC, and in that context the Court drew support from an early ECSC case concerned with an analogous provision of that Treaty (Case 6/60 *Humblet* v. *Belgium* [1960] ECR 559).

The Court was equally brief on the subject of the conditions for state liability: the right to damages was subjected to a test based on the nature of the provisions, which was similar, but not identical, to the test applied to determine the direct effect of a provision. Three conditions must be satisfied: the result prescribed by the provision must involve the conferring of rights on individuals; the content of the rights must be capable of definition on the basis of the directive; and there must be a causal link between the violation of the Treaty obligation by the Member States and the loss suffered by the individual. In applying these conditions the national court is bound to apply national procedural rules which are no less favourable than those governing similar actions. The provisions of Directive 80/987 would appear to satisfy these tests, since the beneficiary of the rights and the nature of the rights were defined; the Directive failed only to define the subject of the obligation, namely the precise nature of the guarantee fund.

The *Francovich* or 'state liability' action quickly received a warm welcome from most observers of the Court's case law (e.g. Steiner, 1993; Curtin, 1992). It presents numerous advantages. It avoids the need to make the provisions of the directive themselves justiciable before the national courts using direct effect, or to achieve an uncomfortable resolution between irreconcilable provisions of EU law and national law through strained constructions under the doctrine of indirect effect. It also avoids the possibility that either increasingly marginal 'emanations of the state' (through the *Foster* doctrine) or even private parties (through the medium of indirect effect) will be asked to carry the principal burden of giving effect to the substantive rights for individuals contained in directives. Instead it concentrates on what has always been the primary obligation of the Member State under a directive, namely the obligation to implement, and attaches a rigorous sanction to failure to fulfil that obligation. It is arguable that this mechanism may be a much more effective way of securing compliance on the part of Member States in the implementation of EU law than either direct effect or indirect effect. Certainly it represents a very neat coupling of the principle of 'responsibility' conceived of as one way of instrumentalising the constitutional qualities of EU law, and the principle of 'effective national remedies'.

On the other hand, just as quickly new questions were raised (e.g. Bebr, 1992; Ross, 1993; Craig, 1993), both about the basis of the action itself and about its practical instrumentalisation in the national legal orders. The Court of Justice had simply given insufficient detail in *Francovich I* itself, and it was inevitable that further references would follow. Four questions have preoccupied commentators in particular:

– What are the limits of the state liability principle? What provisions of EU law does it apply to? Can the principle of responsibility extend to subjects of EU law other than states?
– What, if any, should be the relationship between the state liability imposed on the Member States and any similar 'non-contractual' liability falling upon the EU itself by virtue of the principles contained in Article 288 EC (Chapter 17)?
– Following that question, it is pertinent to enquire what standard of liability should be imposed; should it be the same standard of liability which governs the liability of the EU institutions under Article 288 EC?
– Finally, the principal difficulty with the *Francovich* action would appear to be that it drives a coach and horses through the formulations of national procedural autonomy which govern the impact of EU law on national law at the third level of analysis identified in Figure 12.1. A number of Member States simply do not recognise actions against the state for loss caused by legislative action or inaction; it is difficult, therefore, to imagine how analogies can be drawn between the *Francovich* action and the national procedural rules governing non-existent similar actions. The national courts may be required to invent *de novo* a cause of action against the state.

Moreover, the welcome was not universal, with the judgment in *Francovich I* attracting the label of being over-activist from some of the Court's more 'conservative' critics. Sir Patrick Neill described it as being 'novel', and a surprising conclusion for the Court to reach that there was indeed an EU law principle of state liability, since it had previously argued for such a principle to be included in the Treaties by means of formal amendment (Neill, 1995: 230). Hartley described the legal reasoning in *Francovich I* as 'not impressive' (Hartley, 1999: 60). Coming from a different direction, Harlow (1996) finds the theoretical underpinnings of state liability within the EU legal order to be weak, and the dangers which it raises for the EU's system of liability to be serious, bearing in mind the interaction with the national legal orders.

12.18 The Clarification of Francovich I

The expected clarification came in March 1996 in two judgments (Cases 46, 48/93 *Brasserie du Pêcheur* v. *Germany, R* v. *Secretary of State for Transport, ex parte Factortame Ltd (Factortame III)* [1996] ECR I-1029 and Case C-392/93 *R* v. *HM Treasury, ex parte British Telecom* [1996] ECR I-1631). In *Brasserie du Pêcheur/Factortame III*, the Court dealt with two separate references which it had put together for the sake of convenience. The first case was brought by a French brewery which claimed damages for loss of profits for the period 1981–87 from the German authorities, allegedly caused by the German authorities' unlawful failure to revise the Beer Purity laws which were held by the Court in 1987 to constitute a restriction on the free movement of goods, contrary to what is now Article 28 EC (Case 178/84 *Commission* v. *Germany* [1987] ECR 1227) (i.e. an omission on the part of the German legislature). During the period covered by the claim it had been forced to discontinue exports of beer to Germany. The second case was the continuation of the litigation brought about by the adoption by the UK of the Merchant Shipping Act 1988, which prevented a number of Spanish fishing boats from fishing out of the UK until a new registration system was introduced which no longer restricted Spanish-owned vessels (see 8.17, 12.13, 13.3) (i.e. an act of the UK legislature). The applicants now claimed damages from the UK government in respect of the documented breach of what is now Article 43 EC (right of establishment).

The Court began by clarifying the scope of the principle of state liability and delimiting its relationship to direct effect. It firmly claimed jurisdiction over the right to create through judicial action a right to reparation, in the absence of express Treaty or legislative provisions, reiterating that the right of reparation is 'inherent in the system of the Treaty' (para. 31). It also rejected an argument that state liability can only occur in circumstances where the relevant EC provisions are not directly effective. In other words, it is not a residual, but a complementary, technique of protection:

'The Court has consistently held that the right of individuals to rely on the directly effective provisions of the Treaty before national courts is only a minimum guarantee and is not sufficient in itself to ensure the full and complete implementation of the Treaty. The purpose of that right is to ensure that provisions of Community law prevail over national provisions. It cannot, in every sense, secure for individuals the benefit of the rights conferred on them by Community law and, in particular, avoid their sustaining damage as a result of breach of Community law attributable to a Member State ... [T]he full effectiveness of Community law would be impaired if individuals were unable to obtain redress when their rights were infringed by a breach of Community law' (para. 20).

It then concluded that state liability could attach not only to a failure to transpose a directive, as in *Francovich I*, but also to a breach by a Member State – by action or inaction – of:

'a right directly conferred by a Community provision upon which individuals are entitled to rely before the national courts. In that event, the right to reparation is the necessary corollary of the direct effect of the Community provision whose breach caused the damage sustained' (para. 22).

In these cases, that meant two EC Treaty provisions – Article 28 and Article 43. State liability can attach to any organ of the state, and no exclusion can be claimed on the basis of domestic rules as the division of powers between constitutional authorities. In particular, the Court stressed that national legislatures are responsible under the state liability principle.

It then went on to address the circumstances in which national legislatures could be liable for acts or omissions in breach of EU law, here drawing heavily upon its own case law on the 'non-contractual' liability of the EU legislature governed by Article 288 EC. In that context, the Court went on to reformulate and slightly revise the three conditions for liability set out in *Francovich I*, bearing in mind that the circumstances of the two cases were rather different to that case, and did not involve the tightly constrained duty of implementation which Articles 10 and 249 EC impose on Member States in respect of directives, but broader questions of legislative policy and discretion. We shall discuss these aspects of the judgment in 13.6 as they concern primarily the interaction of the EU and national legal orders within the framework of the effective national remedies principle, and the extent to which EU law fetters national procedural autonomy. Similarly, in Case C-392/93 *R* v. *HM Treasury, ex parte British Telecom*, the Court of Justice provided a small reformulation of the conditions of liability in respect of the implementation of directives (here a 'mis-implementation' of a public procurement directive by the UK government), in the light of the detailed discussion of *Francovich I*, in *Brasserie du Pêcheur/Factortame III*.

The judgment in *Brasserie du Pêcheur/Factortame III* concluded with a refusal by the Court to impose a temporal limitation upon its effects, despite a request from the German government. The Court pointed out that the principle of legal certainty, which underlies the possibility of imposing a temporal limitation, would be built in to the national substantive and procedural conditions which would govern the precise availability of damages in cases like *Brasserie du Pêcheur/Factortame III*. Hence, there was no need for a temporal limitation. In *Francovich I*, it had likewise ignored without comment the plea of AG Mischo for a temporal limitation in the event that it decided in favour of a principle of state liability.

State liability engages 'the state'. It should normally follow that as with the scope of enforcement actions under Article 226 EC, no public authority would automatically be exempted from coverage including judicial authorities (8.4). However, such a decision by a national court would undoubtedly be of considerable sensitivity, and the Court of Justice is likewise rather likely to shy away from such a determination (but cf. Toner, 1997).

One question of principle remains unresolved, and that is whether the notion of 'responsibility' identified in this chapter as one of four principal means for giving effect is limited to 'state liability', or whether it extends in appropriate cases to cover individuals as well, where they are directly subject to duties imposed by EU law. This arises particularly – but not solely – in relation to the application of Articles 81 and 82 EC. The Court of Justice has never had occasion to determine whether or not there exists a right to damages for aggrieved individuals harmed by private action in breach of those provisions, as a matter of EU law. Clearly such an action may exist at national law, as one of a range of sanctions made available to give effect to the direct effect of those provisions. However, there is an arguable case – made out in detail by AG van Gerven in his opinion in Case C-238/92 *Banks & Co. Ltd.* v. *British Coal Corporation* ([1994] ECR I-1209), and extra-judicially in van Gerven (1994b) – for an EC right to damages in appropriate cases, subject to the procedural conditions of national law (see Shaw, 1995: 138–145). In the event, the Court of Justice did not find it necessary to consider this question, as it concluded that the relevant competition law provision (Article 65 ECSC) was not capable of giving rise to rights which national courts must enforce, in the absence of a Commission decision finding an infringement. In this respect the ECSC Treaty differs sharply from the EC Treaty. Since the only means by which EU law can impose duties on individuals (as opposed to the State which is bound by the general provisions of the Treaty, including Article 10) is through the medium of direct effect, it seems difficult to argue with the conclusion that direct effect must be a prerequisite of 'individual responsibility', in contradistinction to state liability. Given that in a number of circumstances individuals can rely directly upon EC Treaty provisions which guarantee their right to free movement, notably Article 39 EC, and that these provisions cover also certain types of restrictions imposed by individuals, actions against individuals for damages for breach of EU law may not be too long following upon the heels of the state liability case law. It was said, after his successful action under Article 39 EC that this would be the approach taken against the football authorities by Jean-Marc Bosman, the Belgian footballer who has revolutionised the transfer system in Europe (Case C-415/93 *Union Royale belge des Sociétés de football association ASBL* v. *Bosman* ([1995] ECR I-4921). However, nothing has yet transpired before the Court of Justice to raise this issue.

Summary

1   The impact of the EU legal order on the national legal orders is mediated principally through three main policy objectives of the Court of Justice:
    – ensuring the effectiveness of EU law;
    – ensuring the uniformity of EU law;
    – ensuring the legal protection of individuals as legal subjects.

2   These policy objectives, and the implications for the national legal orders, were made clear by the Court of Justice in a number of early pronouncements about the nature of the future EU legal order.

3   EU law has two principal constitutional qualities:
    – it is a superior source of law;
    – it penetrates into the national legal orders.
    – it bases these on a thesis of the transfer of sovereign powers by the Member States to the EU, on accession.

4   Four main techniques are available for the ensuring that these constitutional qualities are given effect to by national courts:
    – direct effect;
    – the 'pre-emptive' qualities of EU law;
    – indirect effect or the 'interpretative obligation';
    – the responsibility of the Member States in respect of violations of EU law 'state liability'.

5   These developments have occurred not as a result solely of unilateral action by the Court of Justice, but through a continuing constitutional dialogue between the EU and national legal orders, at the constitutional level.

6   There are particular theoretical difficulties with reconciling membership of the EU with a strict view of the sovereignty of the Westminster Parliament, but for the most part the European Communities Act 1972 offers the UK courts the means whereby they can resolve any practical difficulties that arise.

7   The justiciability, or direct effect, of EU law in national courts is well established, and depends on a construction of the individual provision at issue. Provisions of EU law which are sufficiently precise and unconditional may

be enforced in national courts at the instance of individuals to whom they grant rights. Directives are not capable of giving rise to horizontal direct effect, and so do not bind individuals.

8   As EU law prevails over all national law, including national constitutions, it also limits the law-making powers of the Member States and imposes duties to enforce EU law on the authorities of the Member States, including the courts.

9   The interpretative duties of national courts in relation to EU law are extensive, and extend to interpreting all national law in the light of the text and spirit of relevant EU law, and to do everything possible to achieve a resolution of the two.

10 There is no interpretative obligation on national courts to interpret national law in the light of an unimplemented directive where a Member State seeks to rely upon it. Where a Member State adopts a national measure in violation of the procedural requirements laid down by a directive, that measure may be unenforceable in national courts.

11 The principle of state liability for breaches of EU law is still evolving. Since *Francovich I* and *Brasserie du Pêcheur/Factortame III*, the principle now seems firmly established, although some details of its application remain to be worked out. It rests partly on Article 10 EC, and partly on the notion that the responsibility of the Member States is 'inherent' to the system of the Treaty.

Questions

1   In what ways do the statements of principle by the Court of Justice in *Van Gend en Loos* and *Costa* v. *ENEL* define the fundamental relationship between EU law and national law?

2   Why is it important to distinguish the different levels at which EU law and national law interact?

3   Do you agree with the argument that the relationship between EU law and national law is based on a dialogue, rather than on the unilateral statements of the Court of Justice?

4   How can the right of individuals to rely upon potentially any provisions of EU law which can give rise to justiciable rights in national courts be justified?

5   Why might direct effect be said to be an 'infant disease' of the EU? What other mechanisms exist to give effect to the constitutional qualities of EU law?

6   Why is indirect effect a difficult principle for national courts to give effect to?

7   What advantages and disadvantages are offered by the principle of state liability?

8   In 2.1 it was suggested that there was often a time lag between significant developments in the political arena led by the Member States, and the achievement of comparably important legal goals. Assess this assertion,

by reference to the historical surveys in Chapters 2 and 3 and the pattern of judicial development of the EU legal order which emerges in this chapter.

Workshop (for Chapters 12 and 13)

In July 1997, the Council of Ministers adopted (fictitious) Directive 93/8000 requiring Member States to introduce a principle of strict liability for personal injury and property damage on the part of occupiers for the escape of toxic substances from their premises. It also requires Member States to establish a guarantee fund out of which compensation is to be paid to victims of accidents resulting from the escape of toxic substances where the occupier is unable, because of inadequate insurance, to satisfy a judgment debt. The Directive does not determine the details of the operation and funding of the guarantee fund. Finally, it requires Member States to establish the framework for training programmes on safety matters to be delivered to employees working with toxic substances. Directive 97/8000 was to be implemented by 31 December 1999.

Consider the following sets of circumstances:

1 The UK has not implemented the directive by the due date. On 2 January 2000, Anna is injured by the escape of a toxic chemical from a Government Research Institute situated near to her house. Discuss the nature of her claim for damages under EU law.

   Would your answer be any different if the toxic chemical escaped from (a) a University or (b) a pharmaceutical company?

2 The UK believes that the directive is fully implemented by the existing (fictitious) Toxic Substances (Occupiers Liability) Act 1970, under which occupiers are subject to a reversal of the burden of proof requiring them to prove that any escapes of toxic substances from their premises are not the result of any lack of reasonably care on their part. Bert claims that his garden has been contaminated by the escape of contaminated substances during a flood from the premises of Rip Off plc, a manufacturer of chemicals. Assess the likelihood that Bert will succeed with his claim.

   Would your answer be any different if Rip Off plc has gone into liquidation, and it is discovered that it had no insurance to cover the loss such as that caused to Bert?

3 The UK is fundamentally opposed to the directive, believing it to be inconsistent with the principle of subsidiarity. Parliament adopts the (fictitious) Toxic Substances (Derogation) Act 1999 under which it specifically prohibits the UK courts from giving effect to the directive. Advise the Community Rights Group, a pressure group concerned with the proper enforcement and implementation of EU law, of the likelihood of a successful challenge to the Act in the UK courts.

   In the event that you conclude that a challenge would be possible in principle, consider whether the Community Rights Group could properly be denied standing to challenge the Act on the grounds that it has suffered no damage.

4 The UK has not introduced the necessary framework for training programmes on safety matters to be delivered to employees working with toxic substances. In February 2000, the Health and Safety Board issues a warning notice under national health and safety legislation to a company called Farmers' Friend which makes pesticides for farm use highlighting the dangers which its factory poses to a neighbouring housing estate and indicating that failure to do a thorough safety audit and introduce new training procedures within ten weeks may result in a compulsory closure order being issued by the court. In its warning notice it refers to Directive 93/8000.

Further Reading

A. Arnull (1999a), Ch. 3, 'The Relationship between Treaty Provisions and the National Laws of the Member States', and Ch. 4, 'The Direct Effect of Community Legislation'.

G. Bettlem (1995), 'The Principle of Indirect Effect of Community Law', (1995) 3 *European Review of Private Law* 1.

D. Curtin and K. Mortelmans (1994), 'Application and Enforcement of Community Law by the Member States: Actors in Search of a Third Generation Script', in Curtin and Heukels (1994).

R. Dehousse (1998a), Ch. 2, 'The Constituitonalization of the Community Legal Order'.

W. van Gerven (1994a), 'The Horizontal Effect of Directive Provisions Revisited: The Reality of Catchwords', in Curtin and Heukels (1994).

C. Harlow (1996), 'Francovich and the Problem of the Disobedient State', 2 *European Law Journal* 199.

C. Hilson and T. Downes (1999), 'Making Sense of Rights: Community Rights in EC Law', 24 *European Law Review* 121.

N. Maltby (1993), 'Marleasing: What is All the Fuss About?' 109 *Law Quarterly Review* 301.

P. Pescatore (1983), 'The Doctrine of 'Direct Effect': An Infant Disease of Community Law', 8 *European Law Review* 155.

M. Ross (1993), 'Beyond Francovich', 56 *Modern Law Review* 55.

F. Snyder (1993b), 'The Effectiveness of European Community Law: Institutions, Processes, Tools and Techniques', 56 *Modern Law Review* 19.

T. Tridimas (1994), 'Horizontal Effect of Directives: A Missed Opportunity?', 19 *European Law Review* 621.

B. de Witte (1999b), 'Direct Effect, Supremacy and the Nature of the Legal Order', in Craig and de Búrca (1999).

D. Wyatt (1982), 'New Legal Order or Old?', 7 *European Law Review* 147.

Key Websites

For a comprehensive collection of materials on the principle of state liability:
http://www.asser.nl/er/fran/francovi.htm

13 The National Dimension: Domestic Remedies for Breach of EC Law and National Reactions to the Challenge

13.1 Introduction

This chapter makes use of the argument developed in both Chapter 11 and in earlier discussions of EU constitutionalism, that the relationship between EU law and national law possesses two dimensions. It can be viewed not only from the perspective of the Court of Justice, but also from the perspective of the national courts (Slaughter *et al.*, 1998). The chapter looks at two key facets of the 'national dimension': it examines first the third level of analysis identified in Figure 12.1 (the availability of national remedies within the constraints of the principles of non-discrimination and effectiveness articulated by the Court of Justice), and then turns briefly to the responses of some national courts to the principal conceptual and practical challenges posed by EC law, with a focus upon the UK.

13.2 National Remedies and Breach of EU Law

National courts are under a duty to give comprehensive remedies to individuals seeking redress against national law in conflict with EU law, or seeking to enforce EC rights (Case 811/79 *Amministrazione delle Finanze dello Stato* v. *Ariete SpA* [1980] ECR 2545). Rights granted to individuals by directives or other EU provisions must be capable of protection by judicial process (Case 222/84 *Johnston* v. *Chief Constable of the Royal Ulster Constabulary* [1986] ECR 1651; Case 222/86 *UNECTEF* v. *Heylens* [1987] ECR 4097). These points have already emerged earlier in the discussion of general principles of EU law (9.4).

The nature of the remedies granted are a matter for national courts and the national legal order, under the principle of national procedural autonomy; but they must be no less favourable than those accorded by the court in respect of violations of similar rights arising under national law (the principle of non-discrimination). Moreover, the procedural conditions, such as limitation periods or *locus standi* rules, which govern actions for the enforcement of EU law are a matter for national law and are not subject to the control of EU law (at least until they have been harmonised by the EU legislature), unless such:

> 'conditions and time limits made it impossible in practice to exercise the rights which the national courts are obliged to protect' (Case 33/76 *Rewe-Zentralfinanz* v. *Landwirtschaftskammer für das Saarland* [1976] ECR 1989 at 1998) (see also to the same effect Case 45/76 *Comet* v. *Produktschap* [1976] ECR 2043).

In many cases since then, the Court has referred to these principles, stating them to be an articulation of the principle of cooperation contained in Article 10 EC (formerly Article 5 EC, and referred to in these terms in some quotations below). In Cases 46, 48/93 *Brasserie du Pêcheur/Factortame III* ([1996] ECR I-1029), the Court reiterated the point once more, stating that:

> 'the conditions for reparation of loss and damage laid down by national law must not be less favourable than those relating to similar domestic claims and must not be such as in practice to make it impossible or excessively difficult to obtain reparation' (para. 67).

It will be apparent that two extra words have crept in over the years: 'excessively difficult'. Perhaps those extra words crept in because the Court of Justice became impatient at some points with some of the inadequacies of the national remedial systems and the reaction of some national courts to the demands of EU law. Meanwhile, there have been clear 'ebbs and flows' in the case law, as the Court has intruded at various times to greater or lesser degrees into national procedural autonomy. This variation is especially evident in relation to the requirement of adequate sanctions and the scrutiny of national procedural conditions placed on remedies for breach of EU law such as time limits. Many of the Court's rulings have required national courts to 'exercise a degree of creativity', and one consequence of its case law has been a higher degree of uncertainty for both litigants and national courts (Craig and de Búrca, 1998: 226). At the present time, the case law appears to be in a phase where the Court lays greater stress upon the value of national procedural autonomy rather than minimum harmonisation of national procedural conditions through the imposition of uniform supranational requirements. The Court's heady activism of the middle stage in the development of the case law has eased off (Craufurd Smith, 1999).

None the less, despite that relatively hands-off approach, just as the formula on national procedural autonomy has evolved over the years, so the

Court can be shown to have changed its position on another fundamental principle of national autonomy: that the effect of EU law within the national legal order is not such as to require the creation of new legal remedies in addition to those which exist already, although every type of action available under national law must be available also for the protection of EC rights (Case 158/80 *Rewe-Handelsgesellschaft Nord mbH* v. *Hauptzollamt Kiel* [1981] ECR 1805). This point is difficult to sustain since the development of the concept of state liability.

13.3   National Remedies and the Disapplication of National Law

Case 106/77 *Amministrazione delle Finanze dello Stato* v. *Simmenthal SpA (Simmenthal II)* ([1978] ECR 629) tells national courts that they are responsible for 'disapplying' national law which comes into conflict with EU law (12.13). The idea of disapplying an Act of Parliament is a novel concept for a UK judge, accustomed to occupying a subordinate position in relation to the legislature. However, as the Court made clear in its ruling on the reference from the House of Lords in Case C-213/89 *R* v. *Secretary of State for Transport, ex parte Factortame Ltd (Factortame I)* ([1990] ECR I-2433), it is inherent in the system of EU law that national courts must be able, in either final or interim proceedings, to issue appropriate orders to give effect to EU law. It held (at p. 2473):

> 'In accordance with the case law of the Court, it is for the national courts, in application of the principle of co-operation laid down in Article 5 of the EEC Treaty, to ensure the legal protection which persons derive from the direct effect of provisions of Community law ...
> The Court has also held that any provision of a national legal system and any legislative, administrative or judicial practice which might impair the effectiveness of Community law by withholding from the national court having jurisdiction to apply such law the power to do everything necessary at the moment of its application to set aside national legislative provisions which might prevent, even temporarily, Community rules from having full force and effect are incompatible with those requirements, which are the very essence of Community law ...
> It must be added that the full effectiveness of Community law would be just as much impaired if a rule of national law could prevent a court seised of a dispute governed by Community law from granting interim relief in order to ensure the full effectiveness of the judgment to be given on the existence of the rights claimed under Community law. It follows that a court which in those circumstances would grant interim relief, if it were not for a rule of national law, is obliged to set aside that rule.'

On these grounds the House of Lords was obliged to abrogate, at least as regards matters of Community competence, the rule prohibiting the granting of interim injunctions against the Crown, as it had indicated in its judgment prior to ordering a reference that it would be prepared to do if required by the Court (*R* v. *Secretary of State for Transport, exparte Factortame Ltd* [1990] 2 AC 85; [1989] 3 CMLR 1; award of interim relief: [1991] 1 All ER 70; [1990] 3 CMLR 375). The Court also held that a national court must be prepared to grant such a remedy even in advance of an authoritative ruling by the Court on the existence of an infringement of EU law. Consequently, the House of Lords was required to contemplate two novelties: first, removing a procedural bar on interim relief against the Crown, and second, giving interim relief which effectively disapplied an Act of Parliament. The effect of the ruling must be regarded as coming very close to requiring the creation of new remedies (Ross, 1990).

13.4 Adequate Sanctions and EU Law

One of the most important aspects of the 'effective remedies' principle has been the Court's approach to the issue of the adequacy of sanctions. This point was initially addressed in Case 14/83 *Von Colson and Kamann* v. *Land Nordrhein-Westfalen* ([1984] ECR 1891) (see 12.10 and 12.14). In the context of a provision of the Equal Treatment Directive which the Court had found allowed Member States to choose from a range of sanctions, the Court concluded:

'if a Member State chooses to penalize breaches of that prohibition by the award of compensation, then in order to ensure that it is effective and that it has a deterrent effect, that compensation must in any event be adequate in relation to the damage sustained and must therefore amount to more than purely nominal compensation ...' (p. 1909).

This conclusion led easily onto a challenge in Case C-271/91 *Marshall* v. *Southampton and South West Hampshire AHA (Marshall II)* ([1993] ECR I-4367) to the UK's then applicable compensation limits on sex discrimination claims, which limited the maximum amount to £6,250 and appeared to deny a right to interest on compensation awarded (12.10). The Court concluded that 'full' compensation was the only appropriate remedy where the Member State had chosen monetary compensation as the means of sanctioning the discriminatory act, and that this must include also a right to interest; this was necessary to ensure 'real and effective judicial protection' and to 'have a real deterrent effect on the employer' (p. 4407). Only then could 'real equality of opportunity' be ensured through adequate reparation (p. 4409).

However, subsequent case law has indicated that the Court will not pursue the full implications of this judgment. In *R* v. *Secretary of State for Social Security, ex parte Sutton* ([1997] ECR I-2163), it refused to extend this approach to UK rules on the retrospective payment of state benefits. Sutton claimed a benefit for caring for her sick daughter which she would have been paid if she had been a man of the same age, but which she was denied because of the difference between the pensionable ages for men and women (she made the claim when 63). She was able to establish that this was discriminatory under the Social Security Directive which guarantees equal treatment on grounds of sex and was awarded the contested benefit, backdated to one year before the date of her application. At issue was whether interest should be paid on the benefits payable to Sutton when she won her claim, something for which there was no provision in the relevant national law. The Court drew a distinction between awards of compensation for discriminatory dismissal and the payment of benefits by the public authorities, subject to the conditions laid down in national law. It denied that the payment of interest on the award was 'an essential component of the right' to non-discrimination and to adequate sanctions, even though the wording of the two directives was on this point identical. Under Directive 79/7, the limit of the private party's entitlement was to the benefit to which they would have been entitled had there been no discrimination. In the final part of the judgment, however, the Court suggested that there was no reason why an applicant could not pursue an action for that part of their claim via the principle of state liability. The national court could, therefore, apply the principles of state liability to ascertain whether Sutton was entitled to reparation on those grounds. This suggestion – made in other cases as well (e.g. Case C-192-218/95 *Comateb* [1997] ECR I-165) – gives national courts more influence over the outcome of the action (Arnull, 1999a: 186). By refusing to condemn national rules on the payment of interest (and indeed time limits, as the next paragraph will show), the Court of Justice is preserving both national procedural autonomy and a higher degree of legal certainty, but the approach should leave the claimant still able to claim her loss in full *if* she can show that the state has acted wrongfully within the meaning of the state liability principle and can demonstrate a causal link with her loss. The Member State remains in a position to defend itself by showing that it has not committed a sufficiently serious breach.

13.5   Effective Remedies and the Procedural and Jurisdictional Conditions Applying to National Remedies

The general trend in the case law on national remedies and procedural and jurisdictional conditions in the late 1980s and early 1990s was for the Court to take an increasingly interventionist line. For example, it has held that the rights granted by EU law may not be limited by the application of additional substantive conditions. For example, in Case C-177/88 *Dekker* v. *Stichting Vormingscentrum voor Jong Volwassenen* ([1990] ECR I-3941) the Court held that national provisions may not subject liability for sex discrimination in employment matters arising under the Equal Treatment Directive to the requirement that the victim show fault on the part of the employer since all that is required under the Directive is proof of the objective fact of discrimination. In similar vein, in Case C-377/89 *Cotter and McDermott* v. *Minister for Social Welfare (No. 2)* ([1991] ECR I-1155), the Court held that the state may not defeat a claim to a social benefit based on the right to non-discrimination on grounds of sex based on the Social Security Directive, by claiming that the applicant would be unjustly enriched by the receipt of the benefit because she had received an equivalent benefit via her husband. Unjust enrichment may not, therefore, be a valid defence to a claim based on EC rights – an argument reminiscent, not of the effective national remedies principle, but of the 'estoppel' argument often put forward to justify the direct effect of directives (12.11).

In a further case also concerned with rights under the same Directive, the 'estoppel' argument once more came to the fore: in Case C-208/90 *Emmott* v. *Minister for Social Welfare* ([1991] ECR I-4269) the Court held that the application of time limits which preclude the applicant from bringing a claim can only occur as from date when the provision of EU law in question had been transparently implemented by that state. Only from that date could the applicant be in a position to know what her EC rights were; hence time should not begin to run until that date. Until then the national authorities were precluded from relying upon the ordinary national time limits relating to the bringing of proceedings in the national courts. In recent cases, however, the Court does appear to have resiled somewhat from that approach to the Social Security Directive; the application of this measure for the benefit of women has proved to be exceedingly problematic in the context of widespread welfare benefit cuts across many Member States. In a series of rulings, the Court has found itself forced to accept arguments from the Member States effectively bringing about levelling down, in the name of equality, rather than levelling up.

In Case C-338/91 *Steenhorst-Neerings* v. *Bestuur van de Bedrijfsvereniging voor Detailhandel* ([1993] ECR I-5475) and Case C-410/92 *Johnson* v. *Chief Adjudication Officer* ([1994] ECR I-5483) the Court refused to apply the *Emmott* principle to national provisions which limited not the right to bring an action, but the length of time for which a claim could be backdated. The Court applied the two limb national remedies test, and concluded that the national conditions were not discriminatory and did not make it 'virtually impossible' for an action to be brought on the basis of EU law (*Johnson*, p.

5510). The tenor of these judgments and later ones has been that *Emmott* should be very much regarded as an exceptional case, restricted to its facts.

That is not to say that the Court has taken an approach to time limits which allows complete national autonomy. In Case C-246/96 *Magorrian* v. *Eastern Health and Social Services Board* ([1997] ECR I-7153) the rule at issue was one which restricted membership of an occupational pension scheme, from which the applicants had previously been excluded on indirectly discriminatory grounds. Although membership was opened up, it would take effect from a date no earlier than two years before the proceedings were instituted. The Court found that this was not compatible with EU law. It illustrates the difference between a limitation period that allows the claim but restricts it to the losses incurred within a specific time period, and a limitation period which restricts the entitlement to membership of a pension scheme and thus to acquire, for the future, an entitlement to benefits; such a rule strikes at the 'very essence of the right conferred by the Community legal order' (para. 44).

Many of the cases before the Court of Justice have been concerned with the reclaiming of taxes and charges levied in breach of EU law. In principle such taxes can be reclaimed from the national authorities, although typically national law will restrict recovery through restrictions on the payment of interest and time limits for the bringing of claims under the system of administrative justice which tend to be shorter for such public law claims than for claims between two private parties under the law of obligations. For example the 1969 Capital Duty Directive on permissible indirect taxes upon the raising of capital for companies restricts what fees and charges a Member State may make on the registration of companies and on the registration of increases in the capital of the companies. Case law before the Court had already clarified the scope of permissible action by Member States. The applicants in Case C-188/95 *Fantask* v. *Industriministeriet* ([1997] ECR I-6783) sought recovery from the Danish authorities of unlawful charges which had been levied upon them. They encountered a Danish rule time-barring actions for the recovery of debts after five years. The contention that a Member State could not rely upon a limitation period under national law until after the Directive had been properly transposed into national law because until then the applicants would be unable to ascertain the full extent of their rights under the Directive was rejected. The Court acknowledged the importance of the principle of legal certainty within the national system of remedies and recovery, and provided the national time limits did not make it virtually impossible or excessively difficult for an applicant to bring a claim, it would not interfere with national procedural autonomy. It found the Danish time limit of five years to be reasonable. One aspect of the Danish rules was, however, found to be incompatible with EU law; this was a national rule which established that actions for the recovery of charges would be dismissed if they were imposed as a result of an excusable error on the part of the national authorities in as much as they were levied over a long period without either those authorities or the person liable to them having being aware that they were unlawful. The Court pointed out that such a rule would indeed make recovery excessively difficult, and would have the effect of encouraging infringements of EU law which were committed over a long period of time.

One final illustration serves to demonstrate the Court's approach to national procedural rules. In Case C-231/96 *Ediliza Industriale Siderurgica* v. *Ministero delle Finanze* [1998] ECR I-4951, one of a series of cases on recovery in the Italian courts of charges wrongfully levied under the Capital Duty Directive, the rules at issue were a three year limitation period applying to time bar claims and a relatively low interest rate on arrears payable. The Court applied the *Fantask* case law to find that the national time limits were reasonable, and in relation to the rules on the payment of interest it ruled that the principle of equivalence between actions based on national law and those based on EU law did not mean that a Member State had to extend its most favourable rules governing recovery under national law to all actions for repayment of charges or ducs levied in breach of EU law. These cases highlight that the 'practical impossibility' test has not been wholly superseded by an effectiveness test (Craufurd Smith, 1999), although effectiveness will clearly remain a relevant policy issue which the Court must consider.

A separate question addressed by the Court has been national procedural rules which restrict the ability of national judges to consider questions of EU law. In two judgments decided on the same day (Case C-312/93 *Peterbroeck* v. *Belgian State* [1995] ECR I-4599 and Cases 430, 431/93 *van Schijndel* v. *Stichting Pensioenfonds voor Fysiotherapeuten* [1995] ECR I-4705), the Court was asked to consider the status of national procedural rules which limit the ability of national courts to raise of their own motion questions of EU law which the parties have failed to raise themselves within the relevant national time limits. *Peterbroeck* was a taxation action, brought against a state authority, and the Court concluded that such a national procedural provision would contravene the 'effective remedies' principle by making the application of EU law virtually impossible or excessively difficult. The Court offered some useful further general guidance on judging national procedural provisions in the light of the 'effectiveness' principle:

'Each case ... must be analysed by reference to the role of that provision in the procedure, its progress and special features, viewed as a whole, before the various national instances. In the light of that analysis the basic principles of the domestic judicial system, such as the protection of the rights of the defence, the principle of legal certainty and the proper conduct of procedure, must, where appropriate, be taken into consideration' (para. 14).

In that case, a 60-day time limit after which new points of law could not be raised by the parties or by the court was objectionable because it had expired before the referring court (which was the first court in the national hierarchy capable of making a reference under the applicable domestic appeals system: see Case C-24/92 *Corbiau* [1993] ECR I-1277 (11.4)) had even held its hearing, and no other national court further up the judicial hierarchy could of its own motion raise the point of EU law.

In contrast, in *van Schijndel*, although a substantial part of the judgment was identical to that in *Peterbroeck*, the Court applied different reasoning to a general principle of the Dutch legal system that a court in civil proceedings should normally take a passive role, leaving the conduct of litigation to the parties, and should take the initiative only in exceptional circumstances. Whatever EU principle there is that national courts should be able to raise points of EU law of their own motion, it does not override such a fundamental national principle of procedural economy such as to generate an obligation to raise points of EU law in cases involving the resolution of rights and obligations in private law. Prechal (1998: 705) comments that *van Schijndel* makes clear:

> 'that the full effectiveness of Community law is not an overpowering principle. It must be reconciled with the application of national procedural, remedial and other – written and unwritten – rules and principles'.

Despite the numerous cases decided by the Court of Justice, it is noticeable how vague many of the general principles guiding the national courts have remained. This is well illustrated by the fact that it was not until 1998 that the Court offered clear guidance to national courts on the operation of the principle of *equivalence*, which is the other limb of the *Rewe* criteria governing national remedies. In Case C-326/96 *Levez* v. *T. H. Jennings (Harlow Pools) Ltd* [1998] ECR I-7385, the Court instructed the national court to:

> 'consider both the purpose and the essential characteristics of allegedly similar domestic actions ... Furthermore, whenever it falls to be determined whether a procedural rule of national law is less favourable than those governing similar domestic actions, the national court must take into account the role played by that provision in the procedure as a whole, as well as the operation and any special features of that procedure before the different national courts' (paras. 43 and 44).

13.6   The Conditions Governing the Principle of State Liability

It is difficult to argue against the proposition that the development of a principle of state liability, based on a uniform EC principle of reparation, represents a rupture in the distinction drawn hitherto – and highlighted in Figure 12.1 – between the ways in which the fundamental constitutional qualities of EU law are given effect within the EU legal order, and the practical enforcement of those techniques at national level. This point is particularly clear because, having articulated the general principle in a judgement (Cases 6, 9/90 *Francovich I*) described by one commentator as 'extremely brief and sweeping' and 'terse and laconic' (Bebr, 1992: 568, 575), the Court was forced by the demand for clarification from below to look in much more detail at the precise conditions under which this particular remedy should be available in the national legal orders. In other words, although the Court refers at several points in its judgement in Cases 46, 48/93 *Brasserie du Pêcheur/ Factortame III* to national procedural autonomy, it has in effect laid out in some detail the terms under which liability will arise. In so doing, it also slightly reformulated the original three conditions which it articulated in *Francovich I* which were the only guidance it offered on implementing this remarkable new principle (12.17), drawing heavily, quite probably in response to comments and suggestions made by observers including the Commission, a number of Member States and many academic commentators, on its own case law on the non-contractual liability of the EU institutions for unlawful acts in order to create a parallelism between state liability and EU liability. This paragraph will discuss these revised formulations; the facts of *Brasserie du Pêcheur/Factortame III* are set out in 12.18.

In *Brasserie du Pêcheur/Factortame III* the Court identified four factors which affect the conditions under which liability will arise:

- the nature of the breach of EU law giving rise to the damage;
- the principle of the full effectiveness of EC rules and the effective protection of EC rights;
- the obligation of cooperation imposed on Member States under Article 10 EC; and
- the relevance of the Court's own case law on Article 288 EC, acknowledging that without particular justification there cannot be a difference between the conditions under which the EU institutions and the Member State governments are liable.

The Court then went on to apply the principles that it applies to actions for damages in respect of loss arising as a result of the legislative acts of the EU institutions, where it takes into account factors such as the complexity of the situation, difficulties in the interpretation or application of legal texts, and particularly the margin of discretion given to legislative actors. This leads to a test under which the EU institutions (and now the Member States) can only be held liable for an act taken in a legislative context characterised by the exercise of wide discretion where they have 'manifestly and gravely disregarded the limits' on the exercise of their powers (para. 45) (17.9). On the other hand, in many circumstances Member States do not have a wide discretion when they act 'in a field governed by Community law' (para. 46). EU law imposes many obligations of conduct or result on Member States that reduce their margin of discretion – in particular the obligation to implement a directive. In contrast, the German and UK legislatures in the two cases at issue in *Brasserie du Pêcheur/Factortame III* were in a situation comparable to the EU legislature, faced with a wide range of choices in fields lacking harmonisation measures or an exhaustive set EU regulations (beer contents, and implementation of the common fisheries policy). On the basis of this the Court concluded that the three conditions for liability should now be reformulated for such cases as follows:

- the rule of law infringed must be intended to confer rights on individuals;
- the breach must be sufficiently serious; and
- there must be a direct causal link between the breach of the obligation resting on the State and the damage sustained by the injured parties.

The Court felt easily able to conclude for itself that the first condition was satisfied in respect of both Articles 28 and 43 EC (free movement of goods and freedom of establishment). On the second condition, the Court concluded that this was a matter for the national court, but offered some guidance to the national courts on its reading of seriousness of the breaches manifested by the legislative measures in question. The circumstances to be considered by the national court include the degree of clarity and precision of the rule breached, the measure of discretion which it provides for, the intentional or involuntary nature of the infringement, the excusable or inexcusable nature of any actual error of law by the Member State, the contributory role of any positions taken by the Community institutions, and the adoption of national measures or practices especially where these contravene settled case law of the Court of Justice.

In the case of the Merchant Shipping Act 1988, the Court offered the view that the introduction of provisions making registration of trawlers subject to a nationality condition constituted 'direct discrimination manifestly contrary to Community law' (para. 61). Other provisions on residence and domicile, while *prima facie* contrary to Article 43 were arguably justifiable by reference to the objectives of the common fisheries policy, although the Court rejected that argument in Case C-221/89 *Factortame II* [1991] ECR I-3905 (the judgment on the substance of the case on Article 43, made on the basis of questions referred by the Divisional Court in the UK). Furthermore in assessing the seriousness of a breach, it is important to take into account the promptness of any national reaction to a finding of a violation of EU law by the Court of Justice. Failure to observe such a finding would be determinative of the question of the seriousness of the breach; this is a matter of fact to be determined by the national court. A number of other points arose for consideration in *Brasserie du Pêcheur/Factortame III*. The Court concluded – unsurprisingly in view of its decision in Case C-177/88 *Dekker* (13.5) – that beyond the concept of a 'serious' breach, the national court could not demand an additional element of 'fault' in the action under national law. It referred to the fact that the national legal systems have very different concepts of 'fault'. Finally, it held that the principle of 'full' compensation should apply, subject to the duty to mitigate with due diligence – incumbent also on plaintiffs in actions under Article 288. None the less a number of questions relating to compensation remain inconclusive, especially the possibility of exemplary damages.

While clarifying the position in relation to breach of EU primary law (see also Case C-5/94 *R* v. *MAFF, ex parte Hedley Lomas* [1996] ECR I-2553), *Brasserie du Pêcheur/Factortame III* left open a number of questions about the applicability to the state liability principle to circumstances involving failure to implement, misimplementation or failure to enforce a directive. *Hedley Lomas* itself was a case of breach of the EC Treaty, notably Article 29 which prohibits restrictions on exports in circumstances where the UK authorities had been systematically refusing export licences for live animals to Spain because of the risk that their treatment in Spanish slaughterhouses would not be conform with the relevant EU rules under a directive. However, the Court highlighted the fact that if at the time it committed the infringement the defendant state was:

'not called upon to make any legislative choices and had only considerably reduced, or even no, discretion, the mere infringement of Community law may be sufficient to establish the existence of a sufficiently serious breach' (para. 28).

A fortiori, this applies to the complete failure to take any measures to implement a directive, which amounts to a manifest and grave disregard by the Member State of the limits of its discretion in the exercise of its rule-making powers. In Case C-178/94, etc. *Dillenkofer and others* v. *Germany* ([1996] ECR I-4845), Germany failed to implement the Package Travel Directive until eighteen months after the time limit for its implementation had expired, and limited the protection of travellers against the insolvency of the travel agent which had to be established under the Directive due to commence two years after implementation had been due. This prompted a flood of claims for state liability in Germany, and in *Dillenkofer* the Court concluded not only that the relevant provisions of the directive were such as to confer rights on individuals, but also that a sufficiently serious breach had taken place. The implementation of the Package Travel Directive has also caused difficulties for the Austrian authorities, and in Case C-140/97 *Rechberger* v. *Austria* [1999] ECR I-3449, a transposition of the Directive which deliberately limited its coming into force to a period some four months after it should have been implemented was a sufficiently serious breach. On the other hand, in Case C-392/93 *R* v. *HM Treasury, ex parte British Telecommunications* ([1996] ECR I-1631) the Court concluded that the UK government could not be liable in damages in respect of loss allegedly caused by its good faith (if incorrect) interpretation and misimplementation of a provision in a public procurement Directive. Such an act was not a sufficiently serious breach of EU law. It is notable in such cases that the Court of Justice is not leaving the issue of whether the breach is sufficiently serious to the national court, but deciding it for itself. In *Brasserie du Pêcheur/ Factortame III* the issue of whether the breach of EU primary law was sufficiently serious was left to the national court (13.8). These cases also leave a question mark over the incorrect 'deeming' of existing national law to be a sufficient implementation of a directive, as occurred in Case 334/92 *Wagner Miret* v. *Fondo de Garantía Salarial* ([1993] ECR I-6911) (12.14) where the Court specifically referred the national court to the *Francovich I* case.

Beyond the application of the three conditions of state liability, which are a matter of EU law, albeit to be decided in some cases on the facts by the national court, the remaining questions about the implementation of the state liability principle are matters of national procedural autonomy. In Case C-66/95 *Sutton*, the Court pointed out that:

> 'While the right to reparation is founded directly on Community law where the three conditions set out above are fulfilled, the national law on liability provides the framework within which the State must make reparation for the consequences of the loss and damage caused, provided always that the conditions laid down by national law relating to reparation of loss and damage must not be less favourable than those relating to similar domestic claims and must not be so framed as to make it virtually impossible or excessively difficult to obtain reparation' (para. 33).

One issue about national procedural autonomy in this context raised by Case C-302/97 *Konle* v. *Austria* [1999] ECR I-3099 concerned responsibility for making reparation in the context of states with a federal structure, such as Austria. The Court found that it was a matter for each Member State to ensure that individuals can obtain reparation, regardless of which public authority is responsible for the breach and which is responsible for providing reparation. EU law does not interfere with the divisions of powers and responsibilities at national level, except to impose the principle that the domestic system must provide remedies which effectively allow individuals to protect the rights they derive under EU law.

13.7 The Alternative: Legislative Action

The parallels drawn between Article 288 and the principle of state liability may, in the view of some, presage the emergence of a 'Common Law' of Europe in the field of legal remedies (e.g. van Gerven, 1994b, 1995; Caranta, 1995; Beatson and Tridimas, 1998). The Court has been eager, as in *Brasserie du Pêcheur/Factortame III*, to refer to both Article 288 and state liability as:

> 'simply an expression of the general principle familiar to the legal systems of the Member States that an unlawful act or omission gives rise to an obligation to make good the damage caused' (para. 29).

In view of that conclusion, there may be arguments in favour of moving fairly rapidly towards a harmonisation of the conditions on the basis of which that general principle is given effect, in the interests of improving individual legal protection and reducing the complexity of the systems which EU citizens currently face. Back in 1976, in Case 33/76 *Rewe-Zentralfinanz* (13.2) the Court seemed to indicate that the EU had competence – on the basis of what were then Articles 100–102 and 235 EEC (now Articles 94, 96, 97 and 308 EC) – to adopt harmonisation measures in the procedural field in order to:

> 'remedy differences between the provisions laid down by law, regulation or administrative action in Member States if they are likely to distort or harm the functioning of the Common Market' (p. 1998).

There are a number of pieces of evidence which indicate a gradual movement towards harmonisation, although the balance between judicial action and legislative action remains uncertain (Himsworth, 1997). These include the Remedies Directive operating in the field of public procurement (Directive 89/665 OJ 1989 L395/33), which specifically recognised in its preamble that in some Member States the absence or inadequacy of existing remedies, at least in that field, might deter undertakings from submitting tenders for public procurement contracts. It would not be so difficult to extrapolate outwards from that argument in favour of harmonisation of remedies in other fields, or across the board. Second, there are a series of measures taken to protect the financial interests of the EU, which aim specifically at the creation of adequate penalties in the criminal field to deter and punish those involved in fraud against the EU, significantly bolstered by the specific law-making competence in this area added by the Treaty of Amsterdam (Article 280 EC) (7.16). Again this is a sectoral measure, but it is an indication of a willingness to intervene with binding measures in fields which appear at first sight to be within the sphere of national sovereignty in order to achieve an important EU objective. However, in mid-1995 the Council did adopt a general measure on effective uniform application of EU law and on remedies, but it took the form of a non-binding resolution (OJ 1995 C188/1). The Resolution referred throughout to the importance of Article 10, the need for effective remedies, and the essential element of cooperation. The Council concluded by agreeing to examine 'openly and constructively' proposals on effective penalties put forward by the Commission in the future. Finally, the provisions on civil cooperation were introduced into the EC Treaty by the Treaty of Amsterdam, having previously been third-pillar matters (Article 65 EC). This is primarily concerned with matters of private international law and matters of civil procedure where these represent an obstacle to the internal market, but the gradual convergence or harmonisation of remedial systems at national level certainly cannot be ruled out.

13.8   Domestic Responses to the Challenges of EU Law

Details were given in 12.4 and 12.5 regarding the differing constitutional responses made by the national legal systems to the demands of EU law. These were in effect the responses to the first level of analysis identified in Figure 12.1. In the spirit of the dialogue which underlies the constitutionalisation of the EU legal order, we shall now concentrate principally on the progress made towards a complete acceptance of the approaches taken by the Court of Justice at the second and third levels in national courts. Ideally the Court should always seek to balance its approach between the need to promote dynamism within the EU legal order, and the need to avoid accelerating beyond the bounds of what national courts consider acceptable. It is from the reactions of the national courts that it is possible to discern whether the Court has achieved that balance.

For example, some courts such as the French *Conseil d'Etat* (Supreme Administrative Court) and the German Federal Finance Court have been unwilling to accept that Directives could give rise to rights justiciable at the instance of individuals. The views of the two courts in *Minister of the Interior* v. *Cohn-Bendit* ([1980] 1 CMLR 543) and *Kloppenburg* v. *Finanzamt Leer* ([1989] 1 CMLR 873) were founded on an analysis of Article 189 which focused on the differences between regulations and directives, and which has found support among academic commentators also (e.g. Hamson, 1976). It is ironic how the Court itself has turned to a similar analysis in Case C-91/92 *Faccini Dori* ([1994] ECR I-3325) (12.11).

The *Conseil d'Etat* has also experienced difficulties accepting the full consequences of the superior nature of EU law. However, in later cases such as *Boisdet* ([1991] 1 CMLR 3) it accepted an interpretation of the Article 55 of the French Constitution which allows EU law to take precedence over subsequent French laws, an interpretation which accords with the position already long adopted by the highest French court in the private law field, the *Cour de Cassation* (*Café Jacques Vabre* ([1975] 2 CMLR 336).

In the UK, much of the debate has centred around key provisions of the European Communities Act 1972. These should ensure the effective application and enforcement of EU law in the UK. Section 2(1) enshrines the concept of direct effect:

'All such rights, powers, liability, obligations and restrictions from time to time created or arising by or under the Treaties, and all such remedies and procedures from time to time provided for by or under the Treaties, as in accordance with the Treaties are without further enactment to be given legal effect or used in the United Kingdom shall be recognised and available in law, and be enforced, allowed and followed accordingly.'

The supremacy of EU law appears to be guaranteed by the rather obscurely worded section 2(4) which contains the text:

'any enactment passed or to be passed, other than one contained in this Part of this Act, shall be construed and have effect subject to the foregoing provisions of this section.'

The best view of section 2(4) is as a rule of construction for national law aimed at avoiding conflicts with EU law. According to Lord Bridge in *Factortame* ([1989] 2 All ER 692 at p. 701) section 2(4):

'has precisely the same effect as if a section were incorporated in [Part II of the Merchant Shipping Act 1988] which in terms enacted that the provisions with regard to registration of British fishing vessels were to be without prejudice to the directly enforceable rights of nationals of any Member States of the EEC.'

At the practical level, the House of Lords in *Factortame* complied fully with the requirements of EU law as laid down by the Court, with Lord Bridge remarking on the rehearing of the case following the judgment of the Court ([1990] 3 CMLR 375) on the misconceived comments of those who regarded the requirement that the courts override national legislation in violation of EU law as a novel and dangerous invasion of the sovereignty of the UK. He regarded the approach taken by the Court as mandated by the supremacy of EU law; a concept well entrenched in the EU legal order before even the UK acceded to the Treaties.

However, achieving the enforcement of EU law through the medium of interpretation rather than through simple acceptance of the direct applicability principle (12.2) caused a number of difficulties for the UK courts, particularly when they were asked to apply the EU interpretative obligation –

the principle of indirect effect. The judges generally showed themselves willing to give sympathetic interpretations of national provisions introduced with the specific purpose of implementing EU legislation. In *Pickstone* v. *Freemans plc* ([1988] 2 All ER 813) the House of Lords interpreted section 1(2)(c) of the Equal Pay Act 1970, which was introduced by the Equal Value Regulations 1983 in order to bring UK law into conformity with the requirements of what was then Article 119 EEC on equal pay (now Article 141 EC), in order to give effect to what it saw as the purpose of Parliament. This meant that it was permissible to give an interpretation of the words in the light of the purpose of the equal value principle and to allow it to function effectively to deal with the 'mischief' which it was introduced to counter. In an equal value claim, one group of workers is compared against another group of workers in order to assess the respective value of the work done by each group of workers. Sec. 1(2)(c) should not be rendered inoperative by the employment of one token man among what is normally a disadvantaged group of female workers; it should be sufficient that the group of workers disadvantaged was predominantly female (or, exceptionally, male). A similar approach was taken in *Litster* v. *Forth Dry Dock and Engineering Co Ltd* ([1989] 1 All ER 1134) to the Transfer of Undertakings Regulations 1981, passed to implement the Acquired Rights Directive 77/187.

However, in a case where there was at the time when the facts arose no specific implementing legislation, the House of Lords found itself unable to adopt the same approach. In *Duke* v. *GEC Reliance* ([1988] 1 All ER 626) the House was asked to interpret the provisions of the Sex Discrimination Act 1975 on retirement ages in accordance with the provisions of the Equal Treatment Directive 76/207, in order to give a remedy to a woman working in the private sector who was made redundant earlier than a man in the same position, on grounds of having reached a (discriminatory) retirement age. This would have equalised the position of private and public sector workers, since the latter had a remedy based on the direct effect of the Directive as interpreted by the Court of Justice in Case 152/84 *Marshall* v. *Southampton and South West Hampshire AHA (Marshall I)* ([1986] ECR 723) (12.11). The House of Lords used the European Communities Act 1972 to draw a much stronger distinction between EU law which is and is not justiciable than is probably tenable in the light of the case law of the Court of Justice on indirect effect, holding that section 2(4) only applies the supremacy principle to directly effective EU law, and that no other principle of EU law required it to give what it considered to be a strained interpretation of the Sex Discrimination Act in order to achieve a reconciliation with the terms of the Equal Treatment Directive. In the absence of specific implementing legislation the House regarded itself as outside the duty of sympathetic interpretation which it was fulfilling in *Pickstone* and *Litster*. It is difficult to reconcile the position in *Duke* with the subsequent judgment of the Court of Justice in Case C-106/89 *Marleasing* (12.14).

Although *Duke* has not been formally overruled, there is evidence that some of its harshest effects were quietly dropped by the House of Lords in subsequent cases. In its judgment in *Webb* v. *EMO Cargo Ltd* ([1993] 1 WLR 49), ordering a reference on the question of pregnancy discrimination to the Court of Justice, the House of Lords appeared no longer to see a difficulty in applying an interpretative obligation to national legislation (again the Sex Discrimination Act 1975) which preceded an EU Directive (Equal Treatment Directive). It did not refer a question to the Court of Justice on the interpretative obligation, perhaps somewhat to the surprise of the Court of Appeal which had found itself in the same case unable to find an interpretation of the Sex Discrimination Act which did not distort its meaning ([1992] 2 All ER 43). When the case returned to the House of Lords following the Court of Justice judgment (Case C-32/93 *Webb* v. *EMO Cargo Ltd* [1994] ECR I-3567) which was wholly concerned with the question of what constitutes 'pregnancy discrimination', the House of Lords did find a way to fit the ruling of the Court of Justice into the Sex Discrimination Act – without discussing exactly how it was achieved within the framework offered by either the European Communities Act or the principle of indirect effect – albeit one which commentators may find a little narrow in scope ([1995] 4 All ER 577; see Szyszczak, 1996).

This line of case law reveals most clearly the difficulties which flow in the UK from the dualist inheritance under which the authority of EU law is seen as deriving its force from the European Communities Act 1972, rather than from its inherent qualities as interpreted by the Court of Justice using the theory of the transfer of sovereign powers.

Perhaps the most notable 'success story' in terms of the enforcement of EU law in the UK has been the *Factortame* litigation, which has stretched over a period of more than ten years as it has moved towards the final resolution of the compensation issue. In *R.* v *Secretary of State for Transport, Ex parte Factortame Ltd. and Others (No. 5)* ([1999] 3 CMLR 597) the House of Lords unanimously confirmed that the breach of EU law committed by the UK authorities when it adopted and applied the Merchant Shipping Act 1988 was sufficiently serious to give rise to an action in damages for state liability on the part of the applicant trawler owners and companies. The full sum of damages likely to be paid by the British State has been estimated in some quarters at £80 million.

One indirect consequence of that litigation has been the resolution of a difficult *locus standi* issue relating to the powers of the Equal Opportunities Commission to enforce sex discrimination law. In *R* v. *Secretary of State for Employment, ex parte EOC* ([1994] 1 All ER 910), the House of Lords relied upon *Factortame* to assist in holding that the EOC can bring judicial review proceedings in a matter of public importance and in relation to which it was given a role under public law, notwithstanding that it had no direct personal interest in the outcome of the proceedings that there was no 'decision' which it wished to challenge but merely a legislative policy (which discriminated against part-time workers). This ruling opens up the possibilities of 'public interest' actions in the UK courts not only by the EOC, but also potentially by a range of interested groups concerned with the effective enforcement of EU law. On the issue of substance, it is useful to note that the House of Lords felt able to decide for itself that there had been a breach of EU law, without recourse to an Article 234 reference. This is an indication, perhaps, that UK judges are becoming more adept at handling the substantive law of the EU, albeit that they remain still a little wary of some of its procedural and remedial implications.

Chalmers (2000a) notes the continuing patchiness of coverage in the UK courts of issues of EU law. Litigation has tended to cluster in specific pockets of EU law, such as social law and environmental law. Moreover, he notes the need for a sophisticated understanding of the legal framework, environment and cultural context, within which national judges apply EU law. As he concludes (Chalmers, 2000a: 128):

> 'the particular context of each individual case embeds the national court in a network of idiosyncratic relations – all of which pull in different directions. Inevitably, within this milieu it is possible to find a number of decision given by the British courts, which one doubts would have been given by the Court of Justice in the rarefied climate in Luxembourg. Yet a common feature of even these decisions is that such relations are constructed in terms of how they relate to EC law. It is true that the relationship is an adaptive one, so that the norms of EC law are often contoured around these relations. Nevertheless, they are examined through the prism of EC law. And that, in a complex and imperfect world, is possibly the mark of a relatively settled legal order.'

Summary

1 National courts must give comprehensive remedies for breach of EU law, and although subject to national procedural conditions, these must be at least as generous as those applicable in equivalent national actions and not such as to render rights under EU law incapable of enforcement in practice.

2 Although in principle there is no obligation on the part of national courts or national legal orders to create new remedies for the enforcement of EU law, in reality the effect of the Court's case law, particularly in *Factortame I*, *Francovich I* and *Brasserie du Pêcheur/Factortame III*, requires this to occur.

3 Where compensatory sanctions are chosen by the national legislature as the means to ensure that rights arising under EU law are effectively enforced, the sanction of damages must be adequate.

4   In determining the extent to which EU law imposes itself upon national procedural conditions the Court of Justice has balanced the requirements of the effective remedies principle against the autonomy of national law.

5   Damages for state liability for breach of EU law will be available – subject to national procedural rules – if the following conditions are satisfied:
– the rule of law infringed must be intended to confer rights on individuals;
– the breach must be sufficiently serious; and
– there must be a direct causal link between the breach of the obligation resting on the State and the damage sustained by the injured parties.

6   The Court has introduced a parallelism between the liability of the Member States and the non-contractual liability of the EU institutions under Article 288 EC.

7   The record of national legal systems in giving effect to the case law of the Court of Justice is mixed. In the UK particular difficulties centre around the right to damages, and the willingness of the courts to make use of the indirect effect principle, the latter problem resulting from the interpretation of the European Communities Act 1972, and the continued insistence of the courts upon that Act as the foundation for the enforcement in the UK of EU law, rather than its inherent qualities, as interpreted by the Court of Justice.

Questions

1   Has the Court of Justice struck the right balance in policing the 'effective' and 'non-discriminatory' national remedies principles?

2   How does *Brasserie du Pêcheur/Factortame III* differ from *Francovich I*, both as regards the facts of the cases, and the principle of state liability as determined by the Court of Justice? Has the Court of Justice now given sufficiently clear advice to the national courts so that they will be able to apply the principle in future?

3   Is the record of the higher English courts in the application of EU law satisfactory?

Further Reading

A. Arnull (1999a), Ch. 5, 'European Rights, National Remedies'.

A. Biondi (1999), 'European Court of Justice and Certain National Procedural Limitations: Not such a Tough Relationship', 36 *Common Market Law Review* 1271.

C. Boch (2000), Ch. 11, 'Specific Community Rules for the Enforcement of Community Law'.

D. Chalmers (2000a), 'The Application of Community Law in the United Kingdom, 1994–1998', 37 *Common Market Law Review* 83.

D. Chalmers (2000b), 'The Much Ado about Judicial Politics in the United Kingdom: A Statistical Analysis of Reported Decisions of the United Kingdom

Courts Invoking EU Law 1973–1998', 23 *Western European Politics* no.2, forthcoming.

R. Craufurd Smith (1999), 'Remedies for Breaches of EU Law in National Courts: Legal Variation and Selection', in Craig and de Búrca (1999).

W. van Gerven (1994b), 'Non-contractual Liability of Member States, Community Institutions and Individuals for Breaches of Community Law with a View to a Common Law for Europe', 1 *Maastricht Journal of European and Comparative Law* 6.

W. van Gerven (2000), 'Of Rights, Remedies and Procedures', 37 *Common Market Law Review* 501.

C. Himsworth (1997), 'Things Fall Apart: The Harmonisation of Community Judicial Procedural Protection Revisited' 22 *European Law Review* 291.

M. Hoskins (1998), 'Rebirth of the Innominate Tort?', in Beatson and Tridimas (1998).

F. Jacobs (1997), 'Enforcing Community Rights and Obligations: Striking the Balance', in Lonbay and Biondi (1997).

I. Maher (1994), 'National Courts as European Community Courts', 14 *Legal Studies* 226.

I. Maher (1995a), 'A Question of Conflict: The Higher English Courts and the Implementation of European Community Law', in Daintith (1995b).

E. Szyszczak (1990), 'Sovereignty: Crisis, Compliance, Confusion, Complacency', 15 *European Law Review* 480.

T. Tridimas (1998), 'Member State Liability in Damages for Breach of Community Law: An Assessment of the Case Law', in Beatson and Tridimas (1998).

A. Ward (1995), 'Effective Sanctions in EC Law: A Moving Boundary in the Division of Competence', 1 *European Law Journal* 204.

Part VI

The Judicial Control of the EU Institutions

14 Introduction to the Judicial Control of the EU Institutions

14.1 Introduction

Every developed legal system needs a system of judicial control which places fetters upon the exercise of state power. In the EU the clear mandate for such a system lies in the task of the Court under Article 220 EC (formerly Article 164 EC) to ensure that the law is observed. The system is structured, in EU law, in terms of the system of remedies provided by Articles 230, 232, 234, 241 and 288 EC (formerly Articles 173, 174, 177, 184 and 215 EC: note some of the quotations in this and the following chapters use the old numbers). The Court explained the system and the principle in Case 294/83 *Parti Ecologiste 'Les Verts'* v. *Parliament* ([1986] ECR 1339) in the following terms (at p. 1365):

'It must first be emphasised in this regard that the European Economic Community is a Community based on the rule of law, in as much as neither its Member States nor its institutions can avoid a review of the question whether the measures adopted by them are in conformity with the basic constitutional charter, the Treaty. In particular, in Articles 173 and 184, on the one hand, and in Article 177, on the other, the Treaty established a complete system of legal remedies and procedures designed to permit the Court of Justice to review the legality of measures adopted by the institutions. Natural and legal persons are thus protected against the application to them of general measures which they cannot contest directly before the Court by reason of the special conditions of admissibility laid down in the second paragraph of Article 173 of the Treaty. Where the Community institutions are responsible for the administrative implementation of such measures, natural or legal persons may bring a direct action before the Court against implementing measures which are addressed to them or which are of direct and individual concern to them and, in support of such an action, plead the illegality of the general measure on which they are based. Where implementation is a matter for the national authorities, such persons may plead the invalidity of general measures before the national courts and cause the latter to request the Court of Justice for a preliminary ruling.'

The system of judicial control extends also to a system of reparation for tortious acts (what the Treaty terms 'non-contractual' liability); according to the Court in Cases 46, 48/93 *Brasserie du Pêcheur/Factortame III* [1996] ECR I-1029:

> 'The principle of the non-contractual liability of the Community expressly laid down in Article 215 of the Treaty is simply an expression of the general principle familiar to the legal systems of the Member States that an unlawful act or omission gives rise to an obligation to make good the damage caused. That provision also reflects the obligation on public authorities to make good damage caused in the performance of their duties' (para. 29).

In the last part of this book we will show how these principles have been put into effect, with separate chapters on the judicial review of EU action, on the review of wrongful omissions by the institutions, and on the availability of compensation for loss caused by the EU institutions. It will assess the extent to which the 'state' authorities (i.e. EU institutions and, where appropriate, the national authorities acting under EU law) are bound by the rule of law in their enforcement of EU law *vis-à-vis* individual subjects. It will also provide some assessment of how the balance between the requirements of administrative efficiency and protection of the individual is achieved by the Court of Justice.

This introductory chapter puts in place some essential background for the understanding of this field of EU law, by laying out the key Treaty provisions, and explaining the many functions which these provisions have to fulfil. As will be apparent, the variety of functions fulfilled by Articles 230 and 234 EC in particular are such that aside from vague generalities such as 'the protection of the rule of law' it is hard sometimes to see what these functions share in common with each within the framework of the EU legal order. It is this 'multifunctionalism' which makes this field of EU law sometimes difficult to understand. In this chapter and the ones which follow, the terms 'Court of Justice' and 'Court' should be understood to include both EU courts, as the 'Community judicature', until a distinction is explicitly drawn between the different functions which they now fulfil, by virtue of the current division of jurisdiction. This chapter will also reflect briefly upon some aspects of the development of administrative law in the EU context, especially in the context of the evolving role of the European Ombudsman.

14.2 The Framework of Treaty Provisions

It should be recalled that the Court of Justice is a court of limited jurisdiction, exercising only the powers conferred upon under the Treaties. Occasionally, it has moved to fill small lacunae in the system of judicial protection offered by the Treaty (notably by introducing the *locus standi* of the Parliament under Article 230, and an extended possibility for imposing temporal restrictions on the impact of its rulings under Article 234). However, in general terms, any actions brought before the Court must come under one of the heads of claim contained in the Treaty.

For the purposes of the judicial review of unlawful EU action, the Treaty offers both direct and indirect means of challenge. The main means of direct challenge is Article 230, which we have discussed already in many contexts in this book (e.g. inter-institutional litigation: 7.18; individual complainants and the Commission's enforcement powers: 8.5 and 8.16). Article 230 (formerly Article 173 EC) provides:

'The Court of Justice shall review the legality of acts adopted jointly by the European Parliament and the Council, of acts of the Council, of the Commission and of the ECB, other than recommendations and opinions, and of acts of the European Parliament intended to produce legal effects *vis-à-vis* third parties.

It shall for this purpose have jurisdiction in actions brought by a Member State, the Council or the Commission on grounds of lack of competence, infringement of an essential procedural requirement, infringement of this Treaty or of any rule of law relating to its application, or misuse of powers.

The Court shall have jurisdiction under the same conditions in actions brought by the European Parliament, by the Court of Auditors and by the ECB for the purpose of protecting their prerogatives.

Any natural or legal person may, under the same conditions, institute proceedings against a decision addressed to that person or against a decision which, although in the form of a regulation or a decision addressed to another person, is of direct and individual concern to the former.

The proceedings provided for in this Article shall be instituted within two months of the publication of the measure, or of its notification to the plaintiff, or, in the absence thereof, of the day on which it came to the knowledge of the latter, as the case may be.'

In the event of a finding by the Court of Justice that these principles of legality have been breached, the consequence is annulment. Article 231 EC (formerly Article 174 EC) provides:

'If the action is well founded, the Court of Justice shall declare the act concerned to be void.

In the case of a regulation, however, the Court of Justice shall, if it considers this necessary, state which of the effects of the regulation which it has declared void shall be considered as definitive.'

Article 232 EC (formerly Article 175 EC) provides a direct complement to Article 230. It covers unlawful inaction, and makes provision for challenges to unlawful omissions:

> 'Should the European Parliament, the Council or the Commission, in infringement of this Treaty, fail to act, the Member States and the other institutions of the Community may bring an action before the Court of Justice to have the infringement established.
>
> The action shall be admissible only if the institution concerned has first been called upon to act. If, within two months of being so called upon, the institution concerned has not defined its position, the action may be brought within a further period of two months.
>
> Any natural or legal person may, under the conditions laid down in the preceding paragraphs, complain to the Court of Justice that an institution of the Community has failed to address to that person any act other than a recommendation or an opinion.
>
> The Court of Justice shall have jurisdiction, under the same conditions, in actions or proceedings brought by the ECB in the areas falling within the latter's competence and in actions or proceedings brought against the latter.'

The consequences of a successful action under Articles 230 or 232 are dealt with in Article 233 EC (formerly Article 176 EC) which provides:

> 'The institution (or institutions) whose act has been declared void or whose failure to act has been declared contrary to this Treaty shall be required to take the necessary measures to comply with the judgment of the Court of Justice.
>
> This obligation shall not affect any obligation which may result from the application of the second paragraph of Article 288 [the obligation to pay compensation for wrongful acts causing loss].
>
> This Article shall also apply to the ECB.'

On the basis of these provisions, the following summary can be given: a successful direct action to challenge an unlawful act or omission presupposes three basic requirements:

(a) a reviewable act or omission;
(b) *locus standi* on the part of the applicant;
(c) illegality on the part of the defendant (i.e. the presence of the grounds for review in Article 230 or the violation of a duty to act in the context of Article 232).

In the event that a general measure of the EU is at issue, Article 241 EC (formerly Article 184 EC) makes provision for indirect challenge in the context of other proceedings:

> 'Notwithstanding the expiry of the period laid down in the fifth paragraph of Article 230, any party may, in proceedings in which a regulation adopted jointly by the European Parliament and the Council, or a regulation of the Council, of the Commission, or of the ECB is at issue, plead the grounds specified in the second paragraph of Article 230, in order to invoke before the Court of Justice the inapplicability of that regulation.'

The possibility also exists for mounting indirect challenges to EU measures through the medium of an action in the national court, which raises a question about the validity of an EU measure. In that context, the national court is under an obligation to make a reference on the question of validity, if it has reason to doubt the validity of the EU measure. It cannot itself in any circumstances invalidate an EU measure (11.7). Of course, neither Article 241 nor Article 234 in themselves constitutes a separate 'cause of action' against unlawful EU action, but are mechanisms whereby the Court of Justice can, in the context of other proceedings, review the legality of underlying EU acts, particularly those of a general legislative nature.

The jurisdiction in relation to compensation actions follows from Article 235 EC (formerly Article 178 EC) which provides that 'in disputes relating to the compensation of damage provided for in the second paragraph of Article 288'. The latter provision sets out the conditions governing non-contractual liability:

> 'In the case of non-contractual liability, the Community shall, in accordance with the general principles common to the laws of the Member States, make good any damage caused by its institutions or by its servants in the performance of their duties.'

Again, as we shall see, actions in national courts have a role to play in this context. Frequently, where the issue raised is one of the return of monies unlawfully levied or unlawfully denied, the correct action for an applicant to bring will be one in the national court against the national implementing authority, which so often is the body which has direct contact with those who are being 'administered'. On the other hand, as the EU institutions – particularly, of course, the Commission – become increasingly directly involved in certain fields of redistributive social policy, through the disbursement of aids and subsidies for example through the various funds, then the proper course will be through the medium of an action in the Court of Justice.

Two further provisions should be cited to complete the basic framework for judicial offered by the Treaty. Article 242 EC (formerly Article 185 EC) provides:

'Actions brought before the Court of Justice shall not have suspensory effect. The Court of Justice may, however, if it considers the circumstances so require, order that application of the contested act be suspended.'

Consequently, one category of actions before the Court will be applications for suspension of contested measures. Likewise, the Court will hear applications for interim measures – under the same jurisdiction which covers interim measures in the case of Article 169 enforcement actions (8.14). Article 243 EC (formerly Article 186 EC) provides:

'The Court of Justice may in any cases before it prescribe any necessary interim measures.'

14.3   The Many Functions of the System of Judicial Protection

Article 230 in particular conceals behind its text a whole multitude of different functions, which highlight the many different ways in which various actors – institutions, Member States, 'individuals' (all natural or legal persons, including any potential applicants such as pressure groups, trade or other types of associations, sub-national governments) – interact with the EU legal order. The different types of interactions are expressed according to the various conditions which Article 230 imposes upon each actor, in particular:

- the extent of *locus standi* (limited or unlimited);
- the range of EU measures which can be challenged (all acts having legal effects including legislative measures, or only certain categories of 'decisions' or individual measures);
- finally, we shall see that in some cases Article 230 interacts with other provisions of the Treaty, in particular the Article 234 preliminary reference provisions.

It would be useful to summarise the numerous uses of the action for annulment:

(a) The action brought by one institution against another for annulment of any legal act, ranging from general legislative measures, through administrative acts, to even the most informal act which can be characterised as having legal effects. Only the Parliament, the Court of Auditors and the ECB have limited *locus standi* (to protect their prerogatives). The

Council and Commission are in contrast presumed always to have an interest in taking action – doubtless because they represent most directly the 'supranational' and 'intergovernmental' elements in the EU. As we saw in the examination of inter-institutional litigation in 7.18, these types of actions could properly be termed constitutional in so far as they raise fundamental questions about the division of competence, inter-institutional balance, and principles such as democracy, and institutional accountability and legitimacy.

(b) Also constitutional in nature are the many actions brought by Member States against the institutions. In the example of legal basis litigation, here too the preoccupation is very much with questions of competence and inter-institutional balance. The same could be said of the various actions that Luxembourg has taken against the Parliament in order to enforce its right to host the seat of that institution and to prevent it moving wholesale to Strasbourg or Brussels. Alternatively, a Member State may be arguing that an EU measure was taken in violation of general principles of law, or even fundamental rights. This situation is more likely to arise with increased use of QMV, perhaps as an alternative to the veto which unanimity gives each Member State. A good example would be the attempt by Germany, which had already expressed its bitter opposition within the political forum, to obtain annulment of the EU's banana regime, established in 1993 by means of Council Regulation (Case C-280/93 *Germany* v. *Council* [1994] ECR I-4873; 5.13, 7.11). Germany argued vehemently, but unsuccessfully, that the regulation breached both international trade law (the GATT), and fundamental rights of economic actors involved (banana traders) (15.13). As with the Council and the Commission, there are no problems of *locus standi* for the Member States.

(c) From time to time, however, the Member States may become involved in litigation – particularly with the Commission – which is administrative rather than constitutional in character. That is, it contests the use of executive power by the Commission, rather than fundamental constitutional principles of the legal order. It would normally arise in instances where the Commission has the power, by decision, to apply the Treaty rules to an individual situation (4.4, 8.12). Examples arise commonly in relation to the management of the CAP, especially the disbursement of monies under the European Agricultural Guidance and Guarantee Fund and to the management of other structural funds (Social Fund, Regional Development Fund, etc.). The Commission also has direct executive powers in many fields of customs law, especially the use of Article 134 EC to prevent distortions in the internal market, under Article 86(3) on the application of the competition rules to highly regulated markets, and under Article 95(4)–(7) and (9) in relation to the management of national derogations from harmonisation measures. All of these provisions have given rise to actions based on Article 230 EC, but provided there are no difficulties for the applicant in identifying the reviewable act, and provided the action is brought within the correct time limits, there will be no problems of admissibility as Member States have unlimited *locus standi*. Moreover, many such actions deal with small questions of technical detail on the powers of the Commission, rather than large issues of principle.

(d) Then there are a number of categories of cases which arise because of the involvement of 'individuals' (i.e. anyone who is not an institution or a Member State) in the Commission's executive processes. Outside a narrow range of circumstances, as we shall see in Chapter 15, such persons will have great difficulty satisfying the *locus standi* requirement. Essentially, the system of the Treaty sees these types of actions as protecting an individual, 'private' (and normally economic) interest, and not as operating for the broader public interest:

– in the fields of customs law and agricultural law, difficulties tend to arise either because the measure challenged (e.g. an import quota arrangement) does not have a sufficiently individuated impact upon the applicant, or because the Commission's procedures do not directly affect the applicant (e.g. in a case of indirect administration, involving the national authorities: 8.1); the rules preclude individuals in such circumstances challenging by means of actions under Article 230 allegedly unlawful legislative measures which form the framework for the executive rules;

– in cases of 'direct administration', e.g. in relation to the structural funds or development aid provided to the countries of Central and Eastern Europe or in the developing world individual applicants such as those who tender to run projects using EU monies are more likely to be able to establish *locus standi*, providing, that is, that they are not trying to challenge the general legislative framework;

– the cases of competition law, anti-dumping law and state aid law are *sui generis*, as they both involve the Commission in a 'quasi-judicial' role which impacts directly on individuals, investigating alleged instances of breaches of the EU rules by individual or groups of undertakings. Rights of 'due process' arise in these areas, both for those subject to investigation and those who make complaints, which can be protected by means of direct actions for annulment. In the case of competition law where the Commission also takes all of the relevant decisions, the Court explicitly has 'unlimited jurisdiction' (Article 229 EC, formerly Article 172 EC) in relation to the fines and penalties which the Commission can impose.

(e) However, Article 230 does not normally offer the basis for the judicial review of unconstitutional legislation at the instance of individual applicants (that is legislation which was adopted *ultra vires*, or in breach of some general principle or fundamental right upheld under the Treaty). It makes no difference that the applicant may be alleging a very serious infringement of his or her fundamental rights. Even so, the system of EU law does recognise the principle of constitutional supremacy, under which the Court of Justice (but not national courts) can invalidate unconstitutional EU legislation. Challenges by individual applicants to general legislative measures should be brought against the implementing measures of the national authorities in the national courts (or brought about by resisting the application of such rules at national level, again in the national court), and the challenge to the underlying EU measure effected indirectly via a reference on validity under Article 234. This system has been heavily criticised as 'letting individuals down' by making them 'explore the highways and byways of national procedural law' (Mancini and Keeling, 1994: 189). A certain level of illogicality is introduced into the system because the Court will hear claims by individuals for damages under Article 288 in respect of loss suffered, even as the result of general legislative measures where the relevant measures cannot be challenged by means of a direct action under Article 230. However, such actions will only very rarely succeed. One of the main focuses of discussion in these chapters on the judicial control of the institutions, therefore, will be the question of the access of individual applicants to the Court of Justice.

In comparison to Article 230, Article 232 does not have so many functions to perform. The relative lack of complexity reflects partly the fact that it is not used as the basis for actions anywhere near as often. Even less often are actions actually successful, as Article 232 will only apply where an institution is under a duty to act. For non-privileged applicants, the utility of Article 232 has been clearest in the field of competition law (where it is especially useful for complainants (8.16)). In the inter-institutional sphere it is the Parliament which has been able to make greatest use of the provision, with a successful claim against the Council in respect of failure to adopt a number of measures relating to the Common Transport Policy (Case 13/83 *Parliament* v. *Council* ([1985] ECR 1513).

For each of the situations identified above there will be a different set of policy factors operating; these will underlie the view which the Court takes of the actions of the EU institutions, determining very often the 'intensity' of the review to which it will subject these actions. In other words, policy factors may influence how closely the Court enquires into the actions of the institution under challenge. As a final point about the complexity and difficulty of this field of EU law, a note should be made of the highly technical and often impenetrable frameworks of EU legislation, which are the subject of claims in fields such as agriculture and customs. These will frequently make it more difficult for the reader to identify readily the precise policy point which is emerging from any given case, and reduce the sense of a coherent body of law controlling the exercise of public power in the EU.

14.4   Articles 230 and 232 and Public Interest Litigation

A notable feature of many modern legal systems has been the development of public interest litigation, where either one litigant takes action on behalf of a number of others, or a representative association takes action on behalf of its members, or of some 'abstract' interest which it represents (e.g. the environment) (Harlow and Rawlings, 1992; Harlow, 1999b; Micklitz and Reich, 1996). Public interest litigation has proved to be particularly useful as a strategy to be followed in relation to some areas of EU law, notably the private enforcement of sex discrimination law and environmental law (Harlow, 1992a), and some 'repeat players' such as the UK Equal Opportunities Commission have achieved some important successes (Barnard, 1995). These successes have occurred, however, in the national courts, using the medium of Article 234 references in order to secure an authoritative pronouncement by the Court of Justice (Reich, 1996).

In contrast, because of the restrictive standing rules in the Court of Justice itself, public interest litigation has had almost no impact in relation to direct actions brought by individuals. There have been some attempts to bring cases that have sought to raise some 'public interest' which was more than the aggregate of the 'private interests' of those directly involved. Few have succeeded. Virtually the sole successes outside the field of competition law have been in relation to the 'transparency' rules or document disclosure. For example, Case T-194/94 *Carvel and Guardian Newspapers* v. *Council* ([1995] ECR II-2765; 10.8) was brought by a journalist and his newspaper as an attack upon the Council's so-called 'transparency arrangements' for allowing public access to documents, and a number of subsequent cases. In all these cases, the litigants have been the direct addressees of the decisions they wish to contest. However, they can be an effective weapon to address public interest issues. In Case T-105/95 *WWF International* v. *Commission* ([1997] ECR II-313) the action related to a campaign to prevent Ireland destroying a beauty spot, and to ensure that the Commission enforced the relevant provisions of EU law, if necessary through an enforcement action. EU structural funds had been awarded to fund a visitors' centre in an area of outstanding natural beauty, and the complaint was that EU environmental standards had been breached in the use of those funds. After a complaint by the Irish National Trust and the World Wildlife Fund, the Commission decided to take no action. The complainants requested certain documents and were refused under the relevant Commission decision on access to documents. They brought a challenge before the Court of First Instance, and although the Commission's use of a public interest exception was upheld, none the less the Commission's decision was annulled for lack of proper reasoning because of the failure to weigh up the interests of the complainants against the public interest. It gave the groups 'a little space in which to fight and manoeuvre' (Harlow, 1999b: 28).

Competition law has brought some successes, notably for consumer groups. This is due to the very specific participatory rights which many of the actors in the process have under the EU rules, and the ease with which a non-participant can become a participant through the presentation of a complaint. The role of BEUC (the *Bureau Européen des Consommateurs*, an umbrella group partly funded by the Commission) has been particularly important. In Cases 228, 229/82 *Ford of Europe Inc* v. *Commission* ([1984] ECR 1129) two groups – BEUC and the UK Consumers' Association – were granted the right by the Court of Justice to intervene in an appeal by Ford against an unfavourable decision of the Commission under the competition rules. However, in Case C-170/89 *BEUC* v. *Commission* ([1991] ECR I-5709) the Court rejected an attempt by BEUC to gain access to confidential documentation in an anti-dumping case concerning the importation of audiocassettes from the Far East. Significantly, the Court did not dispose of the action by holding that BEUC had no standing to challenge a Commission ruling denying the access to documentation, but dismissed the arguments on their merits, observing in its conclusions that it was for the EU legislature to consider the introduction of the types of procedural rights which BEUC was claiming. It would be interesting to speculate what difference the access to documents rules might make in such circumstances. In Case T-37/92 *BEUC* v. *Commission* ([1994] ECR II-285), BEUC took action again, this time before the Court of First Instance, and successfully challenged a decision of the Commission not to pursue a complaint which BEUC had lodged regarding certain restrictive practices between British and Japanese car manufacturers relating to the British car market.

The possibility of an amendment to Article 230 has often been raised, either to extend *locus standi* for private parties, or possibly to allow a specific right of action to certain types of representative associations. The need for amendment will be discussed in greater detail below, as the weaknesses of the standing rules emerge clearly only from a full discussion of how they operate. Such a question needs to be seen, however, in the context of considering whether a formal right of 'access to justice' needs to be instituted.

14.5 The Division of Jurisdiction and the Appellate Role of the Court of Justice

Since its establishment, the Court of First Instance has acquired a particularly important role in relation to EC 'administrative' law, as it now hears all direct actions brought by non-privileged applicants (i.e. under Articles 230, 232 and 288 EC). It will from time to time decline jurisdiction in circumstances where the same measure has been challenged in proceedings before the Court of Justice. This has occurred in the fields of merger control (Case T-88/94 *Société Commerciale des Potasses et de l'Azote* v. *Commission* [1995] ECR II-222) and state aid (Case T-490/93 *Bremer Vulkan Verbund AG* v. *Commission* [1995] ECR II-477). To ensure the protection of the interests of the individuals concerned, they will exceptionally be permitted leave to intervene in the proceedings before the Court of Justice where the same measures are challenged.

As we shall see, the continuing refusal of the Court of First Instance to loosen the standing rules means that it rejects as inadmissible all actions brought against general EU acts. It therefore has relatively little role to play in respect of the 'constitutional' aspects of the judicial protection scheme identified above (but compare its role in relation to Article 288). In the first years of its operation, the Court of First Instance was widely acknowledged to be underemployed, as it took only staff cases and competition cases. It now has a heavy workload – comparable with that of the Court of Justice itself – and that may change the way in which, so far, it has been able to deal with cases by handing down rather fuller and more detailed reviews of the facts and law in the cases it decides. These have compared favourably with the judgments of the Court of Justice itself, whose pronouncements are notably delphic. Obviously a widening of the standing rules would have as dramatic an impact upon the Court of First Instance as the transfer of additional categories of case, although the latter seems unlikely to occur in the very near future. The Court of Justice is likely to continue to have responsibility for most constitutional aspects of the system of judicial control, as well as for overall review of the system through the exercise of its appellate jurisdiction.

The exercise of that jurisdiction is governed by the Statute of the Court of Justice and the Rules of Procedure of the Court of Justice. Article 51 provides:

> 'An appeal to the Court of Justice shall be limited to points of law. It shall lie on the grounds of lack of competence of the Court of First Instance, a breach of procedure before it which adversely affects the interests of the appellant as well as the infringement of Community law by the Court of First Instance.'

If the appeal is well founded, the Court of Justice can either quash the judgment and remit it to the Court of First Instance for decision, or, where the state of the proceedings so permits, it may decide the case itself (as it did in Case C-137/92 P *Commission* v. *BASF* [1994] ECR I-2555, which concerned Commission procedures for taking decisions in competition cases; 4.2, or in Cases C-174 & 189/98 P *Netherlands and van der Wal* v. *Commission*,

11 January 2000, a fundamental rights/access to documents case discussed in 9.6). So long as much of the work of the Court of First Instance consisted of staff cases, the level of appeals was bound to remain low, as there are financial disincentives in staff cases against appealing. This will undoubtedly change as the Court of First Instance now deals with a much wider range of cases, and a number of the cases discussed in the chapters which follow are under appeal. However, as it takes nearly two years for the Court of Justice to decide appeals, it would appear that there are disincentives other than mere questions of money.

In their joint contribution to the 2000 IGC, the Court of Justice and the Court of First Instance suggested making amendments to Article 225 EC which establishes the Court of First Instance to allow a filtering system for appeals to be set up by means of the Statute of the Court of Justice. This is especially contemplated for staff cases, and for trademark cases. In each case, the Court of First Instance would become the effective appellate jurisdiction, with first-instance jurisdiction in the hands of a judicial board of appeal separately established and given the status of an independent tribunal. Proposals such as these are made in the knowledge of the already heavy burden faced by the two Courts, especially in relation to direct actions, and the anticipated surge in new actions resulting from appeals against determinations in the intellectual property field, once the systems in relation to trademarks and patents are full established and operating.

14.6 Reviewing Administrative Processes and the Role of the Ombudsman

The Ombudsman (4.15) now has a significant role to play in reviewing the work of the EU institutions, especially the Commission's management of its executive and administrative functions. While complaining to the Ombudsman and obtaining a 'critical remark' or even generating the adoption of an own initiative Special Report on the topic of the complaint by the Ombudsman, may seem less spectacular than obtaining formal judicial review, it can be just as effective. In the first place, as it is the Ombudsman's basic role within the system to review cases of maladministration, he is specialised in his task. He offers a continuous focus for reform initiatives, and in practice he has been effective in a 'rule-making' capacity, even if the rules are 'soft' in nature (Bonnor, 2000). Areas where he has been forced – by the dilatory conduct of the institutions – to take a particularly active role have been transparency (10.8), pushing the institutions towards the adoption of a code of good administrative practice, forcing the Commission's hand in its treatment of complaints seeking action under Article 226 (8.16), and, most recently, chastising the Commission because it is a very slow payer of its debts and bills.

Summary

1   The Court of Justice attaches great importance to the system of remedies for judicial control of the actions of the EU institutions under the Treaties, aiming to ensure that the European Community is a Community based on the rule of law.

2   The system of remedies is principally based on Articles 230, 232, 234, 241 and 288 EC. Many of these provisions fulfil a number of different constitutional and administrative functions, depending upon the nature of the litigants before the Court, the type of provision under challenge, and whether the litigation began in the national court, the Court of First Instance or the Court of Justice.

3   For the EU institutions and the Member States, Article 230 offers a mechanism for maintaining the constitutional checks and balances offered by the separation of powers and functions within the EU, and between the EU and its Member States.

4   Individuals wishing to challenge general EU measures must normally begin their challenge in the national court, and seek a reference on validity from the national court under Article 234. Individual measures may be challenged in the Court of First Instance. Compensation claims rarely succeed.

5   The Court of Justice exercises an important appellate jurisdiction in relation to the judgments of the Court of First Instance.

Questions

See Chapters 15–17.

Workshop (for Chapters 14–17)

What changes (if any) would you introduce in the text of Articles 230 and 232 EC to increase the level of individual access to the Court of First Instance and the Court of Justice?

Further Reading

See Chapters 15–17.

Key Websites

The Ombudsman's contribution to 'good administration' is detailed on his website:
http://www.euro-ombudsman.eu.int
Searching for case law on judicial review is possible via the Court's website:
http://curia.eu.int/en/index.htm

15 Judicial Review of the Acts of the Institutions

15.1 Introduction

This chapter examines the main elements of annulment actions brought under Article 230, concentrating on the following questions:

- concept of 'reviewable act';
- the difficulties of establishing *locus standi* for 'non-privileged applicants';
- the basic approach which the Court of Justice takes to the grounds for review.

All of these elements are essential to a successful action for annulment. The text of Article 230 is set out in 14.2. The chapter also examines the conditions governing the availability of indirect review, through the medium of a national court reference on the validity of an EU measure under Article 234, as well as on the basis of Article 241. The different approaches which the Court takes to the cases it encounters, in particular the types of policy factors which it applies, have to be viewed in the light of the typology of cases outlined in 14.3. Perhaps the most important variable concerns the identity of the parties to the litigation: EU institutions, Member States or 'private' parties.

15.2 The Notion of 'Reviewable Act'

Article 230 provides for the Court of Justice to review the legality of certain 'acts' of the institutions. The exclusion in the original Treaty of acts of the Parliament did cause problems in the context of the increased role and powers of the Parliament. Judicial recognition of these changes was gradually given by the Court. The terms of Article 230, as amended by the Treaties of Maastricht and Amsterdam, are now clear: certain acts of the Parliament are explicitly included, along with those of the Council and the Commission, and of the Council and the Parliament acting jointly as legislator using the co-decision procedure.

In Case 230/81 *Luxembourg* v. *Parliament* ([1983] ECR 255) the Court had already annulled a resolution of the Parliament concerning the moving of its seat from Luxembourg to Strasbourg and Brussels which obviously affected the Parliament's role under all three founding Treaties. However, the annulment was effected under Article 38 ECSC alone, which explicitly recognises the power to annul acts of the Parliament. The Court went one stage further in Case 294/83 *Parti Ecologiste 'Les Verts'* v. *Parliament* ([1986] ECR 1339) annulling the decision of the Bureau of the Parliament allocating money to parties for campaigning in the 1984 direct elections. It stated (p. 1365):

> 'It is true that, unlike Article 177 of the Treaty, which refers to acts of the institutions without further qualification, Article 173 refers only to acts of the Council and the Commission. However, the general scheme of the Treaty is to make a direct action available against "all measures adopted by the institutions ... which are intended to have legal effects", as the Court has already had occasion to emphasise in [Case 22/70 *Commission* v. *Council (ERTA)*] ... The European Parliament is not expressly mentioned among the institutions whose measures may be contested because, in its original version, the EEC Treaty merely granted it powers of consultation and political control rather than the power to adopt measures intended to have legal effects *vis-à-vis* third parties.'

After a comparison with the system of judicial control under the ECSC Treaty, the Court went on:

> 'An interpretation of Article 173 of the Treaty which excluded measures adopted by the European Parliament from those which could be contested would lead to a result contrary both to the spirit of the Treaty as expressed in Article 164 and to its system. Measures adopted by the European Parliament in the context of the EEC Treaty could encroach on the powers of the Member States or of the other institutions, or exceed the limits which have been set to the Parliament's powers, without it being possible to refer them for review by the Court. It must therefore be concluded that an action for annulment may lie against measures adopted by the European Parliament intended to have legal effects *vis-à-vis* third parties.'

In application of these principles, and in recognition of the role of the European Parliament in relation to the budget, the Court also held that the Order of the President of the Parliament adopting the 1986 budget could be annulled in Case 34/86 *Council* v. *Parliament* ([1986] ECR 2155). The inclusion of the words of the Court verbatim in the revised third paragraph of Article

230 is testimony to the role of the Court as the originating force of many of the institutional developments contained in the Treaty of Maastricht.

The most important element of a reviewable act has already been referred to in the quotations from *'Les Verts'*, and that is the requirement that it be one which produces 'legal effects'. Although Article 230 refers to this as a requirement only in relation to acts of the Parliament, it applies likewise to both the Council and the Commission, and was read into Article 230 by the Court in recognition that it has been faced with annulment proceedings concerned with acts of the institutions which do not fit neatly into the typology of legal acts offered by Article 189. An early example of such a *sui generis* act is provided by the challenge to the minutes of the Council incorporating a resolution which determined the negotiation procedures for the European Road Transport Agreement brought by the Commission in Case 22/70 *Commission* v. *Council (ERTA)* ([1971] ECR 263). The reason the Commission sought the annulment was in order to demonstrate that these negotiations were matters falling within Community rather than national competence. The Court held that it was not an obstacle to judicial review that a legal act does not formally fall within the system set up by what was then Article 189 EEC (now Article 249 EC), but that there is a category of *sui generis* legal acts. The only question is whether the act has legal effects. *Sui generis* acts are very much an open category, as the cases that follow will show.

There is an obvious case for the application of these principles to the many internal management measures of the institutions:

- staffing decisions (Case 15/63 *Lassalle* v. *Parliament* [1964] ECR 31);
- the decision of the Parliament Bureau in *'Les Verts'* concerning the allocation of electoral campaign funds.

In two cases, the Court has construed internal Commission measures as reviewable acts, even though they were essentially non-binding in nature. France was successful in challenges both to instructions on the management of the EAGGF (Case C-366/88 *France* v. *Commission* ([1990] ECR I-3571) and to a Code of Conduct concerning the management of the structural funds issued by the Commission (Case C-303/90 *France* v. *Commission* [1991] ECR I-5315). What was notable was that in each case the Commission precisely lacked the competence to adopt the type of measures which purported to have legal effects. The cases therefore illustrate the interaction between the basic structural requirements for a successful action and the grounds for review that the Court must apply. Similarly, France proved itself once again a reliable challenger of the outer limits of the Commission's competence when it sought the annulment of a Commission communication which purported to have legal effects (Case C-57/95 *Commission* v. *France* [1997] ECR I-1627). It was issued after a failure to reach agreement on a

Commission proposal for a directive relating to the freedom of management and investment of pension funds, and it was very similar to the withdrawn proposal. The Court examined whether the communication purported to lay down specific obligations, and the mandatory language in the communication along with frequent use of the term 'the Member States shall...' proved decisive. Once it was established that it was a reviewable act by reference to those terms, it was a simple deduction that it should be annulled, as the Commission has no competence to adopt such dispositive measures.

Finally, the concept of a 'reviewable act' has proved particularly important in the context of the control of the legality of competition proceedings under Articles 81 and 82 EC, where the Court has found it important to identify the stages at which undertakings may legitimately challenge preliminary decisions taken during the course of such proceedings, without waiting for the final decision. The Court decided in Cases 8-11/66 *Cimenteries* v. *Commission (Noordwijks Cement Accoord)* ([1967] ECR 75) that a decision under Article 15(6) of Regulation 17 whereby the Commission removes from undertakings, after a preliminary investigation, the protection from fines accorded to them if they notify their arguably anti-competitive agreements to the Commission, could be challenged under Article 230. The Court held (at p. 91):

> 'this measure deprived them of the advantages of a legal situation which Article 15(5) attached to the notification of the agreement, and exposed them to a grave financial risk. Thus the said measure affected the interests of the undertakings by bringing about a distinct change in their legal position. It is unequivocally a measure which produces legal effects touching the interests of the undertakings concerned and which is binding on them. It constitutes not a mere opinion but a decision.'

The Court repeated substantially the same arguments in holding in Case 60/81 *IBM* v. *Commission* ([1981] ECR 2639) that a letter informing IBM that the Commission was of the opinion that it had abused a dominant position in breach of Article 82 and a 'statement of objections' containing the Commission's allegations were not reviewable acts. A reviewable act must be one which definitively lays down the position of the institution in question on the conclusion of a procedure, and is not merely a provisional or preparatory measure which itself could be challenged if the final decision was challenged.

In the context of complaints, the procedural equivalent of a statement of objections is the 'Article 6' letter, named after the provision which requires the Commission to inform complainants if it intends to reject their complaint, and to give them an opportunity to make known their views. An

Article 6 letter is not a reviewable act (Case T-64/89 *Automec* v. *Commission (Automec I)* [1990] ECR II-367). The letter rejecting a complaint, and informing the complainant that the Commission believes there are no grounds for the application of Articles 81 and 82 is reviewable (Case T-186/94 *Guérin Automobiles* v. *Commission* [1995] ECR II-1753), and even if the letter from the Commission is not couched in particularly formal terms the Court will not hesitate to construe it as a reviewable act, in order to protect the complainant's right to a judicial review (Case C-39/93 P *SFEI* v. *Commission* [1994] ECR I-2681).

The field of merger control also offers an example of just how informal an act can be (or at least its means of public communication), while still being construed as reviewable on the 'legal effects' test. In Case T-3/93 *Société Anonyme à Participation Ouvrière Nationale Air France* v. *Commission (Air France)* ([1994] ECR II-121) the Court of First Instance held that an oral statement by the spokesman for the competition Commissioner could be the basis of an annulment action. The Court found that there was a definitive 'act' that had been made public.

The act must none the less be an act *of* the institutions. Two cases involving the Parliament illustrate this point. In Case C-316/91 *Parliament* v. *Council (Lomé Convention)* ([1994] ECR I-6250) the Parliament brought an action against the Council for annulment of a financial regulation granting development aid under the Fourth ACP-EEC Convention. The basis of the development aid was an 'internal agreement' relating to the financing and administration of EU aid, adopted by the representatives of the governments of the Member States, 'meeting in Council'. It wished to establish the principle that such aid ought to be provided as Community expenditure under Article 209 EC, with the Parliament involved in the legislative process. It failed on this point, but succeeded in establishing that it could at least bring a challenge against a financial regulation adopted by the Council acting under 'intergovernmental' powers. In contrast, the action in Cases C-181, 248/91 *Parliament* v. *Council and Commission (Aid to Bangladesh)* ([1993] ECR I-3685) was declared inadmissible, because the act in question was one involving the Member States acting not as the Council, but simply as the representatives of their governments. It involved an agreement among the Member States to pay special aid to Bangladesh after the 1991 cyclone, aid which was paid directly by every Member State but Greece, rather than through a special bank account opened by the Commission for that purpose. It was construed as an independent decision of the Member States who happened to be meeting in the Council. In addition, as they are not 'institutions', 'acts' of the European Council and of COREPER cannot be annulled (Case T-584/93 *Roujansky* v. *European Council* [1994] ECR II-585; Case C-25/94 *Commission* v. *Council (FAO)* ([1996] ECR I-1469).

In certain exceptional circumstances an act may be so vitiated by defects that it is 'non-existent' (4.2), and therefore incapable of annulment by the Court. Such an act is not reviewable; neither, however, does it have legal effects. The definition of a non-existent act has not been extensively discussed in the Court, but in Cases 1, 14/57 *Société des Usines à Tubes de la Sarre* v. *High Authority* ([1957] ECR 105) the Court held that the absence of reasons renders an act non-existent. In a more recent application of this doctrine (4.2), the Court of First Instance held a Commission Decision imposing heavy fines on a number of chemical companies in respect of an alleged cartel to be so vitiated by defects of form and procedure as to be non-existent (Cases T-79, etc./89 *BASF AG et al.* v. *Commission* [1992] ECR II-315). The judgment was overturned by the Court of Justice which did not consider the defects, on the facts, to be sufficiently serious to merit the application of this exceptional doctrine, which operates as an exception to the principle that acts of the EU institutions are presumed to be lawful and accordingly to produce legal effects, even if tainted with irregularities, until such time as they are annulled or withdrawn (Case C-137/92 P *Commission* v. *BASF* [1994] ECR I-2555). In so doing the Court suggested the following definition of acts which would be 'inexistent', and therefore having no legal effect, even provisional:

> 'acts tainted by an irregularity whose gravity is so obvious that it cannot be tolerated by the Community legal order' (at p. 2647).

15.3   Locus Standi

Applicants under Article 230 now fall into three categories. There are privileged applicants (Commission, Council and Member States) who may challenge any measures adopted by any of the institutions. They need prove no specific interest in the act challenged, but must be presumed to have a general interest to act. At the opposite end of the scale are the non-privileged applicants – any natural or legal person – who are subject to restrictive rules on standing. An intermediate category was created by judicial evolution of the standing of the Parliament, and has since been confirmed by the terms of the Treaty of Maastricht, which allows three bodies – the Parliament, the Court of Auditors and the ECB – to take action against the other institutions only for the purpose of protecting their prerogatives.

This is an example of institutional developments in the Treaty of Maastricht directly shadowing the developments promoted by the Court. However, the position now confirmed by the Treaty was not reached without a change of heart by the Court (see also 7.18). The Court initially denied the standing of the Parliament in Case 302/87 *Parliament* v. *Council (Comitology)* ([1988] ECR 5615), refusing to draw parallels with either

Article 232 which has always recognised the right of the Parliament to bring actions for failure to act, or with its decision in *'Les Verts'* in which it confirmed that the Parliament was capable of being a defendant in Article 230 proceedings. It asserted that the Parliament was adequately protected by Commission's general right to take action on behalf of the 'Community' interest, working on the assumption that the Commission would always have an interest and desire to take action to protect the interests of the Parliament. The Parliament had to be content with this and the right to intervene in Article 230 proceedings brought by other parties (Article 37 of the Statute of the Court) (see Case 138/79 *Roquette Frères* v. *Council* [1980] ECR 3333 – failure to consult the Parliament before the adoption of a Regulation). Less than two years later the Court reviewed its position, and adopted the halfway house offered by Advocate General Darmon in *Comitology*, and since incorporated in the Treaty of Maastricht, namely that the Parliament is treated as a special case able to take action only in order to protect its own prerogatives (Case C-70/88 *Parliament* v. *Council (Chernobyl)* [1990] ECR I-2041).

15.4   Locus Standi: Non-Privileged Applicants

The rules governing the *locus standi* of non-privileged applicants are to be found in the fourth paragraph of Article 230, and are designed to restrict access to judicial review in the Court of Justice to measures which are in essence individual rather than general, and in which the applicant has a personal interest. Consequently, the reference in Article 230 to 'decision' means a decision in the material sense of an individual measure having legal effects, regardless of its formal designation or the formalities which have necessarily attended its adoption. Challenge is restricted to:

- decisions addressed to the applicant;
- decisions addressed to third parties which are of 'direct and individual concern' to the application;
- decisions 'in the form of' regulations, which are of 'direct and individual concern' to the applicant.

In general, the provisions have been narrowly interpreted by the Court, but there have been inconsistencies in its approach such that it is not possible to identify a single line of authority. In particular, there are special rules governing standing to challenge measures adopted by the Council and the Commission which are the result of quasi-judicial procedures, such as anti-dumping regulations, and competition and state aid decisions. There are also a number of anomalous cases that will be highlighted in this discussion, where the result achieved by the Court has been clearly determined by policy considerations. Where judicial review is not possible within the Court itself, an alternative route can normally be taken via the national court and the indirect review of the measure in question using Article 234, providing national implementing measures which can form the immediate subject of the national challenge can be found. There are a number of cases where the Court has rejected the standing of the applicant in an Article 230 case only to examine the validity of the offending measure in the context of an Article 234 ruling. An example is offered by the *'Berlin butter'* cases: in Case 97/85 *Union Deutsche Lebensmittelwerke* v. *Commission* ([1987] ECR 2265) an Article 230 challenge was unsuccessfully brought against a Commission scheme based for the sale of cheap butter in Berlin. The scheme was adopted in the form of a Decision addressed to Germany, which the applicant had no standing to challenge. However, in Case 133-6/85 *Walter Rau* v. *BALM* ([1987] ECR 2289), in the context of a challenge in the German courts to the German implementing measures, which was based on the argument that the originating Commission measure was invalid, the Court was prepared to review the legality of the underlying act in the context of an Article 234 reference. It held the measure valid.

The simplest case is that of the decision addressed to the applicant. Decisions of the Commission adopted under the procedures laid down in Regulation 17 are frequently challenged by their addressees – the alleged infringers of the competition rules. In this context, the Court also has the power to review the fines imposed by the Commission (Article 229 EC).

Decisions addressed to third parties can only be challenged by those who are directly and individually concerned. Proving direct and individual concern involves more than simply showing some sort of legal interest in the measure. These criteria must be examined separately.

15.5   Direct Concern

A measure will be of direct concern provided that there is a relationship of cause and effect between the act and its impact on the applicant. The question must be asked whether there is any intervening discretion between the decision and the applicant, for example, on the part of a Member State.

In Case 69/69 *Alcan* v. *Commission* ([1970] ECR 385) the applicant importers were held to be not directly concerned by a Commission Decision refusing a request from the Belgian government for a quota of unwrought aluminium imports at a reduced rate of duty. The Belgian government could have declined to use the quota once it had received it, or could have granted it to other importers. In contrast, the applicant in Case 62/70 *Bock* v. *Commission* ([1971] ECR 897) was held to be directly concerned. Bock had applied to the German authorities for a permit to import Chinese mushrooms and was told that the request would be refused as soon as the authorisation had been obtained from the Commission. When the Commission took a Decision addressed to the German government authorising the refusal of the application, Bock was able to challenge the decision. The Court held that there was direct concern because the German government had already made it clear what it would do with the authorisation once received. A further example of direct concern is Case 11/82 *Piraiki-Patraiki* v. *Commission* ([1985] ECR 207), a case which is notable for its generous interpretation of the rules on individual concern, where the possibility that the French government would not take advantage of a Commission authorisation to impose restrictions on imports of cotton yarn from Greece was held to be 'purely theoretical' when the measures were challenged by Greek manufacturers.

The criterion of direct concern precludes challenges to measures adopted by the EU which grant discretionary powers to the Member States, such as the Commission Decision authorising Luxembourg to grant aids to steel firms which undertook reductions in capacity, which was unsuccessfully challenged in Case 222/83 *Municipality of Differdange* v. *Commission* ([1984] ECR 2889).

Two decisions of the Court of First Instance on the Merger Regulation seemed to add a new layer to the test of direct concern. In Case T-96/92 *Comité central d'entreprise de la Société générale des grande sources* v. *Commission* ([1995] ECR II-1213) and Case T-12/93 *Comité central d'entreprise de la Société anonyme Vittel* v. *Commission* ([1995] ECR II-1247) the Court was faced with a challenge to a Commission Decision declaring the takeover of Perrier by Nestlé compatible with the common market, subject to compliance by Nestlé with certain conditions such as the sale of Perrier's Vittel subsidiary. Actions were brought by the Works Councils of Perrier and Vittel, who were both held to be individually concerned by the decision (see below). However, they were not directly concerned by the decision: as representatives of the employees, their 'own rights' were not prejudiced by the Decision approving the merger. The Court denied that a reduction in the workforce, or indeed the closure of plant would adversely affect the rights of the Works Councils. According to the Court in Case T-12/93, the fact that the closure of one plant leading, by virtue of the operation of French law, to the end of the central enterprise Works Council did not mean that the applicants were directly concerned by the decision as:

> 'the central works council has not demonstrated an interest in the preservation of its functions where by reason of a change in the structure of the undertaking concerned the conditions under which the applicable national law provides for it to be set up are no longer met' ([1995] ECR I-1247 at p. 1271).

The Court also refused to base direct concern on an argument that the merger Decision would directly prejudice the interests of Perrier employees, including the loss of jobs and collective benefits, pointing, perhaps over-optimistically, to the existence of legislation, including legislation at EU level, intended to safeguard the rights of employees in the event of a transfer of undertaking (including a takeover). That would appear to break the causal link between the Decision of the Commission and any adverse employment consequences for employees and their representatives. Effectively, therefore, the Court is denying any responsibility on the part of the Commission for the employment consequences of the merger.

15.6 **Individual Concern**

In Case 25/62 *Plaumann* v. *Commission* ([1963] ECR 95), an early case which set the tone of restrictive interpretation for the entire system of direct judicial review in the Court of Justice, a German importer of clementines sought to challenge a Commission Decision addressed to Germany refusing it an authorisation to levy only 10 per cent duty on imports of clementines into the European Community from third countries, in place of the full duty of 13 per cent. On the question of admissibility the Court held that (at p. 107):

> 'Persons other than those to whom a decision is addressed may only claim to be individually concerned if that decision affects them by reason of certain attributes which are peculiar to them or by reason of circumstances in which they are differentiated from all other persons and by virtue of these factors distinguishes them individually just as in the case of the person addressed. In the present case the applicant is affected by the disputed decision as an importer of clementines, that is to say, by reason of a commercial activity which may at any time be practised by any person and is not therefore such as to distinguish the applicant in relation to the contested decision as in the case of the addressee.'

In practice, in the course of an extensive case law in which many cases have been declared inadmissible on the grounds of no individual concern, it has emerged that the Court requires the applicant to be part of a closed class, membership of which is fixed and ascertainable at the date of the adoption of the contested measure. An example is provided by Cases 106-107/63 *Toepfer* v. *Commission* ([1965] ECR 405) where the applicant was held to be individually concerned by a Commission Decision confirming the decision of the German government to refuse licences for imports of cereals from France, since the measure applied only to a closed class of importers who had applied for an import licence on a particular day. This test can also explain the distinction between cases such as Case 62/70 *Bock*, where the applicant was held to be individually concerned by a Commission Decision adopted in response to its request to the German government for an import licence and authorising the refusal of that licence, and Case 231/82 *Spijker Kwasten* v. *Commission* ([1983] ECR 2559), where the action failed. In *Spijker Kwasten*, the applicant sought annulment of a Commission Decision addressed to the Dutch government authorising it to ban imports of Chinese brushes for six months following the applicant's submission of a request for a licence. The applicant's difficulty was that although there was some evidence that the Decision was passed specifically to deal with its position, and indeed it was the only importer of Chinese brushes into the Benelux countries at that time, the ban was imposed for a period subsequent to the application for a licence, a period during which, hypothetically, other persons could have made an application for an import licence. Consequently, the action was held inadmissible on grounds of no individual concern.

It will be seen from these cases that there is a clear focus in terms of subject matter on areas like customs and agriculture, reflecting particularly strongly the nature of the Commission's involvement in administering these fields – in conjunction with the Member States as appropriate. The nature of the subject matter of the cases may, it is argued, perhaps best explain the Court's reluctance to give a broader interpretation of the concept of individual concern. It has protected the Commission's scope for discretionary determinations, particularly under the CAP (Craig, 1994).

Even as the EU has extended the range of its activities, however, the general thrust of the approach to Article 230 taken by first the Court of Justice and, more recently, the Court of First Instance has not changed. This is well illustrated by more recent cases. From the field of merger control comes Case T-83/92 *Zunis Holdings SA* v. *Commission* ([1993] ECR II-1169) in which the Court of First Instance rejected as inadmissible for lack of individual concern an action brought by shareholders in a company against a Decision by the Commission, using discretionary powers under the Merger Control Regulation, that the acquisition of a shareholding of 12 per cent did not constitute a merger under the terms of the Regulation. In Case T-117/94 *Associazione Agricoltori della Provincia di Rovigo et al.* v. *Commission (Po Delta)* ([1995] ECR II-455 (confirmed on appeal by the Court of Justice: Case C-142/95 P [1996] ECR I-6669), the applicant associations and agriculturists objected to a Commission Decision approving an Italian government plan for actions related to the protection of the environment in the Po Delta funded by an EU financial instrument. They argued that they had not been consulted in the process of drawing up the plan, and the Commission had therefore disregarded their interests in approving it. The Court rejected the applications as inadmissible on the grounds that those of the applicants who were agriculturists were not affected in any way other than all other residents of the Po Delta by the Decision. None of the rules governing the disbursement of monies put the Commission under a duty to take account of the particular situation of either the agriculturists or indeed the associations representing them. No special rules apply to the situation of representative associations – in contrast to the situation under Italian law where the associations were recognised as having a special status. The Court stated (at p. 466):

> 'It cannot be accepted as a principle that an association, in its capacity as the representative of a category of traders, is individually concerned by a measure affecting the general interests of that category.'

Consequently, the associations had to prove individual concern in the same way as the individual agriculturists, and, like them, failed at that hurdle. On appeal, the Court of Justice rejected arguments that the applicants had tried to derive from the EU's Fifth Environmental Action Programme. They argued that they had acquired participation rights from their participation within the framework of the Environmental Action Programme. However, the Court held that the Action Programme was designed to provide a framework for defining and implementing Community environmental policy and did not lay down mandatory rules. Hence the adoption of that programme did not trigger any consultation obligations or participation rights through which *locus standi* could be generated. Other bodies finding themselves in exactly the same situation in having to prove direct and individual concern include autonomous sub-central governmental authorities (Case T-288/97 *Regione autonoma Fruili Venezia Giulia* v. *Commission* [1999] ECR II-1693) and representatives of management or labour (Case T-135/96 *UEAPME* v. *Council* [1998] ECR II-2335 (6.9)).

Case T-585/93 *Stichting Greenpeace Council* v. *Commission* ([1995] ECR II-2205; on appeal Case C-321/95 P [1998] ECR I-1651) concerned the disbursement of aid from the EU under the structural policies. Greenpeace challenged a Commission Decision addressed to Spain granting aid under the regional development programme for the building of two power stations in the Canary Islands. The concerns raised by Greenpeace were whether the aid was being disbursed to projects that were in keeping with the EU's other policies, particularly its environmental policies, as required by the relevant Regulations. There was some question as to whether the Spanish government had carried out the proper environmental impact assessment measures. The actions were held inadmissible, on the grounds that none of the applicants – who included residents of the Canaries, Greenpeace International, and a number of local environmental organisations – had shown individual concern. Notably the Court of First Instance refused to take any particular cognisance of the fact that the interests involved were environmental, not economic, so

that the principles of *Plaumann* which are principally predicated on a particular perception of economic interest should not apply in their full rigour. As
in the *Po Delta* case the Court also refused to draw any distinction between
the interests of individual applicants and those of representative associations.

One final example will demonstrate that the EU courts represent exceedingly stony ground for public interest litigation. In Case T-219/95R
Danielsson v. *Commission* ([1995] ECR II-3051) the President of the Court
of First Instance rejected an application for interim measures brought by
residents of Tahiti. They were concerned about the Commission's refusal to
apply Article 34 Euratom to the programme of underground nuclear tests
then being undertaken by France in the Pacific Ocean. The application of
Article 34 could have given the Commission grounds even for ordering the
suspension of the tests on health and safety grounds. In the event, the Commission concluded that the tests did not constitute 'particularly dangerous
experiments', and so Article 34 did not apply. The application for interim
measures was rejected on the grounds that the applicants had not established the *prima facie* admissibility of their case. Demonstrating the possibility or even likelihood of (physical or economic) harm or serious detriment
was in itself insufficient to show individual concern, because the applicants
were not affected in any way which differed from other residents of Tahiti.
Nor were they protected because they were part of the 'general public' in
whose interests additional health and safety precautions might be sought by
the Commission under Article 34 Euratom.

More 'generous' interpretations of the rules tend to be explicable on special grounds, or because they belong to a number of specific categories identified below (15.9). In Case 11/82 *Piraiki-Patraiki*, certain Greek yarn manufacturers who had already entered into contracts to export cotton to France
were held to be individually concerned by the Commission Decision permitting France to impose restrictions on imports. This was because Article 130
of the Greek Act of Accession, which empowered the Commission to adopt
such a measure, required it to take into account the interests specifically of
those who were bound by contractual arrangements. It could be argued that
the evidence derived from the Act of Accession distinguished the applicants
from a wider group of persons who might suffer prejudice as a consequence
of the measure in question. This case was distinguished in Case C-209/94 P
Buralux v. *Council* ([1996] ECR I-615) where there was no need for the defendant institution to examine to what extent its actions impacted upon
pre-existing contractual arrangements.

Case 294/83 *'Les Verts'* must also be taken as an exceptional application of
the rules on individual concern. On the face of it, the French Green Party
was affected by the decision of the Bureau of the Parliament concerning the
allocation of electoral funds only as a member of an indeterminate class,

namely parties which might stand in the elections and were not already represented in the Parliament. On policy grounds the Court granted standing, since the applicants had a good case on the merits, and there was no obvious alternative route whereby the applicants could enforce the principle of equality in the context of the Parliament's organisation of its own business.

15.7 Challenges to Regulations

The wording of the standing rules in Article 230 would seem to indicate that individuals may only challenge regulations which are in essence decisions. It has proved almost impossible, in practice, for applicants to prove that what is in form a general normative measure is in truth a bundle of individual measures although the applicants in Cases 41-44/70 *International Fruit Co* v. *Commission* ([1971] ECR 411) succeeded in precisely this task when they challenged a Commission Regulation laying down the rules for granting or refusing licences for the importation of apples from non-Member States. At that time, the national authorities received the applications for licences and passed them on to the Commission. The Court held that the Regulation establishing the rules for licences to be granted in a particular week, which was framed directly in response to the number of applications received by the Member States, was in truth a bundle of individual decisions and held the actions by the applicants who had requested licences to be admissible. The Court of First Instance has explained this aspect of Article 230 in the following terms:

> 'the objective of [Article 230(4)] is in particular to prevent the Community institutions from being able, merely by choosing the form of a regulation, to preclude an individual from bringing an action against a decision which concerns him directly and individually' (Case T-476/93 *FRSEA and FNSEA* v. *Council* [1993] ECR II-1187 at p. 1195).

In practice, however, applicants have generally found it extremely difficult to establish that measures based on the exercise of discretion in the economic policy context are in truth individual measures, since the Court has consistently held that individuals should not be able to use Article 230 to challenge 'true' regulations, that is abstract, normative measures. It defined such measures in Cases 16 and 17/62 *Confédération Nationale des Producteurs des Fruits et Légumes* v. *Council* ([1962] ECR 471) as being:

> 'essentially of a legislative nature, ... applicable not to a limited number of persons, defined or identifiable, but to categories of persons viewed abstractly and in their entirety.'

The Court then went on apparently to conflate the question of whether a measure is individual or general with the question of individual concern, as discussed in the previous paragraph. However, in reality, the Court has not always consistently applied this test, and in some cases has additionally imposed a test which looks at the terminology of the measure rather than the persons affected by it.

For example in Cases 789-790/79 *Calpak SpA* v. *Commission* ([1980] ECR 1949) the Court held inadmissible a challenge to a Regulation governing the grant of production aid in respect of certain pears in the following terms (at p. 1961):

'A provision which limits the granting of production aid for all producers in respect of a particular product to a uniform percentage of the quantity produced by them during a uniform preceding period is by nature a measure of general application within the meaning of Article 189 of the Treaty. In fact the measure applies to objectively determined situations and produces legal effects with regard to categories of persons described in a generalised and abstract manner. The nature of the measure as a regulation is not called in question by the mere fact that it is possible to determine the number or even the identity of the producers to be granted the aid which is limited thereby.'

Thus even where they have been able to establish that the measures affect only small and easily identifiable groups (e.g. the isoglucose regulations affecting only isoglucose producers, a small class unlikely to grow because of the major investment required – Case 101/76 *KSH* v. *Commission* [1977] ECR 797) or indeed a closed category of persons (e.g. Cases 103-9/78 *Beauport* v. *Council and Commission* [1979] ECR 17 – a measure affecting only sugar refineries which had previously been granted a sugar quota), direct actions to challenge regulations implementing the policies of the EU have been unsuccessful, although some of the policies pursued have appeared manifestly unfair to particular groups and have proved vulnerable to indirect challenge (e.g. Cases 103, 145/77 *Royal Scholten Honig Holdings Ltd* v. *Intervention Board for Agricultural Produce* [1978] ECR 2037 – isoglucose regulation held invalid for breach of the principle of equality in the context of Article 234 reference). It is in this type of situation which Mancini and Keeling (1994: 188–189) see the Court of Justice as failing the individual, describing its construction of 'what is in any event a restrictive provision' as 'bizarre and paradoxical, if not downright perverse'.

The exceptions to this approach have tended once more to be special cases, either where the Commission is involved more directly in the administration of EU law as in *International Fruit Company*, or where the applicant is in some way specifically identified by the measure. In Case 138/79 *Roquette Frères* v. *Council* the applicant was one of a number of producers named in an annex to a Regulation. The action in Case C-152/88 *Sofrimport*

Sarl v. *Commission* ([1990] ECR I-2477) was to challenge a Commission Regulation imposing protective measures which restricted the import of Chilean apples into the Community. Applying only the test of individual concern, and ignoring the abstract terminology test elaborated in *Calpak*, the Court held the actions by importers whose apples were in transit when the measure was adopted admissible on the grounds that the enabling Council Regulation which permitted it to control the imports of fruit into the European Community required it to have special regard to the interests of importers whose products were in transit. The Court held that since the enabling Regulation gave specific protection to such importers, they must be able to enforce observance of that protection and bring legal proceedings for that purpose. Thus there was a direct link between the substance of the applicants' case and the admissibility of their action. There is a parallel between *Sofrimport* and *Piraiki-Patraiki*, since in both cases specific features in the enabling measures distinguished the applicants from other affected persons.

When this group of cases was transferred to the Court of First Instance in the mid-1990s, the hope was expressed by some commentators that the Court of First Instance whose specific task is that of hearing actions brought by individual applicants might be able to develop more flexible criteria on *locus standi* (Mancini and Keeling, 1994: 189). The chance of this occurring appeared to have been considerably enhanced by the approach taken by the Court of Justice to the one of last cases on the question of general/individual measures which it had to decide before the transfer of jurisdiction. For this reason, Case C-309/89 *Codorniu* v. *Council* ([1994] ECR I-1853) attracted a high level of interest and comment (e.g. Usher, 1994; Waelbroeck and Fosselard, 1995). It is regarded as particularly important because it concerns general policy on the regulation of agricultural trade, rather than agricultural licences or anti-dumping policy (see 15.9).

The action brought by Codorniu was against a Council Regulation reserving the word '*crémant*' as a designation for certain quality sparkling wines produced in specified regions of France and Luxembourg. The reservation of a designation in that way is intended to protect traditional descriptions. The applicant also produced quality sparkling wines, but in Spain not France or Luxembourg, and since 1924 had designated one of its wines '*Gran Crémant de Codorniu*'. It was also the holder of a Spanish graphic trademark in the same terms. It was the largest producer in the EU of sparkling wines described as '*crémant*', but a number of other Spanish producers also used the term '*Gran Crémant*' to designate certain quality sparkling wines. Consequently, there was no question of the applicant being the only producer, or even only Spanish producer, affected by the Regulation. Holding that the applicant had *locus standi*, the Court held that the fact that the measure was of a general legislative nature in that it applied to the traders concerned in a general way, did not prevent it being of individual concern to the applicants (a form of reasoning which it has drawn from the field of anti-dumping: see Cases 239, 275/82 *Allied Corporation* v. *Commission* [1984] ECR 1005). The Court concluded that the applicant was affected by reference to certain specific attributes because it had registered the trademark in 1924 and traditionally used that mark before and after registration. In consequence, therefore, the reservation to French and Luxembourg producers brought about by the Council Regulation interfered with the applicant's property rights. It may well be, therefore, that the Court's judgment was directly influenced by Article 295 EC which provides that the Treaty shall operate without prejudice to the rights of the Member States to regulate property rights. It is not clear that the Court would have found the application admissible simply on the grounds of the impact upon the applicant's competitive situation (which was undoubtedly severe, but probably no more severe than in some of the other cases where the Court has denied standing to challenge Regulations). Even so, it was the case that *Codorniu* went beyond previous approaches to the standing question, since it was not suggested that the contested Regulation was adopted in view of the situation of the applicants, a requirement that the Court had previously imposed in such cases.

As the 'torch' was passed to the Court of First Instance, it was suggested that there might be a significant general relaxation of standing under Article 230. As we saw in 15.6 this has not occurred in relation to 'decisions addressed to another person'. Nor, in the event, has it occurred in relation to challenges to regulations. In Case T-107/94 *Kik* v. *Council and Commission* ([1995] ECR II-1717) the Court rejected a challenge to the language regime instituted by the Council Regulation establishing the Community trademark and the Community trademark office, which excluded the applicant's language (Dutch). The Court refused to accept the application of Article 6 ECHR which guarantees a right to judicial process and which has been cited by the Court in a number of other cases notably involving the exclusion of judicial process by the Member States (e.g. Case 222/84 *Johnston* v. *Chief Constable of the Royal Ulster Constabulary* [1986] ECR 1651; 9.4). According to the Court of First Instance this provision, although part of the body of EU general principles, does not preclude the application of standing rules in provisions such as Article 230. What is unsatisfactory about this judgment is the failure of the Court to indicate the alternative remedies available to the plaintiff, and to offer a convincing justification why such a potentially serious infringement of fundamental rights should not be dealt with directly at the level of the courts of the EU itself.

More pertinent to the scenario which arose in *Codorniu* was Case T-472/93 *Campo Ebro Industrial* v. *Council* ([1995] ECR II-421). In this case the applicants challenged a Council Regulation concerned with the alignment of sugar prices in Spain with those within the Single Market, following the arrangements laid down in the Spanish Act of Accession. Adjustment aid was made available under the Regulation to aid the restructuring in the Spanish sugar industry to assist the process of reducing the Spanish sugar price to the single market level. The applicants, who were the only producers of isoglucose in Spain and who held all the Spanish quotas for isoglucose production, were not granted adjustment aid when the Regulation entered into force, unlike a number of traders producing sugar from beet and cane. The case therefore concerns the continuing disputes concerning the competitive balance between beet and cane sugar and isoglucose (17.9). The Court held the action inadmissible on the grounds that:

> 'even if, following the introduction of the quota system, the present applicants are now the only producers of isoglucose in Spain and even assuming, further, that they are affected by the contested regulation in so far as it applies to future situations, they are in any event affected only in their objective capacity as isoglucose producers in the same way as any other trader in the sugar sector who, actually or potentially, is in an identical situation' (p. 435).

The Court further denied a claim that standing could be based on the impact upon the applicants' particularly disadvantageous competitive situation. As *Campo Ebro* represents an explicit continuation of the Court of Justice's earlier case law on the regulation of markets, it may be that *Codorniu* will turn out to the an exceptional case to be confined to its facts, rather than a new dawn in the approach to *locus standi*. Even where the Court of First Instance has allowed standing in such situations, moreover, its decisions have been quashed by the Court of Justice (Case C-73/97 P *France* v. *Comafrica and Dole* [1999] ECR I-185). It is apparent that a *Codorniu*-type situation will only arise where special rights of the applicants (including where appropriate property rights) have been infringed, or where the defendant institution has breached some duty to the applicants (Case C-10/95 *Asocarne* v. *Council* [1995] ECR I-4149; Case T-480 & 483/93 *Antillean Rice Mills* v. *Commission* [1995] ECR II-2305).

15.8   Can Individuals Challenge Directives?

There is no reason, in principle, why individuals could not challenge directives using Article 230, although they will undoubtedly face formidable hurdles regarding standing. In Case C-298/89 *Government of Gibraltar* v. *Council* ([1993] ECR I-3605), the Court dismissed the application – in which the applicants were treated as 'private' individuals for the purposes of *locus standi* – on the grounds of admissibility, but did not appear to claim that directives as such could not be challenged. This suggests a reworking of

Article 230, similar to that undertaken in relation to Article 241 which is likewise phrased in terms of indirect challenges to regulations only (15.16), towards allowing the annulment of potentially any general legislation, irrespective of its form.

A challenge to a directive gave rise to one of the most intriguing recent cases on the standing rules: Case T-135/96 *UEAPME*. However, the rejection as inadmissible of the action brought by the representative association for small and medium sized business to challenge a Council directive approving a framework agreement adopted by the social partners would seem to indicate that no special measures will be taken by the Court of First Instance to safeguard the possibility of judicial review in the context of the social dialogue. UEAPME had argued that it was wrongfully excluded from the process for adopting the framework agreement. However, while applying the criteria derived from *Codorniu* and *Plaumann* to assess whether the applicants had standing to challenge what it concluded was indeed a legislative measure, the Court did undertake a very careful review of the processes and context of the whole social dialogue. It concluded that the applicant had no general right to participate in the negotiation phase in relation to the social dialogue and it was not distinguished as regards its representativity in terms of that dialogue from all other representatives of management and labour consulted by the Commission who were not parties to the agreement. Hence it was not individually concerned by the Directive and the action was declared inadmissible.

15.9 Quasi-Judicial Determinations

Special features characterise the Court's interpretation of the standing rules under Article 230 in the context of the involvement of the applicants in procedures before or within the EU institutions which are quasi-judicial in nature. These features concern the treatment not only of those who are directly involved in the procedures, e.g. as alleged infringers, and those involved as complainants (cf. 8.16).

In the context of competition proceedings, a disappointed complainant may bring an action challenging a decision granting an exemption or giving negative clearance (Case 26/76 *Metro* v. *Commission* [1977] ECR 1875). Under Regulation 17, provision is made for the participation of complainants with a legitimate grievance in the proceedings; for example, they have a right to be heard which they are entitled to have protected by the Court. Similarly, the applicants in Case T-96/92 *Comité central d'entreprise de la Société générale des grande sources* v. *Commission* and Case T-12/93 *Comité central d'entreprise de la Société anonyme Vittel* v. *Commission* were able to establish individual concern, even though not all of them had actually participated in the administrative process. According to the Court of First Instance:

'in a case more specifically concerning the recognised representatives of
the employees of the undertakings concerned, the number and identity
of which are likely to be known when the decision is adopted, the mere
fact that [the Merger Control Regulation] mentions them expressly and
specifically among the third persons showing a 'sufficient interest' to
submit their observations to the Commission is enough to differentiate
them from all other persons and enough for it to be considered that the
decision adopted under that regulation is of individual concern to them,
whether or not they have made use of their rights during the administrative procedure.' ([1995] ECR I-1213 at p. 1232)

The position of complainants is often made considerably easier because, as
a result of their involvement in the process, they will normally be contesting
decisions addressed to them by the Commission (cf. Case C-39/93 P *SFEI* v.
Commission and Case T-3/93 *Air France*, discussed in 15.2).

   Similar considerations apply in the context of state aid. French fertiliser
producers who had complained to the Commission about an alleged state
aid given to their Dutch competitors by the Dutch government were held to
be individually concerned by a Commission Decision addressed to the
Dutch government terminating the proceedings when the Commission concluded that there was no aid involved (Case 169/84 *COFAZ* v. *Commission*
[1986] ECR 391). In this case, the applicants had been exercising participation rights granted to them under Article 88(2) EC. The Court took the protection of complainants one step further in Case C-198/91 *William Cook plc*
v. *Commission* ([1993] ECR I-2486), holding that a potential participant in
Article 88(2) proceedings has standing to challenge a Decision taken by the
Commission under Article 88(3) following a preliminary examination to the
effect that a particular aid was compatible with the Common Market. The
Court held that the participation rights under Article 88(2) could only be
properly protected by allowing a challenge to such a Decision. Even stronger policy considerations speak in favour of the right of action of the benefi-
ciaries of an aid held to be incompatible with the Common Market, and the
standing of a beneficiary to challenge a Commission Decision addressed to
the Dutch government and requesting it to refrain from granting the aid in
question was confirmed by the Court in Case 730/79 *Philip Morris Holland
BV* v. *Commission* ([1980] ECR 2671). Finally, in the field of state aid it
would appear that representative bodies are given particular consideration:
in Case C-313/90 *CIRFS* v. *Commission* ([1993] ECR I-1125) the Court held
that the applicant association had standing to challenge a decision – addressed to a third party – which adversely affected the interests of its members. The *locus standi* was based on the fact that it had been in close contact
with the Commission.

The case of anti-dumping proceedings is slightly different since in that context the enabling powers provide for the adoption of regulations by the Council imposing countervailing duties intended to offset the effects of subsidies granted in third countries to imports into the EU. These regulations are obviously not 'addressed' to particular persons, although clearly some categories of economic actors may be more seriously affected than others. An unqualified application of the principles set out in 15.7 would doubtless lead to unfairness to those affected by anti-dumping duties by excessively restricting the possibility of judicial review of the procedures in question. The Court has proceeded in this context generally by distinguishing between provisions of anti-dumping regulations which in effect operate as decisions *vis-à-vis* certain categories of interested parties, and those which preserve a general normative nature. In other words, a regulation may be of individual concern to certain applicants, while still retaining its general normative character.

So far the following categories of applicant have been held to be individually concerned by anti-dumping regulations:

– producers named in a regulation (Case 113/77 *NTN Toyo Bearing Co.* v. *Council and Commission* [1979] ECR 1185);
– producers who have been involved in the preliminary investigations (Cases 239, 275/82 *Allied Corporation* v. *Commission*);
– complainants (Case 264/82 *Timex* v. *Council and Commission* [1985] ECR 849).

Generally importers were refused standing, unless they were in some way linked to the manufacturer or exporter, or if their resale prices had been used by the Commission to construct export prices as the basis for the duty imposed (Case C-157/87 *Electroimpex* v. *Council* [1990] ECR I-3021). An attempt by the applicants in Case 307/81 *Alusuisse* v. *Council and Commission* ([1982] ECR 3463) to establish standing by challenging the general nature of anti-dumping regulations was firmly rejected by the Court.

However, in Case C-358/89 *Extramet Industrie SA* v. *Council* ([1991] ECR I-2501) the Court appeared to move towards a more generous approach to the standing of importers. It held that without losing its normative character an anti-dumping regulation may individually concern importers. The applicant was able to establish standing by reference to its specific characteristics as not only the major importer of the product subject to the anti-dumping duty, but also its end user. It was held to be relevant that Extramet's operations were heavily dependent on the imports and were seriously affected by the disputed Regulation, in view of the very small number of manufacturers of the product in question and the difficulty of obtaining supplies from the only EU producer, which was, moreover, Extramet's main competitor in relation to the end product. It would therefore appear that standing to challenge an anti-dumping regulation can be established if the importer can show that the regulation has an impact on its vital economic interests. In his Opinion in *Extramet*, AG Jacobs made very clear that he considered that the EU system of judicial review needed to be able to offer a substantive investigation of this type of case; if not, it would be seriously deficient and inconsistent with the principle of the rule of law.

15.10 **Locus Standi of Non-Privileged Applicants: Conclusions and Critique**

Looking at the remarkable number of cases each year in which the Court of First Instance finds itself declaring actions under Article 230 inadmissible it is difficult to avoid one of three conclusions. Either the rules are so uncertain as to be generating much wasted effort on the part of litigants, or those litigants are very badly advised in their decisions to bring actions, or alternatively there is a great deal of 'pressure from below' for a wider definition of the standing rules. But this issue is obviously not new. The restrictive interpretation of the standing rules under Article 230 has long been a subject for debate (e.g. Rasmussen, 1980; Harding, 1980; Greaves, 1986; from a comparative perspective Stein and Vining, 1976). The types of arguments put forward to explain the Court's approach have included:

- a perceived need (at least in the early days) to protect a nascent 'Community' against challenges to its activities;
- the restrictive terms of Article 230 itself, in which 'individuals' are marginal;
- the need to draw distinctions between the different types of cases, an argument apparently vindicated by the differences between 'discretionary' and 'quasi-judicial' cases highlighted above;
- the availability of indirect review through the medium of the national court and the Article 234 reference (15.17).

More recent work critiquing the approach taken by the Court has placed it within the framework of the broad-based challenge which standing poses for modern administrative law (Harlow, 1992a; Craig, 1994; Arnull, 1995a). For Harlow, the question of standing cannot be separated from the question of the EU's democratic deficit, and the role for the Court within the institutional structure which this consequently leaves. Standing is intimately linked to broader questions of participation (see also Craig and de Búrca, 1998: 486–489), and it would be difficult to conceive of a radically changed approach to standing in the absence of a form of arrangement for administrative procedures which located the individual more centrally within those processes. There is no doubt that the Court's approach to standing is stifling public interest litigation, and it is arguable that in some areas where there are interests to be protected which cannot – as it were – take *themselves* to court, such as the environment, the Court's approach may be very dangerous (Berrod, 1999). Arnull (1995a) suggested a change in EU law to adopt a halfway house for the standing question. He proposed abandoning the restrictive approach involving the search for a concrete interference with a legal right, and the adoption of an approach which looks for an adverse effect on the applicant's interests. In his view, the EU is not yet ready for the broadest approach – the so-called *actio popularis* or citizen's action based on the assumption that the citizen has an interest in any action of a public body. A mature polity, such as the EU claims increasingly to be, could, however, match the progressive relaxations in standing to be seen in many other administrative jurisdictions (Arnull, 1999a: 47). Arnull, like Neuwahl (1996), looked for an attempt to resolve these difficult questions within the framework of the 1996 IGC, but none was forthcoming. It was not placed on the agenda for the 2000 IGC.

15.11 Time Limits

Actions under Article 230 must observe the time limit of two months from 'the publication of the measure, or of its notification to the plaintiff, or, in the absence thereof, of the day on which it came to the knowledge of the latter, as the case may be'. Details of the application in practice of the time limits can be derived from the Rules of Procedure of the Court of Justice.

15.12 Interim Measures

In appropriate cases, the Court may award interim measures in the context of Article 230 actions under its general power in Article 243 EC. The same conditions of a *prima facie* case and urgency which are applied in the context of Article 226 EC (see 8.14) govern the award of interim measures under Article 230. These have been awarded in a number of cases involving anti-dumping regulations (Case 113/77R *NTN Toyo Bearing Co* v. *Commission* [1977] ECR 1721) and decisions taken by the Commission under Article 134 EC authorising Member States to exclude imports from the other Member States of third country goods in free circulation (Case 1/84R *Ilford* v. *Commission* [1984] ECR 423). The field of competition law also offers a number of examples of successful applications for interim measures. In Case T-56/89 R *Publishers Association* v. *Commission* ([1989] ECR 1693) the Court awarded interim measures in relation to the operation of a Commission Decision declaring the UK Net Book Agreement to be in breach of the competition rules, and requiring its termination. The interim measures brought about the suspension of the Commission's Decision pending the final resolution of the action on the merits.

15.13 Grounds for Review

There is considerable overlap between the four grounds for review set out in Article 230 (lack of competence, infringement of an essential procedural requirement, infringement of the Treaty or of any rule of law relating to its application, and misuse of powers). Indeed it could be argued that infringement of the Treaty and of any rule of law relating to its application is potentially a catch-all phrase which encompasses not only the written rules of the Treaty and the various provisions adopted thereunder, but also the body of unwritten general principles of law and fundamental rights, which were discussed as a source of law in Chapter 6 and must now be applied in practice here. What follows is exemplary, and there are many more instances throughout the book of the application of the grounds for review, for example in the discussion of inter-institutional litigation (7.18).

Lack of competence is a ground on occasions in the context of inter-institutional relations, or relations between the Member States and the institutions, especially the Commission. One example is provided by Case C-303/90 *France* v. *Commission*, in which France successfully established that the Commission did not have the power to adopt a legally binding implementation measure (albeit one characterised as a 'Code of Conduct') under the legal regime governing the application of the structural funds (Article 158 EC *et seq.*). Case C-106/96 *UK* v. *Commission (Poverty 4)* ([1998] ECR I-2729) demonstrated that the Commission had no competence to commit monies to expenditure on an anti-poverty programme in the absence of a separate enabling measure properly adopted under the Treaty (7.16).

There are numerous cases on procedural requirements – especially, but not only, in the field of competition law, and the Court has held the following requirements to be essential:

– the requirement to consult the Parliament where required during the legislative process (Case 138/79 *Roquette Frères* v. *Council*);
– a sufficiently full statement of reasons under Article 190 EC (Case 24/62 *Commission* v. *Germany* [1963] ECR 63);
– the requirement of a specific legal basis which is an additional feature of the duty to give reasons (Case 45/86 *Commission* v. *Council (Generalised Tariff Preferences)* [1987] ECR 1493).

Use of the wrong legal basis is designated an infringement of the Treaty, and numerous examples are likewise to be found in 7.18. For further examples of those general principles of law which have been used as the bases for challenges to the legality of EU acts, reference should be made to the discussion in 9.3. It is worth commenting upon the relevance of international law principles as grounds of annulment. It was a controversial move on the part of the Court of Justice to confirm in Case C-280/93 *Germany* v. *Council* ([1994] ECR I-4973) that principles of the (old) GATT could not be invoked as the basis for challenging the legality of EU acts. It has extended this principle further in Case C-149/96 *Portugal* v. *Council* (23 November 1999) in which it held that the Agreement establishing the WTO and the agreements and memoranda annexed to that Agreement were not, having regard to their nature and structure, among the rules in whose light the Court was to review the legality of measures adopted by the EU institutions.

The most infrequently applied ground is the misuse of powers, which constitutes the use of a power for purposes other than that for which it was granted, and is based on the French administrative law concept of *détournement de pouvoir*. In Case 8/55 *Fédéchar* v. *High Authority* ([1956] ECR 292) the ECSC equivalent provision was considered by the Court. It held that a measure will not be annulled simply because one of the reasons for its adoption was improper, if the others are legitimate. Nor will a measure be annulled if the improper purpose had no effect upon the substance of the measure.

The essential question, from the perspective of the development of the judicial control of the EU institutions, is the nature and intensity of the review which the Court of Justice and Court of First Instance apply to their actions. The precise approach taken will depend upon the type of power under which the particular institution is operating. There will be a good deal of difference in the degree of scrutiny applied to the exercise of discretionary legislative powers in a field such as agriculture, compared with the fairly precise procedural requirements which structure the investigatory work of the Commission in the field of competition law. In a sense the exercise of the review can become a dialogue between the institutions concerned with legislation, and the Court of Justice – as the series of cases on the evaluation of the milk quota system in light of the general principles of EU law shows very clearly. Although these cases were decided by means of Article 234 references on validity, and not as direct actions, the principles are the same as they are under Article 230.

In Case 120/86 *Mulder* v. *Minister van Landbouw en Visserij* ([1988] ECR 2321), the Court held that a legislative framework which effectively penalised those who had ceased production of milk – in response to incentives put in place to reduce the surplus production of dairy products – infringed the principle of legitimate expectations (at p. 2352):

'A producer who has voluntarily ceased production for a certain period cannot legitimately expect to be able to resume production under the same conditions as those which previously applied and not to be subject to any rules of market or structural policy adopted in the mean time.

The fact remains that where such a producer, as in the present case, has been encouraged by a Community measure to suspend marketing for a limited period in the general interest and against payment of a premium he may legitimately expect not to be subject, upon the expiry of his undertaking, to restrictions which specifically affect him precisely because he availed himself of the possibilities offered by the Community provisions.'

The Council tried again. The problem was that those who had ceased production had not delivered any milk during what is termed the 'reference year', that is the year chosen by the Netherlands as the basis for calculating milk quotas. Hence on return to production, those who had ceased production lost out. In the revised rules the Council instituted a system whereby this group of producers would receive a special reference quantity equal to 60 per cent of the quantity of milk delivered or sold during the 12 months preceding the month in which the producer applied for the incentive scheme for ceasing production. Again that restriction was challenged on the grounds that it breached legitimate expectations, and the applicants were successful once more (Case C-189/89 *Spagl* [1990] ECR I-4539). The Court again held that the reduction of 40 per cent was a restriction which specifically affected the group of producers who had ceased production precisely because they had undertaken to do just that. The Council was forced to revise the arrangements for a second time, introducing a higher special reference quantity (for a discussion of the compensation claims that resulted from these cases see 17.8).

15.14 The Consequences of Annulment

The consequence of a successful action under Article 230 is a declaration by the Court under Article 231 that a measure is void. A measure may be declared void in part only, provided the offending part can be effectively severed from the rest. In Case 17/74 *Transocean Marine Paint Association* v. *Commission* ([1974] ECR 1063) an onerous condition in an exemption from the prohibition under Article 81 issued by the Commission was annulled on the grounds that the Commission had failed to give the applicant a sufficient hearing on the matter. The Court used Article 233, which requires the institution whose act has been declared void to take the necessary measures to comply with the judgment of the Court, to refer the measure back to the Commission for consideration. The alternative – entire annulment of the Commission's Decision that would have left an earlier exemption standing – might have been too favourable to the applicant.

15.15 Indirect Challenge

The availability of indirect challenge to unlawful acts of the EU institutions completes the system of judicial review as described by the Court in Case 294/83 *'Les Verts'*. The objective is to ensure that illegal 'parent' EU acts can be attacked through the medium of implementing EU or national measures. The availability of two avenues for indirect challenge in EU law – Articles 234 and 241 – was emphasised in 14.2. Although, where Article 234 is used, the proceedings will begin in the national court, in practice indirect challenge is an instrument of judicial control which lies principally in the hands of the Court of Justice, since it has claimed the exclusive right to decide on the invalidity of EU acts (Case 314/85 *Firma Foto-Frost* v. *HZA Lübeck-Ost* [1987] ECR 4199).

The types of case in which an indirect challenge may occur obviously include actions for annulment, where the basis for the action is the illegality of a 'parent' EU act. In particular, Article 241 provides the opportunity in proceedings brought by an individual against an administrative act in the Court of Justice to challenge a normative act on which the administrative act is based and which is not susceptible itself to challenge by individuals. In the national courts, the alleged illegality of an EU act may form the basis of either the cause of action or the defence in the full range of civil, criminal and administrative proceedings (e.g. action for the recovery of money claimed by the authorities on the basis of an unlawful EU act; defence to criminal proceedings where the national criminal provisions are based on an unlawful EU act).

The Court has sought to keep the two remedies separate. In Cases 31, 33/62 *Wöhrmann* v. *Commission* ([1962] ECR 501) it held that Article 241 may only be raised in proceedings before the Court in which the allegedly illegal act is relevant. It cannot be invoked in Article 234 proceedings. However, in Case 216/82 *Universität Hamburg* v. *HZA Hamburg-Kehrwieder* ([1983] ECR 2771), the Court explicitly drew a parallel between Article 241 and Article 234 holding that:

> 'According to a general principle of law which finds its expression in Article 184 of the EEC Treaty, in proceedings brought under national law against the rejection of his application [for duty-free admission of scientific apparatus from the USA into Germany] the applicant must be able to plead the illegality of the Commission's Decision on which the national decision adopted in his regard is based.'

15.16 Article 241 (formerly Article 184): The Plea of Illegality (for text see 14.2)

According to the Court of Justice in Case 92/78 *Simmenthal SpA* v. *Commission* ([1979] ECR 777 at p. 778):

'Article 184 of the EEC Treaty gives expression to a general principle conferring upon any party to proceedings the right to challenge, for the purpose of obtaining the annulment of a decision of direct and individual concern to that party, the validity of previous acts of the institutions which form the legal basis of the decision which is being attacked, if that party was not entitled under Article 173 of the Treaty to bring a direct action challenging those acts by which it was thus affected without having been in a position to ask that they be declared void.'

In view of these conclusions, the Court interpreted the term 'regulation' as used in what is now Article 241 broadly in order to include within the scope of indirect challenge any normative acts which produce similar effects to regulations and which are therefore on those grounds not subject to direct challenge. On the other hand, the raising of a plea of illegality does not in any way exonerate the applicant from satisfying the basic conditions – *locus standi*, observance of time limits, reviewable act – which govern the proceedings in which the plea is raised.

Since it would appear that an Article 241 plea is available first and foremost for the purpose of allowing challenges to measures which the applicant could not have challenged by way of an Article 230 action, it follows that Article 241 cannot be used by applicants to challenge individual acts addressed to them in the context of other proceedings. This would in effect do away with the time limits for challenging such acts and would destroy the coherence and certainty of the remedies system under the Treaty (Case 21/64 *Dalmas* v. *High Authority* [1965] ECR 175). There have been no clear statements from the Court on whether or not Article 241 can be used to challenge measures which the applicant might have had standing to challenge, for example, by application of the rules of direct and individual concern. Nor has the Court decided the extent to which privileged applicants can rely upon Article 241. The logical extension of its views in *Simmenthal* would appear to be that since privileged applicants have unlimited standing to challenge all reviewable EU acts they should not be allowed the second chance of an Article 241 plea once the time limit for direct challenge has expired. In Case 32/65 *Italy* v. *Commission* ([1966] ECR 389), although the Court did not decide the point, AG Roemer inclined to the view that privileged applicants should be allowed to rely upon Article 241 since at the time when the act was adopted they might not have thought it was unlawful. There are certainly restrictions on the use of Article 241 as a defence in enforcement proceedings. In Case 156/77 *Commission* v. *Belgium* ([1978] ECR 1881) the Commission had brought proceedings under Article 88(2) EC for failure by Belgium to comply with a Commission Decision of May 1976 which Belgium had failed to challenge directly. The Court refused to allow Belgium to raise Article 241 as a defence. However, there are some differences between the specific nature of enforcement proceedings in the context of state aids which are based in part on the Commission taking enforcement decisions which the Member State must challenge by annulment proceedings if it objects, and general enforcement proceedings under Article 226, where the onus lies on the Commission to issue a statement of objections and to bring the Member State before the Court. In that context, it might remain possible for the Member State to argue that the policy measure that the Commission is seeking to enforce is in fact unlawful.

The grounds for review under Article 241 are the same as those in Article 230, which is specifically referred to in the terms of Article 241. The effects of a successful indirect challenge are not formally annulment, but for all practical purposes the act must be seen as invalidated and without legal effect.

15.17 The Scope of Indirect Challenge under Article 234

In 11.7 the powers of the Court of Justice in relation to rulings on validity were outlined, and it was indicated that there is an implicit obligation on national courts to make a reference in any proceedings where there is a doubt about the validity of an EU measure. The scope of judicial review via the national court is, as we have seen, much more generous to the individual applicant. This is an important aspect of ensuring that the EU is a 'Community subject to the rule of law', in accordance with the statements of the Court in Case 294/83 *'Les Verts'*.

It was thought that the ability of bringing an indirect challenge operated entirely independently to the issue of an action for annulment under Article 230. In Cases 133-6/85 *Walter Rau* v. *BALM* the Court held that a national court faced with proceedings in which a national act implementing a Commission Decision is being challenged does not need to ascertain before hearing the case whether an action could have been brought against the Decision under Article 230. It is sufficient that the national conditions for the bringing of annulment proceedings are satisfied. There are two reasons for the Court to take this approach: first, the applicant in the national proceedings is unlikely to have been notified of the measure in question, and thus, secondly, it might not have been aware of the expiry of the time limit under Article 230.

There are, however, a range of cases where this principle will not apply. In Case C-188/92 *TWD Textilwerke Deggendorf GmbH* v. *Germany* ([1994] ECR I-833) the question before the Court was whether a national court was bound by a 1986 Commission Decision, addressed to the German government, declaring certain state aids paid to a producer of synthetic yarns situated in Deggendorf (i.e. TWD) to be incompatible with the Common Market. The Commission required the German government to recover the aid, using its enforcement powers. The German government informed TWD of the Decision, and indicated that it would be challengeable under Article 230 (15.9). TWD took no action under Article 230, but challenged the German measure requiring repayment of the aid in the German courts, relying on the alleged unlawfulness of the Commission Decision. In these circumstances, the Court declared that legal certainty required that there should be no further opening up of the question whether the Commission Decision was valid in the context of Article 234 proceedings. Because of the potential for application of these principles outside the narrow field of state aids, Ross argues that 'the *TWD* reasoning only works if the generally messy case law on *locus standi* is itself made more intelligible' (Ross, 1994: 644). In the light of the discussion in this chapter, it must be concluded that this happy state of affairs remains some way off. That this judgment is to be confined to a narrow set of circumstances became apparent when *TWD* was considered, but not applied, by the Court of Justice in Case C-408/95 *EurotunnelSA* v. *SeaFrance* ([1997] ECR I-6315).

The effects of findings of invalidity under Article 234 have already been discussed in 11.8.

Summary

1 A successful Article 230 action requires:
   – a reviewable act;
   – *locus standi* on the part of the applicant;
   – an application within the time limits;
   – substantive or procedural illegality on the part of the adopting institution.

2 A reviewable act is any act with legal effects which brings about a change in the legal position of the applicant.

3 For individual applicants, the need to demonstrate *locus standi* will often be an unassailable hurdle. In particular, the requirement that a decision addressed to another person must 'individually concern' the applicant has often prevented individuals showing standing. Individuals can only very rarely bring actions under Article 230 to challenge regulations. The Court's case law has been criticised as unnecessarily restricting the access of individuals.

4 In a number of areas involving quasi-judicial determinations by the Commission (competition law, state aids, anti-dumping) the Court of Justice has taken a more liberal approach, in the interests of ensuring effective protection of individual rights.

5 The Court applies its case law on general principles of law when assessing whether there are grounds for reviewing an EU act. The intensity of review applied depends upon the circumstances of the case.

6 Indirect challenge occurs under Articles 234 and 241. Article 241 permits challenges to general EU measures in the context of challenges to admin-

istrative measures brought under Article 230. Under Article 234, the Court claims the exclusive right to declare the invalidity of EU measures the legality of which is impugned before the national court.

7　An indirect challenge via the national court and Article 234 will be excluded for an individual applicant who clearly had standing to challenge the relevant measure under Article 230.

Questions

1　What is a reviewable act?

2　In what way has the Court influenced the present text of the judicial review provisions (as amended by the Treaty of Maastricht)?

3　How and why has the Court of Justice interpreted the *locus standi* provisions of Articles 230 in such a way as to restrict the direct access of individuals to remedies in that Court?

4　Why has the Court of First Instance declined to develop a more generous approach to *locus standi* since the case of *Codorniu*?

5　Why is the Court's interpretation of the *locus standi* provisions more generous in cases involving quasi-judicial determinations by the EU institutions?

6　How does the system of indirect challenge to the legality of EU acts complement the system of direct challenge?

Further Reading

A. Albors-Llorens (1996), *Private Parties in European Community Law*, Oxford: Oxford University Press.

A. Arnull (1995a), 'Private Applicants and the Action for Annulment under Article 173 of the EC Treaty', 32 *Common Market Law Review* 7.

F. Berrod (1999), 'Case Note on *Stichting Greenpeace*', 36 *Common Market Law Review* 635.

K. Bradley (1988), 'The Variable Evolution of the Standing of the European Parliament in Proceedings before the Court of Justice', 8 *Yearbook of European Law* 27.

K. Bradley (1991), 'Sense and Sensibility: *Parliament* v. *Council* Continued', 16 *European Law Review* 245.

P. Craig (1994), 'Legality, Standing and Substantial Review in Community Law', 14 *Oxford Journal of Legal Studies* 507.

R. Greaves (1996), 'The Nature and Binding Effect of Decisions under Article 189 EC', 21 *European Law Review* 3.

C. Harlow (1992a), 'Towards a Theory of Access for the European Court of Justice', 12 *Yearbook of European Law* 213.

T. Hartley (1998), Ch. 14, 'Indirect Challenge'.

M. Hedemann-Robinson (1996), 'Article 173 EC, General Community Measures and *Locus Standi* for Private Persons: Still a Cause for Individual Concern?', 2 *European Public Law* 127.

N. Neuwahl (1996), 'Article 173 Paragraph 4 EC: Past, Present and Possible Future', 21 *European Law Review* 17.

H. Rasmussen (1980), 'Why is Article 173 Interpreted against Private Plaintiffs?', 5 *European Law Review* 112.

D. Wyatt (1997), 'The Relationship between Actions for Annulment and References on Validity after TWD Teggendorf', in Lonbay and Biondi (1997).

16 Judicial Control of Failure to Act

16.1 Introduction: Article 230 and Article 232

Articles 230 and 232 EC (formerly Articles 173 and 175 EC; for the text of these provisions see 14.2) are intended to provide complementary remedies: acting illegally and illegally failing to act should be two sides of the same coin. Non-privileged applicants with limited standing under Article 230 should be unable to sue in respect of a failure to adopt a legislative act that they would be unable to challenge if it were in fact adopted. In contrast, privileged applicants, who are entitled to challenge any reviewable acts should be able to challenge the refusal or failure to adopt any acts which the authority is under a legal obligation to adopt. In the context of such actions, therefore, the latter condition will be the crucial determinant of what constitutes a reviewable omission.

The Court's position on the linkage between the two provisions has been slightly inconsistent. In Case 15/70 *Chevalley* v. *Commission* ([1970] ECR 975), given the applicant's uncertainty as to whether the action in question should be under Article 232 or Article 230, for the purposes of a preliminary investigation of admissibility, the Court held that it was unnecessary to distinguish between the two remedies, since they 'merely prescribe one and the same method of recourse'. However, since then the Court has stated that where proceedings are begun under both Articles the applicant must identify the act which it intends to challenge by means of an annulment action (Case 247/87 *Star Fruit Co* v. *Commission* ([1989] ECR 291). In Case 302/87 *Parliament* v. *Council (Comitology)* ([1988] ECR 5615) when initially rejecting the Parliament's standing to sue under Article 230, the Court also denied the linkage between Articles 230 and 232. The fact that the Parliament has a right of action under Article 232 had 'no necessary link to any right of action under Article 173 (now Article 230)'.

Article 232 applies to 'pure omissions', not to refusals to act, which are characterised as negative decisions and actionable under Article 230, if at all. The interplay between the two is illustrated by Case 42/71 *Nordgetreide* v. *Commission* ([1972] ECR 105). The Commission refused to amend a Regulation when requested to do so by Nordgetreide. Article 232 proceedings were barred because the Commission's refusal was held to be a definition of its position, and Article 230 proceedings failed because although the refusal to amend the regulation was in one sense a 'decision', Nordgetreide would have no standing to challenge the Regulation which was a pure normative act and could not therefore challenge the negative act refusing to amend it. In other words, the link between the two provisions will be operated in such a way as to prevent one provision being used to evade the restrictive conditions applying to the other provision.

This was stated expressly by the Court in Cases 10, 18/68 *Eridania* v. *Commission* ([1969] ECR 459). The applicants had requested the Commission to revoke a certain measure, and when it failed to do so, they started proceedings for failure to act under Article 232. They also started an action for annulment against the act which failed because they did not have *locus standi* to challenge the act. The Court held that Article 232 cannot be used to circumvent Article 230 in this way (at p. 483):

> 'To admit, as the applicants wish to do, that the parties concerned could ask the institution from which the measure came to revoke it and, in the event of the Commission's failing to act, refer such a failure to the Court as an illegal omission to deal with the matter would amount to providing them with a method of recourse parallel to that of Article 173, which would not be subject to the conditions laid down by the Treaty.'

Like Article 230, Article 232 was amended by the Treaty of Maastricht to bring the Parliament fully within its terms. This is particularly important in respect of its budgetary, as well as its legislative, activities. Paragraph 4 brings the ECB into the scope of Article 232, as a potential plaintiff or defendant. Unlike Article 230, it does not cover in any way the Court of Auditors.

16.2   Procedure

The procedure must begin with a formal request to the defendant to take action. It must state clearly what action is required, that it is made within the terms of Article 232, and that the applicant considers the defendant legally obliged to take the action required (Case 25/85 *Nuovo Campsider* v. *Commission* [1986] ECR 1531). The defendant has a period of two months to comply. If that period expires without response or action by the defendant, the applicant may take the matter to the Court within a further two months. This procedure puts the defendant formally in default, and also gives it the opportunity to comply. In a case decided under Article 35 ECSC (the equivalent to Article 232 EC) the Court has held that the preliminary procedure must be initiated within a reasonable time. In Case 59/70 *Netherlands* v. *Commission* ([1971] ECR 639) the action was held inadmissible because of a lapse of 18 months between a statement by the Commission to which the Netherlands objected, and the Netherlands submitting a formal request for action.

A definition of position by the authority terminates the Article 232 action. For example, Case 377/87 *Parliament* v. *Council* ([1988] ECR 4017) concerned an alleged failure by the Council to comply with the budget timetable. The Council acted after the action was brought before the Court, but before the judgment of the Court was delivered. The Court held that once an institution has defined its position, the action cannot continue, as its subject matter has ceased to exist. In that sense, the Article 232 action can be contrasted with the Article 226 enforcement action, which the Commission may continue to prosecute notwithstanding compliance by the Member State (8.3). The position is the same for a non-privileged applicant (Cases C-15, 108/91 *Buckl* v. *Commission* [1992] ECR I-6061). If the act refusing the request of the applicant has been adopted by the defendant institution after the application has been submitted to the Court, there will be no need to give a judgment. Moreover, if the institution defines its position by adopting an act other than that requested by the applicant before the application has been submitted to the Court, the application will be rejected as inadmissible (Case C-25/91 *Pesqueras Echebastar* v. *Commission* [1993] ECR I-1719).

In theory, a definition of position which blocks an Article 232 action where the applicant had standing should, according to the unity principle, always be reviewable under Article 230. In fact, that is not the case, as the Court of First Instance reiterated in Case T-186/94 *Guérin Automobiles* v. *Commission* ([1995] ECR II-1753). In the field of competition law, in which Article 232 has proved to be a particularly useful tool for complainants in pushing the Commission to take a position on the complaint, what is termed an 'Article 6' letter in which the Commission expresses its provisional view that it will not take up the complaint, while not a reviewable act (15.2), will none the less be a classed as a 'definition of position' because it constitutes a necessary preliminary step in a procedure which will eventually lead to a reviewable act (the definitive refusal to take up the complaint).

Moreover, distinguishing exactly what constitutes a definition of position is not easy, and consequently proceedings may have to be initiated under both Articles. In the most prominent successful case involving Article 232 which was concerned with the failure of the Council to enact a number of measures under the common transport policy (Case 13/83 *Parliament* v. *Council (Common Transport Policy)* [1985] ECR 1513), the case was able to continue under Article 232, as the Council's definition of position was deemed to be inadequate. For the Parliament, which still does not have full status as a privileged applicant under Article 230 even after the amendments introduced by the Treaty of Maastricht, but whose position under Article 232 is identical to the other institutions and the Member States, the difference between what is and what is not a definition of position – a question of fact, not law – could be crucial. In that case the Council failed either to confirm or to deny the alleged failure to act, and failed also to state what measures it proposed to adopt.

In the event of a finding of failure to act, there is no unlawful act for the Court to annul. The Court will make an order under Article 232 with which the institution in default must comply, but there are no further sanctions for non-compliance. For example, although the Court declined to decide the point expressly in Case 13/83 *Parliament* v. *Council*, it is clear that a legislative failure on the part of the Council does not result in the legislative power reverting to another institution which is willing to act. While changes to Article 228 EC which were introduced by the Treaty of Maastricht have instituted the possibility of imposing financial sanctions for non-compliance on the Member States, similar changes to the obligations of the EU institutions were not contemplated. However, the institutions remain under an obligation to compensate individuals in respect of unlawful conduct which causes damage, and there are a few, although so far unsuccessful, examples of actions against the institutions in respect of unlawful omissions (e.g. Cases 326/86 and 66/88 *Francesconi* v. *Commission* [1989] ECR 2087 (17.5) and Case C-63/89 *Les Assurances du Crédit SA* v. *Council and Commission* ([1991] ECR I-1799 (17.9)).

16.3   Failure to Act: Privileged Applicants

The terms of Article 232 draw a clear distinction – as do those of Article 230 – between actions brought by privileged and non-privileged applicants. The first paragraph refers simply to a 'failure to act', without being specific as to the nature of that act. That raises the question of the range of reviewable omissions which privileged applicants can challenge. One of the few instances of success is Case 13/83 *Parliament* v. *Council* in which the Parliament challenged the Council's failure to introduce a common policy for transport and its failure to reach a decision on sixteen specified proposals submitted by the Commission in relation to transport, which were required in order to secure freedom to provide transport services. The Parliament failed on the first rather more general allegation: there was no legally complete obligation under what was then Article 74 EEC to introduce a common transport policy. However, it succeeded on the second ground, since the Council was legally required to implement these freedoms, as guaranteed by what were then Articles 75, 59, 60 and 61 EEC (now Articles 71, 49, 50 and 51 EC), within the transitional period. The actions sought 'must be sufficiently defined to allow the Court to determine whether ... the failure to adopt them is lawful' (para. 36). This is the mirror image of the requirement in all Article 230 EC actions that there should be a reviewable act which produces legal effects.

It would appear that privileged applicants can seek a review of the failure to adopt certain preparatory or preliminary acts. In Case 377/87 *Parliament* v. *Council*, the Parliament's action was brought to challenge the failure of the Council to present a draft budget under what is now Article 272(4) EC. The action failed because the Court found that the Council had presented a draft budget. However, somewhat strangely the Court commented in a later case (Case 302/87 *Parliament* v. *Council (Comitology)* [1988] ECR 5615) that Case 377/87 'showed' that the Parliament could challenge the failure by the Council to present a draft budget. The position taken is justifiable in the sense that the Parliament is under a legal obligation under the Treaty to adopt the budget, and without a Council draft budget it cannot act. However, the approach taken breaks the unity of Articles 230 and 232, since the draft budget is not a challengeable act itself, under the principles set out in 15.2.

16.4 Failure to Act: Non-Privileged Applicants

The terms of the third paragraph of Article 232 restrict the action for failure to act to circumstances where a natural or legal person can claim that 'an institution of the Community has failed to address to that person any act other than a recommendation or an opinion.' This would seem to indicate that only legally binding measures are covered by the provision, and that the same standing restrictions apply as do under Article 230.

So, for example, in Case 246/81 *Bethell* v. *Commission* ([1982] ECR 2277) the plaintiff found himself wholly without a remedy. At the time of the action brought by Lord Bethell, who was seeking to force stricter application of the competition rules in the air transport sector, air transport was not covered by Regulation 17 which provides enforcement procedures for Articles 81 and 82, or any other similar provisions. As such, he had no protected status as a complainant, and could not therefore lay claim even to the basic investigation of a complaint to which a complainant would otherwise be entitled (8.16). A complainant under the competition, anti-dumping or state aid provisions should be entitled to force the EU authorities adopt a position *vis-à-vis* them which would be reviewable under Article 230, or to obtain the review of a failure to act under Article 232, in particular where the action is brought in order to enforce observance of the complainant's procedural rights. In Case 191/82 *FEDIOL* v. *Commission* ([1983] ECR 2913) a challenge brought by the EU seed crushers and oil processors federation to ensure judicial review of the extent to which their procedural rights, as complainants, to be involved in anti-dumping proceedings had been observed, was held admissible. Although the position of complainants in competition proceedings long remained uncertain, in Case T-24/90 *Automec* v. *Commission (Automec II)* ([1992] ECR II-2223), the Court of First Instance finally resolved that such a complainant is entitled to the adoption of a reviewable act by the Commission. Consequently, Article 232 can be used by the complainant to force the Commission to undertake a basic investigation. On the other hand, complainants cannot force the Commission to take a final decision on the application of the competition rules, provided their procedural rights have been observed (Case 125/78 *GEMA* v. *Commission* [1979] ECR 3173).

In these types of circumstances, involving complainants, the applicant is the would-be addressee. The question that has arisen is whether the same formulation of the standing rules under Article 232 should be used as for Article 230 (i.e. direct and individual concern). Should the '*de facto* addressee' (Hartley, 1998: 396) be able to bring an action. The point appears to have been decided in favour of a parallelism in the standing rules in Case C-107/91 *ENU* v. *Commission* ([1993] ECR I-599), a case brought under Article 148 Euratom (which is materially identical to Article 232 EC). ENU was a Portuguese company producing a form of uranium, which found itself in financial difficulties as a result of a price fall on the market and a lack of demand for its product. It wished the Euratom Supply Agency to make use of its option under Article 57 Euratom to purchase some of its supplies and so relieve its difficulties. Not receiving any satisfactory response from the Agency, ENU turned to the Commission, asking it to use its powers under Article 53 to bring about a resolution of the problem. The Court held that the action was admissible, since any decision addressed by the Commission to the Agency under Article 53 would have concerned the applicant directly and individually, and this was sufficient as a basis for an action for failure to act. In the event, the Court also found that the Commission was guilty of an unlawful failure to act, and made an order accordingly.

A failure by the Commission to put a proposal for legislation has been found to be not reviewable, since it is only a preliminary act. Similar reasoning can be used to explain the decisions in Case 48/65 *Lütticke* v. *Commission* ([1966] ECR 19) and Case 247/87 *Star Fruit Co* v. *Commission* in which the Court held that individuals could not force the Commission to take enforcement proceedings against Member States. Nothing in the enforcement procedure constitutes a binding reviewable act.

It is possible that there may be certain special circumstances in which a broader approach is necessary. These are illustrated by the facts, if not the decision, in Case C-41/92 *The Liberal Democrats* v. *Parliament* ([1993] ECR I-3153), which represents a neat parallel with Case 294/83 *Parti Ecologiste 'Les Verts'* v. *Parliament* ([1986] ECR 1339). In that case, it will be recalled, the Court adopted a generous interpretation of the standing rules in the interests, it may be contended, of protecting and enhancing the democratic basis of the EU (15.6). *Liberal Democrats* involved an action brought by the UK Liberal Democratic Party against the Parliament in respect of its failure to put forward proposals for a uniform electoral procedure under what was then Article 138(3) EEC. It was struck out as inadmissible because the Parliament, after the initiation of the legal proceedings, adopted a resolution on a uniform electoral procedure, proposing a form of proportional representation, but with a formula which would allow states such as the UK to maintain two-thirds of its seats as single member constituencies. AG Darmon suggested that the failure to produce a preparatory act without which another institution cannot produce a definitive act itself has legal effects and justifies an action for failure to act. The question that this does not answer is whether the Liberal Democrats would have had standing to challenge that failure, given the nature of their 'interest' in the eventual legislation (proven when a number of Liberal Democrat MEPs were elected in June 1999 when the UK electoral system was shifted from a 'first-past-the-post' system which privileges the two main parties of the left and right to multi-member constituencies with a party list system).

Summary

1 Article 232 provides a complementary remedy to that available under Article 230, covering failure to act. It has only very rarely been used successfully.
2 A successful Article 232 action requires:
   – *locus standi* on the part of the applicant;
   – a request by the applicant to the defendant to define its position, and a failure by the defendant to define its position;
   – a failure to adopt an act on the part of the defendant institution which it is under a duty to adopt.

Questions

1 What is the unity principle?
2 What is the relationship between a reviewable omission and a reviewable act?
3 Can you explain why Article 232 has proved to be particularly useful to two very different types of applicant: the Parliament, and complainants in the field of competition law?

Further Reading

T. Hartley (1998), Ch. 13, 'Failure to Act'.

17 Non-Contractual Liability and Compensation for Loss Caused by the EU

17.1 Introduction

The framework of rules governing the non-contractual (i.e. tortious) liability of the EU for the acts of its institutions and servants shares many of the complexities and the policy-oriented nature of the rules governing judicial review. The text of the key provisions (Articles 235 and 288(2) EC) is set out in 14.2.

In principle, therefore, the EU must compensate for the damage it causes. Damage may be caused either by an institution (e.g. through a legislative measure, an administrative act or some other action or statement which inflicts loss, or indeed by an omission), or by its servants, in which case the institution will be subject to a form of vicarious liability (e.g. an EU official reveals confidential information about an undertaking to a third party). The nature of the liability (i.e. fault-based or strict liability, nature of the causal link required, scope of damage recoverable) is determined according to principles common to the laws of the Member States, and has been subject to judicial evolution in the hands of the Court of Justice (and now, the Court of First Instance, which is responsible for such actions). As a matter of practice, the EU is represented by the institution alleged, directly or vicariously, to have caused the damage, and not always by the Commission, even though the latter institution does have a number of important representative functions.

17.2 The Conditions of Liability

The judicial evolution of the EU law on non-contractual liability has demonstrated that the following are the necessary conditions of a successful action:

> – a wrongful act or omission which is the responsibility of an institution;
> – damage to the plaintiff;
> – a causal link between the two.

These conditions will be examined in turn.

17.3 The Requirement of a Wrongful Act

It is implicit in much of the Court's case law that some form of 'fault' is a necessary element of liability. The Court was given the opportunity in Cases 9, 11/71 *Compagnie d'Approvisionnement* v. *Commission* ([1972] ECR 391) to adopt the French doctrine of '*égalité devant les charges publiques*' (equal apportionment of public burdens). This means that the state may in certain circumstances be liable even in the absence of fault, as a result of the simple fact that policy measures which it adopts may weigh more heavily on some citizens than on others. Since the Court concluded that the measures under challenge in Cases 9, 11/71, which were intended to offset the effects of the devaluation of the French franc in 1969, and in particular its disruptive effects on the Common Agricultural Policy (CAP), did not in fact impose a burden on the applicants, it was not required to consider this question. In Case T-113/96 *Dubois* v. *Council and Commission* ([1998] ECR II-125) the Court of First Instance again rejected a claim formulated in terms of the principle of *égalité devant les charges publiques*. The applicant was a customs agent who was claiming damage for loss which he alleged he had suffered as a result of the implementation of the Single European Act, which had deprived him of his livelihood as a result of implementing an area without frontiers by 1 January 1993, at least for tax purposes and custom controls. The Court reformulated the general part of the claim as seeking damages in respect of the effects of Article 13 of the Single European Act, which has subsequently become Article 14 EC. This was an act of the Member States as High Contracting Parties to the Treaty and was an instrument of primary EU law in respect of which no strict liability could arise as suggested by the applicant.

A similar requirement of 'wrongfulness' or 'fault' is an essential element of the non-contractual liability of the EU institutions under the ECSC Treaty regime (see Case T-120/89 *Stahlwerke Peine-Salzgitter* v. *Commission* [1991] ECR II-279; Case C-220/91 P *Stahlwerke Peine-Salzgitter* v. *Commission* [1993] ECR I-2393).

17.4 Wrongful Acts: Vicarious Liability and the Responsibility of the Institutions

In the one case in which it has been required to consider the nature of the EU's responsibility for a fault on the part of one of its servants (*faute personnelle*), the Court has given a restrictive interpretation of the extent of EU vicarious liability. Interpreting the equivalent provision of the Euratom Treaty (Article 188(2)) in Case 9/69 *Sayag* v. *Leduc* ([1969] ECR 329) the Court held (at p.335):

'By referring at one and the same time to damage caused by the institutions and to that caused by the servants of the Community, Article 188 indicates that the Community is only liable for those acts of its servants which, by virtue of an internal and direct relationship, are the necessary extension of the tasks entrusted to the institutions.'

In *Sayag*, a reference for a preliminary ruling from a Belgian court, the question concerned whether a person injured in a traffic accident caused by an engineer employed by Euratom who had been travelling on official business in Belgium in his private car should be suing the engineer personally in the Belgian courts or the EU as vicariously liable in the Court of Justice. The restrictive interpretation given by the Court resulted in the conclusion that the driving of a private car on official business would not fall within the concept of *faute personnelle* except in the exceptional circumstances where the EU would not have been able to undertake the tasks entrusted to it without the official using private means of transport.

Clearly, also, the institutions will be liable for forms of employers' and occupiers' liability. For example, in Case C-308/87 *Grifoni* v. *Euratom* ([1990] ECR I-1203), the plaintiff was the proprietor of an Italian construction company who was injured in the course of carrying out maintenance work at the Commission's Ispra Research Centre in Italy. He had not been supplied with a safety harness, and the place where he was working was not fitted with a safety rail, contrary to the requirements of Italian health and safety law. The Court held that the EU was required to comply with Italian law on industrial safety, that this requirement applied also to an independent contractor, and that the EU was therefore liable in damages. The damages were reduced by 50 per cent, on account of contributory negligence on the part of Grifoni, who had agreed to go on the roof in the absence of the necessary protective devices.

17.5   Wrongful Acts: Liability for Administrative Acts

One of the most infamous cases concerning the responsibility of the EU, and one of the relatively few which resulted in a definitive award of damages, involved a clear case of carelessness within the Commission which was not imputable to any one official or to the organisation of the institution as an employer or a contractor, but to the administrative service as a whole (*faute de service*) (Case 145/83 *Adams* v. *Commission* [1985] ECR 3539). Stanley Adams, while working for the Swiss pharmaceutical company Hoffman-La-Roche (HLR), supplied the Commission with documents, on an assurance of confidentiality. The documents showed that HLR was violating EU competition law, and the Commission successfully took proceedings against the company. In the course of the proceedings, the Commission supplied HLR with documents which assisted them in identifying Adams as the informant. Although Adams had left HLR's employment by that time and was living in Italy, he was arrested under the Swiss industrial espionage laws when he returned for a visit. He was held in solitary confinement, unable to communicate with his family, and his wife, who was also interrogated, subsequently committed suicide. He was eventually convicted and given a one-year suspended sentence. When he claimed damages against the Commission, it was found by the Court to have violated its duty towards him, in particular when it failed to warn Adams after it discovered that HLR was planning to prosecute him. The damages payable were reduced by one-half in respect of Adams' own contributory fault in returning to Switzerland, which occasioned his arrest.

A less tragic case is Case 353/88 *Briantex* v. *Council and Commission* ([1989] ECR 3623) where the Commission was said to have misled the plaintiff into thinking that it could conclude contracts with Chinese companies in the context of an 'EEC–China Business Week', when in fact the Italian quota for the relevant good was already exhausted. The claim failed on the facts, as the applicants were unable to prove wrongful conduct on the part of the Commission. The same grounds were given by the Court for dismissing the application in Cases 326/86 and 66/88 *Francesconi* v. *Commission* ([1989] ECR 2087). This was an attempt to make the Commission liable for failure effectively to cooperate with a Member State and for bad management and supervision of the wine sector following the so-called glycol and methanol wine scandals in 1985–86. The claim, although unsuccessful, raises the possibility of an extension of Commission liability in the context of its cooperative and supervisory roles in relation to the implementation of EU law (see also 17.10).

In Case T-231/97 *New Europe Consulting* v. *Commission* (July 9 1999), however, the Court concluded that all the necessary elements of a successful action under Article 288 were present: an unlawful act, damage and a direct causal link. NEC had been involved since 1991 in the PHARE programme, which has provided aid to Central and Eastern European countries and had run a teaching programme for senior officials in Hungary. On the basis of a report from Hungarian officials, a Commission official warned the coordinators of the PHARE programme against suing NEC on the ground that it was financially unsound and systematically failed to pay its suppliers. NEC was removed from the PHARE lists, and suffered considerable loss of business. It brought an action for damages, claiming *inter alia* the principle of good administration. Applying this principle, the Court found that the Commission had acted wrongfully by failing to carry out its own investigation into the allegations before passing the information onto the PHARE programme. It had effectively infringed the rights of the defence of the applicant. The applicant received, *inter alia*, compensation for damage to his reputation. It is interesting to note the success of a claim for damages based on the administrative failures of the Commission in the era of the Ombudsman, who has been seeking the adoption of a code of good administrative behaviour by the institutions (4.15).

17.6   **Acts or Omissions?**

For many years, there was little indication as to whether and to what extent the EU may be liable for omissions. In Cases 19, etc./69 *Richez-Parise* v. *Commission* ([1970] ECR 325) the Commission was held liable for the failure to correct the good faith, but incorrect, interpretation it had given to a number of officials regarding their pensions. However, in Case C-146/91 *KYDEP* v. *Council and Commission* ([1994] ECR I-4199) the Court held that the EU institutions could only be held liable for omissions in circumstances where they had breached a legal duty to act resulting from a provision of EU law. In circumstances where the institutions have a wide discretion as to the nature and form of their action (see 17.7 *et seq.*) it is exceedingly unlikely that an action to establish liability for an omission will succeed. In a recent example (Case T-572/93 *Odigitria AAE* v. *Council and Commission* [1995] ECR II-2025) the applicant failed in a contention that the Council and Commission had unlawfully failed to take into account the existence of a longstanding territorial dispute between Guinea-Bissau and Senegal before the International Court of Justice when they negotiated and concluded fishing agreements with these two countries. The applicant's contention was that this failure had caused it loss when one of its boats inadvertently became involved in this dispute with the result that it was seized and its cargo confiscated by the Guinea-Bissau authorities. The Court found no violation of a superior rule of law (cf. 17.9) by the institutions. On the other hand, the judgment of the Court does seem to indicate that the Commission might have been guilty of an unlawful omission in the conduct of its administrative duties in failing to warn the applicant about an escalation in the dispute which led to the incident in which the applicant's boat was seized (cf. 17.10). However, on the facts the Court found that it could not have been the failure to warn which caused the loss since it appeared that the applicant's captain in fact knew about the escalation (see 17.11). Likewise in Case T-113/96 *Dubois* the Court found that the institutions were under no obligation to take steps to compensate the applicant for loss caused by an international treaty which did not emanate from the institutions themselves. Hence the omission could not be the subject of a compensation claim.

17.7   **Wrongful Acts: Acts having Legal Effects**

In practice, the most important category of cases decided by the Court under Article 288 has concerned alleged liability for damage caused by acts which have legal effects such as an illegal refusal to grant an import or export licence, or measures of economic policy which impose more onerous financial burdens on one product than on a competing product, or which discriminate between producers of the same product. In these cases the wrongful act is quite different in nature to, for example, the breach of confidentiality which caused harm to Stanley Adams.

One of the most difficult questions in this context has been that of distinguishing between actions for annulment and actions for compensation; should recovery be governed by the same conditions which govern the annulment of acts with legal effects? If not, what conditions determine the circumstances in which the wrongful and damaging administrative or legislative actions of an EU institution give rise to an action for compensation?

17.8 The Relationship between Annulment and Compensation

The second paragraph of Article 233 EC states that the obligation on the institution whose act has been declared void to take the necessary measures to comply with the judgment of the Court of Justice 'shall not affect any obligation which may result from the application of the second paragraph of Article 288'. This appears to state clearly that annulment actions and actions for compensation are quite separate.

However, in Case 25/62 *Plaumann* v. *Commission* ([1963] ECR 95) the Court linked the two actions together. It will be recalled that in this case a German importer of clementines sought to challenge a Commission Decision addressed to Germany, refusing it the right to lower the duty on clementines from 13 to 10 per cent. Holding the Article 230 EC annulment action to be inadmissible on the grounds that the importer lacked *locus standi*, the Court went on to declare an Article 288 action for compensation admissible. However, the action failed on the merits (at p.108):

> 'It must be declared that the damage allegedly suffered by the applicant issues from this Decision and that the action for compensation in fact seeks to set aside the legal effects on the applicant of the contested Decision.
> In the present case the contested Decision has not been annulled. An administrative measure which has not been annulled cannot of itself constitute a wrongful act on the part of the administration inflicting damage upon those whom it affects. The latter cannot therefore claim damages by reason of that measure. The Court cannot by way of an action for compensation take steps which would nullify the legal effects of a Decision which, as stated, has not been annulled.'

This doctrine has since been reversed and there is now no need for an applicant under Article 288 to challenge directly or indirectly, via Articles 230, 234 or 184 EC, the legality of administrative or legislative measures in respect of which it claims compensation. In Case 4/69 *Lütticke* v. *Commission*

([1971] ECR 325), in the context of a claim for failure on the part of the Commission to address a directive or decision to Germany requiring it to modify certain taxes which the applicant had to pay, the Court stated (at p. 336):

> 'The action for damages provided for by Article 178 and the second paragraph of Article 215 was established by the Treaty as an independent form of action with a particular purpose to fulfil within the system of actions and subject to conditions for its use, conceived with a view to its specific purpose. It would be contrary to the independent nature of this action as well as to the efficacy of the general system of forms of action created by the Treaty to regard as a ground for inadmissibility the fact that, in certain circumstances, an action for damages might lead to a result similar to that of an action for failure to act under Article 175.'

The clearest statement of the separation of the actions for annulment and compensation came in Case 175/84 *Krohn* v. *Commission* ([1986] ECR 753) where the Court stated expressly that the existence of an individual decision which has become definitive because it had not been challenged under Article 230 was not a bar to the admissibility of a compensation action.

In practice, although annulment, or a declaration of invalidity under Article 234, is by no means a prerequisite of a successful action under Article 288, many actions for compensation are either linked to, or have been preceded by, successful annulment actions or declarations of invalidity (e.g. Case C-152/88 *Sofrimport* v. *Commission* [1990] ECR I-2477 – actions under Article 230 and 288 brought simultaneously; in the *Isoglucose* cases (see 17.9) Article 288 actions were brought at about the same time as actions in the national courts which resulted in references on the validity of the relevant measures under Article 234; in the milk quota cases discussed in the same paragraph the actions for compensation have followed findings of invalidity of a series of Council measures).

17.9   The Elaboration and Application of the Schöppenstedt Formula

The formula for determining whether there has been a breach of EU law in the context of a claim for compensation caused by an act having legal effects is quite different, and in many ways more restrictive, than the criteria which the Court uses to determine the legality of an act for the purposes of annulment or invalidity. It was elaborated by the Court in the first instance in Case 5/71 *Zuckerfabrik Schöppenstedt* v. *Council* ([1971] ECR 975) and it has consistently applied these principles since that time. The *Schöppenstedt* formula, as restated by the Court in Cases 83, etc./76 *Bayerische HNL et al.* v.

Council and Commission (Second Skimmed Milk Powder case) ([1978] ECR 1209 at p. 1224) states that:

> 'The Community does not incur liability on account of a legislative measure which involves choices of economic policy unless a sufficiently serious breach of a superior rule of law for the protection of the individual has occurred.'

This formula applies only to legislative measures of the institutions, that is, to those which are of general application and involve an element of discretionary decision making. Inevitably such measures will impact to varying degrees upon economic actors and, in order to avoid a flood of claims from aggrieved plaintiffs while at the same upholding the constitutional supremacy of the rule of law under the Treaties, the Court has chosen a restrictive definition of wrongfulness. This definition has in turn been applied in such a way as to exclude the majority of claims.

The first requirement is the breach of a superior rule of law for the protection of individuals. This is a reference to the range of general principles and fundamental rights evolved by the Court in its case law. For example, in Case 74/74 *CNTA* v. *Commission* ([1975] ECR 533) the Court held that the abolition with immediate effect and without warning of monetary compensatory amounts (MCAs), used to compensate agricultural traders for fluctuations in exchange rates which made the single pricing system under the CAP unreliable, could constitute a breach of the principle of legitimate expectations which is protected under EU law. In Case C-152/88 *Sofrimport* v. *Commission*, the Court found that importers of Chilean apples which were in transit to the EU had a legitimate expectation that they would be protected against the unfavourable consequences of protective measures against such apples which were introduced by the EU authorities. This was because the enabling Regulation specifically addressed the situation of those whose apples were actually already in transit to the EU, who could not therefore mitigate their loss by arranging for an alternative disposal of the products.

The prerequisite of a breach of a superior rule of law would normally be satisfied by a successful annulment action under Article 230, or a ruling of invalidity under Article 234, although it is arguable that a successful claim for invalidity on the grounds that the wrong legal basis had been used, or that Parliamentary prerogatives had not been observed would not satisfy the requirement that the rule of law which has been breached must be for the protection of individuals. The point was directly addressed by the Court in Case C-282/90 *Vreugdenhil* v. *Commission* ([1992] ECR I-1937). The alleged breach was of a rule governing the exercise of delegated powers by the Commission, and involved the Commission exceeding the powers granted to it by the Council. The Court had already made a ruling of invalidity in respect of the same provision in Case 22/88 *Vreugdenhil* v. *Minister van Landbouw and*

Visserij ([1989] ECR 2049) Faced with an action for damages, the Court held (at p. 1968):

> 'the aim of the system of the division of powers between the various Community institutions is to ensure that the balance between the institutions provided for in the Treaty is maintained, and not to protect individuals. Consequently, a failure to observe the balance between the institutions cannot be sufficient on its own to engage the Community's liability towards the traders concerned.'

In addition, the breach must be sufficiently serious. This is, in practice, the most stringent requirement, and in numerous cases the applicants' cases have failed at this hurdle. Cases 83, etc./76 *Second Skimmed Milk Powder case* concerned the attempt by the Community institutions to get rid of a skimmed milk powder mountain which stemmed from the overproduction of milk, by passing a Regulation obliging producers of animal feed to purchase skimmed milk powder from the intervention agencies. This had a damaging effect on soya, which was the alternative, and cheaper, source of protein in animal feeds. The result was also that farmers would have to pay more for their feed. The farmers succeeded in obtaining a declaration that the Regulation was invalid on the grounds that it infringed the principles of non-discrimination and proportionality (Case 114/76 *Bela-Mühle Josef Bergman* v. *Grows-Farm* [1977] ECR 1211), but failed in their tort actions because the institution concerned had not 'manifestly and gravely disregarded the limits on the exercise of its powers'.

Applying this formulation to the facts, the Court considered both the range of potential plaintiffs – which was a wide category of persons – and the effect of the infringement in terms of its impact on the price of the products in question, as compared to other factors such as fluctuations in world prices. It found this effect to be relatively small. It summed up the effect of the EU's measures as being within the normal range of risk inherent in activities in the economic sector concerned.

Soon after the *Second Skimmed Milk Powder case*, the Court made its first finding of tortious liability in respect of EU legislative acts. In Cases 64, etc./76 *Dumortier et al.* v. *Council and Commission (Quellmehl and Gritz)* ([1979] ECR 3091) the alleged tortious act was a Council Regulation withdrawing subsidies from the production of quellmehl and gritz, products used in baking which are in part in competition with starch, but leaving the subsidies in place for starch. The measure was declared invalid on a reference for a preliminary ruling (Cases 117, etc./76 *Ruckdeschel* v. *HZA Hamburg St-Annen* [1977] ECR 1753) on grounds of infringement of the principle of non-discrimination, and when the subsidies were restored for the future, but not retrospectively, the producers brought proceedings under Article 288 to claim the losses they had suffered during the period when there were no subsidies. In finding for the applicants, the Court pointed out that the producers were a small and ascertainable class, and that the loss they suffered went beyond the risks inherent in the economic activity in question. This was not the beginning of a radical change in approach, however, for shortly thereafter the Court rejected the tortious actions in the *Isoglucose* cases, reinforcing the perception that its judgements in this field are tempered by policy factors which it does not always make very clear.

In the *Isoglucose* cases, the Court ruled that a levy imposed on isoglucose was unlawful in so far as it amounted to discriminatory treatment of isoglucose producers in comparison to the treatment of sugar producers (Cases 103 and 145/77 *Royal Scholten-Honig (Holdings) Ltd* v. *Intervention Board for Agricultural Produce* [1978] ECR 2037). However, in Cases 116, 124/77 *Amylum and Tunnel Refineries* v. *Council and Commission* ([1979] ECR 3479) and Case 143/77 *KSH NV* v. *Council and Commission* ([1979] ECR 3583), it rejected the Article 288 actions. Neither the ruling of invalidity nor the special facts of the case, which showed that the victims were a very small group, that there was some evidence that the measure was aimed at driving isoglucose out of the market by making it uneconomical to produce and that the levy was so severe that it pushed at least one firm into liquidation, were sufficient for the Court to hold that the violation was sufficiently 'grave and manifest'. In that case, the Court appeared to push the definition of 'sufficiently serious' even further by requiring the actions of the institutions to be 'verging on the arbitrary'. It declared that the damage alleged must go beyond the bounds of the normal economic risks inherent in the sector concerned. Unsurprisingly, the *Isoglucose* cases were the subject of extensive criticism, and appear to mark a low point in the Court's unwillingness to interfere in the economic planning of the Council and Commission.

Although, as can be seen, the Court's case law in this area is uneven, it would appear that two factors are central to its evaluation of the nature of the breach: these are the conduct of the defendant and the effect of breach. If, as in Case C-152/88 *Sofrimport* v. *Commission*, the EU 'fails completely' to take into account the interests of a group of applicants which it was specifically mandated to consider 'without invoking any overriding public interest', and the effect of that breach upon a narrowly defined category of economic actors 'goes beyond the limits of the economic risks inherent in the business in issue inasmuch as the purpose of that provision [i.e. the one disregarded by the Commission] is precisely to limit those risks with regard to goods in transit', then the Court will be prepared to make a finding of liability. *Sofrimport* appears to have been the harbinger of a more liberal attitude on the part of the Court to actions for damages.

In Case C-220/91P *Stahlwerke Peine-Salzgitter* v. *Commission*, a case decided under the ECSC Treaty, the Court of First Instance had stated specifically that the harmful conduct did not have to be verging on the arbitrary.

The Court of Justice has also repeated both parts of the formula developed in *Sofrimport* (Case C-152/88) in what is, so far, its most 'generous' finding of tortious liability on the part of the EU (Cases C-104/89 and 37/90 *Mulder and Heinemann* v. *Commission and Council* ([1992] ECR I-3061). In that case, the loss stemmed from a Council Regulation fixing an exemption from levies on the production of dairy products by reference to the quantities which undertakings had marketed in a given earlier year. The applicants in the case had not marketed any dairy products in the reference year, since they had undertaken not to do so as part of the EU's attempts to reduce dairy overproduction. The applicants were not therefore allocated a 'reference quantity' excluded from production levies. The regulation was challenged, by means of actions in the Dutch courts and references on validity to the Court of Justice, which found a violation of the principle of legitimate expectations. Subsequent amendments to the Regulations giving a 60 per cent reference quantity were also successfully challenged. These cases are discussed in 12.13 (Case 120/86 *Mulder* v. *Minister van Landbouw en Visserij* [1988] ECR 2321; C-189/89 *Spagl* [1990] ECR I-4539).

In the action for damages which followed, the Court distinguished between the case where no reference quantity was given, and that where the reference quantity was set at 60 per cent. In the former case, it found the Council liable:

> 'In so far as it failed completely, without invoking any higher public interest, to take account of the specific situation of a clearly defined group of economic agents, that is to say, producers who, pursuant to an undertaking ... delivered no milk during the reference year, the Community legislature manifestly and gravely disregarded the limits of its discretionary power, thereby committing a sufficiently serious breach of a superior rule of law' (at p. 3132).

However, the Court found no liability in respect of the 60 per cent rule, notwithstanding that it had found the same rule to violate the principle of legitimate expectations. It concluded that the breach was not sufficiently serious to merit liability. By adopting the amending regulation: 'the Community legislature made an economic policy choice with regard to the manner in which it was necessary to implement the principles set out in those judgments. That was based, on the one hand, on the 'overriding necessity of not jeopardising the fragile stability that currently obtains in the milk products sector' [a quote from the preamble to the Regulation] and, on the other, on the need to strike a balance between the interests of the producers concerned and the interests of the other producers subject to the scheme ... Accordingly, the Council took account of a higher public interest, without gravely and manifestly disregarding the limits of its discretionary power in this area' (at pp. 3133–3134).

One of the notable aspects of the case is that although the farmers represented a defined group of economic actors, they were none the less a very large group (up to 13,000 strong), and the financial consequences of paying compensation and reorganising the quota structure are considerable.

An attempt failed to use the *Schöppenstedt* formula in order to claim compensation for loss caused by an allegedly unlawful directive harmonising national rules affecting the creation of the internal market. In Case C-63/89 *Les Assurances de Crédit SA* v. *Council and Commission* ([1991] ECR I-1799) the Court held that a Directive harmonising the conditions in which export credit insurance operations could be undertaken, but which did not apply to public sector insurance business, was not unlawful in the sense of giving rise to a claim for compensation. The Court did not accept the argument that the Directive discriminated against the private sector businesses. It held that the Council could validly pass a partial harmonisation measure and possessed complete discretion as to the timetable under which it adopted harmonisation measures.

17.10 Liability in Respect of Other Acts having Legal Effects

The *Schöppenstedt* formula is not used to assess whether individual acts having legal effects can give rise to the liability of the EU. For example, in Cases 5, etc./66 *Kampffmeyer* v. *Commission* ([1967] ECR 245) the Court found that the responsibility of the Commission was engaged by its wrongful and 'improper' application of a safeguard provision allowing protective measures to be taken to prohibit the import of certain agricultural products. The measure in question was a decision addressed to Germany, annulled by the Court in Cases 106, 107/63 *Toepfer* v. *Commission* ([1965] ECR 405).

In Case C-55/90 *Cato* v. *Commission* ([1992] ECR I-2533), the applicant sought to argue that the Commission was liable to compensate for loss caused by the approval, by means of a decision addressed to the UK, of what he considered to be an incorrect implementation of a Council Directive on the awarding of compensation to persons who decommissioned fishing boats. Cato argued that the UK implementing measures placed an excessive burden of proof on the party claiming compensation, and that the Commission should not have approved them. The Court simply referred, without either discussing or disapproving of it, to the applicant's contention that the Commission had committed a sufficiently serious breach of a superior rule of law for the protection of individuals, and was therefore liable to pay compensation, but dismissed the action on the facts for failure on the part of Cato to prove his contentions about the effect of the UK measures. In the event that the Court might hold the Commission liable for its failure adequately to supervise the implementation of EU obligations by Member

States, it is arguable that the test to be used is one which should be different from that governing discretionary legislative activities. If the Commission is subject to a duty, in certain cases, to approve by Decision the correct implementation of particular directives, a failure to fulfil such a duty does not involve a true exercise of discretion. It is in any event unlikely that the Court will encourage the development of a line of cases which seeks to make the Commission responsible for inadequate supervision. It has long been the tendency of the Court to encourage individuals to seek redress in respect of unimplemented or misimplemented Directives from Member States in national courts, and this line of case law was further strengthened by the decision on damages for failure to implement in Cases 6, 9/90 *Francovich* v. *Italian State* ([1991] ECR I-5357).

17.11 **The Requirements of Causation and Damage**

It is for the applicant to prove causation and damage; the Court does not draw an inference from the fact of unlawful conduct that the unlawful conduct caused the damage (Case 253/84 *GAEC* v. *Council and Commission* ([1987] ECR 123). The Court has not applied a 'but for' test in assessing whether there is a factual causal link between the unlawful act on the part of the EU and the alleged damage. Rather it has tended to focus on the fact that it will always be difficult to prove in a market situation that a legislative or other measure is *'the'* cause of any damage due to a reduction of profits, and it has held (e.g. in Cases 64, etc./76 *Dumortier et al.* v. *Council and Commission (Quellmehl and Gritz)* that the damage must be a sufficiently direct consequence of the unlawful conduct of the institution concerned. This in practice has a tendency to restrict the ability of applicants to recover for losses of profit. For example, in Cases 5, etc./66 *Kampffmeyer* v. *Commission* the applicants had applied for permits to import maize from France into Germany at a time when large profits could be made because of a zero rate of levy. The German authorities wrongfully refused to grant the permit and the Commission upheld the refusal. Those applicants who had already concluded contracts and had to cancel them were held entitled to recover their cancellation fees and loss of profits, but with the latter discounted by 90 per cent, because of the speculative nature of the transactions. Those applicants who had not previously concluded contracts recovered nothing.

In a number of cases applicants have failed to recover damages despite establishing liability in principle, because they have been unable to prove damage. In Case 74/74 *CNTA* v. *Commission*, although they were able to establish that the sudden termination of MCAs engaged the tortious responsibility of the Community, the applicants were unable to establish that the currency fluctuations had in fact caused loss. Similarly, in Case 253/84 *GAEC* v. *Council and Commission*, the Court refused to consider the applicant's contention that a Council Decision authorising Germany to grant state subsidies to its farmers was unlawful because it was unable to prove that the effect of the subsidies had been to cause damage to French farmers through a lowering of prices on the French market because of competition from artificially cheaper German products. Statistics were produced by the defendants to demonstrate that prices in France had already begun to fall before the entry into force of the contested Decision.

The Court also applies the defence of contributory negligence (Case 145/83 *Adams* v. *Commission*; Case C-308/87 *Grifoni* v. *Euratom*) and the duty to mitigate losses (Cases C-104/89 and 37/90 *Mulder and Heinemann* v. *Commission and Council*) in order to restrict in practice the level of damages payable by the EU. In the latter case the Court deducted from the damages payable to the aggrieved dairy producers an amount representing what they would have earned if they had reasonably sought to undertake alternative commercial or agricultural activities during the period when they could not produce and sell dairy products. It held that damages had to be calculated on the basis of the:

> 'general principle common to the legal systems of the Member States to the effect that the injured party must show reasonable diligence in limiting the extent of his loss or risk having to bear the damage himself' (at pp. 3136–3137).

Interest can be awarded on damages payable by the EU, since it is in general awarded under the rules common to the Member States (Case C-152/88 *Sofrimport* v. *Commission*).

In each case, the Court states the basis for calculating the damages (e.g. in Case C-152/88 *Sofrimport* v. *Commission* the difference between the price at which the apples were sold after the Court had suspended the protective measures in interim proceedings, and the price the applicants would have got for them had the measures not been imposed), and then sends the parties away to formulate, within a time limit, an agreed amount of damages which they must then communicate to the Court. In the event of a failure to agree, the parties must submit their views to the Court which will itself fix the amount.

17.12 **The Problem of Concurrent Liability: National Court or Court of Justice?**

Not all actions for loss ultimately attributable to unlawful conduct on the part of the EU can be brought in the Court of First Instance. Despite the fact that the EU operates a system of own resources, whereby the levies collected and sums paid by national administrations on behalf of the EU are in truth the EU's own money (see 7.14), the Court none the less refuses to consider certain applications for money damages. A distinction must be drawn to this end between what are essentially restitutionary claims, namely actions for restitution of a sum unlawfully levied and sums withheld in breach of an obligation, and actions for unliquidated damages such as loss of profit.

The case law on these questions was largely developed by the Court of Justice prior to the transfer of jurisdiction over those cases to the Court of First Instance and it is generally consistent with that Court's persistent encouragement to undertakings to begin their actions against unlawful conduct on the part of the EU by challenging the national implementing measures. For example, it requires actions for restitution of a sum unlawfully levied to be brought against the national authority which levied the sums in the national court, even though the sums in question may have been paid into the EU funds (Case 96/71 *Haegemann* v. *Commission* [1972] ECR 1005; Case C-282/90 *Vreugdenhil* v. *Commission*). Consequently, it would be wrong for a national court to deny the liability of the national authority, on account of its role as an 'agent' of the EU. In contrast, it would appear that an action for a sum withheld in breach of a lawful obligation can be brought in either the Court of First Instance or the national court. Since the case law on this point is mixed, however, prudence would seem to suggest that, unless damages at large in addition to the specified sum are claimed, the national court is a better place to start. Exceptionally, of course, there may, for some reason, be no national remedy; an example would be where there is no legal basis in national law for an action for compensation once the unlawful act has been removed from the field.

Similar considerations would appear to apply where the damage is alleged to have occurred as a result of the withholding of some other administrative act on the part of the national authority (e.g. the refusal of a licence as in Case 175/84 *Krohn* v. *Commission*). In its judgment in *Krohn*, the Court of Justice made clear that the Commission was the true author of the unlawful act, and that a national action would not have provided effective protection for the individual concerned against loss, and consequently held the action admissible.

Actions in respect of unliquidated loss, such as the additional loss suffered as a consequence of the unlawful levying of a sum by the national authority, must always be brought in the Court of First Instance in addition to the national action (Case 26/74 *Roquette* v. *Commission* [1976] ECR 677). Since the transfer of jurisdiction this raises difficulties, as any Article 234 reference will be heard by the Court of Justice.

The case law remains unsatisfactory, therefore, since it is wrong to impose an obligation upon an aggrieved undertaking to choose between the national court and the Court of Justice, or to take two actions where one should suffice. In reality, since the implementation of EU measures is frequently a result of a combination of EU and national action, it is difficult for the victim of the loss always to assess to whom in truth the wrongful conduct is attributable. Cases 89, 91/86 *L'Etoile Commerciale* v. *Commission* ([1987] ECR 3005) provide an example of the restrictive application of the rules on the admissibility of Article 288 claims where the alleged wrongful conduct was a decision adopted by the Commission which led a national authority to reclaim certain agricultural subsidies. The Court declared the action under Articles 235 and 288 inadmissible. There is a case for allowing an application of the principles of joint and several liability, widely recognised in the legal systems of the Member States, whereby the victim of a tort may sue one of several or joint tortfeasors in respect of the whole of the obligation, leaving the tortfeasors to recover contributions between themselves (see the analysis of AG van Gerven in Case 201/86 *Spie-Batignolles* v. *Commission* [1990] ECR I-197 where he recognised the wide applicability of the rules on joint and several liability). However, the continuing organic separation of the Community judicature and the national courts, and the failure to recognise either that an EU institution may be a defendant in a national court, or that a Member State may be a defendant in the Court of First Instance in an action brought by an individual, represent conclusive obstacles to this more equitable solution of the problem (Wils, 1992). However, the decision of the Court of Justice to base the liability of Member States for breach of EU law on the same principles as the liability of the EU institutions (12.17, 13.6) might presage a convergence in relation to this question as well.

Summary

1   The non-contractual (i.e. tortious) liability of the EU is governed by Articles 235 and 288(2) EC.

2   The basic prerequisites of a successful action are:
– a wrongful act (i.e. one involving some 'fault' or breach of EU law on the part of the EU institutions); exceptionally a wrongful omission;
– damage to the plaintiff;
– a causal link between the two.

3   The EU can be liable in respect of *fautes de service* (i.e. failures which are imputable to an institution) and *fautes personnelles* (i.e. unlawful acts of officials for which an institution is vicariously liable).

4   Much of the case law of the Court has been concentrated on attempted claims for damages for discretionary legislative acts. The Court applies the rules restrictively in such cases so as to limit access to compensation, although it does not require the applicant to have first successfully challenged the validity of the offending EU act either via an action under Article 230 or an action in the national court and a ruling on validity.

5   To be successful an applicant seeking damages for an allegedly wrongful legislative act involving choices of economic policy must prove a sufficiently serious breach of a superior rule of law intended for the protection of individuals (the *Schöppenstedt* formula).

6　The Court's interpretation of 'sufficiently serious breach' has been particularly restrictive, although there are some signs that the Court may be taking a more liberal view in recent cases.

7　Where the applicant's action consists of a restitutionary claim for money wrongfully paid to or withheld by a national authority acting on the basis of an unlawful EU act, the Court will normally require the applicant to begin the action in the national court. Only actions for unliquidated damages against the EU institutions may be brought in the Court of Justice.

Questions

1　What are the basic elements of a successful damages claim against the EU?

2　What is the difference between a *faute de service* and a *faute personnelle*?

3　Should the Court require an applicant for compensation under Article 288 to challenge first the validity of the act in question?

4　What is the *Schöppenstedt* formula, and how and why has it been restrictively applied by the EU Courts?

5　Are there any policy factors which link together the successful actions for damages against the EU?

6　In what ways would the application of a doctrine of joint and several liability assist applicants who bring the claims in tort against the EU and the national authorities?

Workshop (for Chapters 15–17)

The State of Rubric is the sole source of imports of a rare desert orchid into the EU. The orchid is much in demand for its medicinal properties. Five firms in the EU, including a UK firm Orchids Alive plc, import the orchids from Rubric. The Commission adopts (fictitious) Regulation 6000 of 2000 imposing an additional import levy of 10 per cent *ad valorem* on imports of the orchids, following representations from the World Save the Orchid Campaign. The Campaign produced evidence of the activities of Orchids Alive plc, including allegations about the environmental damage caused to the eco-system in Rubric as a result of the harvesting of the orchids, and of bribery of public officials in Rubric to ensure that other firms based in the EU do not get access to the supplies there. The firm did not know of the Commission's intention to adopt the Regulation until it was published in the *Official Journal*. It is also known that a consortium of EU-based firms is planning to launch the farming under glass of the orchids within the EU, and that a group of officials within the Directorate-General of the Commission which was responsible for the Regulation has a financial interest in the venture.

Advise Orchids Alive plc as to which court or courts it should bring an action in, and assess its chances of obtaining the following forms of redress:

1   annulment of the Regulation, or a declaration of invalidity;
2   recovery of the additional import levy paid to the UK customs authorities;
3   compensation for the loss of profits on long-term supply contracts which it holds within the UK.

Further Reading

A. Arnull (1997), 'Liability for Legislative Acts under Article 215(2) EC', in Heukels and McDonnell (1997).

F. Fines (1997), 'A General Analytical Perspective on Community Liability', in Heukels and McDonnell (1997).

W. van Gerven (1994b), 'Non-contractual Liability of Member States, Community Institutions and Individuals for Breaches of Community Law with a View to a Common Law for Europe', 1 *Maastricht Journal of European and Comparative Law* 6.

W. van Gerven (1998), 'Taking Article 215(2) Seriously', in Beatson and Tridimas (1998).

W. Wils (1992), 'Concurrent Liability of the Community and a Member State', 17 *European Law Review* 191.

M. van der Woude (1997), 'Liability for Administrative Acts under Article 215(2) EC', in Heukels and McDonnell (1997).

Bibliography

Academy of European Law (ed.) (1998), *Collected Courses of the Academy of European Law. 1995, European Community Law, Vol. VI, Book 1*, The Hague: Martinus Nijhoff.

Albors-Llorens, A. (1996), *Private Parties in European Community Law*, Oxford: Oxford University Press.

Alston, P. (ed.) (1999), *The EU and Human Rights*, Oxford: Oxford University Press.

Alston, P. and Weiler, J.H.H. (1999), 'An 'Ever Closer Union' in Need of a Human Rights Policy: The European Union and Human Rights', in Alston (1999).

Alter, K. (1996), 'The European Court's Political Power', 19 *West European Politics* 458.

Alter, K. (1998a), 'Explaining National Court Acceptance of European Court Jurisprudence: A Critical Evaluation of Theories of Legal Integration', in Slaughter, Stone Sweet and Weiler (1998).

Alter, K. (1998b), 'Who are the "Masters of the Treaty"?: European Governments and the European Court of Justice', 52 *International Organization* 121.

Andersen, S. and Eliassen, S. (eds) (1996), *The European Union: How Democratic Is It?*, London: Sage.

Anderson, D. (1994), 'The Admissibility of Preliminary References' 14 *Yearbook of European Law* 179.

Armstrong, K. (1996), 'Citizenship of the Union? Lessons from *Carvel and The Guardian*', 59 *Modern Law Review* 582.

Armstrong, K. (1998), 'Theorizing the Legal Dimension of European Integration', 36 *Journal of Common Market Studies* 155.

Armstrong, K. and Bulmer, S. (1998), *The Governance of the Single European Market*, Manchester: Manchester University Press.

Armstrong, K. and Shaw, J. (eds) (1998), *Integrating Law*, Special Issue of the *Journal of Common Market Studies*, Vol. 36, No. 2.

Arnull, A. (1990a), 'Does the Court of Justice have Inherent Jurisdiction?', 27 *Common Market Law Review* 683.

Arnull, A. (1990b), 'References to the European Court', 15 *European Law Review* 375.

Arnull, A. (1993), 'Owning up to Fallibility: Precedent and the Court of Justice', 30 *Common Market Law Review* 47.

Arnull, A. (1995a), 'Private Applicants and the Action for Annulment under Article 173 of the EC Treaty', 32 *Common Market Law Review* 7.

Arnull, A. (1999a), *The European Union and its Court of Justice*, Oxford: Oxford University Press.

Arnull, A. (1997), 'Liability for Legislative Acts under Article 215(2) EC', in Heukels and McDonnell (1997).

Arnull, A. (1999b), 'Taming the Beast? The Treaty of Amsterdam and the Court of Justice', in O'Keeffe and Twomey (1999).

Arnull, A. (1999c), 'Judicial Architecture or Judicial Folly? The Challenge Facing the European Union', 24 *European Law Review* 516.

Axtmann, R. (1999), 'Globalization, Europe and the State: Introductory Reflections', in Axtmann, R. (ed.), *Globalization and Europe*, London: Pinter.

Azzi, G.C. (2000), 'The Slow March of European Legislation: The Implementation of Directives', in Neunreither and Wiener (2000).

Bańkowski, Z. and Christodoulidis, E. (1998), 'The European Union as an Essentially Contested Project', 4 *European Law Journal* 341.

Barav, A. (1980), 'Preliminary Censorship? The Judgment of the European Court in Foglia v. Novello', 5 *European Law Review* 443.

Barents, R. (1994), 'The Quality of Community Legislation', 1 *Maastricht Journal of European and Comparative Law* 101.

Barnard, C. (1995), 'A European Litigation Strategy: The Case of the Equal Opportunities Commission', in Shaw and More (1995).

Barnard, C. (1997), '*P* v. *S*: Kite Flying or a New Constitutional Approach?', in Dashwood and O'Leary (1997).

Barnard, C. (1999), 'Article 13: Through the Looking Glass of Union Citizenship', in O'Keeffe and Twomey (1999).

Beatson, J. and Tridimas, T. (eds) (1998), *New Directions in European Public Law*, Oxford: Hart Publishing.

Beaumont, P. and Walker, N. (eds) (1999), *Legal Framework of the Single European Currency*, Oxford: Hart Publishing.

Bebr, G. (1982), 'The Possible Implications of Foglia v. Novello II', 9 *Common Market Law Review* 421.

Bebr, G. (1988), 'The Reinforcement of the Constitutional Review of Community Acts under Article 177 EEC', 25 *Common Market Law Review* 684.

Bebr, G. (1992), 'Case Note on Francovich v. Italy', 19 *Common Market Law Review* 559.

Beetham, D. and Lord, C. (1998), *Legitimacy and the European Union*, Harlow: Longman.

Begg, I. (1999), 'Reshaping the EU Budget: Yet another Missed Opportunity', ESRC One Europe or Several Programme Policy Paper 1/99.

Bellamy, R. and Castiglione, D. (eds) (1996), *Constitutionalism in Transformation*, Oxford: Blackwell.

Bermann, G. (1989), 'The Single European Act: A New Constitution for the Community?' 27 *Columbia Journal Transnational and International Law* 529.

Berrod, G. (1999), 'Case Note on *Stichting Greenpeace*', 36 *Common Market Law Review* 635.

Bettlem, G. (1995), 'The Principle of Indirect Effect of Community Law', 3 *European Review of Private Law* 1.

Beveridge, F. and Nott, S. (1998), 'A Hard Look at Soft Law', in Craig and Harlow (1998).

Bieber, R. (1984), 'The Settlement of Institutional Conflicts on the Basis of Article 4 of the EEC Treaty', 21 *Common Market Law Review* 505.

Bieber, R. et al. (eds) (1988), *1992: One European Market? A Critical Analysis of the Commission's Single Market Policy*, Baden-Baden: Nomos.

Biermann, R. (1999), *The Stability Pact for South Eastern Europe – Potential, Problems and Perspectives*, ZEI Discussion Paper, C 56, 1999 (www.zei.de).

Biondi, A. (1999), 'European Court of Justice and Certain National Procedural Limitations: Not such a Tough Relationship', 36 *Common Market Law Review* 1271.

Boch, C. (2000), *EC Law in the UK*, Harlow: Longman.

den Boer, M. (1999), 'An Area of Freedom, Security and Justice: Bogged Down by Compromise', in O'Keeffe and Twomey (1999).

von Bogdandy, A. (1999), 'The Legal Case for Unity: The European Union as a Single Organisation with a Single Legal System', 36 *Common Market Law Review* 887.

von Bogdandy, A. (2000), 'The European Union as a Supranational Federation: A Conceptual Attempt in the Light of the Amsterdam Treaty', 6 *Columbia Journal of European Law* forthcoming.

von Bogdandy, A. and Nettesheim, M. (1996), 'Ex Pluribus Unum: Fusion of the European Communities into the European Union', 2 *European Law Journal* 267.

Bonnie, A. (1998), 'Commission Discretion under Article 171(2) EC', 23 *European Law Review* 537.

Bonnor, P.G. (2000), 'The European Ombudsman: a Novel Source of Soft Law in the European Union', 25 *European Law Review* 39.

van den Bossche, P. (1996), 'In Search of Remedies for Non-compliance: The Experience of the European Community', 3 *Maastricht Journal of European and Comparative Law* 371.

Boyron, S. (1998), 'The Co-decision Procedure: Rethinking the Constitutional Fundamentals', in Craig and Harlow (1998).

Bradley, K. (1988), 'The Variable Evolution of the Standing of the European Parliament in Proceedings before the Court of Justice', 8 *Yearbook of European Law* 27.

Bradley, K. (1991), 'Sense and Sensibility: Parliament v. Council Continued', 16 *European Law Review* 245.

Bradley, K. (1992), 'Comitology and the Law: Through a Glass, Darkly', 29 *Common Market Law Review* 693.

Bradley, K. (1995), 'Administrative Justice: A Developing Human Right?', 1 *European Public Law* 347.

Bradley, K. (1999), 'Reflections on the Human Rights Role of the European Parliament', in Alston (1999).

Buitendijk, G. and van Schendelen, M. (1995), 'Brussels Advisory Committees: A Channel for Influence', 20 *European Law Review* 37.

Bulmer, S. and Scott, A. (eds) (1994), *Economic and Political Integration in Europe. Internal Dynamics and Global Context*, Oxford: Blackwell.

Bunyan, T. (1999), *Secrecy, Democracy and the Third Pillar of the European Union*, London: Kogan Page.

de Búrca, G. (1993a), 'The Principle of Proportionality and its Application in EC Law', 13 *Yearbook of European Law* 105.

de Búrca, G. (1993b), 'Fundamental Human Rights and the Reach of EC Law', 13 *Oxford Journal of Legal Studies* 283.

de Búrca, G. (1995), 'The Language of Rights and European Integration', in Shaw and More (1995).

de Búrca, G. (1997), 'The Role of Equality in European Community Law', in Dashwood and O'Leary (1997).

de Búrca, G. (1998), 'The Principle of Subsidiarity and the Court of Justice as an Institutional Actor', 36 *Journal of Common Market Studies* 155.

de Búrca, G. (1999a), 'The Institutional Development of the EU: A Constitutional Analysis', in Craig and de Búrca (1999).

de Búrca, G. (1999b), 'Reappraising Subsidiarity's Significance after Amsterdam', Harvard Jean Monnet Working Paper no. 8/99.

de Búrca, G. and Scott, J. (eds) (2000), *Constitutional Change in the European Union: From Uniformity to Flexibility*, Oxford: Hart Publishing.

Burley, A.-M. and Mattli, W. (1993), 'Europe Before the Court: A Political Theory of Legal Integration', 47 *International Organization* 41.

Burns, T. (1996), 'Law Reform in the European Community and its Limits', 16 *Yearbook of European Law* 243.

Cafruny, A. and Rosenthal, G. (eds) (1993), *The State of the European Community. Vol. 2. The Maastricht Debates and Beyond*, Boulder, CO: Lynne Rienner.

Canor, I. (2000), '*Primus inter pares*. Who is the Ultimate Guardian of Fundamental Rights in Europe?', 25 *European Law Review* 3.

Cappelletti, M. (1987), 'Is the European Court of Justice "Running Wild"?', 12 *European Law Review* 3.

Caranta, R. (1995), 'Judicial Protection Against Member States: A New Jus Commune Takes Shape', 32 *Common Market Law Review* 703.

Cecchini, P. (1988), *The European Challenge: 1992, the Benefits of a Single Market*, Aldershot: Wildwood House/Gower.

Chalmers, D. (1998), *European Union Law: Volume One: Law and EU Government*, Aldershot: Dartmouth.

Chalmers, D. (2000a), 'The Application of Community Law in the United Kingdom, 1994–1998', 37 *Common Market Law Review* 83.

Chalmers, D. (2000b), 'The Much Ado about Judicial Politics in the United Kingdom: A Statistical Analysis of Reported Decisions of the United Kingdom Courts invoking EU Law 1973-1998', 23 *Western European Politics* no.2, forthcoming.

Chalmers, D. and Szyszczak, E. (1998), *European Union Law: Volume Two: Towards a European Polity?* Aldershot: Dartmouth.

Cheyne, I. (1994), 'International Agreements and the European Community Legal System', 19 *European Law Review* 581.

Chiti, E. (2000), 'The Emergence of a Community Administration: the Case of European Agencies' 37 *Common Market Law Review* 309

Cockfield, Lord (1994), *The European Union: Creating the Single Market*, Chichester; Wiley/Chancery Law.

Commission (1985), *Completing the Internal Market, White Paper from the Commission to the European Council*, COM(85) 310.

Commission (1993a), *White Paper on Growth, Competitiveness and Employment*, Bull. EC, Supp. 6/93.

Commission (1993b), *Green Paper on European Social Policy*, COM(93) 551.

Commission (1994), *White Paper on European Social Policy*, COM(94) 333.

Commission (1995a), *White Paper on the Preparations of the Associated Countries of Central and Eastern Europe for Integration into the Internal Market of the Union*, COM(95) 163.

Commission (1995a), *European Union Public Finance. The Characteristics, Rules and Operation of the European Financial System*, OOPEC, Luxembourg.

Commission (1997), Action Plan for the Single Market – need better reference.

Commission (1999a), Communication on *The Stabilisation and Association Process*, COM(99) 235 (Chapter 1).

Commission (1999b), Communication on a Strategy for the Internal Market, 24 November 1999.

Commission (1999c), *Action Plan of the Council and the Commission on how best to implement the provisions of the Treaty of Amsterdam on an area of freedom, security and justice*, OJ 1999 C19/1.

Commission (2000a), Communication on *Strategic Objectives 2000–2005: 'Shaping the New Europe'*, COM(2000) 154, 9 February 2000.

Commission (2000b), *Reforming the Commission: A White Paper*, COM(2000) 200.

Commission (2000c), Commission Report to the European Council: *Better Law Making 1999*, COM(99) 562.

Commission (2000d), *Adapting the Institutions to Make a Success of Enlargement: Commission Opinion to the IGC*, COM(2000) 34.

Coppel, J. and O'Neill, A. (1992), 'The European Court of Justice: Taking Rights Seriously?', 12 *Legal Studies* 227.

Court of Justice (1999), *The Future of the Judicial System of the European Union (Proposals and Reflections)*, Luxembourg.

Craig, P. (1993), 'Francovich, Remedies and the Scope of Damages Liability', 109 *Law Quarterly Review* 595.

Craig, P. (1994), 'Legality, Standing and Substantial Review in Community Law', 14 *Oxford Journal of Legal Studies* 507.

Craig, P. (1998), 'Report on the United Kingdom', in Slaughter, Stone Sweet and Weiler (1998).

Craig, P. (1999a), 'The Nature of the Community: Integration, Democracy and Legitimacy', in Craig and de Búrca (1999).

Craig, P. (1999b), 'EMU, the European Central Bank, and Judicial Review', in Beaumont and Walker (1999).

Craig, P. (2000), 'The Fall and Renewal of the Commission: Accountability, Contract and Administrative Organisation', 6 *European Law Journal* 98.

Craig, P. and de Búrca, G. (1998), *EU Law. Text, Cases and Materials* (2nd edn), Oxford: Oxford University Press.

Craig, P. and de Búrca, G. (eds) (1999), *The Evolution of EU Law*, Oxford: Oxford University Press.

Craig, P. and Harlow, C. (1998), *Lawmaking in the European Union*, London/The Hague: Kluwer Law International.

Cram. L. (1999), 'The Commission', in Cram, Dinan and Nugent (1999).

Cram. L., Dinan, D. and Nugent, N. (eds) (1999), *Developments in the European Union*, London: Macmillan.

Craufurd Smith, R. (1999), 'Remedies for Breaches of EU Law in National Courts: Legal Variation and Selection', in Craig and de Búrca (1999).

Cremona, M. (1994), 'The "Dynamic and Homogeneous" EEA: Byzantine Structures and Variable Geometry', 19 *European Law Review* 508.

Cremona, M. (1999), 'External Relations and External Competence: The Emergence of an Integrated Policy', in Craig and de Búrca (1999).

Cullen, H. and Charlesworth, A. (1999), 'Diplomacy by Other Means: The Use of Legal Basis Litigation as a Political Strategy by the European Parliament and Member States', 36 *Common Market Law Review* 1243.

Curtin, D. (1990), 'Directives: The Effectiveness of Judicial Protection of Individual Rights', 27 *Common Market Law Review* 709.

Curtin, D. (1992), 'State Liability under Private Law: A New Remedy for Private Parties', 21 *Industrial Law Journal* 74.

Curtin, D. (1993), 'The Constitutional Structure of the Union: A Europe of Bits and Pieces', 30 *Common Market Law Review* 17.

Curtin, D. (1996), 'Betwixt and Between: Democracy and Transparency in the Governance of the European Union', in Winter *et al.* (1996).

Curtin, D. (1999), 'The Fundamental Principle of Open Decision-Making and EU (Political) Citizenship', in O'Keeffe and Twomey (1999).

Curtin, D. (2000), 'Citizens' Fundamental Rights of Access to EU Information: An Evolving Digital *Passepartout*?', 37 *Common Market Law Review* 7.

Curtin, D. and Dekker, I. (1999), 'The EU as a "Layered" International Organisation: Institutional Unity in Disguise', in Craig and de Búrca (1999).

Curtin, D. and Heukels, T. (eds) (1994), *Institutional Dynamics of European Integration: Liber Amicorum Henry G. Schermers*, Dordrecht: Martinus Nijhoff.

Curtin, D. and Mortelmans, K. (1994), 'Application and Enforcement of Community Law by the Member States: Actors in Search of a Third Generation Script', in Curtin and Heukels (1994).

Cutler, T. *et al.* (1989), *1992 – The Struggle for Europe*, London: Berg.

Dagtoglou, D. (1981), 'The Legal Nature of the European Community' in Commission of the European Communities (ed.), *Thirty Years of Community Law*, Luxembourg: OOPEC.

Daintith, T. (1995a), 'European Community Law and the Redistribution of Regulatory Power in the United Kingdom', 1 *European Law Journal* 134.

Daintith, T. (ed.) (1995b), *Implementing EC Law in the United Kingdom: Structures for Indirect Rule*, Chichester: Wiley/Chancery Law.

Dashwood, A. (1994), 'The Role of the Council of the European Union', in Curtin and Heukels (1994).

Dashwood, A. (1998), 'States in the European Union', 23 *European Law Review* 201.

Dashwood, A. (1999), 'External Relations Provisions of the Amsterdam Treaty', in O'Keeffe and Twomey (1999).

Dashwood, A. and O'Leary, S. (eds) (1997), *The Principle of Equal Treatment in EC Law*, London: Sweet and Maxwell.

Dashwood, A. and White, R. (1989), 'Enforcement Actions and Article 169 and 170', 14 *European Law Review* 388.

Dehaene, J.-L., von Weizsäcker, R. and Simon, D. (1999), *The Institutional Implications of Enlargement*, Report to the European Commission.

Dehousse, F. (1999), 'The IGC Process and Results', in O'Keeffe and Twomey (1999).

Dehousse, R. (ed.) (1994a), *Europe after Maastricht. An Ever Closer Union?*, Munich: Law Books in Europe.

Dehousse, R. (1994b), 'Community Competences: Are there Limits to Growth?', in Dehousse (1994a).

Dehousse, R. (1997), 'Regulation by Networks in the European Community: The Role of European Agencies', 4 *Journal of European Public Policy* 246.

Dehousse, R. (1998a), *The European Court of Justice*, London: Macmillan.

Dehousse, R. (1998b), 'European Institutional Architecture after Amsterdam: Parliamentary System or Regulatory Structure?', 35 *Common Market Law Review* 595.

Demetriou, M. (1995), 'When is the House of Lords not a Judicial Remedy?', 20 *European Law Review* 628.

Denza, E. (1999), 'Two Legal Orders: Divergent or Convergent?' 48 *International and Comparative Law Quarterly* 257.

Dinan, D. (1999), *Ever Closer Union: An Introduction to European Integration* (2nd edn), London: Macmillan.

Docksey, C. (1995), 'Case Note on Johnson v. Chief Adjudication Officer', 32 *Common Market Law Review* 1447.

Docksey, C. and Fitzpatrick, B. (1991), 'The Duty of National Courts to Interpret Provisions of National Law in Accordance with Community Law', 20 *Industrial Law Journal* 113.

Douglas-Scott, S. (1998), 'In Search of Union Citizenship', 18 *Yearbook of European Law* 29.

Duff, A. (ed.) (1997), *The Treaty of Amsterdam: Text and Commentary*, London: Federal Trust/Sweet and Maxwell.

Dwyer, C. (1994), 'When should a United Kingdom Court Refer Questions to Luxembourg?', *Journal of Business Law* 528.

- Dyrberg, P. (1999), 'Current Issues in the Debate on Public Access to Documents', 24 *European Law Review* 157.

Dyson, K. and Featherstone, K. (1999), *The Road to Maastricht*, Oxford: Oxford University Press.

Earnshaw, D. and Judge, D. (1993), 'The European Parliament and the Sweeteners Directive: From Footnote to Inter-Institutional Conflict', 31 *Journal of Common Market Studies* 103.

Earnshaw, D. and Judge, D. (1997), 'The Life and Times of the European Union's Co-operation Procedure', 35 *Journal of Common Market Studies* 35.

Editorial (1997), 'The Treaty of Amsterdam: Neither a Bang nor a Whimper', 34 *Common Market Law Review* 767.

Edward, D. (1995), 'How the Court of Justice Works', 20 *European Law Review* 539.

Edwards, G. and Pijpers, A. (eds) (1997), *The Politics of European Treaty Reform*, London: Pinter.

Edwards, G. and Spence, D. (eds) (1994), *The European Commission*, Harlow: Longman.

Ehlermann, C.-D. (1984), 'How Flexible is Community Law? An Unusual Approach to the Concept of Two Speeds', 82 *Michigan Law Review* 1274.

Ehlermann, C.-D. (1996), 'Increased Differentiation or Stronger Uniformity', in Winter *et al.* (1996).

Ehlermann, C.-D. (1998), 'Differentiation, Flexibility, Closer Co-operation: the New Provisions of the Amsterdam Treaty', 4 *European Law Journal* 246.

El-Agraa, A. (ed.) (1998), *The European Union*, London: Prentice-Hall.

Eleftheriadis, P. (1996), 'Aspects of European Constitutionalism', 21 *European Law Review* 32.

Eleftheriadis, P. (1998), 'Begging the Constitutional Question', 36 *Journal of Common Market Studies* 255.

Ellis, E. and Tridimas, T. (1995), *Public Law of the European Community: Text, Materials and Commentary*, London: Sweet & Maxwell.

Emiliou, N. (1993), 'Treading a Slippery Slope: The Commission's Original Legislative Powers', 18 *European Law Review* 305.

Emiliou, N. (1996), *The Principle of Proportionality in European Law*, The Hague: Kluwer.

Eriksen, E.O. and Fossum, J.E. (eds) (2000), *Democracy in the European Union: Integration through Deliberation?* London: Routledge.

Eurostat (1999), *Millennium Round: The European Union Figures for the Seattle Conference*, Memo 9/99, 18 November 1999 (available from Eurostat website).

Everling, U. (1984), 'The Member States of the European Community before their Court of Justice', 9 *European Law Review* 315.

Everling, U. (1992), 'Reflections on the Structure of the European Union', 29 *Common Market Law Review* 1053.

Everling, U. (1994), 'The Maastricht Judgment of the German Federal Constitutional Court and its significance for Development of European Union', 14 *Yearbook of European Law* 1.

Everling, U. (1996), 'Will Europe Slip on Bananas? The Bananas Judgement of the Court of Justice and National Courts', 33 *Common Market Law Review* 401.

Everson, M. (1995), 'Independent Agencies: Hierarchy Beaters?', 1 *European Law Journal* 180.

Farrell, M. (1999), *WTO and EU Regulatory Frameworks*, London: Kogan Page.

Fines, F. (1997), 'A General Analytical Perspective on Community Liability', in Heukels and McDonnell (1997).

Fitzpatrick, B. (1989), 'The Significance of EEC Directives in UK Sex Discrimination law', 9 *Oxford Journal of Legal Studies* 336.

Flynn, L. (1995), 'Telecommunications and EU Integration', in Shaw and More (1995).

Flynn, L. (1999), 'The Implications of Article 13 EC – After Amsterdam, Will Some Forms of Discrimination be More Equal than Others?', 36 *Common Market Law Review* 1127.

Føllesdal, A. and Koslowski, P. (eds) (1998), *Democracy and the European Union*, Berlin: Springer Verlag.

Foster, N. (ed.) (1999), *Blackstone's EC legislation 1999/2000*, London: Blackstones.

Fries, S. and Shaw, J. (1998), 'Citizenship of the Union: First Steps in the Court of Justice', 4 *European Public Law* 533.

Gaja, G. (1990), 'New Developments in a Continuing Story: The Relationship between EEC Law and Italian Law', 27 *Common Market Law Review* 83.

Garman, G. and Hilditch, L. (1998), 'Behind the Scenes: An Examination of the Importance of the Informal Processes at Work in Conciliation', 2 *Journal of European Public Policy* 271.

Garton Ash, T. (1999), *History of the Present*, London: Penguin Press.

Geddes, A. (2000), *Immigration and European Integration*, Manchester: Manchester University Press.

George, S. (1996), *Politics and Policy in the European Union* (3rd edn), Oxford: Oxford University Press.

van Gerven, W. (1994a), 'The Horizontal Effect of Directive Provisions Revisited: The Reality of Catchwords', in Curtin and Heukels (1994).

van Gerven, W. (1994b), 'Non-contractual Liability of Member States, Community Institutions and Individuals for Breaches of Community Law with a View to a Common Law for Europe', 1 *Maastricht Journal of European and Comparative Law* 6.

van Gerven, W. (1995), 'Bridging the Gap Between Community and National Laws: Towards a Principle of Homogeneity in the Field of Legal Remedies?', 32 *Common Market Law Review* 579.

van Gerven, W. (1996), 'The Role and Structure of the European Judiciary Now and in the Future', 21 *European Law Review* 211.

van Gerven, W. (1998), 'Taking Article 215(2) Seriously', in Beatson and Tridimas (1998). Van Gerven, W. (2000), 'Managing the European Union: For Better or for Worse?', in Markesinis, (2000).

van Gerven, W. (2000), 'Of Rights, Remedies and Procedures', 37 *Common Market Law Review* 501.

Gil Ibáñez, A.J. (1998a), 'A Deeper Insight into Article 169', Harvard Jean Monnet Working Paper 11/98.

Gil Ibáñez, A.J. (1998b), 'Commission Tools for the Supervision and Enforcement of EC Law other than Article 169 EC Treaty: An Attempt at Systematisation', Harvard Jean Monnet Working Paper 12/98.

Gil Ibáñez, A.J. (1999), *The Administrative Supervision and Enforcement of EC Law*, Oxford: Hart Publishing.

Gil Ibáñez, A.J. (2000), 'Exceptions to Article 226: Alternative Administrative Procedures and the Pursuit of Member States', 6 *European Law Journal* 148.

Gormley, L. (1999), 'Reflections on the Architecture of the European Union after the Treaty of Amsterdam', in O'Keeffe and Twomey (1999).

Gormley, L. and de Haan, P. (1996), 'The Democratic Deficit of the European Central Bank', 21 *European Law Review* 95.

Greaves, R. (1986), 'Locus Standi under Article 173 EEC when Seeking Annulment of a Regulation', 11 *European Law Review* 119.

Greaves, R. (1996), 'The Nature and Binding Effect of Decisions under Article 189 EC', 21 *European Law Review* 3.

Green Cowles, M. and Smith, M. (eds) (2000), *State of the Union, Volume 5, Risks, Reforms, Resistance of Revival*, Oxford: Oxford University Press.

Greenwood, J. (1997), *Representing Interests in the European Union*, London: Macmillan.

Grief, N. (1991), 'The Domestic Impact of the ECHR as Mediated through Community Law', *Public Law* 555.

Grimm, D. (1995), 'Does Europe Need a Constitution?' 1 *European Law Journal* 282.

Gustavsson, S. (1996), 'The European Union: 1996 and Beyond – A Personal View from the Side-line', in Andersen and Eliassen (1996).

Habermas, J. (1995), 'Comment on the Paper by Dieter Grimm: 'Does Europe Need a Constitution?' 1 *European Law Journal* 303.

Hall, S. (2000), 'Tales from the Vienna Woods: EU Constitutional Law and Democracy in the Member States', *Challenge Europe*, Issue no. 1: url: http://www.theEPC.be/ChallengeEurope/Journal/hall.htm

Hamson, J. (1976), 'Methods of Judicial Interpretation', in Proceedings of a Judicial and Academic Conference, Luxembourg: OOPEC.

Harden, I., White, S. and Donnelly, K. (1995), 'The Court of Auditors and Financial Control and Accountability in the European Community', 1 *European Public Law* 599.

Harding, C. (1980), 'The Private Interest in Challenging Community Action', 5 *European Law Review* 354.

Harlow, C. (1992a), 'Towards a Theory of Access for the European Court of Justice', 12 *Yearbook of European Law* 213.

Harlow, C. (1992b), 'A Community of Interests? Making the Most of European Law', 55 *Modern Law Review* 331.

Harlow, C. (1996), 'Francovich and the Problem of the Disobedient State', 2 *European Law Journal* 199.

Harlow, C. (1999a), 'European Administrative Law and the Global Challenge', in Craig and de Búrca (1999).

Harlow, C. (1999b), 'Citizen Access to Political Power in the European Union', EUI RSC Working Paper 99/2.

Harlow, C. and Rawlings, R. (1992), *Pressure Through Law*, London: Routledge.

Harmsen, R. (1994), 'A European Union of Variable Geometry: Problems and Perspectives', 45 *Northern Ireland Legal Quarterly* 109.

Hartley, T. (1996), 'The European Court, Judicial Objectivity and the Constitution of the European Union', 112 *Law Quarterly Review* 95.

Hartley, T. (1998), *Foundations of European Community Law* (4th edn), Oxford: Oxford University Press.

Hartley, T. (1999), *Constitutional Problems of the European Union*, Oxford: Hart Publishing.

Hayes-Renshaw, F. (1999), 'The European Council and the Council of Ministers', in Cram, Dinan and Nugent (1999).

Hayes-Renshaw, F. and Wallace, H. (1997), *The Council of Ministers*, London: Macmillan.

Hayton, D. (ed.), *Law(s) Futures*, Oxford: Hart Publishing.

Hayward, J. (1995), 'Governing the New Europe', in Hayward and Page (1995).

Hayward, J. and Page, E. (eds) (1995), *Governing the New Europe*, Cambridge: Polity.

Hedemann-Robinson, M. (1996), 'Article 173 EC, General Community Measures and *Locus Standi* for Private Persons: Still a Cause for Individual Concern?', 2 *European Public Law* 127.

Hedemann-Robinson, M. (1999), 'The Area of Freedom, Security and Justice with Regard to the UK, Ireland and Denmark: The 'Opt-in Opt-outs' under the Treaty of Amsterdam', in O'Keeffe and Twomey (1999).

Herdegen, M. (1994), 'Maastricht and the German Constitutional Court: Constitutional Restraints for an "Ever Closer Union"', 31 *Common Market Law Review* 235.

Hervey, T. (1999), 'Putting Europe's House in Order: Racism, Race Discrimination and Xenophobia after the Treaty of Amsterdam', in O'Keeffe and Twomey (1999).

Hesse, J.J. and Johnson, N. (eds) (1995), *Constitutional Policy and Change in Europe*, Oxford: Oxford University Press.

Heukels, T., Blokker, N. and Brus, M. (eds) (1998), *The European Union after Amsterdam : a legal analysis*, The Hague/Boston : Kluwer Law International.

Heukels, T. and McDonnell, A. (eds) (1997), *The Action for Damages in Community Law*, The Hague: Kluwer Law International.

Hilson, C. and Downes, T. (1999), 'Making Sense of Rights: Community Rights in EC Law', 24 *European Law Review* 121.

Himsworth, C. (1997), 'Things Fall Apart: The Harmonisation of Community Judicial Procedural Protection Revisited' 22 *European Law Review* 291.

Hix, S. (1999), *The Political System of the European Union*, London: Macmillan.

Høegh, K. (1999), 'The Danish Maastricht Judgment', 24 *European Law Review* 80.

Holland, S. (1993), Ch. 1, 'Integration and the Ideas of Jean Monnet: Federalism versus Intergovernmentalism'.

Hoskins, M. (1998), 'Rebirth of the Innominate Tort?', in Beatson and Tridimas (1998).

Hunt. J. and Shaw, J. (2000), 'European Union Legal Studies: Then and Now', in D. Hayton (ed.), *Law(s) Futures*, Oxford: Hart Publishing.

Hurwitz, C. and Lesquesne, C. (eds) (1991), *The State of the European Community. Vol. 1. Policies, Institutions and Debate in the Transition Years*, Boulder, CO: Lynne Rienner.

Inghelram, J. (2000), 'The European Court of Auditors; Current Legal Issues', 37 *Common Market Law Review* 129.

Jacobs, F. (1997), 'Enforcing Community Rights and Obligations: Striking the Balance', in Lonbay and Biondi (1997).

Jackson, J. (1992), 'Status of Treaties in Domestic Legal Systems: A Policy Analysis', 86 *American Journal of International Law* 311.

Jacqué, J.-P. and Weiler, J.H.H. (1990), 'On the Road to European Union – A New Judicial Architecture: An Agenda for the Intergovernmental Conference', 27 *Common Market Law Review* 493.

Joerges. C. and Vos, E. (eds) (1999), *EU Committees: Social Regulation, Law and Politics*, Oxford: Hart Publishing.

Kennedy, S. (1998), *Learning European Law*, London: Sweet & Maxwell.

Keohane, R. and Hoffmann. S. (eds) (1991), *The New European Community: Decision making and Institutional Change*, Boulder, CO: Westview.

van Kersbergen, K. and Verbeek, B. (1994), 'The Politics of Subsidiarity in the European Union', 32 *Journal of Common Market Studies* 215.

Kilpatrick, C., Novitz, T. and Skidmore, P. (eds) (2000), *The Future of Remedies in Europe*, Oxford: Hart Publishing, forthcoming.

King, T. (2000), 'Ensuring Human Rights Review of Intergovernmental Acts in Europe', 25 *European Law Review* 79.

Kohler-Koch, B. (1999), 'A Constitution for Europe?' Working Paper of the Mannheim Centre for European Social Research, 8/1999.

Kokott, J. (1998), 'Report on Germany', in Slaughter *et al.* (1998).

Koopmans, T. (1991a), 'The Birth of European Law at the Crossroads of Legal Traditions', 39 *American Journal of Comparative Law* 493.

Koopmans, T. (1991b), 'The Future of the Court of Justice of the European Communities', 11 *Yearbook of European Law* 15.

'Kortenberg' (a pseudonym) (1998), 'Closer Cooperation in the Treaty of Amsterdam', 35 *Common Market Law Review* 833.

Kreher, A. (1997), 'Agencies in the European Community: A Step towards Administrative Integration in Europe', 4 *Journal of European Public Policy* 225.

Kutscher, H. (1976), 'Methods of Interpretation as Seen by a Judge at the Court of Justice', in *Proceedings of a Judicial and Academic Conference*, Luxembourg: OOPEC.

Laffan, B. (1993), 'The Treaty of Maastricht: Political Authority and Legitimacy', in Cafruny and Rosenthal (1993).

Laffan, B. (1996), 'The Politics of Identity and Political Order in Europe', 34 *Journal of Common Market Studies* 81.

Laffan, B. (1997), *The Finances of the European Union*, London: Macmillan.

Laffan, B. (1999a), 'Democracy and the European Union', in Cram *et al.* (1999).

Laffan, B. (1999b), 'Becoming a 'Living Institution': The Evolution of the European Court of Auditors', 37 *Journal of Common Market Studies* 251.

Laffan, B., O'Donnell, R. and Smith, M. (2000), *Europe's Experimental Union*, London: Routledge.

Langrish, S. (1998), 'The Treaty of Amsterdam: Selected Highlights', 23 *European Law Review* 3.

Laurent, P.-H. and Maresceau, M. (eds) (1998), *The State of the European Union, Vol. 4. Deepening and Widening*, Boulder, CO: Lynne Rienner.

Lenaerts, K. (1991a), 'Some Reflections on the Separation of Powers in the European Community', 28 *Common Market Law Review* 11.

Lenaerts, K. (1991b), 'Fundamental Rights to be Included in a Community Catalogue', 16 *European Law Review* 367.

Lenaerts, K. (1993), 'Regulating the Regulatory Process: "Delegation of Powers" in the European Community', 18 *European Law Review* 23.

Lenaerts, K. (1994), 'Form and Substance of the Preliminary Rulings Procedure', in Curtin and Heukels (1994).

Lenaerts, K., Arts, D. and Bray, R. (1999), *Procedural law of the European Union*, London: Sweet & Maxwell.

Lenaerts, K., van Nuffel, P. and Bray, P. (1999), *Constitutional law of the European Union*, London: Sweet and Maxwell.

Lenaerts, K. and de Smijter, E. (1996), 'The Question of Democratic Representation', in Winter, Curtin, Kellermann and de Witte (1996).

Lenaerts, K. and Verhoeven, A. (2000), 'Towards a Legal Framework for Executive Rile-Making in the EU? The Contribution of the New Comitology Decision' 37 *Common Market Law Review* 645.

Lonbay, J. and Biondi, A. (eds) (1997), *Remedies for Breach of EC Law*, Chichester: John Wiley.

Lord, C. (1998), *Democracy in the European Union*, Sheffield: Sheffield Academic Press.

Lyons, C. (1997) 'A Voyage around Article 8: An Historical and Comparative Evaluation of the Fate of European Union Citizenship', 17 *Yearbook of European Law* 135.

McAllister, R. (1997), *From EC to EU: An Historical and Political Survey*, London: Routledge.

McCormick, J. (1999), *Understanding the European Union. A Concise Introduction*, London: Macmillan.

MacCormick, N. (1993), 'Beyond the Sovereign State', 56 *Modern Law Review* 1.

MacCormick, N. (1995), 'The Maastricht-Urteil: Sovereignty Now', 1 *European Law Journal* 259.

MacCormick, N. (1999), *Questioning Sovereignty. Law, State, and Nation in the European Commonwealth*, Oxford: Oxford University Press.

McGoldrick, D. (1997), *International Relations Law of the European Union*, Harlow: Longman.

McGoldrick, D. (1999), 'The European Union after Amsterdam: An Organisation with General Human Rights Competence?', in O'Keeffe and Twomey (1999).

MacLoed, I., Hendry, I. and Hyett, S. (1996), *External Relations of the European Communities*, Oxford: Oxford University Press.

Maher, I. (1994), 'National Courts as European Community Courts', 14 *Legal Studies* 226.

Maher, I. (1995a), 'A Question of Conflict: The Higher English Courts and the Implementation of European Community Law', in Daintith (1995b).

Maher, I. (1995b), 'Legislative Review by the EC Commission: Revision without Radicalism', in Shaw and More (1995).

Maltby, N. (1993), 'Marleasing: What is All the Fuss About?', 109 *Law Quarterly Review* 301.

Mancini, G.F. (1989), 'The Making of a Constitution for Europe', 26 *Common Market Law Review* 595.

Mancini, G.F. (1998), 'Europe: The Case for Statehood', 4 *European Law Journal* 29.

Mancini, G.F. and Keeling, D. (1991), 'From *CILFIT* to *ERT*: The Constitutional Challenge Facing the European Court', 11 *Yearbook of European Law* 1.

Mancini, G.F. and Keeling, D. (1994), 'Democracy and the European Court of Justice', 57 *Modern Law Review* 175.

de la Mare, T. (1999), 'Article 177 in Social and Political Context', in Craig and de Búrca (1999).

Markesinis, B. S. (ed.) (2000), *The Clifford Chance Millennium Lectures: The Coming Together of the Common Law and the Civil Law*, Oxford: Hart Publishing.

Marks, G., Scharpf, F., Schmitter, P. and Streeck, W. (1996), *Governance in the European Union*, London: Sage.

Marshall, T.H. (1950), *Citizenship and Social Class*, Cambridge: Cambridge University Press.

Martin, S. (1994), *The Construction of Europe. Essays in Honour of Emile Noël*, Dordrecht: Kluwer.

Mattli, W. and Slaughter, A.-M. (1998), 'The Role of National Courts in the Process of European Integration: Accounting for Judicial Preferences and Constraints', in Slaughter, Stone Sweet and Weiler (1998).

Mazey, S. and Richardson, J. (1994), 'The Commission and the Lobby', in Edwards and Spence (1994).

Mazey, S. and Richardson, J. (1995), 'Promiscuous Policymaking: the European Policy Style?', in Rhodes and Mazey (1995).

Mazey, S. and Richardson, J. (1999), 'Interests', in Cram et al. (1999).

McLaughlin, A. and Greenwood, J. (1995), 'The Management of Interest Representation in the European Union', 33 *Journal of Common Market Studies* 43.

Meads, P. (1991), 'The Obligation to Apply European Law: Is Duke Dead?', 16 *European Law Review* 490.

Mendrinou, M. (1996), 'Non-compliance and the European Commission's Role in Integration', 3 *Journal of European Public Policy* 1.

Micklitz, H.W. and Reich, N. (eds) (1996), *Public Interest Litigation before European Courts*, Baden-Baden: Nomos.

Millett, T. (1989), 'Rules of Interpretation of EEC Legislation', 10 *Statute Law Review* 163.

Mitchell, J.D.B. (1979), 'The Sovereignty of Parliament: The Stumbling Block that isn't There', *International Affairs* 33.

Mitchell, J.D.B., Kuipers, S. and Gall, B. (1972), 'Constitutional Aspects of the Treaty and Legislation Relating to British Membership', 9 *Common Market Law Review* 134.

Monar, J. (1994), 'Inter-institutional Agreements: The Phenomenon and its New Dynamics After Maastricht', 31 *Common Market Law Review* 693.

More, G. (1999), 'The Principle of Equal Treatment: From Market Unifier to Fundamental Rights?', in Craig and de Búrca (1999).

Munro, C. (1987), *Studies in Constitutional Law*, London: Butterworths.

Neill, P. (1995), 'The European Court of Justice. A Case Study in Judicial Activism', in House of Lords Select Committee on the European Communities: 1996 Intergovernmental Conference, Minutes of Evidence, HL Session 1994–95, 18th Report.

Nelsen, B. and Stubb, A. (eds) (1998), *The European Union: Readings on the Theory and Practice of European Integration* (2nd edn), London: Macmillan.

Neuhold, C. (2000), 'Into the New Millennium: The Evolution of the European Parliament from Consultative Assembly to Co-legislator', *Eipascope*, issue no. 1, p.3.

Neunreither, K.-H. (1999), 'The European Parliament', in Cram, Dinan and Nugent (1999).

Neunreither, K.-H. and Wiener, A. (eds) (2000), *European Integration after Amsterdam: Institutional Dynamics and Prospects for Democracy*, Oxford: Oxford University Press.

Neuwahl, N. (1996), 'Article 173 Paragraph 4 EC: Past, Present and Possible Future', 21 *European Law Review* 17.

Neyer, J. (2000), 'Justifying Comitology: The Promise of Deliberation', in Neunreither and Wiener (2000).

Nicoll, T. (1993), '"Note the Hour – and File the Minute"', 31 *Journal of Common Market Studies* 559.

Nicoll, T. (1994), 'The European Parliament's Post-Maastricht Rules of Procedure', 32 *Journal of Common Market Studies* 403.

Nugent, N. (1999a), *The Government and Politics of the European Union* (3rd edn), London: Macmillan.

Nugent, N. (1999b), 'Decision Making', in Cram, Dinan and Nugent (1999).

Öberg, U. (1998), 'Public Access to Documents after the Entry into Force of the Amsterdam Treaty: Much Ado about Nothing', 2 *European Integration online Papers* no. 8 (http://eiop.or.at/eiop/texte/1998-008.htm).

Obradovic, D. (1996), 'Policy Legitimacy and the European Union', 34 *Journal of Common Market Studies* 191.

O'Keeffe, D. (1994), 'Union Citizenship', in O'Keeffe and Twomey (1994).

O'Keeffe, D. (1998), 'Is the Spirit of Article 177 under Attack? Preliminary References and Admissibility', 23 *European Law Review* 509.

O'Keeffe, D. (1999), 'Can the Leopard Change its Spots? Visas, Immigration and Asylum – Following Amsterdam', in O'Keeffe and Twomey (1999).

O'Keeffe, D. and Twomey, P. (eds) (1994), *Legal Issues of the Maastricht Treaty*, Chichester: Chancery.

O'Keeffe, D. and Twomey, P. (eds) (1999), *Legal Issues of the Amsterdam Treaty*, Oxford: Hart Publishing.

d'Oliveira, H.U.J. (1994a), 'European Citizenship: Its Meaning, its Potential', in Dehousse (1994a).

d'Oliveira, H.U.J. (1994b), 'Expanding External and Shrinking Internal Borders: Europe's Defence Mechanisms in the Areas of Free Movement, Immigration and Asylum', in O'Keeffe and Twomey (1994).

O'Neill, M. (1996), *The Politics of European Integration: A Reader*, London: Routledge.

O'Neill, M. (1998), The Right of Access to Community-Held Documentation as a General Principle of EC Law', 4 *European Public Law* 403.

Österdahl, I. (1999), 'Case Note on *Interporc, van der Wal* and *Svenska Journalistförbundet*', 36 *Common Market Law Review* 36.

Peers, S. (1999a), 'Constitutional Principles and International Trade', 24 *European Law Review* 185.

Peers, S. (1999b), 'Banana Split: WTO Law and Preferential Agreements in the EC Legal Order', 4 *European Foreign Affairs Review* 195.

Peers, S. (2000a), *EU Justice and Home Affairs Law*, Harlow: Longman.

Peers, S. (2000b), 'Justice and Home Affairs: Decision Making after Amsterdam', 25 *European Law Review* 183.

Pernice, I. (1999), 'Multilevel Constitutionalism and the Treaty of Amsterdam: European Constitution-Making Revisited?', 36 *Common Market Law Review* 703.

Pescatore, P. (1983), 'The Doctrine of 'Direct Effect': An Infant Disease in Community Law', 8 *European Law Review* 155.

Pescatore, P. (1987), 'Some Critical Remarks on the Single European Act', 24 *Common Market Law Review* 9.

Peterson, J. (1994), 'Subsidiarity: A Definition to Suit Any Vision?', 47 *Parliamentary Affairs* 116.

Peterson, J. (1995), 'Decision-making inthe European Union: towards a frame-work for analysis', 2 *Journal of European Public Policy* 69.

Peterson, J. (1999), 'Jacques Santer: The EU's Gorbachev', *ECSA Review*, Vol. XII, No. 4, p. 4.

Peterson, J. (2000), 'Romano Prodi: Another Delors?', *ECSA Review*, Vol. 13, No. 1, p. 1.

Peterson, J. and Bomberg, E. (1999), *Decision-Making in the European Union*, London: Macmillan.

Phelan, D.R. (1992), 'Right to Life of the Unborn v. Promotion of Trade in Services: The European Court of Justice and the Normative Shaping of the European Union', 55 *Modern Law Review* 670.

Philippart, E. and Edwards, G. (1999), 'The Provisions on Closer Cooperation in the Treaty of Amsterdam: the Politics of Flexibility in the European Union', 37 *Journal of Common Market Studies* 87.

Piris, J.C. (1999), 'Does the European Union have a Constitution? Does it Need One?' 24 *European Law Review* 557.

Poiares Maduro, M. (2000), 'Europe and the Constitution: *What if this is as Good as it Gets?*' in Weiler and Wind (2000).

Pollack, M. (2000), 'A Blairite Treaty: Neo-Liberalism and Regulated Capitalism in the Treaty of Amsterdam', in Neunreither and Wiener (2000).

Prechal, S. (1998a), 'Community Law in National Courts: The Lessons from *van Schijndel*', 35 *Common Market Law Review* 681.

Prechal, S. (1998b), 'Institutional Balance: A Fragile Principle with Uncertain Contents', in Heukels, Blokker and Brus (1998).

Preuss, U. (1995), 'Problems of a Concept of European Citizenship', 1 *European Law Journal* 267.

Rasmussen, H. (1980), 'Why is Article 173 Interpreted against Private Plaintiffs?', 5 *European Law Review* 112.

Rasmussen, H. (1986), *On Law and Policy in the European Court of Justice*, Dordrecht: Martinus Nijhoff.

Rawlings, R. (2000), 'Engaged Elites: Citizen Action and Institutional Attitudes in Commission Enforcement', 6 *European Law Journal* 4.

Rees, W., Neuwahl, N. and Lynch, P. (2000), *Reforming the European Union*, Harlow: Longman.

Reich, N. (1996a), 'Judge-made 'Europe à la carte': Some Remarks on Recent Conflicts between European and German Constitutional Law Provoked by the Banana Litigation', 7 *European Journal of International Law* 103.

Reich, N. (1996b), 'Public Interest Litigation Before European Jurisdictions', in Micklitz and Reich (1996).

Rhodes, C. and Mazey, S. (eds) (1995), *The State of the European Union. Vol. 3. Building a European Polity?*, Boulder, CO: Lynne Rienner.

Rhodes, M., Heywood, P. and Wright, V. (eds) (1997), *Developments in West European Politics*, London: Macmillan.

Richardson, J. (ed.) (1996), *European Union: Power and Policy-Making*, London: Routledge.

Rosamund, B. (1999), *Theories of European Integration*, London: Macmillan.

Ross, M. (1990), 'Refining Effective Enjoyment', 15 *European Law Review* 476.

Ross, M. (1993), 'Beyond Francovich', 56 *Modern Law Review* 55.

Ross, M. (1994), 'Limits on using Article 177 EC', 19 *European Law Review* 640.

Rudden, B. and Wyatt, D. (eds.) (1999), *Basic Community Laws*, Oxford University Press, Oxford (7th edn).

Ruggeri Laderchi, F.P. (1998), 'Report on Italy', in Slaughter, Stone Sweet and Weiler (1998).

Sack, J. (1995), 'The European Community's Membership of International Organizations', 32 *Common Market Law Review* 1227.

Sandholtz, W. and Stone Sweet, A. (eds) (1998), *European Integration and Supranational Governance*, Oxford: Oxford University Press.

Schermers, H. (1990), 'The Scales in Balance: National Constitutional Court v. Court of Justice', 27 *Common Market Law Review* 97.

Schermers, H. *et al.* (eds) (1987), *Article 177 EEC: Experiences and Problems*, Amsterdam: North-Holland.

Schuppert, G.F. (1995), 'On the Evolution of a European State: Reflections on the Conditions of and the Prospects for a European Constitution', in Hesse and Johnson (1995).

Schwarze, J. (1991), 'Tendencies towards a Common Administrative Law in Europe', 16 *European Law Review* 3.

Scorey, D. (1996), 'A New Model for the Communities' Judicial Architecture in the New Union', 21 *European Law Review* 224.

Scott, J. (1995a), *Development Dilemmas in the European Community. Rethinking Regional Development Policy*, Buckingham: Open University Press.

Scott, J. (1995b), 'GATT and Community Law: Rethinking the "Regulatory Gap"', in Shaw and More (1995).

Scott, J. (1998), 'Law, Legitimacy and EC Governance: Prospects for "Partnership"', 36 *Journal of Common Market Studies* 175.

Shackleton, M. (1998), 'The European Parliament's New Committees of Inquiry: Tiger or Paper Tiger?', 36 *Journal of Common Market Studies* 115.

Shapiro, M. (1992), 'The Giving Reasons Requirement', *University Chicago Legal Forum* 179.

Shaw, J. (1995), 'Decentralization and Law Enforcement in EC Competition Law', 15 *Legal Studies* 128.

Shaw, J. (1996), 'European Union Legal Studies in Crisis? Towards a New Dynamic', 16 *Oxford Journal of Legal Studies* 231.

Shaw, J. (1998a), 'Citizenship of the Union: Towards Postnational Membership', in Academy of European Law (1998).

Shaw, J. (1998b), 'The Interpretation of European Union Citizenship', 61 *Modern Law Review* 293.

Shaw, J. (1998c), 'The Treaty of Amsterdam: Challenges of Flexibility and Legitimacy', 4 *European Law Journal* 63.

Shaw, J. (1999), 'Postnational Constitutionalism in the European Union', 6 *Journal of European Public Policy* 579.

Shaw, J. (2000a), 'Constitutionalism and Flexibility in the EU: Developing a Relational Approach', in de Búrca and Scott (2000).

Shaw, J. (2000b), 'Constitutional Settlements and the Citizen after the Treaty of Amsterdam', in Neunreither and Wiener (2000).

Shaw, J. (2000c), 'Process and Constitutional Discourse in the European Union', 27 *Journal of Law and Society* 4.

Shaw, J. and Hunt, J. (2000), 'European Legal Studies: Then and Now', in Hayton (2000).

Shaw, J. and More, G. (eds) (1995), *New Legal Dynamics of European Union*, Oxford: Oxford University Press.

Shaw, J. and Wiener, A. (2000), 'The Paradox of the "European Polity"', in Green Cowles and Smith (2000); also published as Harvard Jean Monnet Working Paper 10/99.

Slaughter, A.-M., Stone Sweet, A. and Weiler, J.H.H. (eds) (1998), *The European Courts and National Courts. Doctrine and Jurisprudence*, Oxford: Hart Publishing.

Slynn, G. (1992), *Introducing a European Legal Order*, London: Sweet & Maxwell.

Smits, P. (1994), 'A Single Currency for Europe and the Karlsruhe Court', *Legal Issues of European Integration*, Issue 2, 115.

Snyder, F. (1990), *New Directions in European Community Law*, London: Weidenfeld & Nicolson.

Snyder, F. (ed.) (1993a), *European Community Law*, 2 vols, Aldershot: Dartmouth (International Library of Essays in Law and Legal Theory Series).

Snyder, F. (1993b) 'The Effectiveness of European Community Law: Institutions, Processes, Tools and Techniques', 56 *Modern Law Review* 19.

Snyder, F. (1994), 'Soft Law and Institutional Practice in the European Community', in Martin (1994).

Snyder, F. (1998), 'General Course on Constitutional Law of the European Union', in Academy of European Law (1998).

Snyder, F. (2000), 'The Unfinished Constitution of the European Union: Principles, Processes and Culture', in Weiler and Wind (2000).

Söderman, J. (1998), *The Citizen, the Administration and Community Law*, General Report prepared by the European Ombudsman for the 1998 FIDE Congress Stockholm, Sweden, 3–6 June 1998 (available from European Ombudsman website).

Soysal, Y. (1994), *Limits of Citizenship: Migrants and Postnational Membership in Europe*, Chicago: University of Chicago Press.

Spence, D. (2000), 'Plus ça change, plus c'est la même chose? Attempting to Reform the European Commission', 7 *Journal of European Public Policy* 1.

Stein, E. and Vining, G.J. (1976), 'Citizen Access to Judicial Review of Administrative Action in a Transnational and Federal Context', 70 *American Journal of International Law* 219.

Steiner, J. (1993), 'From Direct Effects to Francovich: Shifting Means of Enforcement of Community Law', 18 *European Law Review* 3.

Stone Sweet, A. (1998), 'Constitutional Dialogues in the European Community', in Slaughter, Stone Sweet and Weiler (1998).

Stone Sweet, A. (2000), *Governing with Judges*, Oxford: Oxford University Press.

Stone Sweet, A. and Brunell, T. (1998), 'The European Court and the National Courts: A Statistical Analysis of Preliminary References, 1961–1995', 5 *Journal of European Public Policy* 66.

Stubb, A. (1996), 'A Categorization of Differentiated Integration', 34 *Journal of Common Market Studies* 283.

Stubb, A. (2000), 'Negotiating Flexible Integration in the Amsterdam Treaty', in Neunreither and Wiener (2000).

Szyszczak, E. (1990), 'Sovereignty: Crisis, Compliance, Confusion, Complacency', 15 *European Law Review* 480.

Szyszczak, E. (1996), 'Pregnancy and Sex Discrimination', 21 *European Law Review* 79.

Szyszczak, E. (1999), 'The New Parameters of European Labour Law', in O'Keeffe and Twomey (1999).

Teasdale, P. (1993), 'The Life and Death of the Luxembourg Compromise', 31 *Journal of Common Market Studies* 567.

Temple Lang, J. (1990), 'Community Constitutional Law: Article 5 EEC Treaty', 27 *Common Market Law Review* 645.

Temple Lang, J. (1997), 'The Duties of National Courts under Community Constitutional Law', 22 *European Law Review* 3.

Temple Lang, J. (1998), 'The Duties of National Authorities under Community Constitutional Law', 23 *European Law Review* 109.

Tesauro. G. (1993), 'The Effectiveness of Judicial Protection and Co-operation between the Court of Justice and the National Courts', 13 *Yearbook of European Law* 1.

Toner, H. (1997), 'Thinking the Unthinkable? State Liability for Judicial Acts after *Factortame (III)*', 17 *Yearbook of European Law* 165.

Toth, A. (1994), 'A Legal Analysis of Subsidiarity', in O'Keeffe and Twomey (1994).

Toth, A. (1995), 'Case Note on Air France v. Commission', 32 *Common Market Law Review* 271.

Trachtman, J. (1999), 'Bananas, Direct Effect and Compliance', 10 *European Journal of International Law* 655.

Tridimas, T. (1994), 'Horizontal Effect of Directives: A Missed Opportunity?', 19 *European Law Review* 621.

Tridimas, T. (1996), 'The Court of Justice and Judicial Activism', 21 *European Law Review* 199.

Tridimas, T. (1998), 'Member State Liability in Damages for Breach of Community Law: An Assessment of the Case Law', in Beatson and Tridimas (1998).

Turner, C. (1999), 'Human Rights Protection in the European Community: Resolving Conflict and Overlap between the European Court of Justice and the European Court of Human Rights', 5 *European Public Law* 453.

Twomey, P. (1996), 'Case Note on *Carvel* v. *Guardian*', 33 *Common Market Law Review* 831.

Urwin, D. (1995), *The Community of Europe. A History of European Integration Since 1945* (2nd edn), London: Longman.

Usher, J. (1976), 'The Influence of National Concepts on Decisions of the European Court', 1 *European Law Review* 359.

Usher, J. (1981), *European Community Law and National Law: The Irreversible Transfer?*, London: Allen & Unwin.

Usher, J. (1994), 'Individual Concern in General Legislation – 10 Years On', 19 *European Law Review* 636.

Usher, J. (1998), *General Principles of EC Law*, Harlow: Longman.

Usher, J. (ed.) (2000), *The State of the European Union: Structure, Enlargement and Economic Union*, Harlow: Longman.

Verhoeven, A. (1998), 'How Democratic need European Union Members be? Some Thoughts after Amsterdam', 23 *European Law Review* 217.

Vesterdorp, B. (1994), 'Complaints Concerning Infringements of Competition Law within the Context of European Community Law', 31 *Common Market Law Review* 77.

Vos, E. (1997), 'The Rise of Committees', 3 *European Law Journal* 210.

Vos, E. (1999), *Institutional Frameworks of Community Health and Safety Legislation*, Oxford: Hart Publishing.

Vranken, M. (1996), 'Role of the Advocate General in the Law-Making Process of the European Community', 25 *Anglo-American Law Review* 39.

Waelbroeck, D. and Fosselard, D. (1995), 'Case Note on Codorniu v. Council', 32 *Common Market Law Review* 257.

Wainwright, M. (1994), 'The Future of European Community Legislation in the Light of the Recommendations of the Sutherland Committee and the Principle of Subsidiarity', 15 *Statute Law Review* 98.

Walker, N. (1996), 'European Constitutionalism and European Integration', *Public Law* 266.

Walker, N. (2000), 'Theoretical Reflections on Flexibility and Europe's Future', in de Búrca and Scott (2000).

Wallace, H. (1985), *Europe: The Challenge of Diversity*, Chatham House Paper No. 29, Royal Institute of International Affairs.

Wallace, H. (2000), 'Flexibility: A Tool of Integration or a Restraint on Disintegration?', in Neunreither and Wiener (2000).

Wallace, H. and Wallace, W. (eds) (2000), *Policy-Making in the European Union* (4th edn), Oxford: Oxford University Press.

Wallace, W. (ed.) (1990), The Dynamics of European Integration, London: Pinter.

Wallace, W. (1994), *Regional Integration: The West European Experience*, Washington, DC: The Brookings Institution.

Ward, A. (1995), 'Effective Sanctions in EC Law: A Moving Boundary in the Division of Competence', 1 *European Law Journal* 1204.

Ward, I. (1996a), *A Critical Introduction to European Law*, London: Butterworths.

Ward, I. (1996b), *The Margins of European Law*, London: Macmillan.

Watson, S. (1986), 'Asser Institute Colloquium on European Law 1985: Experiences and Problems in Applying the Preliminary Proceedings of Article 177 EEC', 23 *Common Market Law Review* 207.

Weale, A. and Nentwich, M. (eds) (1998), *Political Theory and the European Union: Legitimacy, Constitutional Choice and Citizenship*, London: Routledge.

Weatherill, S. (1992), 'Regulating the Internal Market: Result Orientation in the House of Lords', 17 *European Law Review* 299.

Weatherill, S. (1994), 'Beyond Pre-emption? Shared Competence and Constitutional Change in the European Community', in O'Keeffe and Twomey (1994).

Weatherill, S. (1995a), *Law and Integration in the European Union*, Oxford: Oxford University Press.

Weatherill, S. (1995b), 'Implementation as a Constitutional Issue', in Daintith (1995b).

Weatherill, S. (1996a), 'Compulsory Notification of Draft Technical Regulations: The Contribution of Directive 83/189 to the Management of the Internal Market', 16 *Yearbook of European Law* 129.

Weatherill, S. (1996b), 'Public Interest Litigation in EC Competition Law', in Micklitz and Reich (1996).

Weatherill, S. (1998), 'Safeguarding the *acquis communautaire*', in Heukels *et al* (1998).

Weatherill, S. (1999), '"If I Had Wanted You to Understand I Would Have Explained it Better": What is the Purpose of the Provisions on Closer Co-operation Introduced by the Treaty of Amsterdam?', in O'Keeffe and Twomey (1999).

Weatherill, S. (2000a), 'Flexibility or Fragmentation? Trends in European Integration', in Usher (2000).

Weatherill, S. (2000b), 'New Strategies for Managing the EC's Internal Market', *Current Legal Problems*, forthcoming.

Weatherill, S. (2000c), 'Addressing Problems of Unbalanced Implementation in EC law: Remedies in an Institutional Perspective', in Kilpatrick, Novitz, and Skidmore (2000).

Weatherill, S. and Beaumont, P. (1999), *EU Law* (3rd edn), Harmondsworth: Penguin.

Weigall, D. and Stirk, D. (1992), *The Origins and Development of the European Community*, Leicester/London: Leicester University Press.

Weiler, J.H.H. (1981) 'The Community System: The Dual Character of Supranationalism', 1 *Yearbook of European Law* 267.

Weiler, J.H.H. (1988), 'The White Paper and the Application of Community Law', in Bieber et al. (1988).

Weiler, J.H.H. (1989), 'Pride and Prejudice – Parliament v. Council', 14 *European Law Review* 334.

Weiler, J.H.H. (1993), 'Journey to an Unknown Destination: A Retrospective and Prospective of the European Court of Justice in the Arena of Political Integration', 31 *Journal of Common Market Studies* 417.

Weiler, J.H.H. (1994a), 'Fin-de-Siècle Europe', in Dehousse (1994a).

Weiler, J.H.H. (1995), 'Does European Need a Constitution? Reflections on Demos, Telos and the German Maastricht Decision', 1 *European Law Journal* 219.

Weiler, J.H.H. (1996), 'Citizenship and Human Rights', in Winter *et al.* (1996).

Weiler, J.H.H. (1997), 'The Reformation of European Constitutionalism', 53 *Journal of Common Market Studies* 97.

Weiler, J.H.H. (1998), 'Europe: The Case against the Case for Statehood', 4 *European Law Journal* 43.

Weiler, J.H.H. (1999a), *The Constitution of Europe*, Cambridge: Cambridge University Press.

Weiler, J.H.H. (1999b), 'Prologue: Amsterdam and the Quest for Constitutional Democracy', in O'Keeffe and Twomey (1999).

Weiler, J.H.H. and Lockhart, N. (1995a), '"Taking Rights Seriously" Seriously: The European Court and its Fundamental Rights Jurisprudence – Part I', 32 *Common Market Law Review* 51.

Weiler, J.H.H. and Lockhart, N. (1995b), '"Taking Rights Seriously" Seriously: The European Court and its Fundamental Rights Jurisprudence – Part II', 32 *Common Market Law Review* 579.

Weiler, J.H.H. and Wind, M. (eds) (2000), *Rethinking European Constitutionalism*, Cambridge: Cambridge University Press.

Wellens, K. and Borchardt, G. (1989), 'Soft Law in European Community Law', 14 *European Law Review* 267.

Westlake, M. (1994), *The Commission and the Parliament: Partners and Rivals in the European Policy-Making Process*, London: Butterworths.

Westlake, M. (1995), *The Council of the European Union*, London: Cartermill/Longman.

Wiener, A. (2000), 'The Embedded *Acquis Communautaire*: Transmission Belt and Prism of New Governance', in Neunreither and Wiener (2000).

Wils, W. (1992), 'Concurrent Liability of the Community and a Member State', 17 *European Law Review* 191.

Wincott, D. (1995a), 'Political Theory, Law and European Union', in Shaw and More (1995).

Wincott, D. (1995b), 'The Role of Law or the Rule of the Court of Justice? An "Institutional" Account of Judicial Politics in the European Community', 2 *Journal of European Public Policy* 583.

Winter, J. (1972), 'Direct Applicability and Direct Effect: Two Distinct and Different Concepts in Community Law', 9 *Common Market Law Review* 425.

Winter, J., Curtin, D., Kellermann, A., and de Witte, B. (eds) (1996), *Reforming the Treaty on European Union – The Legal Debate*, The Hague: Kluwer.

de Witte, B. (1991), 'Community Law and National Constitutional Values', *Legal Issues of European Integration* 1991/2, 4.

De Witte, B. (1995), 'Sovereignty and European Integration: The Weight of Legal Tradition', 2 *Maastricht Journal of European and Comparative Law* 145.

de Witte, B. (1998), 'The Pillar Structure and the Nature of the European Union: Greek Temple or French Gothic Cathedral?', in Heukels *et al.* (1998).

de Witte, B. (1999a), 'The Past and Future Role of the European Court of Justice in the Protection of Human Rights', in Alston (1999).

de Witte, B. (1999b), 'Direct Effect, Supremacy and the Nature of the Legal Order', in Craig and de Búrca (1999).

van der Woude, M. (1997), 'Liability for Administrative Acts under Article 215(2) EC', in Heukels and McDonnell (1997).

Wyatt, D. (1981), 'Following up Foglia: Why the Court is Right to Stick to its Guns', 6 *European Law Review* 447.

Wyatt, D. (1982), 'New Legal Order or Old?', 7 *European Law Review* 147.

Wyatt, D. (1997), 'The Relationship between Actions for Annulment and References on Validity after TWD Teggendorf', in Lonbay and Biondi (1997).

Zuleeg, M. (1997), 'The European Constitution under Constitutional Constraints: The German Scenario', 22 *European Law Review* 19.

Index